The
Rockin'
'60s

The Rockin' '60s

Brock Helander

THE PEOPLE WHO MADE THE MUSIC

SCHIRMER BOOKS

NEW YORK

Schirmer Books
An imprint of Macmillan Library Reference USA
1633 Broadway
New York, NY 10019

Library of Congress Catalog Card Number: 98-49457
Printed in the United States of America

Printing Number
1 2 3 4 5 6 7 8 9 10

Library of Congress Cataloging-in-Publication Data

Helander, Brock.
    The rockin' '60s : the people who made the music / Brock
Helander.
        p.   cm.
    "This volume is a critical and historical discography of rock and
soul musics in the 1960's"—Pref.
    Includes bibliographical references and index.
    ISBN 0-02-864873-0
    1. Rock music—1961–1970—Discography.   2. Soul
music—Discography.   I. Title.   II. Title: Rocking '60s   III. Title:
Rockin' sixties   IV. Title: Rocking sixties
    ML156.4.R6 H46 1999
    106.78166—dc21   98-49457
                                                                                    CIP
                                                                                    MN

This book is dedicated to the victims and the survivors of the '60s.
Specifically, to the victims who never knew what hit them.
And to the survivors who never gave up the dream.

CONTENTS

PREFACE

This book follows the publication of my books *The Rock Who's Who,* Second Edition, in 1996 and *The Rockin' '50s* in 1998. This volume is a critical and historical discography of rock and soul music in the 1960s, covering major musical artists who have contributed significantly to the development of contemporary popular music. In addition to musicians and singers, this volume includes songwriters Burt Bacharach and Carole King, the songwriting teams of Jeff Barry and Ellie Greenwich, Barry Mann and Cynthia Weil, and Brian Holland, Lamont Dozier, and Eddie Holland (H-D-H), FM radio pioneer Tom Donahue, Motown Records founder Berry Gordy, Jr., concert producer Bill Graham, record producer Phil Spector, and publisher Jann Wenner (*Rolling Stone*).

In this book, I include extensive discographies of recordings issued on record albums, cassettes, and compact discs by rock, soul, and pop artists that were regular releases in the United States. Foreign releases are not listed, unless they were normally distributed in this country (e.g., England's Ace Records). So-called "bootleg" albums are not listed.

Recording artists are listed in alphabetical order, by group name for groups and by last name for individual artists. Albums are listed in recording order rather than release order. Albums for the same record label (and their subsidiaries and successor labels) are listed together, unless an artist leaves and later returns to a record label (e.g., Diana Ross, who left and returned to Motown Records), thus resulting in separate chronological listings. Anthology albums are often listed separately. Many entries include a bibliography preceding the discography.

In the discussion of hit singles, the gradation from largest to smallest success is indicated in the following order:

Top: Number 1 hit
Smash: Top 10
Major: Top 25
Moderate: Top 40
Minor: Top 100

Hit singles are discussed in the context of the three major chart categories: pop, rhythm-and-blues/soul, and country-and-western, with occasional reference made to easy-listening.

Brock Helander
Sacramento, California

ACKNOWLEDGMENTS

First, I would like to thank my family, mother Helen, brother Bruce, and my late father Ed, for their support and encouragement with my book-writing projects over the years. I would also like to thank my faithful friends who have supported me, particularly Mark Staneart, Gerry Helland, Tom Partington, and Carol Tozer. Others I gratefully acknowledge for their assistance include the late Frank Kofsky, Joel Selvin of the *San Francisco Chronicle,* record collector Jeff Hughson, and first editor Ken Stuart. I am especially grateful for the faith, patience, and understanding of senior editor Richard Carlin, who tracked me down in 1993 and provided me the opportunity to return to writing about a subject I have studied and enjoyed for twenty years. Finally, I thank the following record companies and their representatives for providing current issues of their record catalogs: Flying Fish, Green Linnet, Kicking Mule, Mobile Fidelity, One Way, Razor & Tie, Relix, Rhino, Rounder, Rykodisc, Sierra, Sugar Hill, Sundazed, and Varēse Sarabande.

The discographies in this book were compiled from the following sources:

Brock Helander. *Rock 'n' Roll to Rock: A Discography.* Privately published, 1978.
Brock Helander. *The Rock Who's Who.* New York: Schirmer Books, 1982.
Brock Helander. *The Rock Who's Who,* Second Edition. New York: Schirmer Books, 1996.

USE OF THE DISCOGRAPHIES

The organization of the discographies is illustrated by the examples below:

Happy Jack	Decca	74892	'67	†
	MCA	2045		†
reissued as A Quick One	MCA	31331		CD†
	MCA	11267	'95	CS/CD
Tommy	Decca	(2)7205	'69	†
	MCA	(2)10005		†
	MCA	10801	'93	CS/CD
	MCA	11417	'96	CS/CD
	Mobile Fidelity	00533	'90	CD

From left to right, the five columns supply the following information:

1. The album title. Other information is included parenthetically following the album title. Such information includes movie soundtrack, original cast, television show recording information, and recording date information.
2. The name of the record label on which the album was released. Albums are often reissued on a label different from the original.
3. The record label's catalog number for the album. When an album is a multiple-record set, the number of LPs, cassettes, or compact discs is indicated parenthetically before the catalog number.
4. The release year. When no information is available, the column is left open. If two dates appear, the second is the year of release on compact disc.
5. The format in which the album was or is available. Formats are LP (vinyl), CS (cassette), and CD (compact disc). If no format information appears in the column, the release was as an LP. A dagger (†) in this column indicates the release was no longer available at regular retail outlets as of the summer of 1998. Occasionally, a title once available as both a cassette and compact disc is currently only available as a CD, thus the notation CS†/CD.

INTRODUCTION

If it had been left up to the major record companies, rock 'n' roll would have never happened. These so-called majors—Columbia, RCA-Victor, Decca, Capitol, Mercury, MGM, and ABC-Paramount in the '50s—were either oblivious or downright hostile to the emergence of rock 'n' roll. The majors believed they controlled the production of popular music, subdividing the task of music production into three elements: (1) songwriters working for established publishing companies working in the Tin Pan Alley tradition of professional, factory-style songwriting; (2) the record company's artist-and-repertoire (A&R) representative, who matched the song to the musical artist and often commissioned the arrangements and musicians used for recordings; and (3) the musical artist, contracted to the record label, who had little or no input into decisions regarding song selection and arrangements. The majors viewed rock 'n' roll as a bastardized form of music of little consequence or longevity. After all, they concluded, rock 'n' roll utilized elements of "minority" musics, rhythm-and-blues (once known as "race" music), and country-and-western (once called "hillbilly" music).

Rock 'n' roll proved them wrong. Rock 'n' roll showed that a "minority" form of popular music could be enjoyed by the affluent white middle-class masses, that tiny record companies independent of the majors could fulfill a widespread musical need, that singers could write their own songs and arrangements, and that rhythm-and-blues, rockabilly, and doo-wop were valid popular music genres which could serve as foundations for further developments in contemporary popular music.

The majors, astounded by the success of a music they did not control, soon sought to control and exploit white rockabilly. Decca successfully recorded Bill Haley and The Comets, while Capitol recorded Gene Vincent. Other majors practiced "corporate raiding," signing rockabilly acts away from independent labels. RCA signed Elvis Presley and Columbia signed Johnny Cash and Carl Perkins. Later, Jerry Lee Lewis moved to the Smash subsidiary of Mercury and Ricky Nelson switched to Decca. To diffuse and capitalize on the rise of rock 'n' roll, record companies promoted their own "teen idols," such as Paul Anka on ABC-Paramount and Neil Sedaka on RCA. Mercury Records became the most successful practitioners of the "cover" record, in which white artists such as Georgia Gibbs, The Crew Cuts, and The Diamonds, recorded tame versions of vital rhythm-and-blues hits. The black genres of rock 'n' roll, rhythm-and-blues, and doo-wop, were essentially left to the independents, although Mercury signed The Platters, ABC signed Ray Charles and B. B. King, and RCA signed Sam Cooke.

By the beginning of the '60s, rock 'n' roll seemed to be in eclipse, owing to corporate raiding, cover records, and the promotion of teen idols. Buddy Holly and Eddie Cochran were dead. Jerry Lee Lewis was in disgrace, Chuck Berry was on trial, and Little Richard was in (and out) of the ministry.

In the late '50s and early '60s, folk music enjoyed an amazing revival, with Joan Baez, Judy Collins, Peter, Paul and Mary, and Bob Dylan leading the way. The Beach Boys introduced surf music and songwriter-producers like Phil Spector and Jerry Leiber and Mike Stoller promoted "girl groups." Detroit's Motown Records reinvigorated rhythm-and-blues as soul, as did New York's Atlantic Records and Memphis' Stax-Volt Records. By the mid-'60s, British groups had recycled American rock 'n' roll with their own distinctive sound and charm, virtually taking over the marketplace. American "garage bands" produced crude but compelling hits that later inspired the development of "punk" music in the '70s. Bob Dylan helped advance the causes of folk-rock and country-rock and inspired the rise of singer-songwriters in the '70s. Others such as Blood, Sweat and Tears and Chicago promoted jazz-rock. In the latter half of the '60s, psychedelic music joined the popular cause, yielding up a myriad of groups from San Francisco, as well as England's Pink Floyd, Traffic, and Cream. Out of the seminal Yardbirds came Led Zeppelin, prime purveyors of heavy metal, which would become one of the dominant forms of popular music in the '70s.

This time, the majors were not caught unaware. Columbia's John Hammond signed Aretha Franklin and Bob Dylan. After the departure of A&R chief Mitch Miller, one of rock 'n' roll's staunchest opponents, Columbia signed Simon and Garfunkel, The Byrds, Paul Revere and The Raiders, Moby Grape, The Chambers Brothers, Leonard Cohen, Laura Nyro, Blood, Sweat and Tears, The Electric Flag, Big Brother and The Holding Company, Chicago, It's A Beautiful Day, and Santana during the course of the decade. The subsidiary label Epic released recordings by Great Britain's Dave Clark Five, The Yardbirds, Donovan, and Jeff Beck, and signed Sly and The Family Stone.

Capitol recorded The Beach Boys and issued the recordings of The Beatles and Peter and Gordon. However, lacking faith in the upstart British quartet, Capitol allowed early releases by The Beatles to be issued on VeeJay and Atco. In the latter part of the decade, Capitol signed The Band, The Steve Miller Band, and Quicksilver Messenger Service, and issued the early recordings of Pink Floyd on its subsidiary Tower and Harvest labels.

Decca recorded Brenda Lee and issued the recordings of The Who, while the London subsidiary released the recordings of The Rolling Stones, Marianne Faithfull, and John Mayall. The Deram subsidiary of British Decca recorded The Moody Blues, as well as Cat Stevens and Ten Years After. MGM issued the recordings of The Animals and Herman's Hermits, while its Verve subsidiary recorded The Blues Project, The Mothers of Invention, Tim Hardin, Richie Havens, Janis Ian, and The Velvet Underground.

ABC signed Ray Charles and B. B. King, recorded The Impressions, and purchased the independent Dunhill label in 1966. Dunhill artists included The Mamas and The Papas, The Grass Roots, Steppenwolf, and Three Dog Night. In the second half of the '60s, RCA recorded Jose Feliciano, The Jefferson Airplane, The Youngbloods, and The Guess Who, while Mercury recorded Jerry Butler and Spanky and Our Gang.

Although the majors signed many of the most popular acts of the decade, independent labels were again important in the evolution of contemporary popular music. The folk labels Vanguard and Elektra, formed in New York in 1948 and 1950, respectively, recorded important folk acts in the first half of the decade. Vanguard's roster included Joan Baez, Ian and Sylvia, The Jim Kweskin Jug Band, Buffy Sainte-Marie, Eric Andersen, and Richard and Mimi Farina, while Elektra recorded Judy Collins, The Dillards, Phil Ochs, Tom Rush, and, later, Tim Buckley. Both expanded into rock in the second-half of the '60s, Vanguard with Country Joe and The Fish, and Elektra with The Paul Butterfield Blues Band, Love, and The Doors.

The "girl group" sound of the early '60s was largely provided by independents, namely Laurie, Scepter, Dimension, Philles, and Red Bird. Formed in New York in 1958 and 1959, respectively, Laurie Records featured The Chiffons (and Dion), while Scepter recorded The Shirelles and Dionne Warwick, as well as B. J. Thomas. Dimension, formed in New York by Don Kirshner in 1962, recorded The Cookies and Carole King. Producer Phil Spector formed Philles Records in 1961, recording The Crystals and The Ronettes, as well as The Righteous Brothers and Ike and Tina Turner's most celebrated album. Songwriter-producers Jerry Leiber and Mike Stoller formed Red Bird Records in 1964, hitting with The Shangri Las, The Dixie Cups, and The Jelly Beans.

A number of important independent labels were significant in the advancement of black popular music. Berry Gordy, Jr. formed Tamla and Motown Records in Detroit in 1960. Tamla recorded Smokey Robinson and The Miracles, The Marvelettes, Marvin Gaye, and Stevie Wonder, while Motown recorded Mary Wells, The Supremes, The Four Tops, and, later, The Spinners and The Jackson Five. Gordy Records, formed in 1962, featured Martha and The Vandellas and The Temptations. By the time of the formation of Soul Records in 1965, with Junior Walker and The All-Stars and Gladys Knight and The Pips, the Motown conglomerate had become the most successful black-owned and operated company in America.

Initially formed as Satellite Records in Memphis in 1960, Stax Records took its name in 1961 and featured one of the most important house bands of the decade, Booker T. and The MGs, as well as The Bar-Kays and The Memphis Horns. The label's roster included Sam and Dave, Eddie Floyd, Johnnie Taylor, and The Staple Singers, while the subsidiary Volt label recorded Otis Redding.

Atlantic Records, the most successful rhythm-and-blues label of the '50s, continued to provide black music in the '60s. The roster included The Drifters, Solomon Burke, Joe Tex, Wilson Pickett, Percy Sledge, Aretha Franklin (after her unsuccessful stint at Columbia), and Roberta Flack. The Atco subsidiary recorded Ben E. King (after his departure from The Drifters) and Donny Hathaway. Atlantic also distributed Stax product until 1968. In the second half of the decade, Atlantic Records expanded into rock, signing The Young Rascals, Led Zeppelin, Crosby, Stills and Nash, and Yes. Atco recorded Sonny and Cher, The Buffalo Springfield, Vanilla Fudge, Iron Butterfly, and Doctor John, and issued the recordings of Cream, The Bee Gees, and Derek and The Dominoes.

Warner Brothers Records enjoyed its earliest success with The Everly Brothers and Peter, Paul and Mary. It expanded into rock in the second half of the decade, signing The Grateful Dead and, later, Little Feat. In 1963, Warner Brothers joined Reprise Records, originally formed by Frank Sinatra and others in 1960. Reprise issued the recordings of The Kinks, Jimi Hendrix, Pentangle, Jethro Tull, and Fleetwood Mac, and recorded Joni Mitchell, Randy Newman, Neil Young, and Frank Zappa and The Mothers of Invention, after they left Verve.

Imperial Records, formed in Los Angeles in 1947, enjoyed its biggest successes in the '50s with Fats Domino and Rick Nelson. In 1963, it was taken over by Liberty Records, formed in Hollywood in 1955. During the decade, Liberty recorded Jan and Dean, Jackie DeShannon, and Canned Heat, while Imperial issued the recordings of Johnny Rivers, The Hollies, and The Bonzo Dog Band. In 1968, Liberty merged with United Artists Records, which had recorded Jay and The Americans and issued the recordings of The Spencer Davis Group and Traffic. United Artists later signed War and Don McLean.

A&M Records was formed in 1962 in Los Angeles by Herb Alpert and Jerry Moss, enjoying its earliest success with Alpert's Tijuana Brass. In the late '60s, A&M expanded into rock, issuing recordings by Procol Harum, The Flying Burrito Brothers, Joe Cocker, Fairport Convention, Free, and, later, Cat Stevens and Sandy Denny.

Other important independent American record labels included King, VeeJay, Monument, Kama Sutra, Buddah, and Fantasy. King recorded James Brown, while VeeJay recorded Jerry Butler and The Four Seasons before its demise in 1966. Monument recorded Roy Orbison during his greatest hit-making period, while Kama Sutra recorded The Lovin' Spoonful and Buddah recorded Captain Beefheart and Melanie. Fantasy, originally a jazz label, enjoyed astounding success with Creedence Clearwater Revival at the end of the decade.

During the '60s, rock 'n' roll became simply rock and soul. The amazingly fertile period, with its wide-open experimentation and various cross pollinations, produced folk-rock, blues-rock, country-rock, jazz-rock, psychedelic rock, and heavy metal. Rhythm-and-blues became funk and doo-wop became soul. Black music even investigated the potential of psychedelic soul. On a foundation provided by '50s rock 'n' roll, rock and soul had succeeded spectacularly. A generation that endured one of the most trying decades in American history, with its civil rights demonstrations, antiwar movement, political assassinations, free love, and psychedelic drugs, would never forget its music.

THE ROCKIN' '60s: A TO Z

THE ANIMALS

Alan Price (born April 19, 1942, in Fairfield, County Durham, England), organ, piano; Eric Burdon (born May 11, 1941, in Newcastle upon Tyne, England), vocals; Bryan "Chas" Chandler (born December 18, 1938, in Newcastle upon Tyne; died July 17, 1996, in London), bass; Hilton Valentine (born May 22, 1943, in North Shields, England), lead guitar; and John Steel (born February 4, 1941, in Gateshead, County Durham, England), drums. Later members included keyboardist Dave Rowberry (born December 27, 1943, in Newcastle upon Tyne, England) and drummer Barry Jenkins (born December 22, 1944, in Leicester, England).

THE ANIMALS, WITH ERIC BURDON (HULTON-DEUTSCH COLLECTION/CORBIS)

The Animals were one of the most important rhythm-and-blues-based bands to emerge from England in the mid-'60s, second in stature to only The Rolling Stones. Rivaling for a time both The Beatles and The Rolling Stones in popularity, The Animals first gained recognition on the basis of Eric Burdon's raw and often compelling vocals and Alan Price's subtle arrangements and inspired organ playing. However, The Animals faded within two years of Price's 1965 departure, and Burdon, after moving to California and recording second-rate psyche-delic music, eventually reemerged in 1970 backed by War, an American soul ensemble that soon went on to success on their own. In the meantime, Animals' bassist "Chas" Chandler "discovered" and managed Jimi Hendrix, while Price pursued a solo career that established him in England. The original Animals reunited briefly in 1977 and 1983, and Burdon toured in the early '90s with Robby Krieger and Brian Auger. The Animals were inducted into the Rock and Roll Hall of Fame in 1994.

Originally formed in 1958 in Newcastle by Alan Price as The Alan Price Combo, the group became known as The Animals sometime after Eric Burdon joined in 1962. Gaining local popularity, the band recorded with bluesman Sonny Boy Williamson at Newcastle's Club A-Go-Go in late 1963. Moving to London in January 1964, The Animals signed with manager-producer Mickie Most, who secured them a recording contract with Columbia Records (with American releases on MGM). They scored a top British and American hit with the blues classic "House of the Rising Sun" (note Price's outstanding arrangement and organ work). They followed up with Price and Burdon's "I'm Crying" and four subsequent major American and smash British hits from *Animal Tracks,* including "Don't Let Me Be Misunderstood" (previously recorded by Nina Simone), "We Gotta Get Out of This Place" (by Brill Building songwriters Barry Mann and Cynthia Weil), and "It's My Life." The Animals also managed moderate hit versions of John Lee Hooker's "Boom Boom" and Sam Cooke's "Bring It on Home to Me."

Alan Price departed for a solo career in May 1965, to be replaced by Dave Rowberry. The Animals hit with Carole King and Gerry Goffin's "Don't Bring Me Down" and Ma Rainey's "See See Rider." John Steel was replaced by Barry Jenkins in early 1966 and the rest of the group left Burdon in September 1966. Retaining The Animals' name, Eric Burdon moved to California at the beginning of 1967 and reconstituted The Animals lineup. They appeared at the Monterey International Pop Festival in June and recorded a number of second-rate psychedelic hits such as "When I Was Young," "San Franciscan Nights," "Monterey" and "Sky Pilot." Andy Summers, later with The Police, was a member of The New Animals beginning in September 1968, but the group disbanded in December.

In the meantime, Alan Price formed The Alan Price Set, hitting with a remake of Screamin' Jay Hawkins' "I Put a Spell on You" in 1966. Their one album, *The Price Is Right,* contained one of the first Randy Newman songs ever recorded, "Simon Smith and His Amazing Dancing Bear." Disbanding the group in 1968, Price teamed with Georgie Fame from 1969 to 1971 for tours and television. Fame had had a major hit with "Yeh Yeh" in 1965. Chas Chandler "discovered" Jimi Hendrix at New York's Cafe Wha in 1966 and became his first manager, producing The Jimi Hendrix Experience's first two albums. In the '70s Chandler managed the English rock band Slade.

Eric Burdon helped form the backup group War with members of Los Angeles' Night Shift and Danish harmonicist Lee Oskar. Recording two albums and the smash hit single "Spill the Wine" with Burdon for MGM, War later became a popular act in its own right. After recording an album with blues singer Jimmy Witherspoon, Burdon formed yet another band, cutting two albums for Capitol.

Alan Price reemerged in 1973 for the soundtrack recording of (and appearance in) the Lindsay Anderson film *O Lucky Man.* He recorded one other album for Warner Brothers before concentrating his activities in Great Britain. By the '80s, Price was well established in Great Britain as a performer and composer, writing scores for movies, television, and a stage musical.

The original Animals reunited for tours and the recording of *Before We Were So Rudely Interrupted* and *Ark* in 1977 and 1983, respectively. Eric Burdon performed the lead role of a downfallen rock star in the 1982 film *Comeback,* wrote an autobiography, and recorded the solo album *Wicked Man* in 1988. He toured with guitarist Robby Krieger in 1990 and keyboardist Brian Auger in 1991. The Animals were inducted into the Rock and Roll Hall of Fame in 1994. Chas Chandler died in London on July 17, 1996, while undergoing tests for an aortic aneurysm. Eric Burdon toured once again in 1997, with his new band The Flying I Band.

THE ANIMALS BIBLIOGRAPHY

Burdon, Eric. *I Used to Be an Animal, but I'm All Right Now.* Boston: Faber and Faber, 1986.

The Animals

In the Beginning	Wand	690		†
In The Beginning: Live in Newcastle	Sundazed	6001		CD
Early Animals	Pickwick	3330	'73	†
Live at the Club A Go Go (recorded 1963 in Newcastle)	Griffin	264		CD†
With Sonny Boy Williamson (recorded 1963)	Griffin	270		CD†
The Animals (with Eric Burdon)	MGM	4264	'64	†
On Tour	MGM	4281	'65	†
Animal Tracks	MGM	4305	'65	†
Best	MGM	4324	'66	†
Animalization	MGM	4384	'66	†
Animalism	MGM	4414	'66	†
Best, Volume 2	MGM	4454	'67	†
Don't Bring Me Down	Polygram	837671		CS
Best of Eric Burdon and The Animals (1966–1968)	Polydor	849388	'86/'91	CS/CD
Best	Abkco	4226	'73	†
	Abkco	4324		LP/CS/CD
Before We Were So Rudely Interrupted	Jet	790	'77	†
Looking Back	Accord	7193	'82	†
Ark	I.R.S.	70037	'83	†
Rip It to Shreds (live 1983)	I.R.S.	70043	'84	†
	I.R.S./A&M	0043	'89	CS/CD
Animal Tracks: Heavy Hits	Special Music	5027	'94	CS/CD

Eric Burdon and The Animals

Eric Is Here	MGM	4433	'67	†
	One Way	31376	'95	CD
Winds of Change	MGM	4484	'67	†
	One Way	30335	'95	CD
Twain Shall Meet	MGM	4537	'68	†
	One Way	30336	'95	CD
Every One of Us	MGM	4553	'68	†
	One Way	30337	'94	CD
Love Is	MGM	(2)4591	'68	†
	One Way	30338	'94	CD
Best	MGM	4602	'69	†

Eric Burdon and War

Eric Burdon Declares War	MGM	4663	'70	†
	Avenue	71050	'92	CS/CD
reissued as Spill the Wine	Lax	37109	'81	†
Black Man's Burdon	MGM	(2)4710	'70	†
	Rhino	(2)71193	'93	CS/CD
Love Is All Around	ABC	988	'76	†
	Rhino	71218	'93	CS/CD
Best	Avenue	71954	'95	CD

Eric Burdon and Jimmy Witherspoon

Guilty!	MGM	4791	'71	†

Eric Burdon Band

Sun Secrets	Capitol	11359	'74	†
	Lax	37110	'81	†
Stop!	Capitol	11426	'75	†

Sun Secrets/Stop	Rhino	71219	'93	CS/CD
That's Live	Inak	1704	'88	CD
Eric Burdon				
Animals' Greatest Hits Sung by Eric Burdon	Special Music	4919		CS/CD
Eric Burdon's Greatest Animal Hits	Pair	1209		CD
Wicked Man	GNP Crescendo	2194	'88	LP/CS/CD
The Unreleased Eric Burdon	Blue Wave	117	'92	CS/CD
Greatest Animal Hits	Avenue	71708	'94	CD
Alan Price				
The Price Is Right	Parrot	71018	'68	†
	London	71018	'73	†
O Lucky Man! (soundtrack)	Warner Brothers	2710	'73	†
	Warner Brothers	46137	'96	CD
Between Today and Yesterday	Warner Brothers	2783	'74	†
Alan Price	United Artists	809	'77	†
Lucky Day	Jet	35710	'79	†
Rising Sun	Jet	36510	'80	†
House of the Rising Sun	Townhouse	7126	'81	†
Hilton Valentine				
All in Your Head	Capitol	330	'70	†

THE ASSOCIATION

Gary "Jules" Alexander (born September 25, 1943, in Chattanooga, Tennessee), lead guitar, vocals; Terry Kirkman (born December 12, 1941, in Salinas, Kansas), brass, reeds, percussion, vocals; Jim Yester (born November 24, 1939, in Birmingham, Alabama), rhythm guitar, keyboards, vocals; Russ Giguere (born October 18, 1943, in Portsmouth, New Hampshire), guitar, vocals; Brian Cole (born September 8, 1942, in Tacoma, Washington; died August 2, 1972, in Los Angeles), bass, vocals; and Ted Beuchel, Jr. (born December 2, 1942, in San Pedro, California), drums.

Hitting in 1966 with the psychedelic classic "Along Comes Mary" on Valiant Records, The Association nonetheless achieved their greatest success with the softer and more urbane sound of pop hits such as "Cherish," "Windy," and "Never My Love" through 1968. The Association suffered a crippling blow with the death of group mentor Brian Cole in 1972, yet Russ Giguere and second-generation member Larry Ramos reconstituted the group for performances well into the '80s.

Debuting at the Ice House in Pasadena, California, in November 1965, The Association signed with the small local label Valiant in 1966. Among the group's members was Terry Kirkman, who had performed in local coffeehouses with Frank Zappa. Their debut single, "Along Comes Mary," became a near-smash pop hit despite its apparent reference to marijuana. They quickly adopted a gentler, romantic sound for the top pop hit "Cherish," written by Kirkman. After Warner Brothers bought Valiant Records in April 1967, the group continued to exploit the formula through 1968 with "Windy," "Never My Love," and "Everything That Touches You."

Alexander left The Association in early 1968, to be replaced by Larry Ramos of The New Christy Minstrels. The group subsequently recorded the soundtrack to *Goodbye Columbus* and experimented with a more progressive sound until disbanding after the death of Brian Cole in 1972. Russ Giguere had left in July 1970 and recorded a solo album for

Warner Brothers. The surviving members of the group reunited in the early '80s, and Giguere and Ramos continued to front the band throughout the decade.

THE ASSOCIATION BIBLIOGRAPHY

The Association. *Crank Your Spreaders.* Los Angeles: Price/Stern/Sloan, 1966, 1969.

The Association

And Then . . . Along Comes The Association	Valiant	5002	'66	†
	Warner Brothers	1702	'69	†
Renaissance	Valiant	5004	'67	†
	Warner Brothers	1704	'69	†
Insight Out	Warner Brothers	1696	'67	†
Birthday	Warner Brothers	1733	'68	†
Greatest Hits	Warner Brothers	1767	'68	CS/CD
Goodbye Columbus (soundtrack)	Warner Brothers	1786	'69	†
The Association	Warner Brothers	1800	'69	†
"Live"	Warner Brothers	1868	'70	†
Stop Your Motor	Warner Brothers	1927	'71	†
Waterbeds in Trinidad	Columbia	31348	'72	†
Songs That Made Them Famous	Pair	1061	'84/'86	CD

Russ Giguere

Hexagram 16	Warner Brothers	1910	'71	†

BURT BACHARACH

Born May 12, 1928, in Kansas City, Missouri.

With Hal David, Burt Bacharach formed one of the most successful professional songwriting teams in popular music history, writing literally dozens of hit songs. Their compositions featured David's Tin Pan Alley—style lyrics and Bacharach's uncommon rhythms and distinctive melodies, bridges and modulations. In arranging horn and string parts for The Drifters in the early '60s and for Dionne Warwick throughout the '60s, Bacharach helped change the sound of contemporary rhythm-and-blues and soul music. After a fallow period during the '70s, Bacharach reemerged in the '80s with a number of huge hit compositions in collaboration with lyricist Carole Bayer Sager, including Dionne Warwick's "That's What Friends Are For."

Burt Bacharach grew up in New York and studied music theory and composition at McGill University in Montreal in the early '50s. He later worked as a pianist and arranger and served as Marlene Dietrich's music director from 1956 to 1958. He subsequently teamed with lyricist Hal David (born May 25, 1921, in New York), who had been writing song lyrics since 1943. Early successful collaborations included "The Story of My Life" for Marty Robbins and "Magic Moments" for Perry Como. Initially, the two often worked separately. They were associated with a number of hits, such as Sarah Vaughan's "Broken-Hearted Melody" (by David and Sherman Edwards), Gene McDaniels' "Tower of Strength" (by Bacharach and Bob Hilliard), and The Shirelles' "Baby, It's You" (by Bacharach, Mack David, and Barney Williams).

In the early '60s, Burt Bacharach arranged and scored sessions for The Drifters, meeting Dionne Warwick. He wrote The Drifters' "Mexican Divorce" (with Bob Hilliard) and Chuck Jackson's smash rhythm-and-blues and major pop hit "Any Day Now." Bacharach and

David began working together regularly in 1962, collaborating on many smash hits. These included Gene Pitney's "Only Love Can Break a Heart" and "Twenty Four Hours from Tulsa," Dusty Springfield's "Wishin' and Hopin,'" and Jackie DeShannon's "What the World Needs Now Is Love." Into the '70s, the duo provided Dionne Warwick with more than thirty chart records, among them being "Anyone Who Had a Heart," "Walk On By," "Message to Michael," "Do You Know the Way to San Jose?" and "I Say a Little Prayer."

Throughout the '60s, Bacharach and David composed for films, providing the title songs to *What's New Pussycat?* (by Tom Jones, 1965) and *Alfie* (by Dionne Warwick, 1967), as well as "The Look of Love" (by Dusty Springfield, 1967) from *Casino Royale,* and the top hit "Raindrops Keep Falling on My Head" (by B. J. Thomas, 1969) from *Butch Cassidy and the Sundance Kid.* In the late '60s, the two collaborated on the smash Broadway musical *Promises, Promises,* from which Dionne Warwick scored two hits, the title song and "I'll Never Fall in Love Again."

Although Burt Bacharach and Hal David provided smash hits for The Carpenters ("Close to You") and The Fifth Dimension ("One Less Bell to Answer") in 1970, they soon broke up the team. Bacharach and Dionne Warwick also ended their professional relationship in the early '70s. During the '70s, Bacharach performed in public to enthusiastic audiences, both live and on television. Having embarked on his own recording career in 1966, Bacharach recorded the symphonic suite, *Woman,* with the Houston Symphony in 1979.

In 1981, Burt Bacharach began collaborating with lyricist Carole Bayer Sager, born in New York City on March 8, 1946. She had provided the lyrics for a number of smash hit songs, including "Groovy Kind of Love" (The Mindbenders, 1966), "Midnight Blue" and "Don't Cry Out Loud" (Melissa Manchester, 1975 and 1978, respectively), "When I Need You" (Leo Sayer, 1977), and "Nobody Does It Better" (Carly Simon, 1977). Their first collaboration, with Peter Allen and Christopher Cross, yielded the top hit "Best That You Can Do" as the theme to the film *Arthur* for Cross in 1981.

The couple married in 1982 and soon composed the hits "Making Love" for Roberta Flack and "Heartlight," with and for Neil Diamond. In 1986, they supplied the top hits "On My Own" to Patti Labelle and Michael McDonald, and "That's What Friends Are For" to Dionne Warwick with Stevie Wonder and others. The profits to "That's What Friends Are For"—over $1.5 million—were donated to the American Foundation for AIDS Research. The following year, Bacharach toured with Warwick, and Bacharach and Sager provided Warwick and Jeffrey Osborne with the major hit "Love Power." Burt Bacharach and Carole Bayer Sager divorced in 1991. In 1995, Burt Bacharach collaborated with Elvis Costello on "God Give Me Strength" from the *Grace of My Heart* soundtrack. Later, the two worked together on 1998's *Painted from Memory.*

Burt Bacharach

Man! His Songs	Kapp	3447	'66	†
Plays His Hits	Kapp	3577	'69	†
	MCA		'65	†
Casino Royale (soundtrack)	Colgems	5005	'67	†
	Varèse Sarabande	5265	'90	CS/CD
Reach Out	A&M	4131	'67	†
	A&M	3102		†
Make It Easy on Yourself	A&M	4188	'69	†
Butch Cassidy and the Sundance Kid (soundtrack)	A&M	3159	'69	CD
Burt Bacharach	A&M	3501	'71	†
Living Together	A&M	3527	'74	†
Greatest Hits	A&M	3661	'74	†
	A&M	3321	'89	CS/CD

Futures	A&M	4622	'77	†
Burt Bacharach	A&M	2521	'87	CD†
The Look of Love: The Burt Bacharach Collection	Rhino	(3)75339	'98	CD
Burt Bacharach with the Houston Symphony				
Woman	A&M	3709	'79	†
Elvis Costello with Burt Bacharach				
Painted from Memory	Mercury	5380022	'98	CS/CD

JOAN BAEZ

Born January 9, 1941, on Staten Island, New York.

JOAN BAEZ (LEIF SKOOGFORS/CORBIS)

One of the finest female vocalists to emerge from the early '60s folk scene, Joan Baez was the first folk singer of the era to achieve massive international success. One of the first solo folk singers to record best-selling albums of traditional folk material, she subsequently helped introduce Bob Ðylan to a wider audience as she became one of the first folk singers to become involved with the "protest" movement. Associated with the protest classic "We Shall Overcome," Baez later enjoyed popularity as a song interpreter before emerging as a singer-songwriter, particularly with 1975's *Diamonds and Rust* album. Although accorded star status in Europe, she was reduced to mere celebrity status in the United States and remained without an American record label for much of the '80s. While continuing to involve herself with protest and freedom movements internationally in the '90s, Joan Baez recorded her first album in years for a major label in 1992.

Joan Baez started performing in public, accompanying herself on guitar, at small clubs around Cambridge and Boston in the late '50s and soon graduated to New York's Greenwich Village. Successful appearances at the 1959 and 1960 Newport Folk Festivals followed, with Baez moving to California in 1961. She met Bob Dylan in April 1961 at Gerde's Folk City in Greenwich Village and spent considerable time with him between 1963 and 1965. Signed to Vanguard Records, her first three albums consisted of standard folk fare, primarily traditional English and American ballads, and her second, *Vol. 2,* proved her commercial breakthrough. Her fourth album, *In Concert, Part 2,* featured "We Shall Overcome," the song that became the protest anthem of the '60s. That and subsequent albums contained her versions of songs by then-unrecognized folk artists such as Dylan ("Don't Think Twice," "It's All Over Now, Baby Blue," and others) and Phil Ochs ("There but for Fortune"). In June 1965, she established the Institute for the Study of Nonviolence in Carmel, California, beginning a lifelong commitment to nonviolence and protest.

With 1967's *Joan,* Joan Baez began recording songs by contemporary songwriters such as Tim Hardin ("If I Were a Carpenter"), Simon and Garfunkel, and Lennon and McCartney. Between 1968 and 1973, she recorded six albums in Nashville. *Any Day Now,* released in 1969, was a double-record set comprised entirely of songs by Bob Dylan. *One Day at a Time* included the labor anthem "Joe Hill," Jagger and Richards' "No Expectations," and Steve Young's "Seven Bridges Road." She also covered material by songwriters such as Willie Nelson, Hoyt Axton, and John Prine, achieving her only major hit in 1971 with Robbie Robertson's "The Night They Drove Old Dixie Down."

Joan Baez began writing her own songs in the early '70s and signed with A&M Records in May 1972. She placed six of her songs on *Come from the Shadows,* including the undisguised "To Bobby," as well as sister Mimi Farina's "In the Quiet Morning." Her 1975 *Diamonds and Rust* album contained her own compositions "Winds of the Old Days" and the hit title song, plus John Prine's "Hello in There" and Janis Ian's "Jesse." During 1975 and 1976, Baez toured with Bob Dylan's curious Rolling Thunder Revue. After two final albums for A&M, she switched to Portrait Records (reissued on Epic) for *Blowin' Away* and *Honest Lullaby.*

Joan Baez confirmed her commitment to humanitarian causes with the 1979 formation of the human rights organization, Humanitas International. During the '80s, she toured internationally in support of human rights organizations, including Poland's Solidarity movement and Palestinian civil disobedience groups. In 1985, she sang on the Amnesty International tour and appeared at Live Aid. Her second autobiography, *And a Voice to Sing With,* was published in 1987, the year she began recording for the small Gold Castle label. In 1992, in order to reinvigorate her musical career, Joan Baez ceased operation of Humanitas International. She recorded her first major label release in thirteen years, *Play Me Backwards,* for Virgin and later recorded *Ring Them Bells* for Guardian Records.

JOAN BAEZ BIBLIOGRAPHY

Baez, Joan. *And a Voice to Sing With: A Memoir.* New York: Summit Books, 1987; New York: New American Library, 1988.

———. *Daybreak.* New York: Dial Press, 1968.

——— and David Harris. *Coming Out.* New York: Pocket Books, 1971.

Fuss, Charles J. *Joan Baez: A Bio-Bibliography.* Westport, CT: Greenwood Press, 1996.

Garza, Hedda. *Joan Baez.* New York: Chelsea House, 1991.

Swanekamp, Joan. *Diamonds and Rust: A Bibliography and Discography of Joan Baez.* Ann Arbor, MI: Pierian Press, 1980.

Joan Baez with Bill Wood and Ted Alvizos

The Best of Joan Baez (recorded 1959)	Squire	33001	'63	†

Joan Baez

Joan Baez	Vanguard	2077	'60	CS/CD
Joan Baez, Volume 2	Vanguard	2097	'61	CS/CD
In Concert	Vanguard	2122	'62/'90	CS/CD

In Concert, Part 2	Vanguard	2123	'63/'90	CS/CD
Joan Baez in Concert	Vanguard	(2)113/14	'88	CD
Very Early Joan (recorded live 1961–1963)	Vanguard	7446/7	'83	CS/CD
Five	Vanguard	79160	'64	CS/CD
Farewell Angelina	Vanguard	79200	'65	CS/CD
Noël	Vanguard	79230	'66/'92	CS/CD
Joan	Vanguard	79240	'67	CS/CD
Baptism	Vanguard	79275	'68/'95	CS/CD
Any Day Now	Vanguard	(2)79306/7	'68	CS
	Vanguard	79306/7		CD
David's Album	Vanguard	79308	'69/'95	CS/CD
One Day at a Time	Vanguard	79310	'70/'96	CS/CD
Blessed Are . . .	Vanguard	6570/1	'71	†
Carry It On (soundtrack)	Vanguard	79313	'71/'96	CS/CD
Come from the Shadows	A&M	4339	'72	†
	A&M	3103		CS/CD†
Where Are You Now, My Son	A&M	4390	'73	†
Gracias a la Vida—Here's to Life	A&M	3614	'74	†
Diamonds and Rust	A&M	4527	'75	†
	A&M	3233	'84	CS/CD
	Mobile Fidelity	646	'95	CD
From Every Stage	A&M	(2)6506	'76	CS
	A&M	6506		CD
Gulf Winds	A&M	4603	'76	†
Blowin' Away	Epic	34697	'77/'90	CD
Honest Lullaby	Epic	35766	'79	†
	Epic/Legacy	35766	'90	CD
Recently	Gold Castle	71304	'87	LP/CS/CD†
Diamonds and Rust in the Bullring	Gold Castle	71321	'89	LP/CS/CD†
Speaking of Dreams	Gold Castle	71324	'89	LP/CS/CD†
Brothers in Arms	Gold Castle	71363	'91	LP/CS/CD†
Play Me Backwards	Virgin	86458	'92	CS†/CD
Ring Them Bells	Guardian	34989	'95	CS/CD

Joan Baez Anthologies

The First Ten Years	Vanguard	6560/1	'70	CS/CD
Hits Greatest and Others	Vanguard	79332	'73	CS/CD
Ballad Book	Vanguard	(2)41/2	'72	CS
Ballad Book, Volume 1	Vanguard	73107		CS
Ballad Book, Volume 2	Vanguard	73115		CS
Contemporary Ballad Book	Vanguard	(2)49/50	'74	CS
Lovesong Album	Vanguard	79/80	'76	CS
The Country Music Album	Vanguard	105/6	'79/'91	CS/CD
The Night They Drove Old Dixie Down	Vanguard	73119	'89	CS
Rare, Live and Classic	Vanguard	(3)125-127	'93	CD†
Selections from *Rare, Live and Classic*	Vanguard	705	'93	CD
Best	A&M	4668	'77	†
	A&M	3234	'84	CS/CD
Joan Baez	A&M	2506	'87	CD
Greatest Hits	A&M	0510	'96	CS/CD

THE BAND

Jaime Robert "Robbie" Robertson (born July 5, 1944, in Toronto, Canada), electric, acoustic, and bass guitars, piano, vocals; Richard Manuel (born April 3, 1944, in Stratford, Ontario; died March 4, 1986, in Winter Park, Florida), keyboards, drums, vocals; Garth Hudson (born August 2, 1942, in London, Ontario), keyboards, accordion, brass, woodwinds; Rick Danko (born December 9, 1943, in Simcoe, Ontario), bass, fiddle, vocals; and Levon Helm (born May 26, 1943, in Marvell, Arkansas), drums, mandolin, vocals.

One of the United States' most popular bands between the late '60s and mid '70s, The Band was ironically manned by four Canadians and only one American. With only an underground reputation despite years of playing together, The Band achieved their first recognition as Bob Dylan's backup band, later breaking through with the landmark *Music from Big Pink* and *The Band* albums. In refreshing contrast to psychedelic music, The Band featured a country-gospel sound supplemented by electric instrumentation and loose yet precise musicianship, combined with oblique vocal harmonies and incisive songwriting. Their songs frequently reflected an Americana of yore, as evidenced by the Robbie Robertson classic, "The Night They Drove Old Dixie Down." Following The Band's dissolution with 1976's *The Last Waltz,* the members pursued individual careers, reuniting without Robertson in the early '80s. The Band was inducted into the Rock and Roll Hall of Fame in 1994.

The evolution of The Band began in the person of Levon Helm when he and several other Arkansans moved to Canada in 1958 to back Ronnie Hawkins as The Hawks. Having pursued an unspectacular career as a country musician, Hawkins turned to rock 'n' roll, hitting with "Forty Days" and "Mary Lou" in 1959. One by one, Canadians Rick Danko, Richard Manuel, Garth Hudson, and Robbie Robertson joined the group. They recorded a stunning version of "Who Do You Love," featuring Robertson's psychedelic lead guitar work, but the group left Hawkins in early 1964 to tour East Coast clubs as Levon and The Hawks, under Helm's leadership. In 1965, Robertson, Hudson, and Helm assisted white blues artist John Hammond, Jr., in recording his *So Many Roads* album for Vanguard.

After the release of his first rock-oriented album, *Bringing It All Back Home,* Bob Dylan recruited the band while in New Jersey in the summer of 1965. Helm, Robertson, and Al Kooper backed Dylan at his controversial Forest Hills concert in late August 1965. Without the recalcitrant Helm, the group toured as Dylan's backup band from the fall of 1965 until the spring of 1966. Following Dylan's much-publicized motorcycle accident in July, Levon Helm was summoned from Arkansas, and the group and Dylan retired to upstate New York to rehearse and record the so-called *Basement Tapes.* Available for years only on bootleg albums of questionable legality, this material was eventually released officially in 1975.

While in upstate New York, the group, known simply as The Band, recorded their first album. Released in mid-1968, *Music from Big Pink* contained one Dylan song, "I Shall Be Released," and two Dylan collaborations, "Tears of Rage" (with Manuel) and "This Wheel's on Fire" (with Danko). It also included several excellent songs by chief songwriter Robertson ("The Weight," "Caledonia Mission," and "Chest Fever") and Manuel ("We Can Talk" and "Lonesome Suzie").

Making their debut in February 1969 at Bill Graham's Winterland in San Francisco, The Band's second album proved their commercial breakthrough and revealed a growing maturation of Robertson's songwriting talents. Generally regarded as the group's masterpiece, *The Band* included his classic "The Night They Drove Old Dixie Down," as well as "Across the Great Divide," "Up on Cripple Creek," a major pop hit, and "Rag Mama Rag," a major British hit. Their next album, *Stage Fright,* yielded only one minor hit, "Time to Kill," yet contained several memorable cuts, including the title song, "The Shape I'm In," and "Just Another Whistle Stop." In 1970, Robertson began his outside musical activities, producing Jesse Winchester's debut album. The Band's *Cahoots* album contained several intriguing

Robertson songs ("Smoke Signal" and "Shootout in Chinatown") as well as the collaborative "Life Is a Carnival." After the live *Rock of Ages* album, the group recorded the amusing *Moondog Matinee,* which consisted primarily of old rock 'n' roll songs. In July 1973, The Band appeared before the largest crowd in rock history with The Grateful Dead and The Allman Brothers at Watkins Glen, New York. Recordings from the show were eventually released in 1995.

In 1974, The Band again backed their old mentor and friend Bob Dylan for his *Planet Waves* album and his first tour since 1965. From the tour came *Before the Flood,* an album combining both Dylan and Band favorites. Subsequently, The Band's first album of original material since 1971, *Northern Lights—Southern Cross,* was critically acclaimed as their best since *The Band.* Consisting entirely of Robertson songs, the album included "Acadian Driftwood," "Ophelia," and "Jupiter Hollow."

Again busy outside the group, Robbie Robertson produced Neil Diamond's *Beautiful Noise* album in 1976. Later that year, The Band announced their retirement after more than 15 years on the road. Only days after recording their final album as a group, *Islands,* they made their final appearance at Bill Graham's Winterland on Thanksgiving night, 1976. Billed as "The Last Waltz," this final show featured performances by a number of stars and superstars of rock, from Bob Dylan and Eric Clapton to Joni Mitchell, Neil Young, and Van Morrison. Both a film and an album from the show were released the following spring.

Subsequently, both Rick Danko and Levon Helm recorded on their own, Helm initially with The RCO All-Stars (which included Steve Cropper, Paul Butterfield, and Dr. John), later with his own group. Helm garnered an Academy Award nomination for his supporting role as Loretta Lynn's father in *Coal Miner's Daughter.* Robbie Robertson cowrote, produced, and costarred in the equivocal 1980 film *Carny* with Gary Busey and Jodie Foster. That year, Robertson began working as director Martin Scorsese's musical supervisor, working on *Raging Bull,* 1983's *The King of Comedy,* and 1986's *The Color of Money.* In the meantime, Garth Hudson became Los Angeles' premier sessions accordion player.

The Band reunited, without Robbie Robertson, for touring in 1983, augmented by the Cate Brothers Band. However, while on tour in Florida, Richard Manuel hanged himself in a motel bathroom in Winter Park on the night of March 4, 1986. Levon Helm continued his film work (*Smooth Talk, End of the Line*), whereas Robertson recorded *Robbie Robertson* and *Storyville.* Helm and Rick Danko toured with Ringo Starr during his 1989 American tour. In 1991, Danko, Helm, and Garth Hudson reunited as The Band with three others to tour and later record *Jericho* for Rhino Records. The Band was inducted into the Rock and Roll Hall of Fame in 1994. During the year, a number of Native American musicians billed as The Red Road Ensemble recorded the music, composed by Robertson, for the three-part, six-hour TBS cable network miniseries *The Native Americans.* In 1998, Capitol Records issued Robertson's *Contact from the Underworld of Red Boy.*

THE BAND BIBLIOGRAPHY

Helm, Levon, with Stephen Davis. *This Wheel's on Fire: Levon Helm and the Story of The Band.* New York: William Morrow, 1993.

Hoskyns, Barney. *Across the Great Divide: The Band and America.* New York: Hyperion, 1993.

Ronnie Hawkins and The Hawks

Ronnie Hawkins	Roulette	25078	'59	†
Mr. Dynamo	Roulette	25102	'60	†
Folk Ballads	Roulette	25120	'60	†
Ronnie Hawkins Sings the Songs of Hank Williams	Roulette	25137	'60	†

Ronnie Hawkins with The Band	Roulette	42045	'70	†
The Best of Ronnie Hawkins and The Hawks	Rhino	70966	'90	CS/CD
The Band				
Music from Big Pink	Capitol	2955	'68	†
	Capitol	46069	'87	CS/CD
	Mobile Fidelity	00527	'90	CD†
The Band	Capitol	132	'69	†
	Capitol	16296	'84	†
	Capitol	46493	'88	CD
Stage Fright	Capitol	425	'70	†
	Capitol	16006		†
	Capitol	93593	'90	CD
Cahoots	Capitol	651	'71	†
	Capitol	16003		†
	Capitol	48420	'94	CD
Rock of Ages	Capitol	(2)11045	'72	†
	Capitol	(2)16008/9		†
	Capitol	(2)93595	'90	CD
Live at Watkins Glen	Capitol	31742	'95	CD
Moondog Matinee	Capitol	11214	'73	†
	Capitol	16004		†
	Capitol	93592	'90	CD
Northern Lights—Southern Cross	Capitol	11440	'75	†
	Capitol	16005		†
	Capitol	93594	'91	CD†
Best	Capitol	11553	'76	†
	Capitol	16331	'85	†
	Capitol	46070	'89	CS/CD
Islands	Capitol	11602	'77	†
	Capitol	16007		†
	Capitol	93591	'91	CD†
Anthology	Capitol	11856	'78	†
	Capitol	48419	'89	CD†
To Kingdom Come: The Definitive Collection	Capitol	(2)92169	'89	CD†
Across the Great Divide	Capitol	(3)89565	'94	CD
The Last Waltz	Warner Brothers	(3)3146	'78	†
	Warner Brothers	(2)3146	'88	CS/CD
Jericho	Rhino	71564	'93	CS/CD
High on the Hog	Pyramid/Rhino	72404	'96	CS/CD
Jubilation	River North	161420	'98	CS/CD
The Band and Bob Dylan				
The Basement Tapes	Columbia	(2)33682	'75	CS/CD
Planet Waves	Asylum	1003	'74	†
	Columbia	37637	'89	CS/CD
Before the Flood	Asylum	(2)201	'74	†
	Columbia	(2)37661	'86	CS/CD
Rick Danko				
Rick Danko	Arista	4141	'77	†
Levon Helm and The RCO All-Stars				
Levon Helm and The RCO All-Stars	ABC	1017	'77	†
	Mobile Fidelity	00761	'92	CD†

Levon Helm

Levon Helm	ABC	1089	'78	†
	Mobile Fidelity	00759	'92	CD†
American Son	MCA	5120	'80	†
Levon Helm	Capitol	12201	'82	†

Robbie Robertson

Robbie Robertson	Geffen	24160	'87	CS/CD
	Mobile Fidelity	618	'94	CD†
Storyville	Geffen	24303	'91	CS†/CD
Contact from the Underworld of Red Boy	Capitol	54243	'98	CS/CD

Robbie Robertson and The Red Road Ensemble

The Native Americans	Capitol	28295	'94	CS/CD

JEFF BARRY AND ELLIE GREENWICH

Jeff Barry (born April 3, 1938, in Brooklyn, New York) and Ellie Greenwich (born October 23, 1940, in Brooklyn, New York).

Jeff Barry and Ellie Greenwich comprised one of the most successful Brill Building songwriting-production teams to supply hit compositions to Phil Spector and Jerry Leiber and Mike Stoller in the early '60s. Their compositions included the classics "Da Doo Ron Ron," "Be My Baby," and "Chapel of Love."

Recording a number of unsuccessful singles between 1959 and 1962, Jeff Barry became a professional songwriter at the beginning of the '60s. His early hit compositions included "Tell Laura I Love Her" for Ray Peterson (1960) and "Chip Chip" for Gene McDaniels (1962). In 1962, he met and married songwriter Ellie Greenwich. The two collaborated on a number of hits in conjunction with producer Phil Spector on the Philles label in 1963: "Da Doo Ron Ron" and "Then He Kissed Me" for The Crystals, "Be My Baby" and "Baby I Love You" for the Ronettes, and "Wait Till My Bobby Gets Home" for Darlene Love. Spector and Greenwich also cowrote Love's "(Today I Met) The Boy I'm Gonna Marry." That year, Barry and Greenwich also recorded an album for Jubilee Records as The Raindrops, hitting with "What a Guy" and "The Kind of Boy You Can't Forget."

Signed to write and produce for Jerry Leiber and Mike Stoller's Red Bird label in 1964, Jeff Barry and Ellie Greenwich composed a number of hits for several different girl groups: "Chapel of Love" (with Phil Spector) and "People Say" for The Dixie Cups, "I Wanna Love Him So Bad" for The Jellybeans, and "Leader of the Pack" (with George "Shadow" Morton) for The Shangri-Las. Additionally, two other Barry-Greenwich songs became hits in 1964: "Maybe I Know" by Lesley Gore and "Do Wah Diddy Diddy" by Manfred Mann.

By 1966, the couple had divorced yet continued to work together. When Red Bird was sold, they took fellow songwriter Neil Diamond to Bert Berns' Bang Records, where they produced his first three albums for the label. During 1966, the Barry-Greenwich composition "Hanky Panky" (an old Raindrops song) became a hit for Tommy James; "River Deep—Mountain High," cowritten with Phil Spector and recorded by Ike and Tina Turner, was conspicuously unsuccessful and led to Spector's withdrawal from the music scene for several years. Subsequent production chores for Barry included The Monkees ("I'm a Believer") and the studio group The Archies, who had a smash hit with Barry and Andy Kim's "Sugar, Sugar" in 1969. Earlier that year, "I Can Hear Music," composed by Barry, Greenwich, and Spector, had become a major hit for The Beach Boys.

Jeff Barry became a producer for A&M Records in 1971, with little success. Ellie Greenwich recorded solo albums for United Artists Records and Verve Records in 1968 and 1973, respectively. Barry later composed the 1977 country hit "I Honestly Love You" for Olivia Newton-John with Peter Allen, and produced Tommy James' *Midnight Rider* album and John Travolta's second album.

Ellie Greenwich continued to write songs in the '80s. In 1984, she became involved in the musical revue *Leader of the Pack,* based on her life and career. An original cast album featuring Greenwich and Darlene Love was issued by Elektra Records the following year.

The Raindrops

The Raindrops	Jubilee	5023	'63	†

Ellie Greenwich

Composes, Produces and Sings	United Artists	6648	'68	†
Let It Be Written, Let It Be Sung	Verve	65091	'73	†
	Verve/Polydor	825531	'85	†

Leader of the Pack

Original Cast	Elektra	(2)60409	'85	†
Excerpts	Elektra	60420	'85	†

THE BEACH BOYS

Brian Wilson (born June 20, 1942, in Hawthorne, California), bass, keyboards, vocals; Dennis Wilson (born December 4, 1944, in Hawthorne; died December 28, 1983, in Marina del Rey, California), drums, vocals; Carl Wilson (born December 21, 1946, in Hawthorne; died February 6, 1998, in Los Angeles), lead guitar, vocals; Mike Love (born March 15, 1941, in Los Angeles), lead vocals, saxophone; and Al Jardine (born September 3, 1942, in Lima, Ohio), rhythm guitar, vocals. Bruce Johnston (born June 27, 1944, in Chicago) joined in 1965, left in 1972, and returned in 1978.

America's most popular group of the '60s, The Beach Boys were perhaps the first white rock 'n' roll group to employ complex vocal arrangements to create a distinctive ensemble sound. The biggest popularizers of surf music, The Beach Boys established themselves with songs of their own creation at a time dominated by artists who recorded songs provided by professional songwriters. With Brian Wilson writing the songs, singing the falsetto parts, arranging the other voices, and producing the group's records, The Beach Boys were one of the first self-contained rock groups, using studios, musicians, and technicians of their own choosing. Wilson's increasing sophistication of production, beginning with the "California Girls" single of 1965 and culminating in "Good Vibrations" and the *Pet Sounds* album, revealed a unique use of a wide range of instrumentation, styles, and sound effects rivaled at the time only by The Beatles (under George Martin) and Phil Spector. Forming one of the first artist's custom labels, Brother, in 1967 (one year before The Beatles' Apple), The Beach Boys experienced their first decline in popularity with Wilson's inability to complete the *Smile* album, one of the most famous unreleased albums of all time. Suffering an even more severe decline with Brian's recession from the group following 1971's *Surf's Up* album, The Beach Boys staged a modest comeback with Brian's return for 1976's *15 Big Ones,* only to recede from the music scene thereafter. Debuting in the Nevada casino arena in 1980, The Beach Boys were inducted into the Rock and Roll Hall of Fame in 1988.

Formed in 1961 by the Wilson brothers, cousin Mike Love, and friend Al Jardine as Kenny and The Cadets and Carl and The Passions, then The Pendletones, The Beach Boys recorded the regional hit "Surfin'" for the small local label X in 1961. They debuted in Long Beach on New Year's Eve 1961, but Jardine soon departed, to be replaced by David Marks for more than a year. Signed to Capitol Records in the summer of 1962, The Beach Boys issued smash hits ad nauseam on the southern California themes of surfing, cars and motorcycles, girls, and high school, virtually all written by Brian Wilson. Early hits included

"Surfin' Safari," the smash remake of Chuck Berry's "Sweet Little Sixteen," and "Surfin' U.S.A.," backed with "Shut Down." Featuring such ballads as the title song (a near-smash hit) and "In My Room" (a major hit) beginning with *Surfer Girl,* the group's first album produced by Brian Wilson, The Beach Boys scored smash hits with "Be True to Your School" and "Fun, Fun, Fun," and the top hit "I Get Around," backed by the major hit ballad "Don't Worry Baby." "Wendy" proved only a moderate hit, but *The Beach Boys Today* contained two near-smash hits, "When I Grow Up (To Be a Man)" and "Dance, Dance, Dance," and the top hit "Help Me, Rhonda."

Conducting their first major U.S. tour in September 1964, The Beach Boys' *Concert* album, recorded in Sacramento, California, became the first live album to top the album charts. However, Brian Wilson suffered a nervous breakdown in December and ceased touring with the group. With Carl Wilson becoming the on-stage leader and Al Jardine taking over Brian's falsetto parts, the group was briefly augmented by sessions guitarist Glen Campbell, who was replaced by Bruce Johnston in April 1965. Johnston, an early associate of Sandy Nelson and Phil Spector, had formed a partnership with Terry Melcher in 1963 that yielded hits under the names The Rip Chords ("Hey Little Cobra") and Bruce and Terry ("Summer Means Fun").

Relieved of his arduous touring duties, Brian Wilson concentrated on writing for The Beach Boys. With Bruce Johnston's recording debut with the group, the smash hit "California Girls," Brian started using elaborate production techniques on the group's recordings. While the rest of The Beach Boys were on tour, Brian began working on his *Pet Sounds* epic, employing scores of studio musicians and utilizing advanced studio techniques. Although perplexed by Brian's work on the album in their absence, the returning group persevered to complete the critically acclaimed masterpiece. However, despite the lush orchestral sound and the inclusion of songs such as "God Only Knows" (with lead vocals by Carl Wilson), "Wouldn't It Be Nice," "I Just Wasn't Made for These Times," "Caroline No," and the folk song "Sloop John B.," *Pet Sounds* sold poorly compared to previous releases.

Severely disappointed, Brian Wilson nonetheless initiated work on the next album, tentatively titled *Smile,* with lyricist Van Dyke Parks. While deeply immersed in the project, Capitol Records issued the monumental single "Good Vibrations." Taking more than six months to complete, using ninety hours of studio time in seventeen sessions, "Good Vibrations," with Carl Wilson on lead vocals, became a top hit in the fall of 1966. Meanwhile, the already troubled Brian, working against the perceived competition of Phil Spector and The Beatles, began behaving erratically as rumors of heavy drug use circulated. For whatever reason, *Smile* was not issued. *Smiley Smile* was released in its place on the group's recently formed custom label, Brother Records, distributed by Capitol. The album contained several songs from the abortive Wilson-Parks collaboration, including the major hit "Heroes and Villains."

Pulling out of a scheduled appearance at the Monterey International Pop Festival in June 1967, The Beach Boys met guru Maharishi Mahesh Yogi in December. Their fascination with his transcendental meditation, particularly in the person of Mike Love, culminated in a near-disastrous tour with the Maharishi in the spring of 1968. *Friends* reflected the group's conversion to TM, while *20/20,* their final album of new material for Capitol, featured the major hit "Do It Again" and a minor hit remake of the Phil Spector–Jeff Barry–Ellie Greenwich song "I Can Hear Music," with lead vocals by Carl Wilson.

The Beach Boys switched to Warner Brothers/Reprise Records in 1970, reestablishing Brother Records under that company's distributorship. The Beach Boys appeared to be emerging from their doldrums that year with a successful performance at the Big Sur Folk Festival and the release of the underrated *Sunflower* album, to which Dennis Wilson contributed four songs. However, Brian's withdrawal from the group as songwriter and producer with the *Surf's Up* album and his traumatizing appearance at the Whiskey-A-Go-Go in November 1970 left the rest to their own devices. Two old *Smile* songs, "Surf's Up" and the hastily completed "Sail on Sailor," were later issued as singles. Dennis Wilson appeared with

James Taylor in the 1971 film *Two Lane Blacktop* and Johnston left the group in early 1972. By the beginning of 1974, producer James William Guercio (Blood, Sweat and Tears, Chicago) had joined on bass.

The Beach Boys enjoyed a revival with the release of older Capitol material on *Endless Summer* (which remained on the album charts nearly three years) and *Spirit of America*. The Beach Boys toured with Chicago in the spring of 1975 and, during 1976, Brian Wilson rejoined the others for an hour-long documentary aired on NBC in August. The album *15 Big Ones,* comprising half new original material and half remade oldies, including a smash hit version of Chuck Berry's "Rock and Roll Music," saw Brian once again producing, though eschewing the production style pioneered with *Pet Sounds*.

Bruce Johnston provided Barry Manilow with the top hit "I Write the Songs" in late 1975 and recorded *Going Public* in 1977. Dennis Wilson recorded *Pacific Ocean Blue,* regarded as a neglected masterpiece, while Mike Love recorded with both Waves and Celebration, who hit with "Almost Summer." For The Beach Boys, neither *M.I.U.* nor *L.A. (Light Album),* recorded with a returned Bruce Johnston on their new Caribou label, fared particularly well. After Dennis Wilson recorded a second solo album, The Beach Boys issued *Keepin' the Summer Alive,* produced by Johnston. In 1981, Carl Wilson became the first Beach Boy to undertake a solo tour, in support of his Caribou debut.

Mike Love became the front man for The Beach Boys during the '80s, as Brian Wilson embarked on an unorthodox rehabilitation program under therapist Eugene Landy between 1983 and 1988. Dennis Wilson, the only actual surfer in the group, drowned off Marina del Rey, California, on December 28, 1983. The Beach Boys performed at Ronald Reagan's Inaugural Gala in January 1985 and Live Aid the following July. In 1987, they scored a major hit with a remake of the surf classic "Wipeout," recorded with the Fat Boys rap group.

The Beach Boys were inducted into the Rock and Roll Hall of Fame in 1988. During the year, Brian Wilson became the last Wilson brother to release a solo album with the critically acclaimed but poor-selling *Brian Wilson* album on Sire Records. However, a second solo album, entitled *Sweet Insanity,* was rejected by Sire. The Beach Boys, without Brian Wilson, scored a top hit with "Kokomo," written by Mike Love, Terry Melcher, John Phillips, and Scott McKenzie, from the soundtrack to the Tom Cruise movie *Cocktail*. Since December 1991, the personal and business affairs of Brian Wilson have been managed by a court-appointed conservator. Producer Don Was directed the film documentary of Brian Wilson's life, *I Just Wasn't Made for These Times,* released in 1995. Wilson also worked with his *Smile* collaborator, songwriter-producer Van Dyke Parks, for *Orange Crate Art* on Warner Brothers Records. Carl Wilson died in Los Angeles on February 6, 1998, from complications of lung cancer at the age of 51.

By 1988, Brian Wilson's daughters Carnie (born April 29, 1968, in Los Angeles) and Wendy (born October 16, 1969, in Los Angeles) had formed the vocal group Wilson Phillips with Chynna Phillips, the daughter of John and Michelle Phillips of The Mamas and the Papas. Their debut album produced five hits, including the top hits "Hold On," "Release Me," and "You're in Love," but the more personal *Shadows and Light* yielded only two hits. By 1993, Wilson Phillips had disbanded. Carnie and Wendy Wilson soon recorded the Christmas album *Hey Santa!* and later recorded as The Wilsons for Mercury Records.

BEACH BOYS BIBLIOGRAPHY

Abbott, Kingsley (editor). *Back to the Beach: A Brian Wilson and The Beach Boys Reader.* London: Helter Skelter, 1997.

Barnes, Ken. *The Beach Boys: A Biography in Words and Pictures.* New York: Sire Books, 1976.

Elliott, Brad. *Surf's Up: The Beach Boys on Record, 1961–1981.* Ann Arbor, MI: Pierian Press, 1982.

Gaines, Steve. *Heroes and Villains: The True Story of The Beach Boys.* New York: New American Library, 1986; New York: Da Capo Press, 1995.

Golden, Bruce. *The Beach Boys: Southern California Pastoral.* San Bernardino, CA: Borgo Press, 1976.

Leaf, David. *The Beach Boys and the California Myth.* New York: Grosset and Dunlap, 1978.

————. *The Beach Boys.* Philadelphia: Courage Books, 1985.

Milward, John. *The Beach Boys: Silver Anniversary.* Garden City, NY: Doubleday, 1985.

Preiss, Byron. *The Beach Boys.* New York: Ballantine, 1979.

Tobler, John. *The Beach Boys.* Secaucus, NJ: Chartwell Books, 1978.

White, Timothy. *The Nearest Faraway Place: Brian Wilson, The Beach Boys, and the Southern California Experience.* New York: H. Holt, 1996.

Williams, Paul. *Brian Wilson and The Beach Boys: How Deep Is the Ocean? Essays and Conversations Exploring the Mysteries of Their Incomparable Musical Accomplishments.* (originally published 1966) London: Omnibus Press, 1997.

Wilson, Brian, with Todd Gold. *Wouldn't It Be Nice—My Own Story.* New York: Harper Collins, 1991.

Early Beach Boys Albums

Lost and Found 1961–1962	DCC	054	'91	CS/CD
Original Surfin' Hits: Their First Recordings	Curb/Atlantic	77747	'95	CS/CD
Surfin' Safari	Capitol	1808	'62	†
	Capitol	16012	'80	†
	Capitol	29661	'94	CS/CD
Surfin' U.S.A.	Capitol	1890	'63	†
	Capitol	16015		†
	Capitol	48422	'94	CS/CD
Shut Down (2 songs)	Capitol	1918	'63	†
Surfer Girl	Capitol	1981	'63	†
	Capitol	16014		†
	Capitol	29628	'94	CS/CD
Little Deuce Coupe	Capitol	1998	'63	†
	Capitol	16013		†
	Capitol	29630	'94	CS/CD
Shut Down, Volume 2	Capitol	2027	'64	†
	Capitol	29629	'94	CS/CD
All Summer Long	Capitol	2110	'64	†
	Capitol	16016		†
	Capitol	29631	'94	CS/CD
Christmas Album	Capitol	2164	'64	†
	Capitol	95084	'91	CS/CD
Live in London (recorded 1964)	Capitol	11584	'76	†
	Capitol	12011		†
	Capitol	16134		†
	Capitol	93695	'90	CS/CD†
	Capitol	29634	'94	CS/CD
Concert	Capitol	2198	'64	†
	Capitol	16154		†
	Capitol	90427	'94	CS/CD

The Hot Doggers (with Bruce Johnston)

Surfin' USA	Epic	26054	'63	†

The Vettes (with Bruce Johnston)

Rev-Up	MGM	4193	'63	†

The De-Fenders (with Bruce Johnston)

The Big Ones	World Pacific	1810	'63	†
Drag Beat	Del-Fi	1242	'63	†

Bruce Johnston

Surfers Pajama Party	Del-Fi	1228	'63	†
	Del-Fi	71228	'96	CD
Surfin' Round the World	Columbia	8857	'63	†
	Sundazed	6100		CD
Going Public	Columbia	34459	'77	†

The Rip Chords (Creation of Bruce Johnston and Terry Melcher)

Hey, Little Cobra (and Other Hot Rod Hits)	Columbia	8951	'64	†
	Sundazed	6098		CD
Three Window Coupe	Columbia	9016	'64	†
	Sundazed	6099		CD

The Catalinas (with Bruce Johnston and Terry Melcher)

Fun, Fun, Fun	Ric	1006	'64	†

Bruce and Terry

The Best of Bruce and Terry	Sundazed	11052	'98	CD

The Beach Boys

Today!	Capitol	2269	'65	†
	Capitol	29632	'94	CS/CD
Summer Days (and Summer Nights)	Capitol	2354	'65	†
	Capitol	29633	'94	CS/CD
Party!	Capitol	2398	'65	†
	Capitol	16272	'82	†
	Capitol	29640	'94	CS/CD
Pet Sounds	Capitol	2458	'66	†
	Capitol	16156	'81	†
	Capitol	48421	'90	CS/CD
	Capitol	37667	'96	CS/CD
	DCC	1035		CD
	DCC	2006	'95	LP
The Pet Sounds Sessions	Capitol	(4)37662	'96	CD
Smiley Smile	Brother	9001	'67	†
	Capitol	2891	'68	†
	Capitol	16158		†
	Capitol	29635	'94	CS/CD
Wild Honey	Capitol	2859	'67	†
	Capitol	16159		†
	Capitol	29636	'94	CS/CD
Stack-O-Tracks	Capitol	2893	'68	†
	Capitol	29641	'94	CS/CD
Friends	Capitol	2895	'68	†
	Capitol	16157		†
	Capitol	29637	'94	CS/CD
20/20	Capitol	133	'69	†
	Capitol	16155		†
	Capitol	29638	'94	CS/CD
Sunflower	Reprise	6382	'70	†
	Caribou	46950	'90	CS/CD†

Surf's Up	Reprise	6453	'71	†
	Caribou	46951	'90	CS/CD†
Carl and The Passions—So Tough	Brother	2090	'72	†
	Caribou	46953		CS/CD†
Holland	Reprise	2118	'72	†
	Caribou	46952	'90	CS/CD†
In Concert	Reprise	(2)6484	'73	†
	Caribou	46954		CS/CD†
15 Big Ones	Reprise	2251	'76	†
	Caribou	46955	'91	CS/CD†
The Beach Boys Love You	Reprise	2258	'77	†
	Caribou	46956		CS/CD†
M.I.U.	Reprise	2268	'78	†
	Caribou	46957	'91	CS/CD†
L.A. (Light Album)	Caribou	35752	'79	CS/CD†
Keepin' the Summer Alive	Caribou	36283	'80/'91	CS/CD†
The Beach Boys	Caribou	39946	'85	CS/CD†
Summer in Paradise	Brother	727	'92	CD

Beach Boys Reissues

Pet Sounds/Carl and The Passions—So Tough	Reprise	(2)2083	'72	†
	Brother	(2)2083	'72	†
	Warner Brothers	(2)2083		†
Wild Honey/ 20/20	Reprise	(2)2166	'74	†
Friends/Smiley Smile	Reprise	(2)2167	'74	†
Surfin' U.S.A./Surfer Girl	Mobile Fidelity	10521	'89	CD†
Surfin' Safari/Surfin' U.S.A.	Capitol	93691	'90	CS/CD†
Surfer Girl/Shutdown, Volume 2	Capitol	93692	'90	CS/CD†
Little Deuce Coupe/All Summer Long	Capitol	93693	'90	CS/CD†
Today/Summer Days (and Summer Nights)	Capitol	93694	'90	CS/CD†
Smiley Smile/Wild Honey	Capitol	93696	'90	CS/CD†
Friends/ 20/20	Capitol	93697	'90	CS/CD†
Party/Stack-O-Tracks	Capitol	93698	'90	CS/CD†

Beach Boys Anthologies and Compilations

Greatest Hits, 1961–1963	ERA	805	'70	†
	Hollywood/IMG	109		CS/CD
Best	Capitol	2545	'66	†
	Capitol	91318		CS/CD†
Best, Volume 2	Capitol	2706	'67	†
	Capitol	16318	'85	†
Deluxe Set	Capitol	(3)2813	'67	†
Best, Volume 3	Capitol	2945	'68	†
Close Up	Capitol	253	'69	†
Good Vibrations	Capitol	442	'70	†
All Summer Long/California Girls	Capitol	(2)500	'70	†
Fun, Fun, Fun/Dance, Dance, Dance	Capitol	701	'71	†
Endless Summer	Capitol	(2)11307	'74	†
	Capitol	46467		CS/CD
	DCC	1076	'95	CD
Spirit of America	Capitol	(2)11384	'75	†
	Capitol	(2)46618		LP/CS/CD†
	DCC	1089	'96	CD

California Girls	Capitol	16017		†
Fun, Fun, Fun	Capitol	16018		†
Dance, Dance, Dance	Capitol	16019		†
Be True to Your School	Capitol	16273	'82	†
Sunshine Dream	Capitol	12220	'82	†
Rarities	Capitol	12293	'83	†
Made in the U.S.A. (1961–1986)	Capitol	12396	'86	
	Capitol	46324	'86	CD†
Gift Set	Capitol	91341	'89	CD†
Still Cruisin'	Capitol	92639	'89	CS/CD
The Absolute Best of The Beach Boys, Volume 1	Capitol	96795	'91	CS/CD†
The Absolute Best of The Beach Boys, Volume 2	Capitol	96796	'91	CS/CD†
Thirty Years of The Beach Boys: Good Vibrations	Capitol	(5)81294	'93	CD
The Greatest Hits	Capitol	29418	'95	CS/CD
The Ultimate Christmas	Capitol	95734	'98	CS/CD
The Beach Boys	Pickwick	3221	'70	†
Good Vibrations	Pickwick	3269	'71	†
Wow! Great Concert	Pickwick	3309	'72	†
High Water	Pickwick	(2)2059	'73	†
Surfer Girl	Pickwick	3351	'73	†
Little Deuce Coupe	Pickwick	3562	'76	†
Best of The Beach Boys	Scepter	18004	'72	†
Pet Sounds	Reprise	2197	'74	†
Good Vibrations	Reprise	2223	'75	†
	Reprise	2280		†
Ten Years of Harmony (1970–1980)	Caribou	(2)37445	'81/'91	CD†
For All Seasons	Pair	1068	'86	†
Golden Harmonies	Pair	1084	'86	CS

Beach Boys Covers

Got You Covered! Songs of The Beach Boys	Risky Business	67312	'95	CS/CD
The Beach Boys: Stars and Stripes Forever, Vol. 1	River North Nashville	1205	'96	CS/CD

Dennis Wilson

Pacific Ocean Blue	Caribou	34354	'77	CS/CD†
One of Those People	Elektra	230	'79	†

Carl Wilson

Carl Wilson	Caribou	37010	'81	†
Youngblood	Caribou	37970	'83	†

Brian Wilson

Brian Wilson	Sire	25669	'88	CS/CD†
I Just Wasn't Made for These Times	MCA	11270	'95	CS/CD

Brian Wilson and Van Dyke Parks

Orange Crate Art	Warner Brothers	44527	'95	CS/CD

Wilson Phillips

Wilson Phillips	SBK	93745	'90	CS/CD
Shadows and Light	SBK	98924	'92	CS/CD

Carnie and Wendy Wilson

Hey Santa!	SBK	27113	'93	CS/CD
The Wilsons	Mercury	536105	'97	CS/CD

THE BEATLES

John Lennon (born October 9, 1940, in Woolton, Liverpool, England; died December 8, 1980, in New York City), rhythm guitar, piano, harmonica, vocals; Paul McCartney (born June 18, 1942, in Allerton, Liverpool), bass, piano, banjo, trumpet, vocals; George Harrison (born February 24, 1943, in Wavertree, Liverpool), lead guitar, sitar, piano, vocals; and Ringo Starr (born Richard Starkey on July 7, 1940, in Dingle, Liverpool), drums, vocals. Early members included Stuart Sutcliffe (born June 23, 1940, in Edinburgh, Scotland; died April 10, 1962, in Hamburg, Germany), bass, and Pete Best (born November 24, 1941, in Madras, India), drums.

THE BEATLES (UPI/CORBIS-BETTMANN)

The most important rock group in history, The Beatles' unprecedented commercial success was paralleled by their masterful artistic achievements and widespread cultural impact. Musically, The Beatles were the group that institutionalized many of the advances pioneered in rock music in the late '50s, from the self-contained music group to the use of sophisticated arrangements and studio production techniques. In encompassing so many diversified forms of music (pop love songs, ballads, novelty songs, folk, country-and-western, rhythm-and-blues) within the basic rock 'n' roll format, The Beatles revitalized rock 'n' roll. Their music exhibited a fresh, clean, exuberant sound that contrasted sharply with the vapid pop ballads and dance songs pervading popular music in the early '60s. Initiating an eclecticism that was to become one of their trademarks with *Something New,* The Beatles went beyond the standard three-chord progression, often utilizing diminished or augmented seventh and ninth chords while devising intriguing melodies and developing engaging vocal harmonies. Particularly after the *Help!* album, songwriters John Lennon and Paul McCartney brought an unprecedented lyric sophistication to rock music, writing songs of a personal and emotionally evocative nature. Their frequent philosophical concerns in lyrics widened the intellectual boundaries of rock in a manner rivaled only by Bob Dylan. Beginning with the *Revolver* album, perhaps the most innovative rock album ever made, The Beatles introduced novel instrumental combinations into rock, explored elaborate electronic production techniques under George Martin, and sparked the use of the East Indian sitar in rock music. The landmark *Sgt. Pepper* album, regarded by many as the first fully realized concept album and certainly an astounding work, may be the best known rock album of all time; its intricate jacket design also set new standards for the developing field of album artwork. When finally released on CD in 1987, *Sgt. Pepper* quickly became one of the best-selling CDs of all time.

Within the music industry, The Beatles' enormous success turned the industry away from its preoccupation with individual singers performing songs written by professional songwriters toward music groups performing original material. The consistency of The Beatles' musical performances switched the focus of the consuming public's attention from singles to albums. The Beatles' rise enabled dozens of other British musicians to express themselves musically and achieve popularity, thereby breaking the American stranglehold on British popular music. Perhaps most significantly, the musical and songwriting advances pioneered by The Beatles led critics to view rock music as a valid art form in and of itself, and induced the public to perceive rock music as a total, internally coherent form of conscious experience. In social terms, The Beatles brought public attention to psychedelic drugs, the peace movement, Indian music, and Eastern spiritualism. Moreover, they helped promote a growing youth culture and inspired many young people to begin playing music by and for themselves, making music an essential part of their lifestyle. The Beatles were inducted into the Rock and Roll Hall of Fame in 1988.

The evolution of The Beatles began in 1956 when John Lennon formed a group called The Quarrymen. In July 1957, he met Paul McCartney, who subsequently joined the group. George Harrison joined in August 1958 and, by 1959, they were down to a trio. The group's name changed several times during that year, eventually becoming The Silver Beatles. Bassist Stu Sutcliffe and drummer Pete Best joined the group in January and August 1960, respectively. Subsequently performing in Hamburg, Germany, for three months as The Beatles, the group later backed singer Tony Sheridan in Hamburg in June 1961 and recordings done with Sheridan were later released on albums. In Hamburg, the group completed their musical apprenticeship, playing rigorous night-long shows to unappreciative audiences; live recordings made at the Star Club in 1962 were eventually issued in 1977.

The Beatles returned to England and took up residence at The Cavern, a club in Liverpool, beginning in February 1961. In April, Stu Sutcliffe left the group; he died of a brain hemorrhage in Hamburg on April 10, 1962. In November 1961, record shop owner Brian Epstein discovered the group at The Cavern and attempted to secure them a recording contract. They were initially rejected by Decca and later picked up by the Parlophone subsidiary of EMI (British Capitol) in May 1962. That August, Ringo Starr quit Rory Storm's Hurricanes and replaced Pete Best on drums. Best later recorded an album for Savage Records and served as "technical advisor" for the 1979 Dick Clark production "The Birth of the Beatles," which aired on ABC-TV. By the late '90s, Pete Best had formed The Pete Best Combo, recording *Best* for Music Club Records.

In September, with George Martin producing, The Beatles conducted their first recording session. In October, their first single, "Love Me Do," was issued in Great Britain on Parlophone Records, becoming a modest hit. Their second single, "Please Please Me," quickly proved a smash hit. The Beatles' first British album, *Please Please Me,* issued in March 1963, remained near the top of the charts for six months. "From Me to You," released in April, initiated a string of eleven consecutive top British hits for The Beatles. Their second album, *With the Beatles,* issued in November, initiated a string of eleven consecutive studio albums of new material to top the British album charts.

In the United States, the next Beatles' single, "I Want to Hold Your Hand," backed with "I Saw Her Standing There," was released in January 1964, with heavy promotion by Capitol. The song became a top hit within two weeks and proved one of the fastest-selling singles of the '60s, eventually selling fifteen million copies worldwide. In February, The Beatles performed on CBS television's *Ed Sullivan Show* before an estimated audience of 73 million and launched their debut U.S. tour, with massive media coverage.

The dam burst. Nothing could stop The Beatles, and, in their wake, followed dozens of British groups. Indeed, Lennon and McCartney provided a number of hit songs to up-and-coming British groups, including "Hello Little Girl" for The Fourmost, "Bad to Me" for Billy J. Kramer and The Dakotas, and "It's for You" for Cilla Black. Peter and Gordon scored with their "World Without Love" (a top British and American hit) and "I Don't Want to See You

Again," and The Rolling Stones' first major British hit came with Lennon and McCartney's "I Wanna Be Your Man."

For many weeks after the release of "I Want to Hold Your Hand," The Beatles dominated the highest chart positions with the top hits "She Loves You" and "Can't Buy Me Love" (on Capitol), "Please Please Me" and "Do You Want to Know a Secret" (on VeeJay), and "Twist and Shout" and "Love Me Do," backed with "P.S. I Love You" (on Tollie). In March 1964, the group began work on their first film, *A Hard Day's Night,* and John Lennon published his first book, *In His Own Write.* The film premiered in July and the British *A Hard Day's Night* album comprised entirely songs written by Lennon and McCartney. The Beatles' second U.S. tour began in August and the following February and March, they recorded and filmed their second movie, *Help!,* which opened in late July. In June, Lennon published his second book, *A Spaniard in the Works.* Through mid-1965, The Beatles continued their string of hit singles with the top hits "A Hard Day's Night," "I Feel Fine" (backed with "She's a Woman"), "Eight Days a Week," and "Ticket to Ride," and the major hits "And I Love Her," "I'll Cry Instead," and Carl Perkins' "Matchbox" backed with "Slow Down."

Increasing sophistication in the lyrics of Lennon and McCartney became evident after mid-1965. The words to the top hits "Help" and "Yesterday," the smash hit "Nowhere Man" and the major hit "Eleanor Rigby," and songs such as "In My Life" (from *Rubber Soul*) possessed a profound emotional intensity not apparent in earlier work. Completing their third North American tour in August 1965, the Beatles scored a top/smash hit with "We Can Work It Out"/"Day Tripper" at year's end. George Harrison's songwriting ability began to be showcased with *Revolver,* which contained three of his songs: "Taxman," "Love You Too," and "I Want to Tell You." The Beatles conducted their final American tour in August 1966 as "Yellow Submarine" (backed with "Eleanor Rigby") was becoming a smash hit.

With the single "Rain" (the flip side of the top hit "Paperback Writer") and songs such as "Tomorrow Never Knows" (from *Revolver*), The Beatles began utilizing involved studio production techniques in their recordings. The contributions of producer-arranger George Martin became particularly strong between 1966 and 1968. Lyrically, the songs of Lennon and McCartney began a tendency toward the bizarre and surreal, often defying logical explanation. This penchant for the surreal, first evident with "Norwegian Wood" (from *Rubber Soul*), continued with "Lucy in the Sky with Diamonds" and the quintessential "A Day in the Life" (from *Sgt. Pepper*) and the singles "Strawberry Fields Forever"/"Penny Lane" and "I Am the Walrus."

Focusing their attention on recording, The Beatles' *Sgt. Pepper's Lonely Hearts Club Band* was issued in June 1967, with advance sales of one million plus. It remained on the American album charts for more than three years and eventually sold more then eight million copies in the United States. The first Beatles album to be identical in its British and American versions, *Sgt. Pepper* entailed 700 hours of studio time. As the music industry's first recognized concept album, the record was highly acclaimed by critics and marked perhaps the high point of The Beatles' recording career. The album included "Lucy in the Sky with Diamonds," "With a Little Help from My Friends" (sung by Ringo), Harrison's self-consciously philosophical "Within You, Without You," and the quintessential '60s production, "A Day in the Life." The singles "All You Need Is Love" and "Hello Goodbye" became top hits before year's end, followed by the smash "Lady Madonna" the next spring.

Individual endeavors by members of The Beatles began in 1967 with the acting debut of John Lennon in the film *How I Won the War* and Paul McCartney's recording of the soundtrack to the film *The Family Way.* During the year, the group scripted, cast, directed, and edited the made-for-television movie *Magical Mystery Tour,* a conspicuous failure in its poor editing and photography. The soundtrack album, released in November in the United States only, included "The Fool on the Hill," "I Am the Walrus," and "All You Need Is Love." In 1968, George Harrison composed, arranged, and recorded his own music for the soundtrack to the film *Wonderwall.* Lennon, now with conceptual artist Yoko Ono, recorded with her the controversial *Two Virgins* album. In July, the animated movie *Yellow Submarine* premiered. It was probably the most artistically successful film with which The Beatles were associated. Furthermore, it was one of the most engaging psychedelic movies of the late '60s. The soundtrack album included the title song and "All You Need Is Love."

In April, The Beatles had formed their own record company, Apple. The first single for the label, "Hey Jude" (backed with "Revolution"), was released in August and became a top hit. The double-record set entitled *The Beatles* (also known as *The White Album*), issued in November, was the first album on Apple. Disjointed and revealing the tell-tale signs of a Lennon-McCartney rift, the album contained such diverse songs as "Back in the U.S.S.R.," "Blackbird," "Revolution," and Harrison's superlative "While My Guitar Gently Weeps" (recorded, without credit, with Eric Clapton). It remained on the American album charts for nearly three years and sold more than seven million copies in the United States.

During most of 1969, the individual Beatles worked apart. Ringo appeared in the movie *The Magic Christian*. The soundtrack album contained a solo McCartney composition, "Come and Get It," a near-smash hit for Badfinger. In March, John Lennon married Yoko Ono and Paul McCartney married Linda Eastman. The marriages seemed to mark the informal end of the Beatles. During the year, The Beatles scored top hits with "Get Back" and "Come Together" (backed with Harrison's smash hit "Something") and the near-smash hit "The Ballad of John and Yoko." John Lennon became the first Beatle to perform publicly outside the group in September with The Plastic Ono Band in Toronto.

The only Beatle album release of 1969, *Abbey Road* (named for the studio in which the group had recorded since 1962), was issued in November and became their most popular album, selling more than nine million copies in the United States. It included Lennon's "Come Together," Harrison's "Something" and "Here Comes the Sun," Ringo's "Octopus' Garden," and "She Came in Through the Bathroom Window." The *Abbey Road* album was actually the final Beatles recording. *Let It Be,* initially produced by George Martin and later reworked by Phil Spector, was held up by remixing disputes and film editing problems and eventually issued in May 1970. The album included the top hits "Let It Be," "Get Back," and "The Long and Winding Road," the Beatles' final single release.

On the last day of 1970, Paul McCartney sued for dissolution of The Beatles' partnership, which legally ended on January 9, 1975. Subsequent Beatles album releases were the live sets *Live at Star Club* and *Live at the Hollywood Bowl* (recorded in 1964 and 1965), *Rarities,* and various anthology sets. The individual members of The Beatles recorded a number of albums for Apple in the first half of the '70s, most notably Paul McCartney's *McCartney* (1970) and *Band on the Run* (1973), George Harrison's *All Things Must Pass* (1970) and *The Concert for Bangladesh* (1972), John Lennon's *Imagine* (1971), and Ringo Starr's *Ringo* (1973).

Throughout the '70s, rumors persisted that The Beatles would reunite for touring or recordings, but such speculation finally and tragically ended with the murder of John Lennon in New York City on December 8, 1980. The remaining three, plus Linda McCartney, jointly recorded the 1981 tribute to Lennon, "All Those Years Ago," written by Harrison.

The public's fascination with The Beatles was sustained in the early '80s through the film documentary *The Compleat Beatles* (1982) and long-time associate Peter Brown's book, *The Love You Make: An Insider's Story of the Beatles* (1983). In August 1985, superstar Michael Jackson purchased the copyrights to 40,000 songs, including over 200 Lennon-McCartney songs. During the twenty-fifth anniversary year of The Beatles first recording, 1987, Capitol Records issued for the first time on CD The Beatles' first seven albums in their British versions (U.S. versions contained one to four fewer songs) and their last five albums (U.S. and British versions were identical). *Sgt. Pepper,* released in June, rapidly became the best-selling CD of all time. The Beatles were inducted into the Rock and Roll Hall of Fame in 1988. Producer George Martin was inducted in 1999.

In 1994, the movie *Backbeat* focused on the early days of The Beatles and Stu Sutcliffe in particular. Late in the year, Apple Records issued The Beatles' *Live at the BBC,* fifty-six songs recorded for broadcast by the radio station between March 1962 and June 1965. Consisting largely of cover songs, the album quickly sold more than five million copies. In November 1995, the three-part special *The Beatles Anthology* aired on ABC television, and the end of the first program featured the debut of "Free as a Bird," a Lennon demonstration record completed by the former Beatles, which became a near-smash hit. Capitol subsequently issued three double-CD sets of *Anthology* albums that demonstrated the remarkable popularity of a group that had disbanded a quarter of a century ago.

BEATLES BIBLIOGRAPHY

Beatlefan: The Authoritative Publication of Record for Fans of The Beatles. Ann Arbor, MI: Pierian Press, 1985.

The Beatles: From Yesterday to Today. Boston: Little, Brown, 1996.

Best, Pete, and Patrick Doncaster. *Beatle! The Pete Best Story.* New York: Dell, 1985.

Blake, John. *All You Needed Was Love: The Beatles After The Beatles.* New York: Perigee Books, 1981.

Brown, Peter, and Steven Gaines. *The Love You Make: An Insider's Story of The Beatles.* New York: McGraw-Hill, 1983.

Buskin, Richard. *The Complete Idiot's Guide to The Beatles.* New York: Alpha Books, 1998.

Carr, Roy, and Tony Tyler. *The Beatles: An Illustrated Record.* New York: Harmony Books, 1975, 1978.

Castleman, Harry, and Walter J. Podrazik. *All Together Now: The First Complete Beatles' Discography 1961–1975.* Ann Arbor, MI: Pierian Press, 1976.

———. *The Beatles Again?* Ann Arbor, MI: Pierian Press, 1977.

———. *The End of The Beatles?* Ann Arbor, MI: Pierian Press, 1985.

Cepican, Robert. *Yesterday—Came Suddenly: The Definitive History of The Beatles.* New York: Arbor House, 1985.

Clifford, Mike. *The Beatles.* New York: Smithmark Publishers, 1991.

Coleman, Ray. *The Man Who Made The Beatles: An Intimate Biography of Brian Epstein.* New York: McGraw-Hill, 1989.

Davies, Hunter. *The Beatles: The Authorized Biography.* New York: McGraw-Hill, 1968.

———. *The Beatles.* New York: McGraw-Hill, 1978, 1985.

Davis, Edward E. *The Beatles Book.* New York: Cowles, 1968.

DiFranco, J. Philip (editor). *The Beatles: A Hard Day's Night.* London, New York: Penguin, 1978.

Dilello, Richard. *The Longest Cocktail Party: A Personal History of Apple.* Chicago: Playboy Press, 1972.

Dowlding, William J. *Beatlesongs.* New York: Simon and Schuster, 1989.

Epstein, Brian. *A Cellarful of Noise.* Garden City, NY: Doubleday, 1964; New York: Pyramid Books, 1965; Ann Arbor, MI: Pierian Press, 1984.

Fast, Julius. *The Beatles: The Real Story.* New York: G. P. Putnam's Sons, 1968.

Friede, Goldie, Robin Titone, and Sue Weiner. *The Beatles A to Z.* New York: Methuen, 1980.

Gross, Edward. *The Fab Films of The Beatles.* Las Vegas: Pioneer Books, 1990.

Guilano, Geoffrey. *The Beatles: A Celebration.* New York: St. Martin's Press, 1986.

——— and Brenda Guilano. *The Lost Beatles Interviews.* New York: Dutton, 1994.

Harrison, George. *I Me Mine.* New York: Simon and Schuster, 1980, 1981.

Harry, Bill (editor). *Mersey Beat: The Beginnings of the Beatles.* London, New York: Omnibus Press, 1977.

———. *The Beatles Who's Who.* London: Aurum Press, 1982.

————. *The Ultimate Beatles Encyclopedia.* New York: Hyperion, 1992.

Hertsgaard, Mark. *A Day in the Life: The Music and Artistry of The Beatles.* New York: Delacorte Press, 1995; New York: Dell, 1996.

Howlett, Kevin. *The Beatles on the Beeb, '62—'65: The Story of Their Radio Career.* Ann Arbor, MI: Pierian Press, 1983.

Lennon, John. *In His Own Write.* New York: Simon and Schuster, 1964.

————. *A Spaniard in the Works.* New York: Simon and Schuster, 1965.

————. *In His Own Write and A Spaniard in the Works.* New York: New American Library, 1967.

————. *Skywriting by Word of Mouth, and Other Writings.* New York: Harper and Row, 1986.

Lewisohn, Mark. *The Beatles Live!* New York: H. Holt, 1986.

————. *Complete Beatles Recording Sessions.* New York: Harmony Books, 1988.

————. *The Beatles: Day by Day, A Chronology 1962—1989.* New York: Harmony Books, 1990.

————. *The Complete Beatles Chronicle.* New York: Harmony Books, 1992.

MacDonald, Ian. *Revolution in the Head: The Beatles' Records and the Sixties.* New York: H. Holt, 1994.

MacKenzie, Maxwell. *The Beatles: Every Little Thing: A Compendium of Witty, Weird and Ever-Surprising Facts about the Fab Four.* New York: Avon Books, 1998.

Martin, George, with Jeremy Hornsby. *All You Need Is Ears.* New York: St. Martin's Press, 1979.

———— with William Pearson. *Summer of Love: The Making of* Sgt. Pepper. London: Pan Books, 1994.

————. *With a Little Help From My Friends: The Making of* Sgt. Pepper. Boston: Little, Brown, 1994.

McCabe, Peter, and Robert Schonfeld. *Apple to the Core: The Unmaking of The Beatles.* New York: Pocket Books, 1972.

McKeen, William. *The Beatles: A Bio-Bibliography.* New York: Greenwood Press, 1989.

Mellers, Wilfrid. *Twilight of the Gods.* New York: Viking Press, 1974.

Miles (compiler). *The Beatles in Their Own Words.* New York: Quick Fox, 1978.

Miles, Barry. *The Beatles: A Diary: An Intimate Day by Day History.* London: Omnibus Press, 1998.

Neises, Charles P. (editor). *The Beatles Reader: A Selection of Contemporary Views, News and Reviews of The Beatles in Their Heyday.* Ann Arbor, MI: Pierian Press, 1984; Ann Arbor, MI: Popular Culture Ink, 1991.

Norman, Philip. *Shout! The Beatles in Their Generation.* New York: Simon and Schuster, 1981.

O'Donnell, Jim. *The Day John Met Paul: A Hour-by-Hour Account of How The Beatles Began.* New York: Penguin Books, 1996.

The Official Price Guide to The Beatles: Records and Memorabilia. New York: House of Collectibles, 1995.

O'Grady, Terence J. *The Beatles, A Musical Evolution.* Boston: Twayne, 1983.

Pawlowski, Gareth L. *How They Became The Beatles: A Definitive History of the Early Years, 1960—1964.* New York: E. P. Dutton, 1989.

Pritchard, David, and Alan Lysaght (compilers). *The Beatles: An Oral History.* New York: Hyperion, 1998.

Reinhart, Charles. *You Can't Do That! Beatles Bootlegs and Novelty Records, 1963—80.* Ann Arbor, MI: Pierian Press, 1981.

Riley, Tim. *Tell Me Why: A Beatles Commentary.* New York: Knopf, 1988.

Russell, Jeff. *The Beatles Album File and Complete Discography.* New York: C. Scribner's Sons, 1982.

Scaduto, Anthony. *The Beatles.* New York: Signet Books, 1968.

Schaffner, Nicholas. *The Beatles Forever.* New York: McGraw-Hill, 1977.

————. *The Boys from Liverpool: John, Paul, George, Ringo.* New York: Methuen, 1980.

Schultheiss, Tom (compiler). *The Beatles: A Day in the Life: The Beatles Day-by-Day, 1960—1970.* Ann Arbor, MI: Pierian Press, 1980.

Shepherd, Billy. *The True Story of The Beatles.* New York: Bantam Books, 1964.

Somach, Denny, Kathleen Somach, and Kevin Gunn. *Ticket to Ride.* New York: Morrow, 1989.

Spignesi, Stephen J. *The Beatles Book of Lists.* Seacaucus, NJ: Carol Publishing Group, 1998.

Stannard, Neville. *The Long and Winding Road: A History of The Beatles on Record.* New York: Avon Books, 1984.

Stokes, Geoffrey. *The Beatles.* New York: Times Books, 1980.

Sulpy, Doug, and Ray Schweighardt. *Get Back: The Unauthorized Chronicle of The Beatles'* Let It Be *Disaster.* New York: St. Martin's Press, 1997.

Taylor, Derek. *As Time Goes By.* San Francisco: Straight Arrow Books, 1973.

————. *It Was Twenty Years Ago.* New York: Simon and Schuster, 1987.

Terry, Carol D. (editor and compiler). *Here, There and Everywhere: The First International Beatles Bibliography, 1962–1982.* Ann Arbor, MI: Pierian Press, 1985.

Tobler, John. *The Beatles.* New York: Exeter Books, 1984.

Toropov, Brandon. *Who Was Eleanor Rigby? And 998 More Questions and Answers About The Beatles.* New York: Harper Perennial, 1996.

Turner, Steve. *A Hard Day's Write: The Stories Behind Every Beatles Song.* New York: Harper Perennial, 1994.

Wallgren, Mark. *The Beatles on Record.* New York: Simon and Schuster, 1982.

Wenner, Jann. *Lennon Remembers: The* Rolling Stone *Interviews.* San Francisco: Straight Arrow Books, 1971; New York: Popular Library, 1972.

Wiener, Allen J. *The Beatles: A Recording History.* Jefferson, NC: McFarland, 1986.

————. *The Beatles: The Ultimate Recording Guide.* New York: Facts on File, 1992; Holbrook, MA: B. Adams, 1994.

Williams, Allan, and William Marshall. *The Man Who Gave The Beatles Away.* New York: Macmillan, 1975.

Woffinden, Bob. *The Beatles Apart.* London, New York: Proteus, 1981.

Early Beatles Recordings

The Beatles with Tony Sheridan and Their Guests (4 songs)	MGM	4215	'64	†
reissued as This Is Where It Started	Metro	563	'66	†
Live at the Star Club	Lingasong	(2)7001	'77	†
Live at the Star Club, 1962, Volume 1	Sony	48544	'91	CS/CD†
Live at the Star Club, 1962, Volume 2	Sony	48604	'91	CS/CD†
In the Beginning	Polydor	244504	'70	†
	Polydor	823701	'87	CD
	Polydor	825073	'87	CS
Introducing . . . The Beatles	VeeJay	1062	'64	†
Jolly What! The Beatles and Frank Ifield	VeeJay	1085	'64	†
Songs, Pictures and Stories of the Fabulous Beatles	VeeJay	1092	'64	†
The Beatles versus The Four Seasons	VeeJay	(2)30	'64	†
Ain't She Sweet	Atco	33169	'64	†
The Early Beatles	Capitol/Apple	2309	'65	†
	Capitol	02309		LP
	Capitol	90451		CS†

Pete Best

Best of The Beatles	Savage	71	'66	†
Beyond The Beatles 1964–66	Griffin	598	'96	CD

Pete Best Combo

Best Music Club		50069	'98	CD

The Beatles

NOTE: The album releases for The Beatles through 1966 were significantly different in Great Britain (on Parlophone) and the United States (on Capitol). Capitol chose to release the British (U.K.) albums on CD, except in the case of *Meet The Beatles*.

Meet The Beatles	Capitol/Apple	2047	'64	†
	Capitol	90441		LP/CS†
Second Album	Capitol/Apple	2080	'64	†
	Capitol	90444		LP/CS†
A Hard Day's Night (American)	United Artists	6366	'64	†
	Capitol	11921	'79	LP/CS†
Something New	Capitol/Apple	2108	'64	†
	Capitol	90443		LP/CS†
The Beatles' Story	Capitol/Apple	(2)2222	'64	†
Beatles' '65	Capitol/Apple	2228	'64	†
	Capitol	90446		LP/CS†
Beatles VI	Capitol/Apple	2358	'65	†
	Capitol	90445		LP/CS†
Help! (American)	Capitol/Apple	2386	'65	†
	Capitol	90454		LP/CS†
Rubber Soul (American)	Capitol/Apple	2442	'65	†
	Capitol	90453		LP/CS†
Yesterday . . . and Today	Capitol/Apple	2553	'66	†
	Capitol	90447		LP/CS†
Revolver (American)	Capitol/Apple	2576	'66	†
	Capitol	90452		LP/CS†
Hey Jude	Apple/Capitol	385	'70	†
	Capitol	90442		LP/CS†
Please Please Me (U.K.)	Capitol	46435	'87	LP/CS/CD
	Capitol	46435	'96	LP
With The Beatles (U.K.)	Capitol	46436	'87	LP/CS/CD
	Capitol	46436	'96	LP
A Hard Day's Night (U.K.)	Capitol	46437	'87	LP/CS/CD
	Capitol	46437	'96	LP
Beatles for Sale (U.K.)	Capitol	46438	'87	LP/CS/CD
	Capitol	46438	'96	LP
Help! (U.K.)	Capitol	46439	'87	LP/CS/CD
	Capitol	46439	'96	LP
Rubber Soul (U.K.)	Capitol	46440	'87	LP/CS/CD
	Capitol	46440	'96	LP
Revolver (U.K.)	Capitol	46441	'87	LP/CS/CD
	Capitol	46441	'96	LP
Sgt. Pepper's Lonely Hearts Club Band	Capitol/Apple	2653	'67	†
	Capitol	46442	'87	LP/CS/CD
	Capitol	46442	'96	LP
Magical Mystery Tour	Capitol/Apple	2835	'67	†
	Capitol	48062		LP/CS/CD
	Capitol	48062	'96	LP
The Beatles (White Album)	Apple/Capitol	(2)101	'68	†
	Capitol	46443	'87	CS/CD
	Capitol	(2)46443	'96	LP
(limited edition)	Capitol	(2)96895	'98	CD
Yellow Submarine (soundtrack)	Apple/Capitol	153	'69	†
	Capitol	46445	'87	LP/CS/CD
	Capitol	46445	'96	LP

Abbey Road	Apple/Capitol	383	'69	†
	Capitol	46446	'87	LP/CS/CD
	Capitol	46446	'96	LP
Let It Be	Apple	34001	'70	†
	Capitol	11922	'79	†
	Capitol	46447	'87	CS/CD
	Capitol	46447	'96	LP
Live at the BBC	Apple	(2)31796	'94	CS/CD†

Beatles Anthologies

1962–1966	Apple/Capitol	(2)3403	'73	†
	Capitol	(2)90435		LP/CS†
	Capitol	(2)97036	'93	CS/CD
1967–1970	Apple/Capitol	(2)3404	'73	†
	Capitol	(2)90438		LP/CS†
	Capitol	(2)97039	'93	CS/CD
Rock 'n' Roll Music	Capitol	(2)11537	'76	†
Rock 'n' Roll Music, Volume 1	Capitol	16020	'76	LP/CS†
Rock 'n' Roll Music, Volume 2	Capitol	16021	'76	LP/CS†
Live at the Hollywood Bowl	Capitol	11638	'77	LP/CS†
Love Songs	Capitol	(2)11711	'77	LP/CS†
Rarities	Capitol	12060	'80	LP/CS†
Reel Music	Capitol	12199	'82	LP/CS†
20 Greatest Hits	Capitol	12245	'81	LP/CS
Past Masters–Volume 1	Capitol	90043	'88	CD
Past Masters–Volume 2	Capitol	90044	'88	CD
Past Masters Volume 1 & 2	Capitol	(2)91135	'88	LP†
	Capitol	91135	'88	CS
The Ultimate Box Set	Capitol	(16)91302	'88	LP/CS/CD
Anthology 1	Capitol	(3)34445	'95	LP
	Capitol	(2)34445	'95	CS/CD
Anthology 2	Capitol	(3)34448	'96	LP
	Capitol	(2)34448	'96	CS/CD
Anthology 3	Capitol	(2)34451	'96	LP/CS/CD

Don Was (composer)

Back Beat (music from soundtrack)	Virgin Movie Music	39413	'94	CS/CD

Tribute Albums

Motown Sings The Beatles	Razor & Tie	2031	'94	CS/CD
Motown Meets The Beatles	Motown	0410	'95	CS/CD
Come Together: America Salutes The Beatles	Liberty	31712	'95	LP/CS/CD

Symphonic Beatles

The London Symphony Orchestra Plays the Music of The Beatles	Esx	7066	'95	CS/CD
London Starlight Orchestra: 20 Beatles Greatest Hits	Star	86021	'96	CD

Paul McCartney

The Family Way (soundtrack)	London	82007	'67	†
	Philips	528922	'95	CS/CD
McCartney	Apple/Capitol	3363	'70	†
	Columbia	36478	'80	†
	Capitol	46611	'87	CS/CD
	DCC	1029		CD

Paul and Linda McCartney

Ram	Apple/Capitol	3375	'71	†
	Columbia	36479	'80	†
	Capitol	46612	'87	CS†/CD
	DCC	1037		CD

Paul McCartney and Wings

Wild Life	Apple/Capitol	3386	'71	†
	Columbia	36480	'80	†
	Capitol	52017	'89	CS†/CD
Red Rose Speedway	Apple/Capitol	3409	'73	†
	Columbia	36481	'80	†
	Capitol	52026	'88	CS†/CD
Band on the Run	Apple/Capitol	3415	'73	†
	Columbia	36482	'80	†
	Capitol	46675	'87	CS/CD
	DCC	1030		CD

George Harrison

Wonderwall Music	Apple	3350	'68	†
	Apple	98706	'92	CS/CD†
Electronic Sound	Apple	3358	'69	†
All Things Must Pass	Apple/Capitol	(3)639	'70	†
	Capitol	(3)00639		LP
	Capitol	(3)46688		CS
	Capitol	(2)46688		CD
Living in the Material World	Apple/Capitol	3410	'73	†
	Capitol	16216		†
	Apple	94110	'91	CS/CD
Dark Horse	Apple/Capitol	3418	'74	†
	Capitol	16055		†
	Apple	98079	'91	CS/CD
Extra Texture	Apple/Capitol	3420	'75	†
	Capitol	16217		†
	Apple	98080	'91	CS/CD
The Best of George Harrison	Capitol	11578	'76	CS
	Capitol	46682		CD

George Harrison and Friends

The Concert for Bangladesh	Apple	(3)3385	'72	†
	Columbia/Legacy	(2)48616	'91	CS†
	Capitol	(2)93265	'95	CD

John Lennon and Yoko Ono

Unfinished Music #1: Two Virgins	Apple	5001	'68	†
Unfinished Music #2: Life with the Lions	Zapple	3357	'69	†
Wedding Album	Apple	(2)3361	'69	†

John Lennon/Plastic Ono Band

Live Peace in Toronto 1969	Apple	3362	'69	†
	Capitol	12239	'82	†
	Capitol	90428	'95	CD
Plastic Ono Band	Apple/Capitol	3372	'70	†
	Capitol	03372		LP
	Capitol	46770		CS†/CD

Sometime in New York	Apple/Capitol	(2)3392	'72	†
	Capitol	(2)93850	'90	CD

Yoko Ono/Plastic Ono Band

Plastic Ono Band	Apple	3373	'70	†
Fly	Apple	(2)3380	'71	†

John Lennon

Imagine	Apple/Capitol	3379	'71	†
	Capitol	03379		LP
	Capitol	46641	'86	CS/CD
Mind Games	Apple/Capitol	3414	'73	†
	Capitol	16068		†
	Capitol	46769		CS†/CD
Walls and Bridges	Capitol	3416	'74	†
	Capitol	03416		LP
	Capitol	46768		CS†/CD
Rock 'n' Roll	Apple/Capitol	3419	'75	†
	Capitol	16069		†
	Capitol	46707		CD
Menlove Avenue (recorded 1974–1975)	Capitol	12533		LP/CS†
	Capitol	46576	'86	CD
Shaved Fish	Apple/Capitol	3421	'75	†
	Capitol	03421		LP
	Capitol	46642		CS/CD

Yoko Ono

Approximate Infinite Universe	Apple	(2)3399	'73	†
Feeling the Space	Apple	3412	'73	†

Ringo Starr

Sentimental Journey	Apple/Capitol	3365	'70	†
	Capitol	16218		†
	Capitol	98615	'95	CD
Beaucoups of Blues	Apple/Capitol	3368	'70	†
	Capitol	16235	'81	†
	Capitol	32675	'95	CD
Ringo	Apple/Capitol	3413	'73	†
	Capitol	16114		†
	Capitol	95637	'91	CD
	DCC	1066	'95	CD
Goodnight Vienna	Apple/Capitol	3417	'74	†
	Capitol	16219		†
	Capitol	80378	'93	CS/CD
Blast from Your Past	Apple/Capitol	3422	'75	†
	Capitol	46663		CD

JEFF BECK

Born June 24, 1944, in Wallington, Surrey, England.

British lead guitarist extraordinaire, Jeff Beck is one of rock music's most intelligent, innovative, and respected guitarists. One of the first electric guitarists to utilize a fuzztone device and make extensive use of feedback while playing, Beck introduced both modal and East Indian tonalities into rock with The Yardbirds. The debut album by his first Jeff Beck Group introduced American audiences to Rod Stewart and, along with Led Zeppelin's debut album six months later, helped define '70s heavy-metal music. Moreover, with his *Blow by Blow* album, Beck helped redefine and revitalize the more challenging and ambitious sound of fusion music, a '70s phenomenon not strictly classifiable as jazz or rock, but containing elements of both. Taking regular extended breaks from recording and touring throughout his career, Jeff Beck is regarded as a musician's musician.

A competent pianist and guitarist by the age of eleven, Jeff Beck performed with early '60s British bands such as The Nightshifts and The Tridents before replacing Eric Clapton in The Yardbirds in March 1965. Beck played lead guitar with the group through its greatest hit-making period ("Heart Full of Soul," "I'm a Man," "Over Under Sideways Down") and pioneered the use of feedback and effects, particularly with "The Shapes of Things" from 1966. Leaving The Yardbirds that November, he recorded several singles, including the major British hit "Hi Ho Silver Lining," and formed the first of several Jeff Beck Groups with Rod Stewart (vocals), Ron Wood (bass, harmonica), and Mickey Waller (drums). The group proved enormously successful with its blues-oriented material during an American tour in 1968. The tour also introduced American audiences to Rod Stewart, who had been singing almost anonymously with various blues aggregations in Britain for years.

The Jeff Beck Group's debut album for Epic, *Truth,* included "I Ain't Superstitious," "Rock My Plimsoul," and "Beck's Bolero," and helped pioneer heavy-metal music. The group expanded in October 1968 with the addition of sessions keyboardist Nicky Hopkins. After a second album, *Beck-ola,* and the recording of Donovan's major British and moderate American hit "Goo Goo Barabajagal (Love Is Hot)," the group fragmented, with Stewart and Wood joining The Faces, and Hopkins moving to California to join Quicksilver Messenger Service.

An attempt to form a new band with Tim Bogert and Carmine Appice of Vanilla Fudge failed, and a car crash later left Jeff Beck out of commission for 18 months. He reemerged in late 1971 with his second Jeff Beck Group, featuring keyboardist Max Middleton and drummer Cozy Powell. This group recorded two undistinguished albums before disbanding in 1972. With the demise of their second-generation band Cactus, Tim Bogert (bass) and Carmine Appice (drums) joined Beck for the short-lived Beck/Bogert/Appice group, which disbanded in early 1974.

Jeff Beck returned in 1975 with his *Blow by Blow* album, a surprising yet intriguing change of musical direction for Beck. Made with former Beatles producer George Martin, the all-instrumental album had a distinctive jazz (and occasionally disco) flavor and sold remarkably well. *Wired,* recorded with Czech jazz keyboard wizard Jan Hammer, was also well received. Beck subsequently toured with Hammer, releasing a live set from the tour in 1977. After another sabbatical, Beck returned with a new band, the album *There and Back,* and another round of touring as an all-instrumental unit.

In 1983, Jeff Beck joined Eric Clapton, Jimmy Page, and a cast of established British musicians for a brief tour in support of Ronnie Lane's Appeal for Action Research into Multiple Sclerosis. The following year, Beck played on Rod Stewart's *Camouflage* album and its smash hit single "Infatuation," and toured with Stewart before leaving due to "artistic differences." Later he toured and recorded a mini-CD as The Honeydrippers with Robert Plant, Jimmy Page, Brian Setzer, and Cozy Powell. Beck also played on Tina Turner's smash hit "Private Dancer" and Mick Jagger's *She's the Boss* and *Primitive Cool* albums. In 1985, Epic issued his first solo album in five years, *Flash,* which featured Rod Stewart on vocals on "People Get Ready," a minor hit.

Jeff Beck again took several years off, reemerging in 1989 with *Jeff Beck's Guitar Shop,* an all-instrumental album recorded with keyboardist Tony Hymas and drummer Terry Bozzio, and his first major tour in nearly a decade, this time co-headlining with Texas blues guitarist Stevie Ray Vaughan. In 1993, with an ad hoc Big Town Playboys, Beck recorded fifteen Gene Vincent songs for *Crazy Legs,* his tribute to the rockabilly star and his guitarist, Cliff Gallup. Jeff Beck toured with Carlos Santana in 1995.

The Jeff Beck Group

Truth	Epic	26413	'68	†
	Epic/Legacy	47412		CS/CD
Beck-ola	Epic	26478	'69	†
	Epic/Legacy	47411		CD
Truth/Beck-ola	Epic	(2)33779	'75	†
	Epic	33779		CD
Rough and Ready	Epic	30973	'71	CS/CD
Jeff Beck Group	Epic	31331	'72	CS/CD

Beck, Bogert and Appice

Beck, Bogert and Appice	Epic	32140	'73	CS/CD

Jeff Beck

Early Anthology	Accord	7141	'81	†
Blow by Blow	Epic	33409	'75	CS/CD
	Epic	53442	'93	CD
	Mobile Fidelity	00727	'98	CD
Wired	Epic	33849	'76	CS/CD
	Mobile Fidelity	00531	'90	CD†
Wired/Blow by Blow	Epic	38227	'86	CS
There and Back	Epic	35684	'80	CS/CD
3-Pak: Blow by Blow/Wired/There and Back	Epic	(3)64808		CD†
Flash	Epic	39483	'85	CS/CD
Jeff Beck's Guitar Shop	Epic	44313	'89	CS/CD
Beckology	Epic/Legacy	(3)48661	'91	CS/CD†

Jeff Beck and Jan Hammer

Live	Epic	34433	'77	†
	Epic/Legacy	34433		CS/CD

The Honeydrippers

Volume 1	Atlantic (mini)	90220	'84	CS/CD

Jeff Beck and the Big Town Playboys

Crazy Legs	Epic	53562	'93	CS/CD

BOBBY "BLUE" BLAND

Born January 27, 1930, in Rosemont, Tennessee.

One of the most consistent rhythm-and-blues/soul vocalists of the '60s, Bobby "Blue" Bland performed for most of his career on the so-called "chitlin" circuit of small black clubs accompanied by a large band, a feature otherwise maintained by only B. B. King and Ray Charles. Regarded as one of the forerunners of modern soul music, Bland enjoyed his biggest pop success in the first half of the '60s. Subsequently overwhelmed by the rising soul stars of Motown, Stax, and Atlantic Records, Bland endured a fallow period in the late '60s and early '70s, reemerging in the mid-'70s on Dunhill Records both solo and with early associate B. B. King. Bobby Bland was inducted into the Rock and Roll Hall of Fame in 1992.

Moving to Memphis with his mother in 1947, Bobby Bland performed with the gospel group The Miniatures in the late '40s and joined The Beale Streeters, with B. B. King, Johnny Ace, and Rosco Gordon, in 1949. Performing locally with The Beale Streeters, Bland worked for B. B. King and made his first recordings for Chess in 1951 and Modern in 1952. Recording briefly for the Duke label in 1952, Bland served in the Army from 1952 until 1954, by which time Duke had been taken over by Houston's Don Robey. Touring with Little Junior Parker in Blues Consolidated package shows until the early '60s, Bland recorded with a big band for Duke, scoring a top rhythm-and-blues hit with "Farther Up the Road" in 1957 and a major R&B hit with "Little Boy Blue" in 1958.

By the end of the '50s, trumpeter Joe Scott had become Bobby Bland's bandleader and arranger. Scott steered Bland toward more sophisticated material that emphasized Bland's tortured baritone voice. With Scott providing the arrangements and Wayne Bennett supplying dynamic lead guitar, Bland achieved nearly thirty rhythm-and-blues hits from 1959 to 1968. Between 1960 and 1961, he scored a top rhythm-and-blues hit with "I Pity the Fool" and the R&B smashes with "I'll Take Care of You," "Cry Cry Cry," "Don't Cry No More," and the uptempo "Turn on Your Love Light" (a major pop hit). After the near-smash rhythm-and-blues hit "Ain't That Loving You," "Yield Not to Temptation," and "Stormy Monday Blues," "That's the Way Love Is"/"Call on Me" became a two-sided smash R&B and major pop hit in early 1963. Subsequent rhythm-and-blues smashes for Bland included "Ain't Nothing You Can Do" (a major pop hit), "These Hands (Small but Mighty)," "I'm Too Far Gone (To Turn Around)," "Good Time Charlie," "Poverty," and "You're All I Need."

In 1968, Bobby Bland fell into disfavor with Don Robey, the Joe Scott orchestra disbanded, and Bland ceased recording. In 1973, Robey sold Duke to ABC, where Bland enjoyed considerable success on the subsidiary Dunhill label. *His California Album* and *Dreamer,* produced by Steve Barri, yielded smash rhythm-and-blues hits with "This Time I'm Gone for Good" and "I Wouldn't Treat a Dog (The Way You Treated Me)," respectively. He also teamed with B. B. King for *Together for the First Time: Live* for Dunhill. King and Bland toured together in the '70s and '80s, raising Bland's professional profile and bringing him out of the chitlin circuit.

However, subsequent recordings for ABC and its successor, MCA, found Bobby Bland performing pop material with tired and trendy arrangements. He eventually received sympathetic treatment with the small Mississippi-based label Malaco, with which he signed in 1985. Although he failed to achieve popular success on Malaco, Bland continued to tour with longtime associates trumpeter-saxophonist Melvin Jackson (his orchestra leader since 1972) and guitarist Wayne Bennett. Bobby Bland was inducted into the Blues Foundation's Hall of Fame in 1981 and the Rock and Roll Hall of Fame in 1992.

Bobby "Blue" Bland/Junior Parker

Blues Consolidated	Duke	72	'60	†
	MCA	27037	'74	†

Bobby "Blue" Bland

The Soulful Side of Bobby Bland	Kent	044	'86	†
The "3Bs" Blues Boy: The Blues_Years, 1952–1959	Ace	302	'91	CD
Two Steps from the Blues	Duke	74	'61	†
	MCA	27036		LP/CS/CD
Here's the Man	Duke	75	'62	†
	MCA	27038		CS
Call on Me	Duke	77	'63	†
	MCA	27042		CS

Ain't Nothing You Can Do	Duke	78	'64	†
	MCA	27040	'74	CS
The Soul of the Man	Duke	79	'66	†
	MCA	27041		CS
Best, Volume 1	Duke	84	'67	†
	MCA	27013		CS
	MCA	31219		CD
A Touch of the Blues	Duke	88	'67	†
	MCA	27047		CS†
Best, Volume 2	Duke	86	'68	†
	MCA	27045		CS
Spotlighting the Man	Duke	89	'69	†
	MCA	27048		CS†
A Touch of the Blues and Spotlighting the Man	Mobile Fidelity	770		CD†
If Loving You Is Wrong	Duke	90	'70	†
Introspective of Early Years	MCA	(2)4172	'74	CS†
I Pity The Fool: The Duke Recordings, Vol. One	Duke	(2)10665	'92	CS/CD
Turn on Your Love Light: The Duke Recordings, Vol. Two	Duke	(2)10957	'94	CS/CD
The Voice (Duke Recordings 1959–1969)	Ace	323		CD
His California Album	Dunhill	50163	'73	†
	MCA	10349	'91	CS/CD
Dreamer	Dunhill	50169	'74	†
	MCA	10415	'91	CS/CD
Get on Down with Bobby Bland	ABC	895	'75	†
Reflections in Blue	ABC/MCA	1018	'77	†
	MCA	27043		CS
Come Fly with Me	ABC/MCA	1075	'78	†
	MCA	27044		CS†
I Feel Good, I Feel Fine	MCA	3157	'79	†
	MCA	27073		CS
Sweet Vibrations	MCA	5145		†
	MCA	27076		†
Try Me, I'm Real	MCA	5233		†
Here We Go Again	MCA	5297		†
	MCA	883		†
	MCA	22013		CD
Tell Mr. Bland	MCA	5425		†
	MCA	884	'84	†
Members Only	Malaco	7429	'85	LP/CS
After All	Malaco	7439	'86	LP/CS
Blues You Can Use	Malaco	7444	'87	LP/CS/CD
First Class Blues	Malaco	5000	'87	LP/CS/CD
Midnight Run	Malaco	7450	'89	LP/CS/CD
Portrait of the Blues	Malaco	7458	'91	LP/CS/CD

B. B. King and Bobby "Blue" Bland

Together for the First Time: Live	Dunhill	(2)50190	'74	†
	MCA	(2)4160	'82	LP/CS
	MCA	4160		CD
Together Again	Impulse	9317	'76	†
	MCA	27012		CS/CD

BLOOD, SWEAT AND TEARS

Al Kooper (born February 5, 1944, in Brooklyn, New York), keyboards, vocals; Steve Katz (born May 9, 1945, in Brooklyn), guitar, vocals; Jerry Weiss (born May 1, 1946, in New York City) and Randy Brecker (born November 27, 1945, in Philadelphia), trumpets, flugelhorns; Fred Lipsius (born November 19, 1944, in New York City), alto saxophone, piano; Dick Halligan (born August 29, 1943, in Troy, New York), trumpet, flute, keyboards; Jim Fielder (born October 4, 1947, in Denton, Texas), bass; and Bobby Colomby (born December 20, 1944, in New York City), drums, vocals. Al Kooper, Jerry Weiss, and Randy Brecker left after the first album, to be replaced by David Clayton-Thomas (born David Tomsett on September 13, 1941, in Surrey, England), vocals; Lew Soloff (born February 20, 1944, in Brooklyn) and Chuck Winfield (born February 5, 1943, in Monessen, Pennsylvania), trumpet, flugelhorn; and Jerry Hyman (born May 19, 1947, in Brooklyn), trombone, recorder.

The first major rock group to successfully augment its sound with horns, Blood, Sweat and Tears displayed an early amalgamation of jazz, rock, and, later, classical music. Following the departure of keyboardist-vocalist Al Kooper after their first album, Blood, Sweat and Tears evolved into an enormously popular, highly arranged pop band fronted by vocalist David Clayton-Thomas that set the standard for the blending together of rock, pop, and jazz music.

Blood, Sweat and Tears was formed in 1968 by Al Kooper, Steve Katz, and Bobby Colomby following Katz and Kooper's departure from The Blues Project. These founders recruited additional musicians Jim Fielder, Jerry Weiss, Randy Brecker, Fred Lipsius, and Dick Halligan. Although their debut album on Columbia, *Child Is Father to the Man,* failed to generate any hit singles, it contained a number of excellent Al Kooper compositions ("I Love You More Than You'll Ever Know," "My Days Are Numbered," and "I Can't Quit Her"), as well as early versions of Harry Nilsson's "Without Her" and Randy Newman's "Just One Smile."

In mid-1968, Kooper left Blood, Sweat and Tears to accept a lucrative offer from Columbia Records to become a producer. Weiss and Brecker also left, to be replaced by Lew Soloff, Chuck Winfield, and Jerry Hyman. The lead vocalist role was taken over by David Clayton-Thomas. Clayton-Thomas had worked around Toronto for ten years, recording five Canadian gold-award records with The Bossmen. The new lineup's first album exploded onto the music scene in early 1969. In addition to including Steve Katz's beautiful "Sometimes in Winter" and a remake of Billie Holiday's "God Bless the Child," the album yielded *three* smash hit singles with Laura Nyro's "And When I Die," Brenda Hollway's "You've Made Me So Very Happy" and Clayton-Thomas' "Spinning Wheel." Blood, Sweat and Tears' next album contained two hit singles, "Hi-De-Ho" and "Lucretia MacEvil," plus the elaborately arranged "Symphony/Sympathy for the Devil" and "40,000 Headmen." Their next album included only one moderate hit, "Go Down Gamblin.'"

A series of defections soon struck Blood, Sweat and Tears, effectively crippling the group. Clayton-Thomas and Lipsius departed at the end of 1971, with Clayton-Thomas pursuing an undistinguished solo career. Halligan also left, followed by Katz and Winfield in 1973. The group persevered with new personnel and a succession of lead vocalists—Bobby Doyle, Jerry Fisher, and Jerry La Croix.

David Clayton-Thomas subsequently rejoined Blood, Sweat and Tears in July 1974. By then, only Bobby Colomby remained from the original group. Personnel shifts continued to plague Blood, Sweat and Tears, and, in 1976, Colomby left. On January 31, 1978, one-year member Gregory Herbert was found dead in an Amsterdam hotel room during the group's European tour. By 1980, David Clayton-Thomas was the only "original" member left in Blood, Sweat and Tears. Yet another edition of the group toured the United States in 1988. Blood, Sweat and Tears also appeared at Woodstock '94.

Blood, Sweat and Tears

Child Is Father to the Man	Columbia	9619	'68	†
	Columbia/Legacy	64214	'94	CD
Blood, Sweat and Tears	Columbia	9720	'69	CS/CD
	Mobile Fidelity	00559	'92	CD
	Mobile Fidelity	251	'96	LP
Blood, Sweat and Tears 3	Columbia	30090	'70/'86	CD
Blood, Sweat and Tears 4	Columbia	30590	'71	†
	Columbia/Legacy	66422	'96	CD
Greatest Hits	Columbia	31170	'72	CS/CD
New Blood	Columbia	31780	'72	†
No Sweat	Columbia	32180	'73	†
Mirror Image	Columbia	32929	'74	†
New City	Columbia	33484	'75	†
More Than Ever	Columbia	34233	'76	†
Live and Improvised	Columbia/Legacy	(2)46918	'91	CS†/CD
What Goes Up! The Best Of (rec. 1967–1975)	Columbia/Legacy	(2)64166	'95	CD
Brand New Day	ABC	1015	'78	†
Blood, Sweat and Tears	MCA	3227	'80	†
Greatest Hits	Hollywood/IMG	738	'92	CS†
Nuclear Blues (recorded 1980)	Avenue	71922	'95	CD
Live (recorded 1982)	Avenue	71287	'94	CS/CD
Collection	Griffin	379		CD

David Clayton-Thomas

I Got a Woman	Decca	75146	'69	†
Magnificent Sanctuary Band	Columbia	31000	'72	†
Tequila Sunrise	Columbia	31700	'72	†
Harmony Junction	RCA	0173	'73	†
Clayton	ABC/MCA	1104	'78	†

MIKE BLOOMFIELD

Born July 28, 1944, in Chicago; died February 15, 1981, in San Francisco.

In the forefront of the late '60s blues revival with The Paul Butterfield Blues Band and The Electric Flag, Mike Bloomfield became established as an American guitar hero (and rival to Eric Clapton) through his recordings with Butterfield and Bob Dylan. Helping pioneer the extended guitar solo, Bloomfield later recorded with Al Kooper (the landmark *Super Session* album that set the precedent for "supergroup" recordings) and pursued a variety of independent musical projects. He became a stalwart of the San Francisco Bay Area blues scene, but died of a drug overdose on February 15, 1981.

Mike Bloomfield obtained his first guitar at age thirteen and was soon frequenting Chicago area blues clubs. He played guitar at local blues and folk clubs with vocalist Nick Gravenites and harmonica player Charlie Musselwhite in the early '60s and became a respected sessions musician. In 1964, he joined The Paul Butterfield Blues Band, whose earliest recordings were eventually released in 1995 as *The Lost Elektra Sessions*. In June 1965, the Butterfield band brought electric guitar to the Newport Folk Festival both on their own and behind Bob Dylan. During the year, Bloomfield and Al Kooper helped record Bob Dylan's monumental "Like a Rolling Stone" single and *Highway 61 Revisited* album. Bloomfield remained with The Paul Butterfield Blues Band for two albums, their debut and *East-West,* before departing in early 1967 to form The Electric Flag with Gravenites, keyboardist Barry Goldberg, bassist Harvey Brooks, drummer Buddy Miles, and a horn section. Debuting at the Monterey International Pop Festival in June 1967, The Electric Flag recorded the soundtrack to the psychedelic movie *The Trip*. Their debut album featured "Killing Floor," "Over-Lovin' You," and "Groovin' Is Easy." However, the band disintegrated before the release of its second album.

Mike Bloomfield returned to the studio to work with Moby Grape (*Grape Jam*) and Barry Goldberg (*Two Jews Blues*) and recorded one side of the landmark *Super Session* album with Al Kooper. Bloomfield recorded *Live Adventures* with Al Kooper, and later joined Paul Butterfield and others to record Muddy Waters' *Fathers and Sons*. Recording his first solo album for Columbia in 1969, Bloomfield joined Dr. John and John Paul Hammond in the short-lived Triumvirate group in 1973. The Electric Flag reformed with Bloomfield, Gravenites, Goldberg, and Miles, among others, in 1974, enduring one tour and one ill-received album. Bloomfield subsequently recorded another solo album before vocalist Ray Kennedy, Goldberg, and Bloomfield formed the short-lived group KGB in 1976. Bloomfield subsequently became a mainstay of the San Francisco blues scene, recording albums for several labels, primarily John Fahey's Takoma Records. Bloomfield was found dead of a drug overdose in San Francisco on February 15, 1981.

MIKE BLOOMFIELD BIBLIOGRAPHY

Ward, Ed. *Mike Bloomfield: The Rise and Fall of an American Guitar Hero*. New York: Cherry Lane Books, 1983.

The Paul Butterfield Blues Band

The Original Lost Elektra Sessions (recorded 1964)	Rhino/Elektra	73505	'95	CD
The Paul Butterfield Blues Band	Elektra	7294	'65	CD
East-West	Elektra	7315	'66	CD

The Electric Flag

The Trip (soundtrack)	Sidewalk	5908	'67	†
	Curb/Atlantic	77863	'96	CS/CD
A Long Time Comin'	Columbia	9597	'68	CD
An American Music Band	Columbia	9714	'68	†
Best	Columbia	30422	'71	†
The Band Kept Playing	Atlantic	18112	'74	†
Groovin' Is Easy	Magnum America	29	'96	CD

Bloomfield, Kooper and Stills

Super Session	Columbia	9701	'68	CS/CD

Mike Bloomfield and Al Kooper

Live Adventures of Mike Bloomfield and Al Kooper	Columbia	(2)6	'69	†
	Columbia/Legacy	(2)64670	'98	CD

Mike Bloomfield

It's Not Killing Me	Columbia	9883	'69	†
	Harmony	30395	'71	†
Don't Say That I Ain't Your Man: Essential Blues, 1964–1969	Columbia/Legacy	57631	'94	CS/CD
Try It Before You Buy It	Columbia	33173	'75	†
Bloomfield	Columbia	(2)37578	'83	†
Live at the Old Waldorf	Columbia/Legacy	65688	'98	CS/CD

If You Love These Blues	Guitar Player	3002	'77	†
	Kicking Mule	166		CS
Analine	Takoma	7059	'77	†
	Takoma	72759		†
Michael Bloomfield	Takoma	7063	'78	†
	Takoma	72763		†
Between the Hard Place and the Ground	Takoma	7070	'79	†
	Takoma	72770		†
	Magnum America	12	'95	CD
Cruisin' for a Bruisin'	Takoma	7091	'81	†
	Takoma	72791		†
Best	Takoma	72815	'87	CD†
Count Talent and The Originals	Clouds	8805	'78	†
Living in the Fast Lane	Waterhouse	11	'81	†
	ERA	5006	'92	CS/CD
Junko Partner	Intermedia	5068		LP/CS
Blues, Gospel and Ragtime Guitar Instrumentals	Shanachie	99007	'93	CS/CD

Mike Bloomfield, John Paul Hammond and Dr. John

Triumvirate	Columbia	32172	'73	CD

Mike Bloomfield with KGB

KGB	MCA	2166	'76	†

Mike Bloomfield and Woody Harris

Gospel Guitar Duets	Kicking Mule	164	'80	CS
Mike Bloomfield with Woody Harris	Sky Ranch	2328	'92	CD

BLUE CHEER

Dickie Peterson (born 1948 in Grand Forks, North Dakota), bass, lead vocals; Bruce "Leigh" Stephens, guitar; and Paul Whaley, drums. Later members included guitarists Randy Holden, Bruce Stephens, and Gary Yoder, drummer Norman Mayell, and keyboardist Ralph Burns Kellogg.

Dismissed on the East Coast and ignored in Great Britain, Blue Cheer was one of the loudest bands of the late '60s and probably the first American heavy metal band. Modeled after The Jimi Hendrix Experience, Blue Cheer was one of the first American power trios. Scoring a major pop hit with a bombastic version of Eddie Cochran's "Summertime Blues" in 1968, Blue Cheer endured a series of personnel changes and dissolved in 1971, although principal Dick Peterson has since reunited the group several times.

Bassist Dick Peterson, a veteran of Boston's psychedelic Group B, recruited lead guitarist Bruce "Leigh" Stephens and drummer Paul Whaley of Sacramento's Oxford Circle for the formation of Blue Cheer. Based in San Francisco by 1967, the group enjoyed airplay of a demonstration tape of Eddie Cochran's "Summertime Blues" on "underground" FM radio station KMPX and soon signed a recording contract with Philips Records. The song and their debut album became major hits in early 1968, and "Just a Little" proved a minor hit from their second album.

Personnel changes subsequently plagued Blue Cheer. Leigh Stephens was dismissed and keyboardist Ralph Kellogg was added, with Bruce Stephens quickly succeeding Randy Holden on guitar. Soon Whaley was replaced by Norman Mayell, leaving Peterson the only original member still in the group. The group dissolved after 1971's *Oh! Pleasant Hope*.

In the meantime, Leigh Stephens recorded a solo album for Philips and a group album with Silver Metre. He later joined Bruce Stephens in Pilot. Peterson reunited Blue Cheer in 1979, 1984 (with Paul Whaley), and again in the late '80s, recording *The Beast Is Back.* In the early '90s, Blue Cheer recorded two German-released albums.

Blue Cheer

Vincebus Eruptum	Philips	600264	'68	†
	Philips	9001	'79	†
	Mercury	514685	'93	CD
Outsideinside	Philips	600278	'68	†
	Mercury	514683	'93	CD
New! Improved! Blue Cheer	Philips	600305	'69	†
Louder Than God (The Best of Blue Cheer, 1968–1969)	Rhino	70130	'86	CS
Blue Cheer	Philips	600333	'70	†
The Original Human Being	Philips	600347	'70	†
Oh! Pleasant Hope	Philips	600350	'71	†
Good Times Are So Hard to Find (The History of Blue Cheer)	Mercury	834030	'88	CD
The Beast Is Back	Megaforce/Caroline	1395	'89	LP/CS/CD

Leigh Stephens

Red Weather	Philips	600294	'69	†

Silver Metre

Silver Metre	National General	2000	'69	†

Pilot (with Leigh and Bruce Stephens)

Pilot	RCA	4730	'72	†
Point of View	RCA	4825	'73	†

THE BLUES PROJECT

Tommy Flanders, vocals; Danny Kalb (born September 19, 1942, in Brooklyn, New York), guitar; Andy Kulberg (born June 1944 in Buffalo, New York), bass, flute; and Roy Blumenfeld, drums. Flanders left after the first album and keyboardist-vocalist Al Kooper (born February 5, 1944, in Brooklyn) and guitarist Steve Katz (born May 9, 1945, in Brooklyn) were added.

Perhaps the first white band to use electric instruments in playing folk music and the blues, The Blues Project, along with The Butterfield Blues Band, helped spark the blues revival of the late '60s. New York's first "underground" group, The Blues Project featured Al Kooper on its second and third albums. Members Andy Kulberg and Roy Blumenfeld later formed Seatrain, one of the first rock bands to play country-style material.

Formed by folk guitarist Danny Kalb, The Blues Project debuted at Greenwich Village's Cafe Au Go Go in the summer of 1965. Playing a curious admixture of folk, blues, and jazz, the group signed with Verve Records. Tommy Flanders left after their first album and the group soon added guitarist Steve Katz and the multitalented Al Kooper. Kooper contributed the underground favorite "Flute Thing" and "No Time Like the Right Time" (a minor pop hit), but he and Katz left The Blues Project in 1968 to form Blood, Sweat and Tears.

Andy Kulberg and Roy Blumenfeld recruited violinist Richard Greene and saxophonist Don Kretmar for *Planned Obsolescence,* but the group subsequently recorded for A&M Records as Seatrain. With Kalb, Blumenfeld, and Kretmar as principals, The Blues Project reunited for two more albums for Capitol in the early '70s. Around 1971, Seatrain re-grouped in California with Kulberg, Greene, bluegrass veteran Peter Rowan, and drummer

Larry Atamanuik for two Capitol albums. The group recorded a wide range of material, including country, as evidenced by their recordings of "Orange Blossom Special" and Lowell George's "Willin.'"

The Blues Project (without Flanders, but with Al Kooper) reunited for a live concert in Central Park in 1973. Steve Katz helped form American Flyer with Eric Kaz, Craig Fuller, and Doug Yule in 1976. The Blues Project again reunited for Al Kooper's fiftieth birthday party at New York's Bottom Line in 1994.

The Blues Project

"Live" at the Cafe Au Go Go	Verve/Folkways	3000	'66	†
	Verve	833346	'89	CS†/CD
Projections	Verve/Folkways	3008	'66	†
	Verve	827918	'89	CD
"Live" at Town Hall	Verve/Forecast	3025	'67	†
	One Way	30010	'94	CD
Planned Obsolescence	Verve/Forecast	3046	'68	†
	One Way	32642	'96	CD
Kooper, et al. of The Blues Project	Verve/Forecast	3069	'69	†
Best	Verve/Forecast	3077	'69	†
The Blues Project	MGM	118	'70	†
Archetypes	MGM	4953	'74	†
Lazarus	Capitol	782	'71	†
The Blues Project	Capitol	11017	'72	†
Reunion in Central Park	MCA	(2)8003	'73	†
	One Way	22186	'95	CD
Best: "No Time Like the Right Time"	Rhino	70165	'89	CS/CD†

Danny Kalb and Stefan Grossman

Crosscurrents	Cotillion	9007	'69	†

Tommy Flanders

Moonstone	Verve/Forecast	3075	'69	†

Seatrain

Seatrain	A&M	4171	'69	†
Seatrain	Capitol	659	'71	†
	Capitol	29800	'94	CS†
Marblehead Messenger	Capitol	829	'71	†
	One Way	57661		CD
Watch	Warner Brothers	2692	'73	†

American Flyer

American Flyer	United Artists	650	'76	†
Spirit of a Woman	United Artists	720	'77	†

THE BONZO DOG BAND

Vivian Stanshall (born March 21, 1943, in Shillingford, Oxfordshire, England; died March 5, 1995, in London), trumpet, vocals; Neil Innes (born December 9, 1944, in Danbury, Essex, England), keyboards, guitar, bass, vocals; Roger Ruskin Spear (born June 29, 1943, in Hammersmith, London), reeds, sound effects; Rodney Slater (born November 8, 1941, in Crowland, Lincolnshire, England), reeds; and "Legs" Larry Smith (born January 18, 1944, in Oxford, England), drums, percussion, tap dancing.

One of the first groups to explore the visual, the theatrical, and the absurd within the rock format, The Bonzo Dog Band parodied '50s rock-and-roll, pretentious folk music, and the English music hall tradition while satirizing many aspects of contemporary life. Sometimes compared to The Mothers of Invention for their combination of rock music and satire, The Bonzo Dog Band were particularly important in Great Britain, where they proved to be particularly influential on the creators of British television's *Monty Python's Flying Circus.*

Formed by art students at London's Goldsmiths College, The Bonzo Dog Doo Dah Band began performing their demented brand of music and satire in pubs in 1965. They graduated to cabarets and clubs in 1966, signed with British Liberty (Imperial in the United States) in 1967, and appeared briefly in The Beatles' television film *Magical Mystery Tour.* With Vivian Stanshall and Neil Innes as the chief songwriters, the group's debut album included the underground favorite "The Intro and the Outro," in which various historical figures and musicians from a mythical band were introduced. Foreshortening their name to The Bonzo Dog Band and adding bassist Dennis Cowan, the group's second album included "Humanoid Boogie," "Can Blue Men Sing the Whites?" and "I'm the Urban Spaceman," a near-smash British hit produced by Paul McCartney under the pseudonym Apollo C. Vermouth. *Tadpoles* contained "Canyons of Your Mind," "Tubas in the Moonlight," and the favorite "Mr. Apollo."

Recognized only by "underground" FM radio in the United States, The Bonzo Dog Band persevered until early 1970, reuniting around Vivian Stanshall, Neil Innes, and Dennis Cowan for 1972's *Let's Make Up and Be Friendly.* Stanshall subsequently led a variety of groups, while Innes recorded extensively, both solo and with various groups, as well as an accompanist. He later worked as a composer for British television shows such as *Monty Python's Flying Circus* and *Rutland Weekend Television.* In 1978 Innes joined Monty Python's Eric Idle for the irreverent Beatles parody *AllYou Need Is Cash,* broadcast on NBC television, and the album *The Rutles,* later reuniting for 1996's *Archeology.* Vivian Stanshall died in a fire at his London apartment on March 5, 1995.

The Bonzo Dog Doodah Band

Gorilla	Imperial	12370	'68	†
	One Way	17370		CD

The Bonzo Dog Band

Urban Spaceman	Imperial	12432	'69	†
	One Way	17430		CD
Tadpoles	Imperial	12445	'69	†
	One Way	17431		CD
Keynsham	Imperial	12457	'70	†
	One Way	17432		CD
The Beast of the Bonzoes	United Artists	5517	'71	†
Let's Make Up and Be Friendly	United Artists	5584	'72	†
	One Way	17795	'94	CD
The History of the Bonzo Dog Band	United Artists	(2)321	'74	†
Best	Rhino	71006	'90	CD†

Roger Ruskin Spear

Electric Shocks	United Artists	097	'72	†

Grimms (with Neil Innes)

Grimms Rockin' Duck	Antilles	7012	'76	†

Neil Innes and Eric Idle

Rutland Weekend Songbook	Passport	98018	'76	†

The Rutles (with Neil Innes and Eric Idle)

The Rutles	Warner Brothers	3151	'78	†
	Rhino	75760	'90	CD
Archaeology	Virgin	42200	'96	CD†
	Rhino	90679	'98	CD

BOOKER T. AND THE MGs

Booker T. Jones (born November 12, 1944, in Memphis, Tennessee), keyboards, guitar, bass; Steve Cropper (born October 21, 1941, in Willow Springs, Missouri), lead and rhythm guitar; Donald "Duck" Dunn (born November 24, 1941, in Memphis), bass; and Al Jackson, Jr. (born November 27, 1935, in Memphis; died October 1, 1975, in Memphis), drums.

Best remembered historically as the studio band for Stax-Volt Records during the '60s, Booker T. and The MGs created the so-called "Memphis Sound" behind hit recordings by Carla and Rufus Thomas, Otis Redding, and Sam and Dave, among others. The group featured a cohesive yet spare sound on hits of their own such as "Green Onions," "Hang 'Em High," and "Time Is Tight," and were perhaps the last rock band to issue albums entirely comprising instrumentals. Members Booker T. Jones ("Born Under a Bad Sign") and Steve Cropper ("In the Midnight Hour," "Knock on Wood," and "Dock of the Bay") also proved effective songwriters for others artists. Booker T. and The MGs were inducted into the Rock and Roll Hall of Fame in 1992.

Booker T. Jones began working at Stax Records in Memphis as a saxophonist in 1960. In 1962, Booker T. and The MGs (for *M*emphis *G*roup) formed as the "house band" for the label. Steve Cropper and Donald "Duck" Dunn had been members of The Mar-Keys since the late '50s and both played on the group's 1961 smash rhythm-and-blues and pop instrumental hit "Last Night." Dunn remained with The Mar-Keys until 1964, when he replaced original bassist Lewis Steinberg in The MGs. In the early '60s, Booker T. and The MGs provided the instrumental backing for smash rhythm-and-blues and pop hits by Carla Thomas ("Gee Whiz") and her father Rufus Thomas ("Walking the Dog"). Their reputation as a band in their own right was established in 1962 with the top rhythm-and-blues and smash pop instrumental hit "Green Onions."

Over the next seven years, Booker T. and The MGs recorded independently and backed various Stax-Volt artists while individual members pursued solo projects. Jones worked with artist-producer William Bell and co-wrote the oft-recorded blues classic "Born Under a Bad Sign" with him for Albert King. In 1966, Booker T. received a degree in music from Indiana University. In the meantime, Steve Cropper supervised the recordings of Otis Redding and cowrote top rhythm-and-blues hits by Wilson Pickett ("In the Midnight Hour"), Eddie Floyd ("Knock on Wood"), and Redding ("Dock of the Bay"). Al Jackson produced recordings by blues guitarist Albert King. Booker T. and The MGs also served as the backing band for Sam and Dave's "Hold On! I'm Coming" and "Soul Man," both top R&B hits.

On their own, Booker T. and The MGs scored near-smash rhythm-and-blues hits with "Hip Hug-Her," "Groovin'," "Soul Limbo," and "Time Is Tight." "Groovin' " and "Soul Limbo" proved major pop hits, while "Hang 'Em High" and "Time Is Tight" became near-smash pop hits. The latter song came from the soundtrack to *Uptight,* scored by Booker T. Jones. In 1967, Booker T. and The MGs toured Great Britain in support of Otis Redding, Sam and Dave, Eddie Floyd, Carla Thomas, and others, later performing and backing Otis Redding at the Monterey International Pop Festival in June. In 1969, Steve Cropper recorded *With a Little Help from My Friends* and, with Albert King and gospel patriarch "Pop" Staples, *Jammed Together.*

By 1970, Booker T. and The MGs had abandoned their role as the Stax house band, officially disbanding in 1972. Jones moved to California and joined A&M Records as a staff producer. There he supervised recording sessions for Rita Coolidge, his wife Priscilla (Rita's sister), and Bill Withers. In the early '70s, Jones recorded three albums with his wife, plus the solo album *Evergreen*. Cropper continued with sessions and production chores at Stax-Volt Records until 1975, when Stax-Volt folded. He then moved to Los Angeles.

The original members of Booker T. and The MGs were planning a reunion when Al Jackson was shot to death in Memphis on October 1, 1975. The band did reunite, with Willie Hall succeeding Jackson on drums, for *Universal Language,* and Jones later recorded three solo albums for A&M. Jones, Cropper, and Dunn recorded with others as The RCO All-Stars behind The Band's Levon Helm. Cropper and Dunn recreated their distinctive '60s sound behind The Blues Brothers (John Belushi and Dan Aykroyd) on tours and albums, as well as in the popular *Blues Brothers* movie of 1980. Booker T. Jones also produced Willie Nelson's 1978 album *Stardust*. In 1988, Booker T., Steve Cropper, and "Duck" Dunn reunited with drummer Anton Fig to perform at Atlantic Records' fortieth anniversary show at Madison Square Garden, and the quartet subsequently stayed together for several years to perform as Booker T. and The MGs. The group was inducted into the Rock and Roll Hall of Fame in 1992 and, that October, Booker T. Jones, Cropper, and Dunn joined sessions drummer Jim Keltner to serve as the house band for the four-hour Bob Dylan tribute staged at Madison Square Garden. In 1994, Booker T., Cropper, and Dunn recorded their first album in seventeen years, *That's the Way It Should Be,* with sessions drummers. Cropper and Dunn reunited in the Blues Brothers Band for the 1998 movie *Blues Brothers 2000*.

The Mar-Keys

Last Night	Atlantic	8055	'61	†
Do the Pop-Eye	Atlantic	8062	'62	†
The Great Memphis Sound	Stax	707	'66	†
	Atlantic	82339	'91	CS/CD
Damifiknew	Stax	2025	'69	†
The Memphis Experience	Stax	2036	'71	†
Damnifiknew/The Memphis Experience	Stax	88021	'94	CD

Booker T. and the MGs/The Mar-Keys

Back to Back	Stax	720	'67	†
	Atlantic	90307	'91	CS/CD

Various Artists

The Complete Stax-Volt Singles 1959–1968	Atlantic	(9)82218	'91	CD
The Complete Stax-Volt Singles Volume 2	Atlantic	(9)4411	'93	CD

Booker T. and the MGs

Green Onions	Stax	701	'62	†
	Atlantic	7701		†
	Atlantic	82255	'91	CS/CD
Soul Dressing	Stax	705	'65	†
	Atlantic	7705		†
	Atlantic	82337	'91	CS†/CD
And Now!	Stax	711	'66	†
	Atlantic	7711		†
	Rhino	70297	'92	CS/CD
In the Christmas Spirit	Stax	713	'66	†
	Atlantic	7713	'69	†
	Atlantic	82338	'91	CS/CD

Hip Hug-Her	Stax	717	'67	†
	Atlantic	7717		†
	Rhino	71013	'92	CS/CD
Doin' Our Thing	Stax	724	'68	†
	Atlantic	7724		†
	Rhino	71014	'92	CS/CD
Soul Limbo	Stax	2001	'68	†
	Stax	4113	'78	CS/CD
Uptight (soundtrack)	Stax	2006	'69	†
	Stax	8562		CS/CD†
The Booker T. Set	Stax	2009	'69	†
	Stax	8531	'87	LP/CS/CD
McLemore Avenue	Stax	2027	'70	†
	Stax	8552	'90	CS/CD
Greatest Hits	Stax	2033	'70	†
	Stax	8505		CS
Melting Pot	Stax	2035	'71	†
	Stax	8521	'90	CS/CD
Free Ride	Stax	4104	'78	†
Best	Stax	60004		CD
	Atlantic	8202	'68	†
	Atlantic	81281	'85	CS/CD
Universal Language	Asylum	1093	'77	†
Groovin'	Rhino	71234	'93	CS/CD
Very Best	Rhino	71738	'94	CS/CD
That's the Way It Should Be	Columbia	53307	'94	CS/CD

Steve Cropper

With a Little Help from My Friends	Volt	6006	'69	†
	Stax	8555	'90	LP/CD
Playin' My Thang	MCA	5171	'81	†
Night After Night	MCA	5340	'82	†

Steve Cropper/Albert King/Pop Staples

Jammed Together	Stax	2020	'69	†
	Stax	8544	'90	LP/CS/CD

Priscilla Jones

Gypsy Queen	A&M	4297	'71	†

Booker T. and Priscilla Jones

Booker T. and Priscilla	A&M	(2)3504	'71	†
Home Grown	A&M	4351	'72	†
Chronicles	A&M	4413	'73	†

The MGs

The MGs	Stax	3024	'73	†

Booker T. Jones

Evergreen	Epic	33143	'74	†
Try and Love Again	A&M	4720	'78	†
The Best of You	A&M	4798	'80	†
Booker T. Jones	A&M	4874	'81	†
The Runaway	MCA	6282	'89	LP/CS/CD†

Levon Helm and The RCO All-Stars

Levon Helm and The RCO All-Stars	ABC	1017	'77	†
	Mobile Fidelity	761	'92	CD†

The Blues Brothers

Briefcase Full of Blues	Atlantic	19217	'78	†
	Atlantic	82788	'95	CS/CD
The Blues Brothers (music from the soundtrack)	Atlantic	16017	'80	CS/CD
	Atlantic	82787	'95	CS/CD
Made in America	Atlantic	16025	'80	†
	Atlantic	82789	'95	CS/CD
Best	Atlantic	19331	'81	†
	Atlantic	82790	'95	CS/CD
The Definitive Collection	Atlantic	82428	'92	CS/CD
Red, White and Blues	Turnstyle	14206	'92	CS/CD†
Blues Brothers 2000	Universal	53116	'98	CS/CD

JAMES BROWN

Born May 3, 1928, in Macon, Georgia (although some sources claim May 3, 1933, in Barnwell, South Carolina).

Probably the single most popular black artist among blacks until the mid '70s, James Brown may very well be the last vaudeville performer, with his high-powered, histrionic, and intensely dramatic stage show. In fact, his performance style influenced generations of performers, from Mick Jagger and Sly Stone to Michael Jackson and Prince. His classic 1962 album, *Live at the Apollo,* is regarded by some as the greatest in-concert album ever recorded and was likely the first album bought in mass quantities by blacks. With his unique mixture of gospel, blues, and even jazz, and the powerful choreographed playing of The Fabulous Flames, Brown reinvigorated soul music in the '60s and opened the door for soul shouters such as Wilson Pickett and Otis Redding. One of the first rock entertainers to gain complete control over his career, James Brown was certainly the first black artist to achieve independence from his record company in matters of arrangements, production, and packaging. In emphasizing polyrhythms from the late '60s to early '70s with instrumentalists Maceo Parker, Fred Wesley, and William "Bootsy" Collins, Brown Africanized American rhythm-and-blues and originated funk music later pursued by Sly Stone and George Clinton. That influence extended into the '80s and '90s with the development of hip-hop and rap music, which regularly mimicked his style and sampled his early recordings. Moreover, Brown was one of the first blacks to champion black self-pride and political consciousness in the '60s, while at the same time establishing himself as one of the nation's first black entrepreneurs. Inducted into the Rock and Roll Hall of Fame in its inaugural year, 1986, James Brown endured a rocky period of health, financial, and legal problems in the late '80s.

Raised in Augusta, James Brown took up keyboards, then drums and bass, at an early age. Dropping out of school in the seventh grade, Brown spent a delinquent youth, serving four years in reform school for petty theft beginning in 1949. Upon release, he joined pianist Bobby Byrd's Gospel Starlighters. Evolving into the Famous Flames and concentrating on rhythm-and-blues music, the group played around Georgia and came to the attention of Ralph Bass of Cincinnati's King Records. He signed them to a recording contract in January 1956 after hearing their first demonstration record. Rerecorded with Byrd and former Gospel Starlighters Sylvester Keels and Nafloyd Scott, the song, "Please, Please, Please," became a smash rhythm-and-blues hit in April.

JAMES BROWN (NEAL PRESTON/CORBIS)

James Brown quickly became the undisputed leader of the Famous Flames. Their next hit, 1958's "Try Me," topped the R&B charts and filtered into the pop charts. A series of smash rhythm-and-blues hits began in 1960 with "Think," followed by "I Don't Mind," "Baby, You're Right," "Lost Someone," and "Night Train." Brown organized the James Brown Revue with dozens of singers, musicians, and dancers, and, with a tightly rehearsed and choreographed stage act polished to near perfection, they played to sellout, box-office record audiences in ghetto areas across the country in the early '60s. The live recording of their show at Harlem's Apollo Theater on October 24, 1962, reflected Brown's mastery of showmanship and effectively established him as an important artist, and the resulting album is regarded as a classic.

During 1962, James Brown reluctantly recorded several songs with vocal chorus and strings at the insistence of King Records. One of the songs, "Prisoner of Love," became a major pop hit. By 1964, however, Brown had deemphasized vocals in favor of strong hard polyrhythms. He brought a set of recently recorded songs to the Smash subsidiary of Mercury Records in Chicago. One of them, "Out of Sight," became a major pop hit and Brown's first record to sell in large quantities to whites. Brown eventually returned to King with complete control over all aspects of his recording career, with releases on Smash restricted to instrumentals and recordings by members of the Revue.

With The Famous Flames, James Brown became perhaps the earliest purveyor of bottom-heavy funk music. Over the years, his groups included saxophonists Maceo Parker (1964–1970, 1973–1976, and 1984–1988, the last as band director) and Alfred "Pee Wee" Ellis (1965–1970), guitarist Jimmy Nolen (1965–1970, 1972–1983), trombonist Fred Wesley (1968–1976), and bassist William "Bootsy" Collins (1969–1971). All except Nolen recorded albums on their own after leaving Brown.

Eschewing club engagements in favor of concert auditoriums, Brown scored a top rhythm-and-blues and near-smash pop hit in 1965 with the seminal "Papa's Got a Brand New Bag," recorded with Nolen, Parker, and new band leader Nat Jones. Adding Ellis, Brown followed up with the top R&B and smash pop hits "I Got You (I Feel Good)" and "It's a Man's World," and the rhythm-and-blues smashes "Ain't That a Groove (Part 1)," "Don't Be a Drop-Out," "Bring It Up," and "Let Yourself Go." Ellis took over as musical director and chief musical collaborator in 1967. Buying three Southern radio stations, Brown subsequently achieved top R&B and near-smash pop hits with the funk masterpiece "Cold Sweat" and "I Got the Feelin,'" and rhythm-and-blues smashes with "I Can't Stand Myself (When You Touch Me)"/"There Was a Time," and "Licking Stick—Licking Stick."

By the late '60s, James Brown was producing the entire show for the Revue—songs, costumes, routines, choreography, and lighting. Credited with helping quell riots after the assassination of Dr. Martin Luther King, Jr., Brown issued one of the first anthems of black pride in 1968, "Say It Loud I'm Black and I'm Proud," a top R&B and major pop hit. Performing at President Richard Nixon's inaugural celebration in January 1969, Brown scored the top R&B and major pop hit "Give It Up or Turnit A Loose" and the smash R&B and major pop hit "I Don't Want Nobody to Give Me Nothing." He next returned to more conventional hits based on the dance style called the Popcorn, beginning with the top R&B and major pop hit "Mother Popcorn," followed by the smash R&B and major pop hit "Ain't It Funky Now (Part 1)" and the seminal "Funky Drummer."

In mid-1970, the Famous Flames broke up, to be replaced by The JBs, centered around pianist Bobby Byrd, guitarist Jimmy Nolen, saxophonist "Pee Wee" Ellis, trombonist Fred Wesley, and new bassist William "Bootsy" Collins. Scoring his final smash R&B hits on King with "Get Up I Feel Like Being a Sex Machine," "Super Bad," "Get Up, Get Into It, Get Involved," and "Soul Power," Brown switched to Polydor Records in 1971, bringing with him his entire back catalog and forming his own label, People, for the classic "Hot Pants" and recording by the JBs. However, Ellis and Collins soon left the JBs, with Fred Wesley replacing Ellis as band leader. Nonetheless, top rhythm-and-blues hits continued through 1974 with "Make It Funky (Part 1)," "Talking Loud and Say Nothing (Part 1)," "Get on the Good Foot (Part 1)," "The Payback (Part 1)," "My Thang," and "Papa Don't Take No Mess (Part 1)." Smash R&B hits of the era included "King Heroin," "There It Is (Part 1)," "I Got a Bag of My Own," "I Got Ants in My Pants," and "Funky President (People It's Bad)." In 1973, Brown and Wesley scored the music to the movies *Black Caesar* and *Slaughter's Big Rip-Off.*

In the early '70s, Maceo Parker, Pee Wee Ellis, and Fred Wesley recorded as Maceo and The King's Men and Maceo and The Macks. The JBs recorded a number of albums for People Records in the first half of the '70s. Parker, Wesley, and Bootsy Collins all joined George Clinton's Parliament-Funkadelic aggregation in the '70s, with Wesley recording one spin-off album as The Horny Horns. Collins later went on to his own successful funk career, and Parker, Wesley, and Ellis recorded successful jazz albums in the '90s.

James Brown began having tax disputes with the Treasury Department in 1975 and scored his last smash rhythm-and-blues hit for twelve years with "Get Up Offa That Thing" in 1976. Enduring diminished popularity, particularly with the rise of disco music, Brown even utilized the services of an outside producer for the first time for *The Original Disco Man* in 1979. Touring the rock club circuit for the first time in 1980, he was introduced to a new generation of fans with his appearance in *The Blues Brothers* movie. He began playing the supper club circuit in 1983, but long-time guitarist Jimmy Nolen died in Atlanta on December 18, 1983. Brown scored a minor R&B hit with hip-hop pioneer Afrika Bambaataa on "Unity" in 1984 and experienced a revival of interest in his music with the 1986 smash pop and near-smash R&B hit "Living in America" from the movie *Rocky IV.*

In 1986, James Brown was inducted into the Rock and Roll Hall of Fame and switched to Scotti Brothers Records. He soon became beset by personal, health, and financial troubles, yet scored a smash rhythm-and-blues hit with "I'm Real" in 1988. However, his September 1988 arrest in South Carolina following a two-state car chase by police resulted in a prison term of more than two years beginning in December. Paroled in February 1991, James Brown quickly resumed touring and recording.

JAMES BROWN BIBLIOGRAPHY

Brown, James, with Bruce Tucker. *James Brown: The Godfather of Soul.* New York: Macmillan, 1986; New York: Thunder's Mouth Press, 1990, 1997.

Rose, Cynthia. *Living in America: The Soul Saga of James Brown.* London: Serpents' Tail, 1990.

James Brown

Please, Please, Please	King	610	'59	†
	King	909	'64	†
	Polydor	1016	'96	CS/CD
Try Me	King	635	'60	†
	Polydor	1017	'96	CS/CD
reissued as "The Unbeatable James Brown"	King	919	'64	†
Think!	King	683	'60	†
	Polydor	1018	'96	CS/CD
The Always Amazing James Brown	King	743	'61	†
Jump Around/Night Train	King	771	'62	†
Shout and Shimmy/Good Good Twistin'	King	780	'62	†
Tour the U.S.A.	King	804	'62	†
"Live" at the Apollo	King	826	'63	†
reissued as "Lowdown at the Apollo, Volume 1"	Solid Smoke	8006	'80	†
reissued as "Live at the Apollo: October 24, 1962"	Polydor	843479	'90	CS/CD
	Mobile Fidelity	00583	'93	CD†
Prisoner of Love	King	851	'63	†
Pure Dynamite!	King	883	'64	†
Papa's Got a Brand New Bag	King	938	'65	†
	Polygram	847982	'92	CS/CD
I Got You (I Feel Good)	King	946	'66	†
Mighty Instrumentals	King	961	'66	†
It's a Man's World	King	985	'66	†
Christmas Songs	King	1010	'66	†
Raw Soul	King	1016	'67	†
	Polydor	3081	'96	CS/CD
Live at the Garden	King	1018	'67	†
Cold Sweat	King	1020	'67	†
Live at the Apollo, Volume 2	King	(2)1022	'68	†
	Polydor	823001	'87	CS/CD
Live at the Apollo, Volume 2, Part 1	Rhino	70217	'85	CS†
Live at the Apollo, Volume 2, Part 2	Rhino	70218	'85	CS†
I Can't Stand Myself When You Touch Me	King	1030	'68	†
I Got the Feelin'	King	1031	'68	†
Nothing but Soul	King	1034	'68	†
Thinking About Little Willie John and A Whole New Thing	King	1038	'68	†
A Soulful Christmas	King	1040	'68	†
Say It Loud, I'm Black and I'm Proud	King	1047	'69	†
	Polydor	1992	'96	CS/CD
Gettin' Down to It	King	1051	'69	†
Popcorn	King	1055	'69	†
It's a Mother	King	1063	'69	†
Ain't It Funky	King	1092	'70	†
It's a New Day	King	1095	'70	†

Soul on Top	King	1100	'70	†
Sex Machine	King	(2)1115	'70	†
	Polydor	517984	'93	CS/CD
Sho Is Funky Down Here	King	1110	'71	†
Hey America!	King	1124	'71	†
Super Bad	King	1127	'71	†
Showtime	Smash	67054	'64	†
Grits and Soul	Smash	67057	'65	†
Today and Yesterday	Smash	67072	'65	†
Plays New Breed	Smash	67080	'66	†
Handful of Soul	Smash	67084	'66	†
Presenting . . . The James Brown Show	Smash	67087	'66	†
Plays the Real Thing	Smash	67093	'67	†
Sings Out of Sight	Smash	67109	'68	†
reissued as Out of Sight	Polydor	3080	'96	CS/CD
The JBs				
Food for Thought	People	5601	'72	†
Doing It to Death	People	5603	'73	†
Damn Right I Am Somebody	People	6602	'74	†
Breakin' Bread	People	6604	'75	†
Hustle with Speed	People	6606	'75	†
Funky Good Time: The Anthology (recorded 1970–1976)	Polydor	(2)527094	'95	CS/CD
Maceo and The King's Men				
Doin' Their Own Thing	House	1	'71	†
Maceo and The Macks				
Maceo	People	6601	'74	†
Maceo Parker				
For All the King's Men	4th & Broadway	4027	'90	CS/CD
Roots Revisited	Verve	843751	'90	CS†/CD
Mo' Roots	Verve	511068	'91	CS†/CD
Life on Planet Groove	Verve	517197	'92	CS/CD
Southern Exposure	Novus	63175	'94	CS/CD
Maceo and All The King's Men				
Funky Music Machine	Southbound	087	'93	CD
Fred Wesley and The Horny Horns				
A Blow for Me, A Toot for You	Atlantic	18214	'77	†
The King All Stars (with Fred Wesley, Pee Wee Ellis, Bootsy Collins, and Bobby Byrd)				
The King All Stars	After Hours	4116	'91	LP/CS/CD
Fred Wesley				
New Friends	Antilles	848280	'91	CS/CD
Comme Ci Comme Ca	Antilles	512002	'92	CS/CD
Swing and Be Funky	Minor Music	801027	'93	CD
Amalgamation	Minor Music	801045	'95	CD
Pee Wee Ellis				
Twelve and More Blues	Minor Music	801034	'93	CD
Sepia Tonality	Minor Music	801040	'95	CD
The JB Horns				
I Like It Like That	Instinct	296	'94	CS/CD

James Brown

Funk Power 1970: A Brand New Thang	Polydor	531684	'96	CS/CD
Hot Pants	Polydor	4054	'71	†
	Polydor	517985	'93	CS/CD
Revolution of the Mind (Live at the Apollo, Vol. III)	Polydor	(2)3003	'71	†
	Polydor	517983	'93	CS/CD
Love Power Peace: Live at the Olympia, Paris, 1971	Polydor	513389	'92	CS/CD
There It Is	Polydor	5028	'72	†
	Polydor	517986	'93	CS/CD
Get on the Good Foot	Polydor	(2)3004	'72	†
	Polydor	523982	'95	CS/CD
Black Caesar (music from the soundtrack)	Polydor	6014	'73	†
	Polydor	517135	'92	CS/CD
Slaughter's Big Rip-Off (music from the soundtrack)	Polydor	6015	'73	†
	Polydor	517136	'92	CS/CD
The Payback	Polydor	(2)3007	'74	†
	Polydor	517137	'92	CS/CD
It's Hell	Polydor	(2)9001	'74	†
	Polydor	523983	'95	CS/CD
Reality	Polydor	6039	'75	†
	Polydor	523981	'95	CS/CD
Sex Machine Today	Polydor	6042	'75	†
Everybody's Doin' the Hustle	Polydor	6054	'75	†
Hot	Polydor	6059	'76	†
Get Up Offa That Thing	Polydor	6071	'76	†
Body Heat	Polydor	6093	'77	†
Mutha's Nature	Polydor	6111	'77	†
Sex Machine Recorded Live at Home	Polydor	(2)9004	'77	†
Jam 1980s	Polydor	6140	'78	†
Take a Look at Those Cakes	Polydor	6181	'79	†
The Original Disco Man	Polydor	6212	'79	†
People	Polydor	6258	'80	†
Live . . . Hot on the One	Polydor	(2)6290	'80	†
Soul Jubilee (recorded 1984)	Magnum	43	'96	CD
Living in America	Scotti Brothers	75467	'85/'94	CS/CD
Gravity	Scotti Brothers	40380	'86	CS/CD†
	Scotti Brothers	5212	'91	CS/CD
I'm Real	Scotti Brothers	44241	'88	LP/CS/CD†
	Scotti Brothers	5213	'91	CS/CD
James Brown and Friends: Soul Session Live	Scotti Brothers	45164	'89	LP/CS/CD†
	Scotti Brothers	5214	'91	CS/CD
Love Overdue	Scotti Brothers	75225	'91	CS/CD
Universal James	Scotti Brothers	75274	'92	CS/CD
Live at the Apollo 1995	Scotti Brothers	75480	'95	CS/CD
Hooked on Brown	Scotti Brothers	75508	'96	CS/CD

James Brown Anthologies and Compilations

Soul Classics, Volume 1	Polydor	5401	'72	†
Soul Classics, Volume 2	Polydor	5402	'73	†
Solid Gold: 30 Golden Hits	Polydor	(2)829254	'77	LP†
	Polydor	829254	'77	CS†

Best (1956–1971)	Polydor	6340	'81	†
Roots of a Revolution (1956–1964)	Polydor	(2)817304	'84/'95	CD
Ain't That a Groove (1966–1969)	Polydor	821231	'84	CS†
Doin' It to Death (1969–1973)	Polydor	821232		CS†
The CD of JB: Sex Machine and Other Soul Classics (1956–1973)	Polydor	825714	'85	CD†
Dead on the Heavy Funk (1974–1976)	Polydor	827439	'85	CS†
James Brown's Funky People (recorded 1971–1975)	Polydor	829417	'86	CS/CD†
In the Jungle Groove	Polydor	(2)829624	'86	LP†
	Polydor	829624	'86	CS/CD†
The CD of JB II (Cold Sweat and Other Soul Classics)	Polydor	831700	'88	CD†
James Brown's Funky People, Part II	Polydor	835857	'88	LP/CS/CD†
Motherlode	Polydor	837126	'88	LP/CS/CD†
Messing with the Blues (1957–1975)	Polydor	(2)847258	'90	CD†
	Polydor	(2)7258	'95	CD
Star Time	Polydor	(4)849108	'91	CS/CD
20 All-Time Greatest Hits	Polydor	511326	'91	CS/CD
Soul Pride: The Instrumentals (1960–1969)	Polydor	(2)517845	'93	CS/CD
James Brown's Funky Christmas	Polydor	7988	'95	CS/CD
Foundations of Funk: A Brand New Bag, 1964–1969	Polydor/Chronicles	(2)1165	'96	CS/CD
Make It Funky/The Big Payback: 1971–1975	Polydor/Chronicles	3052	'96	CS/CD
JB40: 40th Anniversary Collection	Polydor/Chronicles	3409	'96	CD
1975–1983: Dead on the Heavy Funk	Polydor/Chronicles	(2)7901	'98	CS/CD
Say It Live and Loud	Polydor/Chronicles	7668	'98	CD
Spank	Polygram	837726		CS
Federal Years, Volume 1	Solid Smoke	8023	'84	†
Federal Years, Volume 2	Solid Smoke	8024	'84	†
Greatest Hits (1964–1968)	Rhino	219	'86	†
	Rhino	70219		CS†
Santa's Got a Brand New Bag	Rhino	70194	'88	CS/CD
Soul Syndrome	Rhino	70569	'91	CS/CD
James Brown Is Back	Hollywood/IMG	458	'91	CS/CD
Greatest Hits of the Fourth Decade	Scotti Brothers	75259	'92	CS/CD
Sex Machine	ITC Masters	1080	'98	CS/CD

THE BUFFALO SPRINGFIELD

Neil Young (born November 12, 1945, in Toronto, Canada), first lead guitar, vocals; Stephen Stills (born January 3, 1945, in Dallas, Texas), second lead guitar, keyboards, vocals; Richie Furay (born May 9, 1944, in Yellow Springs, Ohio), rhythm guitar, vocals; Bruce Palmer (born in September 1946, in Liverpool, Nova Scotia, Canada), bass; and Dewey Martin (born September 30, 1942, in Chesterville, Ontario, Canada), drums. Jim Messina (born December 5, 1947, in Maywood, California) sang and played bass with the group during its last months of existence.

One of the first American groups to combine electric instrumentation and drums with distinctive, incisive songwriting and intricate vocal harmonies, The Buffalo Springfield (along with The Byrds) pioneered both folk-rock and country-rock. Although the group featured three excellent singer-songwriter-guitarists, they failed to garner major commercial success during their existence, perhaps due to their inability to transfer the tension and excitement of their live shows onto recordings. The Buffalo Springfield nonetheless produced the masterful *Buffalo Springfield Again* and became a rock legend, and the influence of its key members is still felt today through various aggregations and solo endeavors. The Buffalo Springfield were inducted into the Rock and Roll Hall of Fame in 1997.

Also known as The Herd in their early days, The Buffalo Springfield formed in Los Angeles in the spring of 1966. Neil Young had played in several Canadian groups, including The Squires, and manned The Mynah Birds with Bruce Palmer and future funk star Rick James in the Detroit area before moving to Los Angeles in 1965. Stephen Stills and Richie Furay had been members of the New York–based Au Go-Go Singers. Canadian Dewey Martin had played with the bluegrass group The Dillards and toured with Roy Orbison.

Performing an extended engagement as the house band at Los Angeles' Whiskey A-Go-Go, The Buffalo Springfield were featured at a July 1966 Hollywood Bowl concert and later toured with The Byrds and The Beach Boys. Signed to the Atco subsidiary of Atlantic Records, their third single, Stills' "For What It's Worth," became the group's best-selling single and launched their popular recording career. Their debut album contained seven Stills songs, including the country-flavored "Go and Say Goodbye" and "Hot Dusty Roads," and five Neil Young songs, including the beautiful love song "Do I Have to Come Right Out and Say It" and "Flying on the Ground Is Wrong," both sung by Richie Furay. Relations between Stills and Young grew increasingly tense and Young left the group in the spring of 1967 for several months. Thus, The Buffalo Springfield performed at the June 1967 Monterey International Pop Festival without Young.

Neil Young returned for the gutsier *Buffalo Springfield Again,* which contained a wider range of material, from the rock 'n' roll of Young's psychedelic "Mr. Soul" and Stills' "Bluebird" and "Rock and Roll Woman" to the major production efforts of Young's "Expecting To Fly" and "Broken Arrow." Jim Messina handled part of the engineering duties along with playing some bass. Palmer departed in early 1968, and, amidst reports of dissension and group infighting, *Last Time Around* was produced by Jim Messina, who also played bass, sang, and contributed "Carefree Country Day." Other outstanding songs on the album included "On the Way Home" and "I Am a Child" by Young, "Pretty Girl Why" and "Four Days Gone" by Stills, and Furay's "Kind Woman." The Buffalo Springfield performed their last concert at Long Beach in May 1968.

Subsequently, Jim Messina and Richie Furay formed Poco, whereas Neil Young recorded solo before joining Steve Stills in Crosby, Stills, Nash and Young. Stills later recorded solo and Messina dueted with Kenny Loggins. In the mid '70s Furay helped form the Souther-Hillman-Furay Band. Young has enjoyed an incredibly diverse solo career. The Buffalo Springfield were inducted into the Rock and Roll Hall of Fame in 1997.

The Au Go-Go Singers (with Steve Stills and Richie Furay)

They Call Us the Au Go-Go Singers	Roulette	25280	'64	†
The Buffalo Springfield				
Buffalo Springfield	Atco	33200	'67	CS/CD
Buffalo Springfield Again	Atco	33226	'67	CS/CD
Last Time Around	Atco	33256	'68	†
	Atco	90393	'92	CD
Retrospective	Atco	33283	'69	†
	Atco	38105	'88	CS/CD
Buffalo Springfield	Atlantic	(2)806	'73	CS
Dewey Martin				
Medicine Ball	Uni	73088	'70	†
Bruce Palmer				
The Cycle Is Complete	Verve/Forecast	3086	'71	†

JERRY BUTLER

Born December 8, 1939, in Sunflower, Mississippi.

One of the most engaging soul music singer-songwriters to emerge in the late '50s, Jerry Butler, along with Curtis Mayfield, helped define the sound of Chicago soul in the '60s. Possessing a powerful mellifluous baritone voice, Butler achieved his initial success with Mayfield in The Impressions. He later scored a number of pop and rhythm-and-blues hits in the early '60s with Mayfield as his guitarist and songwriting partner, and, later, was in the forefront of the Philadelphia sound of producer-songwriters Kenny Gamble and Leon Huff.

Moving to Chicago with his family at the age of three, Jerry Butler began singing in gospel groups as a child. He sang with Curtis Mayfield in the Northern Jubilee Gospel Singers and, during 1957, he and Mayfield joined The Roosters. By 1958, they had changed their name to The Impressions and signed with VeeJay Records. Featuring Butler's soothing baritone, The Impressions' first single, "For Your Precious Love" (coauthored by Butler) became a smash rhythm-and-blues and major pop hit.

Leaving The Impressions after the solitary hit, Jerry Butler scored a top rhythm-and-blues and smash pop hit in late 1960 with "He Will Break Your Heart," cowritten by Butler and Mayfield. Butler and Mayfield also cowrote the near-smash rhythm-and-blues and major pop hits "Find Another Girl" and "I'm-a Telling You." Through his success with Henry Mancini's "Moon River" and Burt Bacharach's "Make It Easy on Yourself" (both major crossover hits), Butler was established as a purveyor of smooth soul ballads on the American supper club circuit. Subsequent hits included "Need to Belong" and "Let It Be Me," recorded with Betty Everett. Butler's moderate hit, "I Don't Want to Hear It Anymore," was one of the first Randy Newman songs to make the charts and Butler later wrote "I've Been Loving You Too Long (To Stop Now)" for and with Otis Redding.

With the demise of VeeJay Records in 1966, Jerry Butler moved to Mercury Records, where he worked with songwriter-producers Kenny Gamble and Leon Huff. The collaboration resulted in a number of hits for Butler through 1969. These included the top rhythm-and-blues hits "Hey Western Union Man" and "Only the Strong Survive" (also a smash pop hit), as well as the smash rhythm-and-blues and major pop hits "Never Give You Up," "Moody Woman," and "What's the Use of Breaking Up." His 1969 album *The Ice Man Cometh,* the most successful of his career, contained three of the hits and provided Butler with his nickname, denoting his cool sophisticated style.

Jerry Butler stayed with Mercury Records when Kenny Gamble and Leon Huff moved to Columbia Records in 1970. He established the Songwriters' Workshop in Chicago and recorded an album with Gene Chandler. With Brenda Lee Eager, Butler scored a major rhythm-and-blues hit with "Power of Love" and his last major pop hit with "Ain't Understanding Mellow" (a rhythm-and-blues smash hit). "If It's Real What I Feel" and "One Night Affair" also became R&B smashes on Mercury in the early '70s. Butler subsequently switched to Motown Records, where he achieved a rhythm-and-blues smash hit with "I Wanna Do It to You" and recorded two albums with Thelma Houston. In 1978, he reunited with Kenny Gamble and Leon Huff at Philadelphia International Records for two albums and the major rhythm-and-blues hit "(I'm Just Thinking About) Cooling Out." Elected as a Cook County (Chicago) commissioner in 1986, Jerry Butler returned to recording in the '90s with *Time and Faith* and *Simply Beautiful.*

The Impressions with Jerry Butler

For Your Precious Love	VeeJay	1075	'63	LP/CS
The Impressions/Jerry Butler	Dominion	324		CS/CD†

Jerry Butler

Jerry Butler Esquire	Abner	2001	'59	†
	VeeJay	1027	'61	†
He Will Break Your Heart	VeeJay	1029	'61	†
Love Me	VeeJay	1034	'61	†
Aware of Love	VeeJay	1038	'62	†
Moon River	VeeJay	1046	'63	†
Folk Songs	VeeJay	1057	'63	†
Giving Up on Love/Need to Belong	VeeJay	1076	'63	†
Soul Artistry	Mercury	61105	'67	†
Mr. Dream Merchant	Mercury	61146	'68	†
Golden Hits (Live)	Mercury	61151	'68	†
The Soul Goes On	Mercury	61171	'68	†
The Iceman Cometh	Mercury	61198	'69	†
Ice on Ice	Mercury	61234	'69	†
You and Me	Mercury	61269	'70	†
Sings Assorted Sounds	Mercury	61320	'70	†
Sagittarius Movement	Mercury	61347	'71	†
Power of Love	Mercury	689	'74	†
Sweet Sixteen	Mercury	1006	'74	†
Melinda (soundtrack)	Pride	0006		†
Love's on the Menu	Motown	850	'76	†
	Motown	5479	'90	CS/CD†
Suite for the Single Girl	Motown	878	'77	†
	Motown	5476	'90	CS/CD†
It All Comes Out in My Song	Motown	892	'77	†
Nothing Says I Love You Like I Love You	Philadelphia Int'l	35510	'78	†
The Best Love I Ever Had	Philadelphia Int'l	36413	'80	†
Time and Faith	Ichiban	1151	'92	CS/CD†
Simply Beautiful	Valley Vue	22006	'95	CS/CD

Jerry Butler Anthologies and Compilations

Best	VeeJay	1048	'63	†
More of the Best	VeeJay	1119	'64	†
Gold	VeeJay	(2)1003	'87	†
The Iceman	VeeJay	700	'92	CS/CD
Gift of Love	Sunset	5216	'68	†
Starring Jerry Butler	Tradition	2068		†
Very Best	Buddah	4001	'69	†
Best	Mercury	61281	'70	†
	Mercury	810639		CS
Spice of Life	Mercury	(2)7502	'72	†
Only the Strong Survive—The Great Philadelphia Hits	Mercury	822212	'84	†
Very Best	Mercury	510967	'92	CS/CD
Iceman: The Mercury Years Anthology	Mercury	(2)510968	'92	CS/CD
Hey Western Union Man	Polygram	838170		CS
Best, 1958–1969	Rhino	70216	'85	CS
	Rhino	75881	'85	CD
All Time Hits	Up Front	124		†
Jerry Butler	Pickwick	3202		†
All Time Hits	Trip	(2)8011		†

Best	United Artists	498	'76	†
Greatest Hits	Curb/Warner Brothers	77419	'91	CS/CD
Jerry Butler and Betty Everett				
Delicious Together	VeeJay	1099	'64	†
Starring Jerry Butler and Betty Everett	Tradition	2073	'68	†
Together	Buddah	7507	'70	†
Jerry Butler and Gene Chandler				
One and One	Mercury	61330	'71	†
Jerry Butler and Brenda Lee Eager				
The Love We Have	Mercury	660	'73	†
Jerry Butler and Thelma Houston				
Thelma and Jerry	Motown	887	'77	†
Two to One	Motown	903		†

PAUL BUTTERFIELD

Born December 17, 1942, in Chicago; died May 4, 1987, in North Hollywood, California.

With The Paul Butterfield Blues Band, Paul Butterfield legitimized white blues with their debut album and laid the foundation for the blues revival of the late '60s. One of the first white bands to play the blues with rock instrumentation, The Paul Butterfield Blues Band brought much-deserved recognition to black blues performers and paved the way for blues-rock bands such as Cream and The Electric Flag. The Paul Butterfield Blues Band was the first band to bring electric instrumentation to the Newport Folk Festival in 1965 (on their own and behind Bob Dylan) and Butterfield became known as one of America's leading white blues harmonica players. The band's *East-West* album was one of the first recordings to explore the fusion of Western and Eastern musical styles and feature extended guitar improvisation. The Butterfield Blues Band's *Pigboy Crabshaw* album was one of the first to augment electric instrumentation with horns, several months before Blood, Sweat and Tears. Furthermore, members Mike Bloomfield, Elvin Bishop, and Mark Naftalin later moved to the San Francisco Bay Area, where they helped establish a regional blues scene second only to that of Chicago.

Paul Butterfield grew up in Chicago and studied classical flute as a child. He later took up guitar and harmonica, mastering blues harmonica by his late teens. Meeting vocalist Nick Gravenites, the two began playing on college campuses. Butterfield subsequently met guitarist Elvin Bishop (born October 21, 1942, in Tulsa, Oklahoma), who was attending the University of Illinois on a scholarship, and the two began frequenting Chicago area black blues clubs, where they were befriended by Muddy Waters. In 1963, Butterfield, Bishop, bassist Jerome Arnold, and drummer Sam Lay began playing at Big John's on Chicago's North Side. Mike Bloomfield, a respected blues guitarist, joined the group in late 1964. Signed to Elektra Records in 1964, The Paul Butterfield Blues Band's initial recordings were not issued until 1995.

The Paul Butterfield Blues Band brought electric instrumentation to the Newport Folk Festival in June 1965, both on their own and behind Bob Dylan. Augmented by keyboardist Mark Naftalin (who subsequently became a permanent member), the group's debut album featured Chicago blues fare played with rock instruments and pioneered blues-rock. Replacing Sam Lay with jazz drummer Billy Davenport, their second album, *East-West,* included more blues standards and Gravenite's "Born in Chicago" plus Mike Bloomfield's exotic thirteen-minute title cut, which explored both Eastern and Western music and popularized extended guitar improvisation. In early 1967, Bloomfield departed to form The Electric Flag with Nick Gravenites and Buddy Miles. The Paul Butterfield Blues Band performed at the Monterey International Pop Festival in June 1967 and the remaining original members (Butterfield, Bishop, and Naftalin) regrouped, adding a three-piece horn section for *The Resurrection of Pigboy Crabshaw* in one of the first instances of horns augmenting a rock band.

Mark Naftalin left The Paul Butterfield Blues Band after *Pigboy Crabshaw* and Elvin Bishop left after *In My Own Dream*. In 1969, Butterfield, Mike Bloomfield, and Sam Lay helped record Muddy Waters' *Fathers and Sons*. That August, The Paul Butterfield Blues Band performed at the Woodstock Music and Art Fair. As the only original member left, Butterfield persevered with a series of guitarists, bassists, and drummers, eventually disbanding the group in the fall of 1972. He then moved to Woodstock, New York, and formed Paul Butterfield's Better Days with vocalist-guitarist Geoff Muldaur and guitarist Amos Garrett, recording two albums for Bearsville Records. Better Days broke up in 1974. Butterfield appeared at The Band's *Last Waltz* in 1976 and later toured with Levon Helm and The RCO All-Stars and the Danko-Butterfield Band, with The Band's Rick Danko. Paul Butterfield died of drug-related heart failure on May 4, 1987, in his apartment in North Hollywood, California.

Elvin Bishop and Mark Naftalin had moved to the San Francisco Bay area by 1968. Elvin Bishop recorded two albums for Bill Graham's short-lived Fillmore label before switching to Epic in 1972 and Capricorn in 1974. His Capricorn debut, *Let It Flow,* featured favorites like "Stealin' Watermelons" and the minor hit "Travelin' Shoes." His biggest success came in 1976 with the smash hit "Fooled Around and Fell in Love," sung by Mickey Thomas, who later joined The Jefferson Starship. Playing West Coast engagements during the '80s, Bishop ultimately returned to recording in 1988 with the Chicago-based blues label Alligator Records.

Mark Naftalin pursued sessions work, recording over 100 albums with others, including John Lee Hooker, Percy Mayfield, James Cotton, and Big Joe Turner. He also put together his own Rhythm & Blues Revue and produced concerts, festivals, and radio shows. His *Blues Power Hour* radio show (on San Francisco's KALW-FM since 1984) has run almost continuously since 1979. Naftalin served as associate producer of the Monterey Jazz Festival's Blues Afternoon from 1982 to 1991 and produced the Marin County Blues Festival beginning in 1981. In the '90s, Naftalin's Winner Records issued archival recordings of The Paul Butterfield Blues Band.

The Paul Butterfield Blues Band

The Original Lost Elektra Sessions (recorded 1964)	Rhino/Elektra	73505	'95	CD
The Paul Butterfield Blues Band	Elektra	7294	'65	CD
East-West	Elektra	7315	'66	CD
The Resurrection of Pigboy Crabshaw	Elektra	74015	'67/'89	CD
In My Own Dream	Elektra	74025	'68	†
Keep on Moving	Elektra	74053	'69	†
Live	Elektra	(2)2001	'70	†
Sometimes I Feel Like Smiling	Elektra	75013	'71	†
Golden Butter	Elektra	(2)2005	'72	†
Born in Chicago—The Best of the Butterfield Blues Band:				
The Elektra Years	Elektra	62124	'98	CD
Strawberry Jam (recorded 1966–1968)	Winner	446	'95	CD
East-West Live (recorded 1966–1967)	Winner	447	'96	CD

Paul Butterfield's Better Days

Better Days	Bearsville	2119	'73	†
	Rhino	70877	'87	CS/CD

It All Comes Back	Bearsville	2170	'73	†
	Rhino	70878	'87	CS/CD
Paul Butterfield				
Put It in Your Ear	Bearsville	6960	'76	†
	Rhino	70879	'87	CS†
North South	Warner Brothers	6995	'81	†
	Rhino	70880	'87	CS†
The Legendary Paul Butterfield Rides Again	Amherst	3305	'86	LP†
	Amherst	53305	'86	CS
	Amherst	93305	'86	CD
Sam Lay				
In Bluesland	Blue Thumb	14	'70	†
Stone Blues	Evidence	26081	'96	CD
Sam Lay Blues Band				
Shuffle Master	Appaloosa	6106	'93	CS/CD†
Elvin Bishop				
Elvin Bishop	Fillmore	30001	'69	†
	Columbia	30001		†
Feel It!	Fillmore	30239	'70	†
Rock My Soul	Epic	31563	'72	†
Best: Crabshaw Rising	Epic	33693	'75	LP/CS†
	Epic/Legacy	33693	'96	CS/CD
Tulsa Shuffle: The Best of Elvin Bishop	Epic/Legacy	57630	'94	CS/CD
Let It Flow	Capricorn	0134	'74	†
	Polygram	839142		CS
	One Way	32647	'96	CD
Juke Joint Jump	Capricorn	0151	'75	†
	One Way	32646	'96	CD
Struttin' My Stuff	Capricorn	0165	'75	†
Hometown Boy Makes Good!	Capricorn	0176	'76	†
Live! Raisin' Hell	Capricorn	(2)0185	'77	†
	One Way	32648	'96	CD
Sure Feels Good: The Best	Polydor	513307	'92	CS/CD
Big Fun	Alligator	4767	'88	LP/CS/CD
Don't Let the Bossman Get You Down!	Alligator	4791	'91	LP/CS/CD
Ace in the Hole	Alligator	4833	'95	CS/CD

THE BYRDS

Jim McGuinn (born July 13, 1942, in Chicago), lead electric twelve-string guitar, vocals; Gene Clark (born November 17, 1941, in Tipton, Missouri; died May 24, 1991, in Sherman Oaks, California), rhythm guitar, harmonica, vocals; David Crosby (born David Van Cortland on August 14, 1941, in Los Angeles), rhythm guitar, vocals; Chris Hillman (born December 4, 1942, in Los Angeles), bass, mandolin, vocals; and Mike Clarke (born June 3, 1943 or 1944, in New York City; died December 19, 1993, in Treasure Island, Florida), drums. Gene Clark left in March 1966. David Crosby left in October 1967. Gram Parsons (born Cecil Connor III on November 5, 1946, in Winter Haven, Florida; died September 19, 1973, in Joshua Tree, California) was a member in 1968. Other later members included guitarist-vocalist Clarence White (born June 7, 1944, in Lewiston, Maine; died July 14, 1973, in Palmdale, California), bassists

John York (born August 3, 1946, in White Plains, New York) and Skip Battin (born February 2, 1934, in Gallipolis, Ohio), and drummers Kevin Kelly and Gene Parsons.

THE BYRDS (HULTON-DEUTSCH COLLECTION/CORBIS)

The most important group in the creation of both folk-rock and country-rock, The Byrds are often considered as influential as The Beatles and The Rolling Stones. Producing a remarkable body of work between 1965 and 1968, The Byrds were noteworthy for their spirit of adventure and innovation, and they were one of the first rock groups to experiment with studio technology. Presenting the first substantial challenge to the popularity of The Beatles and The Rolling Stones in the mid-'60s, The Byrds' recording of Bob Dylan's "Mr. Tambourine Man" marked the first time his still-acoustic music had been adapted to rock and launched folk-rock. Ostensibly, their recording inspired Dylan to take up electric guitar. The Byrds' 1966 hit "Eight Miles High" was the first hit psychedelic song and showcased Roger McGuinn's chiming 12-string electric guitar playing (a sound later emulated by Tom Petty and R.E.M.). The song was also one of the first to be banned for radio airplay due to its supposed reference to drugs. Anchored by the excellent songwriting of Roger McGuinn, David Crosby, Gene Clark, and Chris Hillman, The Byrds were an inspiration to the singer-songwriter movement that proved so popular in the '70s. Moreover, their attention to melody and harmony opened rock to the gentle sophistication later explored by groups such as Crosby, Stills and Nash. The Byrds' 1968 *Sweetheart of the Rodeo* album, one of the first albums recorded in Nashville by an established rock group, introduced Gram Parsons to rock audiences and pioneered country-rock. The Byrds were inducted into the Rock and Roll Hall of Fame in 1991. Although talented songwriter Gene Clark languished in obscurity after leaving the group, others, particularly Gram Parsons, Chris Hillman, and David Crosby went on to spectacularly influential and successful careers. Parsons and Hillman formed The Flying Burrito Brothers, the group that laid the foundation for dozens of bands that explored country and rock during the '70s. David Crosby helped found Crosby, Stills and Nash, who blended acoustic instrumentaion with electric backing on engaging melodies and impeccable harmonies and helped define the singer-songwriter movement of the '70s.

The Byrds formed in Los Angeles in the summer of 1964. Jim McGuinn had made his debut at The Gate of Horn in Chicago in the late '50s, later backing The Limeliters and Judy Collins. He performed as a solo folk artist in Greenwich Village and played as accompanist to The Chad Mitchell Trio beginning in 1960, helping record their *Mighty Day on Campus* and *At the Bitter End* albums. After working with Bobby Darin in New York in 1962, he returned to solo work at the Troubadour in Los Angeles, where he met Gene Clark in 1964. Gene Clark had played in bands since the age of thirteen and been a member of The

New Christy Minstrels in the early '60s. McGuinn and Clark began working as a duo and were later joined by David Crosby. Crosby had sung in coffeehouses in New York and California in the early '60s and served a short-lived stint in Les Baxter's Balladeers. Crosby introduced them to producer Jim Dickson and the trio recorded "The Only Girl I Adore."

McGuinn, Clark, and Crosby subsequently formed The Jet Set, recording "You Movin'" and "The Only Girl" with sessions musicians. They subsequently recruited drummer Michael Clarke and bluegrass prodigy Chris Hillman. Hillman had formed The Scottsville Squirrel Barkers in 1961, and, later, The Hillmen with Gosdin brothers Vern and Rex. Recordings made by The Hillmen between 1963 and 1964 were later issued on Together Records after the success of The Byrds.

In 1964, with the assistance of Jim Dickson, the group recorded a demonstration tape at World Pacific Studios (later issued as *Preflyte*). Initially signed to Elektra Records as The Beefeaters, the group's first single, "Please Let Me Love You," flopped and they subsequently signed with Columbia Records in November 1964, thus becoming the first rock act signed by the mainstream label. Soon changing their name to The Byrds, the group recorded Bob Dylan's "Mr. Tambourine Man" at the urging of Dickson. Ironically, only McGuinn actually played an instrument on the recording, his electric twelve-string guitar. With McGuinn singing lead and Crosby and Clark providing harmonies, the instrumentation was done by Los Angeles studio stalwarts Leon Russell, Larry Knechtel, and Hal Blaine. The single, issued in March 1965, became a top British and American hit and launched The Byrds into international prominence. Debuting that month at Ciro's in Los Angeles, the original group remained far more effective as a recording group than as performers.

All of The Byrds actually played on their debut album, save the songs "Mr. Tambourine Man" and "I Knew I'd Want You." The album contained four Dylan songs, including the moderate American and near-smash British hit "All I Really Want to Do," Gene Clark's classic "I'll Feel a Whole Lot Better," and Jackie DeShannon's "Don't Doubt Yourself, Babe." Their second album yielded a top American hit with the title song, "Turn! Turn! Turn!" (adapted from the Biblical Book of Ecclesiastes by Pete Seeger), and contained two more Dylan songs, McGuinn's "It Won't Be Wrong," and Clark's "Set You Free This Time," a minor hit.

Conflicts in the group soon became apparent as Crosby and McGuinn frequently disagreed on The Byrds' direction, often coming to actual blows. However, the first defection was Gene Clark in March 1966. He soon recorded his debut album with Gosdin brothers Vern and Rex, augmented by Hillman, Clarke, Clarence White, and Doug Dillard. It included "Echoes," "Tried So Hard," and "So You Say You Lost Your Baby." With Dillard, Clark subsequently formed Dillard and Clark, recording two neglected albums for A&M Records regarded as the earliest example of newgrass, a progressive variation of traditional bluegrass. Their debut, recorded with future Flying Burrito Brother and Eagle Bernie Leadon, featured the Clark-Leadon composition, "Train Leaves Here This Mornin.'" Fiddler Byron Berline joined for the second album. Never afforded the attention of other former Byrds, Clark recorded the solo albums *White Light, No Other,* and *Two Sides to Every Story* during the '70s.

Having lost one of their singers and their principal songwriter, The Byrds realigned, with Hillman taking up vocals and McGuinn and Crosby writing more songs. At the same time, the group started experimenting with a more sophisticated sound, as McGuinn immersed himself in the music of jazz saxophonist John Coltrane. The result was the major hit single "Eight Miles High," written by McGuinn, Crosby, and Gene Clark and recorded shortly before Clark's departure. With three-part harmony and an almost imperceptible melody, the song featured McGuinn playing his electric twelve-string modally (rather than in a major or minor scale). The first hit psychedelic song, with its apparent reference to the LSD experience, "Eight Miles High" had the dubious distinction of being one of the first singles of the '60s to be banned from airplay. The eclectic *Fifth Dimension* album also included McGuinn and Crosby's psychedelic "I See You," the moderate hit "Mr. Spaceman," and the bluesy "Hey Joe."

The Byrds' increasing musical sophistication was evident with the release of *Younger Than Yesterday*. Although marred by two overdone production numbers, the album yielded two hits with Dylan's "My Back Pages" and McGuinn and Hillman's bitterly satiric "So You Want to Be a Rock 'n' Roll Star." It contained Crosby's beautiful "Everybody's Been Burned," two McGuinn-Crosby collaborations, "Why" and "Renaissance Faire," and four Hillman songs, including the country-flavored "Time Between." The Byrds performed at the Monterey International Pop Festival in June 1967, but, by then, the rift between McGuinn and Crosby had become irreparable. When Crosby refused to sing two Gerry Goffin–Carole King compositions, he was summarily paid off and fired in October. Crosby later produced Joni Mitchell's debut album and helped form the quintessential '60s acoustic guitar-vocal harmony group, Crosby, Stills and Nash. Crosby's subsequent career is chronicled under Crosby, Stills and Nash.

Recorded with the assistance of outside musicians, *The Notorious Byrd Brothers* was critically hailed and marked the beginning of a trend toward simplicity rather than sophistication in the music of The Byrds. The album contained the two disputed Goffin-King songs, "Wasn't Born to Follow" and "Goin' Back," a minor hit, and McGuinn and Hillman's "Change Is Now." Mike Clarke departed in late 1967, to be replaced by Hillman's cousin Kevin Kelly.

McGuinn, now using the first name Roger, recruited singer-songwriter-guitarist Gram Parsons in February 1968, lending a country music orientation to The Byrds. They soon appeared at the Grand Ole Opry in Nashville and their next album, *Sweetheart of the Rodeo,* openly embraced country-and-western music. Hailed as the first country-rock album, the album was years ahead of its time and proved a commercial flop. It contained Dylan's "Nothing Was Delivered" and "You Ain't Going Nowhere," a minor hit, and two excellent Parsons' songs, "Hickory Wind" and "One Hundred Years from Now." The Byrds subsequently began to deteriorate. Gram Parsons quit in July 1968, followed in October by Chris Hillman. The two soon formed The Flying Burrito Brothers with Chris Ethridge. Hillman's career with and after The Flying Burrito Brothers is chronicled under The Flying Burrito Brothers.

McGuinn, the only original member left, put together a new group with another bluegrass prodigy, Clarence White. White had been playing bluegrass music with his brothers Roland and Eric since the mid-'50s, initially as the Three Little Country boys, later as The Country Boys. By the early '60s, The Country Boys had evolved into The Kentucky Colonels, one of the most popular West Coast bluegrass bands, rivaled only by Chris Hillman's groups. After The Kentucky Colonels disbanded around 1967, Clarence White had pursued sessions work before joining Gene Parsons, Gib Guilbeau, Sneaky Pete Kleinow, and others in Nashville West. For McGuinn's newest Byrds, Clarence recommended John York (bass, vocals) and Gene Parsons (guitar, bass, drums, vocals). Parsons (no relation to Gram) had played with Guilbeau in the duo Cajun Gib and Gene before joining Nashville West.

The new lineup of The Byrds recorded *Dr. Byrds and Mr. Hyde,* which included McGuinn's "Bad Night at the Whiskey," McGuinn and Gram Parsons' "Drug Store Truck Driving Man," and the instrumental "Nashville West." The Byrds' nose-dive into obscurity was arrested briefly by the surprise popularity of the Peter Fonda–Dennis Hopper film *Easy Rider.* The best-selling soundtrack album contained three songs sung by McGuinn, including the minor hit "The Ballad of Easy Rider." The obvious follow-up album *The Ballad of Easy Rider* yielded The Byrds' final (minor) hit, "Jesus Is Just All Right."

John York left in September 1968, to be replaced by Skip Battin. Years earlier, Battin had been half of the duo Skip and Flip, who hit with a remake of Marvin and Johnny's "Cherry

Pie" in 1960. (*Untitled*), half live and half studio material, included "Truck Stop Girl" (written by Lowell George and Bill Payne of Little Feat) and several McGuinn–Jaques Levy collaborations, most notably "Lover of the Bayou" and "Chestnut Mare." Defections continued and, finally, in February 1973, McGuinn disbanded The Byrds. The original Byrds did reassemble briefly for 1973's rather crassly commercial reunion album, which featured McGuinn's "Born to Rock 'n' Roll." The Byrds were inducted into the Rock and Roll Hall of Fame in 1991.

Clarence White quickly joined David Grisman, Peter Rowan, Richard Greene, and others in Muleskinner, recording one album on Warner Brothers. He formed The New Kentucky Colonels with brother Roland, touring Sweden, and started work on a solo album. However, on July 14, 1973, he was killed when struck by a drunk driver while loading equipment in Palmdale, California.

Gene Parsons recorded the impressive *Kindling* album before joining the later-day edition of The Flying Burrito Brothers for *Flying Again* and *Airborne*. He joined Sierra Records in 1980 and later recorded with Meridian Green, whom he married in 1986.

Roger McGuinn recorded a number of albums for Columbia in the '70s, most notably the overlooked *Cardiff Rose*. Produced by Mick Ronson, the album contained two previously unrecorded songs, Joni Mitchell's "Dreamland" and Bob Dylan's "Up to Me." McGuinn toured with Dylan's Rolling Thunder Revue in late 1975, forming a new band, Thunderbyrd, in 1977. That spring Chris Hillman's band toured Europe with Gene Clark's band and McGuinn's Thunderbyrd, leading to a jam session among the three at London's Hammersmith Odeon. Later, Clark joined McGuinn onstage at The Troubadour in Los Angeles. They later toured as a duo, becoming a trio when Hillman joined. The three, playing acoustic guitars, opened the Canadian leg of Eric Clapton's *Slowhand* tour. In late 1978, the three recorded the highly polished *McGuinn, Clark and Hillman* album for Capitol Records, and managed a moderate hit with McGuinn's "Don't Write Her Off."

Gene Clark toured with John York and others as The Byrds from 1985 to 1987. In 1987, he recorded the solo album *Firebyrd* for Takoma Records and *So Rebellious a Lover* with Carla Olson of The Textones. In January 1989, David Crosby, Roger McGuinn, and Chris Hillman played three California club dates to establish their right to The Byrds' name and prevent Gene Clark and Mike Clarke from touring under the name. On May 24, 1991, Clark was found dead in his home in Sherman Oaks. Roger McGuinn, who did not record during the '80s, finally reemerged in 1991 with *Back from Rio*, recorded with the assistance of Elvis Costello and Tom Petty. Michael Clarke died of liver failure on December 19, 1993, in Treasure Island, Florida.

THE BYRDS BIBLIOGRAPHY

Fong-Torres, Ben. *Hickory Wind: The Life and Times of Gram Parsons.* New York: Pocket Books, 1991; New York: St. Martin's Griffin, 1998.

Rogan, John. *Timeless Flight: The Definitive Biography of The Byrds.* London: Scorpion/Dark Star, 1981.

Scoppa, Bud. *The Byrds.* New York: Scholastic, 1971.

The Chad Mitchell Trio (with Jim McGuinn)

A Mighty Day on Campus	Kapp	3262	'62	†
Live at the Bitter End	Kapp	3281	'62	†

The Scottsville Squirrel Barkers (with Chris Hillman)

Blue-Grass Favorites	Crown	5346	'63	†

The Hillmen

The Hillmen (recorded 1963–1964)	Together	1012	'69	†
	Sugar Hill	3719	'95	CS/CD

Early Albums by The Byrds

Preflyte	Together	1001	'68	†
	Columbia	32183	'73	†
In the Beginning	Rhino	70244	'88	CS/CD
Mr. Tambourine Man	Columbia	9712	'65	CS/CD†
	Columbia	64845	'96	CD
Turn! Turn! Turn!	Columbia	9254	'65	CS/CD†
	Columbia	64846	'96	CD
Mr. Tambourine Man/Turn! Turn! Turn!	Columbia	(2)33645	'75	†
Fifth Dimension	Columbia	9349	'66	CD†
	Columbia	64847	'96	CD
Younger Than Yesterday	Columbia	9442	'67	CD†
	Columbia	64848	'96	CD
Notorious Byrd Brothers	Columbia	9575	'68	CD†
	Columbia	65151	'97	CD

Gene Clark

Early L.A. Sessions	Columbia	31123	'72	†
Gene Clark with The Gosdin Brothers	Columbia	9418	'67	†
	Sony	2618		CS/CD†
reissued as Echoes	Columbia/Legacy	48523	'91	CS†/CD
White Light	A&M	4292	'71	†
No Other	Asylum	1016	'74	†
Two Sides to Every Story	RSO	3011	'77	†
	RSO	835739	'88	CD†
Firebyrd	Takoma	72812	'87	LP/CS†

Dillard and Clark

The Fantastic Expedition of Dillard and Clark	A&M	4158	'68	†
Through the Morning, Through the Night	A&M	4203	'70	†
The Fantastic Expedition of Dillard and Clark/ Through the Morning, Through the Night	Mobile Fidelity	00791		CD†

Gene Clark and Carla Olson

So Rebellious A Lover	Rhino	70832	'87	†
	Razor & Tie	1992	'92	CD

The Kentucky Colonels (with Clarence White)

New Sound of Bluegrass	Briar	109	'63	†
Livin' in the Past	Briar	4202	'75	†
	Sierra	4202		LP/CS
	Sierra	7003	'97	CD
Scotty Stoneman with The Kentucky Colonels—Live in L.A.	Briar	4206	'75	LP/CS
Long Journey Home (recorded at Newport Folk Festival 1964)	Vanguard	77004	'64/'91	CS/CD
Appalachian Swing!	World Pacific	1821	'64	†
	Liberty	10185	'90	†
	Rounder	31	'93	CS/CD
The Kentucky Colonels	Rounder	0070	'74	
reissued as 1965–1967	Rounder	0070	'76	LP/CS
The White Brothers (The New Kentucky Colonels) Live in Sweden	Rounder	0073	'77	LP/CS†

The Kentucky Colonels Featuring Clarence White	Rounder	0098	'80	LP/CS
On Stage	Rounder	0199	'84	CS

Nashville West (with Clarence White and Gene Parsons)

Nashville West (recorded 1968)	Sierra	4216	'78	LP/CS
	Sierra	6016	'96	CD
Nashville West Featuring Clarence White	Sierra	7000	'97	CD

Muleskinner (with Clarence White)

Muleskinner	Warner Brothers	2787	'74	†
	Ridge Runner	0016	'90	†
reissued as "A Potpurri of Bluegrass Jam"	Sierra	6009	'95	CS/CD
	Sierra	7017		CD
Live: Original Television Soundtrack (recorded 1973)	Sierra	6000	'92	CD
	Sierra	7016		CD

Later Byrds Albums

Sweetheart Of The Rodeo	Columbia	9670	'68	CD†
	Columbia	65150	'97	CD
Dr. Byrds and Mr. Hyde	Columbia	9755	'69/'91	CD†
	Columbia/Legacy	65113	'97	CD
Ballad Of Easy Rider	Columbia	9942	'69/'91	CD†
	Columbia/Legacy	65114	'97	CD
(Untitled)	Columbia	(2)30127	'70	†
	Columbia	30127		CD
	Mobile Fidelity	722	'98	CD
Byrdmaniax	Columbia	30640	'71	†
	Columbia/Legacy	30640	'92	CD
Farther Along	Columbia	31050	'71	†
Clark, Hillman, Crosby, McGuinn, Clarke	Asylum	5058	'73	†

Byrds Anthologies and Compilations

Greatest Hits	Columbia	9516	'67	CS/CD
The Original Singles (1965–1967)	Columbia	37335	'81	CS/CD
Best (Greatest Hits, Volume 2)	Columbia	31795	'72/'87	CS/CD
The Byrds Play Dylan	Columbia	36293	'79	†
The Byrds: Box Set	Columbia/Legacy	(4)46773	'90	CS/CD
20 Essential Tracks from the Boxed Set: 1965–1990	Columbia/Legacy	47884	'91	CS/CD
Very Best	Pair	1040	'86	LP/CS†

McGuinn, Clark and Hillman

McGuinn, Clark and Hillman	Capitol	11910	'79	†
	Capitol	16280	'83	†
	Capitol	96355	'91	CS/CD†
City	Capitol	12043	'80	†
	One Way	18503	'96	CD

McGuinn and Hillman

McGuinn and Hillman	Capitol	12108	'80	†
	One Way	18498	'96	CD

Skip Battin

Skip Battin	Signpost	8408	'73	†

Gene Parsons

Kindling	Warner Brothers	2687	'73	†

Melodies	Sierra	8703	'80	†
	Sierra	4217		LP/CS
	Sierra	6010	'96	CD
The Kindling Collection	Sierra	6007	'95	CS
Gene Parsons and Meridian Green				
Birds of a Feather	Sierra	4223	'87	LP/CS†
	Sierra	6004	'96	CS/CD
Roger McGuinn				
Roger McGuinn	Columbia	31946	'73	†
Peace on You	Columbia	32956	'74	†
Roger McGuinn and Band	Columbia	33541	'75	†
Cardiff Rose	Columbia	34154	'76	†
	Columbia/Legacy	34154	'92	CD
Thunderbyrd	Columbia	34656	'77	†
Born to Rock & Roll	Columbia/Legacy	47494	'91	CD
Back from Rio	Arista	8648	'90	CS/CD
Live from Mars	Hollywood	62090	'96	CS/CD

CANNED HEAT

Bob "The Bear" Hite (born February 26, 1945, in Torrance, California; died April 5, 1981, in North Hollywood, California), vocals, harmonica, guitar; Alan "Blind Owl" Wilson (born July 4, 1943, in Boston, Massachusetts; died September 3, 1970, in Topanga, California), guitar, harmonica, vocals; Henry Vestine (born December 25, 1944, in Washington, D.C.; died October 20, 1997, in Paris, France), guitar; Larry Taylor (born June 26, 1942, in Brooklyn, New York), bass; and Frank Cook, drums. Cook was replaced by Adolpho "Fito" de la Parra (born February 8, 1946, in Mexico City, Mexico) in 1968 and Vestine was replaced by Harvey Mandel (born March 11, 1945, in Detroit, Michigan) in 1969. In 1970, Mandel departed and Vestine returned.

An exciting late '60s American blues-and-boogie band, Canned Heat created its own distinctive style without the use of horns, a practice favored by New York and Chicago blues bands. Favoring country blues rather than urban blues, the group's popularity was bolstered through appearances at the Monterey, Woodstock, and Isle of Wight Festivals. However, Canned Heat's momentum was irrevocably stalled with the death of Alan Wilson in 1970, yet they later recorded *Hooker 'N' Heat* with blues legend John Lee Hooker. After the 1981 death of Bob Hite, Canned Heat persevered in the person of Fito de la Parra.

Formed in Los Angeles as a jug band in 1965, Canned Heat transformed into a popular white blues-and-boogie band and played local clubs. Members Bob "The Bear" Hite and Alan "Blind Owl" Wilson were blues scholars and record collectors, and the group's recordings reflected their enthusiasm for the music. Debuting at the Monterey International Pop Festival in June 1967, Canned Heat signed with Liberty Records. Their debut album featured "Rollin' and Tumblin,'" while their second and most successful, with new drummer Fito de la Parra, included "Amphetamine Annie" and yielded a major hit with "On the Road Again." The album remained on the album charts for an entire year. Touring Europe in the fall of 1968, the band scored a near-smash hit with "Going up the Country." However, Henry Vestine departed in July 1969, to be replaced by Harvey Mandel.

Canned Heat appeared at the Woodstock Music and Art Fair in August 1969, and the following spring Taylor left and Vestine returned. The group appeared at the Isle of Wight Festival in August 1970, but, on September 3, founding member Alan Wilson was found dead of a drug overdose in the garden of Hite's Topanga Canyon home. Their version of Wilbert Harrrison's "Let's Work Together" soon became a major hit, but the group was subsequently plagued by personnel changes. In 1971, they backed blues great John Lee Hooker for *Hooker 'N' Heat*. Nonetheless, the band's popularity faded and they were without a major record label following 1974's *One More River to Cross* for Atlantic. Since Bob Hite's death of a drug-related heart attack on April 5, 1981, Canned Heat has been led by Fito de la Parra for engagements on the California bar circuit. The group released several albums on small labels in the '90s. While touring with the group, Henry Vestine died of apparent respiratory failure in a hotel near Paris, France, on October 20, 1997, at the age of 52.

Canned Heat

Live at Topanga	Wand	693	'70	†
	Pickwick	3364		†
Canned Heat	Liberty	7526	'67	†
Boogie with Canned Heat	Liberty	7541	'68	†
	Liberty	10105	'80	†
	Pickwick	3614	'78	†
Livin' the Blues	Liberty	27200	'68	†
	United Artists	9955	'71	†
Hallelujah	Liberty	7618	'69	†
Cookbook (Best)	Liberty	11000	'69	†
	Liberty	10106	'81	†
Future Blues	Liberty	11002	'70	†
Live in Europe	United Artists	5509	'71	†
Historical Figures and Ancient Heads	United Artists	5557	'72	†
The New Age	United Artists	049	'73	†
Very Best	United Artists	431	'75	†
Best	EMI America	48377	'87	CS/CD
Vintage Canned Heat	Janus	3009	'70	†
Collage	Sunset	5298	'71	†
One More River to Cross	Atlantic	7289	'74	†
Canned Heat	Springboard Int'l	4026	'75	†
Human Condition	Takoma	7066	'79	†
	Takoma	72766	'87	LP/CS†
In Concert (recorded 1979)	King Biscuit			
	Flower Hour	88005	'96	CD
Captured Live	Accord	12179	'81	†
Reheated	Chameleon	89022	'90	†
Internal Combustion	River Road	61794	'94	†
Gamblin' Woman	Mausoleum	60026	'96	CD
The Ties That Bind	Archive	80002	'97	CD
Boogie Up the Country	Inak	88042	'98	CD
Live!	Griffin	1104		CD

Canned Heat and John Lee Hooker

Hooker 'N' Heat	Liberty	(2)35002	'71	†
	EMI America	(2)97896	'91	CD
	Mobile Fidelity	(2)676	'96	CD
The Best Of Hooker 'N' Heat	EMI	38207	'96	CD
Infinite Boogie (recorded 1970)	Rhino	71105	'87	CS†
Recorded "Live" at the Fox Venice Theatre	Rhino	801		CS
	Rhino	75776		CD

CAPTAIN BEEFHEART

Born Don Van Vliet on January 15, 1941, in Glendale, California.

An early associate of both Frank Zappa and Ry Cooder, Captain Beefheart and His Magic Band played a curious mix of delta blues, rock 'n' roll, and avant-garde jazz that explored the farthest reaches of rock music in the '60s and '70s. The band's unique sound, passed over by all but the most progressive of fans, was characterized by Beefheart's incredible voice (growling and gravely, with a range of more than four octaves), intricate arrangements, enigmatic lyrics (generally written by Beefheart), and early use of the theremin, an electronic instrument. Perhaps best known for 1969's *Trout Mask Replica,* Captain Beefheart and His Magic Band are an acknowledged influence on punk and new wave music.

Captain Beefheart moved with his family to the desert town of Lancaster at age thirteen and became friends with Frank Zappa in high school. Teaching himself harmonica and saxophone, Beefheart performed with several rhythm-and-blues bands before forming the first edition of His Magic Band in 1964. Gaining a reputation in area desert towns, the group recorded Bo Diddley's "Diddy Wah Diddy" for A&M Records, and the single became a regional hit. However, material for a first album was rejected by A&M as "too negative," and Van Vliet retreated to Lancaster. By 1965, he had assembled a new Magic Band with guitarist Ry Cooder and drummer John French to rerecord the material for Buddah Records, which released it as *Safe as Milk.* Winning considerable critical acclaim in the United States and Europe, the album spurred a successful tour of Europe in early 1966.

With the departure of lead guitarist Ry Cooder, Captain Beefheart and His Magic Band were crippled, since the lead guitar parts, complex and erratic, were personally taught by Van Vliet over long periods of time. Nonetheless, with new guitarist Jeff Cotton, sessions for the next album began in April 1968. The album was ultimately released in altered form as *Strictly Personal.* Most of the album's contents were reissued in unaltered form as *I May Be Hungry but I Sure Ain't Weird* in 1992. *Mirror Man,* recorded around the same time, was not issued until 1970.

A disappointed Don Van Vliet subsequently accepted Frank Zappa's offer to make a new album, free of all artistic restrictions, for Zappa's Straight Records. Following Van Vliet's lead, the members of the reorganized Magic Band took on bizarre names: guitarist-flutist Bill Harkleroad became Zoot Horn Rollo; guitarist Jeff Cotton became Antennae Jimmy Semens; and bassist Mark Boston became Rockette Morton. Joining them was an unidentified drummer (John French, known as Drumbo) and the Mascara Snake on vocals and clarinet. *Trout Mask Replica,* produced by Frank Zappa, was hailed as one of the most advanced concepts in rock music but proved a commercial failure.

Captain Beefheart subsequently performed the vocals on "Willie the Pimp" from Zappa's *Hot Rats,* switching the group to Reprise for *Lick My Decals Off, Baby.* In 1971, they made one of their infrequent tours of the United States to befuddled fans. Art Tripp (also known as Ed Marimba) was added on drums and marimba for *The Spotlight Kid* and *Clear Spot.* Moving to Mercury Records, the band recorded the softer and more accessible *Unconditionally Guaranteed.* Thereafter, the band quit and Beefheart recorded *Bluejeans and Moonbeams* with sessions musicians.

On May 20 and 21, 1975, Captain Beefheart recorded *Bongo Fury* with Frank Zappa and The Mothers at the Armadillo World Headquarters in Austin, Texas. By 1976, Beefheart had assembled a new Magic Band for occasional club appearances. During 1977 and 1978, the group successfully toured Europe and played sold-out engagements at New York's Bottom Line and Hollywood's Roxy. Subsequent album releases were *Shiny Beast (Bat Chain Puller), Doc at the Radar Station* (hailed as perhaps the best of Beefheart's later career), and *Ice Cream for Crow.* The group successfully toured Europe and the United States in 1980, but the group disbanded in 1982. Van Vliet, an accomplished artist for many years, retired from music in 1985 to pursue painting as a full-time profession. He has since exhibited his works at galleries in the United States and Europe, including the San Francisco Museum of Modern Art in 1989.

Captain Beefheart and His Magic Band

The Legendary A&M Sessions	A&M (EP)	12510		LP/CS†
Safe as Milk	Buddah	5001	'65	†
	Buddah	5063	'69	†
	One Way	29088		CD†
Strictly Personal	Blue Thumb	1	'68	†
I May Be Hungry but I Sure Ain't Weird	Griffin	215	'92	CD
Mirror Man	Buddah	5077	'70	†
	One Way	22166		CD†
Trout Mask Replica	Straight	(2)1053	'69	†
	Reprise	(2)2027	'70	LP†
	Reprise	52027		CS†
	Reprise	2027		CD†
Lick Off My Decals, Baby	Reprise	6420	'70	
	Enigma/Retro	73394	'89	CS/CD†
	Bizarre/Straight	70364	'91	CS/CD†
The Spotlight Kid	Reprise	2050	'72	†
Clear Spot	Reprise	2115	'72	†
The Spotlight Kid/Clear Spot	Reprise	26249	'91	CD†
Unconditionally Guaranteed	Mercury	709	'74	†
	Blue Plate	1633		CD†
Bluejeans and Moonbeams	Mercury	1018	'74	†
	Blue Plate	1631		CD†
Shiny Beast (Bat Chain Puller)	Warner Brothers	3256	'78	†
	Enigma/Retro	73548	'90	CS/CD†
	Bizarre/Straight	70365	'91	CS/CD†
Doc at the Radar Station	Virgin	13148	'80	†
	Blue Plate	1824	'92	CD
Ice Cream for Crow	Virgin/Epic	38274	'82	†
	Blue Plate	1632		CD
The Best Beefheart	Pair	1232	'89	CD†
Captain Beefheart at His Best	Special Music	4922		CS/CD

Captain Beefheart/Frank Zappa/The Mothers

Bongo Fury	DiscReet	2234	'75	†
	Barking Pumpkin/ Capitol	74220	'89	CS†
	Rykodisc	10097	'89	CD†
	Rykodisc	10522	'95	CD

JOHNNY CASH

Born February 26, 1932, in Kingsland, Arkansas.

Achieving his initial success recording gentle rockabilly at Sun Records, John Cash graduated to Columbia Records in 1958, scoring his earliest major pop hit with "Ring of Fire" in 1963. He later recorded folk-oriented material in the mid-'60s, bringing an unprecedented social consciousness to country music with 1964's "Ballad of Ira Hayes" from *Bitter Tears,* his monumental tribute to the American Indian. Helping to broaden the scope of country-and-western music and popularize country music with rock and pop fans, Johnny Cash became the first international country star and may have done more to popularize country music than anyone since Hank Williams. Indeed, his television series (1969–1971) was instrumental in widening the audience for country music. Additionally, he was instrumental in introducing Bob Dylan and Kris Kristofferson to broader public acceptance. Johnny Cash scored his most recent success with Kristofferson, Willie Nelson, and Waylon Jennings in The Highwaymen. Inducted into the Rock and Roll Hall of Fame in 1992, Cash achieved his first album chart entry in eighteen years with *American Recordings* in 1994.

Johnny Cash grew up in Dyess, Arkansas, where he had moved at the age of three. Following his discharge from the Air Force in July 1954, he traveled to Memphis and eventually auditioned for Sam Phillips of Sun Records in March 1955. Signed to Sun, Cash managed pop hits with his own "I Walk the Line," "Ballad of a Teenage Queen," "Guess Things Happen That Way," and "The Ways of a Woman in Love." In 1957, W. S. Holland joined his backup band, becoming one of the first drummers in country music. In August 1958, Johnny Cash switched to Columbia Records and soon hit with "Don't Take Your Guns to Town." Moving to California, Cash started working with June Carter, of the legendary Carter Family, in 1961. He began feeling the strain of constant touring and the collapse of his first marriage and grieved the death of friend Johnny Horton. As a consequence, Cash started taking amphetamines and tranquilizers to cope with his hectic life.

In 1963, Johnny Cash scored his first major pop hit on Columbia with "Ring of Fire." He soon began hanging out on the periphery of the Greenwich Village folk music scene, and his next hit, "Understand Your Man," had a distinctive folk feel to it. In 1964, he appeared with Bob Dylan at the Newport Folk Festival. During this time, Cash recorded a number of folk songs, including Peter LaFarge's "Ballad of Ira Hayes" and Dylan's "Don't Think Twice, It's Alright," and, with June Carter, "It Ain't Me, Babe," another country and pop hit.

Despite increasing popular success, Johnny Cash's life seemed to deteriorate. In October 1965, he was arrested at El Paso International Airport in possession of hundreds of stimulants and tranquilizers. After being found near death in a small Georgia town in 1967, Cash decided to reform. With June Carter providing moral support, he cleaned up his act. The couple scored a smash country hit with "Jackson" in 1968, the year they married. In 1970, they hit the pop charts with Tim Hardin's "If I Were a Carpenter."

Johnny Cash began a series of successful television appearances in 1967, and his 1968 *Johnny Cash at Folsom Prison* remained on the album charts for more than two years and revitalized his career. The album yielded a top country hit and moderate pop hit with "Folsom Prison Blues." In early 1969, Cash scored another top country and moderate pop hit with Carl Perkins' "Daddy Sang Bass." Cash's penchant for novelty songs culminated in his biggest pop hit, "A Boy Named Sue," from *Johnny Cash at San Quentin,* another best-seller. The 1969 debut show for his ABC network television series featured a film of Cash and Bob Dylan recording "Girl from the North Country." The song later appeared on Dylan's first country album, *Nashville Skyline.* Later shows featured artists such as Gordon Lightfoot, Kris Kristofferson, Waylon Jennings, and Joni Mitchell. During the 1969 Newport Folk Festival, Johnny Cash introduced Kris Kristofferson, later recording his "Sunday Morning Coming Down" and bolstering his early career.

Johnny Cash again demonstrated his social consciousness in the early '70s with the hits "What Is Truth" and "Man in Black." He also narrated and coproduced the soundtrack to the Christian epic *Gospel Road* and assisted in the production of *The Trail of Tears,* a dramatization of the tragedy of the Cherokee Indians, broadcast on public television (PBS). Cash scored another pop novelty hit with "One Piece at a Time" in 1976 and hit the country charts in 1978 with "There Ain't No Good Chain Gangs," recorded with Waylon Jennings. His last major country hit came in 1981 with "The Baron." Future country star Marty Stuart was a member of Cash's band from 1979 to 1985.

In 1985, Johnny Cash joined Waylon Jennings, Willie Nelson, and Kris Kristofferson to tour and record as The Highwaymen. They hit the top of the country charts with Jimmy Webb's "The Highwayman." The following year, Cash reunited with old Sun Records alumni Carl Perkins, Jerry Lee Lewis, and Roy Orbison for *Class of '55,* contributing "I Will Rock & Roll with You." Cash was dropped from the Columbia Records roster in 1986 and he subsequently signed with Mercury Records, switching to American Records in 1993. In 1990, he joined Jennings, Nelson, and Kristofferson as The Highwaymen for another album and round of touring. Inducted into the Rock and Roll Hall of Fame in 1992, Cash later sang "The Wanderer" with U2, included on their *Zooropa* album. In 1994, he recorded the moody, acoustic *American Recordings* album for American Records under producer Rick Rubin, best known for his work with Run-D.M.C., Public Enemy, and The Red Hot Chili Peppers. The following year, Cash once again joined The Highwaymen, to tour and record for Liberty Records *The Road Goes on Forever,* which included Steve Earle's "The Devil's Right Hand," Stephen Bruton's "It Is What It Is," Billy Joe and Eddie Shaver's "Live Forever," and Robert Earl Keen's title song.

Over the years, Johnny Cash has appeared in films (*A Gunfight* with Kirk Douglas), on television (1986's *Stagecoach* with the other Highwaymen, 1988's *Davy Crockett*) and even written a novel (1986's *Man in White*). Despite health problems (he had a double-bypass heart operation in 1988), Johnny Cash continued to tour with his wife June and son John Carter Cash.

JOHNNY CASH BIBLIOGRAPHY

Cash, Johnny. *Man in Black.* Grand Rapids, MI: Zondervan, 1975.

————. *Man in White: A Novel.* San Francisco: Harper and Row, 1986.

————, with Patrick Carr. *Cash: The Autobiography.* San Francisco: HarperSanFrancisco, 1997.

Conn, Charles P. *The New Johnny Cash.* New York: Family Library, 1973; Old Tappan, NJ: F. H. Revell, 1978.

Govoni, Albert. *A Boy Named Cash.* New York: Lancer Books, 1970.

Smith, John L. (compiler). *The Johnny Cash Discography 1954–1984.* Westport, CT: Greenwood Press, 1985.

————. *The Johnny Cash Discography 1984–1993.* Westport, CT: Greenwood Press, 1994.

————. *The Johnny Cash Record Catalog.* Westport, CT: Greenwood Press, 1994.

Wren, Christopher. *Winners Got Scars, Too: The Life and Legends of Johnny Cash.* New York: Dial Press, 1971.

Johnny Cash on Columbia Records

The Fabulous Johnny Cash	Columbia	1253	'58	†
	Columbia	8122	'59	†
	Sony	8122		CS/CD†
	K-tel	75024	'95	CS/CD
Hymns By Johnny Cash	Columbia	8125	'59	†
Songs of Our Soil	Columbia	8148	'59	†
Ride This Train	Columbia	8255	'60	†
	Sony	8255		CS/CD†
	K-tel	75026	'95	CS/CD
Now, There Was a Song!	Columbia	8254	'60	†
	Columbia/Legacy	66506	'94	CD
Hymns from the Heart	Columbia	8522	'62	†

The Sound of Johnny Cash	Columbia	8602	'62	†
Blood, Sweat and Tears	Columbia	8730	'63	†
	Columbia/Legacy	66508	'94	CD
Ring of Fire	Columbia	8853	'63	†
Christmas Spirit	Columbia	8917	'63	†
I Walk the Line	Columbia	8990	'64	†
Bitter Tears—Ballads of the American Indian	Columbia	9048	'64	†
	Columbia/Legacy	66507	'94	CD
3-Pak: Ring of Fire/Blood, Sweat and Tears/Johnny Cash Sings the Ballads of the American Indian: Bitter Tears	Columbia	64812	'95	CD†
Orange Blossom Special	Columbia	9109	'65	†
Ballads of the True West	Columbia	(2)838	'65	†
Mean as Hell	Columbia	9246	'66	†
Everybody Loves a Nut	Columbia	9292	'66	†
That's What You Get for Lovin' Me	Columbia	9337	'66	†
From Sea to Shining Sea	Columbia	9447	'67	†
Greatest Hits	Columbia	9478	'67	CS/CD
At Folsom Prison	Columbia	9639	'68	†
The Holy Land	Columbia	9726	'69	†
At San Quentin	Columbia	9827	'69	CS
At Folsom Prison and San Quentin	Columbia	(2)33639	'75	†
	Columbia/Legacy	33639		CS/CD
Hello, I'm Johnny Cash	Columbia	9943	'70	†
The World of Johnny Cash	Columbia	(2)29	'70	†
The Johnny Cash Show	Columbia	30100	'70	†
I Walk the Line (soundtrack)	Columbia	30397	'70	†
Man in Black	Columbia	30550	'71	†
Greatest Hits, Volume 2	Columbia	30887	'71	CS
A Thing Called Love	Columbia	31332	'72	†
America: A 200-Year Salute in Story and Song	Columbia	31645	'72	†
Any Old Wind That Blows	Columbia	32091	'73	†
Gospel Road (soundtrack)	Columbia	(2)32253	'73	†
	Priority	(2)32253	'82	†
That Ragged Old Flag	Columbia	32917	'74	†
Five Feet High and Rising	Columbia	32951	'74	†
The Junkie and the Juicehead Minus Me	Columbia	33086	'74	†
Sings Precious Memories	Columbia	33087	'75	CS
	Priority	33087	'84	†
John R. Cash	Columbia	33370	'75	†
Look at Them Beans	Columbia	33814	'75	†
Strawberry Cake	Columbia	34088	'76	†
One Piece at a Time	Columbia	34193	'76	†
Last Gunfighter Ballad	Columbia	34314	'77	†
The Rambler	Columbia	34833	'77	†
I Would Like to See You Again	Columbia	35313	'78	†
Greatest Hits, Volume 3	Columbia	35637	'78	†
Gone Girl	Columbia	35646	'78	†
Silver	Columbia	36086	'79	†
A Believer Sings the Truth	Cachet	9001	'79	†
	Priority	38074	'82	†
	Columbia	38074		CS†

Rockabilly Blues	Columbia	36779	'80	†
Classic Christmas	Columbia	36866	'80	†
The Baron	Columbia	37179	'81	†
Encore	Columbia	37355	'81	†
The Adventures of Johnny Cash	Columbia	38094	'82	†
Biggest Hits	Columbia	38317	'82	CS/CD
Johnny 99	Columbia	38696	'83	†
Columbia Records 1958–1986	Columbia	40637	'87	CS/CD†
Patriot (recorded 1964–1976)	Columbia	45384	'90	CS/CD
The Essential Johnny Cash (1955–1983)	Columbia	(3)47991	'92	CS/CD
The Gospel Collection	Columbia/Legacy	48952	'92	CS/CD
Personal Christmas Collection	Columbia/Legacy	64154	'94	CS/CD
The Man in Black	Bear Family	15588	'96	CD

Johnny Cash Budget Releases

Johnny Cash	Harmony	11342	'69	†
Walls of a Prison	Harmony	30138	'70	†
Johnny Cash Songbook	Harmony	31602	'72	†
Ballad of the American Indians	Harmony	32388	'73	†
Folsom Prison Blues	Hilltop	6116	'72	†
I Walk the Line/Rock Island Line	Pickwick	(2)2045		†
Johnny Cash	Pickwick	(2)2052		†
I Walk the Line	Pickwick	6097		†
Rock Island Line	Pickwick	6101		†
Big River	Pickwick	6118		†
Country Gold	Power Pak	246		†
Johnny Cash	Archive of Folk and Jazz Music	278		†
This Is Johnny Cash	RCA-Camden	3014	'81	CS
Classic Cash	Pair	(2)1107	'86	†

Johnny Cash and June Carter

Carryin' On	Columbia	9528	'67	†
The Johnny Cash Family	Columbia	31754	'72	†
Johnny Cash and His Woman	Columbia	32443	'73	†
Super Hits	Columbia	66773	'94	CS/CD
Give My Love to Rose	Harmony	31256	'72	†

Recent Johnny Cash Releases

Believe in Him	Word	8333	'86	†
Johnny Cash Is Coming to Town	Mercury	832031	'87	LP/CS/CD†
Classic Cash	Mercury/Nashville	834526	'88	CS/CD
Water from the Wells of Home	Mercury	834778	'88	LP/CS/CD†
Boom Chick a Boom	Mercury	842155	'90	CS/CD†
The Mystery of Life	Mercury	848051	'91	CS/CD†
Wanted Man	Mercury/Nashville	522709	'94	CS/CD
Greatest Hits	CSI	40195	'91	CD†
Best	Curb/Warner Brothers	77494	'91	CS/CD
American Recordings	American	45520	'94	CS/CD†
	American/Columbia	69402	'98	CS/CD
Unchained	American/Columbia	69404	'98	CS/CD
Live Recording	Fat Boy	235	'96	CD
Golden Hits	ITC Masters	1002	'98	CS/CD

Johnny Cash, Jerry Lee Lewis and Carl Perkins

The Survivors	Columbia	37961	'82	LP/CS†
	Razor & Tie	2077	'95	CS/CD

Johnny Cash and Waylon Jennings

Heroes	Columbia	40347	'86	LP/CS†
	Razor & Tie	2078	'95	CS/CD

Johnny Cash, Jerry Lee Lewis, Roy Orbison and Carl Perkins

Class of '55	America/Smash	830002	'86	LP/CS/CD†
	Mercury	830002	'94	CS/CD

Johnny Cash, Willie Nelson, Waylon Jennings and Kris Kristofferson

The Highwaymen	Columbia	40056	'85	CS/CD†
Highwayman II	Columbia	45240	'90	CS/CD
The Road Goes on Forever	Liberty	28091	'95	CS/CD

RAY CHARLES

Born Ray Charles Robinson on September 23, 1930, in Albany, Georgia.

After pioneering soul music on Atlantic Records in the '50s, Ray Charles applied his gospel-oriented style to country-and-western material on ABC Records in the early '60s, becoming the first black artist to score hits in the country field *and* the first male black singer to make a major impact on the white adult market. He also garnered popularity with jazz audiences through recordings with Betty Carter and the Count Basie Band and appearances at jazz festivals around the world. Additionally, Charles established himself as an important black music entrepreneur, running his own independent record label, music publishing house, and recording studio. Ray Charles was inducted into the Rock and Roll Hall of Fame in its inaugural year, 1986.

Ray Charles grew up in Greenville, Florida, and was blinded by glaucoma at the age of six. From 1937 to 1945, he attended the St. Augustine (Florida) School for the Blind, where he learned piano and, later, clarinet and alto saxophone, plus composing and arranging. Orphaned at fifteen, Charles struck out on his own, performing in bands around the South and later touring with blues artist Lowell Fulson. In 1948, he moved to Seattle and formed a trio that scored a rhythm-and-blues hit with "Confession Blues" on the Downbeat label. In 1951 and 1952, Charles had rhythm-and-blues hits with "Baby Let Me Hold Your Hand" and "Kiss Me Baby" on the small, Los Angeles–based Swingtime label. Around 1952, Ray Charles' recording contract was sold to the New York–based Atlantic label, where he adapted gospel music techniques to blues lyrics. In early 1955, his new sound hit in both the popular and rhythm-and-blues fields with his own composition, "I've Got a Woman." Charles scored consistently on the rhythm-and-blues charts through the late '50s with songs such as "A Fool for You," "Drown in My Own Tears," and "Hallelujah I Love Her So." Finally, in 1959, Charles established himself as a popular recording artist with the release of his own top rhythm-and-blues and smash pop hit composition, "What'd I Say."

Sensing that Atlantic was still basically a rhythm-and-blues organization, Ray Charles switched to ABC-Paramount Records in late 1959. Through 1961, he scored a top pop and smash rhythm-and-blues hit with "Georgia on My Mind," a top pop and rhythm-and-blues hit with "Hit the Road Jack," and the major pop hits "Ruby" and "Unchain My Heart" (another top rhythm-and-blues hit). He also recorded *Genius+Soul=Jazz* for Impulse, with arrangements by Quincy Jones played by the Count Basie Band. Yielding a top rhythm-and-

RAY CHARLES (MIROSLAV ZAJIČ)

blues and near-smash pop hit with the instrumental "One Mint Julep," this album and one recorded with Betty Carter for ABC-Paramount brought him an increasing measure of popularity with jazz fans, black and white.

By 1962, Ray Charles was utilizing forty-piece orchestras and large vocal choruses for his recordings. With this full, commercial sound, his *Modern Sounds in Country and Western* became phenomenally popular, producing the top pop and rhythm-and-blues hit "I Can't Stop Loving You" (backed with "Born to Lose") and the smash pop and rhythm-and-blues hit "You Don't Know Me." Within a year, *Volume II* of country-and-western material was released, yielding smash pop and rhythm-and-blues hits with "You Are My Sunshine" (backed with "Your Cheating Heart") and "Take These Chains from My Heart." Through 1966, Charles scored smash pop and rhythm-and-blues hits with "Busted" and "Crying Time," and major pop hits with "That Lucky Old Sun," "Together Again," and "Let's Go Get Stoned" (a top rhythm-and-blues hit). He later hit with "Here We Go Again" and The Beatles' "Yesterday" and "Eleanor Rigby."

Ray Charles formed his own independent Crossover label in 1973 and returned to Atlantic in 1977, moving to Columbia in the '80s and Warner Brothers in the '90s. During 1976, he recorded *Porgy and Bess* with English songstress Cleo Laine for RCA Records. Charles achieved a major country hit with "Born to Love Me" in 1982 and later recorded duets with country stars on *Friendship*. The album yielded five major country hits, including "We Didn't See a Thing" (with George Jones), "Seven Spanish Angels" (with Willie Nelson), and "Two Old Cats Like Us" (with Hank Williams, Jr.). In late 1989, Charles had his first major pop hit in over twenty years with the Quincy Jones recording "I'll Be Good to You," featuring Chaka Khan. During the '90s, Ray Charles appeared in a series of stylish commercials for Pepsi and was the subject of a PBS documentary.

In the '90s, Ray Charles continued to work about eight months a year, touring with a large orchestra. He lived in Los Angeles, where he was involved with RPM International, a corporation that included Crossover Records, the music publishing companies Tangerine and Racer Music, and RPM Studios, where he recorded. In 1990, Ray Charles began recording for Warner Brothers Records, recording 1993's *My World* with Eric Clapton, Billy Preston, Mavis Staples, and June Pointer.

RAY CHARLES BIBLIOGRAPHY

Charles, Ray, and David Ritz. *Brother Ray: Ray Charles' Own Story.* New York: Dial Press, 1978; New York: Da Capo Press, 1992.

Ritz, David. *Ray Charles: Voice of Soul.* New York: Chelsea, 1994.

Winski, Norman. *Ray Charles.* Los Angeles: Melrose Square, 1994.

Ray Charles on ABC Records

The Genius Hits the Road	ABC	335	'60	†
Dedicated to You	ABC	355	'61	†
Modern Sounds in Country and Western	ABC	410	'62	†
	Rhino	70099	'88	CS/CD
Greatest Hits	ABC	415	'62	†
Modern Sounds in Country and Western, Volume II	ABC	435	'62	†
Ingredients in a Recipe for Soul	ABC	465	'63	†
	DCC	047		CS/CD†
	DCC	1027		CD†
	Sandstone	33074	'92	CD†
Sweet and Sour Tears	ABC	480	'64	†
Have a Smile with Me	ABC	495	'64	†
Live in Concert	ABC	500	'65	†
Together Again	ABC	520	'65	†
Crying Time	ABC	544	'66	†
Ray's Moods	ABC	550	'66	†
A Man and His Soul	ABC	(2)590	'67	†
Invites You to Listen	ABC	595	'67	†
A Portrait of Ray	ABC	625	'68	†
I'm All Yours	ABC	675	'69	†
Doing His Thing	ABC	695	'69	†
Love Country Style	ABC	707	'70	†
Volcanic Action of My Soul	ABC	726	'71	†
25th Anniversary Salute	ABC	(3)731	'71	†
Cryin' Time	ABC	744	'71	†
A Message from the People	ABC	755	'72	†
Through the Eyes of Love	ABC	765	'72	†
All-Time Greats	ABC	(2)781/2	'73	†
My Kind of Jazz	Tangerine/ABC	1512	'70	†
Jazz Number II	Tangerine/ABC	1516	'73	†

Ray Charles and Betty Carter

Ray Charles and Betty Carter	ABC	385	'61	†
	DCC	039	'88	CS/CD†
	DCC	2005	'95	LP†
	Rhino	75259	'98	CD

More Ray Charles

Genius + Soul = Jazz	Impulse	2	'61	†
	DCC	038	'88	CS/CD†
	Sandstone	33073	'92	CD†
Rock + Soul = Genius (recorded 1961)	Jazz Music Yesterday	1009	'91	CD
Original Ray Charles	Hollywood	504	'62	†
Fabulous Artistry	Hollywood	505	'63	†

Great Ray Charles	Premier	2004	'62	†
Fabulous Ray Charles	Premier	2005	'62	†
Ray Charles	Design	145	'62	†
Berlin, 1962 (recorded March 6, 1962)	Pablo	5301	'96	CD
Come Live with Me	Crossover	9000	'74	†
Renaissance	Crossover	9005	'75	†
My Kind of Jazz, Part 3	Crossover	9007	'75	†
True to Life	Atlantic	19142	'77	†
Love and Peace	Atlantic	19199	'78	†
Ain't It So	Atlantic	19251	'79	†
Brother Ray Is at It Again	Atlantic	19281	'80	†
Wish You Were Here Tonight	Columbia	38293	'83	†
Do I Ever Cross Your Mind	Columbia	38990	'84	†
Friendship	CBS	39415	'84	CD†
The Spirit of Christmas	Columbia	40125		LP/CS/CD†
From the Pages of My Mind	Columbia	40338	'86	CS†
Just Between Us	Columbia	40703	'89	CS/CD†
Seven Spanish Angels and Other Hits (1982–1986)	Columbia	45062	'89	CS/CD†
Would You Believe?	Warner Brothers	26343	'90	CD
My World	Warner Brothers	26735	'93	CS/CD
Strong Love Affair	Qwest/ Warner Brothers	46107	'96	CS/CD

Ray Charles Anthologies and Compilations

20 Golden Pieces of Ray Charles	Bulldog	2012	'79	LP/CS
Greatest Hits, Volume I	DCC	036	'87	CD
Greatest Hits, Volume II	DCC	037	'87	CD
Greatest Hits, Volumes I and II	DCC	(2)36/37		CD†
Greatest Country and Western Hits	DCC	040	'88	CS/CD†
	DCC	2012	'95	LP†
	DCC	1086	'95	CD†
Greatest Hits, Volume 1	Rhino	70097	'88	CS
Greatest Hits, Volume 2	Rhino	70098	'88	CS
Anthology	Rhino	75759	'88	CD
Blues + Jazz	Rhino	(2)71607	'94	CD†
Classics	Rhino	71874	'95	CS/CD
Genius & Soul—The 50th Anniversary Collection	Rhino	(5)72859	'98	CS/CD
Standards	Rhino	75210	'98	CD
Complete Country and Western Recordings 1959–1986	Rhino	(4)75328	'98	CD
Ray Charles	Bella Musica	89904	'90	CD†
Greatest Hits	CSI	40141	'91	CD†
His Greatest Hits	Sandstone	(2)33079	'92	CD†
The Session, Volume 2	Royal Collection	83154	'92	CD
C. C. Rider	Drive	3233	'95	CD
See See Rider	Musketeer	9011	'95	CD
Walkin and Talkin	Fat Boy	325	'96	CD
Going Down Slow	CMA	8020	'96	CD
The Great Ray Charles	Goldies	63117	'96	CD
Best of Easy Listening	Richmond	2154		CS
Goin' Down Slow	Intermedia	5013		LP/CS

Ray Charles and Cleo Laine

Porgy and Bess	RCA	(2)1831	'76	†

CHICAGO

Robert Lamm (born October 13, 1944, in Brooklyn, New York), keyboards, vocals; Terry Kath (born January 31, 1946, in Chicago; died January 23, 1978, in Woodland Hills, California), guitar, vocals; Peter Cetera (born September 13, 1944, in Chicago), bass, guitar, vocals; James Pankow (born August 20, 1947, in Chicago), trombone; Lee Loughnane (born October 21, 1946, in Chicago), trumpet, percussion, vocals; Walt Parazaider (born March 14, 1945, in Chicago), saxophone, clarinet, flute; and Danny Seraphine (born August 28, 1948, in Chicago), drums. Keyboardist-guitarist-vocalist Bill Champlin joined in 1982.

A big-band rock group that initially featured compelling jazz-style improvisation, Chicago launched their career by issuing three double-record sets in two years, saturating the market and perhaps overextending the group's creativity. Sustained by a series of hit singles (including the smash hits "25 or 6 to 4," "Saturday in the Park," and "Just You 'N' Me") and best-selling albums through the mid-'70s, Chicago became perhaps the second most successful American rock band of all time, excelled by only The Beach Boys. Degenerating into purveyors of melodic but inconsequential ballads and pop songs, Chicago suffered a lapse of popularity following the departure of mentor-producer James William Guercio in 1977. Rebounding under producer-writer David Foster beginning in 1982, Chicago continued to score smash pop and easy-listening hits through the '80s despite the departure of lead vocalist Peter Cetera for a solo career in 1985.

Self-taught guitarist Terry Kath and saxophonist-clarinetist Walt Parazaider were members of Jimmy and The Gentleman in 1966. While studying classical clarinet at Chicago's DePaul University, Parazaider met fellow music students James Pankow, Lee Loughnane, and Danny Seraphine. Parazaider, Kath, Pankow, and Seraphine subsequently decided to form their own band, the Missing Links, recruiting Loughnane and Robert Lamm. Lamm had moved to Chicago at the age of fifteen and studied piano and composition at Roosevelt University. Renamed the Big Thing, the group began rehearsals in early 1967, making their concert debut in May. In August, Parazaider's friend James William Guercio spotted the group playing the Midwest bar and club circuit. They added bassist-vocalist Peter Cetera at the end of 1967, as Guercio relocated to Los Angeles, where he produced the Buckinghams' *Portraits* and Blood, Sweat and Tears' second album.

Moving to Los Angeles in 1968 at the behest of Guercio, who renamed the group Chicago Transit Authority, the band recorded their debut album at the beginning of 1969. It featured two long and exciting jams on Lamm's "Beginnings" and Steve Winwood's "I'm a Man" and yielded a minor hit with "Questions 67 and 68." The album remained on the album charts for more than three years and eventually sold more than two million copies. Shortening their name to Chicago in July 1969, the group toured the United States during 1970, scoring smash hits with Pankow's "Make Me Smile" and Lamm's "25 or 6 to 4" from *Chicago II* and Lamm's "Does Anybody Really Know What Time It Is?" and "Beginnings" from their debut album. *Chicago III* included the hits "Free" and "Lowdown."

Chicago continued to record successfully under manager-producer James William Guercio through 1977, moving toward mainstream pop as the decade progressed. Their stint as the first rock group to play at New York's Carnegie Hall in April 1971 resulted in a live four-record set (their fourth multirecord set in a row). *Chicago V* yielded the smash hit "Saturday in the Park" and the major hit "Dialogue," while *Chicago VI* featured two smash hits, Cetera and Pankow's "Feelin' Stronger Every Day" and Pankow's "Just You 'N' Me." Touring the world in 1972, Chicago permanently added percussionist Laudir de Oliveira in 1974, when Lamm recorded the solo album *Skinny Boy*. The near-smash hits for Chicago continued with "(I've Been) Searchin' So Long," Loughnane's "Call on Me," and Cetera's "Wishing You Were Here" (a top easy-listening hit) from *Chicago VII,* and Lamm's "Harry Truman" and Pankow's "Old Days" from *Chicago VIII.* Touring with The Beach Boys in 1975, Chicago's subsequent hits included the top pop and easy-listening hit "If You Leave Me Now" and the smash pop hit "Baby, What a Big Surprise," both written by Cetera.

Chicago's career momentum stalled after James William Guercio ceased managing and producing the group in 1977. On January 23, 1978, Terry Kath died of an accidental self-inflicted gunshot wound in Woodland Hills, California. *Hot Streets,* coproduced by Phil Ramone and recorded with guitarist Donnie Dacus, yielded two major hits with "Alive Again" and "No Tell Lover," but the group would not score another major hit for more than three years. In 1995, virtually all Chicago albums originally released on Columbia were reissued on the group's own Chicago label.

Chicago eventually began a remarkable comeback on Full Moon Records in 1982 under producer David Foster. Joined by singer-songwriter-keyboardist Bill Champlin, the longtime leader of Northern California's Sons of Champlin who had just released the solo album *Runaway,* Chicago scored a top pop and easy-listening hit with Cetera and Foster's "Hard to Say I'm Sorry." *Chicago 17* and *18* (the latter on Warner Brothers Records) each yielded four hits, most notably "Hard Habit to Break," "You're the Inspiration," and "Will You Still Love Me?" *Chicago 19,* produced by Ron Nevison for Reprise Records, contained five hits, including the top pop and easy-listening hit "Look Away," the smashes "I Don't Wanna Live Without Your Love" and "What Kind of Man Would I Be?" and the near-smash "You're Not Alone." However, Seraphine soon left the group and Chicago never achieved another major hit. In 1995, with Champlin, Parazaider, Lamm, Loughnane, and Pankow as mainstays, they recorded their versions of big-band standards on *Night and Day* for Giant Records.

Peter Cetera recorded a solo album for Full Moon Records in 1982 and left Chicago for a solo career in early 1985 following *Chicago 17.* In 1986, *Solitude/Solitaire* yielded a top pop and easy-listening hits with "Glory of Love" (included in the movie *Karate Kid Part II*) and "The Next Time I Fall," recorded with Amy Grant. "One Good Woman" and "After All" (recorded with Cher) became top easy-listening and smash pop hits in 1988 and 1989, and "Restless Heart" was a top easy-listening and moderate pop hit in 1992. By the end of 1993, Cetera had switched to the Chicago-based independent label River North Records.

Chicago

Live in Toronto	Special Music	4818		CS/CD
Live in Toronto	Magnum America	26	'96	CD
Chicago Transit Authority	Columbia	(2)8	'69	†
	Columbia	00008	'89	CS/CD†
	Chicago	3001	'95	CS/CD
Chicago II	Columbia	(2)24	'70	†
	Columbia	00024		CS/CD†
	Chicago	3002	'95	CS/CD
Chicago III	Columbia	(2)30110	'71	†
	Columbia	30110	'86	CD†
	Chicago	3003	'95	CD
Live at Carnegie Hall	Columbia	(4)30865	'71	†
At Carnegie Hall, Volumes 1–4	Columbia	(3)30865		CD†
	Chicago	(3)3004	'95	CS/CD
Chicago V	Columbia	31102	'72	CS/CD†
	Chicago	3005	'95	CS/CD
Chicago VI	Columbia	32400	'73	CS/CD†
	Chicago	3006	'95	CS/CD
Chicago VII	Columbia	(2)32810	'74	†
	Columbia	32810	'86	CD†
	Chicago	3007	'95	CS/CD

Chicago VIII	Columbia	33100	'75	CD†
	Chicago	3008	'95	CS/CD
Greatest Hits, Volume 1	Columbia	33900	'75	CS/CD†
	Chicago	3009	'95	CS/CD
Chicago X	Columbia	34200	'76	CD†
	Chicago	3010	'95	CS/CD
Chicago XI	Columbia	34860	'77	CS/CD†
	Chicago	3011	'95	CS/CD
Hot Streets	Columbia	35512	'78	†
Chicago (XIII)	Columbia	36105	'79/'90	CS/CD†
	Chicago	3013	'95	CS/CD
Chicago XIV	Columbia	36517	'80	†
	Chicago	3014	'95	CS/CD
Greatest Hits, Volume 2	Columbia	37682	'81	CS/CD†
	Chicago	3015	'95	CS/CD
If You Leave Me Now	Columbia	38590	'83	CS/CD†
	Chicago	3016	'95	CS/CD
Take Me Back to Chicago	Columbia	39579	'85	CD
Group Portrait	Columbia/Legacy	(4)47416	'91	CS/CD†
	Chicago	(4)3018	'95	CS/CD
Chicago 16	Full Moon/Asylum	23689	'82	CS†/CD
Chicago 17	Full Moon/Asylum	25060	'84	CS/CD
Chicago 18	Warner Brothers	25509	'86	CS/CD
Chicago 19	Reprise	25714	'88	CS/CD
Greatest Hits, 1982–1989	Reprise	26080	'89	CS/CD
Twenty 1	Reprise	26391	'91	CS/CD
Night and Day	Giant	24615	'95	CS/CD
Live	Richmond	2188		CS
Beginnings	Griffin	1034		CD
Robert Lamm				
Skinny Boy	Columbia	33095	'74	†
Bill Champlin				
Single	Full Moon	35367	'78	†
Runaway	Elektra	563	'82	†
Peter Cetera				
Peter Cetera	Full Moon	3624	'82	†
Solitude/Solitaire	Warner Brothers	25474	'86	CS/CD
One More Story	Warner Brothers	25704	'88	CS/CD
World Falling Down	Warner Brothers	26894	'92	CS/CD
One Clear Voice	River North	1110	'95	CS/CD

THE DAVE CLARK FIVE

Dave Clark (born December 15, 1942, in Tottenham, London, England), drums; Mike Smith (born December 12, 1943, in Edmonton, London), keyboards, lead vocals; Lenny Davidson (born May 30, 1944, in Enfield, Middlesex), lead guitar; Denny Payton (born August 11, 1943, in Walthamstow, London), saxophone, harmonica, guitar; and Rick Huxley (born August 5, 1942, in Dartford, Kent), rhythm guitar and bass.

One of the few '60s rock groups led by a drummer, The Dave Clark Five were an enormously successful singles band from 1964 to 1966, briefly challenging The Beatles in popularity, particularly in the United States. Despite featuring three songwriters and a potent lead vocalist, The Dave Clark Five never progressed beyond their raucous rockers and gentle ballads, disbanding in 1970, although principals Mike Smith and Dave Clark continued to perform until 1973.

Originally formed as a semiprofessional band in 1958 by Dave Clark and Rick Huxley, The Dave Clark Five comprised Clark, Huxley, Mike Smith, Lenny Davidson, and Denny Payton by 1961. Debuting in Tottenham, London, in early 1962, the group first recorded for the Pye subsidiary of Picadilly Records later that year. The group switched to Columbia Records (Epic in the United States) in 1963.

With Clark, Smith, and Davidson providing many of the songs, The Dave Clark Five achieved more than twenty British and American hits in the '60s. They began their string of successes with the smash British and American hits "Glad All Over," "Bits and Pieces," and "Can't You See That She's Mine," written by Clark and Smith. Conducting a highly successful American tour in the spring of 1964, the group made the first of eighteen appearances on the *Ed Sullivan Show* on May 31. They scored major American hits with the ballads "Because" (by Clark) and "Everybody Knows," and the originals "Anyway You Want It" and "Come Home" became major British and American hits. The group appeared in the 1965 film *Having a Wild Weekend* and toured America during the summer.

Later in 1965, The Dave Clark Five scored a smash British and American hit with "Catch Us if You Can" (by Clark and Davidson) and a top American hit with Bobby Day's "Over and Over." Major American hits continued with "At the Scene" and "Try Too Hard," and the group once again toured the United States in the summer of 1966. The hits subsequently slowed down and, after the smash American hit "You Got What It Takes" in the spring of 1967, The Dave Clark Five never achieved another major American hit. Major British hits continued into 1970 with "Red Balloon," "Good Old Rock and Roll," and "Everybody Get Together."

The Dave Clark Five announced their intention to disband in August 1970, yet Clark and Smith continued to perform as Dave Clark and Friends until 1973. Mike Smith recorded a British-only album with former Manfred Mann vocalist Mike D'Abo in 1975, as Dave Clark concentrated on business activities that included music publishing. In 1986, Clark cowrote and produced the modestly successful London stage musical *Time*. The original cast recording of the show included performances by Cliff Richard, Dionne Warwick, Leo Sayer, and Freddie Mercury. The hit recordings of The Dave Clark Five, unavailable for years, were eventually issued on the 1993 anthology set *The History of the Dave Clark Five*.

The Dave Clark Five

Glad All Over	Epic	26093	'64	†
Return!	Epic	26104	'64	†
American Tour	Epic	26117	'64	†
Coast to Coast	Epic	26128	'65	†
Weekend in London	Epic	26139	'65	†
Having a Wild Weekend (soundtrack)	Epic	26162	'65	†
I Like It Like That	Epic	26178	'65	†
Greatest Hits	Epic	26185	'66	†
Try Too Hard	Epic	26198	'66	†
Satisfied with You	Epic	26212	'66	†
More Greatest Hits	Epic	26221	'66	†
5 by 5	Epic	26236	'67	†
You Got What It Takes	Epic	26312	'67	†
Everybody Knows	Epic	26354	'68	†

The Dave Clark Five	Epic	30434	'71	†
Glad All Over (All-Time Greatest Hits)	Epic	(2)33459	'75	†
The History of the Dave Clark Five	Hollywood	(2)61482	'93	CS/CD
"Time"				
Time (London original cast)	Capitol	(2)12447	'86	†

JOE COCKER

Born John Cocker on May 20, 1944, in Sheffield, Yorkshire, England.

An English rhythm-and-blues vocal stylist whose jerky body movements brought him notoriety during the late '60s and early '70s, Joe Cocker achieved his biggest successes with his 1969 appearance at the Woodstock Music and Art Fair and his 1970 Mad Dogs and Englishmen tour with Leon Russell and Rita Coolidge.

Joe Cocker joined his first band, The Cavaliers, in 1959 and, by 1963, he was the lead vocalist of Vance Arnold and The Avengers. Forming The Grease Band with musical mentor Chris Stainton in 1966, Cocker scored a minor English hit with Stainton's "Marjorine" in 1968. The follow-up, a slow blues version of Lennon and McCartney's "With a Little Help from My Friends," became a top British and minor American hit. Cocker's debut album for A&M Records featured the playing of Jimmy Page and Stevie Winwood and included a driving version of Dave Mason's "Feelin' Alright."

In 1969, Cocker and Stainton regrouped The Grease Band for a successful U.S. tour that culminated in Cocker's much-heralded appearance at the Woodstock Music and Art Fair in August. During the tour, he met sessions keyboardist Leon Russell, who later produced and played on *Joe Cocker!,* which yielded a minor hit with Russell's "Delta Lady" and a moderate hit with Lennon and McCartney's "She Came in Through the Bathroom Window." Russell subsequently assembled a large revue for Cocker dubbed Mad Dogs and Englishmen, with a full horn section and vocal chorus (which included Rita Coolidge), for an enormously successful 1970 tour. The double-record set of recordings from the tour remained on the album charts for a year and eventually produced two near-smash hit singles with "The Letter" and "Cry Me a River." The tour launched the popular careers of Leon Russell and Rita Coolidge and marked the high point of Cocker's career.

Exhausted physically and financially by the tour, Joe Cocker abandoned England for California, and his subsequent success was limited to the United States. *Joe Cocker,* recorded with Grease Band veterans Chris Stainton and Alan Spenner, yielded two major hits, "High Time We Went" and "Midnight Rider," and two minor hits, "Woman to Woman" and "Pardon Me Sir." However, Stainton quit the band in early 1973 and Cocker's 1974 tour was a virtual disaster due to his excessive drinking. He did not achieve another major success until 1975's "You Are So Beautiful," cowritten by Billy Preston, became a smash hit. Dumped by A&M, Cocker switched to Elektra/Asylum in 1978 and Island in 1982. On Island, he soon scored a top hit with Jennifer Warnes on the love theme from the film *An Officer and a Gentleman,* "Up Where We Belong." By 1984, he had moved to Capitol Records, where he eventually had a major hit with "When the Night Comes" in 1989. In 1994, Cocker switched to 550 Music for *Have A Little Faith.* The 1995 A&M anthology set *Long Voyage Home* featured Joe Cocker's recordings for A&M, Elektra, Island, and Capitol.

Joe Cocker

With a Little Help from My Friends	A&M	4182	'69	†
	A&M	3106		CS/CD
Joe Cocker!	A&M	4224	'69	†
	A&M	3326	'89	CD

Mad Dogs and Englishmen	A&M	(2)6002	'70	CD
	A&M	6002		CS
	Mobile Fidelity	736	'98	CD
Joe Cocker	A&M	4368	'72	†
I Can Stand a Little Rain	A&M	3633	'74	†
	A&M	3175		CD†
Jamaica Say You Will	A&M	4529	'75	†
Stingray	A&M	4574	'76	†
Greatest Hits	A&M	4670	'77	†
	A&M	3257	'84	CS/CD
Joe Cocker	A&M	2503		CS/CD
Box Set	A&M	0018	'92	CD†
The Long Voyage Home	A&M	(4)0236	'95	CD
Luxury You Can Afford	Asylum	145	'78	†
Sheffield Steel	Island	9750	'82	†
	Island	842476	'92	CD
	Mobile Fidelity	631	'95	CD†
One More Time	Island	90096	'83	†
Civilized Man	Capitol	12335	'84	LP/CS/CD†
	Capitol	46038		CS/CD†
Cocker	Capitol	12394	'86	LP/CS/CD†
	Capitol	46268		CS†/CD
Unchain My Heart	Capitol	48285	'87	CS†/CD
One Night of Sin	Capitol	92861	'89	CS/CD
Joe Cocker Live!	Capitol	93416	'90	CS/CD
Night Calls	Capitol	97801	'92	CS/CD
Best	Capitol	81243	'93	CS/CD
Have a Little Faith	550 Music	66460	'94	CS/CD
Across from Midnight	CMC International	86245	'98	CS/CD

LEONARD COHEN

Born September 21, 1934, in Montreal, Canada.

Canadian-born poet and novelist Leonard Cohen was one of the most powerful song poets to emerge in the '60s. Despite the limited musical effectiveness of his gruff monotonic voice and sparse musical settings, his poetics more than compensate for any musical short-comings. His lyrics, legitimately described as brooding and gloomy, even depressing, ultimately succeed through the underlying intensity of their humanity. One of the first artists to bring a spiritual and poetic sensibility to rock music, Cohen became an acclaimed musical figure in Europe, where he was sometimes compared to Jacques Brel. In the United States, he endured years as a cult figure before emerging as a contemporary force with 1988's *I'm Your Man*.

Leonard Cohen studied English literature at McGill and Columbia Universities and published his first book of poetry, *Let Us Compare Mythologies,* in 1956. During the '60s, he published a number of books of poetry as well as two novels, *The Favorite Game* (1963) and *Beautiful Losers* (1966). The latter became standard college literary fare and sold more than 300,000 copies.

Taught the classics of music as a child, Leonard Cohen began playing guitar at age thirteen and singing at fifteen, performing with a barn-dance group called The Buckskin Boys

LEONARD COHEN (FRÉDÈRIC HUIJBREGTS/CORBIS)

during his late teens. His first popular acclaim came when Judy Collins recorded one of his most romantic compositions, "Suzanne," for her 1966 *In My Life* album. Cohen launched his performing career through appearances at the Newport Folk Festival and New York's Central Park (with Collins) in 1967.

Signed to Columbia Records by John Hammond, Leonard Cohen's debut album included "Suzanne," the alienated "Stranger Song," the sorrowful "Hey, That's No Way to Say Goodbye," and the compassionate "Sisters of Mercy." The latter three songs had appeared on Collins' *Wildflower* album. In 1969, Cohen successfully toured North America and Europe and issued *Songs from a Room,* recorded in Nashville. It contained "The Story of Isaac," "Tonight Will Be Fine," and the oft-recorded classic "Bird on a Wire." Retiring from public performance at the end of 1970, he released *Songs of Love and Hate* the following year. It contained "Famous Blue Raincoat," "Joan of Arc," "Dress Rehearsal Rag," "Diamonds in the Mine," and "Love Calls You by Your Name." He also provided the songs for the soundtrack to the 1971 Robert Altman film *McCabe and Mrs. Miller.*

In 1972, Leonard Cohen published another volume of poetry, *The Energy of Slaves,* and toured the United States and Europe with Jennifer Warnes as one of his backup singers. *New Skin for the Old Ceremony,* with "There Is a War" and "Chelsea Hotel," was issued in 1974 and Cohen toured again in 1975. He collaborated with songwriter-producer Phil Spector for the controversial *Death of a Ladies' Man* in 1977 and recorded *Recent Songs* for Columbia in 1979. In 1985, he toured again in support of *Various Positions,* but Columbia did not issue the album, instead leasing it to the small Passport label. The album was quickly deleted, despite the inclusion of "The Broken Hallelujah," "Dance Me to the End of Love," and "Heart with No Companion."

In 1986, longtime associate Jennifer Warnes recorded an entire album of Leonard Cohen songs, *Famous Blue Raincoat,* which became a commercial success and revived interest in his career. Already a well-respected figure in Europe, Cohen's 1988 *I'm Your Man* sold spectacularly there and further reawakened interest in his songs in North America. Hailed as a masterpiece, the album contained a number of haunting, compelling songs such as "First We Take Manhattan," "Ain't No Cure for Love," and "Take This Waltz." The less impressive follow-up, *The Future,* included "Democracy," "Light as a Breeze," and "Waiting for a Miracle." The 1993 book *Stranger Music: Selected Poems and Songs* assembled Cohen's poems, prose, and lyrics.

Contemporary alternative artists such as R.E.M., Nick Cave, and The Pixies paid tribute to Leonard Cohen with 1991's *I'm Your Fan,* while 1995's *Tower of Song* tribute featured mainstream artists such as Elton John, Willie Nelson, and Billy Joel. Cohen's son Adam moved to the United States from Europe in 1992 and began concentrating on his music in New York the following year. In 1998, he made his recording debut on Columbia Records and conducted his first national tour.

LEONARD COHEN BIBLIOGRAPHY

Dorman, L. S., and C. L. Rawlins. *Leonard Cohen: Prophet of the Heart*. London: Omnibus Press, 1990.

Gnarowski, Michael (editor). *Leonard Cohen: The Artist and His Critics*. Toronto / New York: McGraw-Hill Ryerson, 1976.

Morley, Patricia A. *The Immoral Moralists*. Toronto: Clarke, Irwin, 1972.

Nadel, Ira Bruce. *Various Positions: A Life of Leonard Cohen*. New York: Pantheon Books, 1996.

Norris, Ken, and Michael Fournier (editors). *Take This Waltz: A Celebration of Leonard Cohen*. Ste-Anne-de-Bellevue, Quebec: The Muses' Co., 1994.

Scobie, Stephen. *Leonard Cohen*. Vancouver: Douglas and McIntyre, 1978.

LEONARD COHEN BOOKS

The Spice Box of Earth. New York: Viking Press, 1961, 1965.

The Favorite Game, A Novel. New York: Viking Press, 1963; Toronto: McClelland and Stewart, 1970.

Flowers for Hitler. Toronto: McClelland and Stewart, 1964.

Parasites of Heaven. Toronto: McClelland and Stewart, 1966.

Let Us Compare Mythologies. Toronto: McClelland and Stewart, 1966, 1970.

Beautiful Losers. New York: Viking Press, 1966; New York: Bantam Books, 1967; New York: Random House, 1993.

Selected Poems, 1956–1968. New York: Viking Press, 1968.

The Energy of Slaves. New York: Viking Press, 1973.

Death of a Lady's Man. Toronto: McClelland and Stewart, 1978; New York: Viking Press, 1979.

Book of Mercy. Toronto: McClelland and Stewart, 1984; New York: Villard Books, 1984.

Stranger Music: Selected Poems and Songs. New York: Pantheon, 1993.

Leonard Cohen Albums

Songs of Leonard Cohen	Columbia	9533	'68	CS/CD
Songs from a Room	Columbia	9767	'69	†
	Columbia/Legacy	9767		CD
Songs of Love and Hate	Columbia	30103	'71	†
	Columbia	66951		CS/CD
Live Songs	Columbia	31724	'73	†
New Skin for the Old Ceremony	Columbia	33167	'74	†
Best	Columbia	34077	'76	CS/CD
Death of a Ladies' Man	Warner Brothers	3125	'77	†
	Columbia	44286	'88	CD
Recent Songs	Columbia	36264	'79	CD
Various Positions	Passport	6045	'85	†
	Columbia	66950		CS/CD
I'm Your Man	Columbia	44191	'88	CS/CD
The Future	Columbia	53226	'92	CS/CD
Cohen Live—Leonard Cohen in Concert	Columbia	66327	'94	CS/CD

Jennifer Warnes

Famous Blue Raincoat: The Songs of Leonard Cohen	Cypress	0100	'86	LP/CS/CD†
	Private Music	82092	'91	CS/CD

Tribute Albums (Various Artists)

I'm Your Fan—The Songs of Leonard Cohen	Atlantic	82349	'91	CS/CD

Tower of Song: The Songs of Leonard Cohen	A&M	0259	'95	CS/CD
Adam Cohen				
Adam Cohen	Columbia	67957	'98	CS/CD

JUDY COLLINS

Born May 1, 1939, in Seattle, Washington.

As a guitarist, pianist, and singer with a clear soprano voice, Judy Collins, along with Joan Baez, set the standard for female folk artists in the early '60s. Popular as a protest singer after her second album, Collins demonstrated impeccable taste in her selection of material during the middle and late '60s, popularizing the songs of then-obscure songwriters such as Gordon Lightfoot, Joni Mitchell, Randy Newman, Leonard Cohen, and others. She was instrumental in launching the careers of Cohen and Mitchell with her recordings of "Suzanne" and "Both Sides Now" in 1966 and 1967, respectively. Toward the late '60s, she began writing her own songs and, with the success of "Send in the Clowns," became a mainstream pop star.

Judy Collins moved as a child to Los Angeles, then Denver, Colorado, with her family. She began classical piano lessons at the age of five, and studied for eight years under female symphony conductor Antonia Brico. Making her classical piano debut at thirteen, she took up guitar at fifteen and began singing in Boulder, Colorado, folk clubs at nineteen. At the beginning of the '60s, Collins moved to Chicago, then New York, where she immersed herself in the burgeoning Greenwich Village folk music scene. Signed to Elektra Records in 1961, she recorded two albums of standard folk fare before recording protest songs such as Bob Dylan's "Masters of War" and Woody Guthrie's "Deportees." She subsequently began recording the songs by then-unknown songwriters. *Concert* contained Tom Paxton's "The Last Thing on My Mind," and her *5th Album* included Richard Farina's "Pack Up Your Sorrows," Eric Andersen's "Thirsty Boots," Gordon Lightfoot's "Early Morning Rain," as well as three Bob Dylan songs.

With *In My Life,* Judy Collins broke away from the folk singer role and established herself as a performer of a wide range of contemporary material. The album contained Dylan's "Tom Thumb's Blues," Farina's "Hard Lovin' Loser" (her first albeit minor hit), Randy Newman's "I Think It's Gonna Rain Today," and two Leonard Cohen songs. The popularity of one of those songs, "Suzanne," effectively launched the musical career of poet and novelist Cohen. *Wildflowers,* the best selling album of her career, included two of her own songs, plus two more Cohen songs and two songs by Joni Mitchell. One of these, "Both Sides Now," became Collins' first major hit and spurred the career of Mitchell. *Who Knows Where the Time Goes* continued the presentation of outstanding contemporary material with the inclusion of Cohen's "Bird on a Wire," Robin Williamson's "The First Boy (Girl) I Loved," Ian Tyson's "Someday Soon," and Sandy Denny's title song.

After *Whales and Nightingales,* which yielded her second major hit with the traditional gospel song "Amazing Grace," and two other albums, Judy Collins withdrew from music to produce and codirect a documentary film on the life of her former piano teacher, Antonia Brico. The film, entitled *Antonia: A Portrait of the Woman,* premiered in September 1974 and garnered an Academy Award in 1975.

Judy Collins moved fully into the pop field with her recording of Stephen Sondheim's "Send in the Clowns," a moderate hit in 1975 and a major hit upon rerelease in 1977. She achieved a minor hit with "Hard Time for Lovers" in 1979, the year she debuted in the Nevada casino circuit.

She continued to perform six months a year, appearing with symphony orchestras and at concerts and supper clubs around the country. Following 1984's *Home Again,* Elektra Records dropped Collins from its roster and she subsequently recorded two albums for the small Gold Castle label, including *Trust Your Heart,* which also served as the title to her autobiography. In 1990, Collins switched to Columbia for *Fires of Eden,* moving to Geffen for 1993's *Judy Sings Dylan.* In 1995, Pocket Books published Judy Collins' first novel, *Shameless,* the title of her second album for yet another label, Mesa Records.

JUDY COLLINS BIBLIOGRAPHY

Claire, Vivian. *Judy Collins.* New York: Flash Books, 1977.
Collins, Judy. *Trust Your Heart: An Autobiography.* Boston: Houghton Mifflin, 1987.
————. *Shameless.* New York: Pocket Books, 1995.
————. *Singing Lessons: A Memoir of Love, Loss, Hope and Healing.* New York: Pocket Books, 1998.

Judy Collins

A Maid of Constant Sorrow	Elektra	7209	'61	†
Golden Apples of the Sun	Elektra	7222	'62	†
# 3	Elektra	7243	'63	†
Concert	Elektra	7280	'64	†
5th Album	Elektra	7300	'65	CD
In My Life	Elektra	7320	'66	†
	Elektra	74027		CD
Wildflowers	Elektra	74012	'67	CD
Who Knows Where the Time Goes	Elektra	74033	'68	CD
Recollections	Elektra	74055	'69	†
	Elektra	61350	'92	CD
Whales and Nightingales	Elektra	75010	'70	CS/CD
Living	Elektra	75014	'71	CD
Colors of the Day	Elektra	75030	'72	CS/CD
True Stories and Other Dreams	Elektra	75053	'73	CD
Judith	Elektra	1032	'75	†
	Elektra	111		CS/CD
Bread and Roses	Elektra	1076	'76	CS/CD†
So Early in the Spring: The First Fifteen Years	Elektra	(2)6002	'77	†
	Elektra	6002		CS
Hard Time for Lovers	Elektra	171	'79	CD
Running for My Life	Elektra	253	'80	CS/CD†
Times of Our Lives	Elektra	60001	'82	CD
Home Again	Elektra	60304	'84	CD
False True Lovers	Folkways	3564	'67	†
Trust Your Heart	Gold Castle	71302	'87	LP/CS/CD†
Sanity and Grace	Gold Castle	71318	'89	LP/CS/CD†
Fires of Eden	Columbia	46102	'90	CS/CD
Judy Sings Dylan: Just Like a Woman	Geffen	24612	'93	CS/CD
Come Rejoice! A Judy Collins Christmas	Mesa	79085	'94	CS/CD
Shameless	Mesa	92584	'95	CS/CD

Richard Stoltzman and Judy Collins

Innervoices	RCA	7888	'89	CS/CD

COUNTRY JOE AND THE FISH

"Country" Joe McDonald (born January 1, 1942, in El Monte, California), vocals, guitar, harmonica; Barry Melton (born in 1947 in Brooklyn, New York), guitar; David Cohen (born in 1942 in Brooklyn), keyboards; Bruce Barthol (born in 1947 in Berkeley, California), bass; and Gary "Chicken" Hirsh (born in 1940 in California), drums.

The most overtly political band to emerge from the San Francisco psychedelic scene of the '60s, Country Joe and The Fish are best remembered for their "Fish Cheer," the antiwar song "I-Feel-Like-I'm-Fixin'-to-Die Rag," and their appearance at the Woodstock Festival in 1969. After the group's breakup in 1970, Country Joe McDonald pursued a solo career on Vanguard and Fantasy Records before becoming show business' most outspoken activist for Vietnam veterans.

Born into a left-wing family, Joe McDonald taught himself guitar as a youth, later serving in the Navy and attending college in the Los Angeles area. In 1962, he moved to Berkeley, where he met Barry Melton in 1965. They formed the folk-style jug band Country Joe and The Fish and published a recorded issue of the political newspaper *Ragbaby* that included the group's "I-Feel-Like-I'm-Fixin'-to-Die Rag." Adding a rhythm section and keyboardist David Cohen to become a rock band, they played up and down the West Coast and issued another EP in July 1966 that included "Bass Strings," "Love," and the mesmeric instrumental "Section 43."

By 1967, Country Joe and The Fish had added Bruce Barthol and "Chicken" Hirsh and signed with Vanguard Records, recording their remarkable *Electric Music for the Mind and Body* album, which included "Section 43," "Grace" (written for Grace Slick), and the minor hit "Not So Sweet Martha Lorraine." They appeared at the Monterey International Pop Festival and recorded their second album, which introduced "The Fish Cheer" and "I-Feel-Like-I'm-Fixin'-to-Die Rag" to a national audience and included "Janis," written by McDonald for Janis Joplin. *Together* featured "Rock and Soul Music," but Barthol departed in September 1968, followed by Cohen and Hirsh in early 1969. Thereafter, fronted by McDonald and Melton, Country Joe and The Fish did not stir the nation's attention until McDonald's heralded appearance at the Woodstock Music and Art Fair in August 1969. Nonetheless, the group broke up in June 1970, briefly reuniting in 1977.

Through 1975, Country Joe McDonald recorded folk, protest, and country albums for Vanguard Records while establishing himself in Europe. He switched to Fantasy Records in 1975 and even managed a minor hit with "Breakfast for Two." Involved with the "Save the Whales" movement in the late '70s, McDonald revived the Rag Baby label and took up the cause of Vietnam veterans in the '80s. He eventually reemerged in 1991 with his first record in over twelve years on a label other than his own with *Superstitious Blues* on Rykodisc.

Barry Melton recorded several solo albums in the '70s and eventually became a lawyer in 1982. During the '80s and into the '90s, he manned The Dinosaurs with veteran Bay Area musicians such as John Cippollina (Quicksilver), Peter Albin (Big Brother), and Spencer Dryden (Jefferson Airplane). In 1994, he became a deputy public defender in Mendocino County, California. Late that year, the original members of Country Joe and The Fish reunited briefly. In 1996, Shanachie Records issued McDonald's most recent album, *Carry On*.

Country Joe and The Fish

Collector's Items: The First Three EP's	One Way	30990	'94	CD
Electric Music for the Mind and Body	Vanguard	79244	'67	CS/CD
I Feel Like I'm Fixin' to Die	Vanguard	79266	'67	CS/CD
Together	Vanguard	79277	'68	CS/CD

Here We Are Again	Vanguard	79299	'69	†
Live! Fillmore West 1969	Vanguard	(2)139/140	'96	CD
Greatest Hits	Vanguard	6545	'70	†
C. J. Fish	Vanguard	6555	'70/'94	CS/CD
Life and Times—From Haight-Ashbury to Woodstock	Vanguard	(2)27/8	'71	CS/CD
The Collected Country Joe and The Fish (1965–1970)	Vanguard	111	'87	CS/CD
Reunion	Fantasy	9530	'77	†

Barry Melton

Bright Sun Is Shining	Vanguard	6551	'70	†
Melton, Levy and The Dey Brothers	Columbia	31279	'72	†
We Are Like the Ocean	Music Is Medicine	9007	'78	†
Level with Me	Music Is Medicine	9014	'80	†

Country Joe McDonald

The Early Years	Piccadilly	3309	'80	†
Thinking of Woody Guthrie	Vanguard	6546	'70	†
Tonight I'm Singing Just for You	Vanguard	6557	'70	†
	One Way	31000	'95	CD
Quiet Days in Clichy (soundtrack)	Vanguard	79303	'71	†
Hold On It's Coming	Vanguard	79314	'71	†
	One Way	30998	'95	CD
War, War, War	Vanguard	79315	'71	†
	One Way	30995	'94	CD
Incredible! Live!	Vanguard	79316	'72	†
	One Way	30996	'95	CD
Paris Sessions	Vanguard	79328	'73	†
	One Way	30999	'96	CD
Country Joe	Vanguard	79348	'75	†
	One Way	30997	'96	CD
Essential	Vanguard	(2)85/6	'76	†
The Best of Country Joe McDonald: The Vanguard Years (1969–1975)	Vanguard	(2)119/20	'90	CS/CD
Paradise with an Ocean View	Fantasy	9495	'75/'94	CD
Love Is a Fire	Fantasy	9511	'76	†
Goodbye Blues	Fantasy	9525	'77	†
Rock 'n' Roll Music from Planet Earth	Fantasy	9544	'78	†
Leisure Suite	Fantasy	9586	'80	†
Classics	Fantasy	7709		CD
On My Own	Rag Baby		'81	LP†
	One Way	31372	'97	CD
Into the Fray	Rag Baby	(2)	'82	LP†
	One Way	31370	'96	CD
Child's Play	Rag Baby	1018	'83	LP
	One Way	34431	'97	CD
Peace on Earth	Rag Baby		'84	LP†
	One Way	31369	'95	CD
Vietnam Experience	Rag Baby	(2)	'86	LP†
	One Way	30991	'94	CD
Superstitious Blues	Rykodisc	10201	'91	CS/CD
Carry On	Shanachie	8019	'96	CD
Classics	Big Beat	108		CD

CREAM

Eric Clapton (born Eric Clapp on March 30, 1945, in Rippley, Surrey, England), lead guitar, vocals; Jack Bruce (born May 14, 1943, in Glasgow, Scotland), bass, keyboards, harmonica, vocals; and Peter "Ginger" Baker (born August 19, 1939, in Lewisham, London), drums, vocals.

Possibly the second most influential British group of the '60s, Cream was the first rock band to improvise extensively and perform extended pieces, thus elevating virtuoso instrumental playing within rock to an art form. Although all three members of Cream demonstrated exceptional talent on their respective instruments, Jack Bruce was the real musical pioneer—he established the use of the repeated musical figure or ostinato (the so-called "heavy riff") on bass, around which he played lead lines, thus liberating the instrument from its strictly rhythmic role. Additional credit for Cream's success must be given to lyricist Peter Brown, who wrote many of the group's best remembered songs, often with Bruce. Ginger Baker instituted the long drum solo into rock and Eric Clapton unwittingly created the cult of the superstar lead guitarist. In openly acknowledging their debt to many obscure black American bluesmen (Robert Johnson, in particular), Cream helped inspire the blues revival of the late '60s. As the first major rock group to utilize the power trio format, Cream established the viability of the three-man instrumental lineup. Along with The Beatles and The Jimi Hendrix Experience, Cream became one of the most popular rock acts in the world by 1968 but disbanded by year's end, leading to the formation of the first "supergroup," Blind Faith, and subsequent solo careers by Clapton, Baker, and Bruce. Cream was inducted into the Rock and Roll Hall of Fame in 1993.

Cream was formed in June 1966 by lead guitarist Eric Clapton, bassist Jack Bruce, and drummer Peter "Ginger" Baker. Clapton had previously played with The Yardbirds and John Mayall's Bluesbreakers, whereas Baker had played with Alexis Korner and Graham Bond, and Bruce with Bond, Mayall, and Manfred Mann. Signed almost immediately by Atlantic Records, Cream's first album, *Fresh Cream,* was issued in early 1967. Although the album contained little of the improvisation that characterized the group in performance, it included the British hit "I Feel Free," written by Bruce and lyricist Peter Brown, and Baker's "Toad," as well as Muddy Waters' "Rollin' and Tumblin'" and Skip James' "I'm So Glad."

Undeniably more exciting in concert than on records, Cream soon completed enormously successful tours of Great Britain and the United States. Produced by Felix Pappalardi, *Disraeli Gears* established Cream's improvisational format. Rather that playing a song straight through, Clapton, Bruce, and Baker would set up the basic "riff" to a song, then take off into individual improvisatory jams. The album consisted of standard blues fare plus original songs composed by Bruce and Clapton, often with Peter Brown, with Bruce handling most of the lead vocals. "Sunshine of Your Love," written by Clapton, Bruce, and Brown, was a moderate hit from the album, later to become a major hit when rereleased in the summer of 1968. Other outstanding cuts included "Strange Brew" (written by Clapton, Pappalardi, and his wife-to-be, Gail Collins), "Tales of Brave Ulysses," "Take It Back," and "S.W.L.A.B.R.," again by Bruce and Brown.

Wheels of Fire, produced by Felix Pappalardi, was a double-record set, one from the studio and one recorded live at the Fillmore Auditorium in San Francisco. Among the extended live pieces were Robert Johnson's "Crossroads" (a major hit), Willie Dixon's "Spoonful," and "Toad," on which Baker soloed for more than ten minutes. Pappalardi played on the studio record, which contained Booker T. Jones' "Born Under a Bad Sign," and "Politician" and "White Room" (a near-smash hit), both written by Bruce and Brown. By mid-1968, internal strains within the group became increasingly evident and, coupled with the limited amount of mutually acceptable material, Cream announced their intention to disband. After a farewell tour of America in October and November and a final album,

Goodbye (which included "Badge," written by Clapton and George Harrison), Cream made their final appearance at London's Royal Albert Hall on November 26, 1968. Cream was inducted into the Rock and Roll Hall of Fame in 1993.

Almost immediately, Eric Clapton and Ginger Baker formed the "supergroup" Blind Faith with Traffic's Stevie Winwood (keyboards) and Family's Rick Grech (bass). Completing one British and one American tour, the group recorded one interesting, if flawed, album. It included Winwood's "Sea of Joy" and "Can't Find My Way Home" and Clapton's "In the Presence of the Lord." Clashes between Winwood and Baker tore the group apart, and Blind Faith disbanded at the end of 1969. Clapton subsequently performed sessions work, formed Derek and The Dominoes, and pursued a spectacular solo career.

Jack Bruce, the odd-man-out in the formation of Blind Faith, briefly toured with keyboardist Mike Mandel, guitarist Larry Coryell, and drummer Mitch Mitchell before pursuing a solo career in conjunction with lyricist Peter Brown, recording two albums for Atco, including *Songs for a Tailor,* and two albums for RSO. (Material from these albums and 1978's unreleased *Jet Set Jewel* were issued on 1989's *Willpower* album.) Bruce also joined Tony Williams Lifetime with former Miles Davis drummer Tony Williams, organist Larry Young, and guitarist extraordinaire John McLaughlin for touring and the album *Turn It Over.* Peter Brown later formed Battered Ornaments (with Chris Spedding) and Piblokto!, and worked with British blues pioneer Graham Bond in Bond and Brown. He reunited with Bruce for 1989's *A Question of Time.*

Producer-bassist Felix Pappalardi, who produced The Youngbloods' first two albums, was assigned by Atlantic Records to produce the New York group The Vagrants in 1968. Although recordings proved unsuccessful, Pappalardi was sufficiently impressed by the group's lead guitarist Leslie West to produce his debut solo album. In 1969, Pappalardi and West formed Mountain with keyboardist Steve Knight and drummer Corky Laing. They scored a major hit in 1970 with "Mississippi Queen," but disbanded in 1972. West and Laing then joined former Cream bassist Jack Bruce for West, Bruce, and Laing. That group broke up in 1973, and West and Pappalardi briefly reformed Mountain in 1974. Pappalardi later organized and produced the Japanese heavy-metal group Creation around 1975. On April 17, 1983, Felix Pappalardi was shot to death by his wife Gail in their New York apartment.

At the beginning of 1970, drummer Ginger Baker formed Ginger Baker's Air Force with Stevie Winwood, Rick Grech, Chris Wood, and a host of others. Recordings by the group were reissued in 1989. Baker later pursued an interest in African music, building a recording studio in Nigeria, which opened in January 1973, and recording with Fela Kuti. From late 1974 until 1976, he manned The Baker-Gurvitz Army with Gurvitz brothers Adrian and Paul. Baker was out of the limelight during the first half of the '80s, having settled in Italy. He eventually relocated to California and reemerged with *Horses and Trees,* later recording *Middle Passage* with former George Clinton/Talking Heads keyboardist Bernie Worrell and forming the hard-rock group Masters of Reality.

In addition to his solo albums, Jack Bruce recorded with a number of jazz artists during the '70s, including Carla Bley and Mike Mantler, while playing sessions for Lou Reed, John McLaughlin, and Frank Zappa. In the early '80s, he recorded *B.L.T.* with erstwhile Procol Harum lead guitarist Robin Trower and his drummer Bill Lordan and *Truce* with Trower. *No Stopping Anytime,* from 1989, compiled these recordings. Jack Bruce recorded *A Question of Time* for Epic in 1989 and *Somethinels* for Creative Music in 1993. In 1994, Ginger Baker recorded with Bill Frisell and Charlie Haden as The Ginger Baker Trio and formed BBM with Jack Bruce and Gary Moore for *Around The Next Dream.*

CREAM BIBLIOGRAPHY

Platt, John A. *Disraeli Gears: Cream.* New York: Schirmer Books, 1998.

Cream

Fresh Cream	Atco	33-206	'67	†
	RSO	3009	'77	†
	Polydor	827576		CS/CD
	DCC	1022		CD
	DCC	2015	'96	LP
Disraeli Gears	Atco	33-232	'67	†
	RSO	3010	'77	†
	Polydor	823636	'84	CS/CD
	Mobile Fidelity	562	'92	CD†
Wheels of Fire	Atco	(2)700	'68	†
	RSO	(2)3802	'77	†
	Polydor	(2)827578	'86	CS/CD
	DCC	(2)1020		CD
Goodbye	Atco	7001	'69	†
	RSO	3013	'77	†
	Polydor	823660		CS/CD
	Mobile Fidelity	681		CD
Best	Atco	33-291	'69	†
Live Cream, Volume 1	Atco	33-328	'70	†
	RSO	3014	'77	†
	Polydor	827577		CD
Live Cream, Volume 2	Atco	7005	'72	†
	RSO	3015	'77	†
	Polydor	823661		CS/CD
Live Cream Volume I and II	Mobile Fidelity	(2)625	'94	CD
Heavy Cream	Polydor	(2)3502	'72	†
Off the Top	Polydor	5529	'73	†
Strange Brew: The Very Best of Cream	Polydor	811639	'83	CS/CD
Very Best	Polydor	523752	'95	CS/CD

Blind Faith

Blind Faith	Atco	33-304	'69	†
	RSO	3016	'77	†
	Polydor	825094		CS/CD
	Mobile Fidelity	00507	'89	CD†

Ginger Baker

Ginger Baker's Air Force	Atco	(2)703	'70	†
	Polydor	837349	'89	CD†
Ginger Baker's Air Force — 2	Atco	33-343	'70	†
Stratavarious	Atco	7013	'72	†
Fela Ransome-Kuti and Africa '70 with Ginger Baker — Live!	Signpost	8401	'72	†
At His Best	Polydor	(2)3504	'72	†
11 Sides of Baker	Sire	7532	'77	†
Horses and Trees	Celluloid	6126	'86	CS/CD
Middle Passage	Axiom	846753	'89	CS/CD†

Baker-Gurvitz Army

Baker-Gurvitz Army	Janus	7015	'75	†
Elysian Encounters	Atco	36-123	'75	†
Hearts on Fire	Atco	36-137	'76	†

Masters of Reality

Masters of Reality	Delicious Vinyl	842904	'90	CS/CD†
	Delicious Vinyl	92195		CS/CD
Sunrise on the Sufferbus	Chrysalis	21976	'93	CS/CD†

The Ginger Baker Trio

Going Back Home	Atlantic	82652	'94	CS/CD

Jack Bruce

At His Best	Polydor	(2)3505	'72	†
Songs for a Tailor	Atco	33-306	'69	†
	Polydor	835242	'88	CD†
Harmony Row	Atco	33-365	'71	†
	Polydor	835243	'88	CD†
Things We Like	Polydor	835244	'88	CD†
Out of the Storm	RSO	4805	'74	†
	Polydor	835284	'88	CD†
How's Tricks	RSO	3021	'77	†
	Polydor	835285	'88	CD†
I've Always Wanted to Do This	Epic	36827	'80	†
A Question of Time	Epic	45729	'89	CS/CD†
Willpower: A Twenty Year Retrospective	Polydor	(2)837806	'89	LP†
	Polydor	837806	'89	CS/CD
Somethinels	Creative Music	1001	'93	CS/CD
Monkjack	Creative Music	1010	'96	CD

Tony Williams' Lifetime (with Jack Bruce)

Turn It Over	Polydor	244021	'70	†

Mountain (Felix Pappalardi, Leslie West, Corky Laing)

Mountain	Windfall	4500	'69	†
	Columbia/Legacy	66439	'96	CD
Mountain Climbing	Windfall	4501	'70	†
	Columbia/Legacy	47361	'92	CS/CD
Nantucket Sleighride	Windfall	5500	'71	†
	Columbia/Legacy	47362	'92	CS/CD
Flowers of Evil	Windfall	5501	'71	†
	Columbia/Legacy	52749	'96	CD
The Road Goes Ever On	Windfall	5502	'72	†
Best	Windfall	32079	'73	†
	Columbia	32079		CS/CD
Twin Peaks	Windfall	32818	'74	†
	Columbia	32818		CD
Avalanche	Windfall	33088	'74	†

West, Bruce and Laing

Why Dontcha	Windfall	31929	'72	†
	Columbia	31929	'89	CD
Whatever Turns You On	Windfall/Columbia	32216	'73	†
Live 'N' Kickin'	Windfall/Columbia	32899	'74	†

Carla Bley (with Jack Bruce)

Escalator Over the Hill	JCOA	(3)3	'73	†
	ECM/Watt	839310		CD†

Jack Bruce, Bill Lordan and Robin Trower

B.L.T.	Chrysalis	1324	'81	†
	Chrysalis	21324	'91	CS/CD†

Jack Bruce and Robin Trower

Truce	Chrysalis	1352	'82	†
	Chrysalis	21352		CS†
	One Way	17609		CD
No Stopping Anytime	Chrysalis	21704	'89	CD

BBM (Jack Bruce, Ginger Baker and Gary Moore)

Around the Next Dream	Virgin	39728	'94	CD

Jack Bruce and Friends

Sitting on Top of the World	Times Square	90032	'97	CD

CREEDENCE CLEARWATER REVIVAL

John Fogerty (born May 28, 1945, in Berkeley, California), lead guitar, lead vocals, keyboards, harmonica; Tom Fogerty (born November 9, 1941, in Berkeley; died September 6, 1990, in Scottsdale, Arizona), rhythm guitar, piano, vocals; Stu Cook (born April 24, 1945, in Oakland, California), bass, piano; and Doug Clifford (born April 24, 1945, in Palo Alto, California), drums.

Perhaps the most popular American rock band of the late '60s, Creedence Clearwater Revival was the greatest American singles band of the era, scoring nine smash hits and six two-sided hits between 1969 and 1971. Leader John Fogerty's narrative-style rock 'n' roll songs often explored Americana, much like The Band, and provided a refreshing contrast to the British and psychedelic music then dominating popular music. After Creedence disbanded in 1972, the various members pursued careers of their own, but only John Fogerty's proved particularly successful, as evidenced by 1984's *Centerfield* and 1997's *Blue Moon Swamp*. Creedence Clearwater Revival was inducted into the Rock and Roll Hall of Fame in 1993.

John Fogerty obtained his first guitar at the age of twelve. With fellow El Cerrito, California, junior high school students Stu Cook and Doug Clifford, he formed The Blue Velvets in 1959. Joined by John's brother Tom, the band played local engagements for years and recorded unsuccessfully for the Orchestra label before securing a recording contract with Berkeley's Fantasy Records in 1964. With a name change to The Golliwogs, the group released a series of singles between 1965 and 1967, including "Brown-Eyed Girl" and "Walking on the Water." Subsequently, Saul Zaentz took over Fantasy Records and the group changed their name to Creedence Clearwater Revival.

Creedence Clearwater Revival's self-titled debut album, released in the middle of 1968, contained a mixture of rock standards and John Fogerty originals. The first single release, a reworking of Dale Hawkins' "Suzie Q," became a major hit and launched the band on its successful career as a singles band. Their breakthrough album *Bayou Country* produced the smash hit classic "Proud Mary" (covered by Ike and Tina Turner in 1971) and included "Born on the Bayou." Creedence Clearwater Revival played at the Woodstock Music and Art Fair in August 1969, when *Green River* was released. It contained the ballad "Wrote a Song for Everyone" and yielded two smash two-sided hits, "Bad Moon Rising" (a top British hit!) backed with the classic "Lodi," and "Green River" backed by "Commotion." The hits continued with "Down on the Corner"/"Fortunate Son" and three two-sided smash hits from *Cosmo's Factory:* "Travelin' Band"/"Who'll Stop the Rain," "Up Around the Bend"/"Run Through the Jungle," and "Lookin' Out My Back Door"/"Long as I See the Light." "Have You Ever Seen the Rain"/"Hey Tonight" became a near-smash hit in early 1971.

John Fogerty's creative dominance of the group led to dissension among the other members, with Tom Fogerty leaving in February 1971. The remaining trio subsequently toured and recorded *Mardi Gras,* which yielded the hit singles "Sweet Hitchhiker" and "Someday Never Comes." In October 1972, Creedence Clearwater Revival disbanded. The group was inducted into the Rock and Roll Hall of Fame in 1993.

During the '70s, the members of Creedence Clearwater Revival pursued a variety of projects. Tom Fogerty recorded five solo albums and two albums with Ruby. He moved to Arizona in the mid-'80s and died in Scottsdale on September 6, 1990, of respiratory failure. Doug Clifford recorded a solo album and two albums with The Don Harrison Band, which included Stu Cook. Only John Fogerty enjoyed any measure of success. He played all instruments and sang all parts on *Blue Ridge Rangers,* an album comprising primarily country material. The album yielded two hits with "Hearts of Stone" and Hank Williams' "Jambalaya." He later recorded an album for Asylum Records that produced the major hit "Rockin' All Over the World" and the minor hit "Almost Saturday Night."

Embroiled in lawsuits with the group's accountants and Fantasy Records for years, John Fogerty withdrew to a family farm in Oregon for ten years. He eventually reemerged in 1985, playing all instruments on *Centerfield,* which contained the baseball classic "Centerfield" and the major hits "The Old Man Down the Road" and "Rock and Roll Girls." He toured between 1985 and 1986 for the first time since 1972, but the follow-up album *Eye of the Zombie* sold only moderately.

Stu Cook joined the country-rock band Southern Pacific after their debut album, which had yielded the country-only hits "Thing About You" (written by Tom Petty), "Perfect Stranger," and "Reno Bound." The group included John McFee (guitar, pedal steel guitar, fiddle) and Keith Knudsen (drums), formerly with The Doobie Brothers. Featuring intricate, multipart harmonies, Southern Pacific scored major country-only hits with "A Girl Like Emmylou" and "Midnight Highway," and the country smashes "New Shade of Blue," "Honey I Dare You," and "Any Way the Wind Blows" through 1989. The group disbanded in 1991. Cook joined Doug Clifford and three others in the formation of Creedence Clearwater Revisited in 1995.

After another hiatus, John Fogerty spent more than four years recording 1997's *Blue Moon Swamp,* which featured "Walking in a Hurricane" and "A Hundred and Ten in the Shade." He toured in support of the album with a four-piece band, performing Creedence Clearwater Revival material for the first time in twenty-five years.

CREEDENCE CLEARWATER REVIVAL BIBLIOGRAPHY

Bordowitz, Hank. *Bad Moon Rising: The Unofficial History of Creedence Clearwater Revival.* New York: Schirmer Books, 1998.

Hallowell, John. *Inside Creedence.* New York: Bantam Books, 1971.

The Golliwogs				
Pre-Creedence	Fantasy	9474	'75	†
Creedence Clearwater Revival				
Creedence Clearwater Revival	Fantasy	8382	'68	†
	Fantasy	4512		CS/CD
Bayou Country	Fantasy	8387	'69	†
	Fantasy	4513		LP/CS/CD
	DCC	1038		CD
Green River	Fantasy	8393	'69	†
	Fantasy	4514		LP/CS/CD

Willy and the Poor Boys	Fantasy	8397	'69	†
	Fantasy	4515		LP/CS/CD
	DCC	1070	'95	CD
	Acoustic Sounds	2019		LP
The Concert (recorded 1970)	Fantasy	4501	'80	CS/CD
Cosmo's Factory	Fantasy	8402	'70	†
	Fantasy	4516		LP/CS/CD
	DCC	1031		CD
Pendulum	Fantasy	8410	'70	†
	Fantasy	4517		LP/CS/CD
Mardi Gras	Fantasy	9404	'72	†
	Fantasy	4518		CS/CD
Creedence Gold	Fantasy	9418	'72	LP/CS/CD
More Creedence Gold	Fantasy	9430	'73	LP/CS/CD
Live in Europe	Fantasy	(2)79001	'73	†
	Fantasy	(2)CCR1		†
	Fantasy	4526		LP/CS/CD
Chronicle	Fantasy	(2)CCR2	'76	LP/CS
	Fantasy	CCR2		CD
	Fantasy	22	'95	CD
1968/1969	Fantasy	(2)68	'78	LP/CS
1969	Fantasy	(2)69	'78	LP/CS
1970	Fantasy	(2)70	'78	LP/CS
Chooglin'	Fantasy	9621		CS
Creedence Country	Fantasy	4509		CS
The Movie Album	Fantasy	4522	'85	LP/CS
Chronicle, Volume 2	Fantasy	(2)CCR3	'86	LP/CS
	Fantasy	CCR3	'86	CD
	Fantasy	23	'95	CD
Tom Fogerty				
Tom Fogerty	Fantasy	9407	'72	†
Excalibur	Fantasy	9413	'73	†
Zephyr National	Fantasy	9448	'74	†
Myopia	Fantasy	9469	'74	†
Deal It Out	Fantasy	9611	'81	†
Ruby (with Tom Fogerty)				
Ruby	PBR International	7001	'77	†
Rock and Roll Madness	PBR International	7004	'78	†
Tom Fogerty/Kevin Oda				
Sidekicks	Fantasy	9664	'93	CD
Doug Clifford				
Cosmo	Fantasy	9411	'72	†
The Don Harrison Band (with Doug Clifford and Stu Cook)				
The Don Harrison Band	Atlantic	18171	'76	†
Red Hot	Atlantic	18208	'77	†
Southern Pacific (with Stu Cook)				
Killbilly Hill	Warner Brothers	25409	'86	†
Zuma	Warner Brothers	25609	'88	CS/CD†
Country Line	Warner Brothers	25895	'90	CS/CD†

Greatest Hits	Warner Brothers	26582	'91	CS/CD
Creedence Clearwater Revisited (with Doug Clifford and Stu Cook)				
Recollection	Fuel 2000	(2)1015	'98	CD
John Fogerty				
Blue Ridge Rangers	Fantasy	9415	'73	†
	Fantasy	4502		LP/CS/CD
John Fogerty	Asylum	1046	'75	CS
Hoodoo	Asylum	1081	'76	†
Centerfield	Warner Brothers	25203	'85	CS/CD
Eye of the Zombie	Warner Brothers	25449	'86	CS/CD
Blue Moon Swamp	Warner Brothers	45426	'97	CS/CD

CROSBY, STILLS, NASH (AND YOUNG)

David Crosby (born David Van Cortland on August 14, 1941, in Los Angeles), guitar, tenor vocals; Stephen Stills (born January 3, 1945, in Dallas, Texas), guitar, keyboards, vocals; Graham Nash (born February 2, 1942, in Blackpool, Lancashire, England), guitar, high tenor vocals; and Neil Young (born November 12, 1945, in Toronto, Canada), guitar, vocals.

GRAHAM NASH, DAVID CROSBY, AND STEPHEN STILLS (HENRY DILTZ/CORBIS)

The quintessential close harmony, acoustic-guitar songwriting trio of the late '60s and early '70s, Crosby, Stills and Nash combined their considerable talents to produce an outstanding album of gentle melodic songs before adding the harder-edged sound of Neil Young. Relying more on their voices than their instruments, each member retained his own distinctive musical personality and became the darlings of the hippie movement with songs alternately mystical, communal, political, and romantic. More an aggregation of three (and four) individuals than a group, Crosby, Stills, Nash (and Young) created an unmistakable sound emulated by other groups for years. One of rock's first "supergroups," Crosby, Stills, Nash (and Young) were one of the first rock groups to embrace political and environmental causes, as evidenced by Young's "Ohio" and Nash's involvement with the antinuclear movement. During the '70s, each member pursued separate recording projects while occasionally regrouping. However, during the first half of the '80s, Crosby was embroiled in personal and legal difficulties that made him one of rock's most tragic figures of the era. He eventually dealt with his drug and legal problems and reemerged in the late '80s with a solo album and another Crosby, Stills, Nash and Young album. Crosby, Stills and Nash were inducted into the Rock and Roll Hall of Fame in 1997.

Ex—Byrd David Crosby and ex—Buffalo Springfield Stephen Stills met Graham Nash of The Hollies in 1968. An informal jam session in Los Angeles that July so impressed the three that they decided to form a group as soon as Nash could sever relations with the English group. Nash performed his last engagement with The Hollies on December 8, 1968. Signing with Atlantic Records in January 1969, their debut album *Crosby, Stills and Nash* yielded two moderate hits with Nash's "Marrakesh Express" and Stills' "Suite: Judy Blue Eyes," written for Judy Collins. With Crosby on rhythm guitar and Stills overdubbing lead guitar, organ, and bass, the album featured precise three-part harmonies. Included were two excellent Crosby songs, "Long Time Gone" and "Guinnevere," Nash's "Lady of the Island," Stills' "Helplessly Hoping," and the mystical "Wooden Ships," composed by Crosby, Stills, and (uncredited) Paul Kantner.

In an effort to fill out their acoustic sound, Crosby, Stills and Nash recruited ex—Buffalo Springfield Neil Young, already pursuing a successful solo career. They debuted at New York's Fillmore East less than a month before the quartet's celebrated appearance at the Woodstock Music and Art Fair in August 1969. By the end of the year, however, the "good vibes" that had produced the magnificent results on the first album were dashed, as Stills broke up with Judy Collins, Nash broke up with Joni Mitchell, and Crosby's girlfriend Christine Hinton was killed in an auto crash. Young admirably took up the slack for *Deja Vu,* the group's most successful album. It featured three hits, an electric version of Joni Mitchell's "Woodstock," and two Nash songs, "Teach Your Children" and "Our House." The album also contained Crosby's title song and "Almost Cut My Hair," Stills' "Carry On" and "4 and 20," and Young's three-part production effort "Country Girl." By the fall of 1970, the group had shattered in four directions, but not before issuing Young's brilliant "Ohio," an outraged response to the Kent State student murders of May 1970. Nash subsequently compiled the double-record live set *Four Way Street,* which included Young classics such as "On the Way Home," "Cowgirl in the Sand," and "Southern Man," and two beautiful Crosby songs, "Triad" and "The Lee Shore."

Stephen Stills had already recorded one side of the *Super Session* album with Al Kooper. Stills' debut solo album, consisting entirely of his own songs, yielded his only major hit with "Love the One You're With" and the moderate hit "Sit Yourself Down." The album also contained "We Are Not Helpless" and the inebriated "Black Queen," plus the instrumental "Old Times, Good Times" (featuring Jimi Hendrix) and "Go Back Home" (with Eric Clapton on second lead guitar). Stills' second solo album included "Sugar Babe" and "Singin' Call" and yielded moderate hits with "Change Partners" and "Marianne." Conducting his first major solo tour in July 1971, Stills subsequently formed Manassas in October with former Byrd and Flying Burrito Brother Chris Hillman and pedal steel guitarist Al Perkins. The group toured extensively and recorded two albums before disintegrating in September 1973.

In the meantime, David Crosby recorded his debut solo album *If I Could Only Remember My Name.* Featuring several songs composed of wordless vocal harmonies, the album contained Crosby's "Laughing" and "Traction in the Rain," as well as Nash, Young, and Crosby's "Music Is Love" and the conspiratorial "What Are Their Names." Graham Nash's debut solo album, *Songs for Beginners,* produced moderate hits with the political songs "Chicago" and "Military Madness," and included Nash's "Better Days" and the old Hollies' song "I Used to Be a King."

In 1972, David Crosby and Graham Nash teamed for touring and an album that yielded a moderate hit with Nash's "Immigration Man." Nash recorded a second solo album in 1973, and Crosby, Stills, Nash and Young conducted a summer-long stadium tour in 1974. Crosby and Nash subsequently recorded *Wind on the Water* and *Whistling Down the Wire* for ABC (later MCA), whereas Stills recorded three albums for Columbia through 1978. During 1976, Stills and Neil Young formed the short-lived Stills-Young Band for one album on

Reprise and an aborted tour. Crosby, Stills and Nash then regrouped for touring and 1977's *CSN,* which included Stills' "Dark Star" and the near-smash "Just a Song Before I Go" (by Nash). Nash was a founding director of the antinuclear power Musicians United for Safe Energy (MUSE) and organizer of the "No Nukes" concerts of September 1979.

Crosby, Stills and Nash regrouped in 1982 for touring and *Daylight Again,* which yielded the near-smash hit "Wasted on the Way" and the major hit "Southern Cross." The three continued to tour and record, while Stills recorded *Right By You.* Nash reunited with The Hollies' Allan Clarke, Tony Hicks, and Bobby Elliott for the album *What Goes Around* in 1983 and recorded *Innocent Eyes* solo in 1986. Crosby, Stills, Nash and Young appeared at Live Aid in 1985.

David Crosby was arrested several times on drug and weapons charges in the early '80s, leading to his imprisonment in Texas in 1985 and 1986. Breaking his addiction to cocaine while in prison, he was paroled in September 1986 and exonerated of charges in November 1987. Putting his life back together, Crosby married longtime girlfriend Jan Dance in May 1987 and published the autobiography *Long Time Gone* in 1988.

Crosby, Stills, Nash and Young subsequently recorded their first studio release in eighteen years, *American Dream,* and later Crosby recorded *Oh Yes I Can* solo for A&M Records. During the '90s, Crosby, Stills and Nash recorded *Live It Up* and *After the Storm* and conducted an all-acoustic tour in 1992. Crosby recorded *Thousand Roads,* which included "Yvette in English," cowritten with Joni Mitchell, and "Hero," a moderate hit cowritten with Phil Collins. He underwent a liver transplant operation in November 1994. Crosby, Stills and Nash toured again in 1996 and 1997, the year they were inducted into the Rock and Roll Hall of Fame.

In 1995, David Crosby met his heretofore unknown son, James Raymond, with whom he formed the ironically named group CPR with Jeff Pevar. In 1998, Steve Stills' son by actress Veronique Sanson, Chris, launched his solo recording career with *100 Year Thing* on Atlantic Records.

CROSBY, STILLS AND NASH BIBLIOGRAPHY

Crosby, David, and Carl Gottlieb. *Long Time Gone: The Autobiography of David Crosby.* New York: Doubleday, 1988.

Zimmer, Dave. *Crosby, Stills and Nash: The Authorized Biography.* New York: St. Martin's Press, 1984.

Crosby, Stills and Nash

Crosby, Stills and Nash	Atlantic	8229	'69	†
	Atlantic	19117		CS/CD†
	Atlantic	82522	'94	CD
	Atlantic	82651	'94	CS/CD
CSN	Atlantic	19104	'77	CS/CD†
	Atlantic	82650	'94	CS/CD
Replay	Atlantic	16026	'81	†
	Atlantic	82679	'94	CS/CD†
Daylight Again	Atlantic	19360	'82	CS/CD†
	Atlantic	82672	'94	CS/CD
Live It Up	Atlantic	82107	'90	CD
Crosby, Stills and Nash	Atlantic	(4)82319	'91	CD
After the Storm	Atlantic	82654	'94	CS/CD

Crosby, Stills, Nash and Young

Deja Vu	Atlantic	7200	'70	†
	Atlantic	19118		CS/CD†
	Atlantic	82649	'94	CS/CD
4 Way Street	Atlantic	(2)902	'71	†
	Atlantic	82408	'92	CS
	Atlantic	(2)82408	'92	CD
So Far	Atlantic	18100	'74	†
	Atlantic	19119		CS/CD†
	Atlantic	82648	'94	CS/CD
American Dream	Atlantic	81888	'88	CS/CD

Kooper, Bloomfield, and Stills

Super Session	Columbia	9701	'68	CS/CD

Stephen Stills

Stephen Stills	Atlantic	7202	'70	CS/CD†
	Atlantic	82809	'95	CS/CD
Stephen Stills 2	Atlantic	7206	'71/'92	CD
Manassas	Atlantic	(2)903	'72	CS†
	Atlantic	903		CD†
	Atlantic	82808	'95	CS/CD
Down the Road (with Manassas)	Atlantic	7250	'73	CD
Live	Atlantic	18156	'75	CS/CD
Best	Atlantic	18201	'77	†
Right by You	Atlantic	80177	'84	CD
Stills	Columbia	33575	'75/'92	CD
Illegal Stills	Columbia	34148	'76/'90	CD
Thoroughfare Gap	Columbia	35380	'78	†

The Stills-Young Band

Long May You Run	Reprise	2253	'76	CD

Chris Stills

100 Year Thing	Atlantic	83022	'98	CS/CD

David Crosby

If I Could Only Remember	Atlantic	7203	'71	CS/CD
Oh Yes I Can	A&M	5232	'89	LP/CS/CD†
David Crosby (recorded April 1989)	King Biscuit Flower Hour	88018	'96	CD
Thousand Roads	Atlantic	82484	'93	CS/CD
It's All Coming Back to Me Now . . .	Atlantic	82620	'95	CS/CD

CPR

CPR	Samson	145	'98	CS/CD

Graham Nash

Songs for Beginners	Atlantic	7204	'71	CS/CD
Wild Tales	Atlantic	7288	'73/'88	CD
Earth and Sky	Capitol	12014	'80	†
Innocent Eyes	Atlantic	81633	'86	LP/CS/CD†

The Hollies (with Graham Nash)

What Goes Around	Atlantic	80076	'83	†

David Crosby and Graham Nash

Graham Nash/David Crosby	Atlantic	7220	'72	†

Live		Atlantic	19150	'75	CS†
Best		Atlantic	19203	'78	CS†
Wind on the Water		ABC	902	'75	†
		MCA	37007		†
		MCA	31251		CD
Whistling Down the Wire		ABC	956	'76	†
Live		ABC	1042	'77	†
Best		ABC	1102	'78	†
		MCA	37008		†

THE CRYSTALS

Barbara Alston, Delores "Dee Dee" Kennibrew, Mary Thomas, Pattie Wright, and Merna Girard, replaced by Dolores "La La" Brooks in 1962.

DARLENE LOVE

Born Darlene Wright on July 26, 1938, in Los Angeles.

Producer Phil Spector's first girl group, The Crystals recorded his first million-selling single ("He's a Rebel") and were the object of his increasingly adventuresome productions in the early '60s before he turned his attention to The Ronettes and The Righteous Brothers. Darlene Love, the actual lead vocalist on "He's a Rebel," sang with Bob B. Soxx and The Blue Jeans and performed background vocals for Dionne Warwick during the '70s, eventually establishing her own career in the '80s, most notably in the musical *Leader of the Pack*.

Formed in Brooklyn in late 1960 by teenagers Barbara Alston, Delores "Dee Dee" Kennibrew, Mary Thomas, Pattie Wright, and Merna Girard, The Crystals were discovered by producer Phil Spector in March 1961 and the first signing to his Philles label. With Barbara Alston on lead vocals, the group soon scored major pop and rhythm-and-blues hits with "There's No Other (Like My Baby)" and "Uptown," written by Barry Mann and Cynthia Weil.

Dolores "La La" Brooks replaced Girard in 1962, but The Crystals' next two singles, the top pop and smash rhythm-and-blues hit classic "He's a Rebel" (written by Gene Pitney) and the major pop and R&B hit "He's Sure the Boy I Love," were actually recorded by The Blossoms. Originally formed in Los Angeles as The Dreamers in 1954, The Blossoms comprised lead vocalist Darlene Wright, Fanita James, and Gloria Jones by 1960. They sang backup for Sam Cooke and Duane Eddy, but never managed a hit under their own name. From 1964 to 1966, with Jeannie King replacing Gloria Jones, The Blossoms were regulars on ABC-TV's *Shindig*. The group recorded for a variety of labels until 1972 and toured with Elvis Presley in the early '70s.

Subsequent smash pop and rhythm-and-blues hits for The Crystals included the classic Spector, Ellie Greenwich, and Jeff Barry compositions "Da Doo Ron Ron" (recorded by La La Brooks and The Blossoms) and "Then He Kissed Me" (actually recorded by The Crystals). Their next singles failed to sell significantly and, by 1965, The Crystals were recording for United Artists Records. They broke up around 1967, but reunited for tours in the early '70s. In 1986, Dee Dee Kennibrew and La La Brooks recorded an album for Jango Records with two others. Kennibrew continued to perform with two new Crystals into the '90s.

In the meantime, Darlene Wright had taken the name Darlene Love at the behest of Phil Spector in 1963. With Bobby Sheen and Fanita James, she recorded for Philles as Bob B. Soxx and The Blue Jeans, scoring a near-smash pop and rhythm-and-blues hit with "Zip-A-Dee Doo-Dah," a moderate pop hit with "Why Do Lovers Break Each Other's Heart?" and a minor pop hit with "Not Too Young to Get Married." Darlene Love also had solo pop hits with "(Today I Met) The Boy I'm Gonna Marry" and "Wait Til My Bobby Gets Home."

Throughout the '70s, Darlene Love worked as backup vocalist to Dionne Warwick, later backing Aretha Franklin. In 1981, she began pursuing her own career, touring with background vocalist Gloria Jones and appearing in the Tony-nominated 1985 Broadway musical *Leader of the Pack,* based on the songs of Ellie Greenwich. However, the original cast recording of the musical was quickly deleted, as were live recordings of Love issued on Rhino in 1985 and her 1988 Columbia album. Darlene Love appeared in all three *Lethal Weapon* films and recorded *Bringing It Home* with Lani Groves in 1992.

The Crystals

Twist Uptown	Philles	4000	'62	†
He's a Rebel	Philles	4001	'63	†
Greatest Hits	Philles	4003	'63	†
Best	Abkco	7214	'92	CS/CD
He's a Rebel (recorded 1986)	Jango	777	'87	LP/CS/CD†

Bob B. Soxx and The Blue Jeans

Zip-A-Dee-Doo-Dah	Philles	4002	'63	†

Darlene Love

Live	Rhino	855	'85	†
Paint Another Picture	Columbia	40605	'88	†
Best	Abkco	7213	'92	CS/CD

Leader of the Pack

Original Cast	Elektra	(2)60409	'85	†
Excerpts	Elektra	60420	'85	†

Darlene Love and Lani Groves

Bringing It Home	Shanachie	9003	'92	CS/CD

JACKIE DESHANNON

Born Sharon Myers on August 21, 1944, in Hazel, Kentucky.

A prolific songwriter since the beginning of the '60s, Jackie DeShannon wrote more than 600 songs, including the smash hits "Dum Dum" (Brenda Lee) and "Bette Davis Eyes" (Kim Carnes). One of the first female songwriters to turn to performing, DeShannon's early hit "Needles and Pins" evinced the sound that would become known as folk-rock. Additionally, in the first half of the '60s, she worked with then-obscure artists such as Ry Cooder, The Byrds, Jimmy Page, and Randy Newman. Scoring her most conspicuous success with her smash hit recordings of "What the World Needs Now Is Love" and "Put a Little Love in Your Heart," DeShannon recorded occasionally in the '70s but not at all since and has never received the recognition she so richly deserves.

Born into a musical family, Sharon Myers was singing on the radio at the age of six and performing her own radio show by the age of eleven. In the late '50s, she recorded as Jackie Dee ("Buddy") and Jackie Shannon ("Trouble"). She moved to California in 1960 and teamed with Sharon Sheeley to write "Dum Dum," a smash pop hit for Brenda Lee, and "He's the Great Impostor," a moderate pop hit for The Fleetwoods, both from 1961, the year she composed the theme music for the film *Splendor in the Grass.* Signed to Liberty Records in 1962, DeShannon achieved minor hits with Jack Nitzche and Sonny Bono's "Needles and Pins" and her own "When You Walk in the Room." The English group The Searchers scored a top British and major American hit with "Needles and Pins" in 1963 and a smash British and moderate American hit with "When You Walk in the Room" in late 1964.

Jackie DeShannon formed a short-lived band with Ry Cooder in 1963 and opened for The Beatles on their first American tour in February 1964. She toured and recorded demonstration records with The Byrds, who later recorded her "Don't Doubt Yourself Babe" for their debut album. She later met guitarist Jimmy Page in England and he played on her recordings of "Dream Boy" and "Don't Turn Your Back on Me." The two also wrote several songs recorded by Marianne Faithfull, who scored a smash British and major American pop hit with DeShannon's "Come and Stay with Me" in early 1965. DeShannon also worked with Randy Newman, cowriting "She Don't Understand Him" with him and recording his "Did He Call Today Mama."

Switching to Imperial Records, Jackie DeShannon scored a near-smash pop hit with Burt Bacharach and Hal David's "What the World Needs Now Is Love" in the spring of 1965. Moving to the supper club circuit, her next major hit did not come until her *Put a Little Love in Your Heart* album yielded a smash hit with the title song and a moderate hit with "Love Will Find a Way," both of which she cowrote. DeShannon continued to record for Imperial until 1970, switching to Capitol, then Atlantic, where she recorded the acclaimed but poor-selling *Jackie* and *Your Baby Is a Lady* albums. In 1973, she provided background vocals for Van Morrison's *Hard Nose the Highway* album and her 1975 *New Arrangement* album featured "Bette Davis Eyes," cowritten with Donna Weiss, which became a top pop hit for Kim Carnes in 1981. DeShannon recorded her last album for the small Amherst label in 1977. Annie Lennox and Al Green scored a near-smash pop hit with "Put a Little Love in Your Heart" in 1988 and Pam Tillis achieved a near-smash country hit with "When You Walk in the Room" in 1994.

Jackie DeShannon

Jackie DeShannon	Liberty	7320	'63	†
Breakin' It Up on The Beatles Tour	Liberty	7390	'64	†
C'mon Let's Live a Little (soundtrack)	Liberty	7430	'66	†
This Is Jackie DeShannon	Imperial	12286	'65	†
You Won't Forget Me	Imperial	12294	'65	†
In the Wind	Imperial	12296	'65	†
Are You Ready for This?	Imperial	12328	'66	†
New Image	Imperial	12344	'67	†
For You	Imperial	12352	'67	†
What the World Needs Now Is Love	Imperial	12404	'67	†
Laurel Canyon	Imperial	12415	'68	†
Me About You	Imperial	12386	'68	†
Put a Little Love in Your Heart	Imperial	12442	'69	†
To Be Free	Imperial	12453	'70	†
Lonely Girl	Sunset	5225		†
Jackie DeShannon	Sunset	5322		†
Very Best	United Artists	434		†
	EMI	91473		CS/CD†
The Definitive Collection	EMI	29786	'94	CD
Songs	Capitol	772	'71	†
Jackie	Atlantic	7231	'72	†
Your Baby Is a Lady	Atlantic	7303	'74	†
New Arrangement	Columbia	33500	'75	†
You're the Only Dancer	Amherst	1010	'77	†
Good as Gold	Pair	1284	'90	CS/CD
Best	Rhino	70738	'91	CS/CD

DION (DIMUCCI)

Born July 18, 1939, in the Bronx, New York.

Achieving his earliest success as lead singer of Dion and The Belmonts, one of the most successful white doo-wop vocal groups, Dion launched a solo career in 1960, hitting with gutsy, conflict-ridden, even antagonistic and arrogant songs that bore sharp contrast to the pop fluff of the early '60s. Reuniting with The Belmonts in 1967 and 1972, Dion played the coffeehouse circuit after scoring a smash hit with the classic tribute song "Abraham, Martin and John" in 1968. He later recorded a British-only album under Phil Spector in 1973 and recorded Christian music in the '80s, reemerging with *Yo Frankie* in 1989, the year he was inducted into the Rock and Roll Hall of Fame.

In 1958, Dion DiMucci formed Dion and The Belmonts, who signed with the newly established Laurie Records label. The group soon scored major pop hits with "I Wonder Why" and "No One Knows" and smash hits with Doc Pomus and Mort Shuman's "A Teenager in Love" and the Rodgers and Hart classic "Where or When." Dion left the group to pursue a solo career in the fall of 1960, quickly hitting with "Lonely Teenager." He appeared in the 1961 film *Teenage Millionaire* and began working with songwriter Ernie Maresca and the backing vocal group The Del Satins. Adopting a harsh aggressive vocal style, he achieved a top pop and smash rhythm-and-blues hit with "Runaround Sue" (cowritten with Maresca) and subsequently scored smash hits with "The Wanderer" (written by Maresca) and "Lovers Who Wander" (cowritten with Maresca). Dion also managed a smash hit with his own "Little Diane" and major hits with "Love Came to Me" and "Sandy."

Moving to Columbia Records and retaining The Del Satins, Dion scored smash pop hits with "Ruby Baby" (a smash rhythm-and-blues hit) and "Drip Drop," both previously recorded by The Drifters, and "Donna the Prima Donna" (cowritten with Maresca). Dropping The Del Satins in late 1963, he began exploring blues material around 1965, with little commercial success. He reunited with The Belmonts for 1967's *Together Again* on ABC and the live Warner Brothers set *Reunion,* recorded June 2, 1972, at Madison Square Garden.

In 1968, Dion moved to Florida, kicked a heroin habit that he had initiated as an early teenager, and returned to Laurie Records. *Dion,* regarded as his most fully realized album, contained songs by contemporary artists such as Bob Dylan, Leonard Cohen, Fred Neil, and Joni Mitchell, and yielded a smash pop hit with Dick Holler's ode to assassinated leaders, "Abraham, Martin and John." Dion subsequently toured the college-and-coffeehouse circuit playing acoustic guitar, switching to Warner Brothers Records in 1970, with little success. He recorded *Born to Be with You* under producer-extraordinaire Phil Spector in 1973; however, the album was released in England only.

For much of the '80s, Dion recorded modern Christian music. He returned to rock 'n' roll in June 1987 with a series of sold-out concerts at Radio City Music Hall. He published his autobiography *The Wanderer* in 1988 and was inducted into the Rock and Roll Hall of Fame in 1989. Also that year, with the assistance of Paul Simon, Lou Reed, and k.d. lang, Dion recorded *Yo Frankie* under producer Dave Edmunds, managing a minor hit with "And the Night Stood Still." In 1990, Dion toured with Edmunds, Graham Parker, and Kim Wilson of The Fabulous Thunderbirds. By the mid '90s, Dion had moved back to New York and formed the group Little Kings with guitarist Scott Kempner of The Dictators and The Del Lords, bassist Mike Mesaros of The Smithereens, and drummer Frank Funaro of The Del Lords for engagements on the East Coast.

DION BIBLIOGRAPHY

Dion, with Davin Seay. *The Wanderer: Dion's Story.* New York: Beech Tree Books, 1988.

Dion and The Belmonts

Presenting	Laurie	1002	'60	†
	Collectables	5025	'84	LP/CS
When You Wish Upon a Star	Laurie	2006	'60	†
	Collectables	5026	'84	LP/CS
By Special Request: Together On Record	Laurie	2016	'66	†
Everything You Always Wanted to Hear by Dion and The Belmonts	Laurie	4002	'76	CS
60 Greatest Hits of Dion and The Belmonts	Laurie	(3)6000		LP
	Laurie	(2)6000		CS
Together Again	ABC	599	'67	†
Reunion: Live at Madison Square Garden, 1972	Warner Brothers	2664	'73	†
	Rhino	70228	'87	CS/CD
Doo-Wop	Pickwick	3521	'76	†
Best	Pair	1142	'86	CS
20 Golden Classics	Collectables	5041		LP/CS
The Wanderer	3C Records	105		CD
The Fabulous Dion and The Belmonts	Ace	002		CS/CD

Dion on Laurie Records

Alone with Dion	Laurie	2004	'60	†
	Ace	115		†
Runaround Sue	Laurie	2009	'61	†
	Ace	148		†
	Collectables	5027		LP/CS
	The Right Stuff	27304	'93	CS/CD
Lovers Who Wander	Laurie	2012	'62	†
	Ace	163		†
	The Right Stuff	27305	'93	CS/CD
Love Came to Me	Laurie	2015		†
15 Million Sellers	Laurie	2019		†
More Greatest Hits	Laurie	2022		†
Dion	Laurie	2047	'68	†
	The Right Stuff	29667	'94	CS/CD
reissued as Abraham, Martin and John	Ace	204	'87	†
Dion Sings the Hits of the 50s and 60s	Laurie	4013		CS
Hits	Ace	176		LP/CD†
Runaround Sue: The Best of the Rest	Ace	915		CD†

Dion/Dion and The Belmonts

Sings His Greatest Hits	Laurie	2013	'62	†
Dion Sings to Sandy	Laurie	2017	'63	†
Greatest Hits	Columbia	31942	'73/'87	CS†
Lovers Who Wander/So Why Didn't You Do That the First Time	Ace	943		CD
When You Wish Upon a Star/Alone with Dion	Ace	945		CD
Presenting Dion and The Belmonts/Runaround Sue	Ace	966		CD

Later Dion (DiMucci)

Ruby Baby	Columbia	8810	'63	†
	Columbia	35577	'79	†
Donna, The Prima Donna	Columbia	8907	'63	†
	Columbia	35995	'79	†
Wonder Where I'm Bound	Columbia	9773	'69	†
Bronx Blues: The Columbia Recordings	Columbia/Legacy	46972	'91	CD

Sit Down Old Friend	Warner Brothers	1826	'70	†
You're Not Alone	Warner Brothers	1872	'71	†
Sanctuary	Warner Brothers	1945	'71	†
Suite for Late Summer	Warner Brothers	2642	'72	†
Streetheart	Warner Brothers	2954	'76	†
The Return of the Wanderer	Lifesong	35356	'78	†
	Ace	294		†
	DCC	049		CS/CD†
Yo Frankie	Arista	8549	'89	CS/CD
A Rock and Roll Christmas	The Right Stuff	66718	'93	CS/CD

Dion Compilations and Reissues

24 Original Classics	Arista	(2)8206	'84	†
The Fabulous Dion	Ace	008		CS/CD
Return of the Wanderer/Fire in the Night	Ace	936		CD
Dion at His Best: Classic Old and Gold, Volume 3	3C Records	102		CD
Dion at His Best: Classic Old and Gold, Volume 4	3C Records	103		CD

Christian Music by Dion

Inside Job	DaySpring	4022	'80	†
I Put Away My Idols	DaySpring	4109	'83	†
	DaySpring	8111	'85	†
Seasons	DaySpring	8112	'85	†
Kingdom in the Streets	Word	8285	'85	†
Velvet and Steel	Word	8372	'87	†
	Word/Epic	47798	'91	CS/CD

TOM DONAHUE

Born May 21, 1928, in South Bend, Indiana; died April 28, 1975, in San Francisco.

As a disc jockey at San Francisco FM radio station KMPX, "Big Daddy" Tom Donahue created America's first alternative to banal AM-radio programming in 1967. By playing album cuts, reintroducing live music broadcasts, and utilizing the airwaves as a true public service to its listeners, Donahue founded "underground radio." The popularity of KMPX and its successor KSAN-FM (with Donahue as program director) demonstrated that radio audiences would gratefully accept radio programming that eschewed limited playlists, the use of offensive and inane commercials, and the abhorrence of controversy and public access to the airwaves. The stations' success inspired the formation of underground FM radio stations across the country, virtually forced AM radio stations to revise their programming, and encouraged the development of album-oriented rock (AOR) radio, a format that continues to dominate to this day, though with tighter playlists.

Tom Donahue first worked as a disc jockey during the late '40s in Charleston, West Virginia. He later worked at Washington, D.C.'s WINX and Philadelphia's WIBG before being hired by San Francisco radio station KYA in 1961. Known as "Big Daddy" for his 400-pound girth, Donahue and fellow disc jockey Bobby Mitchell formed Autumn Records in early 1964, hiring Sylvester Stewart (Sly Stone) as its principal producer. Autumn scored a smash hit with Bobby Freeman's "C'mon and Swim" in 1964 and issued the earliest hits of San Francisco's first major group, The Beau Brummels. The label also recorded Grace Slick's first group, The Great Society. Donahue and Mitchell also presented rock concerts in the Bay Area at least two years before Bill Graham, including The Beatles' final public performance on August 29, 1966.

On April 7, 1967, Tom Donahue took over the 8 P.M.-to-midnight shift at FM radio station KMPX. The station allowed Donahue to play album cuts, broadcast live music, refuse to air certain commercials, make public announcements of a political or general-interest nature, and generally get involved with the community at large and its concerns. KMPX soon became the nation's first full-time, album-oriented FM radio station. The format proved enormously popular and was adopted by FM radio stations across the country, thus liberating contemporary music fans of the banality and myopia of AM radio programming. After a bitter strike against KMPX management, Donahue and nearly the entire staff defected to KSAN-FM on his fortieth birthday, May 21, 1968. The station was virtually unchallenged as the area's top progressive rock station for years, and Donahue became the station's general manager in 1972. On the verge of becoming the general manager and part-owner of the recently sold KMPX station, "Big Daddy" Tom Donahue died of a heart attack on April 28, 1975, at the age of 46. He was inducted into the Rock and Roll Hall of Fame in 1996.

Tom Donahue

The Golden Age of Underground Radio with Tom Donahue				
(1968–1972)	DCC	045	'89	CS/CD

DONOVAN

Born Donovan Leitch on May 10, 1946, in Glasgow, Scotland.

Initially appearing in the mid-'60s as an English (actually Scottish) folk artist strongly resembling America's Bob Dylan, Donovan later embraced beneficent psychedelia and naive spiritualism for a series of self-penned hit singles and best-selling albums during the late '60s.

Donovan moved to the London area at the age of ten, taking up guitar as a teenager. Becoming a regular on BBC-TV's *Ready, Steady, Go* in early 1965, he signed with Pye Records (Hickory Records in the United States), hitting with the title cut to *Catch the Wind*. *Fairy Tale* produced hits with "Colours" and Buffy Sainte-Marie's "Universal Soldier," and included "Sunny Goodge Street," recorded by Judy Collins for her *In My Life* album. Donovan made his American debut at the Newport Folk Festival in 1965 but subsequently abandoned the Dylan-like image and switched to Epic Records under producer Mickie Most for a number of psychedelic, quasi-mystical hits through the late '60s. His debut Epic album, *Sunshine Superman,* yielded a top American and smash British hit with the title cut (featuring guitarist Jimmy Page) and included perhaps his finest composition, the ominous "Season of the Witch," with Steve Stills as lead guitarist.

Donovan's *Mellow Yellow* produced a smash hit with the title song and included the haunting "Young Girl Blues." After the subdued hits "Epistle to Dippy," "There Is a Mountain," and "Wear Your Love Like Heaven," *Hurdy Gurdy Man* produced one mellow hit, "Jennifer Juniper," and one hard-driving hit with the title cut. *Barabajagal* yielded three hits with "Goo Goo Barabajagal" (recorded with The Jeff Beck Group), "To Susan on the West Coast Waiting," and the inane "Atlantis."

By the middle of 1970, Donovan had split from Mickie Most and formed his own band, but he soon retreated to Ireland. He reemerged in 1974 and continued to record for Epic until 1976, with little success. In virtual retirement from the mid-'70s to the early '80s, Donovan toured again in the late '80s and eventually recorded for American Records in 1995. By the '90s, he was perhaps better known as the father of actress Ione Skye and model-actor-singer Donovan Leitch, Jr., than as a musician in his own right. The glitter rock group Nancy Boy, with lead singer Donovan Leitch, Jr., and guitarist Jason Nesmith (son of Michael Nesmith), released their major label debut album in 1996.

DONOVAN BIBLIOGRAPHY

Donovan. *Dry Songs and Scribbles.* Garden City, NY: Doubleday, 1971.

Donovan

Catch the Wind	Hickory	123	'65	†
	Garland	016	'65	†
	Sandstone	33077	'92	CD†
Fairy Tales	Hickory	127	'65	†
The Real Donovan	Hickory	135	'66	†
Like It Is, Was and Evermore Shall Be	Hickory	143	'67	†
Best	Hickory	149	'69	†
Donovan P. Leitch	Janus	(2)3022	'70	†
History of British Pop	Pye	502	'76	†
History of British Pop, Volume 2	Pye	507	'76	†
The Early Years	Griffin	0837		CD†
Sunshine Superman	Epic	26217	'66	†
	Epic/Legacy	26217	'90	CD
Mellow Yellow	Epic	26239	'67	†
A Gift from a Flower to a Garden	Epic	(2)171	'67	†
Wear Your Love Like Heaven	Epic	26349	'67	†
For Little Ones	Epic	26350	'67	†
In Concert	Epic	26386	'68	†
Sunshine Superman/In Concert	Epic	(2)33734	'75	†
Hurdy Gurdy Man	Epic	26420	'68/'86	CD
Greatest Hits	Epic	26439	'69	CS/CD
Barabajagal	Epic	26481	'69/'87	CD
Barabajagal/Hurdy Gurdy Man	Epic	(2)33731	'75	†
Open Road	Epic	30125	'70	†
World—Physical/Spiritual	Epic	(2)31210	'72	†
Cosmic Wheels	Epic	32156	'73	†
Essence to Essence	Epic	32800	'74	†
7-Tease	Epic	33245	'74	†
Slow Down World	Epic	33945	'76	†
Troubadour: The Definitive Collection 1964–1976	Epic/Legacy	(2)46986	'92	CS/CD
Donovan	Arista	4143	'77	†
Lady of the Stars	Allegiance	72857	'87	LP/CS/CD†
The Classics Live	Great Northern	61007	'91	CS/CD
Donovan	WMO/Qualiton	90323	'96	CD
Sunshine Superman—20 Songs Of Love and Freedom	Remember	75059	'96	CD
Sutras	American Recording	43075	'96	CS/CD

Nancy Boy

Nancy Boy	Sire	61895	'96	CS/CD

THE DOORS

Jim Morrison (born December 8, 1943, in Melbourne, Florida; died July 3, 1971, in Paris, France), lead vocals; Ray Manzarek (born February 12, 1935, in Chicago), keyboards, vocals; Robby Krieger (born January 8, 1946, in Los Angeles), guitar; and John Densmore (born December 1, 1945, in Los Angeles), drums.

THE DOORS (UPI/CORBIS-BETTMANN)

One of the first groups to achieve "underground" popularity by means of extensive FM radio airplay, The Doors were one of the first rock groups to have an extended album cut edited down for release as a single ("Light My Fire"). An excellent improvisatory group, The Doors' sound was grounded in the keyboard playing of Ray Manzarek, who became one of the few rock keyboardists to be recognized for his individual style. Fronted by vocalist Jim Morrison, who contributed powerful pieces of surreal poetry often preoccupied with sex and death, The Doors explored the dark and forbidding side of life years before heavy-metal and punk artists did. In acting out Morrison's poetry with carefully orchestrated performances in concert, The Doors became perhaps the first rock group to consciously inject serious and often compelling theatrics into their act. Furthermore, like Bob Dylan and John Lennon, Morrison was able to use his musical success as a springboard for recognition as a literary poet. As Morrison's later-day performances turned into self-indulgent spectacle, he set the stage for the mythologizing of his persona that occurred after his unexpected death in 1971. Much like actor James Dean, his image and talent became magnified after his death and evoked the fascination of fans too young to have viewed him first hand. Morrison's mystery and notoriety were renewed in the early '80s with the publication of his biography and in the early '90s with the movie *The Doors*. The Doors were inducted into the Rock and Roll Hall of Fame in 1993.

Jim Morrison was born into a naval family and eventually enrolled in the theater arts department of UCLA in 1964, majoring in film. In 1965, he met classically trained keyboardist Ray Manzarek while attending film classes at UCLA. The two quickly contacted jazz drummer John Densmore about forming a music group, and The Doors' lineup was completed with the addition of Densmore's acquaintance Robbie Krieger. After several months of rehearsal, The Doors were hired to play at Los Angeles' Whiskey-A-Go-Go for four months. Recommended to Jac Holzman of Elektra Records by Love's Arthur Lee, the group signed with the label and recorded their debut album in 1966. A stunning blend of rock and aural theater, *The Doors* was an instant success through widespread FM radio airplay, thus becoming one of the first rock albums popularized by the "alternative" media. The album contained Morrison's psychosexual epic "The End" and sported a number of hard-driving rock songs such as "Break on Through," "Take It as It Comes" and Krieger's "Light My Fire." Shortened from its original seven-minute length for release as a single, "Light My Fire" became a top hit in 1967 and broadened The Doors' base of popularity beyond the underground. The album remained on the album charts for more than two years.

Exhibiting more sophisticated musical arrangements, *Strange Days* contained another extended Morrison piece, the eleven-minute "When the Music's Over," the potent rock song "My Eyes Have Seen You," and the haunting ballads "Strange Days" and "Unhappy Girl." "People Are Strange" and "Love Me Two Times" became the hits from the album. *Waiting for the Sun* included the printed words to the epic Morrison poem "The Celebration of the

Lizard," and featured "Not to Touch the Earth," Krieger's puerile top hit "Hello, I Love You," and the moderate hit "Unknown Soldier." Morrison's anarchistic "Five to One" bore stark contrast to the album's otherwise shallow ballads.

In the meantime, given Morrison's penchant for drama in performance, The Doors became an enormous concert attraction by the end of 1968. As audiences grew larger, Morrison increased the theatricality, but his performances became erratic in 1969, culminating in his arrest for indecent exposure in Miami that March. Many subsequent concerts turned into outrageous fiascos due to Morrison's antics.

The Soft Parade was dominated by Krieger's juvenile lyrics and produced one major hit with "Touch Me." The Doors returned to rock with "Roadhouse Blues" and "You Make Me Real" from *Morrison Hotel*. Following the album's release, The Doors completed a successful tour largely free of untoward incidents. *L.A. Woman,* The Doors' final album with Jim Morrison, included the excellent title song and yielded two hits with "Love Her Madly" and "Riders on the Storm."

In March 1971, a disillusioned and weary Jim Morrison, beset by legal problems and years of alcohol and drug abuse, moved to Paris, France, for rest and recuperation, intent on devoting himself to his poetry. He died under mysterious circumstances on July 3, 1971, and was buried in Pere Lachaise cemetery without an autopsy. News of his death was withheld until after his burial and speculation began that he died of a heroin overdose, although the cause of death was listed as a heart attack. The three remaining Doors persevered for two albums before disbanding at the end of 1972.

Ray Manzarek recorded two obscure albums for Mercury before forming Nite City with vocalist Noah James for one album on 20th Century. Manzarek subsequently produced the first four albums by the Los Angeles band X. Robbie Krieger and John Densmore formed The Butts Band for two albums on Blue Thumb. Krieger later recorded the jazz-rock album *Robbie Krieger and Friends* before working with the Los Angeles band X, Iggy Pop, and Phillip Glass. In 1989, he recorded the all-instrumental album *No Habla* for the I.R.S. label and toured with Eric Burdon in 1990. Beginning in the late '80s, Manzarek collaborated with poet Michael McClure, resulting in the poetry and music set *Love Lion* in 1993. By the mid-'90s Manzarek was involved in a variety of film projects.

In 1978, Robbie Krieger, Ray Manzarek, and John Densmore edited over twenty hours of Jim Morrison's recited poetry for *An American Prayer,* for which they provided the musical backdrop. The opening sequence to Francis Ford Coppola's epic 1979 Vietnam War film *Apocalypse Now* used The Doors' "The End." Interest in the career of Jim Morrison and The Doors was fully revived in 1980 with the publication of long time Doors' associate Danny Sugarman's Morrison biography *No One Here Gets Out Alive* (with Jerry Hopkins) and the release of *The Doors Greatest Hits,* which stayed on the album charts for nearly two years. Volumes of Jim Morrison's poetry were published in 1988 and 1990, and another surge of interest in the group took place with the release of the Oliver Stone movie *The Doors* in 1991. The Doors were inducted into the Rock and Roll Hall of Fame in 1993.

THE DOORS BIBLIOGRAPHY

Butler, Patricia. *Angels Dance and Angels Die: The Tragic Romance of Pamela and Jim Morrison.* New York: Schirmer Books, 1998.

Clarke, Ross. *The Doors: Dance on Fire.* Chessington, Surrey, England: Castle Communications, 1993.

Dalton, David. *Mr. Mojo Risin': Jim Morrison, The Last Holy Fool.* New York: St. Martin's Press, 1991.

Densmore, John. *Riders on the Storm: My Life with Jim Morrison and The Doors.* New York: Delacorte Press, 1990.

Hopkins, Jerry. *The Lizard King: The Essential Jim Morrison*. New York: Charles Scribner's Sons, 1992.

————— and Danny Sugerman. *No One Here Gets Out Alive*. New York: Warner Books, 1980.

Jahn, Mike. *Jim Morrison and The Doors*. New York: Grosset and Dunlap, 1969.

Lisciandro, Frank. *Morrison: A Feast of Friends*. New York: Warner Books, 1991.

—————. *Jim Morrison, An Hour of Magic*. London, Plexus, 1996.

Manzarek, Ray. *Light My Fire: My Life with The Doors*. New York: G.P. Putnam's Sons, 1998.

JIM MORRISON

Morrison, Jim. *The Lord and the New Creatures*. New York: Simon and Schuster, 1970, 1987.

—————. *Wilderness: The Lost Writings of Jim Morrison*. New York: Villard Books, 1988; New York: Vintage Books, 1989.

—————. *The American Night: The Writings of Jim Morrison*. New York: Villard Books, 1990.

Riordan, James, and Jerry Prochnicky. *Break on Through: The Life and Death of Jim Morrison*. New York: Morrow, 1991.

Rocca, John M. (editor). *The Doors Companion: Four Decades of Commentary*. New York: Schirmer Books, 1997.

Sugerman, Danny. *The Doors: An Illustrated History*. New York: Morrow, 1983.

Tobler, John, and Andrew Doe. *The Doors: In Their Own Words*. London: Omnibus Press, 1988; New York: Perigee Books, 1991.

The Doors

The Doors	Elektra	74007	'67	CS/CD
	DCC	1023		CD
Strange Days	Elektra	74014	'67	CS/CD
	DCC	1026		CD
Live at the Hollywood Bowl (recorded July 5, 1968)	Elektra	60741	'87	†
Waiting for the Sun	Elektra	74024	'68	CS/CD
	DCC	1045		CD
The Doors/Waiting for the Sun	Elektra	60156		CS
Live in Europe 1968	Vision	(2)50298	'91	CS
	Vision	(2)50299	'91	CD
The Soft Parade	Elektra	75005	'69	CS/CD
Morrison Hotel	Elektra	75007	'70	CS/CD
Absolutely Live	Elektra	(2)9002	'70	†
13	Elektra	74079	'70	†
L.A. Woman	Elektra	75011	'71	CS/CD
	DCC	1034		CD
Strange Days/L.A. Woman	Elektra	60274		CS
Other Voices	Elektra	75017	'71	†
Weird Scenes Inside the Gold Mine	Elektra	(2)6001	'71	†
Full Circle	Elektra	75038	'72	†
Best	Elektra	5035	'73	†
An American Prayer	Elektra	502	'78	†
	Elektra	61812	'95	LP/CS/CD
Greatest Hits	Elektra	515	'80/'91	CS
Alive She Cried	Elektra	60269	'83/'84	CD†
Classics	Elektra	60417	'85	CS
Best	Elektra	(2)60345	'87	CS/CD
The Doors (music from the soundtrack)	Elektra	61047	'91	CS/CD
In Concert	Elektra	(2)61082	'91	CS/CD

The Doors Box Set	Elektra	(4)62123	'97	CD
The Ultimate Collected Spoken Words: 1967–1970	Cleopatra	(2)0191		CD
The Butts Band				
The Butts Band	Blue Thumb	63	'74	†
Hear and Now	Blue Thumb	6018	'75	†
The Complete Recordings	One Way	30993	'95	CD
Robbie Krieger				
Robbie Krieger and Friends	Blue Note	664	'77	†
	World Pacific	96101	'91	CD†
Door Jams (recorded 1977–1985)	I.R.S./MCA	82014	'89	CS/CD†
No Habla	I.R.S./MCA	82004	'89	LP/CS/CD†
	I.R.S.	13004		CS/CD†
RKO Live	One Way	31371	'94	CD
Ray Manzarek				
The Golden Scarab	Mercury	703	'74	†
	Mercury	512445	'92	CD
The Whole Thing Started with Rock and Roll	Mercury	1014	'75	†
Carmina Burina	A&M	4945	'83	LP/CS/CD†
Nite City				
Nite City	20th Century	528	'77	†
Michael McClure/Ray Manzarek				
Love Lion	Shanachie	5006	'93	CS/CD

THE DRIFTERS

Ben E. King (born Benjamin Nelson on September 23, 1938, in Henderson, North Carolina), lead baritone; Charles Thomas (born April 7, 1937), tenor; Doc Green (born October 8, 1934; died March 10, 1989, in New York), baritone; and Ellsbury Hobbs (born August 4, 1936), bass vocals. Later members included Rudy Lewis (born May 27, 1935, in Chicago; died 1964) and Johnny Moore (born 1934 in Selma, Alabama; died December 30, 1998, in London).

The Drifters, initially featuring lead vocalist Ben E. King, helped create and define the sound of soul music under producer-songwriters Jerry Leiber and Mike Stoller with gospel-style singing, pop-oriented material, and lush orchestral backgrounds. Although they were not the first rhythm-and-blues vocal group to utilize strings for recordings (that claim probably goes to The Orioles with 1953's "Crying in the Chapel"), The Drifters did popularize the format, a format subsequently adopted by many rhythm-and-blues and soul acts. The Drifters were inducted into the Rock and Roll Hall of Fame in 1988.

The original Drifters were formed in 1953 around lead vocalist Clyde McPhatter. He departed the group in late 1954, to be replaced by Johnny Moore. Manager George Treadwell, owner of The Drifters' name, fired the group in June 1958 and recruited The Five Crowns as the "new" Drifters. The Five Crowns had formed with Doc Green in Harlem in 1952 and recorded for Rainbow Records from 1952 to 1955. By 1956, the group included Ellsbury Hobbs and Benjamin Nelson, who later became Ben E. King.

Lead baritone Ben E. King coauthored The Drifters' first hit single "There Goes My Baby" with manager George Treadwell. The recording, a top rhythm-and-blues and smash pop hit in 1959, was written and produced by the legendary songwriting-production team of Jerry Leiber and Mike Stoller, who produced their subsequent hits into 1963. Following the smash rhythm-and-blues and major pop hit "Dance with Me," cowritten by Treadwell,

Brill Building professional songwriters "Doc" Pomus and Mort Shuman provided The Drifters with their next four hits: "(If You Cry) True Love, True Love," "This Magic Moment," "Save the Last Dance for Me" (a top rhythm-and-blues and pop hit), and "I Count the Tears."

In May 1960, Ben E. King left The Drifters to pursue a solo career. His first hit came with a song written by Jerry Leiber and then-apprentice producer Phil Spector, "Spanish Harlem," which became a top rhythm-and-blues and smash pop for Aretha Franklin in 1971. Later rhythm-and-blues and pop hits included the smash "Stand by Me" (cowritten by King), "Amor," "Don't Play That Song," and "I (Who Have Nothing)."

In the meantime, The Drifters were enjoying their greatest hit-making period with Rudy Lewis on lead vocals. Through 1963, the group scored major pop and rhythm-and-blues hits with songs provided by Brill Building professional songwriters. These included Carole King and Gerry Goffin's "Some Kind of Wonderful," "When My Little Girl Is Smiling," and "Up on the Roof" (a pop and R&B smash), Doc Pomus and Mort Shuman's "Sweets for My Sweet," and two Barry Mann–Cynthia Weil compositions, "On Broadway" and "I'll Take You Home." Rudy Lewis died in the summer of 1964 and early Drifter Johnny Moore (who had returned in April 1963) took over on lead vocals for the group's final pop hits, "Under the Boardwalk" (by Mann, Weil, Leiber, and Stoller) and "Saturday Night at the Movies" (by Mann and Weil). The Drifters continued to record into the early '70s. Around 1972, Johnny Moore, with a new group of Drifters, moved to England, toured the club and cabaret circuit, and signed with British Bell, for whom they scored a series of British hits through 1975. Several different groupings of The Drifters perform today. Johnny Moore died in London on December 30, 1998, at age sixty-four. The Drifters were inducted into the Rock and Roll Hall of Fame in 1988.

Ben E. King reemerged in 1974 with the top rhythm-and-blues and smash pop funk hit "Supernatural Thing" and later recorded with The Average White Band. His popularity subsequently diminished and he rejoined The Drifters for European tours in the early '80s. King enjoyed renewed popularity (and a near-smash hit) with the title song to the 1986 movie *Stand by Me* and thereafter recorded for EMI Manhattan and Ichiban.

THE DRIFTERS BIBLIOGRAPHY

Millar, Bill. *The Drifters: The Rise and Fall of the Black Vocal Group.* London: Studio Vista, 1971; New York: Macmillan, 1971.

Treadwell, Faye, with Tony Allan. *Save the Last Dance for Me: The Musical Legacy of the Drifters, 1953–1993.* Ann Arbor, MI: Popular Culture Ink, 1993.

The Five Crowns

The Rainbow Sessions (1952–1955)	Relic	5030		LP†
	Relic	7081	'94	CD

The Drifters

Greatest Hits	Atlantic	8041	'60	†
Save the Last Dance for Me	Atlantic	8059	'62	†
Up on the Roof	Atlantic	8073	'63	†
Our Biggest Hits	Atlantic	8093	'64	†
Under the Boardwalk	Atlantic	8099	'64	†
The Good Life	Atlantic	8103	'65	†
I'll Take You Where the Playing Music's Playing	Atlantic	8113	'65	†
Golden Hits 1959–1965: All Time Greatest Hits and More	Atlantic	8153	'67	CS/CD
	Atlantic	(2)81931	'88	CS/CD
The Drifters Now	Bell	219		†

Best	Arista	4111	'77	†
Greatest Hits	Dominion	3000	'91	CS/CD
Bringing You Their Best	Pair	1305	'91	CS/CD
Very Best	Rhino	71211	'93	CS/CD
Up on the Roof, On Broadway and Under the Boardwalk	Rhino	71230	'93	CS/CD
Rockin' and Driftin': The Drifters Box	Rhino	(3)72417	'96	CD
Under the Boardwalk	Musketeer	9016	'95	CD
Golden Hits	ITC Masters	1009	'98	CS/CD
Greatest Hits	Hollywood/IMG	119		CS/CD
16 Greatest Hits	Deluxe	7818		CS/CD
	Deluxe	7898		CS

Ben E. King and The Drifters

Best	Dominion	3272	'94	CS/CD

Ben E. King

Spanish Harlem	Atco	33-133	'61	†
Sings for Soulful Lovers	Atco	33-137	'62	†
Don't Play That Song	Atco	33-142	'62	†
Greatest Hits	Atco	33-165	'64	†
7 Letters	Atco	33-174	'65	†
Rough Edges	Maxwell	88001	'70	†
Beginning of It All	Mandala	3007	'72	†
Supernatural	Atlantic	18132	'75	†
I Had a Love	Atlantic	18169	'76	†
Let Me in Your Life	Atlantic	19200	'78	†
Music Trance	Atlantic	19269	'80	†
Street Tough	Atlantic	19300	'81	†
Stand by Me ("Best")	Atlantic	81716	'86	CS
The Ultimate Collection	Atlantic	80213	'87	CD
Save the Last Dance for Me	EMI Manhattan	46904	'88	LP/CS/CD†
What's Important to Me	Ichiban	1133	'92	CS/CD
Best	Curb/Warner Brothers	77594	'92	CS/CD
Anthology	Rhino	71215	'93	CS/CD
Very Best	Rhino	72970	'98	CD

Ben E. King/The Average White Band

Benny and Us	Atlantic	19105	'77	†

BOB DYLAN

Born Robert Zimmerman on May 24, 1941, in Duluth, Minnesota.

Certainly the single most important figure in contemporary music during the '60s, comparable in impact to Elvis Presley in the '50s, Bob Dylan was the first and most significant singer-songwriter to emerge from the folk music scene, inspiring a whole generation of folk (and later rock) artists to explore the vast potential of songwriting in matters socially conscious, personal, spiritual, philosophical and intellectual. With his second and third albums and such songs as "Blowin' in the Wind" and "The Times They Are A-Changin,'" Dylan revitalized folk music and songwriting with his highly personal, intense song poetics permeated with acute literary and philosophical references. Seemingly one step ahead of his audience at critical philosophical, personal, and musical junctures, Bob Dylan eschewed type-casting by fans and critics alike at progressive stages of his career to maintain his status as contemporary music's most independent, elusive, and enigmatic figure.

BOB DYLAN (UPI / CORBIS-BETTMANN)

The prime mover in the development of folk-rock music during 1965, Bob Dylan alienated folk fans with his move into rock music with his Newport Folk Festival performance backed by the electrified Paul Butterfield Blues Band and his *Bringing It All Back Home* album. While the album reinvigorated rock with its evocative, vituperative, and surrealistic song poetics and vastly expanded the concepts of contemporary music and songwriting, it also virtually demolished the standard a-b-a song structure and instituted almost single-handedly the free-verse stanza. Challenging an entire generation to reexamine their values and attitudes, Dylan soon came to be hailed by the media as the spokesman for his generation. With *Bringing It All Back Home,* Dylan established the album as the unit of personal musical expression and set the stage for the singer-songwriter movement of the '70s.

With *Highway 61 Revisited,* Bob Dylan brought song-poetry into the classrooms and onto the streets and, with The Beatles, made rock music intellectually respectable and validated it as an art form. With the six-minute "Like a Rolling Stone," his first major hit single and perhaps his finest composition, Dylan permanently challenged the recording industry's preoccupation with the three-minute song and encouraged other musical artists to explore the format. Dylan's *Blonde on Blonde* album, one of the first double-record sets released for a major contemporary artist, revealed an unprecedented level of performance and lyrical invention. It also marked the beginning of Dylan's break with the rock 'n' roll crowd in favor of a more sophisticated and intellectual audience, and brought an existential stance to rock music. Winning popularity despite singing in a harsh, strident, adenoidal voice lacking polished musical nuance, Dylan's success encouraged a number of artists with marginally adequate singing voices to sing on recordings, most notably Jimi Hendrix, Neil Young, and Bruce Springsteen, as well as entire generations of subsequent artists.

While convalescing from injuries received in a 1966 motorcycle accident, Bob Dylan recorded the seminal *Basement Tapes* album with his most recent touring unit, eventually known as The Band. The recordings, somehow pirated and issued illegally on so-called "bootleg" albums, became some of the earliest and best-selling of the genre. Dylan eventually reemerged at the beginning of 1968 with *John Wesley Harding,* an album that perplexed many of his fans, as he eschewed his earlier vituperation and anger in favor of a conscious and mature concern with vanity, arrogance and pride, resignation, perseverance, and resurrection in the real world. His next album, *Nashville Skyline,* contained simple, gentle songs that rejected both the profound personal and philosophical concerns of *John Wesley Harding* and the vitriolic and alienated vision of his three previous classic albums. Although not the first country-rock album, *Nashville Skyline* nonetheless represented a reconciliation between country and rock music and encouraged the popular acceptance of this new genre.

With his career in eclipse during the early '70s, Bob Dylan was being dismissed as a major force in popular music. Yet he again confounded his critics with his 1974 tour with The Band and the powerful *Blood on the Tracks* album. In the late '70s, Dylan once more bewildered and mystified fans and critics by recording Christian material. During the '80s, Dylan was better known for his tours than his solo recordings, although *Infidels, Empire Burlesque,* and *Oh Mercy!* were favorably compared by some to *Blood on the Tracks.* His 1985 anthology set *Biograph* pioneered the boxed-set retrospective. Touring with Tom Petty and The Heartbreakers and The Grateful Dead, Dylan later recorded with the supergroup The Traveling Wilburys. Inducted into the Rock and Roll Hall of Fame in 1988, Bob Dylan once again drew unequivocal critical plaudits in 1997 for the intensely honest and profoundly challenging *Time out of Mind* album.

Robert Zimmerman moved with his family to Hibbing, Minnesota, when he was six. Taking up guitar and harmonica at the age of twelve, he later formed several rock bands, including The Golden Chords, while still in high school. After graduation, he attended the University of Minnesota for several months, dropping out to concentrate on his music. Adopting the name Bob Dylan, he traveled to New York at the beginning of 1961 to visit his early idol Woody Guthrie, who was hospitalized with Huntington's disease. Dylan debuted that April in the Greenwich Village folk club Gerde's Folk City, where he first met Joan Baez, who would become one of the first artists to record his songs. Playing harmonica on recording sessions for Harry Belafonte and Carolyn Hester, Dylan received his first public recognition from *New York Times* critic Robert Shelton that September. Signed to Columbia Records by John Hammond in October, Dylan's first album featured traditional folk and blues songs such as "Man of Constant Sorrow" and "House of the Rising Sun," as well as Eric Von Schmidt's "Baby, Let Me Follow You Down" and his own "Song to Woody." His first single, the rock 'n' roll–styled "Mixed Up Confusion," backed with "Corrina, Corrina," failed to sell.

Dylan's second album, *The Freewheelin' Bob Dylan,* was dominated by his own material and effectively established him as a leader in the burgeoning folk singer–songwriter and youth protest movements. Displaying an astonishing range of material, the album included a number of potent protest songs such as "Masters of War," "A Hard Rain's A-Gonna Fall," and "Blowin' in the Wind," as well as "Girl from the North Country" and "Don't Think Twice, It's Alright." His triumphant appearance at the 1963 Newport Folk Festival with Joan Baez and the subsequent success of his "Blowin' in the Wind" (a major British hit) and "Don't Think Twice, It's All Right" as performed by Peter, Paul and Mary launched him into international prominence.

The Times They Are A-Changin' featured the powerful protest songs "The Lonesome Death of Hattie Carroll," "Only a Pawn in Their Game," and "With God on Our Side," and the anthemic title song, as well as the gentler "One Too Many Mornings" and "Boots of Spanish Leather." The more personal *Another Side of Bob Dylan,* his last entirely acoustic album, included a number of songs later recorded by others in the folk-rock style: "It Ain't Me Babe" (The Turtles), "All I Really Want to Do" (The Byrds and Cher), and "Chimes of Freedom" and "My Back Pages" (The Byrds).

Bob Dylan left the folk and protest movements behind with 1965's *Bringing It All Back Home* album. Half acoustic and half electric, the album contained a number of songs written in a stream-of-consciousness style, pervaded with incisive, evocative, and surreal images, such as "Gates of Eden" and "Subterranean Homesick Blues," his first albeit moderate American hit and a near-smash British hit. Other inclusions were the provocative "It's Alright Ma (I'm Only Bleeding)" and "It's All Over Now, Baby Blue," the caustic "Maggie's Farm," the underrated love songs "She Belongs to Me" and "Love Minus Zero/No Limit," and "Mr. Tambourine Man." The Byrds soon recorded "Mr. Tambourine Man," a top American and British hit, as the first folk-rock song. Dylan's brief May 1965 tour of Great Britain was documented by filmmaker D. A. Pennebaker and released as the film *Don't Look Back* in May 1967. By now an international celebrity, Dylan was being hailed by critics as the spokesman of his disillusioned and alienated generation.

Already dismayed by the electric rock sound of "Subterranean Homesick Blues," folk fans and critics were positively outraged by the *Highway 61 Revisited* album, the smash American and British "Like a Rolling Stone" hit single, and Dylan's performance at the Newport Folk Festival in June 1965 backed by keyboardist Al Kooper and members of the electrified Paul Butterfield Blues Band. The album, recorded with Kooper and electric guitarist Mike Bloomfield, showcased an unmistakable sound and featured some of Dylan's most startling songwriting efforts. Filled with surreal images, stimulating existential observations, and evocative song-poetry, the album contained a number of classics of '60s songwriting: "Ballad of a Thin Man," "Queen Jane Approximately," and the masterpiece "Desolation Row." Indeed, the album was remarkably consistent in its high level of songwriting and performance, and effectively made the entire album the unit of Dylan's expression. The quintessential "Like a Rolling Stone," arguably his finest composition, became Dylan's first smash American (as well as British) hit single and established his credibility with a new rock audience. "Positively 4th Street" soon became a smash American and British hit, followed by the minor hit "Please Crawl Out Your Window."

During the summer of 1965, Bob Dylan contacted a Canadian group known as Levon and The Hawks, then touring the United States' East Coast. Between the fall of 1965 and the summer of 1966, the group (Robbie Robertson, Richard Manuel, Rick Danko, Garth Hudson, and Levon Helm), later known simply as The Band, toured internationally with Dylan, although Helm left mid-tour. Dylan's infamous "Royal Albert Hall" concert, actually recorded in Manchester, England, on May 17, 1966, became perhaps the most famous bootleg record of all time and was eventually released in its entirety by Columbia in 1998.

In the summer of 1966, Columbia issued Dylan's *Blonde on Blonde* as one of the first non-anthology double-record sets in rock history. Another masterpiece, the album was recorded with outstanding Nashville sessions musicians such as Wayne Moss, Charlie McCoy, Kenny Buttrey, and Hargus "Pig" Robbins, as well as Al Kooper and The Band's Robbie Robertson. An immensely wide-ranging album in terms of the songwriting, *Blonde on Blonde* yielded four hits with "Rainy Day Women # 12 & 35" (a smash American and British hit), "I Want You," "Just Like a Woman," and "Leopard-Skin Pill-Box Hat." Another strikingly consistent set in terms of musical performance and lyrical invention, the album included "Just Like Tom Thumb's Blues," the desolate "Visions of Joanna," the vituperative "Most Likely You'll Go Your Way and I'll Go Mine," and the side-long "Sad Eyed Lady of the Lowlands," ostensibly composed in the studio as the musicians waited.

In late July 1966, Bob Dylan was seriously injured in a motorcycle accident. He subsequently retreated to upstate New York to recuperate amidst a variety of wild and irresponsible rumors. He summoned the members of The Band and rehearsed and recorded with them during his public absence. The recordings, made between June and September of 1967, were somehow pirated and released on so-called "bootleg" albums, most notably *Great White Wonder,* one of the first such records to sell in significant quantities. The material included a number of previously unrecorded Dylan songs such as "Million Dollar Bash," "Lo and Behold!" and "Please, Mrs. Henry." Several of the songs were later recorded by other groups: "Too Much of Nothing" by Peter, Paul and Mary, "The Mighty Quinn" by Manfred Mann, "Million Dollar Bash" by Fairport Convention, and "You Ain't Goin' Nowhere" and "Nothing Was Delivered" by The Byrds on their landmark *Sweetheart of the Rodeo* album. The Band's debut album featured "Tears of Rage," written with Richard Manuel, and "This

Wheel's on Fire," written with Rick Danko. The recordings were eventually released in 1975 as *The Basement Tapes*.

Bob Dylan reemerged in January 1968 with an appearance at the Woody Guthrie memorial concert at Carnegie Hall and the release of *John Wesley Harding,* yet another album that befuddled many of his fans. The harsh strident voice was replaced by a mellow pleasing voice, and the songs contained little of the vituperation and anger of his previous albums. Instead, the songs were concerned with resignation, regeneration, and resurrection, and an almost religious wariness. Moreover, the songs exhibited little of the rock 'n' roll raunch evident earlier. Recorded with Charlie McCoy on bass, Kenny Buttrey on drums, and the assistance of steel guitarist Pete Drake, the album yielded no hit singles, yet featured a number of profoundly moving existential pieces, including "Dear Landlord," "Drifter's Escape," "The Wicked Messenger," and "All Along the Watchtower," later recorded in its definitive version by Jimi Hendrix. The album's final two songs, "Down Along the Cove" and "I'll Be Your Baby Tonight," introduced another stylistic shift fully realized with 1969's *Nashville Skyline*—a decisive move toward country music.

Recorded with the same basic personnel as used earlier (Buttrey, McCoy, and Drake as well as Charlie Daniels), *Nashville Skyline* once again turned critics' and fans' heads in confused dismay. Attacked as sentimental and simplistic, the album included a duet with Johnny Cash on "Girl from the North Country" and a number of songs written in a country-pop style. "Lay Lady Lay" became a near-smash American and British hit from the album, which also contained ""I Threw It All Away," "To Be Alone with You," and "Tonight I'll Be Staying Here with You." In June, Dylan appeared in an ABC-TV special recorded at the Grand Ole Opry in Nashville with Johnny Cash. Foregoing the Woodstock Festival, he and The Band headlined late August's Isle of Wight Festival.

The disjointed *Self Portrait* contained a variety of different material, including live recordings from the Isle of Wight with The Band ("Like a Rolling Stone" and "The Mighty Quinn") and cover versions of songs by Paul Simon and Gordon Lightfoot. Universally panned, the album was hastily followed by *New Morning,* which contained ditties such as "If Dogs Run Free," "Time Passes Slowly," and "If Not For You." For several years after *New Morning,* Dylan was largely out of the public eye. Macmillan published his novel *Tarantula* in late 1970 and he appeared at George Harrison's August 1971 Concert for Bangladesh. His only recordings of the period were five songs for *Greatest Hits, Volume II* and the singles "Watching the River Flow" and "George Jackson," both moderate hits. In 1973, he appeared in a minor role in the Sam Peckinpah–directed film *Pat Garrett and Billy the Kid,* for which he wrote and performed the soundtrack music. The album yielded a major hit with the plaintive "Knockin' on Heaven's Door," but his next album, *Dylan,* consisted of outtakes from the *Self Portrait* sessions such as Jerry Jeff Walker's "Mr. Bojangles" and Joni Mitchell's "Big Yellow Taxi."

After his Columbia contract expired in September 1973, Bob Dylan signed with Asylum Records in November. Bob Dylan was soon back, first with *Planet Waves,* recorded with The Band. Again, Dylan received a critical drubbing, although some of the songs, such as "Going, Going, Gone," "Something There Is About You," and "Forever Young," were finely crafted. In January and February 1974, he toured for the first time in eight years, again with The Band. The tour was an instant sell-out and yielded the double-record set *Before the Flood.*

Re-signing with Columbia in August 1974, Bob Dylan convincingly reestablished himself as a powerful songwriter with *Blood on the Tracks.* The album included diverse material, from the vituperative "Idiot Wind" to moving songs such as "Tangled Up in Blue," "Simple Twist of Fate," and "Shelter from the Storm," as well as the epic Western tale, "Lily, Rosemary and the Jack of Hearts." In an effort to reestablish himself as a performer, Dylan assembled the Rolling Thunder Revue for engagements in the Northeast in late 1975.

Participants varied greatly, with appearances by Roger McGuinn, Joan Baez, Ramblin' Jack Elliott, Ronnie Hawkins, Mick Ronson, and others. The tour culminated in the December 8, 1975, benefit performance at Madison Square Garden for ex-boxer Rubin "Hurricane" Carter, who was alleged to have been unjustly convicted of three New Jersey murders in 1974. The companion single "Hurricane" became a moderate hit and the tour resumed in the spring of 1976, yielding *Hard Rain*.

Recorded with the assistance of harmony vocalist Emmylou Harris and violinist Scarlet Rivera, Bob Dylan's next album *Desire,* largely a collaborative effort with Jacques Levy, featured "Romance in Durango" and "Black Diamond Bay." Dylan appeared at The Band's "Last Waltz" at San Francisco's Winterland in November 1976 and released the three-hour fifty-two-minute movie *Renaldo and Clara,* shot during the Rolling Thunder Revue tour, in early 1978. Written, produced, directed, and coedited by Dylan, the film assembled fifty-six songs from the tour within a series of confusing and widely careening parables revolving around Renaldo (Dylan), Clara (then-wife Sara), The Woman in White (Joan Baez), and Dylan (Ronnie Hawkins). Greeted by disparaging reviews, the film was later withdrawn for reediting.

Beginning in February 1978, Bob Dylan made his first appearances outside the United States in more than eleven years at concerts in Japan, Australia, New Zealand, and Europe. The tour produced *Bob Dylan at Budokan,* recorded in March. At mid-year, the erratic *Street Legal,* with "Changing of the Guard" and "Is Your Love in Vain," was issued to mixed reviews and his subsequent three-month North American tour was the subject of negative criticism.

Bob Dylan next recorded three overtly religious albums that reflected his conversion to Christianity. The best-selling *Slow Train Coming,* recorded with Dire Straits guitarist Mark Knopfler, yielded a major hit with "Gotta Serve Somebody" while containing "When You Gonna Wake Up," "Gonna Change My Way of Thinking," and "When He Returns." *Saved* sold less well, but included two intriguing secular songs, "What Can I Do for You" and "Solid Rock." *Shot of Love* featured "Every Grain of Sand."

Bob Dylan did not record for two years. *Infidels,* released in 1983, was greeted by mixed reviews, hailed by some as a powerful comeback and his best album since *Blood on the Tracks.* Coproduced by Dylan and Dire Straits guitarist Mark Knopfler, the album included pointed songs such as "Man of Peace" and "Neighborhood Bully," as well as the gentle "Don't Fall Apart on Me" and the rousing "Sweetheart Like You," his last albeit minor hit. His 1984 European tour with Santana yielded *Real Live.* During 1985, he appeared at the Live Aid and inaugural Farm Aid benefits and joined in the recording of the benefit singles "We Are the World" and "Sun City." *Empire Burlesque,* recorded with members of Tom Petty's Heartbreakers, was received equivocally, again acclaimed by some as his strongest album since *Blood on the Tracks.* The album included the ballad "Dark Eyes" and "Emotionally Yours," covered by The O'Jays in 1991. The retrospective boxed-set *Biograph* was greeted enthusiastically, especially by Dylan collectors. The album contained fifty-three songs recorded between 1962 and 1981, including eighteen previously unreleased tracks and three hard-to-find singles, plus a fascinating thirty-six-page booklet written by Cameron Crowe.

In 1986, Dylan conducted his first major American tour in seven years, backed by Tom Petty and The Heartbreakers, the most skilled band he had played with since The Band. Petty and The Heartbreakers also helped record his *Knocked Out Loaded* album, which contained a number of collaborative efforts, including "Got My Mind Made Up" (with Petty), "Under Your Spell" (with Carole Bayer Sager), and "Brownsville Girl" (with playwright Sam Shepard). In the later part of the year, Dylan acted in the movie *Hearts of Fire,* but the film was released in Europe only in 1987 and panned upon U.S. release in 1990. During June 1987, he played six stadium shows with The Grateful Dead that yielded *Dylan and The Dead* in 1989. His 1988 tour was neither well attended nor well received, and *Down in the Groove* failed to sell, despite the assistance of Eric Clapton, Mark Knopfler, and Jerry Garcia and the inclusion of two songs cowritten by Grateful Dead lyricist Robert Hunter.

Bob Dylan contributed to *Folkways: A Vision Shared—A Tribute to Woody Guthrie and Leadbelly* and was inducted into the Rock and Roll Hall of Fame in 1988. He also recorded with George Harrison, Jeff Lynne, Tom Petty, and Roy Orbison as The Traveling Wilburys, contributing "Tweeter and the Monkey Man" and "Congratulations." A second Traveling Wilburys set, without Orbison, was released in 1990. His well-received *Oh Mercy* album, produced by Daniel Lanois and recorded in New Orleans with backing by the Neville Brothers, included "Shooting Star" and "Most of the Time." Lanois also produced 1990's disappointing *Under the Red Sky,* recorded with David Crosby, George Harrison, Al Kooper, and the Vaughan Brothers.

In an effort to thwart long-active bootleggers, Columbia issued *The Bootleg Series—Volumes 1–3* in 1991. The three-CD set contained fifty-eight songs never before officially released, including "Quit Your Lowdown Ways," "She's Your Lover Now," and "Seven Days." Later in the year, Rhino released *I Shall Be Unreleased: The Songs of Bob Dylan,* with selections by Rod Stewart, Joan Baez, Rick Nelson, and Roger McGuinn, among others. In October 1992, "Columbia Records Celebrates the Music of Bob Dylan" was staged at New York's Madison Square Garden. Musicians who played one or more Dylan songs included Neil Young, George Harrison, Eric Clapton, Tom Petty, Willie Nelson, and Tracy Chapman.

Bob Dylan next recorded two albums of folk and blues material performed solo and acoustically, *Good as I Been to You* and *World Gone Wrong.* He appeared at the Woodstock II concert-festival in Saugerties, New York, in August 1994, and recorded a performance with his current band—guitarist John Jackson, multi-instrumentalist Bucky Baxter, bassist Tony Garnier, and drummer Winston Watson—for the MTV cable network series "Unplugged," aired in December. Recordings from the show were released as an album in 1995. In February 1995, Bob Dylan was the subject of the CD-ROM *Bob Dylan: Highway 61 Interactive,* which included several rare early recordings and a brief clip from his 1965 Newport Folk Festival performance.

By late 1995, Bob Dylan was enjoying an amazing revitilization of his career owing, in part, to performing more than 100 engagements a year with his exceptional band. He formed his own record label, Egyptian Records, in 1996 and played before 200,000 fans and Pope John Paul II in Bologna, Italy, in September 1997. That same month, Columbia issued Dylan's *Time Out of Mind,* recorded with Baxter, Garnier, Winston, organist Augie Meyer, blues guitarist Duke Robillard, and guitarist-producer Daniel Lanois. Unequivocally his most engaging work since *Blood on the Tracks,* the album featured a number of incisive, intense, and demanding reflections on the limits of faith, love, and patience in face of life's inevitable failures and disappointments. Outstanding songs included "Standing in the Doorway," "Tryin' to Get to Heaven," "'Til I Fell in Love with You," and "Not Dark Yet." After more than thirty-five years of recording, including at least four classic albums, Dylan finally won his first Grammy Award for the album.

In the late '80s, Bob Dylan's son Jakob formed a group that evolved into The Wallflowers. Featuring guitarist Toby Miller and keyboardist Rami Jaffee, the group's debut 1992 album for Virgin failed to sell and, by 1995, the group had realigned with Dylan and Jaffee as mainstays. Recorded for Interscope Records, *Bringing Down the House* featured "6th Avenue Heartache" and "One Headlight" and sold more than three million copies.

BOB DYLAN BIBLIOGRAPHY

Bauldie, John (editor). *Wanted Man: In Search of Bob Dylan.* Secaucus: Citadel Press, 1991.

Bowden, Betsy. *Performed Literature:Words and Music by Bob Dylan*. Bloomington, IN: Indiana University Press, 1982.

Cable, Paul. *Bob Dylan: His Unreleased Works*. London: Scorpion/Dark Star, 1978.

Cott, Jonathan. *Dylan*. Garden City, NY: Doubleday, 1984.

Dowley, Tim, and Barry Dunnage. *Bob Dylan: From a Hard Rain to a Slow Train*. New York: Hippocrene Books, 1982.

Dylan, Bob. *Tarantula*. New York: Macmillan, 1971.

————. *Writings and Drawings*. New York: Alfred A. Knopf, 1973.

————. *Lyrics, 1962–1985*. New York: Alfred A. Knopf, 1985.

Gray, Michael. *Song and Dance Man:The Art of Bob Dylan*. London: Hart-Davis, MacGibbon, 1972.

Hampton, Wayne. *Guerilla Minstrels: John Lennon, Joe Hill, Woody Guthrie, and Bob Dylan*. Knoxville: University of Tennessee Press, 1986.

Herdman, John. *Voice Without Restraint:A Study of Bob Dylan's Lyrics and Their Background*. New York: Delilah Books, 1982.

Heylin, Clinton. *Dylan — Behind the Shades:A Biography*. New York: Summit Books, 1991.

————. *Bob Dylan: The Recording Sessions (1960–1994)*. New York: St. Martin's Press, 1996.

————. *Bob Dylan:A Life in Stolen Moments: Day by Day 1941–1995*. New York: Schirmer Books, 1996.

Humphries, Patrick. *Oh No! Not Another Dylan Book*. New York: Viking Studio Books, 1991.

Kramer, Daniel. *Bob Dylan*. Secaucus, NJ: Citadel Press, 1967.

Marchbank, Pearce (editor). *Bob Dylan in His Own Words*. New York: Quick Fox, 1978.

Marcus, Greil. *Invisible Republic: Bob Dylan's Basement Tapes*. New York: H. Holt, 1997.

McGregor, Craig. *Bob Dylan:A Retrospective*. New York: Morrow, 1972.

McKeen, William. *Bob Dylan:A Bio-Bibliography*. Westport, CT: Greenwood Press, 1993.

Mellers, Wilfrid. *A Darker Shade of Pale:A Backdrop to Bob Dylan*. London, New York: Faber and Faber, 1984; New York: Oxford University Press, 1985.

Pennebaker, D. A. *Bob Dylan: Don't Look Back*. New York: Ballantine Books, 1968.

Pickering, Steve (editor). *Dylan:A Commemoration*. Berkeley, CA: Book People, 1971.

————. *Bob Dylan Approximately*. New York: David McKay, 1975.

Riley, Tim. *Hard Rain:A Dylan Commentary*. New York: Knopf, 1992.

Rinzler, Alan. *Bob Dylan:An Illustrated Record*. New York: Harmony Books, 1978.

Rolling Stone. Knockin' on Dylan's Door: On the Road in 1974. New York: Pocket Books, 1974.

Scaduto, Anthony. *Bob Dylan:An Intimate Biography*. New York: Grosset and Dunlap, 1971; New York: New American Library, 1979.

Shelton, Robert. *No Direction Home:The Life and Music of Bob Dylan*. New York: William Morrow, 1986.

Shepard, Sam. *Rolling Thunder Logbook*. New York: Viking Press, 1977; New York: Limelight Editions, 1987.

Sloman, Larry. *On the Road with Bob Dylan*. New York: Bantam Books, 1978.

Spitz, Bob. *Dylan:A Biography*. New York: McGraw-Hill, 1989.

Thompson, Elizabeth M., and Davie Gurman. *The Dylan Companion*. New York: Delta Books, 1990.

Thompson, Toby. *Positively Main Street:An Unorthodox View of Bob Dylan*. New York: Coward-McCann, 1971.

Williams, Don. *Bob Dylan:The Man, the Music, the Message*. Old Tappan, NJ: F. H. Revell, 1985.

Williams, Paul. *Bob Dylan: Performing Artist:The Middle Years, 1974–1986*. Novato, CA: Underwood-Miller, 1992.

Bob Dylan

Bob Dylan	Columbia	8579	'62	CS/CD
The Freewheelin' Bob Dylan	Columbia	8786	'63	CS/CD
The Times They Are A-Changin'	Columbia	8905	'64	CS/CD
Bob Dylan/The Times They Are A-Changin'	Columbia	38221	'86	CS
Another Side of Bob Dylan	Columbia	8993	'64	CS/CD
	Columbia	53200	'92	CS/CD†
3-Pak: The Freewheelin' Bob Dylan/The Times They Are A-Changin'/				
Another Side of Bob Dylan	Columbia	(3)64811	'95	CD†
Bringing It All Back Home	Columbia	9128	'65	CS/CD
Highway 61 Revisited	Columbia	9189	'65	CS/CD
	DCC	1021		CD
The Bootleg Series, Vol. 4:				
Live 1966 The "Royal Albert Hall" Concert	Columbia	(2)65759	'98	CD
Blonde on Blonde	Columbia	(2)841	'66	†
	Columbia	00841		CS/CD
Greatest Hits	Columbia	9463	'67	CS/CD
John Wesley Harding	Columbia	9604	'68	CS/CD
Nashville Skyline	Columbia	9825	'69	CS/CD
Self Portrait	Columbia	30050	'70	CS/CD
New Morning	Columbia	30290	'70	CS/CD
Greatest Hits, Volume 2	Columbia	(2)31120	'71	CD
	Columbia	31120	'71	CS
Pat Garrett and Billy the Kid (soundtrack)	Columbia	32460	'73	CS/CD
Dylan	Columbia	32747	'73	CS
Blood on the Tracks	Columbia	33235	'75/'84	CS/CD
Desire	Columbia	33893	'76	CS/CD
Hard Rain	Columbia	34349	'76	CS/CD
Street Legal	Columbia	35453	'78	CS/CD
Bob Dylan at Budokan	Columbia	(2)36067	'79	CD
	Columbia	36067	'79	CS
Slow Train Coming	Columbia	36120	'79	CS/CD
Saved	Columbia	36553	'80/'90	CS/CD
Shot of Love	Columbia	37496	'81	CS/CD
Infidels	Columbia	38819	'83	CS/CD
Real Live	Columbia	39944	'84/'85	CS/CD
Empire Burlesque	Columbia	40110	'85	CS/CD
Biograph (1961–1981)	Columbia	(3)38830	'85	CS/CD
Knocked Out Loaded	Columbia	40439	'86	CS/CD
Hearts of Fire (soundtrack)	Columbia	40870	'87	CS/CD
Down in the Groove	Columbia	40957	'88	CS/CD
Oh, Mercy!	Columbia	45281	'89	CS/CD
Under the Red Sky	Columbia	46794	'90	CS/CD
The Bootleg Series, Volumes 1–3				
(Rare and Unreleased) 1961–1991	Columbia	(3)47382	'91	CS/CD
Good as I Been to You	Columbia	53200	'92	CS/CD
World Gone Wrong	Columbia	57590	'93	CS/CD
Greatest Hits, Volume 3	Columbia	66783	'94	CS/CD
MTV Unplugged	Columbia	67000	'95	CS/CD
Highway 61 Interactive	Columbia	67034	'95	CD-ROM

Time Out of Mind	Columbia	68556	'97	CS/CD
Bob Dylan and The Band				
The Basement Tapes (recorded 1967)	Columbia	(2)33682	'75	CD
	Columbia	33682	'75	CS
Planet Waves	Columbia	37637	'74	CS/CD
Before the Flood	Columbia	(2)37661	'74	CD
	Columbia	37661	'74	CS
Bob Dylan and The Grateful Dead				
Dylan and The Dead (recorded 1987)	Columbia	45056	'89	CS/CD
The Traveling Wilburys				
Volume One	Wilbury	25796	'88	CS/CD
Volume Three	Wilbury	26324	'90	CS/CD
Bob Dylan Tribute Albums				
I Shall Be Unreleased: The Songs of Bob Dylan	Rhino	70518	'91	CS/CD
The 30th Anniversary Concert Celebration	Columbia	(3)53230	'93	LP
	Columbia	(2)53230	'93	CS/CD
The Wallflowers (with Jakob Dylan)				
The Wallflowers	Virgin	86293	'92	CS/CD
Bringing Down the House	Interscope/Atlantic	92671	'95	CS/CD

FAIRPORT CONVENTION

Richard Thompson (born April 3, 1949, in Totteridge, London), guitar, vocals; Simon Nicol (born October 13, 1950, in Muswell Hill, London), guitar, banjo, dulcimer, bass, viola, vocals; Ashley "Tyger" Hutchings (born January 26, 1945, in Southgate, Middlesex, England), bass, guitar, vocals; Judy Dyble (born February 13, 1949, in London), piano, vocals; and Martin Lamble (born August 28, 1949, in St. Johns Wood, London; died May 14, 1969), drums. Ian Matthews (born Iain Matthews MacDonald on June 16, 1946, in Scunthorpe, Lincolnshire, England), guitar and vocals, joined in 1967 and left in 1969. Dyble left in May 1968, to be replaced by Sandy Denny (born Alexandra Denny on January 6, 1947, in Wimbledon, London, England; died April 21, 1978, in London), guitar, keyboards, alto vocals.

Later members included Dave Swarbrick (born April 5, 1941, in New Malden, Surrey, England), violin; Dave Mattacks (born March 1948 in Edgware, Middlesex, England), keyboards, drums; Dave Pegg (born November 2, 1947, in Birmingham, West Midlands, England), bass; Trevor Lucas (born December 25, 1943, in Bungaree, Victoria, Australia; died February 4, 1989, in Sydney, Australia), guitar, vocals; Jerry Donahue (born September 24, 1946, in New York City), guitar, vocals; and Bruce Rowland, drums.

Although sorely neglected in the United States, Fairport Convention was perhaps the first British group to combine traditional British folk music, compelling original songs, and rock instrumentation to emerge as the first British folk-rock group. An immensely seminal group with one of rock's most complicated histories, Fairport Convention introduced Ian Matthews, Ashley Hutchings, Sandy Denny, and Richard Thompson to a wider audience. During her tenure with Fairport Convention, Sandy Denny became established as one of the top British female vocalists and won recognition as an outstanding songwriter, primarily on the strength of "Who Knows Where the Time Goes," popularized by Judy Collins. Ian Matthews later pursued a remarkably diverse career, while Ashley Hutchings proved an important purveyor of traditional English folk music set to rock music. Mainstay Dave Swarbrick was one of the first musicians to play violin as a lead instrument within the rock format. After his stint with Fairport Convention, Richard Thompson emerged as a cult figure, recognized by critics and his devoted following as an excellent songwriter and compellingly innovative guitarist (some claim he is one of only a handful of original and creative guitarists working in rock today). Acclaimed for his recordings with one-time wife Linda (particularly *Shoot Out the Lights*) and subsequent solo recordings, Richard Thompson eventually began receiving wider recognition during the '80s.

Officially formed in 1967, Fairport Convention's initial lineup was Richard Thompson, Simon Nicol, and Ashley "Tyger" Hutchings. Richard Thompson had taken up guitar by age eleven, turned professional by fourteen, and turned to folk and traditional British music by his late teens. Around 1965, he began playing with Nicol and Hutchings. Soon augmented by Judy Dyble, Ian Matthews, and Martin Lamble, Fairport Convention played their first major engagement in January 1968 and recorded one album before the departure of Dyble in May. Dyble was replaced by Sandy Denny, who had worked London folk clubs and been a member of The Strawbs for six months. Fairport Convention's next album, *Fairport Convention* (*What We Did on Our Holidays* in Great Britain), came to be regarded as the first British folk-rock album. It featured Denny's stunning contralto voice and included her "Fotheringay," Thompson's "Meet on the Ledge," and a moving version of Bob Dylan's "I'll Keep It with Mine," as well as the obscure Joni Mitchell song "Eastern Rain." Ian Matthews left the group in February 1969 and Martin Lamble died on May 14, 1969, from injuries received in a wreck of the group's van. For *Unhalfbricking,* Fairport Convention was assisted by virtuoso violinist Dave Swarbrick. The album contained Thompson's "Genesis Hall" and an eleven-minute version of the traditional folk song "A Sailor's Life," as well as Denny's best known composition, "Who Knows Where the Time Goes," and their first major British hit, Bob Dylan's "If You Gotta Go, Go Now," sung by Denny in French. Swarbrick, who had previously toured and recorded with Martin Carthy and Simon Nicol, joined Fairport Convention on a permanent basis in September, as did drummer-keyboardist Dave Mattacks.

Liege & Lief won Fairport Convention its first substantial recognition and became their best-remembered album. It included the traditional "Matty Groves" and "Tam Lin" as well as Denny and Hutchings' "Come All Ye" and Thompson's "Farewell, Farewell." However, Hutchings, who favored the traditional English music rather than original material, left in November, as did Denny in December. Bassist Dave Pegg was brought in for Fairport Convention's *Full House,* which included Thompson's "Sloth." Personnel changes continued to plague the group, as Richard Thompson quit the band in January 1971 to work with Matthews and Denny and later record solo. Nicol, Swarbrick, Pegg, and Mattacks recorded two more albums as Fairport Convention.

In the meantime, Ian Matthews recorded *Matthews' Southern Comfort* and subsequently formed the namesake group for recordings in a country-rock vein, eventually scoring a major American and top British hit with a thinly sung version of Joni Mitchell's "Woodstock." He left the group abruptly in late 1970 and recorded two solo albums for Vertigo before forming Plainsong with singer-guitarist Andy Roberts. At the end of 1972, Matthews moved to Los Angeles to work with ex-Monkee Michael Nesmith, who produced his *Valley Hi* album. He subsequently switched to Columbia Records for two albums before moving to Seattle for six years, hitting with "Shake It" on Mushroom Records in 1978. During the '80s, Matthews worked as an artists-and-repertoire representative for Island, then Windham Hill Music. He reemerged in 1988 with the first all-vocal album on the new age Windham Hill label, *Walking a Changing Line,* comprising songs written by Jules Shear, the author of Cyndi Lauper's smash 1984 hit "All Through the Night." Matthews relocated to Austin, Texas, in 1989 and reverted to the Gaelic spelling of his first name, Iain. He reunited with Andy Roberts for *Dark Side of the Room* as Plainsong and later recorded solo albums for Mesa and Watermelon. In 1995, he joined Michael Fracasso and Mark Hamilton in Hamilton Pool.

Ashley Hutchings became a mainstay of traditional English folk music performed by a rock band. He formed Steeleye Span in 1969 with multi-instrumentalist Tim Hart, vocalist Maddy Prior, and, later, Martin Carthy and John Kirkpatrick. After three albums with the group (released in the United States in 1976), Hutchings left to form The Albion Country Band in 1971. He recorded *No Roses* with his then-wife Shirley Collins and, along with Richard Thompson, provided rock instrumentation to the folk dance form known as Morris dancing on *Morris On*. The Albion Country Band's *Battle of the Field* was recorded in 1973 but not released until 1976. With Hutchings as the mainstay, the group became The Albion Dance Band, then simply The Albion Band for British recordings throughout the '70s and '80s. Recent recordings by The Albion Band were issued on Magnum America and M.I.L. Multimedia. Two 1996 sets, *The Guv'nor* and *The Guv'nor, Vol. 2* anthologized Hutchings' long career from Fairport Convention on.

Sandy Denny formed the short-lived Fotheringay in March 1970 with American guitarist Jerry Donahue and two former members of Eclection, guitarist Trevor Lucas and drummer Gerry Conway. Their sole album for A&M featured the excellent Denny-Lucas composition "Peace in the End." Denny subsequently recorded two outstanding solo albums for A&M and assembled The Bunch with Lucas, Conway, Richard Thompson, Ashley Hutchings, and Dave Mattacks for *Rock On,* an album of rock 'n' roll oldies that showcased Denny's duet with Linda Peters on "When Will I Be Loved." She married Lucas in 1973 and switched to Island Records for the excellent *Like an Old Fashioned Waltz* and *Rendezvous.*

In the autumn of 1972, Fairport Convention regrouped with Dave Swarbrick, Jerry Donahue, Trevor Lucas, Dave Mattacks, and Dave Pegg. Augmented by Richard Thompson and Sandy Denny, the group recorded *Rosie*. Denny rejoined Fairport Convention for their late 1973 world tour and stayed until December 1975, recording two more albums with the group. By the end of 1976, the group comprised Simon Nicol, Dave Swarbrick, Dave Pegg, and drummer Bruce Rowland.

On April 21, 1978, Sandy Denny died of a cerebral hemorrhage after suffering a fall. Lucas subsequently returned to Australia and worked as a producer, dying in Sydney on February 4, 1989, of a suspected heart attack. In August 1979, Fairport Convention disbanded. Pegg next joined Jethro Tull as bassist, while Swarbrick formed Whippersnapper.

Beginning in 1980, Dave Pegg organized a Fairport Convention reunion concert every summer. The first reunion featured Richard and Linda Thompson and the second Judy Dyble. Fairport Convention once more reassembled in 1983 with Simon Nicol, Dave Pegg, and Dave Mattacks, who recorded *Gladys' Leap*. The group added violinist Ric Sanders in 1985 and multi-instrumentalist Martin Allcock joined for the all-instrumental album *Expletive Deleted!* The 1987 reunion concert with Ian Matthews was issued as *In Real Time* and during the year Fairport Convention made its first full tour of the United States since 1975 in support of Jethro Tull, with Pegg playing bass for both bands. In the '90s Dave Swarbrick recorded with guitarist Martin Carthy for Green Linnet Records, as did Fairport Convention (Nicol, Pegg, Allcock, and Sanders).

Richard Thompson launched his solo recording career in 1972 with the quirky *Henry, the Human Fly,* recorded with vocalist Linda Peters. The couple soon married and recorded the stunning but overlooked 1974 album *I Want to See the Bright Lights Tonight,* which included "Calvary Cross," "End of the Rainbow," and "When I Get to the Border." Subsequent albums by the team included *Hokey Pokey,* with "I'll Regret It in the Morning" and "A Heart Needs a Home," and *Pour Down Like Silver,* with "For the Shame of Doing Wrong" and "Beat the Retreat." Converting to the Sufi faith, the couple were absent from recording for three years, reemerging in 1978 for two more albums. In the early '80s, Richard recorded the all-instrumental album *Strict Tempo* and the live solo album *Small Town Romance.*

Richard and Linda Thompson's recording career culminated in *Shoot Out the Lights.* Hailed as one of the best albums of the year, *Shoot Out the Lights* was recorded with Fairport veterans Simon Nicol, Dave Pegg, and Dave Mattacks. It included Linda's heartrending "Walking on a Wire" and a number of potent songs by Richard, including "Don't Renege on Our Love," the desperate "Man in Need," and the rocker "Back Street Slide." It also contained the ominous "Did She Jump or Was She Pushed," the ballad "Just the Motion," and the compelling "Shoot Out the Lights," featuring Richard's inspired lead guitar playing. The couple made their debut American tour in support of the album, but it was fraught with mutual hostility and on- and off-stage shouting matches. The couple made their final appearance together in June 1982 and soon divorced, with Linda Thompson reemerging in 1985 with *One Clear Moment,* which included her "Telling Me Lies," a smash country hit for Linda Ronstadt, Dolly Parton, and Emmylou Harris in 1987.

Soon Richard Thompson began recording on his own. *Hand of Kindness,* recorded with Nicol, Mattacks, and Pegg, was Thompson's first American album chart entry. It included "Poisoned Heart and a Twisted Memory," "Both Ends Burning," "Tear Stained Letter" (a near-smash country hit for Jo-El Sonnier in 1988), and the jaunty "Two Left Feet." Thompson's first album on a major label since his days with Fairport Convention, *Across a Crowded Room,* contained more songs of embittered love such as "She Twists the Knife Again" and "When the Spell Is Broken," plus "Fire in the Engine Room" and "Walking in a Wasted Land." In the second half of the '80s, Thompson toured with rhythm guitarist Clive Gregson and vocalist Christine Collister, who later launched their own duo career. *Daring Adventures* included "How Will I Ever Be Simple Again," "Long Dead Love," and the rocker "Valerie," plus the concert favorite "Al Bowlly's in Heaven." With drummer John French, multi-instrumentalist Fred Firth, and guitarist Henry Kaiser, Richard Thompson recorded the avant-garde album *Live, Love, Larf and Loaf* for Rhino in 1987 and *Invisible Means* for Windham Hill in 1990.

Switching to Capitol Records, Richard Thompson next recorded *Amnesia,* which contained "I Still Dream," "Don't Tempt Me," "Reckless Kind," and the upbeat "Turning of the Tide." *Rumor and Sigh* included "Read About Love," "I Feel So Good," and the concert favorite "1952 Vincent Black Lightning." Green Linnet and Capitol Records each issued a compilation album of various artists performing the songs of Richard Thompson in 1993 and 1994. He subseqently recorded *Mirror Blue* and *You? Me? Us?,* a two-disc set consisting of one disc of acoustic ballads and another of dark electrified songs. Richard Thompson has toured the United States annually since 1994, recording 1997's *Industry* with erstwhile Pentangle bassist Danny Thompson for Hannibal Records.

RICHARD THOMPSON BIBLIOGRAPHY

Humphries, Patrick. *Richard Thompson, Strange Affair: The Biography.* London: Virgin, 1996; New York: Schirmer Books, 1997.

Sandy Denny and The Strawbs

Sandy Denny and The Strawbs	Hannibal	1361	'91	CS/CD
Fairport Convention				
Fairport Convention	Cotillion	9024	'70	†
	Polydor	835230	'90	CD
Fairport Convention	A&M	4185	'69	†
What We Did on Our Holidays	Hannibal	4430		CS/CD
Heyday (performances on BBC radio from 1968 and 1969)	Hannibal	1329	'87	CS/CD
Unhalfbricking	A&M	4206	'70	†
	Hannibal	4418		CS/CD
Liege & Lief	A&M	4257	'70	CD

Full House	A&M	4265	'70	†
	Hannibal	4417		CS/CD
House Full (recorded 1970)	Hannibal	1319	'86	CS/CD
Angel Delight	A&M	4319	'71	†
"Babbacombe Lee"	A&M	4333	'72	†
Rosie	A&M	4386	'73	†
Nine	A&M	3603	'74	†
Fairport Chronicles	A&M	(2)3530	'76	†
	A&M	(2)6016		†
A Movable Feast	Island	9285	'74	†
Rising for the Moon	Island	9313	'75	†
Gottle O'Geer	Island	9389	'76	†
	Antilles	7054		†
Gladys' Leap	Varrick	023	'86	CS/CD
Expletive Delighted!	Varrick	029	'87	CS/CD
In Real Time	Island	842856	'88	CD
Jewel in the Crown	Green Linnet	3103	'95	CS/CD
Old New Borrowed Blue	Green Linnet	3114	'96	CD
Red and Gold (live)	M.I.L. Multimedia	6007	'96	CD

Matthews' Southern Comfort

Matthews' Southern Comfort	Decca	75191		†
2nd Spring	Decca	75242	'70	†
Later That Same Year	Decca	75264	'71	†
Best	MCA	10519	'92	CD

Ian Matthews

If You Saw Thro' My Eyes	Vertigo	1002	'71	†
Tigers Will Survive	Vertigo	1010	'72	†
Valley Hi	Elektra	75061	'73	†
Some Days You Eat the Bear . . . and Some Days the Bear Eats You	Elektra	75078	'74	†
Go for Broke	Columbia	34102	'76	†
Hit and Run	Columbia	34671	'77	†
Stealin' Home	Mushroom	5012	'78	†
Walking a Changing Line: The Songs of Jules Shear	Windham Hill	1070	'88	CS/CD
Pure and Crooked	Goldcastle		'90	†
	Watermelon	1029		CD
Skeleton Keys	Mesa	79054	'93	CS/CD
The Dark Ride	Watermelon	1025	'94	CS/CD

Plainsong (with Ian Matthews)

In Search of Amelia Earhart	Elektra	75044	'72	†
Dark Room	Mesa	79065	'93	CS/CD

Iain Matthews

The Seattle Years 1978–1984	Varèse Sarabande	5738	'96	CD

Hamilton Pool (with Iain Matthews)

Return to Zero	Watermelon	1031	'95	CS/CD

Steeleye Span (with Ashley Hutchings)

Hark! The Village Wait (recorded 1970)	Chrysalis	1120	'76	†
	Shanachie	79052	'88	CS/CD

Please to See the King (recorded 1971)	Big Tree	2004		†
	Chrysalis	1119	'76	†
	Shanachie	79075	'90	CS/CD
Ten Man Mop (or Mr. Reservoir Butler Rides Again) (recorded 1971)	Chrysalis	1121	'76	†
	Shanachie	79049	'88	CS/CD

Shirley Collins and The Albion Country Band

No Roses (recorded 1971)	Antilles	7017		†

Morris On

Morris On (recorded 1972)	Carthage	4406		LP/CS/CD†
	Hannibal	4406		CS/CD

The Albion Country Band

Battle of the Field (recorded 1973)	Antilles	7027		†
	Carthage	4420		†
	Hannibal	4420		†

Ashley Hutchings and John Kirkpatrick

The Compleat Dancing Master (recorded 1974)	Antilles	7003		†
	Hannibal	4416		CS

The Albion Band

Rise Up Like the Sun (recorded 1978)	Carthage	4431		†
	Hannibal	4431		CS
Captured (recorded 1990–1992)	Magnum America	9	'95	CD
Acoustic City	M.I.L. Multimedia	6004	'96	CD
Albion Heart	M.I.L. Multimedia	6003	'96	CD

Ashley Hutchings

The History of Ashley Hutchings	Hannibal	4802		LP/CS/CD†
The Guv'nor	Wildcat!	9221	'96	CD
Volume 2	M.I.L. Multimedia	6005	'96	CD

Eclection (with Trevor Lucas and Gerry Conway)

Eclection	Elektra	74023	'68	†

Fotheringay

Fotheringay	A&M	4269	'70	†
	Hannibal	4426		CS/CD

The Bunch

Rock On	A&M	4354	'72	†
	Carthage	4424		†
	Hannibal	4424		CS

Sandy Denny

The North Star Grassman and The Ravens	A&M	4317	'71	†
	Carthage	4429		†
	Hannibal	4429		CS/CD
Sandy	A&M	4371	'72	†
Like an Old-Fashioned Waltz	Island	9340	'74	†
	Island	9258		†
	Carthage	4425		†
	Hannibal	4425		CS/CD

Rendezvous	Island	9433	'77	†
	Carthage	4423		†
	Hannibal	4423		CS/CD
Best	Hannibal	1328	'89	CS/CD
Who Knows Where the Time Goes	Hannibal	(3)5301	'86	CD

Richard and Linda Thompson

I Want to See the Bright Lights Tonight	Carthage	4407	'74	LP/CS/CD†
	Hannibal	4407		CS/CD
Hokey Pokey	Island	9305	'75	†
	Carthage	4408		LP/CS/CD†
	Hannibal	4408	'83	CS/CD
Pour Down Like Silver	Carthage	4404	'76	LP/CS/CD†
	Hannibal	4404		CS/CD
First Light	Chrysalis	1177	'78	†
	Carthage	4412		†
	Hannibal	4412		CS/CD
Sunny Vista	Hannibal	4403	'83	†
Shoot Out the Lights	Hannibal	1303	'82	CS/CD

Linda Thompson

One Clear Moment	Warner Brothers	25164	'85	†
Dreams Fly Away: A History of Linda Thompson	Hannibal	1379	'96	CD

Richard Thompson

Henry the Human Fly	Reprise	2112	'72	†
	Carthage	4405		LP/CS/CD†
	Hannibal	4405		CS/CD
Guitar, Vocal	Carthage	4413	'76	LP/CS/CD†
	Hannibal	4413		CS/CD
Live (More or Less)	Island	(2)9421	'77	†
Strict Tempo!	Carthage	4409	'81	LP/CS/CD†
	Hannibal	4409		CD
Hand of Kindness	Hannibal	1313	'83	CS/CD
Small Town Romance	Hannibal	1316	'84	LP/CS/CD†
Watching the Dark: The History of Richard Thompson	Hannibal	(3)5303	'93	CD
Across a Crowded Room	Polydor	825421	'85	CD
Daring Adventures	Polydor	829728	'86	CS/CD
Amnesia	Capitol	48845	'88	CS/CD
Rumor and Sigh	Capitol	95713	'91	CD
Mirror Blue	Capitol	81492	'94	CS/CD
You?Me?Us?	Capitol	(2)33704	'96	CS/CD

Richard Thompson Tribute Albums

The World Is a Wonderful Place: The Songs of Richard Thompson	Green Linnet	3086	'93	CS/CD
Beat the Retreat: Songs by Richard Thompson	Capitol	95929	'94	LP/CS/CD

John French, Fred Frith, Henry Kaiser and Richard Thompson

Live, Love, Larf and Loaf	Rhino	70831	'87	CS†
	Shanachie	5711	'96	CD
Invisible Means	Windham Hill	1094	'90	CS/CD

Richard Thompson and Danny Thompson

Industry	Hannibal	1414	'97	CD

Dave Swarbrick				
Swarbrick	TransAtlantic	337	'80	†
	Kicking Mule	337		LP
Dave Swarbrick and Martin Carthy				
Martin Carthy and Dave Swarbrick	Antilles	7041		†
Life and Limb	Green Linnet	3052	'91	CS/CD
Skin and Bone	Green Linnet	3075	'93	CS/CD
Dave Swarbrick/Fairport Convention				
50th Birthday Concert	Cooking Vinyl	001	'96	CD
Big Beat Combo (with Richard Thompson, Ashley Hutchings and Simon Nicol)				
Twangin' N' A-Traddin'	Wild Cat	9218	'95	CD

MARIANNE FAITHFULL

Born December 29, 1946, in Hampstead, London, England.

Perhaps better known for her liaison with Rolling Stone Mick Jagger than for her mid-'60s hits (including Jagger and Keith Richards' "As Tears Go By"), Marianne Faithfull endured heroin addiction and a dissolute life to eventually redefine herself as a brazen songwriter and inventive song stylist with 1979's remarkable *Broken English* album. She later authored one of the most harrowing and vivid biographies of rock, *Faithfull,* published in 1994.

Raised in Reading from the age of five, Marianne Faithfull was a student at St. Joseph's Convent School when she met Rolling Stones manager Andrew Loog Oldham at a London party in 1964. Impressed with her beauty, he invited her to record, providing her with Jagger and Richards' as-yet-unrecorded song "As Tears Go By." The song became a near-smash British and major American hit and launched her brief recording career. Through 1965, she scored smash British and major American hits with Jackie DeShannon's "Come and Stay with Me," John D. Loudermilk's "This Little Bird," and "Summer Nights." Essentially abandoning her recording career after 1966, she returned to the studio in 1969 to record a single that included as its B-side "Sister Morphine," which she wrote (uncredited) with Jagger and Richards. The song later appeared on The Rolling Stones' *Sticky Fingers* album.

Marianne Faithfull lived with Mick Jagger from 1966 to 1969. Miscarrying Jagger's baby in 1966, she was present at the infamous drug arrest at Keith Richards' house in 1967 and spent time in a psychiatric hospital in 1969. In the meantime, she had appeared with Alain Delon in the 1968 French film *Girl on a Motorcycle* (*Naked Under Leather* in the United States) and the 1969 London stage production of Anton Chekhov's *Three Sisters*. In 1969, Faithfull attempted suicide in Australia while Jagger was filming *Ned Kelly*. The couple broke up acrimoniously in 1970 and Faithfull withdrew from the public eye as her life devolved into poverty and heroin addiction.

Marianne Faithfull eventually returned to recording with the country album *Faithless*. She signed with Island Records in 1979, recording the stark yet corruscating *Broken English* album, one of the premier comeback albums of the decade. No longer the thin-voiced waif of the '60s, Faithfull sang in a foreboding mezzo-soprano, producing stunning performances on the title song, John Lennon's "Working Class Hero," and the vitriolic tale of sexual infidelity, "Why'd Ya Do It?" She recorded two more albums in the early '80s, eventually conquering her heroin addiction in 1986. She soon recorded an album of standards, *Strange Weather,* that otherwise included Bob Dylan's "I'll Keep It with Mine" and the title song, cowritten by Tom Waits. Her 1990 *Blazing Away* album, recorded in Brooklyn's St. Ann's Cathedral with Doctor John and Garth Hudson of The Band, effectively anthologized her career, from "As Tears Go By" and "Sister Morphine" to "Broken English" and "Why'd Ya Do It?"

Withdrawing to Ireland, Marianne Faithfull appeared in the 1991 Dublin production of Bertolt Brecht and Kurt Weill's *Threepenny Opera*. She later appeared in the films *Turn of the Screw, Shopping,* and *When Pigs Fly*. In 1994, Little, Brown published her uncompromising autobiography *Faithfull*. Her fascination with the works of Bertolt Brecht and Kurt Weill culminated in 1997's *20th Century Blues*.

MARIANNE FAITHFULL BIBLIOGRAPHY

Faithfull, Marianne, with David Dalton. *Faithfull: An Autobiography.* Boston: Little, Brown, 1994.

Marianne Faithfull

Marianne Faithfull	London	423	'65	†
Go Away from My World	London	452	'65	†
Faithfull Forever	London	482	'66	†
Greatest Hits	London	547	'69	†
	Abkco	7547	'88	LP/CS/CD
Faithless	NEMS	6012	'78	†
	Immediate	46963	'91	CS/CD
Broken English	Island	9570	'79	†
	Island	842355		CS/CD
Dangerous Acquaintances	Island	9648	'81	†
A Child's Adventure	Island	90066	'83	†
	Island	811310		CD
Strange Weather	Island	842593	'87	CS†/CD
Broken English and Strange Weather	Mobile Fidelity	00640	'95	CD
Blazing Away	Island	842794	'90	CS/CD
Faithfull: The Best of Marianne Faithfull	Island	524004	'94	CS/CD
	Island	524036	'94	CD
A Secret Life	Island	524096	'95	CS/CD
A Perfect Stranger—The Island Anthology	Chronicles	(2)524579	'98	CD
20th Century Blues	RCA	38656	'97	CD

RICHARD AND MIMI FARINA

Richard Farina (born circa 1937 in Brooklyn, New York; died April 30, 1966, near Carmel, California), guitar, dulcimer, autoharp, vocals; and Mimi Farina (born Mimi Baez on April 30, 1945, in Palo Alto, California), guitar, vocals.

Prominent members of the Greenwich Village folk music scene in the '60s, Richard and Mimi Farina recorded two excellent albums of Richard's songs. However, their career ended tragically when Richard was killed in a motorcycle accident in 1966. Mimi Farina enjoyed her greatest recognition as the founder of the nonprofit Bread and Roses organization that provided entertainment for shut-ins around the San Francisco Bay area since 1974.

Richard Farina was born to parents of Cuban and Irish descent and divided his early life between Brooklyn, Cuba, and Northern Ireland. Involved with the IRA in the mid-'50s, Farina was deported by the British government. He subsequently moved to Cuba, where he supported the rise of Fidel Castro. In 1959, he moved to Greenwich Village, where he was drawn into folk music during his brief marriage to Carolyn Hester. He later met Mimi Baez, Joan's sister, whom he married in 1963. The couple moved to California and formed a performing duo, appearing at folk clubs and festivals, including the 1964 Big Sur Folk Festival and the 1965 Newport Folk Festival. Signed to Vanguard Records, they were ably assisted by sessions guitarist Bruce Langhorne on their debut album. It included Richard's "One-Way Ticket" and "Reno Nevada," and the oft-recorded classic "Pack Up Your Sorrows," cowritten by Richard and Pauline Marden. Their second album, recorded with Langhorne and bassist Felix Pappalardi, comprised entirely Richard's songs save one, Mimi's instrumental "Miles." The songs included the comic protest songs "Mainline Prosperity Blues" and "House Un-American Blues Activity Dream," the beautiful "Reflections in a Crystal Wind," the dynamic "Bold Marauder," and "Hard Loving Loser," Judy Collins' first albeit minor hit from 1967.

Richard Farina, who had been pursuing a literary career since 1963, wrote the underground novel *Been Down So Long It Looks Like Up to Me* for publication in 1966. However, following a party celebrating its release, Richard was killed in a motorcycle accident near Carmel, California, on April 30, 1966.

Mimi Farina subsequently sang briefly with a folk-rock band and joined the San Francisco improvisational comedy group The Committee for one year. In 1971, she recorded an album with Tom Jans that included "In the Quiet Morning (For Janis Joplin)," popularized by sister Joan Baez in 1972. In 1974, Mimi Farina formed the nonprofit Bread and Roses organization in California's Marin County to provide entertainment for shut-ins at local prisons, halfway houses, drug rehabilitation centers, and hospitals. The success of Bread and Roses inspired groups in other communities across the country to set up similar organizations. To fund the group's ongoing expenses, she staged benefit concerts of acoustic music from 1977 to 1982 at Berkeley's Greek Theater. One of the few all-acoustic music festivals of its time, Bread and Roses' participants included Paul Simon, Joni Mitchell, and Peter, Paul and Mary. The festival was resumed in 1989, when David Crosby, Graham Nash, and Kris Kristofferson performed. Participants in 1990 included Jackson Browne, Boz Scaggs, and Michelle Shocked, and the 1991 festival featured Shawn Colvin, Rickie Lee Jones, and Todd Rundgren.

RICHARD FARINA BIBLIOGRAPHY

Farina, Richard. *Been Down So Long It Looks Like Up to Me*. New York: Random House, 1966; New York: Penguin, 1983.

————. *Long Time Coming and a Long Time Gone*. New York: Random House, 1969.

Richard and Mimi Farina

Celebrations for a Grey Day	Vanguard	79174	'65/'95	CS/CD
Reflections in a Crystal Wind	Vanguard	79204	'66/'95	CS/CD
Memories	Vanguard	79263	'69	†
Best	Vanguard	(2)21/22	'71/'89	CS/CD

Mimi Farina and Tom Jans

Take Heart	A&M	4310	'71	†

Bread and Roses

The Bread and Roses Festival of Acoustic Music (recorded 1977)	Fantasy	(2)79009	'79	LP
		79009		CD
The Bread and Roses Festival of Music, Volume 2	Fantasy	(2)79011	'81	LP
The Bread and Roses Festival of Acoustic Music, Greek Theatre, U.C. Berkeley	Big Beat	103		CD

Mimi Farina

Solo	Philo	1102	'86	CS/CD

THE FIFTH DIMENSION

Lamonte McLemore (born September 17, 1939, in St. Louis, Missouri), Marilyn McCoo (born September 30, 1943, in Jersey City, New Jersey), Billy Davis, Jr. (born June 26, 1940, in St. Louis, Missouri), Florence LaRue (born February 4, 1944, in Philadelphia), and Ron Townson (born January 20, 1941, in St. Louis, Missouri).

One of the more popular black vocal groups of the late '60s and early '70s, The Fifth Dimension featured lush, warm harmonies on songs such as Jimmy Webb's "Up, Up and Away" and Laura Nyro's "Wedding Bell Blues" and "Stoned Soul Picnic." Without a major hit after 1972, The Fifth Dimension established themselves on the supper club circuit, while early members Marilyn McCoo and Billy Davis, Jr., enjoyed renewed popularity between 1976 and 1977.

Lamonte McLemore formed the vocal group The Hi-Fi's in Los Angeles during the mid-'60s with Marilyn McCoo, Floyd Butler, and Harry Elston. They toured with the Ray Charles Revue for six months and when they broke up, two new groups were formed. Butler and Elston eventually formed The Friends of Distinction, who scored smash pop and rhythm-and-blues hits with a vocal version of Hugh Masakela's "Grazing in the Grass" and "Love or Let Me Be Lonely," in 1969 and 1970, respectively. McLemore and McCoo formed The Versatiles with Florence LaRue, Ron Townson, and McLemore's cousin, Billy Davis, Jr. Davis had formed his first group while still in high school and later served with The Emeralds and The St. Louis Gospel Singers. Signed to Johnny Rivers' Soul City Records in 1966, they soon changed their name to The Fifth Dimension.

The Fifth Dimension's debut album yielded a major pop hit with John Phillips' "Go Where You Wanna Go" and a near-smash with Jimmy Webb's "Up, Up and Away," a tame recording somehow identified with psychedelic music. Their second album consisted almost entirely of Jimmy Webb songs. During 1968, the group scored a smash pop and rhythm-and-blues hit with Laura Nyro's "Stoned Soul Picnic" and major pop hits with Nyro's "Sweet Blindness" and Nicholas Ashford and Valerie Simpson's "California Soul." The following year, they had top pop hits with the medley "Aquarius/Let the Sun Shine In" (a smash R&B hit) from the Broadway musical *Hair* and Nyro's "Wedding Bell Blues," and major pop hits with "Blowing Away" and Neil Sedaka's "Workin' on a Groovy Thing."

In 1970, The Fifth Dimension switched to Bell Records, managing a major hit with Nyro's "Save the Country" and a pop and rhythm-and-blues smash with "One Less Bell to Answer," written by Burt Bacharach and Hal David. By the early '70s, The Fifth Dimension were established on the supper club circuit. They achieved their final (near-smash) hits with "(Last Night) I Didn't Get to Sleep at All" and "If I Could Reach You" in 1972. With McLemore, Townson, and LaRue as mainstays, The Fifth Dimension moved to ABC, then Motown, while continuing to tour the supper club circuit. In 1995, the group recorded their first album in sixteen years.

Married in 1969, Marilyn McCoo and Billy Davis, Jr., left The Fifth Dimension in November 1975. They scored a top pop and rhythm-and-blues hit with "You Don't Have to Be a Star (To Be in My Show)" and a near-smash hit in both fields with "Your Love." They hosted their own summer CBS-TV variety show in 1977, yet McCoo went solo in 1978, launching her own supper club career while hosting the television show *Solid Gold* from 1981 to 1984. She later appeared in the soap opera *Days of Our Lives* and, in 1991, recorded an album of contemporary gospel music, *The Me Nobody Knows*.

The Fifth Dimension

Up, Up and Away	Soul City	92000	'67	†
The Magic Garden	Soul City	92001	'67	†
Stoned Soul Picnic	Soul City	92002	'68	†

The Age of Aquarius	Soul City	92005	'69	†
Greatest Hits	Soul City	33900	'70	†
The July 5th Album	Soul City	33901	'70	†
Portrait	Bell	6045	'70	†
Love's Lines, Angles and Rhymes	Bell	6060	'71	†
Live!	Bell	(2)9000	'71	†
Reflections	Bell	6065	'71	†
Individually and Collectively	Bell	6073	'72	†
Greatest Hits on Earth	Bell	1106	'72	†
	Arista	4002		†
	Arista	8335		CS/CD
Living Together, Growing Together	Bell	1116	'73	†
Soul and Inspiration	Bell	1315	'75	†
Earthbound	ABC	897	'75	†
Star Dancing	Motown	896	'78	†
High on Sunshine	Motown	914	'79	†
The Glory Days	Pair	(2)1108	'86	†
The Fifth Dimension Anthology (1967–1973)	Rhino	71104	'86	CS†
16 Greats	Fest	4403		CS
The Fifth Dimension Is in the House	Columbia	64375	'95	CS/CD†

Marilyn McCoo and Billy Davis, Jr.

I Hope We Get to Love in Time	ABC	952	'76	†
	Razor & Tie	2098	'96	CD
Two of Us	ABC	1026	'77	†
Marilyn and Billy	Columbia	35603	'78	†

Marilyn McCoo

The Me Nobody Knows	Warner Brothers	26667	'91	CS/CD†

FLEETWOOD MAC

Mick Fleetwood (born June 24, 1942, in London), drums; John McVie (born November 26, 1945, in London), bass; Peter Green (born Peter Greenbaum on October 29, 1946, in Bethnal Green, London), guitar, vocals; and Jeremy Spencer (born July 4, 1948, in West Hartlepool, Lancashire, England), guitar, vocals. Guitarist-vocalist Danny Kirwan (born May 13, 1950, in London) was added in August 1968. Green departed in May 1970. In August 1970, Christine McVie (born Christine Perfect on July 12, 1943, in Birmingham, England), keyboards and vocals, joined. Spencer left in February 1971. Bob Welch (born July 31, 1946, in Los Angeles), lead guitar and vocals, joined in April 1971 and left at the end of 1974. In January 1975, Lindsey Buckingham (born October 3, 1947, in Palo Alto, California), guitar and vocals, and Stephanie "Stevie" Nicks (born May 26, 1948, in Phoenix, Arizona), vocals, joined. Later members included guitarist-vocalists Billy Burnette (born May 8, 1953, in Memphis, Tennessee), Rick Vito (born October 13, 1949, in Darby, Pennsylvania), and Dave Mason (born May 10, 1946, in Worcester, England), and singer Bekka Bramlett.

Undergoing numerous personnel and stylistic changes for over thirty years, Fleetwood Mac was one of the longest lived of the British groups of the '60s, surpassed in terms of longevity by only The Rolling Stones. Formed by two former members of John Mayall's Bluesbreakers in 1967, Fleetwood Mac initially pursued a successful British career as a blues band during the late '60s blues revival. For a time sporting a three-guitar front line of Peter Green, Jeremy Spencer, and Danny Kirwan, the band gradually left the blues behind with the departure of cofounder Green in 1969. At the time of his exit, Peter Green was considered one of Great Britain's premier blues-based guitarists, rivaled by only Eric Clapton in terms of aptitude and stature. Breaking through in the United States with 1970's *Kiln House,* Fleetwood Mac subsequently added singer-keyboardist-songwriter Christine McVie and singer-songwriter Bob Welch, eventually transforming into a British-California soft-rock band with the addition of Californians "Stevie" Nicks and Lindsey Buckingham in 1975. Achieving massive sales with 1975's *Fleetwood Mac* and 1977's *Rumours,* one of the biggest-selling albums of all time, Fleetwood Mac endured into the '90s with Mick Fleetwood and John McVie as the mainstays.

Fleetwood Mac was formed in July 1967 by two former members of John Mayall's Bluesbreakers, Peter Green and Mick Fleetwood, with Jeremy Spencer and Bob Brunning. Green had joined Mayall following Eric Clapton's departure to form Cream in mid-1966 and appeared on Mayall's *A Hard Road* album. Green had previously been a member of Peter B's Looners and Shotgun Express, as had Mick Fleetwood. Fleetwood, a drummer since the age of thirteen, worked with Mayall's group in 1967. Bassist John McVie, a member of The Bluesbreakers since 1963, replaced Brunning in September.

Originally known as Peter Green's Fleetwood Mac, the group debuted at the British National Jazz and Blues Festival on August 12, 1967, and soon signed with Mike Vernon's Blue Horizon label. Issued on Epic in the United States, their debut album included songs by Elmore James, Howlin' Wolf, and Sonny Boy Williamson, as well as blues-based originals by Green and Spencer. Only marginally successful in the United States, the album proved immensely popular in Great Britain and helped spark the British blues explosion of the late '60s. The group soon scored their first (top) British-only hit with Green's instrumental "Albatross." In August 1968, Green brought in a third guitarist-vocalist, Danny Kirwan, and Fleetwood Mac's second American album, *English Rose,* contained songs by all three guitarists, including Green's "Black Magic Woman," popularized by Santana in 1970. Green's "Man of the World" became a smash British hit in 1969, the year Fleetwood Mac recorded two albums in Chicago with blues greats such as Otis Spann and Willie Dixon.

Switching to Reprise Records, Fleetwood Mac next recorded *Then Play On.* One of the most diverse recordings by the group, the album featured a number of pop-style songs by Green. His "Oh Well" became a smash British and minor American hit, but, unexpectedly, he announced his departure from the group, playing his last engagement with them in May 1970. He subsequently recorded an album for Reprise, only to drop out of sight for many years. Green eventually reemerged in the late '70s on Sail Records, only to abandon music once again.

Fleetwood Mac's first album without Peter Green, *Kiln House,* confirmed the group's move toward a softer, more harmonic, and pop-oriented sound. Containing widely divergent material, the album included Spencer's Western parody "Blood on the Floor," Kirwan's rousing "Tell Me All the Things You Do," and "Station Man" and "Jewel-Eyed Judy," both featuring lead vocals by Kirwan. The album became the group's first substantial success in the United States and expanded their popularity beyond the cult following that had attended their American tours since 1968. For the album, Fleetwood Mac was assisted by John McVie's wife Christine. Married in August 1968, the former Christine Perfect had been a member of Chicken Shack from April 1967 to August 1969, playing piano and singing on the group's British-only 1969 hit "I'd Rather Go Blind." She also recorded a solo album in 1970 that was reissued in 1976 as *The Legendary Christine Perfect Album.* She officially joined Fleetwood Mac in August 1970, shortly before the release of *Kiln House.* However, in February 1971, during Christine's first American tour with Fleetwood Mac, Jeremy Spencer abruptly left the group while in Los Angeles.

Fleetwood Mac, now comprising Kirwan, Fleetwood, and the McVies, held auditions for Spencer's replacement, eventually choosing lead guitarist-singer-songwriter Bob

Welch, who joined in April 1971. Welch, a veteran of both the Los Angeles and Las Vegas club scenes, had been a member of the rhythm-and-blues band The Seven Sons. With the departures of original guitarists Peter Green and Jeremy Spencer, Fleetwood Mac switched to ballads and softer-rock songs with *Future Games,* Christine McVie and Bob Welch's debut recording with the group. The follow-up, *Bare Trees,* included Kirwan's "Dust" and "Bare Trees," Christine's "Spare Me a Little," and Welch's "Sentimental Lady." In August 1972, Danny Kirwan was asked to leave Fleetwood Mac. He eventually recorded three albums for DJM Records.

Experiencing several personnel changes over the next few years, Fleetwood Mac recorded *Penguin* and *Mystery to Me,* which sold surprisingly well in the United States. *Heroes Are Hard to Find,* regarded as Fleetwood Mac's first album as a transplanted Los Angeles band, yielded an underground hit with Welch's "Bermuda Triangle." A protracted series of legal and financial problems beset Fleetwood Mac, as their manager, claiming control of the group name, assembled a group of unknowns to tour America as Fleetwood Mac. The matter was litigated as the real Fleetwood Mac moved to Los Angeles and Mick Fleetwood assumed the group's management. Eventually vindicated by the courts, the real Fleetwood Mac suffered the departure of Bob Welch at the end of 1974.

Reduced to a trio, Fleetwood Mac recruited Stephanie "Stevie" Nicks and Lindsey Buckingham. Nicks had been raised in California and ended up in the San Francisco Bay Area after dropping out of San Jose State College. In 1968, she joined a band named Fritz, whose bassist and second vocalist was Buckingham. The two persevered with the group until 1971, later moving to Los Angeles, where they recorded a duet album for Polydor Records. The two had come to the attention of Fleetwood Mac through producer Keith Olsen before Welch's departure. With Buckingham and Nicks joining the group in January 1975, the new lineup recorded *Fleetwood Mac* in Los Angeles. Once again featuring three independent singer-songwriters, Fleetwood Mac had become the quintessential British-California rock band. The album stayed on the charts for nearly three years and yielded three major hits with Christine's "Over My Head" and "Say You Love Me" and Nicks' "Rhiannon," while containing Christine's "Warm Ways" and Nicks' "Landslide." Spurred by the visual and musical focus provided by Christine McVie and Stevie Nicks, the subsequent six-month tour made Fleetwood Mac a massively popular concert attraction and established the group as one of the prime purveyors of pop-oriented, harmonically rich, and extravagantly produced music.

The self-produced follow-up to *Fleetwood Mac, Rumours,* capitalized on the group's burgeoning popularity as the two couples, John and Christine McVie and Lindsey Buckingham and Stevie Nicks, were splitting up. The album produced four hits, Buckingham's "Go Your Own Way," Nicks' top hit "Dreams," and Christine's "Don't Stop" and "You Make Loving Fun." It remained on the American album charts for more than two years and eventually sold more than twenty-five million copies worldwide. Their popularity as a concert attraction was enhanced by a ten-month, ten-country world tour in support of *Rumours.*

Fleetwood Mac's *Tusk,* recorded over a two-year period at the cost of over $1 million, was issued in late 1979. Overlong and disjointed, the highly experimental album marked the creative ascendancy of Lindsey Buckingham, whose odd, near-smash hit title cut was recorded with the U.S.C. Trojan Marching Band. *Tusk* also yielded a near-smash hit with Nicks' "Sara" and a major hit with "Think About Me." The group completed an exhaustive American tour in late 1979 and a nine-month world tour in 1980. They did not return to the studio until 1982.

During 1981, Stevie Nicks and Lindsey Buckingham each launched solo recording careers. Following 1982's *Mirage* (and its hits "Hold Me," "Love in Store," and "Gypsy") and subsequent tour, Fleetwood Mac were generally inactive as a group. Christine McVie's 1984 album produced hits with "Got a Hold on Me" and "Love Will Show Us How," cowritten by guitarist Todd Sharp. She remarried in 1986. The group reassembled for 1987's *Tango in the Night,* which produced smash hits with "Big Love" and "Little Lies" and major hits with "Seven Wonders" and "Everywhere." On the eve of the tour in support of the album, Lindsey Buckingham abruptly quit the group. Guitarist-vocalist Billy Burnette (Dorsey Burnette's son), a member of Mick Fleetwood's side band The Zoo for many years, was added for the tour, as was guitarist-vocalist Rick Vito, a veteran of the touring bands of Jackson Browne and Bob Seger. As full-fledged members, the two recorded *Behind the Mask* with Fleetwood Mac and performed on their subsequent tour. The album failed to produce any major hits and, with their final performance in Los Angeles on December 7, 1990, Christine McVie and Stevie Nicks vowed to never tour with the group again. The two did record several new songs for 1992's *25 Years—The Chain,* but by then Rick Vito had also left the group.

In 1993, the *Rumours* edition of Fleetwood Mac reunited to perform at President Bill Clinton's inauguration. By 1994, Fleetwood Mac (Mick Fleetwood, John and Christine McVie, and Billy Burnette) had recruited Dave Mason, a former member of Traffic, and Bekka Bramlett, the daughter of Bonnie and Delaney Bramlett. In 1997, the *Rumours* edition of Fleetwood Mac reunited yet again for an MTV concert that produced a live album and subsequent support tour. The enormous popularity of *Rumours* resulted in the 1998 release of *Legacy: A Tribute to Fleetwood Mac's Rumours,* recorded by Jewel, Elton John, Shawn Colvin, and The Goo Goo Dolls, among others.

FLEETWOOD MAC BIBLIOGRAPHY

Carr, Roy, and Steve Clarke. *Fleetwood Mac: Rumours 'n' Fax.* New York: Harmony Books, 1978.

Fleetwood, Mick, with Stephen Davis. *Fleetwood: My Life and Adventures in Fleetwood Mac.* New York: William Morrow, 1990.

Graham, Samuel. *Fleetwood Mac: The Authorized History.* New York: Warner Books, 1978.

Early Fleetwood Mac

The Original Fleetwood Mac (recorded 1967)	Sire	6045	'77	†
Vintage Years: Best	Sire	(2)3706	'75	†
	Sire	(2)6006		†
London Live '68	Magnum America	3	'95	CD
Fleetwood Mac	Epic	26402	'68	†
English Rose	Epic	26446	'69	†
Black Magic Woman (reissue of above two)	Epic	(2)30632	'71	†
English Rose/Fleetwood Mac	Epic	(2)33740	'75	†
Blues Jam in Chicago, Volume 1	Blue Horizon	4803	'69	†
Blues Jam in Chicago, Volume 2	Blue Horizon	4805	'69	†
Fleetwood Mac in Chicago (reissue of above two)	Blue Horizon	(2)3801	'70	†
	Sire	(2)3715	'76	†
	Sire	(2)6009		†
	Blue Horizon	(2)45283	'94	CS/CD
Jumping at Shadows (recorded 1969)	Varrick	020	'86	CS
Early Treasures	Pair	1208		CD
The Early Years	Special Music	4915		CS/CD
The Blues Collection	Griffin	216		CD
The Original Fleetwood Mac	Griffin	344		CD
The Early Years	Griffin	0838		CD

Chicken Shack

40 Blue Fingers Freshly Packed and Ready to Serve	Epic	26414	'69	†
O.K. Ken?	Blue Horizon	7705	'69	†

Christine McVie

The Legendary Christine Perfect Album	Sire	7522	'76	†
	Sire	6022		†
Christine McVie	Warner Brothers	25059	'84	†

Peter Green

End of the Game	Reprise	6436	'71	†
In the Skies	Sail	0110	'79	†
Little Dreamer	Sail	0112	'80	†
Green & Guitar: The Best of Peter Green, 1977–1981	Music Club	50001	'96	CD

Jeremy Spencer

Jeremy Spencer and the Children of God	Columbia	31990	'72	†
Flee	Atlantic	19236	'79	†

Danny Kirwan

Second Chapter	DJM	1	'75	†
Danny Kirwan	DJM	9	'77	†
Hello There, Big Boy	DJM	22	'79	†

Fleetwood Mac

Then Play On	Reprise	6368	'69	CS/CD
Kiln House	Reprise	6408	'70	CS/CD
Future Games	Reprise	6465	'71	CS/CD
Bare Trees	Reprise	2080	'72	†
	Reprise	2278		CS/CD
Penguin	Reprise	2138	'73/'90	CD
Mystery to Me	Reprise	2158	'73	†
	Reprise	2279		†
	Reprise	25982	'90	CD
Heroes Are Hard to Find	Reprise	2196	'74/'87	CD
Fleetwood Mac	Reprise	2225	'75	†
	Reprise	2281		CS/CD
Rumours	Warner Brothers	3010	'77/'84	CS/CD
Fleetwood Mac/Rumours	Warner Brothers	23705		CS
Tusk	Warner Brothers	(2)3350	'79	†
	Warner Brothers	3350		CS/CD
	Warner Brothers	2694		CD†
Live	Warner Brothers	(2)3500	'80	CD
	Warner Brothers	3500	'80	CS
Mirage	Warner Brothers	23607	'82/'84	CS/CD
Tango in the Night	Warner Brothers	25471	'87	CS/CD
Greatest Hits	Warner Brothers	25801	'88	CS/CD
Behind the Mask	Warner Brothers	26111	'90	CS/CD
	Warner Brothers	26206	'90	CD†
25 Years—The Chain	Warner Brothers	(4)45129	'92	CS/CD
Time	Warner Brothers	45920	'95	CS/CD
The Dance	Warner Brothers	46702	'97	CS/CD

Tribute Album

Legacy: A Tribute to Fleetwood Mac's *Rumours*	Lava/Atlantic	83054	'98	CS/CD

Lindsey Buckingham and Stevie Nicks

Buckingham/Nicks	Polydor	5058	'73	†

Stevie Nicks

Bella Donna	Modern	38139	'81	CS/CD
The Wild Heart	Modern	90084	'83	CS/CD
Rock a Little	Modern	90479	'85	CS/CD
The Other Side of the Mirror	Modern	91245	'89	CS/CD
Timespace: The Best of Stevie Nicks	Modern	91711	'91	CS/CD
Street Angel	Modern	92246	'94	CS/CD

Lindsey Buckingham

Law and Order	Asylum	561	'81/'84	CS/CD
Go Insane	Elektra	60363	'84	CS/CD
Out of the Cradle	Reprise	26182	'92	CS/CD

Mick Fleetwood

The Visitor	RCA	4080	'81	†
I'm Not Me	RCA	4652	'83	†

John McVie

John McVie's "Gotta Band"	Warner Brothers	26909	'92	CS/CD†

THE FLYING BURRITO BROTHERS

Gram Parsons (born Cecil Connor III on November 5, 1946, in Winter Haven, Florida; died September 19, 1973, at Joshua Tree, California), rhythm guitar, keyboards, vocals; Chris Hillman (born December 4, 1942, in Los Angeles), guitar, mandolin, vocals; "Sneaky" Pete Kleinow (born circa 1934 in South Bend, Indiana), pedal steel guitar; and Chris Ethridge, bass, piano. Later members included Bernie Leadon (born July 19, 1947, in Minneapolis, Minnesota), guitar, vocals; Michael Clarke (born June 3, 1944, in New York City; died December 19, 1993, in Treasure Island, Florida), drums; and Al Perkins, pedal steel guitar. Gram Parsons left in 1970, to be replaced by Rick Roberts (born August 31, 1949, in Clearwater, Florida), guitar, vocals.

Although virtually unrecognized in their own time, The Flying Burrito Brothers, particularly in the person of Gram Parsons, exerted a tremendous influence on rock music in the late '60s and early '70s. Artistically, they successfully combined rock and country instrumentation, rock amplification, and plaintive country-style lyrics, paving the way for the success of country-rock bands such as Poco and The Eagles. Although The Byrds' *Sweetheart of the Rodeo* album (recorded with Parsons) came to be regarded as the first country-rock album, some claim Parsons' International Submarine Band album *Safe at Home* deserves that accolade. Moreover, Parsons' music and songwriting inspired his erstwhile harmony vocalist Emmylou Harris and later encouraged the development of a whole generation of country-style rockers such as Rodney Crowell and Dwight Yoakam, even influencing artists such as The Rolling Stones and Elvis Costello. However, Parsons may be better known to the general public for his early death than for his pioneering contributions to the development of country-rock. Indeed, he never enjoyed even a minor hit in any field. Bandmate Chris Hillman ultimately established himself with The Desert Rose Band in the late '80s, but like Emmylou Harris, Rodney Crowell, and Southern Pacific, their success was largely limited to the country field.

Gram Parsons grew up in Waycross, Georgia, where he learned to play piano and later took up guitar. After playing with several Georgia bands, he formed the folk-style quartet

The Shilos, with whom he performed in the first half of the '60s. Early recordings with The Shilos were eventually issued in 1979 as *Gram Parsons: The Early Years* on Sierra Records. After briefly studying theology at Harvard University, Parsons formed perhaps the first country-rock band, The International Submarine Band, in 1965 in the Cambridge area. The group recorded two obscure singles before relocating to Los Angeles in 1966 and realigning with a new bassist and drummer for *Safe at Home,* recorded for Lee Hazlewood's LHI label. The album included four Parsons originals, including "Luxury Liner."

In 1968, Gram Parsons joined The Byrds for their celebrated *Sweetheart of the Rodeo* album. Hailed as the first country-rock record, the album included two Parsons songs, "Hickory Wind" and "One Hundred Years from Now." Leaving The Byrds after only three months as the group was preparing for a tour of South Africa, Parsons was soon followed by Chris Hillman.

In late 1968, Gram Parsons and Chris Hillman formed The Flying Burrito Brothers with "Sneaky" Pete Kleinow and Chris Ethridge. Signed to A&M Records, their debut album, *The Gilded Palace of Sin,* pictured the members in elaborate country-and-western-style Nudie suits (Parsons' suit prominently featured marijuana leaves). The album contained some of Parsons' finest songwriting efforts, including "Sin City" and "Juanita" (coauthored by Hillman) and "Hot Burrito #1" (coauthored by Ethridge), with lead vocals by Parsons. In September 1969, Chris Ethridge exited for sessions work and was replaced by future Eagle Bernie Leadon, formerly with Dillard and Clark, with Hillman switching to bass. Ex-Byrd Michael Clarke became the group's drummer that year. *Burrito Deluxe* featured a fine countrified version of Mick Jagger and Keith Richard's "Wild Horse," as well as a number of songs written or cowritten by Parsons, including "High Fashion Queen" and "Lazy Days."

Gram Parsons left The Flying Burrito Brothers in April 1970, shortly before the release of *Burrito Deluxe.* He was replaced by Rick Roberts, who led the group through a variety of incarnations until 1972. *The Flying Burrito Brothers* included Roberts' "Colorado" and Gene Clark's "Tried So Hard," but both "Sneaky" Pete Kleinow and Bernie Leadon departed in 1971. By October, the group was reconstituted with Roberts, Hillman, Clarke, pedal steel guitarist Al Perkins, and three members of Country Gazette. This grouping recorded the live *Last of the Red Hot Burritos,* but, before a late 1971 tour undertaken as The Hot Burrito Revue with Country Gazette, Hillman, Perkins, and Clarke dropped out. By June 1972, The Burritos had dissolved, although Roberts assembled a new group for a 1973 European tour.

Spending two years in Europe, often in the company of Keith Richards, Gram Parsons eventually returned to recording in 1972. For his two solo albums, Parsons enlisted vocalist Emmylou Harris, fiddler Byron Berline, steel guitarist Al Perkins, bassist Rick Grech (a former member of Blind Faith), and guitarist extraordinaire James Burton. The debut album *GP* included Parsons' "Kiss the Children," cowritten with Grech, and "She," cowritten with Chris Ethridge. In the spring of 1973, Parsons toured with The Fallen Angels (including Emmylou Harris) and recordings from the tour eventually surfaced on Sierra Records in 1982. Harris stepped to the fore as harmony vocalist for *Grievous Angel,* as evidenced by "Love Hurts" and "Hearts on Fire." The album also contained "In My Hour of Darkness," cowritten by Parsons and Harris, another Parsons-Grech collaboration, "Las Vegas," and the Parsons' originals "Return of the Grievous Angel" and "Brass Buttons." However, several months before the release of the album, Gram Parsons died from apparent multiple drug use at the age of 26 on September 19, 1973, at Joshua Tree, California. Gram Parsons subsequently found life in the work of Emmylou Harris, whose popularity, ironically, was primarily in the country field.

A burgeoning interest in Gram Parsons soon developed and A&M Records scoured their vaults for additional recordings by the group. The 1974 album *Close Up the Honky Tonks* included five out-takes recorded by the Gram Parsons' edition of The Flying Burrito Brothers. The 1976 album *Sleepless Nights* contained out-takes recorded by Parsons in 1973, as well as Flying Burrito Brothers out-takes from 1970.

In 1975, The Flying Burrito Brothers re-formed with "Sneaky" Pete Kleinow, Chris Ethridge, Louisiana fiddler Floyd "Gib" Guilbeau, and others. After one album, Ethridge departed. With guitarist Greg Harris, the group scored a minor country hit in 1980 with "White Line Fever." This edition of The Flying Burrito Brothers disbanded in 1985, but mainstay Gib Guilbeau assembled yet another group that endured until 1988.

After two early '70s albums for A&M, Rick Roberts formed Firefall in Boulder, Colorado, with guitarists Larry Burnett and Jock Bartley, bassist Mark Andes (Spirit), and drummer Mike Clarke. Signed to Atlantic Records, Firefall's eponymous debut yielded two moderate hits, "Cinderella" and "Livin' Ain't Livin'" and the near-smash "You Are the Woman," the latter two written by Roberts. Subsequent major hits included Roberts' "Just Remember I Love You" and "Strange Way," but the group never achieved another hit after 1983's "Always."

In October 1971, Chris Hillman helped form Steve Stills' Manassas with Al Perkins and Stills' touring veterans Paul Harris, Calvin "Fuzzy" Samuels, and Dallas Taylor. The group recorded two albums but disintegrated in September 1973 when Hillman, Perkins, and Harris left. At the behest of David Geffen, the head of Asylum Records, they helped form The Souther-Hillman-Furay Band with John David Souther and Richie Furay. An early associate of Glenn Frey and Jackson Browne, Souther had contributed three songs to Linda Ronstadt's *Don't Cry Now* album and coauthored three songs on The Eagles' *On the Border* album, including "The Best of My Love." Furay had been a member of The Buffalo Springfield and Poco. Intended as a "supergroup" in the tradition of Crosby, Stills and Nash, the group managed only one (major) hit with Furay's "Fallin' in Love" through two albums, disbanding in late 1975.

During the '70s, Chris Hillman recorded three solo albums, one before and two after Souther-Hillman-Furay. In 1978, he joined former Byrds Gene Clark and Roger McGuinn for touring and two albums, recording an album with McGuinn in 1980. In the early '80s, Hillman recorded two albums for the small Sugar Hill label before forming The Desert Rose Band with longtime associate Herb Pedersen in 1986. Favoring country and bluegrass, The Desert Rose Band scored four country-only hits from their debut album, including the smashes "Love Reunited," "One Step Forward," and "He's Back and I'm Blue." Subsequent smash country hits for The Desert Rose Band included "Summer Wind," "I Still Believe in You," "She Don't Love Nobody," and "Start All Over Again." The group disbanded in 1994 and, in 1996, Chris Hillman and Herb Pedersen recorded *Bakersfield Bound* for Sugar Hill Records.

GRAM PARSONS BIBLIOGRAPHY

Fong-Torres, Ben. *Hickory Wind: The Life and Times of Gram Parsons.* New York: Pocket Books, 1991; New York: St. Martin's Griffin, 1998.

The Shilos

Gram Parsons: The Early Years	Sierra	8702	'79	†
	Sierra	4215		LP/CS

The International Submarine Band

Safe at Home	LHI	12001	'68	†
	Rhino	069	'85	†

The Byrds (with Gram Parsons and Chris Hillman)

Sweetheart of the Rodeo	Columbia	9670	'68	CS/CD†
	Columbia	65150	'97	CD

The Flying Burrito Brothers

The Gilded Palace of Sin	A&M	4175	'69	†
	A&M	3122		†
Burrito Deluxe	A&M	4258	'70	†
The Flying Burrito Brothers	A&M	4295	'71	†
	Mobile Fidelity	00772	'91	CD†
Last of the Red Hot Burritos	A&M	4343	'72	CD†
Hot Burritos	A&M	8070		†
Close Up the Honky Tonks	A&M	(2)3631	'74	†
Farther Along: The Best of The Flying Burrito Brothers	A&M	5216	'88	CD
Flying Again	Columbia	33817	'75	†
Airborne	Columbia	34222	'76	†
Sin City (recorded 1976)	Relix	2052		CS/CD
Live From Tokyo	Regency	79001	'78	LP
Encounters from the West (reissue of Live from Tokyo)	Relix	2044	'91	CD
Cabin Fever (recorded 1985)	Relix	2008	'85	CD
Live from Europe	Relix	2022	'86	CD
Live from Amsterdam 1985	Relix	2090		CD
Relix's Best of the Flying Burrito Brothers	Relix	2069	'95	CD
Eye of a Hurricane	One Way	30330	'94	CD

Gram Parsons/The Flying Burrito Brothers

Sleepless Nights	A&M	4578	'76	†

The Burrito Brothers (with Gib Guilbeau)

Double Barrel	Magnum America	31	'95	CD
Back to the Sweetheart of the Rodeo	Magnum America	504	'96	CD

Swampwater and The Flying Burrito Brothers (with Gib Guilbeau and Sneaky Pete Kleinow)

Live at the Cannary	Magnum America	44	'96	CD

Gram Parsons

Cosmic American Music: The Rehearsal Tapes 1972	Magnum Archives	19	'95	CD†
GP	Reprise	2123	'73	†
Grievous Angel	Reprise	2171	'74	†
GP/Grievous Angel	Reprise	26108	'90	CD

Gram Parsons and The Fallen Angels

Live 1973	Sierra	1973	'82	†
	Sierra	4222		LP/CS
	Rhino	72726	'97	CD
Live 1973—Original Unedited Broadcast Recording	Sierra	6002		CD†

Tribute Album

Conmemoritivo: A Tribute to Gram Parsons	Rhino	71269	'93	CS/CD

Rick Roberts

Windmills	A&M	4372	'72	†
She Is a Song	A&M	4404	'73	†

Firefall

Firefall	Atlantic	18174	'76	†
	Atlantic	19125		CS†
	Rhino	70379	'92	CS/CD
Luna Sea	Atlantic	19101	'77	†
	Rhino	71925	'95	CD

Elan	Atlantic	19183	'78	†
	Rhino	71926	'95	CD
Undertow	Atlantic	16006	'80	†
	Rhino	71927	'95	CD
Clouds Across the Sun	Atlantic	16024	'81	†
Best	Atlantic	19316	'81	CS†
Break of Dawn	Atlantic	80017	'83	†
Mirror of the World	Atlantic	80120	'83	†
Greatest Hits	Rhino	71055	'92	CS/CD
You Are the Woman	Rhino	71231	'93	CS/CD

Chris Hillman

Cherokee	ABC	719	'71	†
Slippin' Away	Asylum	1062	'76	†
Clear Sailin'	Asylum	1104	'77	†
Morning Sky	Sugar Hill	3729	'83/'91	LP/CS/CD
Desert Rose	Sugar Hill	3743	'84	LP/CS/CD
Like a Hurricane	Sugar Hill	3878	'98	CD

Manassas (with Chris Hillman)

Manassas	Atlantic	(2)903	'72	†
	Atlantic	903		CD†
	Atlantic	82808	'95	CS/CD
Down the Road	Atlantic	7250	'73	CD

The Souther-Hillman-Furay Band

The Souther-Hillman-Furay Band	Asylum	1006	'74	†
Trouble in Paradise	Asylum	1036	'75	†

McGuinn, Clark and Hillman

McGuinn, Clark and Hillman	Capitol	11910	'79	†
	Capitol	16280	'83	†
	Capitol	96355	'91	CS/CD†
City	Capitol	12043	'80	†
	One Way	18503	'96	CD

McGuinn and Hillman

McGuinn and Hillman	Capitol	12108	'80	†
	One Way	18498	'96	CD

The Desert Rose Band

The Desert Rose Band	MCA	5991	'87	CS/CD†
	Curb/Warner Brothers	77570	'92	CS/CD
Running	Curb/MCA	42169	'88	CS/CD†
	Curb/Warner Brothers	77573	'92	CS/CD
Pages of Life	Curb/MCA	42332	'90	LP/CS/CD†
	Curb/Warner Brothers	77567	'92	CS/CD
One Dozen Roses—Greatest Hits	MCA	10018	'91	CS/CD†
	Curb/Warner Brothers	77571	'92	CS/CD
True Love	MCA	10407	'91	CS/CD†
	Curb/Warner Brothers	77572	'92	CS/CD
Traditional	Curb/Warner Brothers	77602	'93	CS/CD

Chris Hillman and Herb Pedersen

Bakersfield Bound	Sugar Hill	3850	'96	CD

Chris Hillman, Herb Pedersen, Tony Rice, and Larry Rice				
Out of the Woodwork	Rounder	390	'97	CS/CD

THE FOUR SEASONS

Frankie Valli (born Francis Castelluccio on May 3, 1937, in Newark, New Jersey), Bob Gaudio (born November 17, 1942, in the Bronx, New York), Tommy DeVito (born June 19, 1935, in Bellville, New Jersey), and Nick Massi (born Nicholas Macioci on September 19, 1935, in Newark).

One of the most long-lived and successful white doo-wop groups of the '60s, The Four Seasons scored a series of smash hit singles between 1962 and 1967 featuring the shrill piercing falsetto lead voice of Frankie Valli. One of the few American white groups other than The Beach Boys to challenge The Beatles, The Four Seasons became so popular that they were able to launch Valli on a successful simultaneous solo recording career in 1965. The Four Seasons and Frankie Valli enjoyed renewed success in the mid-'70s, but have since been relegated to the oldies revival circuit. The Four Seasons were inducted into the Rock and Roll Hall of Fame in 1990.

Frankie Valli started out as a solo singer in 1952 and formed The Varietones with guitarist brothers Nick and Tommy DeVito and bassist Hank Majewski around 1954. Changing their name to The Four Lovers in 1956, the group signed with RCA Victor Records and scored a minor hit with "You Are the Apple of My Eye." They subsequently languished on the lounge circuit for several years. In the meantime, another New Jersey group, originally formed in 1957, achieved a major hit as The Royal Teens with the novelty song "Short Shorts" in early 1958. Among the members were songwriter-keyboardist Bob Gaudio and, for a brief time in 1959, Al Kooper.

By 1960, Bob Gaudio and Nick Massi had replaced Nick DeVito and Hank Majewski, respectively, in The Four Lovers. With a name change to The Four Seasons around 1961, the group recorded the unsuccessful single "Bermuda" for George Goldner's Gone label before signing with Vee Jay Records with the help of writer-producer Bob Crewe. With Gaudio and Crewe acting as principal songwriters, The Four Seasons scored a top pop and rhythm-and-blues hit with Gaudio's "Sherry" in the late summer of 1962. "Big Girls Don't Cry" and "Walk Like a Man," written by Crewe and Gaudio, became top pop and smash rhythm-and-blues hits, followed by the pop-only hits "Candy Girl" (a smash), "Stay," and "Alone." Near the end of 1964, Vee Jay assembled early recordings by The Beatles and hits by The Four Seasons as *The Beatles Versus The Four Seasons,* today one of the most valuable of all rock collectors' items.

By 1964, The Four Seasons had switched to Philips Records, where the smash hits continued with Crewe and Gaudio's "Ronnie," "Save It for Me," and the top hit classic "Rag Doll," as well as "Dawn (Go Away)," "Let's Hang On," and "Working My Way Back to You." The Four Seasons' sound was so popular that the group was able to score a major hit as The Wonder Who with a dreadful version of Bob Dylan's "Don't Think Twice." They also recorded the album *The Four Seasons Sing Big Hits by Burt Bacharach . . . Hal David . . . Bob Dylan,* certainly one of the worst albums of the '60s, bad enough to make even the most casual Dylan fan cringe.

In 1965, Massi left The Four Seasons, yet the group continued to achieve hits with "I've Got You Under My Skin," "Tell It to the Rain," and "C'mon Marianne," as Valli initiated his solo recording career with the smash hit "Can't Take My Eyes Off You." In 1968, The Four Seasons attempted being progressive and socially conscious with *The Genuine Imitation Life Gazette,* but the album sold poorly. Tommy DeVito retired around 1971 and Bob Gaudio ceased performing with the group in the early '70s, taking over for Crewe as producer.

With Frankie Valli as the mainstay, The Four Seasons recorded for Mowest and Warner Brothers in the early '70s, while Valli recorded for Motown and Private Stock. Between 1974 and 1976, Valli scored smash hits with "My Eyes Adored You" and "Swearin' to God" on Private Stock, while The Four Seasons achieved smashes with "Who Loves You" and "December, 1963 (Oh, What a Night)" on Warner/Curb. The Four Seasons had no more major hits and Frankie Valli scored his last major hit (a top hit!) with the title song to the 1978 movie *Grease*. Valli and Bob Gaudio re-formed The Four Seasons in 1980 and formed FBI Records in 1984. The Four Seasons were inducted into the Rock and Roll Hall of Fame in 1990.

The Four Lovers

Joyride	RCA	1317	'56	†

The Royal Teens

Short Shorts: Golden Classics	Collectable	5094		CS/CD

The Four Seasons on Veejay

Sherry and 11 Others	VeeJay	1053	'62	†
Four Seasons' Greetings	VeeJay	1055	'63	†
Big Girls Don't Cry	VeeJay	1056	'63	†
Ain't That a Shame	VeeJay	1059	'63	†
Golden Hits	VeeJay	1065	'63	†
Stay and Other Great Hits reissued as Folk-Nanny	VeeJay	1082	'64	†
More Golden Hits	VeeJay	1088	'64	†
Girls, Girls, Girls, We Love Girls	VeeJay	1121	'65	†
Recorded Live on Stage	VeeJay	1154	'65	†

The Four Seasons and The Beatles

The Beatles Versus The Four Seasons	VeeJay	(2)30	'64	†

The Four Seasons

Dawn (Go Away)	Philips	600124	'64	†
Born to Wander	Philips	600129	'64	†
Rag Doll	Philips	600146	'64	†
The Four Seasons Entertain You	Philips	600164	'65	†
Sing Big Hits by Burt Bacharach . . . Hal David . . . Bob Dylan	Philips	600193	'65	†
	Rhino	70248	'88	CS/CD
Gold Vault of Hits	Philips	600196	'65	†
Working My Way Back to You	Philips	600201	'66	†
	Rhino	70247	'88	CS/CD
Second Vault of Golden Hits	Philips	600221	'66	†
Lookin' Back	Philips	600222	'66	†
The Four Seasons' Christmas Album	Philips	600223	'66	†
	Rhino	70234	'91	CS/CD
Christmas Album/Born to Wander	Ace	615	'95	CD
New Gold Hits	Philips	600243	'67	†
Edisione D'Oro (Gold Edition) — 29 Golden Hits	Philips	(2)6501	'68	†
The Genuine Imitation Life Gazette	Philips	600290	'68	†
	Rhino	70249	'88	CS/CD
Half and Half	Philips	600341	'70	†
Chameleon	Mowest	108	'72	†
Who Loves You	Warner Brothers	2900	'75	†
Helicon	Warner Brothers	3016	'77	†

Frankie Valli and The Four Seasons

Reunited Live	Warner/Curb	(2)3497	'81	†

Four Seasons Anthologies and Compilations

The Four Seasons Story	Private Stock	(2)7000	'75	†
Brotherhood of Man	Pickwick	3223		†
24 Original Classics	Arista	(2)8208	'84	†
25th Anniversary Collection	Rhino	(3)72998	'87	CD
Anthology	Rhino	(2)71490	'88	CS
	Rhino	71490	'88	CD
Rarities, Volume 1	Rhino	70973	'90	CS/CD
Rarities, Volume 2	Rhino	70974	'90	CS/CD
Greatest Hits, Volume 1	Rhino	70594	'91	CS/CD
Greatest Hits, Volume 2	Rhino	70595	'91	CS/CD
20 Greatest Hits: Live	Curb/Warner Brothers	77319	'90	CD
Greatest His	Curb/Warner Brothers	77304	'91	CS/CD
Hope + Glory	Curb/Warner Brothers	77546	'92	CS/CD
The Dance Album	Curb/CEMA	77634	'93	CS/CD†
Oh What a Night	Curb/Atlantic	77693	'94	CS/CD

Original Classics Collection Series

Volume 1: Sherry and 11 Other Hits	Curb/Atlantic	77695	'95	CS/CD
Volume 2: Big Girls Don't Cry and 12 Other Hits	Curb/Atlantic	77696	'95	CS/CD
Volume 3: Ain't That a Shame and 11 Other Hits	Curb/Atlantic	77697	'95	CS/CD
Volume 4: Dawn (Go Away) and 11 Other Hits	Curb/Atlantic	77698	'95	CS/CD
Volume 5: Rag Doll and 10 Other Hits	Curb/Atlantic	77699	'95	CS/CD
Volume 6: Let's Hang On and 11 Others Hits	Curb/Atlantic	77711	'95	CS/CD
Volume 7: New Gold Hits	Curb/Atlantic	77712	'95	CS/CD
Volume 8: Who Loves You	Curb/Atlantic	77713	'95	CS/CD

Frankie Valli

Solo	Philips	600247	'67	†
Timeless	Philips	600274	'68	†
Inside You	Motown	852	'75	†
Motown Superstar Series, Volume 4	Motown	5104	'81	CS/CD†
Closeup	Private Stock	2000	'75	†
Gold	Private Stock	2001	'75	†
Our Day Will Come	Private Stock	2006	'75	†
Valli	Private Stock	2017	'77	†
Lady Put the Light Out	Private Stock	7002	'78	†
Hits	Private Stock	7012	'78	†
Frankie Valli . . . Is the Word	Warner Brothers	3233	'78	†
Very Best	MCA	3198	'79	†
Heaven Above Me	MCA	5134	'80	†
Greatest Hits	Curb/Atlantic	77714	'96	CS/CD

THE FOUR TOPS

Levi Stubbs (born Levi Stubbles on June 6, 1936, in Detroit), lead vocals; Abdul "Duke" Fakir (born December 26, 1935, in Detroit); Renaldo "Obie" Benson (born circa 1937 in Detroit); and Lawrence Payton, Jr. (born circa 1938 in Detroit; died June 20, 1997, in Southfield, Michigan).

Performing with their original members for over forty years, The Four Tops were the most stable and consistent vocal group to emerge from Motown Records in the '60s. Scoring a series of major pop and smash rhythm-and-blues hits between 1964 and 1967, almost all written by the songwriting-production team of Brian Holland, Lamont Dozier, and Eddie Holland, The Four Tops featured the gruff pleading voice of lead vocalist Levi Stubbs. Acclaimed for their polished close-harmony singing, precise choreography, and complex stage routines, The Four Tops were the most popular Motown act in Great Britain, yet they were overshadowed by The Supremes in the United States. Persevering despite the departure of Holland-Dozier-Holland (H-D-H) from Motown in 1967, the group recorded for a number of different labels beginning in 1972 while maintaining their status as a popular supper club act. The Four Tops were inducted into the Rock and Roll Hall of Fame in 1990.

Born and raised in Detroit, the members of The Four Tops began singing together as high school students and later performed in local nightclubs. Known as The Four Aims since their formation in 1953, the group changed their name to The Four Tops upon signing with Chess Records in 1956. Their sole single for the label failed to sell, and they subsequently recorded for Red Top, Riverside, and Columbia. Performing at top nightclubs since the '50s, The Four Tops toured with the Billy Eckstine revue in the early '60s. Signing with the infant Motown Records aggregation in March 1963, The Four Tops initially recorded for the company's short-lived jazz-oriented Workshop label, but their debut album was never released.

Switching to the parent label Motown and assigned to the songwriting-production team of Brian Holland, Lamont Dozier, and Eddie Holland (known as H-D-H), The Four Tops scored major rhythm-and-blues and pop hits with H-D-H's "Baby I Need Your Loving" and William Stevenson's "Ask the Lonely" from their debut album. Their *Second Album* yielded a top pop and rhythm-and-blues hit with the classic "I Can't Help Myself (Sugar Pie, Honey Bunch)" and smash R&B and major pop hits with "It's the Same Old Song" and "Something About You," all written by H-D-H. "Shake Me, Wake Me (When It's Over)" became a smash R&B and major pop hit and "Reach Out, I'll Be There" proved a top pop and rhythm-and-blues hit, as well as a top British hit. The Four Tops subsequently achieved smash crossover hits with "Standing in the Shadows of Love" and "Bernadette," and major R&B and moderate pop hits with "Seven Rooms of Gloom" and "You Keep Running Away."

The Holland-Dozier-Holland team left Motown in late 1967 and, by 1968, The Four Tops were covering The Left Banke's "Walk Away Renee" and Tim Hardin's "If I Were a Carpenter." They did not achieve another major pop hit until 1970, when they scored with a remake of "It's All in the Game," and Smokey Robinson and Frank Wilson's "Still Water (Love)." In the early '70s, The Four Tops recorded three albums with The Supremes, scoring a major pop and R&B hit with them on a remake of "River Deep—Mountain High."

Renaldo "Obie" Benson coauthored Marvin Gaye's smash "What's Going On" and The Four Tops managed a rhythm-and-blues near-smash with "(It's the Way) Nature Planned It" in 1972. However, when Berry Gordy moved the Motown organization to Los Angeles in 1972, they declined to go. They signed with ABC-Dunhill Records, where they worked with Dennis Lambert and Brian Potter and achieved major pop and smash R&B hits with "Keeper of the Castle," "Ain't No Woman (Like the One I've Got)," and "Are You Man Enough" from the movie *Shaft in Africa*. Subsequent rhythm-and-blues smashes through 1976 included "Sweet Understanding Love," "One Chain Don't Make No Prison," and "Midnight Flower" for Dunhill and "Catfish" for ABC.

The Four Tops scored another top R&B and near-smash pop hit with "When She Was My Girl" in 1981 on Casablanca. Levi Stubbs was the voice of the voracious plant Audrey II in the 1986 musical movie *Little Shop of Horrors.* Following their sensational appearance with The Temptations at the twenty-fifth anniversary celebration of Motown Records in 1983, The Four Tops re-signed with their old label and toured with The Temptations. However, their next moderate hit did not come until "Indestructible" in 1988 on Arista Records. The Four Tops were inducted into the Rock and Roll Hall of Fame in 1990. They recorded a Christmas album for 1995 release, but, on June 20, 1997, Lawrence Payton died at his home in the Detroit suburb of Southfield of liver cancer at the age of 59.

The Four Tops

The Four Tops	Motown	622	'65	†
	Motown	5122	'89	CS/CD†
Second Album	Motown	634	'65	†
	Motown	5264	'89	CS/CD†
On Top	Motown	647	'66	†
	Motown	5444		CS/CD†
Live!	Motown	654	'66	†
	Motown	5258		CS/CD
On Broadway	Motown	657	'67	†
Reach Out	Motown	660	'67	†
	Motown	5149	'89	CS/CD
Yesterday's Dream	Motown	669	'68	†
Now	Motown	675	'69	†
	Motown	5466	'90	CS/CD†
Soul Spin	Motown	695	'69	†
Still Waters Run Deep	Motown	704	'70	†
	Motown	5224	'89	CS/CD
Changing Times	Motown	721	'70	†
	Motown	5478	'90	CS/CD†
Nature Planned It	Motown	748	'72	†
	Motown	5446	'89	CS/CD†
Keeper of the Castle	Dunhill	50129	'72	†
	Motown	5428	'89	CS/CD†
Main Street People	Dunhill	50144	'73	†
Meeting of the Minds	Dunhill	50166	'74	†
Live and in Concert	Dunhill	50188	'74	†
	MCA	20892	'95	CS/CD
Night Lights Harmony	ABC	862	'75	†
Catfish	ABC	968	'76	†
The Show Must Go On	ABC	1014	'77	†
At the Top	ABC/MCA	1092	'78	†
Tonight	Casablanca	7258	'81	†
One More Mountain	Casablanca	7266	'82	†
Back Where I Belong	Motown	6066	'83	†
Magic	Motown	6130	'85	†
Indestructible	Arista	8492	'88	LP/CS/CD†
Christmas Here with You	Motown	0585	'95	CS/CD

Four Tops Reissues, Anthologies, and Compilations

The Four Tops/Second Album	Motown	8127	'86	CD†
Reach Out/The Four Tops	Motown	(2)6075		CS†
Reach Out/Still Waters Run Deep	Motown	8007	'86	CD†
Greatest Hits	Motown	662	'67	†
	Motown	5209		CS/CD
Greatest Hits, Volume 2	Motown	740	'71	†
Best	Motown	(2)764	'73	†

Anthology	Motown	(3)809	'74	LP/CS
	Motown	(2)809		CD
Motown Superstar Series, Volume 14	Motown	5114		CS†
Great Songs and Performances That Inspired the Motown 25th Anniversary TV Show	Motown	5314	'83	CS/CD
Motown Legends	Motown	5363		CS†
Compact Command Performances (19 Greatest Hits)	Motown	9042	'84	CD†
The Ultimate Collection	Motown	0825	'97	CS/CD
Until You Love Someone: More of the Best (1965–1970)	Rhino	71183	'93	CS/CD
Motown Legends	Esx	8528	'95	CS/CD
I Can't Help Myself	Pickwick	3381	'75	†
Greatest Hits (1972–1976)	MCA	27019	'82	CS/CD
When She Was My Girl	Casablanca	514127	'92	CS/CD
The Four Tops and The Supremes				
The Magnificent Seven	Motown	717	'70	†
	Motown	5123		CS/CD†
The Return of the Magnificent Seven	Motown	736	'71	†
Dynamite	Motown	745	'72	†
The Best of The Supremes and The Four Tops	Motown	5491	'91	CS/CD

ARETHA FRANKLIN

Born March 25, 1942, in Memphis, Tennessee.

The most exciting, inspiring, and influential female soul singer of the '60s, Aretha Franklin started her career as a gospel singer touring with her father C. L. Franklin's evangelistic troupe as a teenager. Her secular career, launched in 1960, languished for a number of years at Columbia Records, where her undeniably powerful and emotive vocal style was constricted by inappropriate material, production, and arrangements. She ultimately found sympathetic treatment in the late '60s under veteran producer Jerry Wexler at Atlantic Records, where she recorded a series of classic pop and rhythm-and-blues hits and best-selling albums, including *I Never Loved a Man the Way I Love You* and *Lady Soul*. Acclaimed at that time as the most popular female artist in rock music, Franklin endured a fallow period before coming back in the early '70s with the astonishing *Live at Fillmore West* and gospel *Amazing Grace* albums. Subsequently recording a number of uneven albums under a variety of producers, she reemerged in the mid-'80s with the rocking *Who's Zoomin' Who?* album. Aretha Franklin was inducted into the Rock and Roll Hall of Fame in 1987.

Born the daughter of well-known evangelist preacher Cecil "C. L." Franklin, Aretha Franklin was raised in Buffalo and Detroit, where she began singing in her father's New Bethel Baptist Church Choir with sisters Carolyn and Erma at the age of eight. By fourteen, she was a featured vocalist on his evangelistic tour, performing on the gospel circuit for four years and recording *The Gospel Sound of Aretha Franklin* (now *Aretha Gospel*) for the Checker subsidiary of Chess Records.

In 1960, with the encouragement of her father and Teddy Wilson bassist Major "Mule" Holly, Aretha Franklin auditioned for Columbia Records' John Hammond, who immediately signed her to a five-year contract. She toured the upper echelon of the so-called "chitlin circuit" as Hammond guided her in the direction of classic jazz and blues singers such as Bessie Smith and Billie Holiday. She managed major rhythm-and-blues hits with "Today I Sing the Blues" and "Won't Be Long" from her debut album and "Operation Heartbreak," and a moderate pop hit with "Rock-A-Bye Your Baby with a Dixie Melody," but sub-

ARETHA FRANKLIN (CORBIS-BETTMANN)

sequent recordings of Tin Pan Alley—style material using glossy pop arrangements met with little success. Of her Columbia albums, her tribute to Dinah Washington, *Unforgettable,* was perhaps her best.

In November 1966, Aretha Franklin switched to Atlantic Records, where she was personally supervised by veteran producer Jerry Wexler. Her first Atlantic single, "I Never Loved a Man (The Way I Love You)," recorded in Muscle Shoals, Alabama, with Franklin on piano and King Curtis on saxophone, became a top R&B and near-smash pop hit. Her debut album also contained favorites such as "Do Right Woman—Do Right Man" and "Dr. Feelgood," and yielded the top pop and rhythm-and-blues hit classic "Respect," written by Otis Redding. After the smash pop and R&B hit "Baby I Love You," *Lady Soul,* perhaps her finest album ever, produced four crossover hits: the smashes "(You Make Me Feel Like) A Natural Woman" (by Carole King and Gerry Goffin), "Chain of Fools" (by Don Covay) and "(Sweet, Sweet Baby) Since You've Been Gone" (coauthored by Franklin), and the major hit "Ain't No Way," written by sister Carolyn Franklin.

In the late '60s, Aretha Franklin's sisters Carolyn and Erma inaugurated their own recording careers. Carolyn had written "Baby Baby Baby" (a minor rhythm-and-blues hit for Anna King and Bobby Byrd in 1964) and "Don't Wait Too Long" (a major R&B hit for Bettye Swann in 1965). She managed two moderate R&B hits in 1969 and 1970. Erma scored a smash rhythm-and-blues hit in 1967 with "Piece of My Heart," arranged by Carolyn. The song was later popularized by Janis Joplin.

Aretha Franklin achieved four crossover smashes from *Aretha Now* with her own "Think," "The House That Jack Built," Burt Bacharach and Hal David's "I Say a Little Prayer," and Don Covay and Steve Cropper's "See Saw," but subsequently experienced personal and marital problems. In 1969, she had major pop and smash rhythm-and-blues hits with Robbie Robertson's "The Weight," "I Can't See Myself Leaving You," Lennon and McCartney's "Eleanor Rigby," and "Call Me." In 1970, she hit with "Spirit in the Dark" and Ben E. King's "Don't Play That Song," disbanding her sixteen-piece band that fall in favor of a tighter combo of sessions players directed by saxophonist King Curtis. This unit recorded the astounding *Live at Fillmore West* album, which featured a surprise appearance by Ray Charles and yielded a smash crossover hit with Simon and Garfunkel's "Bridge Over Troubled Water." Following the smash "Spanish Harlem," Franklin registered four hits from *Young, Gifted and Black,* including the smashes "Rock Steady" and "Day Dreaming."

In early 1972, Aretha Franklin returned to her gospel roots, recording the double-record set *Amazing Grace* at the New Temple Missionary Baptist Church in Watts, California, with perennial gospel favorite Reverend James Cleveland and his Southern California

Community Choir. The album was a surprise success, becoming possibly the best-selling gospel album of all time. Smash rhythm-and-blues hits for Franklin continued with "All the King's Horses," "Master of Eyes," Carolyn Franklin's "Angel," Stevie Wonder's "Until You Come Back to Me," "I'm in Love," "Ain't Nothing Like the Real Thing," and "Without Love," but only "Until You Come Back to Me" became a pop smash.

In 1976, Aretha Franklin worked with songwriter-producer Curtis Mayfield on the soundtrack to the movie *Sparkle,* which produced a top R&B and smash pop hit with "Something He Can Feel" and the R&B near-smash "Look into Your Heart." However, subsequent albums for Atlantic sold less well. In 1980, she appeared in *The Blues Brothers* film and switched to Arista Records for the rhythm-and-blues smashes "United Together" and "Love All the Hurt Away," the latter recorded with George Benson. In the early '80s, she scored a major pop and top R&B hit with "Jump to It," written and produced by Luther Vandross.

Aretha Franklin reestablished her popularity with the pop audience with 1985's *Who's Zoomin' Who?* album. It yielded the crossover smashes "Freeway of Love" and "Who's Zoomin' Who" and the major pop hits "Sisters Are Doin' It for Themselves" (recorded with The Eurythmics) and "Another Night." Major pop hits continued in 1986 with "Jumpin' Jack Flash" and "Jimmy Lee," with 1987's duet with George Michael on "I Knew You Were Waiting (For Me)" becoming a top pop and smash rhythm-and-blues hit. Another gospel album, *One Lord, One Faith, One Baptism,* failed to match the success of *Amazing Grace.* Inducted into the Rock and Roll Hall of Fame in 1987, Franklin scored pop hits with "Through the Storm," recorded with Elton John, and "It Isn't, It Wasn't, It Ain't Never Gonna Be," recorded with Whitney Houston, in 1989. She ceased touring in the '90s, yet continued to record and appear on television. In 1994, Aretha Franklin scored a smash rhythm-and-blues and major pop hit with "Willing to Forgive." She subsequently formed her own record labels, World Class Records and Alf Records, in 1995 and 1996, respectively.

ARETHA FRANKLIN BIBLIOGRAPHY

Bego, Mark. *Aretha Franklin: The Queen of Soul.* New York: St. Martin's Press, 1989.

Aretha Franklin

The Gospel Sound of Aretha Franklin	Checker	10009	'64	†
reissued as Aretha Gospel	Chess	91521	'91	LP/CS/CD

Reverend C. L. and Aretha Franklin

Never Grow Old	Chess	91538	'73	CS

Aretha Franklin on Columbia Records

Aretha (with Ray Bryant Trio)	Columbia	8412	'61	†
reissued as The First 12 Sides	Columbia	31953	'73/'88	CS/CD
Electrifying	Columbia	8561	'62	†
Tender, Moving, Swinging	Columbia	8676	'62	†
Laughing on the Outside	Columbia	8879	'63	†
Unforgettable	Columbia	8963	'64	†
Runnin' Out of Fools	Columbia	9081	'64	†
Yeah!!!	Columbia	9151	'65	†
Aretha Sings the Blues (recorded 1961–1965)	Columbia	40105	'85	CS/CD
Aretha After Hours (recorded 1962–1965)	Columbia	40708	'87	CS/CD
Soul Sister	Columbia	9321	'66	†
Take It Like You Give It	Columbia	9429	'67	†
Greatest Hits	Columbia	9473	'67	†

Take a Look	Columbia	9554	'67	†
Greatest Hits, Volume 2	Columbia	9601	'68	†
Aretha Franklin	Columbia	(2)4	'68	†
Soft and Beautiful	Columbia	9776	'69	†
Today I Sing the Blues	Columbia	9956	'70	†
Queen of Soul	Harmony	11274	'68	†
Once in a Lifetime	Harmony	11349	'69	†
2 Sides of Love	Harmony	11418	'70	†
Greatest Hits, 1960–1965	Harmony	30606	'71	†
In the Beginning: The World of Aretha Franklin (1960–1967)	Columbia	(2)31355	'72	†
The Legendary Queen of Soul	Columbia	(2)37377	'81	†
Sweet Bitter Love	Columbia	38042	'82	CS/CD
Jazz to Soul	Columbia/Legacy	(2)48515	'92	CS/CD

Aretha Franklin on Atlantic Records

I Never Loved a Man the Way I Love You	Atlantic	8139	'67	LP/CS/CD†
	Rhino	8139		CS/CD†
	Rhino	71934	'95	CD
	Mobile Fidelity	574	'93	CD
Aretha Arrives	Atlantic	8150	'67	†
	Rhino	71274	'93	CS/CD
Lady Soul	Atlantic	8176	'68	LP/CS/CD†
	Rhino	8176	'88	CS/CD†
	Rhino	71933	'95	CD
Aretha Now	Atlantic	8186	'68	†
	Rhino	71273	'93	CS/CD
Aretha Now/Lady Soul	Mobile Fidelity	623	'95	CD
Aretha in Paris	Atlantic	8207	'68	†
	Rhino	71852	'94	CD
Soul '69	Atlantic	8212	'69	†
	Rhino	71523	'93	CD
Aretha's Gold	Atlantic	8227	'69	†
	Atlantic	81445		CD†
	Rhino	8227		CS/CD†
This Girl's in Love with You	Atlantic	8248	'70	†
	Rhino	71524	'93	CD
Spirit in the Dark	Atlantic	8265	'70	†
	Rhino	71525	'93	CD
Aretha's Greatest Hits	Atlantic	8295	'71	†
Live at Fillmore West	Atlantic	7205	'71	†
	Rhino	71526	'93	CD
Young, Gifted and Black	Atlantic	7213	'72	†
	Rhino	71527	'93	CD
Amazing Grace	Atlantic	(2)906	'72	LP/CS/CD†
	Rhino	(2)906		CS/CD
Hey, Now, Hey (The Other Side of the Sky)	Atlantic	7265	'73	†
	Rhino	71853	'94	CD
Let Me in Your Life	Atlantic	7292	'74	†
	Rhino	71854	'94	CD
With Everything I Feel in Me	Atlantic	18116	'74	†
You	Atlantic	18151	'75	†

Sparkle	Atlantic	18176	'76	†
	Rhino	71148	'92	CS/CD
Sweet Passion	Atlantic	19102	'77	†
Almighty Fire	Atlantic	19161	'78	†
La Diva	Atlantic	19248	'79	†
Aretha's Jazz (reissue of "Soul '69" and "Hey, Now, Hey")	Atlantic	81230	'84	CS/CD†
	Rhino	81230		CS/CD
Best	Atlantic	81280	'85	LP/CS/CD†
	Rhino	81280		CS/CD†
30 Greatest Hits	Atlantic	(2)81668	'86	LP/CS/CD†
	Rhino	(2)81668		CS/CD
The Delta Meets Detroit: Aretha's Blues	Rhino/Atlantic	72942	'98	CD

Aretha Franklin on Arista Records

Aretha	Arista	9538	'79	†
	Arista	8556	'88	CS/CD
Love All the Hurt Away	Arista	9552	'81	†
Jump to It	Arista	9602	'82	†
Get It Right	Arista	8019	'83	†
Who's Zoomin' Who?	Arista	8286	'85	CS/CD
Aretha Franklin	Arista	8442	'86	CD†
One Lord, One Faith, One Baptism	Arista	(2)8497	'87	LP/CS/CD†
Through the Storm	Arista	8572	'89	LP/CS/CD†
What You See Is What You Get	Arista	8628	'91	CS/CD†
Queen of Soul	Arista	18987	'97	CS/CD
A Rose Is Still a Rose	Arista	18987	'98	CS/CD

Aretha Franklin Anthologies and Compilations on Rhino Records

Queen of Soul	Rhino	(4)71063	'92	CS/CD
Chain of Fools	Rhino	71429		CS/CD†
Very Best, Volume 1	Rhino	71598	'94	CS/CD
Very Best, Volume 2	Rhino	71599	'94	CS/CD

THE FUGS

Ed Sanders (born August 17, 1939, in Kansas City, Missouri), guitar, vocals; Naphtali "Tuli" Kupferberg (born September 28, 1928, in New York City), vocals; and Ken Weaver (born Galveston, Texas), vocals, drums.

Organized by two Beat-generation poets, The Fugs sought to stir '60s audiences with outrageous and iconoclastic poetry, satire, and outright obscenity in their songs concerned with sex, drugs, and politics. One of the earliest rock satire groups and certainly the first "underground" group, The Fugs' pioneering efforts paved the way for the premeditated offensiveness of Frank Zappa's Mothers of Invention, Iggy Pop and The Stooges, Alice Cooper, and the late '70s "punk-rockers," as well as the silliness of Flo and Eddie and Cheech and Chong.

Conceived by Beat poets Ed Sanders and Tuli Kupferberg near the end of 1964, The Fugs also included poet-drummer Ken Weaver and a host of guitarists, bassists, keyboard players, and other musicians. Sanders, a former classical languages major at New York University, had published *Poem from Jail* in 1963 and served as editor of *Fuck You* and as owner-manager of the Peace Eye Bookstore on New York's Lower East Side. Kupferberg, an avowed anarchist, had published *Snow Job: Poems: 1946–1959* in 1959.

Debuting at Greenwich Village's Folklore Center, the ever-changing Fugs later occupied the Players Theater on MacDougal Street, logging some 900 consecutive performances there. Aided by multi-instrumentalist Peter Stampfel and guitarist Steve Weber of The Holy Modal Rounders (best known for "If You Want to Be a Bird" from the 1969 soundtrack *Easy Rider*), The Fugs' debut album was recorded for the small Broadside label. It included songs such as "Slum Goddess," "I Couldn't Get High," "Boobs a Lot," and "Nothing." Their second album, recorded for the avant-garde jazz label ESP, contained Sanders' "Group Grope" and "Dirty Old Man," Kupferberg's antiwar "Kill for Peace," and the uncommonly lyrical "Morning, Morning," composed by Kupferberg and recorded by Richie Havens on his *Mixed Bag* album. *The Virgin Fugs* sported Fugs classics such as "Caca Rock," "Coca Cola Douche," and "New Amphetamine Shriek."

Along with the MC5, The Fugs were one of the most politically active rock groups, appearing at demonstrations at the Pentagon and Democratic National Convention in 1968. Seemingly on the verge of a major breakthrough with their signing to the major label Reprise, The Fugs managed only modest sales. Their second album for the label featured "Johnny Pissoff Meets the Red Angel," "Burial Waltz," and "National Haiku Contest." By late 1969, The Fugs had disbanded. Ken Weaver returned to the Southwest, whereas Sanders recorded two obscure country albums for Reprise. Tuli Kupferberg recorded one album before compiling the book *Listen to the Mockingbird: Satiric Songs to Tunes You Know,* published in 1973. Ed Sanders returned to writing with 1971's *The Family,* chronicling the story of the Charlie Manson commune, and *Tales of Beatnik Glory,* published in 1975. Moving to Woodstock, New York, where he involved himself in various social causes, he presented the irreverent two-hour "Karen Silkwood Cantata" locally in 1979. Sanders continued to write poetry in the '80s and '90s, and he and Kupferberg re-formed The Fugs in the mid-'80s, recording for the New Rose and Gazell labels. In 1994, the two reunited to undermine the Woodstock II Festival at an alternative site in upstate New York with Country Joe McDonald and Alan Ginsberg.

TULI KUPFERBERG BIBLIOGRAPHY

Kupferberg, Tuli. *Snow Job: Poems: 1946–1959.* New York: Pup Press, 1959.

————. *First Glance: Childhood Creations of the Famous.* Maplewood, NJ: Hammond, 1978.

————, with Robert Bashlow. *1001 Ways to Beat the Draft.* New York: G. Layton, 1965.

————, and Sylvia Topp. *As They Were: Celebrated People's Pictures.* New York: Links, 1973.

ED SANDERS BIBLIOGRAPHY

Sanders, Ed. *Poem from Jail.* San Francisco: City Lights, 1963.

————. *Peace Eye.* Buffalo: Frontier Press, 1965.

————. *Shards of God.* New York: Grove Press, 1970.

————. *The Family: The Story of Charles Manson's Dune Buggy Attack Battalion.* New York: Dutton, 1971; New York: Avon, 1972.

————. *Tales of Beatnik Glory.* New York: Stonehill, 1975.

————. *Investigative Poetry.* San Francisco: City Lights, 1976.

————. *20,000 A.D.* North Atlantic Books, 1976.

————. *Fame and Love in New York.* Berkeley, CA: Turtle Isle Foundation, 1980.

————. *The Z-D Generation.* Barrytown, NY: Station Hill Press, 1981.

————. *Thirsting for Peace in a Raging Century: Selected Poems, 1960–1985.* Minneapolis: Coffee House Press, 1987.

————. *The Family: The Manson Group and Its Aftermath.* New York: New American Library, 1989.

————. *Hymn To The Rebel Cafe.* Santa Rosa: Black Sparrow Press, 1993.

The Fugs

Ballads of Contemporary Protest, Point of Views, and General Dissatisfaction	Broadside	304	'66	†
reissued as The Fugs' First Album	ESP	1018	'66	†
	Fantasy	9668	'94	CD
also reissued as Slum Goddess	ESP	1018		†
The Fugs	ESP	1028	'66	†
reissued as Kill for Peace	ESP	1028		†
reissued as The Fugs' Second Album	Fantasy	9669	'94	CD
The Virgin Fugs: For Adult Minds Only	ESP	1038	'67	†
Fugs Four, Rounder's Score	ESP	2018	'75	†
Tenderness Junction	Reprise	6280	'68	†
It Crawled Into My Hand, Honest	Reprise	6305	'68	†
Belle of Avenue A	Reprise	6359	'69	†
Golden Filth	Reprise	6396	'70	†
Best of the Fugs	Adelphi	4116		†
Refuse to Be Burnt Out			'85	†
	Fugs	139	'95	CD
Songs from a Portable Forest	Gazell	2003	'91	CS/CD
The Fugs	Fugs	121	'93	CD
The Real Woodstock Festival	Big Beat	160	'96	CD

Tuli Kupferberg

No Deposit, No Return	ESP	1035	'67	†
Tuli and Friends	Shimmy Disc		'89	†

Ed Sanders

Sanders' Truckstop	Reprise	6374	'70	†
Beer Cans on the Moon	Reprise	2105	'72	†
Songs in Ancient Greek	Olufsen	5073	'92	CD

MARVIN GAYE

Born Marvin Gay, Jr., on April 2, 1939, in Washington, D.C.; died April 1, 1984, in Los Angeles.

In a career that spanned the entire history of rhythm-and-blues, from '50s doo-wop to '80s soul, Marvin Gaye helped define the Motown sound and recorded some of the organization's most enduring hits of the '60s and '70s. Recording some of the label's most personal and engaging songs, Gaye made a graceful transition from early gospel-style recordings to a pop-oriented sound that emphasized his smooth, sensual tenor voice. The top sex symbol among black male singers throughout his career, he was one of soul music's most charismatic yet enigmatic figures and one of its most important stylists, influencing both black and white male vocalists. Gaye entered the second phase of his Motown career with 1971's *What's Going On* album, the first by a Motown artist to be produced outside the supervision of the company's staff of songwriter-producers. Opening the door for other independent productions by Motown artists, most notably Stevie Wonder, *What's Going On* was the first "concept" album by a black artist and its success paved the way for other black artists to explore the form. Furthermore, in its poignant and passionate concern with urban decay, ecological crises, and spiritual impoverishment, the album helped expand soul music's boundaries into areas of social concern. Gaye switched to straightforward romantic mate-rial with 1973's *Let's Get It On,* one of the most erotic albums ever recorded. Subsequently experiencing diminished popularity, he reemerged with the potent sensual *Midnight Love* al-bum in 1982, but was killed by his father in 1984. Marvin Gaye was inducted into the Rock and Roll Hall of Fame in 1987.

Raised in Washington, D.C., Marvin Gaye first sang solos with his father's church choir at the age of three. During high school, he studied piano while also learning to play drums. In the mid-'50s, he was a member of the local vocal group, The Rainbows, whose member-ship included Don Covay and Billy Stewart. Gaye made his first recordings in 1957 as a member of The Marquees, who were drafted to replace the original members of The Moonglows in 1958. Spotted performing with the group in 1961 by Berry Gordy, Jr., Gaye was signed to the fledgling family of Motown labels. He initially served as a sessions drum-mer, later toured with The Miracles for six months, and cowrote Martha and The Vandellas' "Dancing in the Streets" with William Stevenson.

Marvin Gaye started recording solo for the Tamla label in 1961, scoring his first near-smash rhythm-and-blues and moderate pop hit with "Stubborn Kind of Fellow," recorded with Martha and The Vandellas, in late 1962. A string of major hits in both the rhythm-and-blues and pop fields followed with "Hitch Hike" and "Pride and Joy" (which he cowrote) and Holland-Dozier-Holland's "Can I Get a Witness." A more pop-oriented sound emerged in 1964 for the crossover hits "Try It Baby" (by Berry Gordy, Jr.) and "You're a Wonderful One," the overlooked "Baby, Don't Do It," and the smash "How Sweet It Is to Be Loved by You," all written by Holland-Dozier-Holland.

Marvin Gaye began a series of recordings with Motown organization female singers in 1964 with Mary Wells. The duo produced the major two-sided hit "What's the Matter with You, Baby"/"Once Upon a Time." Gaye and Kim Weston had a minor hit in late 1964 with "What Good Am I Without You" and a smash crossover hit in 1967 with "It Takes Two."

Established as a singles artist by 1965, Marvin Gaye continued his hit-making ways with "I'll Be Doggone" and "Ain't That Peculiar," both cowritten by Smokey Robinson, and the definitive top-hit version of Barrett Strong and Norman Whitfield's "I Heard It Through the Grapevine," recorded a year earlier by Gladys Knight and The Pips. Subsequent crossover hits included "Too Busy Thinking About My Baby" and "That's the Way Love Is."

In 1967, Marvin Gaye began teaming with Tammi Terrell, recording three albums with her through 1969. Their smash rhythm-and-blues and pop hits of the period included four Nicholas Ashford–Valerie Simpson compositions, "Ain't No Mountain High Enough," "Your Precious Love," "Ain't Nothing Like the Real Thing," and "You're All I Need to Get By," as well as "If I Could Build My World Around You." However, Gaye ceased touring after Terrell collapsed in his arms on stage in 1969. She died from a brain tumor on March 16, 1970, in Philadelphia.

After a protracted period of seclusion, Marvin Gaye reemerged to demand more inde-pendence from the Motown organization. Eschewing the rigid singles format, he recorded and produced *What's Going On,* which featured sophisticated string and horn arrangements. The album, which revealed Gaye's growing social and spiritual concerns, was reluctantly released in mid-1971. With all songs either written or cowritten by Gaye, the album ironi-cally became one of Motown's best-selling albums, yielding top rhythm-and-blues and smash pop singles with "What's Going On," "Mercy, Mercy Me (The Ecology)," and "Inner City Blues (Make Me Wanna Holler)." He followed up the stunning success of *What's Going On* with the largely instrumental soundtrack to the movie *Trouble Man,* which yielded a smash crossover hit with the title song.

In 1973, Marvin Gaye cowrote, coproduced and recorded *Let's Get It On.* A dramatic contrast to his previous effort, the album shunned social commentary in favor of sensual, romantic material. The title song became a top rhythm-and-blues and pop hit, and the al-bum also yielded the two-sided hit "Come Get to This"/"You Sure Love to Ball." Later that year, Gaye teamed with Diana Ross for an album and the hits "You're a Special Part of Me" (a rhythm-and-blues smash), "My Mistake (Was to Love You)" and "Don't Knock My Love."

In early 1974, Marvin Gaye returned to live performance at the Oakland (California) Coliseum, which resulted in *Marvin Gaye Live!*. Subsequent '70s successes included the top R&B and major pop hit "I Want You" and the discofied "Got to Give It Up (Part I)," a top pop and R&B hit taken from his best-selling *Live at the London Palladium* album. During 1979, bankrupt and the subject of divorce proceedings, Marvin Gaye issued the embittered double-record set *Here, My Dear,* with royalties assigned to his ex-wife.

Marvin Gaye moved to Europe in 1980, eventually settling in Belgium. He negotiated his release from his Motown contract and signed with Columbia Records in 1982. His debut for the label, *Midnight Love,* was recorded in Belgium and became his best selling album, yielding a top R&B and smash pop hit with "Sexual Healing." He returned to the United States to tour in support of the album in 1983, but on April 1, 1984, while in the midst of recording material for a new album, he was shot to death by his father at his parents' home in Los Angeles. The posthumous *Dream of a Lifetime* produced a rhythm-and-blues smash with "Sanctified Lady." Marvin Gaye was inducted into the Rock and Roll Hall of Fame in 1987. In 1992, his daughter Nona launched her own recording career on Third Stone Records. Motown Records issued a tribute album to Marvin Gaye in 1995.

MARVIN GAYE BIBLIOGRAPHY

Davis, Sharon. *I Heard It Through the Grapevine: Marvin Gaye, The Biography.* Edinburgh: Mainstream, 1991.

Ritz, David. *Divided Soul: The Life of Marvin Gaye.* New York: McGraw-Hill, 1985.

Marvin Gaye

Soulful Moods of Marvin Gaye	Tamla	221	'62	†
	Motown	0370	'94	CS/CD
That Stubborn Kinda Fellow	Tamla	239	'63	†
	Motown	5218	'89	CD†
Live on Stage	Tamla	242	'63	†
When I'm Alone I Cry	Tamla	251	'64	†
	Motown	0356	'94	CS/CD
How Sweet It Is to Be Loved by You	Tamla	258	'65	†
	Motown	5419	'89	CD†
Hello Broadway	Tamla	259	'65	†
	Motown	5493	'91	CS/CD†
A Tribute to the Great Nat King Cole	Tamla	261	'66	†
	Motown	5216	'89	CS/CD
Moods of Marvin Gaye	Tamla	266	'66	†
	Motown	5296	'89	CS/CD
In the Groove	Tamla	285	'68	†
reissued as I Heard It Through the Grapevine	Motown	5395	'89	CS/CD
M.P.G.	Tamla	292	'69	†
	Motown	5125	'89	CD†
That's the Way Love Is	Tamla	299	'69	†
	Motown	5422	'89	CD†
What's Going On	Tamla	310	'71	†
	Motown	9036		CD†
	Motown	5339		CS/CD†
	Motown	0022	'94	CS/CD

Trouble Man (soundtrack)	Tamla	322	'72	†
	Motown	5241	'89	CS/CD
Let's Get It On	Tamla	329	'73	†
	Motown	9006		CD†
	Motown	5192	'89	CS/CD
Marvin Gaye Live!	Tamla	333	'74	†
	Motown	9004		CD†
	Motown	5181		CS/CD
I Want You	Tamla	342	'76	†
	Motown	5292	'89	CS/CD
Live at the London Palladium	Tamla	(2)352	'77	†
	Tamla	6191		CD†
	Motown	(2)5259		CS
	Motown	5259		CD
Here, My Dear	Tamla	(2)364	'79	†
	Motown	6310	'94	CS/CD
Love Man	Tamla	369	'80	†
In Our Lifetime: The Final Motown Sessions	Tamla	374	'81	†
	Motown	6379	'94	CS/CD
Midnight Love	Columbia	38197	'82/'85	CS/CD
Midnight Love and the Sexual Healing Sessions	Columbia/Legacy	(2)65546	'98	CS/CD
Dream of a Lifetime	Columbia	39916	'85	CS/CD
Romantically Yours	Columbia	40208	'85	CS/CD
The Last Concert Tour	Giant	24436	'91	CS/CD

Marvin Gaye Reissues (2 LPs on 1 CD)

I Heard It Through the Grapevine/I Want You	Motown	8110	'86	CD†
Let's Get It On/What's Going On	Motown	8113	'86	CD†
Trouble Man (ST)/M.P.G.	Motown	8136	'86	CD†
That Stubborn Kinda Fellow/How Sweet It Is to Be Loved by You	Motown	8157		CD†
Moods of Marvin Gaye/That's the Way Love Is	Motown	8161		CD†

Marvin Gaye and Mary Wells

Marvin and Mary Together	Motown	613	'64	†
	Motown	5260		CS/CD

Marvin Gaye and Kim Weston

It Takes Two	Tamla	270	'66	†

Marvin Gaye and Tammi Terrell

United	Tamla	277	'67	†
	Motown	9009		CD†
	Motown	5200		CS/CD†
You're All I Need to Get By	Tamla	284	'68	†
	Motown	5142	'89	CS/CD†
United/You're All I Need To Get By	Motown	8147		CD†
Easy	Tamla	294	'69	†
	Motown	5394	'90	CS/CD†
Greatest Hits	Tamla	302	'70	†
	Motown	9089		CD†
	Motown	5225		CS/CD
Motown Superstar Series, Volume 2	Motown	5102		CS†

Marvin Gaye and Diana Ross

Diana and Marvin	Motown	803	'73	†
	Motown	5124	'87	CS/CD

Marvin Gaye Anthologies

Greatest Hits	Tamla	252	'64	†
	Tamla	348	'76	†
	Motown	9005		CD†
	Motown	5191		CS/CD
Greatest Hits, Volume 2	Tamla	278	'67	†
Marvin Gaye and His Girls	Tamla	293	'69	†
	Motown	5246	'90	CS/CD
Super Hits	Tamla	300	'70	†
	Motown	5301		LP/CS/CD†
Anthology	Motown	(3)791	'74	LP/CS†
	Motown	(2)791		CD†
Every Great Motown Hit of Marvin Gaye	Motown	6058	'83	CS/CD
Motown Superstar Series, Volume 15	Motown	115	'84	†
Great Songs and Performances That Inspired the Motown 25th Anniversary TV Show	Motown	5311	'84	CS/CD
Anthology (music through 1981)	Motown	(2)0529	'95	CS/CD
Marvin Gaye and His Women: Classic Duets	Motown	9053	'85	CD†
Motown Legends	Motown	9084		CD†
	Motown	5359	'85	CS/CD†
Compact Command Performance, Volume 1 (15 Greatest Hits)	Motown	6069	'84	CD†
Compact Command Performance, Volume 2	Motown	6201	'86	CD†
Motown Remembers Marvin Gaye (1963–1972)	Motown	6172	'86	LP/CS†
A Musical Testament 1964–1984	Motown	(2)6255	'88	LP/CS†
	Motown	6255	'88	CD†
The Marvin Gaye Collection	Motown	(4)6311	'90	CS/CD†
The Marvin Gaye Classics Collection	Motown	(4)0320	'94	CS/CD
The Norman Whitfield Sessions	Motown	0355	'94	CS/CD
The Master 1961–1984	Motown	(4)0492	'95	CS/CD
Vulnerable (recorded 1967–1978)	Motown	0550	'97	CD
	Motown	0786	'97	CD
Adults Only	IMG	704	'92	CS
Seek and Ye Shall Find: More of the Best	Rhino	71182	'93	CS/CD
Motown Legends	Esx	8515	'95	CS/CD

Tribute Album

Inner City Blues: The Music of Marvin Gaye	Motown	0452	'95	CS/CD

Nona Gaye

Love for the Future	Third Stone	92181	'92	CS/CD

BERRY GORDY, JR.

Born November 28, 1929, in Detroit, Michigan.

Founder and owner of the Tamla-Motown family of record labels, Berry Gordy, Jr., established Motown Records as one of the most important independent record labels in the early '60s. Assembling an industrious staff of songwriters, producers, and musicians, Motown Records built one of the most impressive rosters of artists in the history of pop music and became the largest and most successful independent record company in the United States by 1964. Aided immeasurably by William "Smokey" Robinson and the Brian Holland-Lamont Dozier-Eddie Holland songwriting-production team, Motown created a sophisticated commercial blend of gospel and pop music. The new sound proved enormously popular with both black and white audiences, rivaled The Beatles in the extent of its appeal, and encouraged the ascendancy of black vocal groups throughout the '60s. Indeed, the company's success was so widespread that it became the largest black-owned company in America. However, by 1966, Berry Gordy's acts were displaying a high degree of homogeneity and being seriously challenged by acts on the Stax-Volt and Atlantic labels. His biggest early setback came with the departure of Holland-Dozier-Holland in late 1967. Personally supervising the career of Diana Ross after she left The Supremes in 1970, Gordy was able to establish her as a solo act and film star. Bolstered by the success of the teen-oriented Jackson Five, Berry Gordy, Jr., moved the Motown family of record labels from Detroit to Hollywood in 1971. He was able to maintain the position of Motown Records by the emergence of Marvin Gaye and Stevie Wonder as album-oriented singer-songwriters in the early '70s. However, in the mid-'70s, many major artists left Motown as a consequence of the company's alleged oppressive, even exploitive, artistic policy. The company was again challenged, this time by Kenny Gamble and Leon Huff's Philadelphia International label, and endured continued defections, introducing few new acts save The Commodores and Rick James. By the '80s, Motown had slipped from its position of prominence in the soul field. Inducted into the Rock and Roll Hall of Fame in 1988, Berry Gordy, Jr., sold Motown Records later that year.

Berry Gordy, Jr., dropped out of high school to become a featherweight boxer. Upon his discharge from the Army in 1953, he set up a record store that soon went bankrupt. Subsequently working on a Ford Motor Company assembly line, Gordy began writing songs during the mid-'50s. His first song sale, to Decca, was "Reet Petite," Jackie Wilson's first albeit minor pop hit in 1957. His earliest major songwriting success came with "Lonely Teardrops," a top rhythm-and-blues and smash pop hit for Wilson in 1958. Gordy formed Jobete Music in 1958 and began producing records for Eddie Holland and Marv Johnson, who scored a smash R&B and pop hit with Gordy's "You Got What It Takes" in 1959.

Encouraged by songwriter-friend William "Smokey" Robinson, Berry Gordy, Jr., borrowed money from his family to found Tammie Records, soon changed to Tamla Records. The label's first significant success occurred as distributor of Barrett Strong's "Money," on his sister's Anna label. Later in 1960, "Shop Around," cowritten by Gordy and Robinson, became Tamla's first smash hit for Robinson's Miracles, establishing the label as an important independent. Eddie Holland's brother Brian subsequently collaborated on early hits by The Marvelettes, as Robinson worked with Mary Wells for a series of hits in 1962 on the newly formed Motown label. Before year's end, The Contours hit with the raucous "Do You Love Me," written by Gordy, on yet another label, Gordy.

As the Motown family of labels developed local Detroit talent, Brian and Eddie Holland teamed with songwriter Lamont Dozier in 1963 to create a distinctive pop sound of widespread appeal. Initially working with the rough-sounding Martha and The Vandellas, Holland-Dozier-Holland (H-D-H) achieved massive songwriting and production success with The Supremes from 1964 to 1967. The team also wrote and produced major hits for Marvin Gaye and The Four Tops. In the meantime, Smokey Robinson was writing hits for Mary Wells, The Temptations, Marvin Gaye, and his own Miracles.

Recognized by 1964 as the largest independent record company through its success in the singles market, Motown diversified into an entertainment complex. The Jobete Music Company handled song publishing and copyrighting, while Hitsville, U.S.A. controlled the company's recording studios and International Talent Management trained artists in matters of deportment. Gordy's unprecedented concern with career management, coupled with the rigorous discipline imposed on artists, alienated some of his acts and led to the company's first defection in 1964 by Mary Wells. Nonetheless, Motown became respectable as acts originally aimed at teen audiences were groomed for the adult pop market. Thus, acts were introduced into the American supper club circuit and prime-time television while the company was establishing itself internationally.

During 1967, to create a higher degree of visibility for several of its singers, Motown renamed three of its acts: The Supremes became Diana Ross and The Supremes; The Miracles, Smokey Robinson and The Miracles; and Martha and The Vandellas, Martha Reeves and The Vandellas. Later Motown experimented with psychedelic soul for The Temptations under producer-songwriter Norman Whitfield. The team of Nicholas Ashford and Valerie Simpson also provided hits to Marvin Gaye and Tammi Terrell, and Diana Ross solo.

Suffering the departure of the Holland-Dozier-Holland team in 1967, Berry Gordy, Jr., concentrated on the career of Diana Ross as a solo act beginning in 1970. Maintaining the company's success with the astounding popularity of the teen-oriented Jackson Five, Gordy moved the operation to Hollywood in 1971 and established Motown Industries, expanding his activities to a Broadway musical and films. Bolstered by the success of Marvin Gaye and Stevie Wonder as album-oriented singer-songwriters, Motown was nonetheless challenged in the pop and soul fields by Kenny Gamble and Leon Huff's Philadelphia International label by 1973, particularly by The O'Jays.

During the first half of the '70s, Diana Ross was established as Motown's first all-around entertainer through her work in supper clubs and films, particularly with 1972's *Lady Sings the Blues.* Other films, including *Mahogany* and *The Wiz,* proved flops between 1975 and 1978. Moreover, Motown suffered a series of defections in the '70s. Martha Reeves began recording solo for other labels in 1974 and The Four Tops switched to ABC/Dunhill. Gladys Knight and The Pips recorded for Buddah beginning in 1974 and, in 1975, The Jackson Five moved to Epic, as did Michael Jackson in 1978. The Miracles (without Smokey Robinson) switched to Columbia in 1977 and The Temptations went to Atlantic. Nonetheless, Motown maintained its position as an important independent label with the recordings of Diana Ross, Marvin Gaye, Stevie Wonder, The Commodores, and Rick James.

During the '80s, Motown struggled to retain its prominence in popular music. Diana Ross moved to RCA in 1981 and Marvin Gaye signed with Columbia in 1982. The Temptations returned in 1980 and The Four Tops were back in the mid-'80s, later switching to Arista. The Gordy label introduced the popular DeBarge family in 1983. The company staged a successful twenty-fifth anniversary celebration in 1983, later broadcast on ABC-TV, and Motown Productions produced *Lonesome Dove,* one of the highest-rated mini-series of the decade, for CBS television in 1989. However, many former employees, including Eddie Holland and members of The Vandellas and Marvelettes, sued Motown, alleging failure to pay royalties.

Inducted into the Rock and Roll Hall of Fame in 1988, Berry Gordy, Jr., sold Motown Records to MCA and Boston Ventures in July for $61 million. Boston Ventures later bought out MCA's interest and sold Motown Records to the Dutch-based Polygram conglomerate for $325 million in August 1993. In late 1994, Warner Books published Gordy's self-serving biography *To Be Loved.*

BERRY GORDY, JR., AND MOTOWN RECORDS BIBLIOGRAPHY

Benjaminson, Peter. *The Story of Motown.* New York: Grove Press, 1979.
Bianco, David. *Heat Wave: The Motown Fact Book.* Ann Arbor, MI: Pierian Press, 1988.

Davis, Sharon. *Motown: The History.* Enfield, Middlesex: Guinness Books, 1988.

Fong-Torres, Ben. *The Motown Album: The Sound of Young America.* New York: St. Martin's Press, 1990.

George, Nelson. *Where Did Our Love Go? The Rise and Fall of the Motown Sound.* New York: St. Martin's Press, 1986.

Gordy, Berry. *To Be Loved: The Music, The Magic, The Memories of Motown: An Autobiography.* New York: Warner Books, 1994.

Morse, David. *Motown and the Arrival of Black Music.* New York: Macmillan, 1971.

Singleton, Raymona Gordy. *Berry, Me and Motown: The Untold Story.* Chicago: Contemporary Books, 1990.

Taraborrelli, J. Randy. *Motown: Hot Wax, City Cool and Solid Gold.* Garden City, NY: Doubleday, 1986.

Waller, Don. *The Motown Story.* New York: C. Scribner, 1985.

BILL GRAHAM

Born Wolfgang Grajonca on January 8, 1931, in Berlin, Germany; died October 25, 1991, near Vallejo, California.

Rock music's most famous and influential concert producer from the mid-'60s through the '80s, Bill Graham established rock's first and most famous hall at San Francisco's Fillmore Auditorium in 1966. In terms of its historical importance to a specific type of popular music, the Fillmore can be compared only to New York's Apollo Theater (rhythm-and-blues) and Nashville's Ryman Auditorium (country-and-western). Along with competitor Chet Helms, who operated the Avalon Ballroom, Graham helped introduce and popularize both light shows and psychedelic poster art during his tenure at the Fillmore. He helped launch the careers of hundreds of rock bands in the '60s while fostering the growth and development of San Francisco bands such as The Jefferson Airplane, The Grateful Dead, and Santana. With the openings of Fillmore West in San Francisco and Fillmore East in New York City in 1968, Bill Graham advanced the ballroom rock concert scene that flourished until the early '70s. Thereafter, he was at the forefront of promoting concerts at large arenas, outdoor stadiums, and parks. Graham was also actively involved in staging benefit concerts for a wide variety of causes throughout his career, from small, local benefits to large-scale extravaganzas such as 1985's Live Aid concert and the Amnesty International tours of 1986 and 1988. He also supervised massive tours for the likes of Bob Dylan, The Rolling Stones, and The Who, and staged the first major rock concert in the Soviet Union in 1987.

Bill Graham escaped the Nazi persecution of Jews as a child, fleeing first to France, then to the United States in 1941, where he was raised in the Bronx by a foster family. He formally changed his name to Bill Graham in 1949, when granted U.S. citizenship. He later served in the U.S. Army in the Korean War and graduated from New York City College with a degree in business administration before moving to California. By 1960, he was an executive with the Allis-Chalmers farm equipment company in San Francisco.

In 1965, Bill Graham quit his position to take over management of the radical street-theater improvisational group, The Mime Troupe. On November 6, 1965, Bill Graham staged a benefit concert for The Mime Troupe at San Francisco's Longshoreman's Hall with various Bay Area musicians. On December 10, he promoted another benefit concert at the 1100-seat Fillmore Auditorium in one of San Francisco's black ghettos with The Jefferson Airplane, The Great Society (with Grace Slick), and The Warlocks (later The Grateful Dead). The financial and artistic success of the benefits, along with his subsequent production of the now-legendary Trips Festival at the Longshoreman's Hall in January 1966, encouraged Graham to regularly present rock shows at the Fillmore Auditorium. By year's end, he was also presenting concerts at the 5400-seat Winterland Arena and managing, if briefly, The Jefferson Airplane. The concerts became astoundingly successful and featured both little-known local talent and big-name outside acts.

Bill Graham presented his last show at the Fillmore Auditorium in July 1968. He opened Fillmore East in New York City in March 1968 and assumed management of the Carousel Ballroom on San Francisco's Market Street in August. The old dance hall, which he renamed Fillmore West, had been run by The Jefferson Airplane and The Grateful Dead since early in the year. Over the next three years, Graham presented virtually every major rock act at the Fillmores, while giving little-known acts a chance to perform and booking a number of nonrock acts such as Miles Davis, Lenny Bruce, and The Staples Singers.

Graham's success with the Fillmores encouraged the establishment of similar venues across the country and marked the heyday of concert rock. He opened a talent booking agency in October 1968, and formed Fillmore and San Francisco Records in February 1969, recording Cold Blood and Elvin Bishop before dissolving the labels at the beginning of 1972. With the demise of the ballroom concert scene following the Woodstock Festival of August 1969, Graham announced his intention to close the Fillmores.

By July 1971, both Fillmore East and Fillmore West had been closed. Graham "retired" for a time, but was back in 1972, producing The Rolling Stones' tour. He booked acts into the Winterland Arena and produced the massive Watkins Glen Pop Festival in upstate New York in 1973, the largest gathering of its kind. In 1974, he staged The Band's celebrated *Last Waltz* and produced George Harrison's tour, Bob Dylan's comeback tour, and the reunion of Crosby, Stills, Nash and Young. By 1978, the Winterland venue had also become obsolete, giving way to impersonal and lucrative festivals and stadium concerts. On New Year's Eve 1978, The New Riders of the Purple Sage, The Blues Brothers, and The Grateful Dead played the final performance at Winterland, a hall once castigated as overly large and acoustically unsound, but now sorely missed.

Bill Graham became the master of arena concert production, supervising The Rolling Stones 1981 world tour and presenting the US Festival near San Bernardino in 1982. He reopened San Francisco's most successful nightclub, the Old Waldorf, as Wolfgang's in 1983. Withdrawing from the day-to-day operation of his organization, Graham appeared in small roles in the films *Apocalypse Now, The Cotton Club,* and *Gardens of Stone* during the '80s. His organization financed outdoor amphitheaters in Sacramento (Cal Expo) and Palo Alto (Shoreline), which opened in 1983 and 1987, respectively. In 1985, he presided over the day-long Live Aid benefit in Philadelphia and later personally supervised the Amnesty International tours of 1986 and 1988. In 1987, Graham presented the first rock concert in Russia at Moscow's Izmajlovo Stadium with Santana, The Doobie Brothers, James Taylor, and Bonnie Raitt. Personal setbacks of the time included fires that destroyed his warehouse offices in 1985 and Wolfgang's in 1987.

In March 1988, the nightclub wing of the Bill Graham organization began presenting shows at the refurbished Fillmore Auditorium once again, but the hall was closed after October 1989's Loma Prieta earthquake. Graham presented three simultaneous benefit concerts for victims of the quake. He also made the final legal arrangements for and produced the Oliver Stone movie *The Doors* and performed the role of Lucky Luciano in the movie *Bugsy,* starring Warren Beatty. In 1990, he helped produce the Gathering of the Tribes concert, which inspired 1991's Lollapalooza tour. However, on October 25, 1991, Graham, companion Melissa Gold, and longtime pilot Steve Kahn were killed in a fiery helicopter crash near Vallejo, California. Bill Graham was inducted into the Rock and Roll Hall of Fame in 1992.

In fitting tribute to the life and memory of Bill Graham, the Fillmore Auditorium reopened on April 27, 1994, after over $1 million in renovations. Mixing widely varying types of music, as Graham had in the early days of The Fillmore, the announced acts were

American Music Club, Ry Cooder and David Lindley, and Smashing Pumpkins, with impromptu performances by Linda Perry and Joe Satriani. An effort to preserve Fillmore East failed in 1995.

BILL GRAHAM BIBLIOGRAPHY

Glatt, John. *Rage and Roll: Bill Graham and the Selling of Rock.* Secaucus, NJ: Birch Lane Press, Carol Publishing Group, 1993.

Graham, Bill, and Robert Greenfield. *Bill Graham Presents: My Life Inside Rock and Out.* New York: Doubleday, 1992.

The Fillmores

Live at Bill Graham's Fillmore West	Columbia	9893	'69	†
Fillmore: The Last Days	Fillmore	(3)31390	'72	†
	Epic/Legacy	(2)31390	'91	CD

THE GRATEFUL DEAD

Jerome "Jerry" Garcia (born August 1, 1942, in San Francisco; died August 9, 1995, in Forest Knolls, California), lead guitar, vocals; Bob Weir (born Robert Hall on October 16, 1947, in Atherton, California), rhythm guitar, vocals; Ron "Pig Pen" McKernan (born September 8, 1945, in San Bruno, California; died March 8, 1973, in Corte Madera, California), keyboards, vocals; Phil Lesh (born March 15, 1940, in Berkeley, California), bass; and Bill Kreutzmann (born May 7, 1946, in Palo Alto, California), drums. The band's full-time lyricist beginning in 1969 was Robert Hunter (born June 23, 1941, in Arroyo Grande, California).

Other members included drummer Michael "Mickey" Hart (born September 11, 1943, in New York); keyboardists Tom Constanten (born March 19, 1944, in Long Branch, New Jersey), Keith Godchaux (born July 19, 1948, in Concord, California; died July 23, 1980, in Ross, California), Brent Mydland (born October 21, 1952, in Munich, West Germany; died July 26, 1990, in Lafayette, California), and Vince Welnick; and vocalist Donna Godchaux.

One of America's best-loved bands since its inception during the heyday of "psychedelia" in San Francisco, The Grateful Dead were challenged in terms of longevity by only The Rolling Stones. As a band, The Grateful Dead staunchly maintained an anticommercial show business stance that nonetheless produced several enduring and popular albums and even a near-smash hit single, 1987's "Touch of Grey." Performing marathon shows of up to five hours, often starting sluggishly and ending spectacularly, The Grateful Dead introduced more free-form music into the body of rock than any other group, based on the often extraordinary lead guitar playing of Jerry Garcia and the virtuoso bass playing of Phil Lesh. Building an underground reputation by playing regularly and often for free, The Grateful Dead favored live performance as most other area bands signed recording contracts. A true people's band, actually living in the Haight-Ashbury district during the "hippie" era, The Grateful Dead approached rock music on their own terms, dividing funds communally and supporting a massive "family" entourage while eschewing the trappings of the rock stars they nonetheless became. Once signed to a recording contract, The Grateful Dead soon added lyricist Robert Hunter for *Aoxomoxoa* and subsequent albums, including their two classic country-flavored albums, *Workingman's Dead* and *American Beauty*. As one of rock music's least-known major songwriters (along with Procol Harum's Keith Reid), Robert Hunter was favorably compared to The Band's Robbie Robertson in his concern with the plight of the "little man" in the history and folklore of America during the last century.

THE GRATEFUL DEAD (UPI/CORBIS-BETTMANN)

The Grateful Dead weathered regular and often virulent criticism for their anarchistic approach to rock improvisation. Live shows could be transcendentally inspiring or excruciatingly boring, sometimes both. Over the years, their live performances and iconoclastic attitude won them the most staunchly devoted and fiercely loyal following in all of rock music. These fanatics—known as Deadheads—revered the group as fountainheads and mainstays of the "hippie" values of humanity, brotherhood, and spirituality. In demonstrating the remarkably independent and democratic nature of the band, the members of the Grateful Dead retained the freedom to work on outside projects, most notably Garcia's collaborations with The New Riders of the Purple Sage and Old and in the Way. Later concentrating on live performances, The Grateful Dead became one of America's leading concert attractions in the '80s. In the '90s, drummer Mickey Hart pursued an interest in non-Western music that bolstered the world-music movement. Additionally, Hart's studies of the myth and meaning of drumming resulted in two books that won him international recognition as an ethnomusicologist. Inducted into the Rock and Roll Hall of Fame in 1994, The Grateful Dead disbanded after Jerry Garcia's untimely death on August 9, 1995.

Jerry Garcia grew up in San Francisco and Menlo Park, obtaining his first guitar, an electric guitar, at the age of fifteen. Dropping out of high school, he served a brief stint in the Army in 1959 before returning to the Palo Alto area and meeting Robert Hunter. He took up banjo in 1960 and formed a series of folk, jug-band, and bluegrass music groups with Hunter for local engagements beginning in early 1962. These included The Thunder Mountain Tub Thumpers, The Asphalt Jungle Boys (with John "Marmaduke" Dawson), and The Hart Valley Drifters (with David Nelson), who won an amateur bluegrass contest at the Monterey Folk Festival in 1963. The group subsequently became The Wildwood Boys and, by 1964, Garcia had formed Mother McCree's Uptown Jug Champions with harmonica player Ron "Pig Pen" McKernan and guitarists Bob Weir and Bob Matthews. By April 1965, Mother McCree's Uptown Jug Champions had gone electric and reemerged as The Warlocks, with Garcia, Weir, and McKernan. Adding drummer Bill Kreutzmann, the group replaced their first bassist with Phil Lesh, a classically trained trumpeter and composer of twelve-tone and electronic music, in June.

Taking the name The Grateful Dead, the group played at Bill Graham's first rock event at the Fillmore Auditorium in November 1965 and, beginning in December, at author Ken Kesey's infamous "acid tests," chronicled in Tom Wolfe's *Electric Kool-Aid Acid Test*. With financial benefactor and LSD manufacturer Augustus Stanley Owsley III acting as manager, the group performed at local venues such as the Fillmore Auditorium and the Avalon Ballroom, as well as in San Francisco's Golden Gate Park for free with The Jefferson Airplane and other area bands. Moving into 710 Ashbury Street in the heart of the Haight-Ashbury district in June 1966, The Grateful Dead recorded a single for the local Scorpio label before briefly signing with MGM Records, which issued the live albums *Vintage Grateful Dead* and *Historic Dead* in the early '70s. In January 1967, they appeared at the first "Human Be-In" in Golden Gate Park with The Jefferson Airplane and Quicksilver Messenger Sevice, soon signing with Warner Brothers Records.

Already a huge cult band, The Grateful Dead's debut album featured Pig Pen's gruff lead vocals on blues-based material such as "Good Morning, Little School Girl" and "Morning Dew," as well as group favorites such as "Beat It on Down the Line" and "New, New Minglewood Blues." Performing at the Monterey International Pop Festival in June 1967, the group added percussionist-drummer Mickey Hart in September, thus freeing Lesh from his strictly rhythmic function on bass. The Grateful Dead recorded their second album, *Anthem of the Sun,* over a six-month period, augmented by keyboardist Tom Constanten. By early 1968, Hart's father Lenny had become their manager.

The Grateful Dead added Robert Hunter as full-time nonperforming lyricist for 1969's *Aoxomoxoa.* It contained several band favorites such as "St. Stephen," "China Cat Sunflower," and "Mountains of the Moon," with lyrics by Hunter. The group performed at the Woodstock Music and Art Fair in August and the ill-fated Altamont Speedway affair in December. Also recorded that year was their first official live set, *Live Dead,* regarded as one of their better live recordings. It featured a twenty-three-minute rendition of "Dark Star" and a rousing version of "Turn on Your Lovelight."

In 1970, The Grateful Dead dropped their blues- and improvisatory-based approach for a country-flavored, vocally rich, and much simplified sound that resulted in what many consider as the group's finest two albums, *Workingman's Dead* and *American Beauty.* Indeed, these two albums featured some of Robert Hunter's most striking efforts as a songwriter. Recorded with the assistance of old associates John Dawson and David Nelson, *Workingman's Dead* contained the group's first albeit minor hit, "Uncle John's Band," as well as "Easy Wind," "Casey Jones," "Cumberland Blues," and "New Speedway Boogie," their "official" statement about the December 1969 debacle at Altamont Speedway with The Rolling Stones. *American Beauty,* recorded with the assistance of David Grisman and The New Riders of the Purple Sage, featured Garcia on pedal steel guitar. The album included a number of Grateful Dead classics such as Pig Pen's "Operator," Weir and Hunter's "Sugar Magnolia," Lesh and Hunter's "Box of Rain," and the Hunter-Garcia collaborations "Candyman," "Ripple," and " 'Till the Morning Comes," and "Truckin,' " the group's second minor hit and one of their anthem songs. Their next Warner Brothers album, entitled simply *The Grateful Dead,* was a live set. It contained favorites such as "Bertha," "Wharf Rat," and "Playing in the Band," as well as Merle Haggard's "Mama Tried," John Phillips' "Me and My Uncle," and Chuck Berry's "Johnny B. Goode."

By 1970, the remarkably diffuse outside activities of the members of The Grateful Dead had started. While performing and recording with keyboardists Howard Wales and Merl Saunders, Jerry Garcia played sessions for Crosby, Stills, Nash and Young and The Jefferson Airplane. Garcia also played pedal steel guitar and banjo with Dave Torbert and former associates David Nelson and John "Marmaduke" Dawson in the countrified New Riders of the Purple Sage that spring. He remained with The New Riders into 1971, appearing on their debut Columbia album. The album included "I Don't Know You," "Whatcha Gonna Do," "Henry," "Dirty Business," and "All I Ever Wanted," all written by Dawson. The New Riders of the Purple Sage continued to record for Columbia with Garcia's replacement, Buddy Cage, through 1975. Their *Adventures of Panama Red* featured Peter Rowan's title song and "Lonesome L.A. Cowboy," and Robert Hunter's "Kick in the Head." The New Riders switched to MCA Records in 1975 and A&M Records in 1981. By

1983, Dawson was the only original member in the lineup, yet they continued to tour and record albums into the '90s.

Mickey Hart quit the Grateful Dead for a solo career in February 1971. During the year, Pig Pen fell ill and seldom toured with The Grateful Dead. He was replaced by key-boardist-vocalist Keith Godchaux in October 1971. In 1972, Jerry Garcia and Bob Weir each issued solo albums that served as effective companions to *Workingman's Dead* and *American Beauty*. Garcia played all instruments except drums on *Garcia,* which included "Sugaree" (a minor hit), "Deal," and "The Wheel," with songs credited to Garcia, Hunter, and drummer Bill Kreutzmann. Weir's *Ace,* essentially a Grateful Dead album, was recorded with Garcia, Lesh, Kreutzmann, keyboardist Keith Godchaux, and his vocalist wife Donna. It contained "Walk in the Sunshine" and "Mexicali Blues," written by Weir and John Barlow, Weir's own "One More Saturday Night," and the classic Weir-Hunter collaboration, "Playing in the Band." Mickey Hart's 1972 *Rolling Thunder* was recorded with Garcia, Weir, Grace Slick, and Steve Stills.

The Grateful Dead's two-month European tour of 1972, with Keith and Donna God-chaux (who had joined in March), yielded the multirecord set *Europe '72.* The album served as a live compendium of the songs of The Grateful Dead. In addition to featuring songs such as "China Cat Sunflower," "Sugar Magnolia," and "Truckin,'" the album introduced "Jack Straw," "Tennessee Jed," "Ramble on Rose," and "Brown-Eyed Woman." The album proved a best-seller, remaining on the album charts for nearly six months. However, founding member Ron "Pig Pen" McKernan died of liver failure on March 8, 1973, at the age of 27.

In 1973, The Grateful Dead financed the establishment of their own independent record label, Grateful Dead Records. The label's first release, *Wake of the Flood,* contained more Hunter-Garcia songs such as "Row Jimmy," "Stella Blue," and "Mississippi Half-Step," as well as "Weather Report Suite," written, in part, with folk singer Eric Andersen. The following year, Round Records was founded for outside recordings by members of the group. By May, Round Records had issued Garcia's second solo album, with Peter Rowan's "Mississippi Moon" and Doctor John's "What Goes Around," and Robert Hunter's first, *Tales of the Great Rum Runners,* which included "It Must Have Been the Roses" and "Keys to the Rain."

During 1973 and 1974, the bluegrass aggregation Old and in the Way played around the San Francisco Bay Area. Comprising Jerry Garcia (banjo), Peter Rowan (guitar), David Grisman (mandolin), Vassar Clements (fiddle), and John Kahn (bass), the group recorded *Old and in the Way* for Round Records in October 1973. A modern bluegrass classic and one of Garcia's most successful endeavors, the album included Peter Rowan's "Land of the Navajo," "Midnight Moonlight," and "Panama Red." A second and third volume were issued in 1996 and 1997, respectively.

During 1974, The Grateful Dead utilized a massive $400,000 state-of-the-art sound system that emitted a loud, clear, and clean sound, rather than the usual distorted, bone-crushing noise normally associated with such a powerful system. That June, the group issued *Live from Mars Hotel,* which featured "U.S. Blues," "Unbroken Chain," "China Doll," and the Dead classic "Ship of Fools." Following a European tour, The Grateful Dead played five consecutive nights at San Francisco's Winterland in October before "retiring" from live performance for over a year. Recorded remote, the shows later yielded the poorly mixed and poorly received *Steal Your Face* album. Filmed by seven camera crews, edited performances from this run were eventually released in film form in June 1977 as *The Grateful Dead Movie.*

In 1975, Round Records issued *Keith and Donna* (by the Godchauxs), *Seastones* (by Phil Lesh and composer-synthesizer wizard Ned Lagin), and Robert Hunter's *Tiger Rose.* Bob Weir assisted in the recording of the debut Round album by Kingfish, formed by Dave Tor-bert, a former member of The New Riders of the Purple Sage. In 1976, Round issued *Diga* by The Diga Rhythm Band, featuring Mickey Hart and tabla player Zakir Hussain, and Garcia's third solo album *Reflections,* again essentially a Grateful Dead album, which featured Hunter's "It Must Have Been the Roses."

In June 1975, The Grateful Dead signed an agreement with United Artists for worldwide distribution of both Round and Grateful Dead Records. With the return of percussionist Mickey Hart, The Grateful Dead recorded *Blues for Allah,* a decidedly jazz-oriented venture that included the minor hit "The Music Never Stopped," by Weir and John Barlow, and the Hunter-Garcia-Kreutzmann collaboration "Franklin's Tower." In 1977, The Grateful Dead switched to Arista Records for a series of commercially oriented albums. For the first time, they used an outside producer, Keith Olsen of *Fleetwood Mac* fame, for *Terrapin Station.* Prominently featuring horns, strings, and vocal choruses, the album included "Estimated Prophet," "Samson and Delilah," and the extended cut "Terrapin."

Bob Weir's *Heaven Help the Fool,* produced by Olsen and recorded with guitarist Bobby Cochran and keyboardist Brent Mydland, was issued on Arista in early 1978, yielding the minor hit "Bombs Away." Soon thereafter, The Jerry Garcia Group's *Cats under the Stars* was released on Arista, again showcasing the lyrics of Robert Hunter. In September, The Grateful Dead spent $500,000 to ship twenty-five tons of equipment to Egypt so they could play at the foot of the Great Pyramids in a benefit performance for the Egyptian Department of Antiquities and the Faith and Hope Society, a charitable organization. Before year's end, the group's *Shakedown Street* was issued. Produced by Lowell George of Little Feat, the album evinced a sophisticated, almost discofied sound, as did *Go to Heaven,* produced by Gary Lyons. It included "Feel Like a Stranger" and "Althea," and yielded a minor hit with the Garcia-Hunter composition "Alabama Getaway."

In February 1979, Keith and Donna Godchaux left The Grateful Dead to pursue solo projects. He was replaced in April by keyboardist Brent Mydland, a former touring and recording partner of Bob Weir. Keith Godchaux died on July 23, 1980, in Ross, California, of injuries suffered in a motorcycle accident two days prior.

Mickey Hart scored, in part, the music for the epic yet equivocal 1979 Vietnam War movie *Apocalypse Now.* Other recordings that were not used in the film (featuring exotic percussion instruments from Hart's extensive collection) surfaced in late 1980 as *The Rhythm Devils Play River Music.* Bobby and The Midnites, fronted by Bob Weir, debuted in June 1980 and signed with Arista Records. With guitarist Bobby Cochran, Dead keyboardist Brent Mydland, and jazz fusion drummer Billy Cobham, the group recorded two albums and toured through 1984. In 1981, The Grateful Dead issued two live sets, the acoustic *Reckoning* and the electric *Dead Set,* recorded in October 1980.

The Grateful Dead concentrated on live performing during the '80s, as Jerry Garcia slipped into heroin addiction. By the mid-'80s, they had become one of the top-grossing touring rock acts and expanded their audience to a new, youthful generation of fans. During this time, Garcia recorded *Run for the Roses,* Bob Weir recorded a second album with Bobby and The Midnites, and Mickey Hart recorded *Dafos* with percussionist Airto Moreira and vocalist Flora Purim. For a time, Robert Hunter performed in The Dinosaurs with Barry Melton, John Cipollina, Peter Albin, and Spencer Dryden, all veterans of psychedelic San Francisco bands. In July 1986, Jerry Garcia nearly died after collapsing in a diabetic coma. The Grateful Dead resumed touring in December, and Garcia and friends staged a three-week run at New York's Lunt-Fontanne Theater in October 1987 with "Garcia on Broadway."

The Grateful Dead emerged spectacularly in 1987. Their first studio album in seven years, *In the Dark,* was hailed as perhaps their best work since *Workingman's Dead* and *American Beauty.* It contained Weir's "Throwing Stones" and Mydland's "Tons of Steels," and yielded their first major hit (a near-smash, in fact) with "Touch of Grey." The engaging MTV video of the song helped introduce them to a whole new generation of fans. They performed with Bob Dylan at six concerts in June, and recordings from the shows were issued in early 1989. Later that year, *Rolling Stone* magazine declared The Grateful Dead the single most successful touring band in rock history.

In 1984, The Grateful Dead set up the nonprofit philanthropic Rex Foundation to oversee contributions to environmental lobbies, social causes, and private ventures. By 1993, the organization had distributed over $4 million. The group's September 24, 1988, concert at Madison Square Garden in New York heralded their commitment to the issue of rain forest preservation, raising $500,000 for Cultural Survival, Greenpeace, and the Rainforest Action Network. In 1993, The Grateful Dead contributed about one-half of the cost of a liver transplant for legendary poster artist Stanley Mouse, who, with Alton Kelley, created the Grateful Dead skull-and-roses logo.

On July 26, 1990, keyboardist Brent Mydland was found dead of a drug overdose in his Lafayette, California, home. He was replaced temporarily by Bruce Hornsby and permanently by Vince Welnick of The Tubes in September 1990.

At the beginning of the '90s, The Grateful Dead began releasing vintage live material on their own label, available only through mail-order. In 1991, they were honored with *Deadicated,* a benefit album of their songs by such artists as Los Lobos, Midnight Oil, Elvis Costello, Jane's Addiction, Doctor John, and Lyle Lovett. The Grateful Dead became the top concert attraction of 1991 and 1993, with U2 intervening. In 1992, The Grateful Dead had canceled an eighteen-date East Coast tour when Jerry Garcia was reported suffering "exhaustion." He subsequently adopted a new vegetarian diet and initiated weight loss and exercise programs that improved his health significantly. In 1993, Grateful Dead Merchandising began issuing live material assembled by Grateful Dead archivist Dick Latvala as *Dick's Picks.* The Grateful Dead were inducted into the Rock and Roll Hall of Fame in 1994.

During the '80s, Mickey Hart had immersed himself in the music of non-Western cultures and initiated a study of the myth and meaning of drumming. He presented and recorded the chants of Gyuto Tibetan Buddhist Monks, released in 1987, and produced albums by Babatunde Olatunji and Kitaro. In 1988, he released six discs of exotic music on Rykodisc as *The World.* The recordings included Sudanese folk music, traditional Jewish music, and the music of Egypt and India. Recognized as one of the world's leading ethnomusicologists by the late '80s, Hart supervised the transfer of the entire catalog of Folkways Records to CD for the Smithsonian Institute. In the '90s, his drum studies produced two books, *Drumming at the Edge of Magic,* a chronicle of his personal quest, and *Planet Drum,* a collection of world drum lore and legend. Each of the books had a companion CD, released on Rykodisc. Bob Weir also became an author in the '90s, writing two children's books with his sister Wendy.

During the '90s Jerry Garcia recorded *Blues from the Rainforest* with keyboardist Merl Saunders and accompanied David Grisman for "beat" wordsmith Ken Nordine's *Devout Catalyst.* He also performed and recorded with mandolinist David Grisman and his own band, while continuing to perform with The Grateful Dead. He died unexpectedly on August 9, 1995, in a Forest Knolls, California, treatment facility at the age of 53. After four agonizing months, the remaining members of The Grateful Dead officially disbanded the group.

During 1996, a number of Grateful Dead tribute albums were released, including *Fire on the Mountain* (by reggae artists such as The Wailing Soul, Toots Hibbert, and Steel Pulse), *Long Live the Dead* (by country artists Billy and Terry Smith), and jazz saxophonist David Murray's *Dark Star.* Before Garcia's death, Grateful Dead keyboard technician Bob Bralove had formed Second Sight with Vince Welnick, guitarist Henry Kaiser, and others, releasing an album on Shanachie Records. Also in 1995, Bob Weir had formed Ratdog with Welnick, harmonica player Matthew Kelly (from Kingfish), bassist Rob Wasserman, and drummer Jay Lane. Bill Kreutzmann moved to Kauai, where he formed the trio Backbone with guitarist-vocalist Rick Barnett and bassist Edd Cook. Mickey Hart became the first former member of The Grateful Dead to release an album of his own, *Mickey Hart's Mystery Box,* recorded with Weir, Bruce Hornsby, percussionists Airto Moreira and Zakir Hussain (among others), and the female vocal sextet The Mint Juleps, with lyrics by Robert Hunter.

Former members of The Grateful Dead launched the Furthur Festival in the summer of 1996, with Mickey Hart's Mystery Box and Bob Weir's Ratdog. By then Ratdog included Weir, Kelly, Wasserman, and Chuck Berry's longtime pianist Johnnie Johnson. That year, Vince Welnick formed The Missing Man Formation with guitarist Steve Kimock, bassist Bobby Vega, and former Tubes and Starship drummer Prairie Prince, releasing their debut album on Arista Records in 1998. The 1998 Furthur Festival tour featured The Other Ones, with Weir, Hart, Kimock, Phil Lesh, Bruce Hornsby, and saxophonist Dave Ellis, among others.

GRATEFUL DEAD BIBLIOGRAPHY

Brandelius, Jerilyn Lee. *Grateful Dead Family Album.* New York: Warner Books, 1989.

Brightman, Carol. *Sweet Chaos: The Grateful Dead's American Adventure.* New York: Clarkson Potter, 1998.

Constanten, Tom. *Between Rock and Hard Places: A Musical Autobiodyssey.* Eugene, OR: Hulogosi, 1992.

Dodd, David G., and Robert G. Weiner. *The Grateful Dead and the Deadheads: An Annotated Bibliography.* Westport, CT: Greenwood Press, 1997.

Gans, David, and Peter Simon. *Playing in the Band: An Oral and Visual Portrait of The Grateful Dead.* New York: St. Martin's Press, 1985, 1996.

———. *Conversation with The Dead: The Grateful Dead Interview Book.* Secaucus, NJ: Carol Publishing Group, 1991.

Garcia, Jerry. *Paintings, Drawings and Sketches.* Berkeley, CA: Celestial Arts, 1992.

Greene, Herb. *Book of The Dead: Celebrating 25 Years with The Grateful Dead.* New York: Delacorte Press, 1990.

Greenfield, Robert. *Dark Star: An Oral Biography of Jerry Garcia.* New York: William Morrow, 1996.

Grushkin, Paul, Cynthia Bassett, and Jonas Grushkin. *Grateful Dead: The Official Book of the Dead Heads.* New York: William Morrow, 1983.

Harrison, Hank. *The Dead Book: A Social History of The Grateful Dead.* New York: Link Books, 1973.

———. *The Dead.* Millbrae, CA: Celestial Arts, 1980.

———. *The Dead: A Social History of the Haight-Ashbury Experience.* San Francisco: Archives Press, 1990.

Hart, Mickey, with Jay Stevens and Frederic Lieberman. *Drumming at the Edge of Magic: A Journey Into the Spirit of Percussion.* San Francisco: Harper, 1990.

———, and Frederic Lieberman, with D. A. Sonneborn. *Planet Drum: A Celebration of Percussion and Rhythm.* New York: HarperSanFrancisco, 1991.

Hunter, Robert. *A Box of Rain.* New York: Viking, 1990; New York: Penguin, 1993.

Jackson, Blair. *Grateful Dead: The Music Never Stopped.* London: Plexus Publishing, 1983.

———. *Goin' Down the Road: A Grateful Dead Traveling Companion.* New York: Harmony Books, 1992.

Jensen, Jamie. *Grateful Dead: Built to Last: Twenty-Five Years of The Grateful Dead.* New York: Plume Books, 1990.

Reich, Charles, and Jann Wenner. *Garcia: A Signpost to New Space.* San Francisco: Straight Arrow Books, 1972.

Rolling Stone. Garcia. Boston: Little, Brown, 1995.

Ruhlmann, William. *The History of The Grateful Dead.* New York: Smithmark Publishers, 1990.

Scully, Rocky, with David Dalton. *Living with The Dead: Twenty Years on the Bus with Garcia and The Grateful Dead.* Boston: Little, Brown, 1996.

Shenk, David, and Steve Silberman. *Skeleton Key: A Dictionary for Deadheads.* New York: Main Street Books/Doubleday, 1994.

Trager, Oliver. *The American Book of The Dead: The Definitive Encyclopedia of The Grateful Dead.* New York: Fireside Books, 1997.

Troy, Sandy. *One More Saturday Night: Reflections with The Grateful Dead, Dead Family and Dead Heads.* New York: St. Martin's Press, 1991.

———. *Captain Trips: A Biography of Jerry Garcia.* New York: Thunder's Mouth Press, 1994.

Weir, Bob and Wendy. *Panther Dream.* New York: Hyperion, 1991.

———. *Baru Bay, Australia.* New York: Hyperion, 1995.

Wybenga, Eric. *Dead to the Core: Al Almanack of The Grateful Dead.* New York: Delta Trade, 1997.

The Grateful Dead

The Grateful Dead	Warner Brothers	1689	'67	CS/CD
Anthem of the Sun	Warner Brothers	1749	'68	CS/CD
Aoxomoxoa	Warner Brothers	1790	'69	CS/CD
Workingman's Dead	Warner Brothers	1869	'70	CS/CD
American Beauty	Warner Brothers	1893	'70	CS/CD
American Beauty/Workingman's Dead	Warner Brothers	23706		CS
Best—Skeletons from the Closet	Warner Brothers	2764	'74	CS/CD
Best—What a Long Strange Trip It's Been	Warner Brothers	(2)3091	'77	†
	Warner Brothers	3091		CS/CD
Wake of the Flood	Grateful Dead	01	'73	†
	Grateful Dead	4002	'90	CS/CD
	Arista	14002	'95	CS/CD
From Mars Hotel	Grateful Dead	102	'74	†
	Grateful Dead	4007		CS/CD
	Arista	14007	'95	CS/CD
Blues for Allah	Grateful Dead	494	'75	†
	Grateful Dead	4001		CS/CD
	Arista	14001	'95	CS/CD
Terrapin Station	Arista	7001	'77	†
	Arista	8065		CD
	Arista	8329		CS
Shakedown Street	Arista	4198	'78	†
	Arista	8228		CD
	Arista	8321		CS
Go to Heaven	Arista	9508	'80	†
	Arista	8181		CD
	Arista	8332		CS
In the Dark	Arista	8452	'87	CS/CD
Dead Zone: The Grateful Dead CD Collection, 1977–1987	Arista	(6)8530	'87	CD†
Built to Last	Arista	8575	'89	CS/CD
1977–1995	Arista	(2)18934	'96	CS/CD
Reckoning	Pair	(2)1053	'86	CS

Live Grateful Dead Recordings (in Recording Order)

Vintage Grateful Dead (recorded 1966)	Sunflower	5001	'70	†
Historic Dead (recorded 1966)	Sunflower	5004	'71	†

History (compilation of the above two)	Pride	0016		†
Two from the Vault (recorded August 1968)	Grateful Dead	(2)4016	'92	CS/CD
	Arista	(2)14016	'95	CS/CD
Fillmore East (recorded February 1969)	Arista	(2)14054	'97	CD
Live/Dead (recorded 1969)	Warner Brothers	1830	'69	CS/CD
History of the Grateful Dead—Bear's Choice (recorded February 1970)	Warner Brothers	2721	'73	CS/CD
The Grateful Dead	Warner Brothers	(2)1935	'71	†
	Warner Brothers	1935		CS/CD
Europe '72	Warner Brothers	(3)2668	'72	CS
	Warner Brothers	(2)2668		CD
Hundred Year Hall (recorded April 1972)	Grateful Dead	(2)4020	'95	CS/CD
	Arista	(2)14020	'95	CS/CD
Steal Your Face (recorded October 1974)	Grateful Dead	(2)104	'76	†
	Grateful Dead	(2)620	'76	†
	Grateful Dead	(2)4006		CS/CD
	Arista	(2)14006	'95	CS/CD
One from the Vault (recorded August 1975)	Grateful Dead	(2)4013	'91	CS/CD
	Arista	(2)14013	'95	CS/CD
Reckoning (recorded 1980)	Arista	(2)8604	'81	†
	Arista	8523	'90	CD
Dead Set (recorded 1980)	Arista	(2)8606	'81	†
	Arista	(2)8112		CS†/CD
Without a Net (recorded 1989, 1990)	Arista	(3)8634	'90	LP†
	Arista	(2)8634	'90	CS/CD
Dozin' at the Knick (recorded March 1990)	Arista	(3)14025	'96	CD
Fallout from the Phil Zone (recorded 1969–1995)	Arista	(2)14052	'97	CD
Infrared Roses	Grateful Dead	4014	'91	CS/CD
	Arista	14014	'95	CS/CD

Dick's Picks (in Release Order)

Volume 1 (recorded December 1973)	Grateful Dead	(2)4018	'93	CD
	Arista	(2)14018	'95	CS/CD
Volume 2 (recorded October 1971)	Grateful Dead	4019	'94	CD
Volume 3 (recorded May 1977)	Grateful Dead	(2)4021	'95	CD
Volume 4 (recorded February 1970)	Grateful Dead	(3)4023	'96	CD
Volume 5 (recorded December 1979)	Grateful Dead	(3)4024	'96	CD
Volume 6 (recorded October 1983)	Grateful Dead	(3)4026	'96	CD
Volume 7 (recorded September 1974)	Grateful Dead	(3)4027	'97	CD
Volume 8 (recorded May 1970)	Grateful Dead	(3)4028	'97	CD
Volume 9 (recorded September 1990)	Grateful Dead	(3)4029	'97	CD
Volume 10 (recorded December 1977)	Grateful Dead	(3)4030	'98	CD

The Grateful Dead/John Oswald

Grayfolded (1969–1995)	Swell Artifact	(2)1969	'95	CD

Bob Dylan and The Grateful Dead

Dylan and The Dead (recorded 1987)	Columbia	45056	'88	CS/CD

Various Artists (Tribute Albums)

Deadicated: A Tribute to The Grateful Dead	Arista	8669	'91	CS/CD
The Music Never Stopped: Roots of The Grateful Dead	Shanachie	6014	'95	LP/CS/CD
Fire on the Mountain	Pow Wow	7462	'96	CS/CD

Billy and Terry Smith

Long Live The Dead	K-tel	3542	'96	CS/CD

David Murray Octet (Tribute Album)

Dark Star (The Music of The Grateful Dead)	Astor Place	4002	'96	CD

New Riders of the Purple Sage

Before Time Began/The Backwards Tapes (recorded 1969)	Relix	2024	'86	CS†/CD
Vintage New Riders of the Purple Sage (recorded February 1971)	Relix	2025	'86	CS†/CD
N.R.P.S. (with Jerry Garcia)	Columbia	30888	'71	CD
Powerglide	Columbia	31284	'72	†
	Columbia/Legacy	64912	'96	CD
Gypsy Cowboy	Columbia	31930	'72	†
The Adventures of Panama Red	Columbia	32450	'73	CS/CD
Home, Home on the Road	Columbia	32870	'74	†
Brujo	Columbia	33145	'74	†
Oh, What a Might Time	Columbia	33688	'75	†
Best	Columbia	34367	'76	CS/CD
Midnight Moonlight	Relix	2050		CS†/CD
Keep on Keepin' On	Relix	2057		CD
Live on Stage (recorded 1975)	Relix	2059		CD
Relix's Best of the Early NRPS (material from *Before Time Began, Vintage* and *Live on Stage*)	Relix	2071		CD
Relix's Best of The New Riders of the Purple Sage	Relix	2082		CD
Live in Japan (recorded 1993)	Relix	2065		CD
New Riders	MCA	2196	'76	†
	One Way	22108		CD
Who Are These Guys?	MCA	2248	'77	†
	One Way	22109		CD
Marin County Line	MCA	2397	'77	†
	MCA	632		†
	One Way	22107		CD
Feelin' All Right	A&M	4818	'81	†
Live (recorded 1982)	Avenue	71289	'95	CD

Jerry Garcia and Howard Wales

Hooteroll?	Douglas	30859	'71	†
	Ryko Analogue	0052	'87	LP/CS
	Rykodisc	10052	'87	CD
	Grateful Dead	4108		CS/CD

Jerry Garcia

Garcia	Warner Brothers	2582	'72	†
	Grateful Dead	4003		CS/CD
	Arista	14003	'95	CS/CD
Compliments of Garcia	Round	102	'74	†
	Grateful Dead	4009	'89	CS/CD
	Arista	14009	'95	CS/CD
Reflections	Round	107	'76	†
	Round	565	'76	†
	Grateful Dead	4008	'90	CS/CD
	Arista	14008	'95	CS/CD
Almost Acoustic	Grateful Dead	4005	'88	CS/CD
	Arista	14005	'95	CS/CD

Cats Under the Stars	Arista	4160	'78	†
	Arista	8535	'88	CS/CD
Run for the Roses	Arista	9603	'82	†
	Arista	8557	'88	CS/CD

Jerry Garcia Band

Jerry Garcia Band	Arista	(2)18690	'91	CS/CD
How Sweet It Is	Arista	4051	'97	CD

Jerry Garcia and Merl Saunders

Live at the Keystone (recorded 1973)	Fantasy	(2)79002	'73	LP†
	Fantasy	79002		CS†
Live at the Keystone, Volume 1	Fantasy	4535	'88	LP/CS†
	Fantasy	7701	'88	CD
Live at the Keystone, Volume 2	Fantasy	4536	'88	LP/CS†
	Fantasy	7702	'88	CD
Keystone Encores, Volume 1	Fantasy	4533	'88	LP/CS†
	Fantasy	7703	'88	CD
Keystone Encores, Volume 2	Fantasy	4534		LP/CS†
Blues from the Rainforest	Grateful Dead	3901	'91	CS/CD

Old and in the Way

Old and in the Way	Round	103	'74	†
	Rykodisc	10009		CD
	Grateful Dead	4104		CD
	Sugar Hill	3746	'93	CS/CD
That High Lonesome Sound	Acoustic Disc	19	'96	CS/CD
	Grateful Dead	3907		CS/CD
Breakdown	Acoustic Disc	28	'97	CD

Jerry Garcia and David Grisman

Garcia/Grisman	Acoustic Disc	2	'91	CS/CD
	Grateful Dead	4123	'92	CS/CD
Not for Kids Only	Acoustic Disc	9	'93	CS/CD
	Grateful Dead	4134		CS/CD
Shady Grove	Acoustic Disc	21	'96	CD

Ken Nordine, Jerry Garcia, and David Grisman

Devout Catalyst	Grateful Dead	4015	'92	CS/CD

Bob Weir

Ace	Warner Brothers	2627	'72	†
	Grateful Dead	4004		CS/CD
	Arista	14004	'95	CS/CD
Heaven Help the Fool	Arista	4155	'78	†
	Arista	8165	'88	CS/CD

Bobby and The Midnites

Bobby and The Midnites	Arista	9568	'81	†
	Arista	8558	'88	CS/CD
Where the Beat Meets the Street	Columbia	39276	'84	†
	Razor & Tie	2177	'98	CD

Keith and Donna Godchaux

Keith and Donna	Round	104	'75	†

Phil Lesh and Ned Lagin

Seastones	Round	106	'75	†
	Rykodisc	40193		CS/CD†
	Grateful Dead	4126		CS/CD

Silver (with Brent Mydland)

Silver	Arista	4076	'75	†

Matthew Kelly

A Wing and a Prayer (recorded 1973)	Relix	2010	'85	CD

Kingfish

In Concert (recorded April 1976)	King Biscuit Flower Hour	(2)88006	'96	CD
Kingfish	Round	108	'76	†
	Round	564	'76	†
	Relix	2005		CS†/CD
	Grateful Dead	4010	'90	CS/CD
	Arista	14010	'95	CS/CD
Live 'n' Kickin'	Jet/United Artists	732	'77	†
	Accord	7128		†
Trident	Jet/Columbia	35479	'78	†
Live at the Roxy	Townhouse	7128	'81	†
A Night in New York (recorded 1977)	Relix	2089		CD
A Wing and a Prayer	Relix	2010		CD
Alive in '85	Relix	2016	'85	CS /CD
Relix's Best of Kingfish	Relix	2084		CD

Mickey Hart

Rolling Thunder	Warner Brothers	2635	'72	†
	Relix	2026	'86	†
	Grateful Dead	4011	'90	CS/CD
	Arista	14011	'95	CS/CD
Diga (with The Diga Rhythm Band)	Round	600	'76	†
as Diga Rhythm Band	Rykodisc	10101	'88	LP/CS/CD
Music to Be Born By	Rykodisc	20112	'89	CS/CD
At the Edge	Rykodisc	10124	'90	CS/CD
Planet Drum	Rykodisc	10206	'91	CS/CD
Mickey Hart's Mystery Box	Rykodisc	10338	'96	CD
	Grateful Dead	4143		CS/CD
Supralingua	Rykodisc	(2)10396	'98	CS/CD

The Rhythm Devils

Play River Music	Passport	9844	'80	†
The Apocalypse Now Sessions	Rykodisc	10109		CS/CD

Mickey Hart, Airto, and Flora Purim

Dafos (recorded 1982, 1983)	Rykodisc	10108	'89	CS/CD

Mickey Hart, Henry Wolff, and Nancy Hennings

Yamantaka	Celestial Harmonies	13003	'83	LP/CS

Robert Hunter

Tales of the Great Rum Runners	Round	101	'74	†
	Grateful Dead	4122		CS/CD
	Rykodisc	10158	'90	CS/CD

Tiger Rose	Round	105	'75	†
	Grateful Dead	4114		
	Rykodisc	10115	'89	CS/CD
Jack O' Roses	Dark Star	8001	'79	†
	Relix	2001	'80	†
Amagamalin Street	Relix	2003	'84	CS/CD
Rock Columbia	Relix	2019	'84	CS/CD
The Flight of the Marie Helena	Relix	2009	'85	LP†
Liberty	Relix	2029	'87	CS/CD
Promontory Rider	Relix	2002	'89	CS/CD
A Box of Rain: Live 1990	Grateful Dead	4125		CD
	Rykodisc	10214	'91	CS/CD
Sentinel (poetry)	Grateful Dead	4135		CD
	Rykodisc	20265	'93	CD
Second Sight (with Vince Welnick and Bob Bralove)				
Second Sight	Shanachie	5716	'96	CS/CD
Vince Welnick and The Missing Man Formation				
Vince Welnick and The Missing Man Formation	Arista	14058	'98	CD
Backbone (with Bill Kreutzmann)				
Backbone	Grateful Dead	4056	'98	CD

THE GUESS WHO

Burton Cummings (born December 31, 1947, in Winnipeg, Manitoba, Canada), lead vocals, keyboards, rhythm guitar; Randy Bachman (born September 27, 1943, in Winnipeg), lead guitar; Jim Kale (born August 11, 1943, in Winnipeg), bass; and Garry Peterson (born May 26, 1945, in Winnipeg), drums. Many personnel changes beginning in 1970.

BACHMAN-TURNER OVERDRIVE

Randy Bachman, vocals, lead guitar; Tim Bachman, rhythm guitar; Robbie Bachman (born February 18, 1953, in Winnipeg), drums; and C. F. Turner (born October 16, 1943, in Winnipeg), bass, vocals. Tim Bachman left in 1973, to be replaced by Blair Thornton (born July 23, 1950, in Vancouver, British Columbia).

Popular North American singles band of the late '60s and early '70s, The Guess Who were the first Canadian band to achieve international success. Superseded by the harder-rocking Bachman-Turner Overdrive in the mid-'70s, The Guess Who disbanded in 1975 when lead vocalist Burton Cummings left to pursue a solo career. Both The Guess Who and Bachman-Turner Overdrive regrouped in the '80s.

The Guess Who began their evolution in Winnipeg, Manitoba, Canada, in 1962 when Chad Allan (born Allan Kobel), Randy Bachman, Bob Ashley, Jim Kale, and Garry Peterson formed The Reflections. Changing their name to Chad Allan and The Expressions in 1964, they scored a top Canadian and major U.S. hit with "Shakin' All Over" in 1965. Burton Cummings joined the group in the summer of 1965 and Bob Ashley and Chad Allan dropped out of the group in 1966. Becoming The Guess Who, the group appeared on the Canadian television show *Where It's At* in 1967, recording over a dozen Canadian singles through 1968. They secured U.S. distribution of their recordings with RCA Records in

1969 and soon scored a smash hit with the Bachman-Cummings composition "These Eyes" from their debut RCA album. Their second RCA album, *Canned Wheat,* yielded the two-sided hit "Laughing"/"Undun" and the smash hit "No Time," another Bachman-Cummings collaboration.

The Guess Who became international stars with 1970's *American Woman* album and top two-sided single "American Woman"/"No Sugar Tonight." Randy Bachman left in July 1970, yet The Guess Who continued to score major hits through 1971 with "Hand Me Down World," "Share the Land," "Albert Flasher," and "Rain Dance." Experiencing a number of personnel changes, The Guess Who achieved two final hits in 1974 with "Clap for the Wolfman" (a smash) and "Dancin' Fool." The group disbanded in 1975.

Burton Cummings pursued a solo career in the late '70s, managing a near-smash hit with "Stand Tall" in 1976. In 1979, Jim Kale reconstituted The Guess Who for a single album and subsequent touring. Burton Cummings and Randy Bachman toured as The Guess Who in 1987 and, by 1989, Garry Peterson had joined Kale's edition of The Guess Who.

After leaving The Guess Who, Randy Bachman formed Brave Belt with Chad Allan. After a sole album with Allan, Brave Belt regrouped with Bachman, his brothers Tim and Robbie, and C. Fred Turner. In 1972, the group became Bachman-Turner Overdrive, replacing Tim Bachman with Blair Thornton in 1973. Signed to Mercury Records, the group scored major hits with "Let It Ride" and "Takin' Care of Business" and a top hit with "You Ain't Seen Nothing Yet" in 1974. The hits continued in 1975 with "Roll on Down the Highway" and "Hey You." Randy Bachman departed in 1977 and the group continued to chart into 1979. Bachman formed Ironhorse, who achieved a modest hit with "Sweet Lui-Louise" in 1979. Randy and Tim Bachman regrouped with Fred Turner in 1984 for a sole album on Compleat.

BACHMAN-TURNER OVERDRIVE BIBLIOGRAPHY

Melhuish, Martin. *Bachman-Turner Overdrive: Rock Is My Life, This Is My Song: The Authorized Biography.* Toronto: Methuen; New York: Two Continents, 1976.

Chad Allan and The Expressions

Shakin' All Over	Scepter	533	'66	†
	MGM	4645	'69	†

The Guess Who

Sown and Grown in Canada	Wand	691	'71	†
The Guess Who Play The Guess Who	P.I.P.	6806	'71	†
Wheatfield Soul	RCA	4141	'69/'89	CS/CD†
	RCA	1171	'75	†
Canned Wheat Packed by The Guess Who	RCA	4157	'69/'89	CS/CD†
	RCA	0983	'75	†
American Woman	RCA	4266	'70	CD†
	RCA	3673		CS†
Share the Land	RCA	4359	'70	†
	RCA	54359	'94	CS/CD
Best	RCA	1004	'71	†
	RCA	3662	'80	CD
	RCA	7623		CS
So Long, Bannatyne	RCA	4574	'71	†
Rockin'	RCA	4602	'72	†
	RCA	2683	'78	†

Live at the Paramount	RCA	4779	'72/'90	CS/CD†
Artificial Paradise	RCA	4830	'73	†
Number 10	RCA	0130	'73	†
Best, Volume 2	RCA	0269	'73	†
Road Food	RCA	0405	'74	†
Flavours	RCA	0636	'75	†
Power in the Music	RCA	0995	'75	†
The Way We Were	RCA	1778	'76	†
The Greatest of The Guess Who	RCA	2253	'77	†
	RCA	3746	'88	CD
	RCA	7622	'88	CS
American Woman, These Eyes and Other Hits	RCA	2076	'90	CS/CD
Track Record: The Guess Who Collection	RCA	(2)61077	'91	CS/CD
These Eyes	RCA	61133	'92	CS/CD
	RCA	61152	'92	CD†
The Guess Who at Their Best	RCA	66200	'93	CS/CD
Shakin' All Over	Springboard Int'l.	4022	'75	†
The Guess Who	Pickwick	3246		†
All This for a Song	Hilltak	19227	'79	†
	Lacindy	22010	'94	CD

Burton Cummings

Burton Cummings	Portrait	34261	'76	†
My Own Way to Rock	Portrait	34698	'77	†
Dream of a Child	Portrait	35481	'78	†

Randy Bachman

Axe	RCA	4348	'70	†
Survivor	Polydor	6141	'78	†

Brave Belt

Brave Belt	Reprise	6447	'71	†
Brave Belt II	Reprise	2057	'72	†
Bachman-Turner-Bachman as Brave Belt	Reprise	2210	'75	†

Bachman-Turner Overdrive

Bachman-Turner Overdrive	Mercury	673	'73	†
	Mercury	838196	'89	CD
Bachman-Turner Overdrive II	Mercury	696	'73	†
	Mercury	822504	'89	CD
Not Fragile	Mercury	1004	'74	†
	Mercury	830178		CS/CD
Four Wheel Drive	Mercury	1027	'75	†
	Mercury	830970	'89	CD
Head On	Mercury	1067	'75	†
	Mercury	838197	'89	CD†
Best of B.T.O. (So Far)	Mercury	1101	'76	†
	Mercury	822786		CS
Freeways	Mercury	3700	'77	†
	Mercury	838199	'89	CD†
Street Action	Mercury	3713	'78	†
Rock n' Roll Nights	Mercury	3748	'79	†
Greatest Hits	Mercury	830039	'86	CD

The Anthology	Mercury	(2)514902	'93	CS/CD
You Ain't Seen Nothin' Yet	Polygram	838165	'91	CS/CD
Bachman-Turner Overdrive	Compleat	1010	'84	†
BTO Live! Live! Live!	MCA/Curb	5760	'86	†
All-Time Greatest Hits: Live	MCA/Curb	10808	'90	CD†
	Curb/Warner Brothers	77328	'90	CD
Best Of: Live	Curb/Warner Brothers	77653	'93	CS/CD
King Biscuit Flower Hour Concert (recorded 1974)	King Biscuit Flower Hour	88039	'98	CD
Ironhorse				
Ironhorse	Scotti Brothers	7103	'79	†

JIMI HENDRIX

Born James Marshall Hendrix on November 27, 1942, in Seattle, Washington; died September 18, 1970, in London, England.

THE JIMI HENDRIX EXPERIENCE

Jimi Hendrix, lead guitar, lead vocals; Noel Redding (born December 25, 1945, in Folkstone, Kent, England), bass, background vocals; and John "Mitch" Mitchell (born July 9, 1946, in London, England), drums.

JIMI HENDRIX (HULTON-DEUTSCH COLLECTION/CORBIS)

One of the two "super-star" rock guitarists of the '60s, Jimi Hendrix is revered by many as *the* master virtuoso of the electric guitar. Undoubtedly the most adventurous and daring electric guitarist of the '60s, Hendrix is regarded by some as rock's single most important instrumentalist and perhaps the most influential guitarist ever. He enormously expanded the possibilities of the electric guitar, masterfully manipulating devices such as the wah-wah pedal, fuzz-box, and tape-delay mechanism to produce sounds alternately gentle and melodic, loud and psychedelic, even extraterrestrial and aquatic. His masterful and imaginative use of studio techniques with equipment that would be regarded as primitive by today's standards vastly extended the potential of recorded electric music. His carefully controlled use of distortion and feedback laid the foundation for *all* the heavy metal guitarists that followed, while inspiring jazz musicians such as Miles Davis to adopt certain elements of rock music, leading to the development of fusion music.

A left-handed guitarist, Jimi Hendrix astoundingly played a right-handed guitar upside down and backwards, rather than using a left-handed guitar. Perhaps rock music's most outstanding and flamboyant showman during his days with The Jimi Hendrix Experience, he resurrected in performance old bluesmen's show-stopping techniques such as playing the guitar behind his back or head, playing the guitar with his teeth, and aggressively caressing, humping, and attacking his guitar with such sexual lewdness as to become instantly notorious. Ironically achieving his first mass popularity in Great Britain rather than his native United States, Jimi Hendrix was essentially launched in America with his breathtaking performance at the 1967 Monterey International Pop Festival. As rock music's first black "superstar," he was the first black musician to shatter the record industry's preoccupation with blacks as singles artists and establish himself as an album artist. Seeking to alter his image of showman and black "super stud" by 1968, Jimi Hendrix sought to be recognized simply as a guitarist while relegating his flamboyance and outrageous stage demeanor to the past, much to the consternation of perplexed and often hostile fans. Moreover, like Chuck Berry, Hendrix' blues-based recordings have been sorely overlooked in favor of his rock 'n' roll. Hendrix' death in 1970 served to amplify his reputation and legend, and, along with Jim Morrison, Elvis Presley, and John Lennon, he became one of the most exploited and mythologized of all dead rock stars. The Jimi Hendrix Experience was inducted into the Rock and Roll Hall of Fame in 1992.

James Hendrix obtained his first acoustic guitar at the age of eleven, graduating to electric guitar at twelve. Playing in a number of Seattle area bands by fourteen, he dropped out of high school at sixteen and eventually joined the Army in 1961. While serving, he became a paratrooper and met and jammed with bassist Billy Cox. Discharged after slightly more than a year because of a back injury sustained in a parachute jump, Hendrix subsequently toured the South's "chitlin" circuit, backing artists such as B. B. King, Sam Cooke, and Jackie Wilson. He moved to New York in 1964 to record with The Isley Brothers and King Curtis. The following year, he was a member of Little Richard's backup band and Curtis Knight's group. In June 1966, Hendrix formed his own group, Jimmy James and The Blue Flames, for engagements in Greenwich Village coffeehouses. "Discovered" there in July by former Animals bassist Bryan "Chas" Chandler, Hendrix went to England at Chandler's behest in September, forming The Jimi Hendrix Experience with two English musicians, Noel Redding and Mitch Mitchell.

The Jimi Hendrix Experience became an immediate success in Great Britain, scoring major hits with "Hey Joe," "Purple Haze," and "The Wind Cries Mary" in the first half of 1967. Commencing their first British tour in March and their first European tour in May, the group's debut album, *Are You Experienced?* was riding high on the British charts when they debuted in the United States at the Monterey Festival in June. Their performance included Dylan's "Like a Rolling Stone" and the awe-inspiring finale "Wild Thing," which culminated in the torching of Hendrix' lighter fluid–drenched guitar. Word of Hendrix's spectacular, flamboyant Monterey performance spread rapidly, and *Are You Experienced?,* upon American release on Reprise Records in August, became an instant best-seller, remaining on the album charts for over two years. Yielding only minor hit singles with the classics "Purple Haze" and "Foxey Lady," the album also included "Hey Joe," "Are You Experienced?," and the poignantly lyrical "The Wind Cries Mary." Following an abortive tour with The Monkees (a mismatch if ever there was one), Hendrix returned to England.

The Jimi Hendrix Experience's *Axis: Bold as Love,* released stateside in early 1968, became another immediate best-seller, producing the minor hit "Up from the Skies" and containing the masterful "Little Wing," the gentle "One Rainy Wish," and the ominous "If 6 Was 9," later used in the breakthrough Peter Fonda–Dennis Hopper movie *Easy Rider. Electric Ladyland,* The Experience's final album and the crowning achievement of their brief recording career, yielded the group's only major hit with Dylan's "All Along the Watchtower" in its definitive version. Included on the double-record set were the vituperative "Crosstown Traffic," the lilting "Rainy Day, Dream Away," the challenging "1983," and the extended jam "Voodoo Chile," featuring Stevie Winwood on organ.

Tours by The Experience in 1968 saw Hendrix retreating from his role as psychedelic, flash guitarist-showman, much to the chagrin of inflexible fans. Chandler stopped managing the group in September and, in November, The Jimi Hendrix Experience announced their intention to disband, although contractual obligations kept the group together through June 1969. Noel Redding formed Fat Mattress in 1969, Road in 1971, and The Noel Redding Band in 1975. Mitch Mitchell continued to play with Hendrix on and off until his death, briefly becoming a member of Ramatam with former Iron Butterfly guitarist Mike Pinera in 1972.

During 1969, Jimi Hendrix began building his own studio, Electric Ladyland, in New York City, while seldom performing publicly. He eventually logged over 600 hours of studio tapes with various participants, including jazz musicians such as John McLaughlin. In August, Hendrix, backed by Mitch Mitchell and Army buddy Billy Cox, played the Woodstock Festival. The performance closed with a stunning version of "The Star Spangled Banner," which appropriately segued into "Purple Haze" (later included on the first *Woodstock* album).

On New Year's Eve 1969, the all-black Band of Gypsys (Hendrix, Cox, and drummer Buddy Miles) debuted at Bill Graham's Fillmore East. The performance, recorded and later released in album form, included Miles' "(Them) Changes" and Hendrix's twelve-minute-plus "Machine Gun." However, the group never really worked out, perhaps due to Buddy Miles' overbearing drum style.

Jimi Hendrix was soon recording his next album, a double-record set tentatively entitled *First Rays of the New Rising Sun,* with Mitch Mitchell and Billy Cox. During the spring and summer of 1970, Hendrix toured with them, opening his Electric Ladyland studio shortly before their August appearance at the Isle of Wight. On September 18, 1970, Jimi Hendrix died of "inhalation of vomit due to barbiturate intoxication" in London at the age of twenty-seven.

Much of the material from *First Rays of the New Rising Sun* was ultimately released on *The Cry of Love* and *Rainbow Bridge,* and reissued on *Voodoo Soup* in 1995. *The Cry of Love* featured Buddy Miles on "Ezy Rider" and Noel Redding on "My Friend" and included two excellent but overlooked slow blues songs, "Drifting" and "Angel." *Rainbow Bridge* contained "Dolly Dagger," "Pali Gap," and the live "Hear My Train A Comin.'" *Hendrix in the West* assembled live recordings such as Chuck Berry's "Johnny B. Goode" and the Hendrix originals "Red House," "Little Wing," and "Voodoo Chile." *War Heroes* contained nearly completed recordings by Hendrix, including "Izabella" and "Stepping Stone." *Soundtrack Recordings from the Film "Jimi Hendrix"* compiled live performances and interviews.

In 1974, the estate of Jimi Hendrix hired producer Alan Douglas to sort through the tape archives left by Jimi Hendrix. For *Crash Landing* and *Midnight Lightning,* Douglas erased the original sidemen and grafted on Los Angeles sessions players, while *Nine to the Universe* was taken from the jam sessions recorded in 1969 and 1970. Subsequent album releases included the live compilation *The Jimi Hendrix Concerts,* the complete *Jimi Plays Monterey, Radio One* (live recordings made for the BBC in 1967), and the 4-CD anthology of alternate takes, demonstration records, live performances, and interviews *Lifelines.* The Jimi Hendrix Experience was inducted into the Rock and Roll Hall of Fame in 1992 and, the following year, Reprise issued the tribute album *Stone Free,* on which various contemporary artists from Ice-T to Eric Clapton, The Pretenders to Nigel Kennedy recorded versions of Jimi Hendrix's songs.

In July 1995, after years of court battles, Jimi Hendrix's father Al was awarded the rights to his son's music.

JIMI HENDRIX BIBLIOGRAPHY

Benson, Joe. *Uncle Joe's Record Guide: Eric Clapton, Jimi Hendrix, The Who.* Glendale, CA: J. Benson Unlimited, 1987.

Boot, Adrian, and Chris Salewicz (compilers). *Jimi Hendrix: The Ultimate Experience.* New York: Macmillan, 1995.

Carey, Gary. *Lenny, Janis and Jimi.* New York: Pocket Books, 1975.

Henderson, David. *Jimi Hendrix: Voodoo Child of the Aquarian Age.* Garden City, NY: Doubleday, 1978.

———. *'Scuse Me While I Kiss the Sky: The Life of Jimi Hendrix.* New York: Bantam Books, 1981, 1996.

Hendrix, Jimi. *Cherokee Mist: The Lost Writings.* New York: HarperCollins, 1993.

Hopkins, Jerry. *Hit and Run: The Jimi Hendrix Story.* New York: Perigee Books, 1983.

Knight, Curtis. *Jimi.* New York: Praeger, 1974.

———. *Jimi Hendrix: Starchild.* Wilmington, DE: Abelard Productions, 1992.

McDermott, John, with Billy Cox and Eddie Kramer. *Jimi Hendrix Sessions: The Complete Studio Recording Sessions, 1963–1970.* Boston: Little, Brown, 1995.

McDermott, John, with Eddie Kramer. *Hendrix: Setting the Record Straight.* New York: Warner Books, 1992.

Mitchell, Mitch. *The Hendrix Experience.* New York: Da Capo Press, 1998.

———, with John Platt. *Jimi Hendrix: Inside The Experience.* New York: Harmony Books, 1990.

Murray, Charles Shaar. *Crosstown Traffic: Jimi Hendrix and the Post-War Rock 'n' Roll Revolution.* New York: St. Martin's Press, 1989, 1991.

Shapiro, Harry, and Caesar Glebbeek. *Electric Gypsy: Jimi Hendrix.* New York: St. Martin's Press, 1991, 1995.

Welch, Chris. *Hendrix: A Biography.* New York: Flash Books, 1973.

Jimi Hendrix and Little Richard

Roots of Rock	Archive of Folk and Jazz Music	296	'74	†
Together	Pickwick	3347		†

Jimi Hendrix with The Isley Brothers

In the Beginning (recorded 1964)	T-Neck	3007	'71	†

Jimi Hendrix and Curtis Knight

Get That Feeling	Capitol	2856	'67	†
Flashing	Capitol	2894	'68	†
Get That Feeling/Flashing	Capitol	(2)659	'71	†

Jimi Hendrix and Lonnie Youngblood

Together	Maple	6004	'71	†

The Jimi Hendrix Experience/Otis Redding

At Monterey	Reprise	2029	'70	†

The Jimi Hendrix Experience

Radio One (recorded 1967)	Rykodisc	20078	'88	CS/CD
Are You Experienced?	Reprise	6261	'67	LP/CS/CD†
	MCA	10893	'93	CS/CD†
	MCA	11602	'97	CS/CD
Axis: Bold as Love	Reprise	6281	'68	LP/CS/CD†
	MCA	10894	'93	CS/CD†
	MCA	11601		CS/CD

Electric Ladyland	Reprise	(2)6307	'68	†
	Reprise	6307		CS/CD†
	MCA	10895	'93	CS/CD†
	MCA	11600		CS/CD
Smash Hits	Reprise	2276	'69	LP/CS/CD†
The Ultimate Experience	MCA	10829	'93	CS/CD
The Experience Collection	MCA	(4)10936	'93	CS/CD
BBC Sessions (recorded 1967–1969)	MCA	(2)11742	'98	CS/CD
Fat Mattress (with Noel Redding)				
Fat Mattress	Atco	33-309	'69	†
Fat Mattress II	Atco	33-347	'71	†
The Noel Redding Band				
Clonkakilty Cowboys	RCA	1237	'75	†
Blowin'	RCA	1863	'76	†
Noel Redding				
The Missing Album	Griffin	371	'95	CD
Ramatam (with Mitch Mitchell)				
Ramatam	Atlantic	7236	'72	†
In April Came the Dawning of the Red Suns	Atlantic	7261	'73	†
The Band of Gypsys				
The Band of Gypsys	Capitol	472	'70	†
	Capitol	16319		†
	Capitol	96414	'95	LP/CS/CD
The Band of Gypsys 2	Capitol	12416	'86	LP/CS†
Live Recordings by Jimi Hendrix (in Release Order)				
Hendrix in the West	Reprise	2049	'72	†
The Jimi Hendrix Concerts	Reprise	(2)22306	'82	†
Jimi Plays Monterey (June 18, 1967)	Reprise	25358	'86	LP/CS/CD†
In Concert	Springboard Int'l	4031		†
Live at Winterland (October 1968)	Rykodisc	20038	'87	CS/CD
	Rykodisc	90038	'88	CD
The Last Experience Concert	Zeta	517		CD†
Woodstock (August 18, 1969)	MCA	11063	'94	CS/CD
Posthumous Jimi Hendrix Releases				
The Cry of Love	Reprise	2034	'71	LP/CS/CD†
Rainbow Bridge	Reprise	2040	'71	†
War Heroes	Reprise	2103	'72	†
Soundtrack Recordings from the Film "Jimi Hendrix"	Reprise	(2)6481	'73	†
Crash Landing	Reprise	2204	'75	LP/CS/CD†
Midnight Lightning	Reprise	2229	'75	†
The Essential Jimi Hendrix	Reprise	(2)2245	'78	†
The Essential Jimi Hendrix, Volume II	Reprise	2293	'79	†
The Essential Jimi Hendrix, Volumes 1 and 2	Reprise	(2)26035		CD†
Nine to the Universe	Warner Brothers	2299	'80	†
Kiss the Sky	Reprise	25119	'84/'85	LP/CS/CD†
Lifelines: The Jimi Hendrix Story	Reprise	(4)26435	'91	CS/CD†
Stages	Reprise	(4)26732	'91	CS/CD†
Blues	MCA	11060	'94	CS/CD

Voodoo Soup	MCA	11236	'95	CS/CD
First Rays of the New Rising Sun	MCA	11599	'97	CS/CD
Experience Hendrix—The Best of Jimi Hendrix	MCA	11671	'97	CS/CD
South Saturn Delta	MCA	11684	'97	CS/CD

Various Other Jimi Hendrix Releases

In the Beginning (recorded 1966)	Shout	502	'72	†
Rare Hendrix (recorded 1966)	Trip	9500	'72	†
Roots of Hendrix (recorded 1966)	Trip	9501	'73	†
The Genius of Jimi Hendrix (recorded 1966)	Trip	9523	'74	†
Superpak	Trip	(2)3509	'76	†
Very Best	United Artists	505	'76	†
Jimi	Pickwick	3528	'76	†
Before London	Accord	7101	'81	†
Free Spirit	Accord	7112	'81	†
Cosmic Feeling	Accord	7139	'81	†
Rock and Roll	Richmond	2153		CS

Tribute Albums

The Gil Evans Orchestra Plays the Music of Jimi Hendrix	RCA	0667	'74	†
	Bluebird	8409	'88	LP/CS/CD†
Stone Free: A Tribute To Jimi Hendrix	Reprise	45438	'93	CS/CD

HERMAN'S HERMITS

Peter "Herman" Noone (born November 5, 1947, in Manchester, Lancashire, England), vocals, piano, guitar; Keith Hopwood (born October 26, 1946, in Manchester), rhythm guitar; Derek "Lek" Leckenby (born May 14, 1946, in Leeds, Yorkshire, England; died June 4, 1994, in Manchester), lead guitar; Karl Green (born July 31, 1947, in Salford, Lancashire, England), bass; and Barry Whitwam (born July 21, 1946, in Manchester), drums.

Following on the heels of The Beatles, Herman's Hermits enjoyed greater popularity in the United States than in Great Britain with their novelty songs, cover songs, and teen-oriented hit singles. Showing greater sophistication in their song selection in the later '60s ("Dandy," "No Milk Today"), the original Herman's Hermits broke up in 1971 as former lead vocalist Peter Noone pursued a varied entertainment career on his own.

Formed in 1962 by Peter Noone as The Heartbeats, Peter became Herman and the group became Herman's Hermits at the behest of producer Mickie Most, with whom they signed in 1964. The group actually played on few of their recordings, as future Led Zeppelin members Jimmy Page and John Paul Jones handled much of the guitar and bass work, respectively. In late 1964, they scored a top British and major American hit with Carole King and Gerry Goffin's "I'm into Something Good." The following year Herman's Hermits achieved smash American hits with "Can't You Hear My Heartbeat," remakes of The Rays' "Silhouettes" and Sam Cooke's "Wonderful World," the ditties "Mrs. Brown You've Got a Lovely Daughter" and "I'm Henry VIII, I Am," and "Just a Little Bit Better." In 1966, the group starred in the movie *Hold On!,* which yielded smash hits with "A Must to Avoid" and Graham Gouldman's "Leaning on a Lamp Post." That year, they also scored smash hits with "Listen People," from the Connie Francis movie *When the Boys Meet the Girls,* and "Dandy," written by The Kinks' Ray Davies.

Following the 1967 smash "There's a Kind of Hush" (backed with "No Milk Today"), Herman's Hermits managed major American hits with "Don't Go into the Rain (You're Going to Melt)" and "I Can Take or Leave Your Loving" through 1968. Major British hits continued into 1970 and the group persevered through 1971, when Noone began a solo career. In 1973, original members Green, Leckenby, and Whitwam reconstituted Herman's Hermits. Leckenby died of non-Hodgkins lymphoma in Manchester on June 4, 1994.

Peter Noone subsequently hosted an English television show for three years before moving to the south of France, where he recorded a number of hit French singles. He later moved to Los Angeles and became a studio musician. In 1980, Noone recorded an album with The Tremblers for Johnston Records, for whom he recorded a solo album in 1982. He played Frederic in *The Pirates of Penzance* on Broadway later that year and launched a five-year comeback plan in 1986. Beginning in 1989, Peter Noone hosted the music video show *My Generation* on cable television's VH-1 channel.

Herman's Hermits

Introducing Herman's Hermits	MGM	4282	'65	†
On Tour	MGM	4295	'65	†
Best	MGM	4315	'65	†
Hold On!	MGM	4342	'66	†
Both Sides Of Herman's Hermits	MGM	4386	'66	†
Best, Volume II	MGM	4416	'66	†
There's a Kind of Hush All Over the World	MGM	4438	'67	†
Blaze	MGM	4478	'67	†
Best, Volume III	MGM	4505	'67	†
Mrs. Brown, You've Got a Lovely Daughter	MGM	4548	'68	†
Their Greatest Hits	Abkco	4227	'73/'88	CS/CD
Greatest Hits	Hollywood/IMG	386		CS/CD
Herman's Hermits Greatest Hits	Griffin	135		CD

The Tremblers

Twice Nightly	Johnston	36532	'80	†

Peter Noone

One of the Glory Boys	Johnston	37369	'82	†

DAN HICKS

Born December 9, 1941, in Little Rock, Arkansas.

THE CHARLATANS

George Hunter, vocals; Mike Wilhelm, guitar; Michael Ferguson, piano; Richard Olson, bass; and Dan Hicks, drums, guitar.

Founding member of The Charlatans, probably the first San Francisco band of the psychedelic era, Dan Hicks later formed Dan Hicks and His Hot Licks for an engaging acoustic blend of Western swing, vocal jazz, and jug band music. Featuring Hicks' own wry, sardonic songs, the violin virtuosity of Sid Page, and the precise vocal harmonies of the female Lickettes, Dan Hicks and His Hot Licks never produced a hit single, yet they inspired later "nostalgia" acts such as Manhattan Transfer, The Pointer Sisters, Bette Midler, and Leon Redbone. The group disbanded in 1973, with Hicks subsequently pursuing his own low-key career. The surviving members of The Charlatans (Mike Wilhelm died in 1979) ultimately reunited briefly in 1997.

Dan Hicks grew up in Santa Rosa, California, taking up drums at the age of eleven and guitar at twenty. He played locally and eventually joined The Charlatans as drummer in 1965. They debuted at a three-month engagement at the Red Dog Saloon in Virginia City, Nevada, that summer before returning to Haight-Ashbury. Recording one album eventually released by Philips, The Charlatans disbanded in 1969. Before the group's breakup, however, Hicks had formed Dan Hicks and His Hot Licks with violinist David LaFlamme, who soon left to form It's a Beautiful Day.

Reconstituted with Hicks, lead guitarist John Weber, violinist Sid Page, bassist Jaime Leopold, vocalist-keyboardist Christina Gaucher, and vocalist Sherry Snow, Dan Hicks and His Hot Licks signed with Epic Records in September 1968. Their debut album, *Original Recordings,* included Hicks' "Canned Music," "I Scare Myself," and the classic "How Can I Miss You When You Won't Go Away." However, the album sold poorly and the group was dropped by Epic in the summer of 1970.

Dan Hicks and His Hot Licks subsequently realigned, retaining Hicks, Page, and Leopold while adding Nicole Dukes (vocals), Maryann Price (vocals, percussion), and Naomi Ruth Eisenberg (vocals, violin) as The Lickettes. Signed to Blue Thumb Records, their live album *Where's the Money* failed to sell despite favorable reviews and the first of a series of national tours. Dukes was dismissed and guitarist John Girton added for *Striking It Rich!,* which contained "Moody Richard," "Walkin' One and Only," and Johnny Mercer's "Old Cow Hand." As *Last Train to Hicksville* was becoming their best-selling album, Dan Hicks disbanded the group.

In 1978, Warner Brothers released Dan Hicks' *It Happened One Bite,* recorded in 1975 with Page, Girton, and Price as the soundtrack to an unreleased film. By 1979, Hicks had formed a musical partnership with guitarist Kenneth "Turtle" Van Demarr, with whom he toured for more than a decade, primarily on the West Coast. Former Charlatan Richard Olsen has led the San Francisco society dance band The Richard Olsen Orchestra since the early '80s. Sid Page resurfaced in 1984 with the jazz album *Odyssey,* recorded with Dave Shelander. Dan Hicks and His Acoustic Warriors eventually recorded *Shootin' Straight* for the On The Spot subsidiary of Private Music.

The Charlatans

The Charlatans	Philips	600309	'69	†
	One Way	31442	'95	CD
First Album and Alabama Bound	ROIR	4014	'96	CD

Dan Hicks and His Hot Licks

Original Recordings	Epic	26464	'69	†
	Sony	26464		CS/CD†
Where's the Money	Blue Thumb	29	'71	†
	MCA	31337	'89	CD
Striking It Rich!	Blue Thumb	36	'72	†
	MCA	31187		CD
Last Train to Hicksville	Blue Thumb	51	'73	†
	MCA	31188		CD
Dan Hicks and His Hot Licks	K-tel	75053		CS/CD

Dan Hicks

It Happened One Bite	Warner Brothers	3158	'78	†

Sid Page and David Shelander

Odyssey	Bainbridge	6257	'84	CD

Dan Hicks and His Acoustic Warriors

Shootin' Straight	On the Spot	62118	'94	CS/CD

HOLLAND-DOZIER-HOLLAND

Eddie Holland (born October 30, 1939, in Detroit), Lamont Dozier (born June 16, 1941, in Detroit), and Brian Holland (born February 15, 1941, in Detroit).

Motown Records' premier songwriting-production team, Brian Holland, Lamont Dozier, and Eddie Holland were largely responsible for the "Motown sound." Utilizing an excellent team of sessions musicians and sophisticated studio equipment, Holland-Dozier-Holland (hereafter referred to as H-D-H) composed and produced over twenty-five top-ten hits that registered popularity with black *and* white audiences and thrust Motown's brand of soul music into the forefront of American popular music in the '60s. Severing relations with Motown in late 1967, H-D-H continued their hit-making ways on their own labels Invictus and Hot Wax in the early '70s. Holland-Dozier-Holland were inducted into the Rock and Roll Hall of Fame in 1990.

Lamont Dozier began singing as a child in his grandmother's church choir, writing his first song at the age of ten. Making his recording debut with The Romeos at fifteen, he met Berry Gordy, Jr., in 1958 and recorded as Lamont Anthony for Anna Records in 1961. Eddie Holland also met Gordy in 1958, dropping out of college to work for him and later scoring one of Motown's first hits with "Jamie" in 1962. Brother Brian Holland collaborated on two early hits for The Marvelettes, "Please Mr. Postman" and "Playboy."

In 1963, Brian and Eddie Holland and Lamont Dozier teamed up as a songwriting-production unit. Between 1963 and the end of 1967, H-D-H wrote and produced the majority of Motown's hit singles, with Brian providing the music, Eddie contributing lyrics, and Lamont supplying both music and lyrics. Their hit compositions included "Heat Wave," "Quicksand," and "Nowhere to Run" for Martha and The Vandellas, "Mickey's Monkey" for The Miracles, and "Can I Get a Witness," "You're a Wonderful One," and "How Sweet It Is (To Be Loved by You)" for Marvin Gaye. Other hit compositions included "Take Me in Your Arms" for Kim Weston and "This Old Heart of Mine" for The Isley Brothers. Eddie Holland later collaborated with Norman Whitfield on several major hits for The Temptations, including "Ain't Too Proud to Beg," "Beauty Is Only Skin Deep," and "(I Know) I'm Losing You."

Much of H-D-H's finest material was reserved for The Four Tops and The Supremes. Their song hits for The Four Tops included "Baby I Need Your Loving," "I Can't Help Myself," "It's the Same Old Song," "Reach Out, I'll Be There," "Standing in the Shadows of Love," and "Bernadette." H-D-H's biggest success came with The Supremes, for whom they wrote and produced at least ten top pop and smash soul hits as well as numerous major hits. These included "Where Did Our Love Go," "Baby Love," "Come See About Me," "Stop! in the Name Of Love," "Back in My Arms Again," "I Hear a Symphony," "My World Is Empty Without You," "Love Is Like an Itching in My Heart," "You Can't Hurry Love," "You Keep Me Hangin' On," and "Love Is Here and Now You're Gone." H-D-H extended their string of hits for the group as Diana Ross and The Supremes in 1967 with "Reflections" and "In and Out of Love."

However, in late 1967, Brian Holland, Lamont Dozier, and Eddie Holland bitterly quit Motown to form their own record labels, Invictus and Hot Wax. A series of lawsuits ensued between Motown and H-D-H, and the team was enjoined from writing songs after May 1969. Nonetheless, they produced a number of hits in the early '70s. Invictus crossover hits included "Give Me Just a Little More Time," "Pay to the Piper," "Chairman of the Board," and "Finder's Keepers" by Chairmen of the Board, and "Band of Gold," "Deeper and Deeper," and the controversial "Bring the Boys Home" by Freda Payne. Pop and rhythm-and-blues hits on Hot Wax included "Somebody's Been Sleeping" by 100 Proof Aged in Soul, and "Girls It Ain't Easy," "Want Ads," "Stick-Up," "One Monkey Don't Stop No Show," and "The Day I Found Myself" by Honey Cone.

Following the out-of-court settlement of the Motown–H-D-H lawsuits in early 1972, Brian Holland and Lamont Dozier returned to active recording, scoring major soul and minor pop hits on Invictus with "Don't Leave Me Starvin' for Your Love" and "Why Can't We

Be Lovers," respectively. Holland and Dozier recorded as a duo in 1973, the year the overall partnership ended, and Dozier subsequently pursued a solo recording career, achieving smash soul and major pop hits with "Trying to Hold on to My Woman" and "Fish Ain't Biting," and a soul smash with "Let Me Start Tonight" on ABC Records in 1974. Dozier later switched to Warner Brothers Records, then Columbia. He produced Aretha Franklin's 1977 album *Sweet Passion* and wrote songs for Simply Red, Boz Scaggs, Eric Clapton, and Phil Collins during the '80s. In 1991, he recorded *Inside Seduction* for Atlantic Records. Holland-Dozier-Holland were inducted into the Rock and Roll Hall of Fame in 1990.

Eddie Holland

Eddie Holland	Motown	604	'63	†

Lamont Dozier

Out Here on My Own	ABC	804	'74	†
Black Bach	ABC	839	'74	†
Love and Beauty	Invictus	33134	'74	†
Right There	Warner Brothers	2929	'76	†
Peddlin' Music on the Side	Warner Brothers	3039	'77	†
Bittersweet	Warner Brothers	3282	'78	†
Working on You	Columbia	37129	'81	†
Inside Seduction	Atlantic	82228	'91	CS/CD†

THE HOLLIES

Allan Clarke (born April 5, 1942, in Salford, Lancashire, England), lead vocals; Graham Nash (born February 2, 1942, in Blackpool, Lancashire), harmony vocals, guitar; Tony Hicks (born December 16, 1943, in Nelson, Lancashire), lead guitar, vocals, banjo; Eric Haydock (born February 3, 1943, in Burnley, Lancashire), bass; and Bobby Elliott (born December 8, 1942, in Burnley, Lancashire), drums. Later members included Bernie Calvert (born September 16, 1942, in Brierfield, Lancashire) and Terry Sylvester (born January 8, 1945, in Liverpool, Lancashire).

One of the most popular British singles bands to emerge in the wake of The Beatles, The Hollies achieved their mid-'60s success on the basis of Allan Clarke's distinctive lead vocals, the whining, high-pitched, and sometimes harsh harmonies of Graham Nash and Tony Hicks, and the songwriting of Graham Gouldman and the Clarke-Hicks-Nash team. More consistently popular in Great Britain than in the United States, The Hollies were never able to make serious inroads as an album group. They persevered after the 1968 departure of Nash, scoring smash hits with "He Ain't Heavy, He's My Brother," "Long Cool Woman (In a Black Dress)," and "The Air That I Breathe" in the '70s. Clarke, Nash, Hicks, and Bobby Elliott reunited briefly as The Hollies in 1983 to tour and record.

Allan Clarke and Graham Nash became friends in elementary school in Manchester and later sang together as The Two Teens, Ricky and Dane, and The Guytones. They added other members and became The Fourtones and then The Deltas. In 1962, the two teamed with Tony Hicks and two others. By 1963, with one replacement, the group had become The Hollies, with Clarke, Nash, Hicks, Eric Haydock, and Bobby Elliott. Signed to Parlophone Records (Imperial in the United States) in early 1963, The Hollies scored British hits with "Searchin'" and "Stay" before achieving their first (minor) American hit with "Just One Look" in 1964. Although "I'm Alive" became a top British hit in 1965, the group did not have even a moderate American hit until "Look Through Any Window," written by Graham Gouldman. The group toured the United States for the first time in the spring of 1965, replacing Haydock with Bernie Calvert in the spring of 1966. Years earlier, Calvert had been a member of The Dolphins with Tony Hicks and Bobby Elliott.

The Hollies' most successful years were 1966 and 1967. After scoring a smash British and American hit with Graham Gouldman's "Bus Stop," they achieved hits in both countries with "Stop! Stop! Stop!," "On a Carousel," "Pay You Back with Interest," and "Carrie Anne," all Clarke-Hicks-Nash collaborations, the last on Epic Records. An attempt to make inroads in the album market with *Dear Eloise/King Midas in Reverse* failed and Nash, unhappy with the prospect of recording an album of Bob Dylan songs, left the group in late 1968 to join David Crosby and Steve Stills. Nash was replaced by vocalist-rhythm guitarist Terry Sylvester, a former member of The Swinging Blue Jeans (1964's "Hippy Hippy Shake").

During 1969 and 1970, the maudlin ballad "He Ain't Heavy, He's My Brother" became a near-smash hit for The Hollies. In October 1971, the group fired Allan Clarke, who pursued a neglected solo career. Nonetheless, he was the lead vocalist on the smash hit "Long Cool Woman (In a Black Dress)" from *Distant Light,* which also produced a major hit with "Long Dark Road." *Greatest Hits,* released in 1973, included the group's hits on both the Imperial and Epic labels. Clarke returned in mid-1973 and helped record *The Hollies,* which contained the smash hit "The Air That I Breathe." The group continued to record for Epic through 1978. In 1983, Hollies mainstays Tony Hicks and Bobby Elliott reunited briefly with Allan Clarke and Graham Nash for *What Goes Around,* a major hit with a remake of The Supremes' "Stop in the Name of Love," and one round of touring. With stalwarts Clarke, Hicks, and Elliott, The Hollies continued to tour into the '90s.

The Hollies

Here I Go Again	Imperial	12265	'65	†
Hear! Here!	Imperial	12299	'66	†
Beat Group	Imperial	12312	'66	†
Bus Stop	Imperial	12330	'66	†
Stop! Stop! Stop!	Imperial	12339	'67	†
Evolution	Epic	26315	'67	†
Dear Eloise/King Midas in Reverse	Epic	26344	'68	†
	Sundazed	6123		CD
Words and Music by Bob Dylan	Epic	26447	'69	†
He Ain't Heavy, He's My Brother	Epic	26538	'70	†
	Columbia	13092	'76	†
Moving Finger	Epic	30255	'71	†
	Sundazed	6125		CD
Distant Light	Epic	30958	'72	†
	Epic/Legacy	30958	'91	CD
Romany	Epic	31992	'73	†
The Hollies	Epic	32574	'74	†
	Epic/Legacy	32574	'91	CD
Another Night	Epic	33387	'75	†
Clarke, Hicks, Sylvester, Elliott, Calvert	Epic	34714	'77	†
Crazy Steal	Epic	35334	'78	†
Live Hits	Epic/Legacy	65286	'98	CS/CD
What Goes Around	Atlantic	80076	'83	†

Hollies Anthologies and Compilations

Greatest Hits	Imperial	12350	'67	†
Greatest Hits	Epic	32061	'73	CS/CD
Epic Anthology: From the Original Master Tapes	Epic	46161	'90	CD
Very Best	United Artists	329	'75	†
The Hollies' Greatest	Capitol	16056	'80	†
Hottest Hits	Pair	(2)1041	'86	†

More Great Hits (1963–1968)	EMI-America	16397	'86	†
The Best of the Hollies	EMI-America	10329	'87	†
	EMI	92882		CS/CD†
Later Hits	EMI-America	16482	'87	†
Best, Volume I	EMI-Manhattan	46584	'88	CS/CD†
Best, Volume II	EMI-Manhattan	48831	'88	CS/CD†
The 30th Anniversary Collection	EMI	(3)99917	'93	CD†
All-Time Greatest Hits	Curb/Warner Brothers	77377	'90	CS/CD
Magic Touch	Hollywood/IMG	706	'92	CS
Allan Clarke				
My Real Name Is 'Arold	Epic	31757	'72	†
I've Got Time	Asylum	1056	'76	†
I Wasn't Born Yesterday	Atlantic	19175	'78	†
Legendary Heroes	Curb	267	'80	†
Terry Sylvester				
Terry Sylvester	Epic	33076	'74	†

THE IMPRESSIONS

Curtis Mayfield (born June 3, 1942, in Chicago), Jerry Butler (born December 8, 1939, in Sunflower, Mississippi), tenors Arthur Brooks and Richard Brooks, and Sam Gooden (born September 2, 1939, in Chattanooga, Tennessee), baritone and bass vocals. Butler left in 1958. Tenor Fred Cash (born October 8, 1940, in Chattanooga) joined in 1961. Arthur and Richard Brooks left in 1962. Mayfield left in 1970, to be replaced by Leroy Hutson (born June 4, 1945, in Newark, New Jersey).

One of the most popular and influential soul groups of the '60s, The Impressions were one of the few soul acts to record for a label other than Motown, Atlantic, or Stax Records. Achieving their success on ABC-Paramount Records, The Impressions were led by Curtis Mayfield, the principal architect of the sound of "Chicago soul" through his songwriting and production efforts for Jerry Butler, The Impressions, Major Lance, Gene Chandler, and others. Furthermore, along with James Brown, Mayfield was one of the first black songwriters to compose politically aware, socially conscious lyrics, as evidenced by the Impressions' hits "We're a Winner," "This Is My Country," and "Choice of Colors." Mayfield was also noted for his exquisite falsetto voice and innovative guitar playing. The Impressions were inducted into the Rock and Roll Hall of Fame in 1991. Mayfield left The Impressions in 1970 and scored his most significant solo success in 1972 with the soundtrack to *Superfly,* often considered one of the finest examples of orchestral soul music and hailed for its honest and compassionate treatment of the ghetto experience. Suffering diminished popularity after the mid-'70s, Curtis Mayfield was on the verge of reemerging when he was paralyzed from the neck down when a lighting rig fell on him in Brooklyn on August 13, 1990. He was inducted into the Rock and Roll Hall of Fame in 1999.

Curtis Mayfield met Jerry Butler at the age of nine at his grandmother's Traveling Souls Spiritualist Church on Chicago's west side. The two later sang in the gospel group The Northern Jubilee Singers. In 1957, Butler and Mayfield joined the transplanted Chattanooga-based vocal group The Roosters, comprising brothers Arthur and Richard Brooks and bass singer Sam Gooden. Under manager Eddie Thomas, the group became The Impressions, scoring a smash rhythm-and-blues and near-smash pop hit in 1958 with "For Your Precious Love," erroneously credited to Jerry Butler and The Impressions. Butler soon left The Impressions for a successful solo career, taking with him Mayfield as guitarist and songwriter. Mayfield cowrote Butler's hits "He Will Break Your Heart," "Find Another Girl," and "I'm A Telling You."

The Impressions reassembled with Mayfield, the Brooks Brothers, Gooden, and tenor Fred Cash, the fourth member of the original Roosters, in 1959 and moved to New York. Signed to ABC-Paramount Records by 1961, The Impressions scored a smash R&B and major pop hit at the end of the year with "Gypsy Woman," with Mayfield providing the high tenor lead. After the Brooks Brothers left in 1962, The Impressions continued as a trio and returned to Chicago. In the fall of 1963, they began an impressive string of pop and rhythm-and-blues hits, virtually all written by Mayfield, with the smash "It's All Right." Subsequent hits through 1965 included "Talking About My Baby," "I'm So Proud," "Keep on Pushing," "You Must Believe Me," "Amen," "People Get Ready," and "Woman's Got Soul." Throughout the '60s, Mayfield also worked with a number of Chicago acts, providing hits to Major Lance ("Monkey Time" and "Um, Um, Um, Um, Um, Um") and Gene Chandler ("Just Be True" and "Nothing Can Stop Me Now") while producing Walter Jackson, Billy Butler, and others.

The Impressions' popularity subsequently waned for a time, but, by the beginning of 1968, they were back with the prideful "We're a Winner," a top rhythm-and-blues and major pop hit. In the spring, Mayfield formed his own record label, Curtom. The Impressions' first two Curtom albums contained a number of socially conscious songs. Their later masterpiece *Young Mod's Forgotten Story* included "Mighty, Mighty (Spade and Whitey)" and the major pop and top rhythm-and-blues hit "Choice of Colors."

In 1970, Curtis Mayfield left The Impressions for a solo career as he continued to record and produce the group for Curtom. Adding Leroy Hutson for two albums, The Impressions scored major rhythm-and-blues hits with "Check Out Your Mind" and "(Baby) Turn on to Me" in 1970. Hutson left the group for a solo career in 1973, scoring modest hits on Curtom through 1978. Fred Cash and Sam Gooden regrouped with two new members in 1974, scoring a top rhythm-and-blues and major pop hit with "Finally Got Myself Together (I'm a Changed Man)" and R&B smashes with "Sooner or Later" and "Same Thing It Took." The Impressions continued to perform into the '90s, with Cash and Gooden as the mainstays.

Curtis Mayfield's debut solo album, *Curtis,* yielded a smash R&B and major pop hit with "(Don't Worry) If There's a Hell Below We're All Going to Go." His biggest critical and commercial success came in 1972 with the soundtrack to the black-oriented movie *Superfly.* Remaining on the charts for nearly a year, the album produced two smash crossover hits with "Freddie's Dead" and "Superfly" and included "Pusherman."

Following 1973's *Back to the World,* Curtis Mayfield's albums sold modestly at best. He composed and produced the score to the 1974 movie *Claudine,* performed by Gladys Knight and The Pips. His *There's No Place Like America Today* was critically acclaimed and yielded a smash R&B hit with "So in Love." In 1975, he scored and wrote the soundtrack to the film *Let's Do It Again,* performed by The Staple Singers, and the title song became a top pop and rhythm-and-blues hit. His next soundtrack album, *Sparkle,* was performed by Aretha Franklin, and produced a top R&B and major pop hit with "Something He Can Feel." In 1977, Mayfield scored the soundtracks to *A Piece of the Action,* performed by Mavis Staples, and *Short Eyes,* in which he appeared. In 1978, Mayfield produced Aretha Franklin's *Almighty Fire* album and Linda Clifford scored a smash rhythm-and-blues hit with "Runaway Love" on Curtom. The following year, Mayfield recorded an album with Clifford.

In 1980, Curtis Mayfield moved his home base to Atlanta, Georgia. He continued to record in the '80s while producing Gene Chandler and gospel artist Kevin Yancy. In 1983, Mayfield, Jerry Butler, Sam Gooden, and Fred Cash reunited as The Impressions for a tour of the United States. In 1990, Mayfield scored the soundtrack to *The Return of Superfly,* which included four Mayfield tunes and rap songs performed by Ice-T, Eazy-E of N.W.A., and Tone Loc, but, on August 13, 1990, he was critically injured when a stage lighting rig fell on him in Brooklyn, paralyzing him from the neck down. The Impressions were inducted into the Rock and Roll Hall of Fame in 1991. Two years later, Shanachie Records issued the tribute album *People Get Ready,* with artists such as Jerry Butler, Bunny Wailer, and Huey Lewis performing his songs. In 1994, Warner Brothers released *A Tribute to Curtis Mayfield,* with performances by Eric Clapton, Whitney Houston, Bruce Springsteen, Stevie Winwood, and Aretha Franklin, among others. Mayfield has since recorded *New World Order* for Warner Brothers Records.

Early Impressions

In the Beginning	Checker	3014		†
For Your Precious Love	VeeJay	1075	'63	LP/CS
Vintage Years	Sire	(2)3717	'77	†

The Impressions

The Impressions	ABC-Paramount	450	'63	†
	Kent	005		†
Never Ending Impressions	ABC-Paramount	468	'64	†
	Kent	008		†
The Impressions/Never Ending Impressions	Kent	126	'95	CD
Keep on Pushing	ABC-Paramount	493	'64	†
	Kent	009		†
People Get Ready	ABC-Paramount	505	'65	†
	Kent	012		†
The Definitive Impressions	Kent	923		CD
Greatest Hits	ABC-Paramount	515	'65	†
	MCA	1500	'82	CS
	MCA	31338	'89	CD
One by One	ABC-Paramount	523	'65	†
Ridin' High	ABC-Paramount	545	'66	†
The Fabulous Impressions	ABC	606	'67	†
We're a Winner	ABC	635	'68	†
Best	ABC	654	'68	†
Versatile	ABC	668	'69	†
16 Greatest Hits	ABC	727	'71	†
	Pickwick	3602	'78	†
This Is My Country	Curtom	8001	'68	†
The Young Mod's Forgotten Story	Curtom	8003	'69	†
	Curtom	2013	'92	CS/CD†
Best Impressions—Curtis, Sam, Fred	Curtom	8004	'70	†
Check Out Your Mind	Curtom	8006	'70	†
Times Have Changed	Curtom	8012	'72	†
Preacher Man	Curtom	8016	'73	†
Finally Got Myself Together	Curtom	8019	'74	†
Three the Hard Way (soundtrack)	Curtom	8602	'74	†
Sooner or Later	Curtom	0103	'75	†
First Impressions	Curtom	5003	'75	†
Loving Power	Curtom	5009	'76	†
Lasting Impressions	Curtom	2006		LP/CS/CD†
The Anthology 1961–1977	MCA	(2)10664	'92	CS/CD

It's All Right	MCA	22175	'95	CD†
It's About Time	Cotillion	9912	'76	†
Come to My Party	20th Century-Fox	596	'79	†
Fan the Fire	20th Century-Fox	624	'81	†
Chartbusters	Pickwick	3502		†
Further Impressions	Hip-O	40002	'96	CS/CD

Leroy Hutson

Love, Oh, Love	Curtom	8017	'73	†
	Curtom	5020	'78	†
Leroy Hutson	Curtom	5002	'75	†
Feel the Spirit	Curtom	5010	'76	†
Hutson II	Curtom	5011	'76	†
Closer to the Source	Curtom	5018	'78	†
Unforgettable	RSO	3062	'80	†
Paradise	Elektra	60141	'82	†

Curtis Mayfield

His Early Years with The Impressions	ABC	(2)780	'73	†
Curtis	Curtom	8005	'70	†
Curtis Live!	Curtom	(2)8008	'71	†
Roots	Curtom	8009	'71	†
Superfly (soundtrack)	Curtom	8014	'72	†
	Curtom	2002		LP/CS/CD
Back to the World	Curtom	8015	'73	†
Curtis in Chicago Live	Curtom	8018	'73	†
Sweet Exorcist	Curtom	8601	'74	†
Got to Find a Place	Curtom	8604	'74	†
There's No Place Like America Today	Curtom	5001	'75	†
	Curtom	2003		LP/CS/CD†
Give, Get, Take and Have	Curtom	5007	'76	†
	Curtom	2011	'92	CS/CD†
Never Say You Can't Survive	Curtom	5013	'77	†
	Curtom	2010	'92	CS/CD†
Short Eyes	Curtom	5017	'77	†
Do It All Night	Curtom	5022	'78	†
Heartbeat	RSO	3053	'79	†
Something to Believe In	RSO	3077	'80	†
	Curtom	2005		LP/CS/CD†
Live in Europe	Curtom	(2)2901	'87	LP/CS/CD†
Take It to the Streets	Curtom	2008	'90	LP/CS/CD†
Of All Time (Classic Collection)	Curtom	(2)2902		LP/CS/CD†
New World Order	Warner Brothers	46348	'96	CS/CD
People Get Ready: The Curtis Mayfield Story	Rhino	(3)72262	'96	CD
Live	Griffin	8038		CD

Curtis Mayfield/The Staple Singers

Let's Do It Again (soundtrack)	Curtom	5005	'75	†

Curtis Mayfield and Linda Clifford

The Right Combination	RSO	3084	'80	†

Curtis Mayfield and Others

The Return of Superfly	Capitol	94244	'90	CS/CD†

Curtis Mayfield Productions				
Curtis Mayfield's Chicago Soul	Okeh	64770	'95	CS/CD
Curtis Mayfield Tribute Albums				
People Get Ready: A Tribute to Curtis Mayfield	Shanachie	9004	'93	CS/CD
A Tribute to Curtis Mayfield	Warner Brothers	45500	'94	CS/CD

IRON BUTTERFLY

Doug Ingle (born September 9, 1946, in Omaha, Nebraska), vocals, keyboards; Erik Braunn (born August 11, 1950, in Boston, Massachusetts), guitar; Lee Dorman (born September 15, 1945, in St. Louis, Missouri), bass; and Ron Bushy (born September 23, 1945, in Washington, D.C.), drums.

One of the first American heavy metal bands, Iron Butterfly burst onto the music scene in 1968 with their seventeen-minute epic "In-A-Gadda-Da-Vida," one of the longest (and most bombastic) album cuts in rock music at the time. More an oddity than a milestone, the song's notoriety was unable to sustain the group's career beyond 1971, yet the group subsequently re-formed a number of times.

Iron Butterfly formed in San Diego, California, in 1966 with Doug Ingle, Ron Bushy, Darryl DeLoach, Danny Weis, and Jerry Penrod. After a modest-selling debut album for Atco Records, the latter three departed, with Weis and Penrod forming Rhinoceros. Ingle and Bushy replaced them with Erik Braunn and Lee Dorman for *In-A-Gadda-Da-Vida*. An edited version of the seventeen-minute title cut became a moderate pop hit in 1968 and the album remained on the charts for well over two years. Their next album yielded minor hits with "Soul Experience" and "In the Time of Our Lives," but Braunn left in late 1969. He was replaced by guitarists Larry "Rhino" Rheinhardt and Mike Pinera, a former member of Blues Image (1970's smash hit "Ride Captain Ride"). The group continued to tour and record until May 1971, when they disbanded. In 1974, Erik Braunn and Ron Bushy revived the group for touring and two albums for MCA Records. Iron Butterfly reunited several times between the late '80s and mid-'90s.

Iron Butterfly				
Heavy	Atco	33227	'68	†
	Rhino	71521	'93	CD
In-A-Gadda-Da-Vida	Atco	33250	'68	CS/CD
	Rhino	72196	'95	CD
	Mobile Fidelity	675	'96	CD
Ball	Atco	33280	'69/'91	CD
Live	Atco	33318	'70	CD
Metamorphosis	Atco	33339	'70	†
	Rhino	71522	'93	CD
The Best of Iron Butterfly/Evolution	Atco	33369	'71	†
Scorching Beauty	MCA	465	'75	†
Sun and Steel	MCA	2164	'75	†
Rare Flight	Pair	1065	'86	CD
Light and Heavy: The Best of Iron Butterfly	Rhino	71166	'93	CS/CD
Rhinoceros				
Rhinoceros	Elektra	74030	'68	†
Satin Chicken	Elektra	74056	'69	†
Better Times Are Coming	Elektra	74075	'70	†

THE ISLEY BROTHERS

Ronald Isley (born May 21, 1941, in Cincinnati, Ohio), O'Kelly Isley (born December 25, 1937, in Cincinnati; died March 31, 1986, in Alpine, New Jersey), and Rudolph Isley (born April 1, 1939, in Cincinnati). In September 1969, they were joined by Ernie Isley (born March 7, 1952), lead guitar, drums; Marvin Isley (born August 18, 1953), bass, percussion; and Chris Jasper, keyboards.

THE ISLEY BROTHERS (HULTON-DEUTSCH COLLECTION/CORBIS)

Matching the record of Johnny Cash, The Isley Brothers scored hits in five decades, including the classics "Shout" (1959), "Twist and Shout" (1962), and "This Old Heart of Mine" (1966), before gaining a large measure of control over their career at T-Neck Records beginning in 1969. The Isley Brothers became a self-contained band that year with the addition of Chris Jasper and younger brothers Ernie and Marvin. Recording a number of smash soul hits and best-selling albums in the funk style, including their 1973 masterpiece *3 + 3* and 1975's *The Heat Is On,* The Isley Brothers adopted a rock-disco sound during the late '70s. The younger members left Isley Brothers Ronald and Rudolph in 1984 for separate careers, with Ernie, Marvin, and Ronald reuniting as The Isley Brothers in 1990. The Isley Brothers were inducted into the Rock and Roll Hall of Fame in 1992.

Isley Brothers Ronald and O'Kelly were performing as gospel singers backed by mother Sallye Isley by the early '50s. Joined by brothers Vernon and Rudolph, the quartet sang at churches in Cincinnati and later toured churches throughout the Midwest. Reduced to a trio by the accidental death of Vernon in 1955 at the age of eleven, The Isley Brothers moved to New York in April 1956, recording unsuccessful singles for Teenage, Cindy, Gone, and Mark X Records. Debuting at the Howard Theater in Washington, D.C., the brothers were later showcased at New York's Apollo Theater and signed to RCA Victor Records. In 1959, they scored a moderate hit with their own composition "Shout," a smash pop hit for Joey Dee and The Starlighters in 1962, and recorded their own "Respectable," later recorded by The Yardbirds and a major hit for The Outsiders in 1966. Later in 1959, the entire Isley family relocated to Teaneck, New Jersey.

Following a single album for RCA, The Isley Brothers recorded for Atlantic Records under producers Jerry Leiber and Mike Stoller with little success. They subsequently joined the Wand subsidiary of Florence Greenberg's Scepter Records, where they scored a smash rhythm-and-blues and major pop hit with the classic "Twist and Shout" (a smash pop hit for The Beatles in 1964) and recorded "Nobody but Me," a near-smash pop hit for The Human

Beinz in 1968. In 1963, The Isley Brothers moved to United Artists Records, where they recorded the original version of "Who's That Lady."

In 1964, The Isley Brothers toured the "chitlin" circuit with then-unknown guitarist Jimi Hendrix and formed their own production company, T-Neck (named after Teaneck, New Jersey). Their solitary release for the company, "Testify" (with Jimi Hendrix on guitar), distributed by Atlantic, fared poorly. By late 1965, the brothers had moved to Motown Records, where they achieved a smash rhythm-and-blues and major pop hit on Tamla with "This Old Heart of Mine (Is Weak for You)" in 1966. However, subsequent success eluded The Isley Brothers at Tamla.

By 1969, The Isley Brothers had revived T-Neck, working out a distribution deal with Buddah Records. Their first release on T-Neck, "It's Your Thing," became a smash rhythm-and-blues and pop hit and "Behind a Painted Smile" became a smash British-only hit. The three vocalizing Isley Brothers were joined by younger brothers Ernie and Marvin and Chris Jasper in September 1969 to form a self-contained band. Hits through the early '70s included the R&B smashes "I Turned You On" and Stephen Stills' "Love the One You're With" (both major pop hits), "Lay-Away," and "Pop That Thang."

The Isley Brothers switched distributorship of T-Neck to Columbia in 1973, firmly establishing themselves as album artists with *3 + 3*, which yielded the pop and R&B smash "That Lady," featuring Ernie's Hendrix-influenced lead guitar work, and the R&B smashes "What It Comes Down To" and "Summer Breeze." Following the R&B smashes "Live It Up" and "Midnight Sky," The Isley Brothers scored their biggest album success with *The Heat Is On,* which produced the top R&B and smash pop hit "Fight the Power" and major hit "For the Love of You."

Adopting a sound with elements of both rock and disco, The Isley Brothers did not score any more major pop hits, yet they continued to achieve rhythm-and-blues smashes through 1983 with "Who Loves You Better," "The Pride," "Livin' in the Life," "Take Me to Your Next Phase," "I Wanna Be with You," "Don't Say Goodnight (It's Time for Love)," "Between the Sheets," and "Choosey Lover." In 1984, Ernie and Marvin Isley and Chris Jasper left The Isley Brothers and began recording as Isley, Jasper, Isley, scoring a top R&B hit with "Caravan of Love" in 1985. Chris Jasper and Ernie Isley each recorded solo later, with Jasper managing a smash rhythm-and-blues hit with "Superbad" in late 1987.

Reduced to a duo with the death of O'Kelly Isley from a heart attack on March 31, 1986, Ronald and Rudolph Isley achieved a smash R&B hit with "Smooth Sailin' Tonight" on Warner Brothers Records in 1987. Ronald scored a major pop and top easy-listening hit in conjunction with Rod Stewart on "This Old Heart of Mine" in 1990. Late that year, Ernie, Marvin, and Ronald Isley reunited as The Isley Brothers, recording for Warner Brothers, Elektra, and Island Records, where they scored a hit with "Let's Lay Together," written and produced by R. Kelly. The Isley Brothers were inducted into the Rock and Roll Hall of Fame in 1992.

The Isley Brothers

The Isley Brothers and Marvin and Johnny	Crown	5352		†
Shout	RCA	2156	'59	†
	Collectables	5103		LP/CS/CD
Shout! The Complete Victor Sessions	RCA	9901		CS/CD†
Shout! The RCA Sessions	RCA	66883	'96	CS/CD
Twist and Shout	Wand	653	'62	†
	Sundazed	6002		CD
Twisting and Shouting	United Artists	6313	'64	†
The Complete UA Sessions	EMI	95203	'91	CS/CD†
Take Some Time Out	Scepter	552		†

This Old Heart of Mine	Tamla	269	'66	†
	Motown	5128	'89	CS/CD
Soul on the Rocks	Tamla	275	'67	†
	Motown	5425	'89	CD†
This Old Heart of Mine/Soul on the Rocks	Motown	8156		CD†
Greatest Hits and Rare Classics	Motown	5483	'91	CS/CD
In the Beginning (with Jimi Hendrix; recorded in 1964)	T-Neck	3007	'71	†
It's Our Thing	T-Neck	3001	'69	†
Brothers Isley	T-Neck	3002	'69	†
Live at Yankee Stadium	T-Neck	(2)3004	'69	†
Get Into Something	T-Neck	3006	'71	†
Givin' It Back	T-Neck	3008	'71	†
Brother, Brother, Brother	T-Neck	3009	'72	†
Live	T-Neck	(2)3010	'73	†
3 + 3	T-Neck	32453	'73	CS/CD
Live It Up	T-Neck	33070	'74	†
The Heat Is On	T-Neck	33536	'75	CS/CD
Harvest for the World	T-Neck	33809	'76/'87	CS
Go for Your Guns	T-Neck	34432	'77	CS/CD
Showdown	T-Neck	34930	'78	CS
Winner Takes All	T-Neck	(2)36077	'79	†
	T-Neck	36077	'86	CS/CD
Go All the Way	T-Neck	36305	'80	CS
Grand Slam	T-Neck	37080	'81	CS
Inside You	T-Neck	37553	'81	†
The Real Deal	T-Neck	38047	'82	†
Between the Sheets	T-Neck	38674	'83/'85	CS/CD
Masterpiece	Warner Brothers	25347	'85	†
Smooth Sailin'	Warner Brothers	25586	'87	CS/CD
Spend the Night (as "The Isley Brothers, Featuring Ronald Isley")	Warner Brothers	25940	'89	CS/CD
Tracks of Life	Warner Brothers	26620	'92	CS/CD
The Isley Brothers Live	Elektra	61538	'93	CS/CD
Mission to Please	Island	4214	'96	CS/CD
Make Your Body Sing	Island	314524	'96	CS/CD

Isley, Jasper, Isley

Broadway's Closer to Sunset Boulevard	CBS Associated	39873	'84	†
Caravan of Love	CBS Associated	40118	'85	CS/CD†
	Epic Associated	40118		CS/CD
Different Drummer	CBS Associated	40409	'87	CS/CD†

Chris Jasper

Superbad	Epic	44053	'88	CS/CD†
Time Bomb	Gold City	45169	'89	CS/CD†

Ernie Isley

High Wire	Elektra	60902	'90	CS/CD†

Various Isley Brothers Anthologies and Compilations

Do Their Thing	Sunset	5257	'69	†
Doin' Their Thing	Tamla	287	'70	†
Motown Superstar Series, Volume 6	Motown	5106		†
This Old Heart of Mine	Pickwick	3398		†

Rock On, Brother	Camden	0126	'73	†
Country/Rock Around the Clock	Camden	0861	'75	†
Best	Buddah	(2)5652	'76	†
Very Best	United Artists	500	'76	†
Greatest Hits	T-Neck	3011	'73	†
Forever Gold	T-Neck	34452	'77	†
Timeless	T-Neck	35650	'78	†
Greatest Hits, Volume 1	T-Neck	39240	'84	CS/CD
This Old Heart of Mine: Isley Brothers Greatest Hits	Curb/Warner Brothers	77333	'90	CS/CD
Isley Brothers Story, Volume 1: Rockin' Soul 1959–1968	Rhino	70908	'91	CS/CD
Isley Brothers Story, Volume 2: T-Neck Years 1969–1985	Rhino	(2)70909	'91	CS/CD
The Isleys Live	Rhino	72284	'96	CS/CD
Beautiful Ballads	Philadelphia Int'l	57860	'94	CS/CD†
Soul Kings, Volume 1	SMS	56	'95	CD
At Their Best	Special Music	4804		CS/CD
Shout	Collectables	5103		LP/CS/CD
16 Greatest Hits	Deluxe	7899		CS
Shout and Twist with Rudolph, Ronald and O'Kelly	Ace	928		CD

JAN AND DEAN

Jan Berry (born April 3, 1941, in Los Angeles) and Dean Torrance (born March 10, 1940, in Los Angeles).

Early '60s purveyors of innocuous fun songs concerned with surfing, cars, girls, and high school, Jan and Dean were second only to The Beach Boys in the promotion of these Southern California themes. In fact, The Beach Boys' Brian Wilson cowrote several of their biggest hits, including "Surf City" and "Dead Man's Curve." Scoring a series of hit singles between 1963 and 1965, Jan and Dean later recorded folk and Beatles songs. However, in April 1966, Jan was nearly killed in a Los Angeles auto wreck that left him in a coma for nearly a year. He eventually recovered, although permanent damage was sustained, as Dean pursued a career as a graphic artist.

Jan Berry and Dean Torrance met at Emerson Junior High School in Los Angeles. Fascinated with the "doo-wop" sound of the '50s, the two formed The Barons in 1957 with Arnie Ginsburg and, for a time, future Beach Boy Bruce Johnston and drummer Sandy Nelson. Reduced to a trio of Berry, Torrance, and Ginsburg, they recorded "Jennie Lee" in Jan's garage. While Dean was serving in the Army Reserve, Jan signed with the Arwin label, owned by Doris Day's husband Marty Melcher. Arwin released "Jennie Lee" under the name Jan and Arnie and the song became a near-smash hit in 1958. When Ginsburg dropped out to join the Navy in late 1958, Jan and Dean signed with the Dore label, managed by Lou Adler and Herb Alpert. They scored a near-smash on Dore with the novelty song "Baby Talk" in 1959, but the duo's next major hit didn't come until 1961, when "Heart and Soul" was released on Challenge Records.

Later in 1961, Jan and Dean signed with Liberty Records. In the summer of 1962, the duo met The Beach Boys, whose Brian Wilson provided them with their first major hit on Liberty, "Linda." Recording with sessions musicians such as Glen Campbell, Leon Russell, Steve Douglas, and Hal Blaine, Jan and Dean scored a top pop hit with Berry and Wilson's "Surf City" in the summer of 1963. Subsequent major hits included "Honolulu Lulu," "Drag City," "Dead Man's Curve," the smash "The Little Old Lady (From Pasadena)," "Ride the Wild Surf," and Wilson's "Sidewalk Surfin'," a precursor of the skateboard rage. In October 1964, Jan and Dean hosted a concert at the Santa Monica Civic Auditorium that became the

1965 film *The T.A.M.I. SHOW,* with performances by The Rolling Stones, The Beach Boys, The Supremes, The Miracles, and others. Later hits for Jan and Dean included "You Really Know How to Hurt a Guy" and "Popsicle," but, by late 1965, they were recording the songs of Bob Dylan and The Beatles.

On April 12, 1966, Jan Berry was nearly killed when his Corvette Stingray, traveling at a high rate of speed, struck a parked truck. In a coma for nearly a year, Jan spent much of the next ten years undergoing intensive physical therapy for a condition that included paralysis of his right side and impaired speech, hearing, vision, and memory. In the meantime, Dean opened Kittyhawk Graphics, where he designed album covers. Jan and Dean recorded for Columbia and Warner Brothers between 1967 and 1968 and Jan recorded solo for Ode Records from 1972 to 1974. The two reunited to perform at Hollywood's 1973 "Surfer's Stomp Reunion." After the airing of the biographical *Dead Man's Curve* special on network television in February 1978, Jan and Dean reunited for performances with The Beach Boys. Jan and Dean continued to tour as an oldies act into the '90s.

Jan and Dean

Jan and Dean	Dore	101	'60	†
reissued as The Dore Album	Sundazed	5040	'96	LP
The Heart and Soul of Jan and Dean	Design	181		†
Jan and Dean Take Linda Surfin'	Liberty	7294	'63	†
Surf City (and Other Swingin' Cities)	Liberty	7314	'63	†
Drag City	Liberty	7339	'63	†
Dead Man's Curve/The New Girl in School	Liberty	7361	'64	†
Ride the Wild Surf	Liberty	7368	'64	†
The Little Old Lady from Pasadena	Liberty	7377	'64	†
	Liberty	10151		
Command Performance—"Live" in Person	Liberty	7403	'65	†
Jan & Dean's Pop Symphony No. 1	Liberty	7414	'65	†
Folk 'n' Roll	Liberty	7431	'65	†
Filet of Soul	Liberty	7441	'66	†
Jan and Dean Meet Batman	Liberty	7444	'66	†
Popsicle	Liberty	7458	'66	†
Save for a Rainy Day	Columbia	9461	'67	†
	Sundazed	(2)5022	'96	LP
	Sundazed	11035	'96	CD

Jan and Dean Reissues

Ride the Wild Surf/Little Old Lady from Pasadena	Liberty	80055	'92	CS/CD†
The Little Old Lady from Pasadena/Filet of Soul	One Way	18448	'96	CD
Dead Man's Curve/The New Girl in School/Popsicle	One Way	18684	'96	CD
Surf City/Folk 'n' Roll	One Way	18685	'96	CD
Jan and Dean Take Linda Surfin'/Ride the Wild Surf	One Way	18686	'96	CD
Command Performance: Live in Person/Jan and Dean	One Way	18687	'96	CD
Drag City/Jan and Dean's Pop Symphony No. 1	One Way	18839	'96	CD

Jan and Dean Anthologies and Compilations

Teen Suite (recorded 1958–1962)	Varèse Sarabande	5590	'95	CD
Golden Summer Days	Varèse Sarabande	5727	'96	CD
Golden Hits	Liberty	7248	'62	†
Drag City	Liberty	7339	'64	†
Golden Hits, Volume 2	Liberty	7417	'65	†
Golden Hits, Volume 3	Liberty	7460	'66	†
Golden Hits, Vols. 1, 2 & 3	One Way	(2)18838	'95	CD

Best	Liberty	10115	'81	†
Jan and Dean	Sunset	5156	'67	†
Legendary Masters	United Artists	(2)9961	'71	†
reissued as Anthology Album	One Way	18683	'96	CD
Gotta Take That One Last Ride	United Artists	(2)341	'74	†
	One Way	18688	'96	CD
Very Best, Volume 1	United Artists	443	'75	†
Very Best, Volume 2	United Artists	515	'76	†
Dead Man's Curve	United Artists	999	'79	†
	United Artists	10011		†
California Gold	Pair	(2)1071		†
I Gotta Drive	EMI-America	16398	'86	LP/CS†
A Surfer's Dream	EMI-America	16399	'86	LP/CS†
Best	EMI-America	10339	'87	CS†
Surf City: The Best of Jan and Dean	EMI	92772	'90	CS/CD†
All the Hits—From Surf City to Drag City	EMI	53730	'96	CD
All-Time Greatest Hits	Curb/Warner Brothers	77374	'91	CS/CD
Jan and Dean	K-tel	5035	'96	CS/CD
Surf City	Dominion	665		CS/CD†
Best	Special Music	4906		CS
The Jan and Dean Story	Hollywood/IMG	379		CS/CD
Surfin' Safari	Griffin	133		CD
Jan Berry				
Second Wave	One Way	4524	'97	CD

JEFFERSON AIRPLANE

Marty Balin (born Martyn Jerel Buchwald on January 30, 1943, in Cincinnati, Ohio), vocals; Signe Tole (born September 15, 1941, in Seattle, Washington), vocals; Paul Kantner (born March 12, 1942, in San Francisco), rhythm guitar, vocals; Jorma Kaukonen (born December 23, 1940, in Washington, D.C.), lead guitar; John "Jack" Casady (born April 13, 1944, in Washington, D.C.), bass; and Alexander "Skip" Spence (born April 18, 1946, in Windsor, Ontario, Canada), drums. Tole and Spence left in 1966, to be replaced by Grace Slick (born Grace Wing on October 30, 1939, in Chicago) and Spencer Dryden (born April 7, 1943, in New York City). Later members included drummers Joe E. Covington and John Barbata, and electric violinist "Papa" John Creach (born May 28, 1917, in Beaver Falls, Pennsylvania; died February 22, 1994, in Los Angeles).

HOT TUNA

Jorma Kaukonen, guitar, and Jack Casady, bass.

JEFFERSON STARSHIP

Paul Kantner, guitar, vocals; Grace Slick, vocals; "Papa" John Creach, violin; David Freiberg (born August 24, 1938, in Boston, Massachusetts), keyboards, bass, vocals; Craig Chaquico (born September 26, 1954, in Sacramento, California), guitar; Pete Sears, keyboard, vocals; and John Barbata, drums. Marty Balin, vocals, joined in 1975. By 1979, The Jefferson Starship comprised Mickey Thomas (born December 3, 1949, in Cairo, Georgia), vocals; Paul Kantner, David Freiberg, Craig Chaquico, Pete Sears, and drummer Aynsley Dunbar.

STARSHIP

Grace Slick, Mickey Thomas, Craig Chaquico, Pete Sears, and drummer Donny Baldwin.

Although not the first band of San Francisco's "hippie" era (that claim probably belongs to The Charlatans), The Jefferson Airplane was the first psychedelic San Francisco group to sign a major label recording contract and achieve national recognition. The group's debut album, *Jefferson Airplane Takes Off,* featured the romantic songwriting of Marty Balin, one of rock's most underrated and expressive vocalists, and contained one of the earliest versions of the love-and-peace anthem, "Let's Get Together." Anchored by lead guitarist Jorma Kaukonen and bassist Jack Casady, two of rock's most neglected instrumentalists, The Jefferson Airplane transformed into San Francisco's most visible and popular psychedelic act with the addition of vocalist Grace Slick, author of "White Rabbit," one of the first drug-oriented hit singles. Grace Slick's first album with The Jefferson Airplane, *Surrealistic Pillow,* launched the so-called "San Francisco sound" into national, indeed international, prominence while elevating Slick to the rank of female "superstar," a position rivaled at the time by only Janis Joplin. Along with The Grateful Dead, San Francisco's other enduring major group, The Jefferson Airplane was a remarkably populist band, quickly establishing itself with the local "counterculture" community and pioneering the free-concert phenomenon in Golden Gate Park. Following Marty Balin's departure in 1971, The Jefferson Airplane endured a chaotic period of personnel changes and solo and joint album releases. Jack Casady and Jorma Kaukonen left to pursue the improvisational side-group Hot Tuna full-time in 1972. With Balin's return in 1975, the group was reconstituted as The Jefferson Starship for their greatest hit-making era, as evidenced by "Miracles" and "Count on Me." Reestablished as one of America's most popular recording bands with *Red Octopus,* The Jefferson Starship suffered the loss of Balin and Slick in 1978 and Kantner in 1984, reemerging as the highly commercial Starship in 1985. The Jefferson Airplane was inducted into the Rock and Roll Hall of Fame in 1996.

Marty Balin recorded for Challenge Records in 1962 and performed with the folk group The Town Criers in Los Angeles in 1964. In San Francisco in 1965, intent on reopening a closed club, Balin assembled a group of musicians, including guitarists Paul Kantner and Jorma Kaukonen and vocalist Signe Tole, to perform at the club. Paul Kantner had been living in Los Angeles with David Crosby and David Freiberg before returning to the Bay Area. Kaukonen, who had accompanied Janis Joplin locally around 1963, met Kantner in Santa Cruz. Kantner later met Balin while performing on twelve-string guitar and banjo at The Drinking Gourd. Named The Jefferson Airplane, the group debuted at The Matrix on August 13, 1965, performing a blend of rock and folk music. The group's original rhythm section was soon replaced by Alexander "Skip" Spence, a rhythm guitarist converted to drummer, and bassist Jack Casady, a childhood friend of Kaukonen's. On December 10, 1965, The Jefferson Airplane performed at the inaugural concert at the Fillmore Auditorium, run by Bill Graham.

Signed to RCA Records, thus becoming the first of many Bay Area bands to secure a major label recording contract, The Jefferson Airplane recorded their debut album in Hollywood. Dominated by Marty Balin's songwriting and smooth rich voice, *Jefferson Airplane Takes Off* featured the distinctive vocal harmonies of Balin, Kantner, and Signe Anderson (now married). The modest-selling album contained an early version of the "hippie" anthem, "Let's Get Together," and Balin's dynamic love song "It's No Secret." Spence left the group in May 1966 to form Moby Grape and Anderson left in October to have a baby.

Drummer Spencer Dryden and vocalist Grace Slick were recruited as replacements. Grace Slick, a former model, had been a member of the recently dissolved Great Society, which had been performing locally since 1964. The Great Society also included Slick's drummer-husband Jerry Slick and his brother Darby Slick. Recordings made by The Great Society for Columbia were eventually issued in 1968, following the success of The Jefferson Airplane.

Surrealistic Pillow, Grace Slick's first album with The Jefferson Airplane, contained two songs she had performed with The Great Society, Darby Slick's "Somebody to Love" and her own "White Rabbit." Both became smash pop hits for The Jefferson Airplane in 1967 and the album effectively launched the "San Francisco sound." It also included two beautiful romantic ballads by Balin, "Comin' Back to Me" and "Today" (coauthored with Kantner), as well as Balin's frenetic "3/5 of a Mile in 10 Seconds" and surreal "Plastic Fantastic Lover." Slick's piercing soprano voice, more rough and powerful than Anderson's, complemented Balin's high sensual tenor, and her flamboyant stage demeanor soon made her the visual and musical focus of The Jefferson Airplane. The group performed at the Monterey International Pop Festival in June and Slick's presence soon began to overwhelm Balin, as evidenced by *After Bathing at Baxter's.* The album contained only one Balin song, "Young Girl Sunday Blues," coauthored with Kantner. Other inclusions were Kantner's "The Ballad of You and Me and Pooneil" (a moderate hit) and the mellow "Won't You Try"/"Saturday Afternoon," Slick's "Two Heads," and psychedelic ruminations by Casady and Kaukonen such as "Spare Chaynge."

Marty Balin contributed more to *Crown of Creation,* but most attention was directed at Kantner's title song, Slick's surreal "Lather" and vitriolic "Greasy Heart," and David Crosby's previously unrecorded "Triad." In the late summer of 1968, The Jefferson Airplane toured Europe for the first time, issuing the live set *Bless Its Pointed Little Head* in early 1969. They performed at the Woodstock Music and Art Fair in August and their next album, *Volunteers,* was again dominated by Slick and Kantner. Although the standout cut was Balin and Kantner's radical political title song, the album featured Kantner's anthemic "We Can Be Together" and David Crosby, Stephen Stills, and Paul Kantner's mystical "Wooden Ships," a forerunner of the science fiction fantasies that Kantner would soon explore.

A chaotic period of solo and joint projects and personnel changes soon engulfed The Jefferson Airplane. Jorma Kaukonen and Jack Casady had been performing together as the blues-oriented Hot Tuna since 1969, often opening shows for The Jefferson Airplane. The first of many Hot Tuna albums appeared in mid-1970. Spencer Dryden quit the parent group in early 1970 to help form The New Riders of the Purple Sage, to be replaced by surf drummer Joe E. Covington. In October, at the urging of Covington, black electric violinist "Papa" John Creach joined The Jefferson Airplane, subsequently performing and recording with both The Airplane and Hot Tuna. In December, *Blows Against the Empire* was released under the name of Paul Kantner and The Jefferson Starship. The first album nominated for the science fiction writers' Hugo award, the album was recorded by Kantner, Slick, Casady, and Covington, with the assistance of Jerry Garcia, David Crosby, Graham Nash, David Freiberg, and Jorma's brother Peter Kaukonen. It featured a number of Kantner science fiction songs, the most accessible of which, "Have You Seen the Stars Tonite," was cowritten by Crosby. Conspicuously absent was Marty Balin, although he was listed as coauthor of two songs.

By the spring of 1971, Marty Balin had left The Jefferson Airplane. By that August, the group had formed their own independent label, Grunt Records, with manufacturing and distribution handled by RCA. The label's first album release, *Bark,* credited to The Jefferson Airplane, yielded a minor hit with Covington's ditty "Pretty as You Feel." Other Grunt releases included "Papa" John Creach's first solo album and *Sunfighter,* credited to Paul Kantner and Grace Slick. The latter album was recorded with members of The Airplane plus Garcia, Nash, and Crosby, and two members of Grunt Records' Steelwind, leader Jack Traylor and sixteen-year-old guitarist Craig Chaquico. By the spring of 1972, Covington had left The Airplane, to be replaced by sessions veteran John Barbata. That summer, The Jefferson Airplane conducted a major American tour with Barbata and bassist-keyboardist-vocalist David Freiberg, a former member of Quicksilver Messenger Service. They played their last engagement at San Francisco's Winterland in September and Jack Casady and Jorma Kaukonen subsequently left the group to pursue Hot Tuna full-time. Subsequent Jefferson Airplane releases included the live set *Thirty Seconds Over Winterland* and *Early Flight,* recordings from 1965 to 1970 that included Signe Anderson's vocal on "High Flying Bird." The Jefferson Airplane was inducted into the Rock and Roll Hall of Fame in 1996.

During 1973, Marty Balin performed and recorded with the Marin County bar band Bodacious D.F. Their overlooked RCA album featured Balin's fine lead vocal on leader Vic Smith's "Drivin' Me Crazy." By mid-1974, the parent group had added keyboardist-vocalist Peter Sears and lead guitarist Craig Chaquico for *Dragonfly,* credited to The Jefferson Starship. The album contained Slick and Sears' "Hyperdrive" and yielded a minor hit with Slick and Kantner's "Ride the Tiger." However, the feature cut was Marty Balin and Paul Kantner's "Caroline," with lead vocals by Balin. Balin rejoined The Jefferson Starship for their spring 1975 tour and stayed with the group for more than three years. The group's best-selling album ever, *Red Octopus,* yielded a smash hit with "Miracles," composed and sung by Balin, and exposed the group to a new wide audience. The album also included the minor hit "Play on Love" and "Tumblin'," written by Balin, Freiberg, and Grateful Dead lyricist Robert Hunter. "Papa" John Creach left the group in August 1975, forming his own band in Los Angeles for an inauspicious recording career. He died there of natural causes on February 22, 1994, at the age of 76.

The Jefferson Starship next recorded *Spitfire,* which contained "Cruisin'" (written by Charlie Hickox of Bodacious D.F.) and the major hit "With Your Love," cowritten by Balin. The follow-up, *Earth,* produced four hit singles, including the near smashes "Count on Me" (written by Jesse Barish) and "Runaway."

During the summer of 1978, The Jefferson Starship toured Europe for the first time in ten years. However, Grace Slick suddenly became ill before a scheduled appearance in Frankfurt, Germany, in June and the subsequent cancellation of the concert led to a riot in which virtually all of the group's equipment was destroyed. Following a poor performance two nights later in Hamburg, Slick returned to the United States, not to perform with the group again until January 1981. In October 1978, drummer John Barbata was critically injured in a northern California automobile accident. He was replaced by well-traveled English drummer Aynsley Dunbar.

The Jefferson Starship was reconstituted in 1979 with former Elvin Bishop vocalist Mickey Thomas ("Fooled Around and Fell in Love"), Kantner, Freiberg, Chaquico, Sears, and Dunbar. The hard-rock *Freedom at Point Zero* produced a major hit with "Jane" and the minor hit "Girl with the Hungry Eyes." After recording two solo albums, Grace Slick returned to The Jefferson Starship in 1981 for the major hits "Find Your Way Back," "Be My Lady," and "No Way Out" through 1984. In late 1979, Marty Balin directed the rock musical *Rock Justice* at the Old Waldorf in San Francisco, later issued as an album on EMI-America. Two years later, he scored a smash hit with "Hearts" and a major hit with "Atlanta Lady" from *Balin* on EMI-America. He recorded another solo album for the label in 1983.

In 1984, Paul Kantner departed The Jefferson Starship acrimoniously. Through lawsuits, he forced the group to rename itself simply Starship. Soliciting songs from outside writers and pursuing a blatantly commercial direction, The Starship regrouped with Slick, Thomas, Chaquico, Sears, and drummer Donny Baldwin, a member since replacing Aynsley Dunbar in October 1982. The new lineup's debut album *Knee Deep in the Hoopla* yielded four hits, including the top hits "We Built This City," cowritten by Elton John associate Bernie Taupin, and "Sara." The group scored another top hit in 1987 with "Nothing's Gonna Stop Us Now," from the movie *Mannequin,* followed by the near-smash "It's Not Over ('Til It's Over)."

Pete Sears left Starship in 1987, followed by Grace Slick in 1988, and Donny Baldwin in late 1989. Their last major hit came in 1989 with "It's Not Enough." Eventually reduced to Craig Chaquico and Mickey Thomas, the group finally disbanded in 1990. Since 1992, Thomas has been performing around the Lake Tahoe region with a set of musicians as Mickey Thomas' Starship. In the '90s, Craig Chaquico recorded three instrumental acoustic albums for Higher Octave Music.

Jorma Kaukonen and Jack Casady persevered as Hot Tuna until 1978. Casady then performed and recorded with the San Francisco heavy-metal band SVT until 1982. He and Kaukonen reunited for a tour as Hot Tuna in 1983, ultimately regrouping in 1986 as an acoustic duo, recording *Pair a Dice Found* for Epic Records in 1990.

In 1985, Paul Kantner, Marty Balin, and Jack Casady formed a new group with guitarist Slick Aguilar and keyboardist Tim Gorman, among others. Debuting at the reopening of the Fillmore Auditorium in December, the Kantner-Balin-Casady Band recorded a sole album for Arista Records in 1986, scoring a minor hit with "It's Not You, It's Not Me." They completed a national tour in 1987, but disbanded in 1988. The following year, Kantner, Balin, and Casady regrouped with Grace Slick and Jorma Kaukonen as The Jefferson Airplane, recording one abysmal album and conducting one ill-received tour. Kantner and Gorman began performing as Paul Kantner's Wooden Ships in 1991 and later performed in Paul Kantner's Jefferson Starship with Jack Casady, "Papa" John Creach, drummer Prairie Prince, and female vocalist Darby Gould. Marty Balin joined the aggregation in 1993. In 1995, Intersound Records issued *Deep Space / Virgin Sky* for The Jefferson Starship, featuring Kantner, Casady, Balin, and Slick, while MonsterSounds released Kantner's spoken word recollection of his years with The Jefferson Airplane, *A Guide Through the Chaos (A Road to the Passion)*.

JEFFERSON AIRPLANE BIBLIOGRAPHY

Gleason, Ralph J. *The Jefferson Airplane and the San Francisco Sound.* New York: Ballantine, 1969.

Rowes, Barbara. *Grace Slick: The Biography.* Garden City, NY: Doubleday, 1980.

Slick, Grace, with Andrea Cagan. *Somebody to Love? A Rock-and-Roll Memoir.* New York: Warner Books, 1998.

Grace Slick and The Great Society

Conspicuous Only in Its Absence	Columbia	9624	'68	†
How It Was—Collector's Item, Volume 2	Columbia	9702	'68	†
Collector's Item	Columbia	(2)30459	'71	†
	Columbia/Legacy	30459	'90	CD
Born to Be Burned	Sundazed	11027	'95	CD

The Jefferson Airplane

Early Flight	Grunt	0437	'74	†
	RCA	0437		CS/CD
	RCA	7419	'97	CD
Jefferson Airplane Takes Off	RCA	3584	'66/'89	CS/CD
	RCA	3739		†
	RCA	66797	'95	CD
Surrealistic Pillow	RCA	3766	'67	CD
	RCA	3738		CS
	RCA	66598	'95	CD

After Bathing at Baxter's	RCA	1511	'67	†
	RCA	4545	'89	CS/CD
	RCA	66798	'95	CD
Crown of Creation	RCA	4058	'68	CS/CD
	RCA	3797		†
	RCA	67561	'98	CD
	Mobile Fidelity	00148	'91	LP†
	Mobile Fidelity	00523		CD†
Bless Its Pointed Little Head	RCA	4133	'69/'89	CS/CD
	RCA	3798		†
	RCA	66801	'95	CD
Volunteers	RCA	4238	'69	CD
	RCA	3867		CS
	RCA	67562	'98	CD
	Mobile Fidelity	00540	'90	CD†
The Worst of The Jefferson Airplane	RCA	4459	'70	CD
	RCA	3661		CS
	RCA	7420	'97	CD
Bark	Grunt	1001	'71	†
	Grunt	4386	'82	†
	RCA	66574	'95	CD
Long John Silver	Grunt	1007	'72	†
	RCA	66800	'95	CD
Thirty Seconds Over Winterland	Grunt	0147	'73	CS/CD
Flight Log (1966–1976)	Grunt	(2)1255	'77	†
2400 Fulton Street—An Anthology	RCA	(2)5724	'87	CS/CD
White Rabbit and Other Hits	RCA	2078	'90	CS/CD
The Jefferson Airplane Loves You	RCA	(3)61110	'92	CS/CD
The Best of The Jefferson Airplane	RCA	66197	'93	CS/CD
Live at the Fillmore East	RCA	67563	'98	CD
Time Machine	Pair	1090	'86	CD
Rock & Roll	Richmond	2176		CS
Jefferson Airplane	Epic	45271	'89	CS/CD

Paul Kantner and The Jefferson Starship

Blows Against the Empire	RCA	4448	'70	†
	RCA	3868	'88	CS/CD

Paul Kantner and Grace Slick

Sunfighter	Grunt	1002	'71	†
	RCA	4385	'82	†

Paul Kantner, Grace Slick and David Freiberg

Baron von Tollbooth and the Chrome Nun	Grunt	0148	'73	†
	RCA	3799		†

"Papa" John Creach

Papa John Creach	Grunt	1003	'71	†
	One Way	34511	'97	CD
Filthy	Grunt	1009	'72	†
Playing My Fiddle for You	Grunt	0418	'74	†
I'm the Fiddle Man	Buddah	5649	'75	†
	One Way	30004	'94	CD†

Rock Father	Buddah	5660	'76	†
	One Way	30005	'94	CD
The Cat and the Fiddle	DJM	11	'77	†
Inphasion	DJM	18	'78	†
Joe E. Covington's Fat Fandango				
Your Heart Is My Heart	Grunt	0149	'73	†
Hot Tuna				
Hot Tuna	RCA	4353	'70	†
	RCA	3864		CS/CD
	RCA	66872	'96	CD
Electric Hot Tuna—Recorded Live ("First Pull Up, Then Pull Down")	RCA	4550	'71	†
	RCA	3865		†
	RCA	66873	'96	CD
Burgers	Grunt	1004	'72	†
	Grunt	2591		†
	RCA	2591		CS/CD
	Grunt	3951		†
Phosphorescent Rat	Grunt	0348	'74	†
	RCA	0348	'89	CS/CD†
America's Choice	Grunt	0820	'75	†
	RCA	0820	'90	CS/CD†
Yellow Fever	Grunt	1238	'75	†
	RCA	1238	'90	CS/CD†
Hoppkorv	Grunt	1920	'76	†
	Grunt	3950		†
	RCA	66874	'96	CD
Double Dose	Grunt	(2)2545	'78	†
Final Vinyl	Grunt	3357	'79	†
Keep on Truckin' and Other Hits	RCA	2164	'90	CS†
In a Can (boxed set)	RCA	66988	'96	CD
Best	RCA	(2)67692	'98	CD
Historic Hot Tuna (recorded 1971)	Relix	2011	'85	CS/CD
Classic Acoustic Hot Tuna (recorded 1971)	Relix	2075	'96	CD
Classic Electric Hot Tuna (recorded 1971)	Relix	2078	'96	CD
Splashdown (recorded 1975)	Relix	2004	'84	CS/CD
Live at Sweetwater (recorded 1992)	Relix	2058	'92	CS/CD
Live at Sweetwater Two	Relix	2062		CD
Pair a Dice Found	Epic	46831	'90	CD
Jorma Kaukonen with Tom Hobson				
Quah	Grunt	0209	'74	†
	Grunt	3747		†
	Relix	2027		CD
Jorma Kaukonen				
Jorma	RCA	3446	'79	†
Too Hot to Handle (recorded 1984)	Relix	2012		CS/CD
Magic (recorded 1985)	Relix	2007		CS/CD
Magic Two (recorded 1986)	Relix	2068		CD
Land of Heroes	Relix	2072		CD
Too Many Years . . .	Relix	2094		CD

Jorma Kaukonen and Vital Parts

Barbeque King	RCA	3725	'81	†

SVT

No Regrets	MSI	2002	'81	†

Bodacious D.F.

Bodacious D.F.	RCA	0206	'73	†
	RCA	4243	'82	†

Marty Balin

Rock Justice (original cast)	EMI-America	17036	'80	†
Balin	EMI-America	17054	'81	†
Lucky	EMI-America	17088	'83	†
Balince—A Collection	Rhino	70968	'90	CD†
Freedom Flight	Trove/Solid Discs	7005	'97	CS/CD

The KBC Band (Kantner, Balin, Casady)

The KBC Band	Arista	8440	'86	LP/CS/CD†

Grace Slick

Manhole	Grunt	0347	'74	†
	Grunt	3736		†
Dreams	RCA	3544	'80	†
Welcome to the Wrecking Ball	RCA	3851	'81	†
Software	RCA	4791	'84	†

The Jefferson Starship

Dragonfly	Grunt	0717	'74	†
	RCA	3796	'88	CS/CD
Red Octopus	Grunt	0999	'75	†
	RCA	0999		CD
	RCA	3660		CS
Spitfire	Grunt	1557	'76	†
	Grunt	3953		†
Earth	Grunt	2515	'78	†
	RCA	6878	'97	CD
Gold	Grunt/RCA	3247	'79	†
	RCA	3247	'91	CS/CD
Freedom at Point Zero	Grunt	3452	'79	†
	RCA	3452		CD†
	RCA	5161	'84	CS†
Modern Times	Grunt	3848	'81	†
	RCA	3848		CS†
Winds of Change	Grunt	4372	'82	†
	RCA	4372		CS/CD
Nuclear Furniture	Grunt	4921	'84	†
	RCA	4921		CD†
The Jefferson Starship at Their Best	RCA	66231	'93	CS/CD
The Collection	Griffin	345		CD

Paul Kantner

The Planet Earth Rock & Roll Orchestra	RCA	4320	'83	†
A Guide Through the Chaos (A Road to the Passion)	MonsterSounds	(2)1017	'96	CS/CD

The KBC Band (Kantner, Balin, Casady)				
The KBC Band	Arista	8440	'86	LP/CS/CD†
Jefferson Starship				
Deep Space/Virgin Sky	Intersound	9151	'95	CD
Starship				
Knee Deep in the Hoopla	Grunt	5488	'85	†
	RCA	5488		CS/CD
No Protection	Grunt	6413	'87	CS/CD
Love Among the Cannibals	RCA	9693	'89	LP/CS/CD†
Greatest Hits (Ten Years and Change)	RCA	2423	'91	CS/CD
Craig Chaquico				
Acoustic Highway	Higher Octave	7050	'93	CS/CD
Acoustic Planet	Higher Octave	7070	'94	CS/CD
A Thousand Pictures	Higher Octave	7084	'96	CS/CD

JETHRO TULL

Ian Anderson (born August 10, 1947, in Edinburgh, Scotland), flute, guitar, saxophone, lead vocals; Mick Abrahams (born April 7, 1943, in Luton, Bedfordshire, England), guitar, vocals; Glenn Cornick (born April 24, 1947, in Barrow-in-Furness, Cumbria, England), bass; and Clive Bunker (born December 12, 1946, in Blackpool, Lancashire, England), drums. Abrahams left in early 1969, to be replaced by Martin Barre (born November 17, 1946).

Glenn Cornick left in 1971, to be replaced by Jeffrey Hammond-Hammond (born July 30, 1946, in Blackpool, England). Keyboardist John Evan(s) (born March 28, 1948, in Blackpool, England) joined in 1971. Clive Bunker left in late 1971, to be replaced by Barriemore Barlow (born September 10, 1949, in Blackpool, England). Hammond-Hammond left in December 1975, to be replaced by John Glascock (born 1952 in London; died November 17, 1979, in London). Glascock was replaced by Dave Pegg (born November 2, 1947, in Birmingham, England).

Starting out in the '60s as a blues-oriented British band, Jethro Tull evolved into one of the most successful progressive rock bands of the '70s. Generally more popular in the United States than in their native country, Jethro Tull became firmly established as an album band with their first of a series of "concept" albums, *Aqualung*. One of the leading live bands of the early '70s, Jethro Tull featured Ian Anderson's jazz-style flute playing and manic stage presence in performance. Jethro Tull's penchant for the theatrical in concert culminated in the critically scorned but enormously popular *A Passion Play* album and tour. Sustaining their popularity as an album band through the '70s and moving toward folk-rock late in the decade, Jethro Tull's slide into obscurity in the '80s was arrested by 1987's *Crest of a Knave*.

Ian Anderson moved to Blackpool, Lancashire, at the age of twelve and formed the Blades in 1963 with bassist Jeffrey Hammond-Hammond and keyboardist John Evans. Performing on the northern England club circuit, the group became the John Evan Band in 1965, with Glenn Cornick replacing Hammond-Hammond. In late 1967, the band moved to Bedfordshire to establish themselves on the nearby London club circuit, but the rest of the group soon left, leaving Anderson and Cornick to persevere. They quickly formed a new band with Mick Abrahams and Clive Bunker, with Abrahams and Anderson as the principal songwriters.

Adopting the name Jethro Tull, the group became an immediate success on the club circuit, gaining a residency at London's Marquee club in June 1968. Well received at August's Sunbury Jazz and Blues Festival, they signed with Island Records (Reprise in the United States). Their blues-oriented debut album *This Was* sold well in Great Britain but only modestly in the United States. However, in late 1968, Abrahams departed to form Blodwyn Pig. Briefly replaced by future Black Sabbath guitarist Tommy Iommi and former Nice guitarist Davy O'List, Abrahams' permanent replacement was guitarist Martin Barre.

Ian Anderson effectively took over as Jethro Tull's leader, developing his songwriting talents for highly melodic folk and classically influenced songs often featuring wry, off-beat lyrics. "Living in the Past" became a smash British hit in the summer of 1969 and *Stand Up* was dominated by Anderson's songwriting, containing group favorites such as the instrumental "Bouree," "Look Into the Sun," and "We Used to Know." Jethro Tull soon scored smash British hits with "Sweet Dream" and "Witches Promise"/"Teacher."

By 1970, Jethro Tull was established as one of the top concert attractions in the United States through regular tours, perhaps to the detriment of their British popularity. Keyboardist John Evans joined Jethro Tull to record *Benefit,* their last blues-based album, and accompanied the others with Jeffrey Hammond-Hammond on their subsequent American tour. Glenn Cornick left the group in late 1970 to form Wild Turkey, later resurfacing in Bob Welch's power trio Paris in 1975. He was replaced on bass by Jeffrey Hammond-Hammond, formerly of The John Evan Band, and Evans himself joined the group on a permanent basis.

Jethro Tull convincingly broke through in the United States as an album band with *Aqualung,* their first "concept" album and certainly their best-known work. Although attacked by some critics as bombastic and pretentious, the album sold well in both Great Britain and the United States and included concert and FM radio favorites such as "Hymn 43" (a minor American hit), "Cross-Eyed Mary," "Locomotive Breath," and "Aqualung."

Clive Bunker departed Jethro Tull in mid-1971 to form Jude with Robin Trower, Frankie Miller, and Jim Dewar, later reemerging with the re-formed Blodwyn Pig. He was replaced on drums by Barriemore Barlow. Jethro Tull conducted extensive tours of the United States in 1971 and 1972, and *Thick as a Brick,* essentially an album-long ballad without individual cuts, sold spectacularly, staying on the American album charts for nearly a year. *Living in the Past* assembled live performances and early songs unreleased in the United States on Jethro Tull's new label Chrysalis, yielding the group's first major American hit, "Living in the Past," their British hit from 1969.

Jethro Tull's final concept album, *A Passion Play,* was critically lambasted by virtually every rock critic and sold poorly in Britain but massively in the United States. The subsequent American tour featuring the theatrically oriented performance of the album was greeted by record-breaking, sellout crowds. However, the group, road weary and disillusioned by hostile press reviews, announced their "retirement" from live performance in August 1973. The group retreated to Switzerland, where they recorded the largely orchestral *War Child* as the soundtrack to a movie. The movie was eventually abandoned as too costly, but the album yielded the group's second (and last) major American hit with "Bungle in the Jungle."

Jethro Tull continued to record best-selling American albums through the '70s, including *Minstrel in the Gallery* and *Songs from the Wood,* which revealed a decidedly folk-rock orientation. By early 1976, Jeffrey Hammond-Hammond had been replaced by John Glascock. The group conducted their first British tour in three years in February 1977 and added keyboardist David Palmer, the orchestrator of virtually all of Jethro Tull's albums, in May. Ian Anderson subsequently became involved in salmon farming. In the fall of 1979, Dave Pegg, a member of Fairport Convention, replaced ailing John Glascock on bass. On November 17, 1979, Glascock died during open-heart surgery in a London hospital at the age of 27.

In 1980, Ian Anderson dismissed Barriemore Barlow, John Evans, and David Palmer. He then recorded *A,* perhaps his most fully realized folk-rock album, with Barre, Pegg, and violinist-keyboardist Eddie Jobson, who left after a single tour. With Anderson, Barre, and Pegg as mainstays, Jethro Tull continued to tour and record in the '80s. In the meantime, Ian Anderson recorded the solo album *Walk Into Light* and rerecorded a number of Jethro Tull classics with David Palmer conducting the London Symphony Orchestra, released as *A Classic Case.* In 1987, the group recorded their best-selling album in years, *The Crest of a Knave,* and toured for the first time in three years, with Fairport Convention as the opening act. Jethro Tull's 1992 world tour produced the acoustic album *A Little Light Music.* In 1995, Anderson recorded the solo instrumental album *Divinities* for Angel Records. The following year, Martin Barre recorded *The Meeting* for Imago Records.

Early Jethro Tull

This Was	Reprise	6336	'69	†
	Chrysalis	1041		†
	Chrysalis	41041	'83	†
	Chrysalis	21041		CS/CD
Stand Up	Reprise	6360	'69	†
	Chrysalis	1042		†
	Chrysalis	41042	'83	†
	Chrysalis	21042		CS/CD
	Mobile Fidelity	00524		CD†
Benefit	Reprise	6400	'70	†
	Chrysalis	1043		†
	Chrysalis	41043	'83	†
	Chrysalis	21043		CS/CD

Blodwyn Pig (with Mick Abrahams)

Ahead Rings Out	A&M	4210	'69	†
	A&M	3180	'82	†
Getting to This	A&M	4243	'70	†

Mick Abrahams

Mick Abrahams	A&M	4312	'71	†

Wild Turkey (with Glenn Cornick)

Battle Hymn	Reprise	2070	'72	†

Jethro Tull

Aqualung	Reprise	2035	'71	†
	Chrysalis	1044		†
	Chrysalis	21044	'84	CS/CD
Aqualung: 25th Anniversary—Special CD	Chrysalis/EMI	52213	'96	CD
Thick as a Brick	Reprise	2072	'72	†
	Chrysalis	1003		†
	Chrysalis	21003	'86	CS/CD
	Mobile Fidelity	00510		CD†
A Passion Play	Chrysalis	1040	'73	†
	Chrysalis	41040	'83	†
	Chrysalis	21040		CS/CD
	Mobile Fidelity	720	'98	CD
War Child	Chrysalis	1067	'74	†
	Chrysalis	41067	'83	†
	Chrysalis	21067		CS/CD

Minstrel in the Gallery	Chrysalis	1082	'75	†
	Chrysalis	41082	'83	†
	Chrysalis	21082		CS/CD
Too Old to Rock 'n' Roll . . . Too Young to Die	Chrysalis	1111	'76	†
	Chrysalis	41111	'83	†
	Chrysalis	21111		CS/CD
Songs from the Wood	Chrysalis	1132	'77	†
	Chrysalis	41132	'83	†
	Chrysalis	21132		CS/CD
	Mobile Fidelity	734	'98	CD
Heavy Horses	Chrysalis	1175	'78	†
	Chrysalis	41175	'83	†
	Chrysalis	21175		CS†/CD
Bursting Out	Chrysalis	1201	'78	†
	Chrysalis	41201	'83	†
	Chrysalis	21201		CS†/CD
Stormwatch	Chrysalis	1238	'79	†
	Chrysalis	41238	'83	†
	Chrysalis	21238		CS/CD
"A"	Chrysalis	1301	'80	†
	Chrysalis	21301		CS/CD
The Broadsword and the Beast	Chrysalis	1380	'82	†
	Chrysalis	21380	'86	CS†/CD
Under Wraps	Chrysalis	41461	'84	†
	Chrysalis	21461		CS/CD
The Crest of a Knave	Chrysalis	21590	'87	CS/CD
Rock Island	Chrysalis	21708	'89	CS/CD
Catfish Rising	Chrysalis	21863	'91	CS/CD†
A Little Light Music	Chrysalis	21954	'92	CS/CD
Roots to Branches	Chrysalis	35418	'95	CS/CD
In Concert (recorded 1991)	Griffin	578	'95	CD

Jethro Tull Anthologies and Compilations

Living in the Past	Chrysalis	(2)1035	'72	†
	Chrysalis	21035		CS/CD
	Mobile Fidelity	(2)708		CD
M.U.: The Best of Jethro Tull	Chrysalis	1078	'75	†
	Chrysalis	21078		CS/CD
Repeat: The Best of Jethro Tull, Volume 2	Chrysalis	1135	'77	†
	Chrysalis	41135	'83	†
	Chrysalis	21135	'86	CS/CD
Original Master	Chrysalis	41515	'85	†
	Chrysalis	21515	'88	CS/CD
20 Years of Jethro Tull: The Definitive Collection	Chrysalis	(3)21653	'88	CD†
20 Years of Jethro Tull (selections)	Chrysalis	21655	'89	CS†/CD
Jethro Tull: 25th Anniversary Box Set	Chrysalis	(4)26004	'93	CD†
The Best of Jethro Tull: The Anniversary Collection	Chrysalis	(2)26015	'93	CD

Ian Anderson

Walk into Light	Chrysalis	41443	'83	†
	Chrysalis	21443	'86	CS/CD†
Divinities: Twelve Dances with God	Angel	55262	'95	CS/CD

The London Symphony Orchestra				
A Classic Case: The Music of Jethro Tull	RCA	9505	'86	LP/CS†
	RCA	7067	'86	CD†
	RCA	62510	'93	CS/CD
Martin Barre				
The Meeting	Imago	23016	'96	CS/CD

JANIS JOPLIN

Born January 19, 1943, in Port Arthur, Texas; died October 4, 1970, in Hollywood, California.

BIG BROTHER AND THE HOLDING COMPANY

Janis Joplin, lead vocals; Sam Andrew (born December 18, 1941, in Taft, California), guitar, piano, saxophone, vocals; James Gurley (born December 22, 1939, in Detroit, Michigan), guitar; Peter Albin (born June 6, 1944, in San Francisco), bass, guitar, vocals; and David Getz (born January 24, 1940, in Brooklyn, New York), drums.

Perhaps the first female "superstar" of rock music, Janis Joplin was regarded by some as the greatest white female blues singer of all time. She certainly redefined the role of the white female vocalist with her gutsy, physically and emotionally wrenching, and virtually sexual delivery, opening the way for female "shouters" in rock music. Along with The Jefferson Airplane and The Grateful Dead, Joplin's first group, Big Brother and The Holding Company, formed the nucleus of San Francisco's burgeoning "counterculture" music scene of the middle to late '60s. Big Brother and The Holding Company exploded out of the June 1967 Monterey International Pop Festival into international prominence, with Joplin emerging as one of the most powerful personalities of the era and essentially becoming a legend in her own time. The group recorded the classic *Cheap Thrills* album before Joplin's departure in late 1968, much to the chagrin of critics and San Francisco associates. She had nearly completed recording her finest later-day album, *Pearl,* when she died from a heroin overdose on October 4, 1970, at the age of 27. Janis Joplin was inducted into the Rock and Roll Hall of Fame in 1995.

Raised in Port Arthur, Texas, Janis Joplin had discovered the blues by the age of seventeen. She began singing locally in 1961, primarily at Ken Threadgill's Austin bar. She sojourned briefly to San Francisco in 1963 to perform at folk clubs and bars with Jorma Kaukonen or Roger Perkins before returning to Texas to attend the University of Texas at Austin. During 1965, musicians Peter Albin, Sam Andrew, and James Gurley were playing at jam sessions hosted by Chet Helms at the Avalon Ballroom. With Helms' encouragement, they formed Big Brother and The Holding Company in September, replacing their original drummer with David Getz. Helms became the group's manager and they debuted at the Trips Festival in January 1966. In June, Helms successfully recruited Texas friend Janis Joplin as vocalist for the band.

Backed by screeching psychedelic guitars, Janis Joplin sang, virtually shouted, in the style of blues singers such as Bessie Smith, investing her performances with intense, agitated passion. Debuting at the Avalon Ballroom in June 1966, Big Brother and The Holding Company signed a recording contract with the small Chicago-based Mainstream label, which released the group's poorly produced debut album in September 1967.

Big Brother and The Holding Company were launched into international prominence with their celebrated appearance at the Monterey International Pop Festival in June 1967.

JANIS JOPLIN (CORBIS-BETTMANN)

Their soon-released Mainstream album featured Janis Joplin's stunning performances of "Women Is Losers" and "Down on Me," as well as the whole band's overlooked "Blindman." Signed to a management contract with Albert Grossman (then Bob Dylan's manager) in January 1968, the group switched to Columbia Records for their only other album with Joplin, *Cheap Thrills*. "Piece of My Heart" became a near-smash from the album, which included "Big Mama" Thornton's "Ball and Chain," Janis' own "Turtle Blues," and a moving rendition of George Gershwin's "Summertime." With Joplin garnering the bulk of the media attention, rumors of the group's breakup began to spread in November and were confirmed in December with Joplin's final appearance with the band at Chet Helms' Family Dog.

Retaining guitarist Sam Andrew, Janis Joplin formed a new band, alternately known as Squeeze and The Janis Joplin Revue, with organist Bill King, bassist Brad Campbell, and two horn players. Debuting equivocally at the Memphis Sound Party on December 18, 1968, the group soon suffered a variety of personnel changes. After recording *Kozmic Blues* with the group, Joplin performed her final concert with this band on December 29, 1969, at Madison Square Garden. In April 1970, she again appeared with Big Brother and The Holding Company, reconstituted by Sam Andrew and blues singer-songwriter Nick Gravenites, at Fillmore West. Big Brother (without Janis Joplin) subsequently recorded two albums for Columbia, the first featuring Gravenites' tongue-in-cheek ode to Merle Haggard, "I'll Change Your Flat Tire, Merle." Disbanding in 1972, the group re-formed in 1987 with vocalist Michelle Bastian.

Forming a new band, Full-Tilt Boogie, in May, Janis Joplin debuted the group at Freedom Hall in Louisville, Kentucky, on June 12, 1970. The members included guitarist John Till (a later-day member of her prior band) and bassist Brad Campbell. By September, they had nearly finished recording their album, but on October 4, 1970, Janis Joplin was found dead in her Hollywood hotel, the victim of a heroin overdose. Released posthumously, *Pearl* yielded a top hit with Kris Kristofferson's "Me and Bobby McGee" and included "Cry Baby," the silly ditty "Mercedes Benz," and one of her theme songs, "Get It While You Can."

Columbia later released the live set *Joplin in Concert* (recorded with Big Brother and Full-Tilt Boogie), a soundtrack album to the 1975 film documentary *Janis,* and *Farewell Song*. The 1979 Bette Midler movie *The Rose* was inspired by the life of Janis Joplin. Joplin was inducted into the Rock and Roll Hall of Fame in 1995.

JANIS JOPLIN BIBLIOGRAPHY

Amburn, Ellis. *Pearl: The Obsessions and Passions of Janis Joplin: A Biography.* New York: Warner Books, 1992.

Carey, Gary. *Lenny, Janis and Jimi.* New York: Pocket Books, 1975.

Caserta, Peggy. *Going Down with Janis.* Secaucus, NJ: Lyle Stuart, 1973; New York: Dell, 1973.

Dalton, David. *Janis.* New York: Simon and Schuster, 1971; New York: Popular Library, 1971.

————. *Piece of My Heart: The Life, Times and Legend of Janis Joplin.* New York: St. Martin's Press, 1986.

Friedman, Myra. *Buried Alive: The Biography of Janis Joplin.* New York: William Morrow, 1973; New York: Harmony Books, 1992.

Joplin, Laura. *Love, Janis.* New York: Villard Books, 1992.

Landau, Deborah. *Janis Joplin: Her Life and Times.* New York: Paperback Library, 1971.

Big Brother and The Holding Company

Big Brother and The Holding Company	Mainstream	6099	'67	†
	Columbia	30631	'71	†
Cheap Thrills	Columbia	9700	'68	CD
	Columbia	00488		CS
Live at Winterland '68	Columbia/Legacy	64869	'98	CD
Be a Brother (with Kathy McDonald)	Columbia	30222	'70	†
How Hard It Is	Columbia	30738	'71	†

Kathy McDonald

Insane Asylum	Capitol	11224	'74	†

Janis Joplin

I Got Dem Ol' Kozmic Blues Again Mama	Columbia	9913	'69	CD
	Columbia	00748		CS
Pearl	Columbia	30322	'71	CS/CD
Pearl/Cheap Thrills	CBS	38219	'86	CS
3-Pak: Cheap Thrills/I Got Dem Ol' Kosmic Blues Again Mama!/Pearl	Columbia	(3)64804	'95	CD
Joplin in Concert	Columbia	31160	'72	CS/CD
Greatest Hits	Columbia	32168	'73	CS/CD
Janis (soundtrack)	Columbia	(2)33345	'75	†
	Columbia	33345		CS
	Columbia/Legacy	65409	'93	CD
Farewell Song	Columbia	37569	'82	CS/CD
Janis Joplin	Columbia/Legacy	(3)48845	'93	CS/CD

Janis Joplin Tribute Album

Songs of Janis Joplin—Blues Down Deep	House Of Blues	1251	'97	CD

B. B. KING

Born Riley B. King on September 16, 1925, near Itta Bena, Mississippi.

One of the most successful blues artists of the '50s, B. B. King became one of the world's most soulful guitar soloists, developing a style of playing that featured his trademark arpeggios and "bent" note improvisations, which influenced virtually every guitarist in the rock and blues fields in the '60s. Perhaps the most influential blues guitarist on white rock gui-

B. B. King (Hulton-Deutsch Collection/Corbis)

tarists (from Eric Clapton and Mike Bloomfield to Johnny Winter and Stevie Ray Vaughan), King ultimately achieved widespread recognition with his 1969 tour with The Rolling Stones and the conspicuous success of "The Thrill Is Gone" in 1970. Subsequently serving as an international ambassador for the blues, B. B. King became the first and only blues singer and guitarist to graduate into extensive mainstream popularity. Elevated to the exclusive Nevada casino and supper club circuit by the '70s, B. B. King was the first black bluesman to tour Russia in 1979. He was inducted into the Rock and Roll Hall of Fame in 1987.

B. B. King grew up in Indianola, Mississippi, and sang in local gospel choirs. He acquired his first guitar while in his early teens and formed his first group, The Elkhorn Singers, for performances in local black clubs. He permanently settled in Memphis in 1949 and secured a ten-minute afternoon show on radio station WDIA. King subsequently formed The Beale Streeters, whose members at various times included Bobby "Blue" Bland and Johnny Ace, and became known as "The Beale Street Blues Boy," later shortened to "B. B."

After initial recordings for the small Nashville-based Bullet label in 1949, B. B. King was signed to the Los Angeles–based Modern/RPM label by Ike Turner. Scoring his first top rhythm-and-blues hit with "Three O'Clock Blues" in 1952, King formed a thirteen-piece band that included a small horn section (a regular feature of his bands throughout his career) and began relentlessly touring the so-called "chitlin" circuit of small black clubs. Through 1954, he scored top rhythm-and-blues hits with "You Know I Love You," "Please Love Me," and "You Upset Me." By 1954, B. B. King had graduated to major black venues such as the Howard Theater in Washington, D.C., and the Apollo Theater in Harlem. Smash rhythm-and-blues hits through 1957 included "Every Day I Have the Blues" (his signature song). With the discontinuation of the RPM label in 1959, King recorded for Kent Records from 1958 to 1962. "Rock Me Baby" became his first moderate pop hit in 1964, after his departure from the label.

In 1962, B. B. King signed with ABC Records, recording for both ABC and its subsidiary BluesWay label. Although early albums did not sell particularly well, his *Live at the Regal* album, recorded November 21, 1964, came to be regarded as one of his finest blues recordings ever made. Playing up to 300 engagements a year through the late '70s, King was performing on the rock concert circuit and receiving airplay on underground FM radio by 1966. He scored smash R&B hits with "Don't Answer the Door" in late 1966 and "Paying the Cost to Be the Boss" (also a moderate pop hit) in 1968. By then, King was successfully appearing at the Fillmore West and East and receiving the laudatory comments regarding his playing from white guitarists such as Eric Clapton and Mike Bloomfield. *Lucille* became King's first album chart entry and he was soon introduced to a new international audience with his tour in support of The Rolling Stones in 1969. He became fully established with white audiences with *Completely Well* and its near-smash crossover hit "The Thrill Is Gone."

Established on the supper club and Nevada casino circuit by the early '70s, B. B. King began recording exclusively for ABC with *Indianola Mississippi Seeds.* In 1971, he recorded *In London* with Peter Green, Alexis Korner, and Ringo Starr. *To Know You Is to Love You* produced major crossover hits with the title song, cowritten by Stevie Wonder, and "I Like to Live the Love." King also enjoyed considerable commercial success in collaboration with Bobby "Blue" Bland on *Together for the First Time: Live.* King recorded for MCA Records after it had absorbed ABC Records in 1979. That spring, he performed thirty shows in Russia, becoming the first black bluesman to tour that country.

B. B. King continued to tour and record for MCA in the '80s and '90s. Noteworthy albums included *There Must Be a Better World Somewhere* and *Live at San Quentin.* In 1985, he appeared in the John Landis film *Into the Night,* achieving a major rhythm-and-blues hit with the title song. Inducted into the Rock and Roll Hall of Fame in 1987, B. B. King managed a minor pop hit in 1989 with "When Love Comes to Town," recorded with the Irish rock band U2.

B. B. KING BIBLIOGRAPHY

King, B. B., with David Ritz. *Blues All Around Me: The Autobiography of B. B. King.* New York: Avon Books, 1996.

Kostelanetz, Richard (editor). *The B. B. King Companion: Five Decades of Commentary.* New York: Schirmer Books, 1997.

Sawyer, Charles. *The Arrival of B. B. King: The Authorized Biography.* Garden City, NY: Doubleday, 1980.

B. B. King on ABC/BluesWay/MCA Records

Mr. Blues	ABC	456	'63	†
Live at the Regal	ABC	509	'65	†
	MCA	724	'71	†
	MCA	27006		CS†
	MCA	31106		CD†
	MCA	11646		CD
	Pickwick	3593	'78	†
	Ace	86	'83	LP
	Mobile Fidelity	00548	'91	CD†
Confessin' the Blues	ABC	528	'65	†
Blues Is King	BluesWay	6001	'67	†
	ABC	704	'77	†
	MCA	31368	'90	CD
Blues on Top of Blues	BluesWay	6011	'68	†
	ABC	709		†
Lucille	BluesWay	6016	'68	†
	ABC	712	'77	†
	MCA	10518	'92	CS/CD
	Mobile Fidelity	659	'96	CD

Electric B. B.—His Best	BluesWay	6022	'69	†
	ABC	813	'77	†
	MCA	27007		CS/CD
Live and Well	BluesWay	6031	'69	†
	ABC	819		†
	MCA	27008		CS
	MCA	31191	'88	CD
Completely Well	BluesWay	6037	'69	†
	ABC	868	'77	†
	MCA	27009		CS†
	MCA	31039	'87	CD†
	MCA	11207	'95	CD†
	MCA	11768	'98	CS/CD
Back in the Alley	BluesWay	6050	'73	†
	ABC	878	'77	†
	MCA	27010		CS/CD
Great Moments with B. B. King (BluesWay recordings)	MCA	(2)4124		CS
	MCA	4124		CD
Indianola Mississippi Seeds	ABC	713	'70	†
	MCA	31343	'89	CS/CD
Live at Cook County Jail	ABC	723	'71	†
	MCA	27005		CS†
	MCA	31080	'88	CD†
	MCA	11769	'98	CS/CD
In London	ABC	730	'71	†
	MCA	10843	'93	CD
L.A. Midnight	ABC	743	'72	†
Guess Who	ABC	759	'72	†
	MCA	10351	'91	CS/CD
The Best of B. B. King	ABC	767	'73	†
	MCA	27074		CS
	MCA	31040		CD
To Know You Is to Love You	ABC	794	'73	†
	MCA	10414	'91	CS/CD
Friends	ABC	825	'74	†
Lucille Talks Back	ABC	898	'75	†
King Size	ABC	977	'77	†
Midnight Believer	ABC/MCA	1061	'78	†
	MCA	27011		CS/CD
Take It Home	MCA	3151	'79	†
Live "Now Appearing" at Ole Miss	MCA	(2)8016	'80	CS/CD
There Must Be a Better World Somewhere	MCA	5162	'81	†
	MCA	27034	'84	CS/CD
Love Me Tender	MCA	5307	'82	†
	MCA	886		CS/CD
Blues 'n' Jazz	MCA	5413	'83	†
	MCA	27119	'87	CS/CD
Six Silver Strings	MCA	5616	'85	CS/CD
Blues 'n' Jazz/The Electric B. B.	MCA	5881	'87	CD†
The King of the Blues: 1989	MCA	42183	'89	CS/CD
Live at San Quentin	MCA	6455	'90	CS/CD

There Is Always One More Time	MCA	10295	'91	CS/CD
The King of the Blues	MCA	(4)10677	'92	CS/CD
Blues Summit	MCA	10710	'93	CS/CD
B. B. King in London	MCA	10843	'94	CD
Got My Mojo Working	MCA	20541	'94	CS/CD
How Blue Can You Get? (1964–94)	MCA	(2)11443	'96	CD
Deuces Wild	MCA	11711	'97	CS/CD
Blues on the Bayou	MCA	11879	'98	CS/CD
Other B. B. King				
Paying the Cost to Be the Boss	Pickwick	3385	'75	†
King Biscuit Flower Hour (recorded 1978)	King Biscuit Flower Hour	88038	'98	CD
Live at the Apollo	GRP	9637	'91	CS/CD
Heart and Soul: A Collection of Blues Ballads	Pointblank/Virgin	40072	'95	CD
Catfish Blues	Drive	3228	'95	CD
	Allegro	3228	'96	CD
B. B. King and Friends	Spotlite	15105	'96	CS/CD
B. B. King and Bobby "Blue" Bland				
Together for the First Time: Live	Dunhill	(2)50190	'74	†
	MCA	(2)4160	'82	LP/CS
	MCA	4160		CD
Together Again	Impulse	9317	'76	†
	MCA	27012		CS/CD

CAROLE KING

Born Carol Klein on February 9, 1942, in Brooklyn, New York. Songwriting partner Gerry Goffin was born February 11, 1939, in Queens, New York.

CAROLE KING (NEAL PRESTON/CORBIS)

Carole King enjoyed two spectacular careers, first as a prolific songwriter in the '60s, later as one of the first and most popular female singer-songwriters of the '70s. In collaboration with Gerry Goffin, she wrote an astounding series of best-selling songs while working at New York's famed Brill Building during the '60s. The team wrote nearly as many hits as did Beatles Lennon and McCartney, scoring over seventy chart entries by 1970, including the top hits "Will You Love Me Tomorrow," "Take Good Care of My Baby," "Go Away, Little Girl," and "The Loco-Motion." Following the breakup of the Goffin-King team in 1967, Carole King embarked on a solo career in 1970.

Her second album, *Tapestry,* sold spectacularly and heralded the rise of the singer-songwriter. The album eventually sold more than fifteen million copies, becoming the best-selling female solo album of all time during its nearly six-year reign on the album charts. Not surprisingly, *Tapestry* overshadowed King's subsequent recording career. Although she largely withdrew from public view in the mid-'70s, she continued to record into the '90s. Gerry Goffin and Carole King were inducted into the Rock and Roll Hall of Fame in 1990.

Carole King began singing and playing piano at the age of four. She formed the female vocal group The Co-Sines at age fourteen and met songwriter Gerry Goffin in 1958 while attending Queens College. Signed as a staff songwriter to Al Nevins and Don Kirshner's Aldon Music at seventeen, she soon married Goffin and initiated their collaborative songwriting career at New York's Brill Building. She was first brought to the attention of the American record-buying public as the subject of Neil Sedaka's 1959 hit "Oh! Carol." King and Goffin scored their first songwriting hit, a top hit, in late 1960 with "Will You Love Me Tomorrow," recorded by The Shirelles.

In the first half of the '60s, Gerry Goffin and Carole King wrote a series of hits recorded by a variety of artists. These included "Some Kind of Wonderful," "When My Little Girl Is Smiling," and the smash "Up on the Roof" for The Drifters; "Sharing You" and the top hit "Take Good Care of My Baby" for Bobby Vee; "Crying in the Rain" (with Howie Greenfield) for The Everly Brothers; "Her Royal Majesty" for James Darren; "Point of No Return" for Gene McDaniels; the smash "One Fine Day" for The Chiffons; "Hey Girl" for Freddie Scott; and "I Can't Stay Mad at You" for Skeeter Davis. In 1963, Goffin and King provided Steve Lawrence and Eydie Gorme with a number of hits, beginning with the top hit "Go Away, Little Girl" by Lawrence. The team also contributed hits to two British groups during the mid-'60s: "I'm Into Something Good" for Herman's Hermits in 1964 and "Don't Bring Me Down" for The Animals in 1966. The duo also collaborated with Phil Spector on "Just Once in My Life" for The Righteous Brothers in 1965.

In 1962, Don Kirshner formed Dimension Records, as Gerry Goffin learned production and Carole King arranging. Dimension's first release, "The Loco-Motion," written by Goffin and King and recorded by Little Eva, became a top hit. Carole King's version of "It Might as Well Rain Until September," originally written for Bobby Vee, was Dimension's second hit, followed by Little Eva's "Keep Your Hands Off My Baby," and two songs recorded by The Cookies, "Chains" and "Don't Say Nothin' (Bad About My Baby)," all written by Goffin and King.

During the mid-'60s, Goffin and King formed their own record label, Tomorrow, but singles by King and The Myddle Class failed to reach the charts. In 1967, they contributed hit songs to Kirshner's Monkees ("Pleasant Valley Sunday") and to Aretha Franklin ("A Natural Woman"), while providing The Byrds with "Goin' Back" and "Wasn't Born to Follow." Gerry Goffin and Carole King were inducted into the Rock and Roll Hall of Fame in 1990.

Carole King subsequently broke up the songwriting team, divorcing Goffin in 1968 and marrying the bass player from The Myddle Class, Charles Larkey. King moved to Los Angeles, where she formed The City with Larkey and guitarist Danny Kortchmar and recorded one album, *Now That Everything's Been Said,* for Lou Adler's Ode Records. Although the album failed to sell, it did include "Wasn't Born to Follow" and Goffin and King's "Hi-De-Ho," a major hit for Blood, Sweat and Tears in 1970.

By 1970, Carole King had initiated a solo career, assisting James Taylor with *Sweet Baby James* and recording her debut solo album, *Writer,* with Larkey, Kortchmar, and Taylor. The album contained the Goffin-King songs "Up on the Roof," "Goin' Back," and "No Easy Way Down," but sold only modestly. In 1971, King recorded the enormously successful *Tapestry* album. As James Taylor's version of King's "You've Got a Friend" was climbing the charts, so was her own double-sided top hit, "It's Too Late"/"I Feel the Earth Move." The album later yielded another major two-sided hit with "So Far Away"/"Smackwater Jack," while including "Way Over Yonder" and two Goffin-King compositions, "Will You Love Me Tomorrow" and "A Natural Woman." This collection of mature, sophisticated songs (in contrast to the prior teen melodramas) appealed to virtually every sector of the record-buying public, remaining on the album charts for nearly six years and eventually selling more than fifteen million copies.

Carole King's next two albums, *Carole King Music* and *Rhymes and Reasons,* became bestsellers, each yielding a major hit single ("Sweet Seasons" and "Been to Canaan," respectively), but somehow lacking *Tapestry*'s magic. *Fantasy* was somewhat more socially conscious, producing moderate hits with "Believe in Humanity" and "Corazon," but *Wrap Around Joy,* with most lyrics supplied by David Palmer, was decidedly jazz oriented. The album's smash hit "Jazzman" featured an exciting saxophone solo by Tom Scott and was followed by "Nightingale." After *Really Rosie,* an animated television show based on the children's books of Maurice Sendak and using Sendak's lyrics, King recorded *Thoroughbred* with the vocal assistance of Graham Nash, David Crosby, and James Taylor. The album included four Goffin-King songs and yielded a major hit with "Only Love Is Real."

At the end of 1976, Carole King severed relations with Lou Adler's Ode Records, switching to Capitol for the moderate hit "Hard Rock Cafe." By then separated from Charles Larkey, she collaborated with Rick Evers and the band Navarro for touring and recording. King later married Evers and moved to Idaho but, on March 21, 1978, he died from a cocaine overdose in Los Angeles. Subsequent albums for Capitol sold only modestly and only *Pearls,* a collection of her versions of the Goffin-King classics of the '60s, yielded a major hit, with "One Fine Day."

Settling into a less public lifestyle, Carole King recorded two albums for Atlantic and made a brief benefit tour for presidential hopeful Gary Hart in 1984. Working for protection of the wilderness since 1984, King provided the title song to *The Care Bears Movie,* acted in several movies and television shows, and starred in the play *Getting Out.* Following an album for Capitol in 1989, Carole King recorded *Colour of Your Dreams* for her own label in 1993, the year she performed at President Clinton's inaugural ball and made her Broadway acting debut in the musical *Blood Brothers.* Gerry Goffin and Carole King's daughter, Louise, started her modest recording career in the late '70s.

CAROLE KING BIBLIOGRAPHY

Cohen, Mitchell S. *Carole King: A Biography in Words and Pictures.* New York: Sire Books, 1976.

The City

Now That Everything's Been Said	Ode	1244012	'69	†
Gerry Goffin				
It Ain't Exactly Entertainment	Adelphi	(2)4102	'73	†
Back Room Blood	Genes	4132	'96	CD
Carole King				
Writer: Carole King	Ode	77006	'70	†
	Ode	34944	'78	†
	Columbia/Legacy	34944	'91	CD
Tapestry	Ode	77009	'71	†
	Ode	34946	'78	CS/CD
	Epic/Legacy	66226	'95	CD
Carole King Music	Ode	77013	'71	†
	Ode	34949	'78	†
	Columbia/Legacy	34949	'91	CD

Rhymes and Reasons	Ode	77016	'72	†
	Ode	34950	'78	†
	Columbia/Legacy	34950	'91	CD
Fantasy	Ode	77018	'73	†
	Ode	34962	'78	†
	Columbia/Legacy	34962	'91	CD
Wrap Around Joy	Ode	77024	'74	†
	Ode	34953	'78	†
	Columbia/Legacy	34953	'91	CD
Really Rosie (TV soundtrack)	Ode	77027	'75	†
	Ode	34955	'78	CS
Thoroughbred	Ode	77034	'76	†
	Ode	34963	'78	†
	Columbia/Legacy	34963	'91	CD
Her Greatest Hits (1972–1978)	Ode	34967	'78/'86	CS/CD
A Natural Woman: The Ode Collection 1968–1976	Epic/Legacy	(2)48833	'94	CS/CD
Simple Things	Capitol	11667	'77	†
	Capitol	16057		†
Welcome Home	Capitol	11785	'77	†
	Capitol	16058	'78	†
Touch the Sky	Capitol	11953	'79	†
	Capitol	16059		†
Pearls—The Songs of Goffin and King	Capitol	12073	'80	†
One to One	Atlantic	19344	'82	†
Speeding Time	Atlantic	80118	'83	LP/CS/CD†
City Streets	Capitol	90885	'89	CS/CD†
Colour of Your Dreams	King's X		'93	†
	Priority	57197		CS/CD
In Concert	King's X	53878	'94	†
Tribute Album				
Tapestry Revisited: A Tribute to Carole King	Atlantic	92604	'95	CS/CD
Louise Goffin				
Kid Blue	Asylum	203	'79	†
This Is the Place	Warner Brothers	25692	'88	LP/CS/CD†

KING CRIMSON

Robert Fripp (born May 16, 1946, in Wimbourne, Dorset, England), guitar; Ian McDonald (born June 25, 1946, in London), reeds, woodwinds, keyboards, mellotron, vocals; Greg Lake (born November 10, 1948, in Bournemouth, Dorset, England), bass, lead vocals; Mike Giles (born March 1, 1942, in Bournemouth), drums, vocals; and lyricist Pete Sinfield. Giles and McDonald left at the end of 1969 and Lake departed in early 1970. Sinfield was dismissed at the end of 1971.

Later members included Raymond "Boz" Burrell (born August 1, 1946, in Lincoln, England), bass, vocals; Ian Wallace (born September 29, 1946, in Bury, Lancashire, England), drums; John Wetton (born June 12, 1950, in Derby, England), bass, vocals; and Bill Bruford (born May 17, 1949, in Sevenoaks, Kent, England), drums. King Crimson disbanded in 1974 and re-formed from 1981 to 1984 and 1993 to present with Fripp, Bruford, bassist Tony Levin, and guitarist Robert "Adrian" Belew.

A seminal British progressive band of the late '60s and '70s, King Crimson attained "superstar" status in England and Europe but remained essentially a cult band in the United States. Showcasing the doom-laden lyrics of Pete Sinfield and the playing of Robert Fripp (guitar) and Ian McDonald (mellotron), King Crimson's debut album *In the Court of the Crimson King* became a classic of the genre. Virtually reconstituted thereafter, King Crimson and Fripp endured a chaotic series of personnel changes for six more studio albums. One-time members of King Crimson included Greg Lake (later with Emerson, Lake and Palmer), Ian McDonald (later with Foreigner), and Boz Burrell (later with Bad Company). Guitarist extraordinaire Fripp recorded several influential albums with synthesizer player Brian Eno in the mid-'70s, as well as on his own, before reconvening King Crimson in the early '80s and again in the '90s with guitarist Adrian Belew.

Robert Fripp started playing the guitar at age eleven and worked with his first music group at fourteen. In Bournemouth, he helped form Giles, Giles and Fripp in 1967 with Giles brothers Mike and Peter on drums and bass, respectively. They never played in public, their sole album for Deram failed to attract any attention, and, by the fall of 1968, the group had disbanded.

Mike Giles and Robert Fripp began rehearsing a new band called King Crimson in January 1969 and debuted in London that April. With Pete Sinfield providing the lyrics, the other members were Greg Lake and Ian McDonald. The group's underground reputation was enhanced by a July appearance before 650,000 in Hyde Park at a free Rolling Stones concert. King Crimson's debut album, *In the Court of the Crimson King,* was greeted with near-unanimous critical acclaim and featured five extended pieces, including "Epitaph," "21st Century Schizoid Man," and the title song, a minor hit.

However, after King Crimson's first tour of the United States, Giles and McDonald left the group in December 1969, later to record an album together for Cotillion. Reduced to a trio, King Crimson began recording their second album, only to see Greg Lake depart to join Emerson, Lake and Palmer during those sessions. *In the Wake of Poseidon* was completed with Gordon Haskell (bass, lead vocals), Mel Collins (reeds), and the Giles brothers, with Fripp taking over on mellotron. Despite its remarkable resemblance to their debut, the album sold quite well.

By late 1970, Mel Collins and Gordon Haskell had become permanent members of King Crimson, as had drummer Andy McCulloch. Nonetheless, Haskell quit shortly before the final sessions for *Lizard,* later to record a solo album for Atco. Ian Wallace replaced McCulloch and Fripp recruited bassist Boz Burrell for *Islands.* Again, after a second American tour in early 1972, King Crimson disintegrated. Collins, Wallace, and Burrell left to join Alexis Korner, and Fripp dismissed lyricist Pete Sinfield. Sinfield later produced Roxy Music's debut album, recorded a solo album, and wrote songs for Emerson, Lake and Palmer.

After several months' layoff, Robert Fripp reconstituted King Crimson with avant-garde percussionist Jamie Muir, violin and mellotron player David Cross, lead vocalist-bassist John Wetton (from Family), and drummer Bill Bruford (from Yes). This aggregation recorded *Larks' Tongue in Aspic,* but Muir dropped out after the first tour. *Starless and Bible Black* was recorded by the remaining quartet, and *Red* was recorded without Cross, but with the assistance of Mel Collins and Ian McDonald. Fripp dissolved King Crimson in September 1974.

Boz Burrell joined in the formation of Bad Company in late 1973. Ian McDonald helped form Foreigner in early 1976. In the mid-'70s Robert Fripp recorded two esoteric albums with Roxy Music synthesizer player Brian Eno. They devised a system of music utilizing two tape recorders and solo guitar called "Frippertronics" that Fripp employed for his 1979 American "anti-tour." He launched his solo recording career that year with the amazing *Exposure* album, later recording with Daryl Hall, his own League of Gentlemen, and two instrumental albums with Andy Summers of The Police. He also played on David Bowie's

Scary Monsters album, produced Peter Gabriel and The Roches, and served as sessions guitarist for Blondie and Talking Heads.

In 1981, Robert Fripp reconvened King Crimson with vocalist-guitarist Adrian Belew, bassist Tony Levin, and drummer Bill Bruford for three albums and two American tours through 1984. In the '90s, Fripp assembled a large group of guitar players for recordings as The League of Crafty Guitarists. By 1994, King Crimson had reunited with Fripp, Belew, Levin, and Bruford and two others for the concept album *THRAK* and a 1995 tour.

Giles, Giles and Fripp

The Cheerful Insanity of Giles, Giles and Fripp	Deram	18019	'68	†
	Deram	820965	'93	CD

King Crimson

In the Court of the Crimson King	Atlantic	8245	'69	†
	Atlantic	19155		†
	Editions EG	1502		LP/CS/CD†
	EG	001		CS/CD
In the Wake of Poseidon	Atlantic	8266	'70	†
	Editions EG	1503		CS/CD†
	EG	002		CS/CD
Lizard	Atlantic	8278	'71	†
	Editions EG	1504		CS/CD†
	EG	004		CS/CD
3 Pack (reissue of the above three)	Blue Plate	(3)1760	'94	CD†
Islands	Atlantic	7212	'72	†
	Editions EG	1505		CS/CD†
	EG	005		CS/CD
Larks' Tongue in Aspic	Atlantic	7263	'73	†
	Editions EG	1506		LP/CS/CD†
	EG	007		CS/CD
Starless and Bible Black	Atlantic	7298	'74	†
	Editions EG	1507		CS/CD†
	EG	012		CS/CD
Red	Atlantic	18110	'74	†
	Editions EG	1508		LP/CS/CD†
	EG	015		CS/CD
U.S.A.	Atlantic	18136	'75	†
The Great Deceiver (Live 1973–1974)	EG	(4)1597	'92	CD
The Compact King Crimson	Editions EG	1509	'89	CS/CD†
	EG	068		CS/CD
reissued as The Concise King Crimson	Blue Plate	1887	'93	CS/CD
Discipline	Warner Brothers	3629	'81	†
	EG	049	'91	CS/CD
Beat	Warner Brothers	23692	'82	†
	EG	051	'91	CS/CD
Three of a Perfect Pair	Warner Brothers	25071	'84	†
	EG	055	'91	CS/CD
The Abbreviated King Crimson	EG	1467	'91	CD
The Essential King Crimson: Frame by Frame	EG	(4)1595	'91	CD
THRAK	Virgin	40313	'95	CS/CD
B'Boom Official Live Bootleg	Discipline	9503	'95	CD
The Night Watch	Discipline	9707	'98	CD

Absent Lovers	Discipline	9804	'98	CD
McDonald and Giles				
McDonald and Giles	Cotillion	9042	'71	†
Pete Sinfield				
Still	Manticore	66667	'73	†
Robert Fripp and Brian Eno				
No Pussyfooting	Island	16	'75	†
	Antilles	7001		†
	Editions EG	1522		CD†
	EG	002		CD
Evening Star	Antilles	7018	'76	†
	Editions EG	103	'81	†
	Editions EG	1560		CD†
	EG	003		CD
The Essential Fripp and Eno	Venture/Caroline	1886	'94	CS/CD
Robert Fripp				
Exposure	Polydor	6149	'79	†
	Editions EG	1557		CS/CD†
	EG	041		CS/CD
God Save the Queen/Under Heavy Manners	Polydor	4266	'80	†
The League of Gentlemen	Polydor	6317	'81	†
Let the Power Fall	Editions EG	1558	'88	CD†
	EG	010		CD
A Blessing of Tears	Discipline	9506	'95	CD
Daryl Hall with Robert Fripp				
Sacred Songs	RCA	3573	'80	†
	RCA	4554		†
Robert Fripp and The League of Gentlemen				
God Save the King	Editions EG	1559	'81	CS/CD†
	Editions EG	09		CS/CD
Robert Fripp and Andy Summers				
I Advance Masked	A&M	4913	'82/'92	CD
Bewitched	A&M	5011	'84/'92	CD
Robert Fripp and The League of Crafty Guitarists				
Live!	Editions EG	1562	'86	CS/CD†
	EG	043		CS/CD
Show of Hands	Editions EG	2102	'91	CS/CD
Intergalactic Boogie Express	Discipline	9502	'95	CD
Robert Fripp and David Sylvian				
The First Day	Virgin	88208	'93	CS/CD†
Damage	Virgin	39905	'94	CD†

THE KINKS

Ray Davies (born June 21, 1944, in Muswell Hill, London, England), lead vocals, rhythm guitar; Dave Davies (born February 3, 1947, in Muswell Hill), lead and rhythm guitar, keyboards, vocals; Peter Quaife (born December 27, 1943, in Tavistock, Devon, England), bass, vocals; and Mick Avory (born February 15, 1944, in Hampton Court, Surrey, England), drums. Quaife left in March 1969, to be replaced by John Dalton (born May 21, 1943). Keyboardist John Gosling was added in 1971, but Gosling and Dalton departed in 1978. Bassist Jim Rodford joined in 1978 and Bob Henrit replaced Avory in 1984.

One of the longest-lived groups of the '60s British invasion (exceeded only by The Rolling Stones), The Kinks endured an erratic career of hit and flop singles, concept albums, and record company changes under leader Ray Davies and his brother Dave. Launched into international prominence by several seminal hard-edged hit singles, including the classic "You Really Got Me," Ray Davies later wrote satirical songs of social comment such as "A Well Respected Man" and "Dedicated Follower of Fashion" and eventually built a remarkably personal and sensitive body of work. Crippled in their pursuit of American success by a performance ban that lasted until late 1969, The Kinks became known for Ray's cocky stage presence and the often combative relationship between Ray and Dave Davies. Stereotyped in Great Britain as a singles band, The Kinks nonetheless produced several significant albums. They recorded one of the first rock operas, *Arthur,* as well as a series of thematically linked albums such as *Village Green Preservation Society, Lola,* and *Muswell Hillbillies.* Additionally, the title song to *Lola* was the first rock song to deal overtly with the issue of tranvestitism. The Kinks eventually established themselves primarily in the United States with theatrically performed versions of their concurrent concept albums and, later, a number of popular nonconcept albums beginning in the late '70s. The Kinks were inducted into the Rock and Roll Hall of Fame in 1990. Ray Davies later garnered considerable acclaim for his acoustic tours based on his autobiography *X-Ray,* published in 1994.

Ray and Dave Davies received guitars from their parents as early teenagers. Dave played in The Bo Weevils with Peter Quaife before forming The Ravens to play the local debutante circuit in 1962, while brother Ray began playing with The Dave Hunt Band in 1963. Ray insinuated his way into The Ravens around December 1963, as the group was renamed The Kinks and "discovered" by American producer Shel Talmy, who secured them a recording contract with Pye Records (Reprise in the United States).

The Kinks' first two singles barely sold, but the third, "You Really Got Me," became a smash British and American hit. The like-sounding "All Day and All of the Night" was a smash hit in early 1965, followed by the slower-paced smash "Tired of Waiting" and "Set Me Free," a major hit. Other early recordings included "Everybody's Gonna Be Happy," "Something Better Beginning," and "See My Friend." They toured the United States in mid-1965, but, for missing a single engagement, they were banned from performing again until 1969 by the American Federation of Musicians.

The moderate hit "Who'll Be the Next in Line" echoed The Kinks' earlier raunchy sound, but "A Well Respected Man" marked the beginning of a new phase of astute satire in Ray Davies' songwriting. "Dedicated Follower of Fashion" poked fun at Carnaby Street fops, and the follow-up, "Sunny Afternoon," satirized the indolent upper class. Their 1967 album *Face to Face* included Ray's "Dandy," a smash hit for Herman's Hermits.

After *Something Else,* The Kinks' final album under producer Shel Talmy, Ray Davies produced their next two albums, including the neglected concept album *Village Green Preservation Society,* and scored the soundtracks to the movies *The Virgin Soldiers* and *Percy.* Dave Davies managed a smash British-only hit with "Death of a Clown" in 1967, and The Kinks scored smash British hits through 1968 with "Dead End Street," "Waterloo Sunset," "Autumn Almanac," and "Days." However, their albums and singles sold poorly in the United States, in part due to the performance ban. In March 1969, Peter Quaife left the group, to be replaced on bass by John Dalton.

The Kinks' ambitious, critically acclaimed, historically conscious concept album *Arthur (Or the Decline and Fall of the British Empire)* sold modestly at best, despite the inclusion of

"Shangri La" and "Victoria," a minor hit. The Kinks resumed touring the United States in late 1969 with their usual sloppy stage presentation, occasionally marred by open hostility between Ray and Dave Davies. Augmented by keyboardist John Gosling beginning in May 1971, The Kinks finally reestablished themselves in the United States in 1971 with *Lola Versus Powerman and The Moneygoround,* an acerbic look at the pop music industry and their situation in it. Songs included "Get Back in Line," "Top of the Pops," the moderate hit "Apeman," and the near-smash "Lola," apparently the first rock song to deal openly with transvestitism.

By 1971, The Kinks had switched to RCA Records. Their RCA debut, the decidedly countrified *Muswell Hillbillies,* sold only modestly, despite the inclusion of Kinks favorites such as "Alcohol," "Acute Schizophrenia Paranoid Blues," and "20th Century Man." The follow-up, *Everybody's in Show-Biz,* included "Sitting in My Hotel" and the excellent "Celluloid Heroes."

Ray Davies and The Kinks next embarked on a program of ambitious concept albums, complete with on-tour theatrical presentations. The character of Mr. Flash from *The Village Green Preservation Society* was resurrected, but *Preservation,* originally released in two separate *Acts,* sold poorly. During 1974, Ray and Dave Davies formed Konk Records as an outlet for productions outside the group, but recordings by Claire Hamill and Cafe Society proved unsuccessful. The Kinks' next two albums, *Soap Opera* and *Schoolboys in Disgrace,* sold rather well despite yielding no hit singles, but concurrent tours featuring theatrical performances of each album's material seemed to perplex rather than amuse American audiences.

During the late '70s, personnel changes plagued The Kinks, with the Davies brothers and Mick Avory remaining as constants. By 1977, they had switched to Arista Records and abandoned the concept album format. *Sleepwalker,* their best-selling album in years, yielded the group's first albeit minor hit in six years with the title song. *Misfits* produced a major hit with "A Rock 'n' Roll Fantasy" and *Low Budget* included the underground favorite "A Gallon of Gas" and the moderate hit "(I Wish I Could Fly Like) Superman."

Following the minor hits "Destroyer" and "Better Things," The Kinks scored a smash hit with the nostalgic "Come Dancing" from *State of Confusion.* Subsequent hits included "Don't Forget to Dance" and "Do It Again." The 1985 made-for-British-TV movie *Return to Waterloo* marked the debut of Ray Davies as a film director/writer. He also appeared in the 1986 movie *Absolute Beginners* and wrote the music and lyrics for *80 Days,* a musical based on Jules Vernes' "Around the World in Eighty Days," performed at the La Jolla Playhouse in southern California in 1988.

With Ray and Dave Davies as the only original members left, The Kinks switched to MCA Records in 1986. *Think Visual* featured Dave's "Rock 'n' Roll Cities," whereas 1989's *UK Jive* included the ballad "Now and Then" and "Aggravation." The Kinks were inducted into the Rock and Roll Hall of Fame in 1990. They conducted their first U.S. tour in more than three years in 1993. In 1996, the group issued a two-CD live retrospective *To the Bone.*

In 1994, Ray Davies published his account of his early life and career with The Kinks through 1973 as *X-Ray.* He mounted a one-man show (accompanied by a second guitarist) performed in New York and London that combined reminiscences, songs, and readings from his book, and presented an abbreviated form of the show as the inaugural edition of cable TV network VH-1's *Storyteller* series. He later refined the presentation into *A Musical Evening with a 20th Century Man* for tours in 1996 and 1997.

THE KINKS BIBLIOGRAPHY

Davies, Dave. *Kink: An Autobiography.* New York: Hyperion, 1996.
Davies, Ray. *X-Ray.* New York: Viking, 1995.

Mendelsohn, John. *The Kinks Kronikles.* New York: Quill, 1984.
Savage, Jon. *The Kinks: The Official Biography.* London, Boston: Faber and Faber, 1984.

The Kinks

You Really Got Me	Reprise	6143	'64	†
	Rhino	70315	'88	CS/CD†
Kinks-Size	Reprise	6158	'65	†
	Rhino	70317	'88	CS†
Kinda Kinks	Reprise	6173	'65	†
	Rhino	70316	'88	CS/CD†
You Really Got Me/Kinda Kinks	Mobile Fidelity	679		CD
Kinks Kinkdom	Reprise	6184	'65	†
	Rhino	70318	'88	CS†
The Kinks Kontroversy	Reprise	6197	'66	†
Face to Face	Reprise	6228	'66	†
The "Live" Kinks	Reprise	6260	'67	CD
Something Else by The Kinks	Reprise	6279	'68	CD
Village Green Preservation Society	Reprise	6327	'69	CD
Arthur (Or the Decline and Fall of the British Empire)	Reprise	6366	'69	CD†
Lola Versus Powerman and The Moneygoround	Reprise	6423	'70	CS/CD
The Great Lost Kinks Album	Reprise	2127	'73	†
Muswell Hillbillies	RCA	4644	'71	†
	Rhino	70934	'90	CS/CD†
Everybody's in Show-Biz	RCA	6065	'72	†
	Rhino	70935	'90	CS/CD
Preservation, Act I	RCA	5002	'73	†
Preservation, Act II	RCA	(2)5040	'74	†
Preservation: A Play in Two Acts	Rhino	(2)70523	'91	CS/CD†
Soap Opera	RCA	5081	'75	†
	RCA	3750		†
	Rhino	70936	'90	CS/CD†
Schoolboys in Disgrace	RCA	5102	'75	†
	RCA	3749		†
	Rhino	70937	'90	CS/CD†
Sleepwalker	Arista	4106	'77	†
	Arista	8068		CD†
Misfits	Arista	4167	'78	†
	Arista	8069		CD†
Low Budget	Arista	4240	'79	†
	Arista	8050	'85	CD†
One for the Road	Arista	(2)8401	'80	†
	Arista	(2)8041		CS
	Arista	8041		CD
Give the People What They Want	Arista	9567	'81	†
	Arista	8224		CD†
State of Confusion	Arista	8018	'83	†
Word of Mouth	Arista	8264	'84	†
Think Visual	MCA	5822	'86	CS/CD†
Live: The Road	MCA	42107	'88	CS/CD†
UK Jive	MCA	6337	'89	LP/CS/CD†
To the Bone	Guardian	(2)37303	'96	CS/CD

Kinks Anthologies and Compilations

Greatest Hits	Reprise	6217	'66	†
	Rhino	70086	'89	CS/CD
Kink Kronikles	Reprise	(2)6454	'72	†
	Reprise	6454		CS/CD
History of British Pop, Volume 1	Pye	505	'75	†
History of British Pop, Volume 2	Pye	509	'76	†
Celluloid Heroes—The Kinks' Greatest	RCA	1743	'76	†
	RCA	3869		†
Second Time Around	RCA	3520	'80	†
	RCA	4719		†
A Compleat Collection	Compleat	(2)2001	'84	†
Another Compleat Collection	Compleat	(2)2003	'84	†
Come Dancing with The Kinks (Best Of, 1977–1986)	Arista	8428	'86	CS/CD
Kinkdom-Size Kinks	Rhino	75769	'88	CD†
Tired of Waiting for You	Rhino	71849	'95	CS/CD
Lost and Found (1986–1989)	MCA	10338	'91	CS/CD

Dave Davies

AFL1-3603	RCA	3603	'80	†
Glamour	RCA	4036	'81	†
Chosen People	Warner Brothers	23917	'83	†

Larry Page Orchestra

Kinky Music—The Larry Page Orchestra Plays Music of The Kinks	Rhino	058	'83	†

AL KOOPER

Born February 5, 1944, in Brooklyn, New York.

One of the most erratic figures in the history of rock music, Al Kooper has been involved in projects great and small as teenage performer, songwriter, sessions musician, group member, solo artist, and producer. He joined one of the earliest white electric blues and folk bands, The Blues Project, and later founded the pioneering jazz-rock band Blood, Sweat and Tears. Kooper was also a key participant in Bob Dylan's adoption of rock instrumentation, backing him at the Newport Folk Festival in 1965 and helping record the landmark "Like a Rolling Stone" single. Recording and producing one of the first "jam session"-style albums with *Super Session,* Al Kooper's subsequent solo recording career failed to bring him any substantial recognition.

An accomplished guitarist by age thirteen, Al Kooper turned professional when he joined The Royal Teens at fifteen, a year after the group scored a novelty smash with "Short Shorts." Kooper subsequently worked as a sessions guitarist for the likes of Connie Francis and Dion and coauthored Gary Lewis and The Playboy's first hit (a smash), "This Diamond Ring," from 1965.

In the mid-'60s, Al Kooper played folk clubs as Al Casey and met Bob Dylan through producer Tom Wilson. He accompanied Dylan on keyboards at his controversial Newport Folk Festival appearance in June 1965 and assisted in the recording of Dylan's *Highway 61 Revisited* album and its classic "Like a Rolling Stone" single, later helping record Dylan's monumental *Blonde on Blonde* album. Kooper joined The Blues Project, one of the earliest white electric blues and folk bands, in 1966 and, with member Steve Katz, formed Blood, Sweat and Tears, probably the first jazz-rock band, in 1968.

After Blood, Sweat and Tear's debut album, Kooper left the group to accept a lucrative offer from Columbia Records to become a producer, although none of his projects proved remotely successful. In 1968, he played sessions for Moby Grape (*Wow/Grape Jam*) and adopted the format for one of the first successful "jam" albums, *Super Session,* recorded with guitarists Steve Stills and Mike Bloomfield. He also played sessions for The Nitty Gritty Dirt Band, Paul Butterfield, Jimi Hendrix, Taj Mahal, and The Rolling Stones, and recorded a live album with Bloomfield. Initiating his own recording career by 1969, Kooper introduced Johnny Otis's guitar-playing son Shuggie in 1970.

In 1972, Al Kooper "discovered" and signed Lynyrd Skynyrd to MCA's newly formed Sound of the South label, producing their first three albums. He organized a reunion of The Blues Project in 1973 and later produced The Tubes' debut album and Nils Lofgren's *Cry Tough.* Releasing his final solo album in more than a decade in 1982, Kooper moved to Nashville in 1990 and subsequently became music director of The Rock Bottom Remainders, comprising authors Steven King and Amy Tan, among others. He returned to recording with 1994's largely instrumental *Rekooperation* and 1995's *Soul of a Man.*

AL KOOPER BIBLIOGRAPHY

Kooper, Al, with Ben Edmonds. *Backstage Passes: Rock 'n' Roll Life in the Sixties.* New York: Stein and Day, 1977.

Kooper, Bloomfield and Stills

Super Session	Columbia	09701	'68	CS/CD

Al Kooper and Mike Bloomfield

Live Adventures of Mike Bloomfield and Al Kooper	Columbia	(2)6	'69	†
	Columbia/Legacy	(2)64670	'98	CD

Al Kooper

I Stand Alone	Columbia	9718	'69	†
You Never Know Who Your Friends Are	Columbia	9855	'69	†
Kooper Session: Al Kooper Introduces Shuggie Otis	Columbia	9951	'70	†
Landlord (soundtrack)	United Artists	5209	'70	†
Easy Does It	Columbia	(2)30031	'70	†
New York City (You're a Woman)	Columbia	30506	'71	†
A Possible Projection of the Future/Childhood's End	Columbia	31159	'72	†
Naked Songs	Columbia	31723	'73	†
Al's Big Deal/Unclaimed Freight: An Al Kooper Anthology	Columbia	(2)33169	'75	†
	Columbia	45386		CD†
Act Like's Nothing's Wrong	United Artists	702	'76	†
	One Way	18565	'96	CD
Championship Wrestling	Columbia	38137	'82	†
Rekooperation	MusicMasters	65107	'94	CD
Soul of a Man: Al Kooper Live	MusicMasters	(2)65113	'95	CS/CD
Soul of a Man: Live	MusicMasters	65159	'96	CD

LED ZEPPELIN

Robert Plant (born August 20, 1948, in West Bromwich, Staffordshire, England), lead vocals; Jimmy Page (born January 9, 1944, in London), lead guitar, mandolin, pedal steel guitar, banjo; John Paul Jones (born John Baldwin on January 3, 1946, in Sidcup, Kent,

England), bass, keyboards; and John Bonham (born May 31, 1947, in Birmingham, England; died September 25, 1980, in Windsor, Berkshire, England), drums.

The prototypical British heavy-metal band of the late '60s and '70s, Led Zeppelin evolved out of one of the most seminal and influential of all British groups, The Yardbirds. In fact, the designation as the *first* heavy-metal band more deservedly belongs to The Yardbirds, The Jimi Hendrix Experience, or the early Who rather than Led Zeppelin, although the term seems to have been devised with the advent of Led Zeppelin. Instantly successful, Led Zeppelin became the most successful and imitated rock band of the '70s and one of the most popular rock bands of all time. Lead guitarist Jimmy Page, generally recognized as the most consistently successful British "superstar" lead guitarist, acquired that accolade as much by default as actual achievement, given the erraticism of Jeff Beck and Eric Clapton. Also noteworthy is the fact that Page never acknowledged his debt to American black blues guitarists. Led Zeppelin quickly inspired a glut of imitators as vocalist Robert Plant established the style for heavy-metal vocalists with his screaming, shrieking, histrionic vocal manner. Additionally, drummer John Bonham became one of the most imitated rock drummers of the '70s with his thunderous, flamboyant style of play. Probably the first foreign rock group to establish a worldwide reputation by concentrating on live engagements in the United States, Led Zeppelin was regularly breaking box office records by 1970. Not a favorite of critics in their early years, Led Zeppelin eventually gained recognition with "Stairway to Heaven," certainly one of the definitive production arrangements of the '70s. Led Zeppelin disbanded after the September 1980 death of John Bonham, yet their reputation and popularity expanded enormously over the ensuing years. The group was inducted into the Rock and Roll Hall of Fame in 1995. Of all the surviving members, only Robert Plant was able to establish an identity distinct from Led Zeppelin, eventually maturing into an artist in his own right with 1993's *Fate of Nations*. In 1994, Robert Plant and Jimmy Page reunited for the ninety-minute MTV special *Unledded* and the consequent *No Quarter* album, touring together in 1995.

Jimmy Page took up guitar in his early teens, later playing with Neil Christian and The Crusaders before attending art college for two years. Upon returning to music, he quickly became a much sought-after sessions guitarist, allegedly playing on more than half of all the records released in Great Britain between 1963 and 1965. Early sessions credits included The Who's "I Can't Explain," Them's "Here Comes the Night," and unspecified recordings by the Kinks (disputed by Ray Davies), The Rolling Stones, and Herman's Hermits. He turned down an offer to join The Yardbirds as Eric Clapton's replacement in 1965, instead serving as house producer-arranger for Andrew Oldham's Immediate label.

In mid-1966, Jimmy Page did join The Yardbirds, replacing departed bass player Paul Samwell-Smith, later to play twin lead guitars with Jeff Beck after Chris Dreja switched to bass. Yardbirds' recordings with Beck and Page apparently included "The Train Kept A-Rollin'" from *Rave Up,* "Stroll On" from the soundtrack to the movie *Blow-Up,* and "Happenings Ten Years Time Ago." Jeff Beck left The Yardbirds at the end of 1966 and Page continued as the group's lead guitarist for another eighteen months. Finally, in July 1968, The Yardbirds broke up, and Page and Dreja unsuccessfully attempted to continue as The New Yardbirds with vocalist-guitarist Terry Reid. Reid, unavailable to join the group, suggested that Robert Plant from the Birmingham group The Band of Joy be recruited as lead vocalist. Plant, in turn, recommended former Band of Joy drummer John Bonham. Dreja later dropped out to pursue a career as a photographer, and sessions bassist-keyboardist John Paul Jones was brought in as his replacement. Essentially formed in October 1968, Led Zeppelin quickly recorded their debut album for Atlantic Records, soon fulfilling The Yardbirds' remaining concert obligations. In the meantime, Page played sessions with Jeff Beck ("Beck's Bolero"), Donovan (*Hurdy Gurdy Man*) and Joe Cocker (*With a Little Help from My Friends*).

Led Zeppelin's debut album became an instant best-seller, remaining on the album charts for nearly two years. The album featured their first American singles chart entry, "Good Times Bad Times" and the classics "Dazed and Confused" and "Communication Breakdown." In 1969, the group completed their first American tour in support of Vanilla Fudge, soon returning as a headline act. Shortly thereafter, a plethora of heavy-metal rock acts developed in the wake of Led Zeppelin. *Led Zeppelin II* included the smash hit classic "Whole Lotta Love," as well as "Living Loving Maid (She's Just a Woman)" and "Ramble On."

Concentrating their activities on the United States (they never released a single in Great Britain), Led Zeppelin was conducting their fifth American tour by March 1970. The transitional *Led Zeppelin III* yielded the major hit "Immigrant Song," yet revealed a more acoustic sound, as evidenced by "That's the Way" and "Tangerine." *Led Zeppelin IV* was the album that finally brought the group critical recognition. In addition to containing the hits "Black Dog" and "Rock and Roll," the album included one of the definitive production arrangements of the '70s, "Stairway to Heaven," which built from a subtle acoustic guitar and vocal to a thundering climax, ending with a gentle acoustic guitar–vocal reprise. *Led Zeppelin IV* stayed on the album charts for nearly five years and sold more than eleven million copies.

During the summer of 1972, Led Zeppelin again toured America, outdrawing The Rolling Stones in a number of cities. *Houses of the Holy* was the first Led Zeppelin album to utilize string arrangements (by Page), yielding a major hit with "D'yer Mak'er." The group's 1973 American tour was an instant sellout, and they broke both the single-artist concert attendance and gross income records with their Tampa, Florida, show. With the rock press finally acknowledging their enormous popularity, Led Zeppelin formed Swan Song Records with manager Peter Grant in 1974 for their own recordings, as well as recordings by Bad Company, Dave Edmunds, and The Pretty Things.

Physical Graffiti contained the mystical "Kashmir" and yielded the moderate hit "Trampled Under Foot," but lead vocalist Robert Plant was seriously injured in an automobile accident in Greece on August 4, 1975, necessitating a layoff of more than a year. *Presence* sold quite well without the benefit of either a tour or a single. The film (and soundtrack album) *The Song Remains the Same,* taken primarily from a 1973 concert at Madison Square Garden, was released as the group's first live album and movie.

During 1977, Led Zeppelin again toured the United States, playing marathon three-hour sets to sellout crowds, but an ugly incident between shows at the Oakland Coliseum (in which three members of promoter Bill Graham's support crew were allegedly beaten up) served to reinforce the notion that Led Zeppelin had become arrogant, insensitive, and smug. The group subsequently maintained a low profile and eventually reemerged in 1979 with *In Through the Out Door* and the major hit "Fool in the Rain." That fall, Led Zeppelin's first British appearance in four years at the Knebworth Festival was reviewed as perfunctory at best, obsolete at worst. On September 25, 1980, drummer John Bonham was found dead in the Windsor home of Jimmy Page, the victim of inhalation of vomit after a drinking spree. On December 4, Led Zeppelin announced that its was disbanding. Led Zeppelin was inducted int the Rock and Roll Hall of Fame in 1995.

By 1982, Robert Plant was collaborating with guitarist Robbie Blount, recording three solo albums with him through 1985. Plant toured with Blount and drummer Phil Collins (of Genesis) in 1983, scoring a major hit with the oddly titled love song "Big Log" and a moderate hit with "In the Mood" from *The Principle of Moments,* the first album released on Plant's own Es Paranza label. In 1984, Plant helped form the short-lived "supergroup" The Honeydrippers with guitarists Jimmy Page, Jeff Beck, and Nile Rodgers, recording rhythm-and-blues material on the mini-album *Volume One* on Es Paranza. The recording yielded a smash hit with "Sea of Love" and a major hit with "Rockin' at Midnight."

In 1982, Jimmy Page recorded the largely instrumental soundtrack to the movie *Death Wish II.* Following benefit performances for Ronnie Lane's Appeal for Action Research Into Multiple Sclerosis in late 1983 with former Bad Company vocalist Paul Rodgers, Page and Rodgers formed The Firm, a rather crass commercial venture, in July 1984. The group remained together until 1986, touring, recording two albums, and scoring a major hit with "Radioactive" in 1985.

In 1988, Jimmy Page recorded *Outrider* and toured with vocalist John Miles and drummer Jason Bonham, John Bonham's son, whereas Robert Plant reconstituted his band and began collaborating with keyboardist Phil Johnstone. Plant's *Now and Zen* produced a major hit with "Tall Cool One" (which sampled several Led Zeppelin guitar riffs) and the minor hit "Ship of Fools." Following 1990's *Manic Nirvana,* Plant expanded his band for 1993's *Fate of Nations,* a remarkably mature and engaging album that finally established him as a solo artist of some import.

In the later half of the '80s, Led Zeppelin reunited briefly twice, once in July 1985 with drummers Phil Collins and Tony Thompson for the Live Aid concert in Philadelphia, and again in May 1988 for Atlantic Records' fortieth anniversary celebration, with Jason Bonham on drums. In 1989, Jason Bonham formed Bonham, recording two albums for WTG Records. Jimmy Page and one-time Deep Purple vocalist David Coverdale recorded *Coverdale/Page,* released in 1993. In August 1994, Plant and Page performed with Egyptian and Moroccan musicians for what became the MTV cable network special *Unledded* (broadcast in October) and *No Quarter* album. The two, accompanied by several other rock musicians and a Middle Eastern ensemble, toured in support of the album in 1995 and later recorded *Walking Into Clarksdale.* That same year, Atlantic Records issued the Led Zeppelin tribute album *Encomium,* recorded by Sheryl Crow, Stone Temple Pilots, and Hootie and The Blowfish, among others.

LED ZEPPELIN BIBLIOGRAPHY

Cole, Richard. *Stairway to Heaven: Led Zeppelin Uncensored.* New York: HarperCollins, 1992.

Cross, Charles R. *Led Zeppelin: Heaven and Hell, An Illustrated History.* New York: Harmony Books, 1991.

Davis, Stephen. *Hammer of the Gods: The Led Zeppelin Saga.* New York: William Morrow, 1985; New York: Boulevard Books, 1997.

Gross, Michael. *Robert Plant.* New York: Popular Library, 1975.

Kendall, Paul. *Led Zeppelin: A Visual Documentary.* New York: Delilah/Putnam, 1982; New York: Perigee Books, 1986.

Lewis, Dave. *Led Zeppelin: A Celebration.* London: Omnibus, 1991.

McSquare, Eddie. *Led Zeppelin: Good Times, Bad Times.* New York: Bobcat Books, 1991.

Mylett, Howard, and Richard Bunton. *Led Zeppelin: In the Light 1968–1980.* London, New York: Proteus, distributed by Scribner, 1981.

Ruhlmann, William. *Led Zeppelin.* Stamford, CT: Longmeadow Press, 1992.

Yorke, Ritchie. *The Led Zeppelin Biography.* Toronto: Metheun, 1976; New York: Two Continents, 1976.

—————. *Led Zeppelin: The Definitive Biography.* Lancaster, PA: Underwood-Miller, 1993.

Led Zeppelin

Led Zeppelin	Atlantic	8216	'69	†
	Atlantic	19126		LP/CS/CD†
	Atlantic	82632	'94	CS/CD
Led Zeppelin II	Atlantic	8236	'69	†
	Atlantic	19127		LP/CS/CD†
	Atlantic	82633	'94	CS/CD
Led Zeppelin III	Atlantic	7201	'70	†
	Atlantic	19128		LP/CS/CD†
	Atlantic	82678	'94	CS/CD
Led Zeppelin IV ("Zoso")	Atlantic	7208	'71	†
	Atlantic	19129		LP/CS/CD†
BBC Sessions (recorded 1969–1971)	Atlantic	(2)83061	'97	CS/CD
Houses of the Holy	Atlantic	7255	'73	†
	Atlantic	19130		LP/CS/CD†
Led Zeppelin	Atlantic	(6)82144	'90	LP†
	Atlantic	(4)82144	'90	CS/CD
Remasters	Atlantic	(3)82371	'92	CS/CD
Boxed Set [2]	Atlantic	(2)82477	'93	CD
Led Zeppelin: The Complete Studio Recordings	Atlantic	(10)82526	'93	CD
Physical Graffiti	Swan Song	(2)200	'75	†
	Swan Song	(2)92442	'94	CS/CD
Presence	Swan Song	8416	'76	†
	Swan Song	92439	'94	CS/CD
The Song Remains the Same (soundtrack)	Swan Song	(2)201	'76	CS/CD
In Through the Out Door	Swan Song	16002	'79	LP/CS/CD†
	Swan Song	92443	'94	CS/CD
Coda	Swan Song	90051	'82	LP/CS/CD†
	Swan Song	92444	'94	CS/CD

Tribute Albums

Encomium: A Tribute to Led Zeppelin	Atlantic	82731	'95	CS/CD
Kashmir—Symphonic Led Zeppelin	Point Music	4145	'97	CS/CD

Robert Plant

Pictures at Eleven	Swan Song	8512	'82	CS/CD
The Principle of Moments	Swan Song	90101	'83	CS/CD
Shaken 'n' Stirred	Es Paranza	90265	'85	CD
Little by Little (Collectors Edition)	Es Paranza	90485	'85	CS
Now and Zen	Es Paranza	90863	'88	CS/CD
Manic Nirvana	Es Paranza	91336	'90	CD
	Es Paranza	91361		CD†
Fate of Nations	Es Paranza	92264	'93	CS/CD

The Honeydrippers

Volume One	Es Paranza (mini)	90220	'84/'85	CS/CD

The Firm

The Firm	Atlantic	81239	'85	CS/CD
Mean Business	Atlantic	81628	'86	CS/CD

Jimmy Page

Special Early Works	Springboard	4038	'72	†
The Early Years	Immediate	52428	'92	CS/CD†
Session Man 1963–1967 Vol. 1	Voxx	10041		LP/CD
Session Man 1963–1967 Vol. 2	Voxx	10053		LP/CD
Death Wish II (soundtrack)	Swan Song	8511	'82	†
Outrider	Geffen	24188	'88	CS/CD†

David Coverdale/Jimmy Page

Coverdale/Page	Geffen	24487	'93	CS/CD

Jimmy Page and Robert Plant

No Quarter	Atlantic	(2)82706	'94	LP
	Atlantic	82796	'94	CS/CD
Walking Into Clarksdale	Atlantic	83089	'98	CS/CD

Jimmy Page and John Paul Jones

The Masters	Eagle Rock	372		CD

Bonham

The Disregard of Timekeeping	WTG	45009	'89	CS/CD†
	550 Music	45009		CS/CD
Mad Hatter	WTG	46856	'92	CS/CD†
	WTG	52853		CS/CD†
	550 Music	52853		CS/CD

BRENDA LEE

Born Brenda Mae Tarpley on December 11, 1944, in Lithonia, Georgia.

Possessing a powerful voice equally adept at mournful ballads and hard-belting rock songs, Brenda Lee was one of the most popular female vocalists of the early '60s, rivaled primarily by the tamer-sounding Connie Francis. Recording rockabilly early in her career, Lee achieved her greatest success under producer Owen Bradley in Nashville, scoring smash hits with the classics "Sweet Nothin's," "I'm Sorry," "I Want to Be Wanted," and "All Alone Am I," plus the Christmas standard "Rockin' Around the Christmas Tree." Managing her last major pop hit with "Coming on Strong" in 1966, Lee successfully made the transition to country music in the '70s, achieving her last country hit in 1985.

Brenda Lee began singing at the age of four, winning an Atlanta television station's children's talent contest at age six and subsequently performing on the local television show *TV Wranglers* for three years. Introduced to country music veteran Red Foley in 1955, she later appeared on his ABC-TV show *Ozark Jubilee*. Signed to Decca Records in 1956, Lee recorded a number of wild rockabilly songs in the '50s, including "Bigelow 6-200," "Dynamite" (a minor pop hit), and "Let's Jump the Broomstick," achieving her first moderate pop (and major country) hit with "One Step at a Time" in early 1957. She soon became known as "Little Miss Dynamite" for her powerful voice and diminutive stature.

Brenda Lee scored her first smash pop hit in 1960 with the seductive "Sweet Nothin's." That song and the top hit "I'm Sorry" were written by rockabilly artist Ronnie Self. The flip side of "I'm Sorry," "That's All You Gotta Do," written by Jerry Reed, also became a smash hit. Her two 1960 albums became best-sellers as her success continued with the top hit "I Want to Be Wanted," the Christmas classic "Rockin' Around the Christmas Tree," and the smashes "Emotions," "You Can Depend on Me," "Dum Dum" (written by Jackie DeShannon), and "Fool #1." Smash hits continued through 1963 with "Break It to Me Gently," "Everybody Loves Me but You" (also written by Ronnie Self), "All Alone Am I," and "Losing You." Subsequent major hits included "My Whole World Is Falling Down," "As Usual," "Is It True?" (featuring guitarist Jimmy Page!), "Too Many Rivers," and "Coming on Strong" through 1966, when Lee reduced her touring schedule.

For Brenda Lee, the moderate pop hit "Johnny One Time" marked her reentry into the country field after twelve years. By 1973, Decca had been absorbed by MCA Records, and country smashes for Lee on MCA during the '70s included Kris Kristofferson's "Nobody Wins," "Sunday Sunrise," "Wrong Ideas," "Big Four Poster Bed," "Rock on Baby," "He's My Rock," and "Tell Me What It's Like." Following the 1980 country smashes "The Cowgirl and the Dandy" and "Broken Trust," Lee continued to have country hits through 1985, most notably with "Hallelujah, I Love Her So," in duet with George Jones. Regularly performing at the country music mecca of Branson, Missouri, Brenda Lee moved to Warner Brothers Records in the '90s.

Brenda Lee

Grandma, What Great Songs You Sang	Decca	78873	'59	†
Brenda Lee	Decca	74039	'60	†
This Is . . . Brenda Lee	Decca	74082	'60	†
Emotions	Decca	74104	'61	†
All the Way	Decca	74176	'61	†
Sincerely	Decca	74216	'62	†
That's All, Brenda	Decca	74326	'62	†
All Alone Am I	Decca	74370	'63	†
Let Me Sing	Decca	74439	'63	†
By Request	Decca	74509	'64	†
Merry Christmas from Brenda Lee	Decca	74583	'64	†
	MCA	232		†
	MCA	15021		†
Top Teen Hits	Decca	74626	'65	†
Versatile	Decca	74661	'65	†
Too Many Rivers	Decca	74684	'65	†
Bye Bye, Blues	Decca	74755	'66	†
Ten Golden Years	Decca	74757	'66	†
	MCA	107		†
Coming on Strong	Decca	74825	'66	†
Reflections in Blue	Decca	74941	'67	†
Johnny One Time	Decca	75111	'69	†
Memphis Portrait	Decca	75232	'70	†
Here's Brenda Lee	Vocalion	73795	'67	†
Let It Be Me	Vocalion	73890		†
	Coral	20044		†
Brenda	MCA	305	'73	†
The Brenda Lee Story	MCA	(2)4012	'73	CS
	MCA	4012		CD
New Sunrise	MCA	373	'74	†
Now	MCA	433	'75	†
Sincerely, Brenda Lee	MCA	477	'75	†
L.A. Sessions	MCA	2233	'76	†
Even Better	MCA	3211	'80	†
Take Me Back	MCA	5143	'80	†

Only When I Laugh	MCA	5278	'81	†
Greatest Country Hits	MCA	5342	'82	†
	MCA	894		CS†
Anthology Volumes One and Two	MCA	(2)10384	'91	CD
	MCA	(2)10405/6	'91	CS†
Brenda Lee	Warner Brothers	26439	'91	CS/CD†
A Brenda Lee Christmas	Warner Brothers	26660	'91	CS/CD
Greatest Hits *Live*	K-tel	3077	'92	CS/CD
Brenda Lee and Pete Fountain				
For the First Time	Decca	74955	'68	†
Brenda Lee, Kris Kristofferson, Willie Nelson and Dolly Parton				
The Winning Hand	Monument	(2)38389	'83	†
	Sony	75067	'95	CS/CD

LOVE

Arthur Lee (born March 7, 1945, in Memphis, Tennessee), guitar, vocals; Bryan Maclean (born 1947 in Los Angeles; died December 25, 1998, in Los Angeles), guitar, vocals; John Echols (born 1945 in Memphis), guitar; Ken Forssi (born 1943 in Cleveland, Ohio), bass; and Alban "Snoopy" Pfisterer (born 1947 in Switzerland), drums. Lee restructured Love with totally new members in August 1968 and disbanded the group in 1971.

With The Doors, the most important group to emerge from Los Angeles during the psychedelic era, Love was the first rock act signed to Elektra Records and inspired a devoted underground following despite seldom performing outside the Los Angeles region. Recording an early version of the rock classic "Hey Joe" and scoring their biggest hit with the garage band classic "Seven and Seven Is," Love achieved their masterpiece with 1967's *Forever Changes,* one of the overlooked classics of '60s rock. An amazing fusion of folk-rock and psychedelia, the album featured Arthur Lee's biting surreal lyrics underscored by his exquisite melodies and was one of the definitive production arrangements of the era. Lee adopted a harder, more aggressive sound when he revamped the group in 1968, but the group disbanded in 1971.

Moving to Los Angeles as a child, Arthur Lee played with The L.A.G.s before forming Love with Bryan Maclean, John Echols, and two others in April 1965. Debuting live at the club Brave New World, the group replaced the two with Ken Forssi and Alban Pfisterer and built up an impressive local reputation through engagements in Sunset Strip clubs. The first rock group signed to Elektra Records, Love's hard-edged debut album included Lee's "Signed D.C." and an early version of "Hey Joe," yielding a minor hit with a pounding version of Burt Bacharach and Hal David's "Little Red Book." With Pfisterer switching to keyboards, Love recorded *Da Capo* with Tjay Cantrelli (flute, saxophone) and Michael Stuart (drums). The album contained the frantic hit single "Seven and Seven Is," excellent Lee songs such as "Stephanie Who Knows" and "She Comes in Colors," and the side-long "Revelation," a cunning parody of Mick Jagger's "Goin' Home."

With the departures of Cantrelli and Pfisterer, Love was reduced to Lee, Maclean, Echols, Forssi, and Stuart for their acknowledged classic, *Forever Changes.* Pervaded by brilliant existential songs such as MacLean's "Alone Again Or" and Lee's "Andmoreagain," "The Daily Planet," "Bummer in the Summer," and "You Set the Scene," the album was largely acoustic rather than electric and featured the outstanding orchestral arrangements and production of Lee. However, the album sold less well than either previous release and, by August 1968, Lee had reconstitued Love with guitarist Jay Donnellan, bassist Frank Fayad, and drummer George Suranovich. *Four Sail,* the group's final album for Elektra included Lee's

"August," "Good Times," and "Always See Your Face." Switching to Blue Thumb Records, Love recorded two albums for the label, including *False Start,* which featured a cameo appearance by Jimi Hendrix on "The Everlasting First."

Love disbanded in 1971 and Lee later recorded solo albums for A&M and RSO Records. However, Lee's songwriting had devolved into cloying self-parody. Lee reunited with Maclean in the late '70s and recorded a solo album for Rhino Records in 1981. By the early '90s, Lee was again performing in the Los Angeles region, even conducting an East and West Coast club tour in 1994. Bryan Maclean's half-sister Maria McKee (born August 17, 1964, in Los Angeles) formed the country-rock band Lone Justice with guitarist Ryan Hedgecock in 1982 and initiated her solo career in 1986. Bryan Maclean died unexpectedly in Los Angeles on December 25, 1998, at age fifty-two.

Love

Love				
Love	Elektra	74001	'66	CD†
Da Capo	Elektra	74005	'66	CD†
Forever Changes	Elektra	74013	'67	CS/CD†
Four Sail	Elektra	74049	'69	†
Revisited	Elektra	74058	'70	†
	Elektra	4058		CS†
Out Here	Blue Thumb	(2)9000	'69	†
	One Way	22030	'90	CD†
reissued as Out There	Big Beat	69	'88	CD
False Start	Blue Thumb	8822	'70	†
	One Way	22029	'90	CD†
Studio/Live	MCA	27025	'82	†
	One Way	22036	'91	CD†
Best (1966–1969)	Rhino	800	'80	†
	Rhino	70175	'87	CS
Love Story (recorded 1966–1972)	Rhino	(2)73500	'95	CD

Arthur Lee

Vindicator	A&M	4356	'72	†
Reel-to-Real	RSO	4804	'74	†
Arthur Lee	Rhino	020	'81	†

Bryan Maclean

Ifyoubelievein (solo acoustic demos recorded 1966–1967)	Sundazed	11051	'97	CD

THE LOVIN' SPOONFUL

John Sebastian (born March 17, 1944, in Greenwich Village, New York), guitar, autoharp, piano, harmonica, vocals; Zalman Yanovsky (born December 19, 1944, in Toronto, Ontario, Canada), lead guitar, vocals; Steve Boone (born September 23, 1943, in Camp Lejeune, North Carolina), bass, piano, vocals; and Joe Butler (born January 19, 1943, in Glen Cove, Long Island, New York), drums, vocals.

One of the prime movers in the New York folk-rock movement of the mid-'60s, The Lovin' Spoonful created a distinctive mixture of acoustic-based folk, blues, and rock music that appropriately became known as "good-time" music. Featuring a zany and extroverted stage act, the group produced a fresh, exuberant, uncluttered sound behind John Sebastian's clever and intelligent pop-style songs. Scoring a series of major hits between 1965 and 1967, including the classics "Do You Believe in Magic," "Summer in the City," and "Darling Be Home Soon," the group disbanded in 1968. John Sebastian endeared himself to the counterculture with his celebrated appearance at the Woodstock Festival in 1969. Achieving his last major hit with "Welcome Back" in 1976, Sebastian continued to tour and worked in film and television until reemerging in 1993 with *Tar Beach.*

John Sebastian was born the son of a renowned classical harmonica player. Taking up harmonica himself as a child and guitar at the age of twelve, he later added piano and auto-harp to his instrumental repertoire. Playing early recording sessions for Tom Rush, Tim Hardin, and Jesse Colin Young, Sebastian joined The Even Dozen Jug band in 1963. That band included Maria Muldaur (1974's "Midnight at the Oasis"), Stefan Grossman, and Steve Katz, who later formed The Blues Project and Blood, Sweat and Tears.

In 1964, Canadian-born Zalman Yanovsky was a member of the short-lived New York—based Mugwumps with singer-songwriter Jim Hendricks, and Denny Doherty and Cass Elliot, who later became half of The Mamas and The Papas. Yanovsky and Sebastian met during recording sessions for The Mugwumps. Sebastian, with the encouragment of producer Erik Jacobsen, formed The Lovin' Spoonful at the beginning of 1965 with Yanovsky, Steve Boone, and Joe Butler.

Playing regular engagements at the Night Owl in Greenwich Village, The Lovin' Spoonful signed with Kama Sutra Records in June 1965. *Do You Believe in Magic* sported a fresh, clean, friendly sound on traditional folk and blues songs and Sebastian originals such as "Younger Girl," and the near-smash hits "Do You Believe in Magic" and "Did You Ever Have to Make Up Your Mind." *Daydream* yielded a smash hit with the title song and contained a number of fine songs such as "Didn't Want to Have to Do It" and "You Didn't Have to Be So Nice." Between soundtrack albums for Woody Allen's *What's Up, Tiger Lily?* and Francis Ford Coppola's *You're a Big Boy Now,* The Lovin' Spoonful issued *Hums,* generally regarded as their most fully realized album. Producing a top hit with the summertime classic "Summer in the City," the album also contained the near-smashes "Rain on the Roof" and "Nashville Cats." Subsequent hits included "Darling, Be Home Soon," one of Sebastian's strongest and most endearing songs, "Six O'Clock," and "She's Still a Mystery."

However, in 1966, two members of The Lovin' Spoonful were arrested on drug charges in San Francisco, and Yanovsky, threatened with deportation, apparently incriminated at least one area resident. He left the group in ignominy in June 1967, and The Lovin' Spoonful's image was permanently tarnished. Jerry Yester was recruited for *Everything Is Playing,* which contained "Six O'Clock," "She Is Still a Mystery," and "Younger Generation," but John Sebastian departed the group in October 1968. Steve Boone also left, and Joe Butler reconstituted the group for one final album before dissolving the group in the summer of 1969.

In August 1969, John Sebastian reestablished himself with members of the counterculture with his renowned, stoned-out appearance at the Woodstock Festival, performing two songs. However, he had become embroiled in legal disputes among his former manager, MGM Records (the distributor of Kama Sutra), and his new label, Reprise. The release of his debut solo album was delayed for a time and, in fact, both MGM and Reprise issued *John B. Sebastian* in early 1970. The best-selling album of Sebastian's solo career, it was recorded with the assistance of Crosby, Stills and Nash, and contained several good-time up-tempo songs, two gentle love songs, "She's a Lady" and "Magical Connection," and two songs of communal good will, "How Have You Been" and "I Had a Dream." He subsequently recorded *The Four of Us* and *Tarzana Kid* for Reprise. The latter album included Jimmy Cliff's "Sitting in Limbo," Lowell George's "Dixie Chicken," Sebastian and George's "Face of Appalachia," and Sebastian's own "Stories We Could Tell," recorded by The Everly Brothers in 1972. In 1976, Sebastian scored a top pop and easy-listening hit with "Welcome Back" from the ABC-TV situation comedy *Welcome Back Kotter.*

For the next decade, John Sebastian toured the concert and festival circuit, playing around 100 engagements a year. He worked on the animated movies *Charlotte's Web* and *The Care Bears Movie,* and briefly reunited The Lovin' Spoonful for Paul Simon's *One-Trick Pony* movie in 1980. Since 1991, Steve Boone, Joe Butler, and Jerry Yester have toured as The Lovin' Spoonful. In the early '90s, Sebastian hosted *The Golden Age of Rock 'n' Roll* series on cable television's Arts and Entertainment network and recorded instructional harmonica and autoharp tapes for Happy Traum's Homespun Tapes. In 1993, he joined Shanachie Records with the help of labelmate Stefan Grossman, recording *Tar Beach,* his first album in seventeen years. Sebastian later recorded *I Want My Roots* for MusicMasters with a jug band dubbed The J-Band.

The Even Dozen Jug Band

The Even Dozen Jug Band	Elektra	7246	'63	†

The Mugwumps

The Mugwumps	Warner Brothers	1697	'67	†

The Lovin' Spoonful

Do You Believe in Magic	Kama Sutra	8050	'65	†
Daydream	Kama Sutra	8051	'66	†
	One Way	22165		CD†
	Buddah/BMG	49508	'96	CS/CD
What's Up, Tiger Lily (soundtrack)	Kama Sutra	8053	'66	†
Hums of The Lovin' Spoonful	Kama Sutra	8054	'66	†
The Lovin' Spoonful (includes *Do You Believe in Magic* and *Hums of The Lovin' Spoonful*)	Buddah	49500	'95	CS/CD
You're a Big Boy Now (soundtrack)	Kama Sutra	8058	'67	†
What's Up, Tiger Lily/You're A Big Boy Now (soundtracks)	Razor & Tie	2167	'98	CD
Everything Is Playing	Kama Sutra	8061	'67	
Revelation: Revolution '69	Kama Sutra	8073	'68	†

Lovin' Spoonful Anthologies and Compilations

Best	Kama Sutra	8056	'67	†
Best, Volume 2	Kama Sutra	8064	'68	†
24 Karat Hits	Kama Sutra	(2)750	'68	†
John Sebastian Song Book	Kama Sutra	2011	'70	†
Very Best	Kama Sutra	2013	'70	†
Once Upon a Time	Kama Sutra	2029	'71	†
The Best	Kama Sutra	(2)2608	'76	†
Distant Echoes	Accord	7196	'82	†
Best, Volume 2	Rhino	114	'84	†
Anthology	Rhino	70944	'89	CS/CD
Best	Rhino	71024	'94	CS/CD
All the Best	Special Music	4916		CS/CD
Best	Pair	1200		CD
Greatest Hits	Hollywood/IMG	115		CS/CD
Rock and Roll	Richmond	2205		CS

Zalman Yanovsky

Alive and Well in Argentina	Kama Sutra	2030	'69	†

John Sebastian

John B. Sebastian	MGM	4654	'70	†
	Reprise	6379	'70	†
Live	MGM	4720	'70	†
Real Live John Sebastian	Reprise	2036	'71	†
The Four of Us	Reprise	2041	'71	†
Tarzana Kid	Reprise	2187	'74	†
Welcome Back	Reprise	2249	'76	†
Best: 1969–1976	Rhino	70170	'89	CS/CD

John Sebastian (recorded 1979)	King Biscuit Flower Hour	88019	'96	CD
Tar Beach	Shanachie	8006	'93	CS/CD
John Sebastian and The J-Band				
I Want My Roots	MusicMasters	65137	'96	CD

THE MAMAS AND THE PAPAS

John Phillips (born August 30, 1935, on Parris Island, South Carolina), guitar, baritone vocals; Denny Doherty (born November 29, 1941, in Halifax, Nova Scotia, Canada), tenor vocals; Cass Elliot (born Ellen Cohen on September 19, 1941, in Baltimore, Maryland; died July 29, 1974, in London, England), contralto vocals; and Michelle Phillips (born Michelle Gilliam on June 4, 1944, in Long Beach, California), soprano vocals.

THE MAMAS AND THE PAPAS (UPI/CORBIS-BETTMANN)

Early purveyors of gentle, harmonically sophisticated folk-rock, The Mamas and The Papas were one of the earliest "hippie" groups, sporting brightly colored attire *before* the crunch of San Francisco's psychedelic rock. Emerging from the Greenwich Village folk music scene, The Mamas and The Papas moved to Los Angeles, where manager Lou Adler applied slick pop-style production to the excellent compositions of John Phillips. Featuring lustrous vocal harmonies arranged by Phillips and the outstanding playing of some of Los Angeles' finest studio musicians, the group was perhaps the most commercially successful folk-rock group of the years 1965 through 1967. Moreover, Phillips and Adler organized the 1967 Monterey International Pop Festival, perhaps the first-ever rock music festival and certainly one of its most significant, launching the American careers of Jimi Hendrix, The Who, and Janis Joplin. Following the group's breakup, Mama Cass Elliot initiated a modest solo career as a cabaret entertainer, and her Laurel Canyon home served as a center of musical and social activities that saw Crosby, Stills and Nash first join voices together. Michelle Phillips later pursued an unspectacular career as an actress, and, in the '80s, Phillips regrouped The Mamas and The Papas with original member Denny Doherty and daughter Mackenzie. The Mamas and The Papas were inducted into the Rock and Roll Hall of Fame in 1998.

John Phillips began performing in Greenwich Village folk clubs during the late '50s with groups such as The Smoothies, which included Scott McKenzie. In 1961, Phillips,

McKenzie, and Dick Weissman formed the folk trio The Journeymen, debuting at Gerde's Folk City that spring and ultimately recording three albums for Capitol Records. In 1962, in San Francisco, Phillips met aspiring teenage model Michelle Gilliam and the couple soon married. Canadian Denny Doherty recorded two albums for Epic while a member of the folk group The Halifax Three. Cass Elliot, her first husband James Hendricks, and Tim Rose formed The Big Three in New York around 1963, recording two albums for FM Records. By the summer of 1964, The Mugwumps had assembled, with Elliot, Hendricks, Doherty, and future Lovin' Spoonful member Zalman Yanovsky, and the group recorded a single album that was eventually released in 1967.

With the dissolution of The Mugwumps, Denny Doherty joined John and Michelle Phillips as The New Journeymen in the Virgin Islands. Subsequently joined by Cass Elliot, the four worked on perfecting their vocal harmonies (Michelle had been singing only briefly) for five months during 1965 before moving to Los Angeles. There, Barry McGuire put them in touch with producer Lou Adler, who signed the group as The Mamas and The Papas to his newly formed Dunhill label.

The Mamas and The Papas recorded their debut album with studio musicians Larry Knechtel (keyboards), Joe Osborn (bass), and Hal Blaine (drums), with Adler providing slick pop-style production. The album, *If You Can Believe Your Eyes and Ears,* quickly yielded smash hits with John and Michelle's "California Dreamin'" and John's "Monday, Monday," while containing John's "Go Where You Wanna Go" and Lennon and McCartney's "I Call Your Name." *The Mamas and The Papas* produced smash hits with John and Denny's "I Saw Her Again" and John's "Words of Love," and included John and Michelle's "Trip Stumble and Fall" and John's "No Salt on Her Tail," "Dancing Bear," and "Strange Young Girls." *Deliver* provided the smash hits "Dedicated to the One I Love" (a 1961 smash for The Shirelles) and John and Michelle's group autobiography "Creeque Alley," and the major hit "Look Through My Window," by John.

In 1967, John Phillips and Lou Adler organized the Monterey International Pop Festival. Coinciding with the smash success of Phillips' insipid "San Francisco (Be Sure to Wear Some Flowers in Your Hair)," as recorded by former associate Scott McKenzie, the festival (and subsequent D. A. Pennebaker film) launched the American careers of Jimi Hendrix, The Who, and Janis Joplin. The original quartet performed live for the last time to close the festival on June 18, 1967. *The Papas and The Mamas* produced a major hit with John's "Twelve Thirty" and a minor hit with his excellent "Safe in My Garden." "Glad to Be Unhappy" became the group's last major hit and, by mid-1968, The Mamas and The Papas had broken up. The Mamas and The Papas were inducted into the Rock and Roll Hall of Fame in 1998.

Cass Elliot's debut solo album for Dunhill yielded the major hit "Dream a Little Dream of Me" and she later scored moderate hits with "It's Getting Better" and "Make Your Own Kind of Music" in 1969. Pursuing a career as a nightclub and television entertainer, she later recorded an ill-received but underrated album with Dave Mason, who was coming off the huge success of his debut solo album, *Alone Together.* John Phillips managed a moderate hit with "Mississippi" in the summer of 1970, the year he and Michelle divorced. The Mamas and The Papas reunited briefly in 1971 for a single album on Dunhill. After successfully completing a two-week engagement at the Palladium Theater in London, Cass Elliot succumbed to a heart attack on July 29, 1974, at the age of 32.

In the meantime, John Phillips composed the music for the flop Broadway musical *Man on the Moon,* produced by Andy Warhol. Michelle Phillips launched a career as an actress with 1973's *Dillinger* and later recorded a solo album for A&M Records. Years later, she was a featured player in CBS-TV's nighttime soap opera *Knots Landing.* John Phillips, mired in drug addiction during the last half of the '70s, was arrested on serious drug charges in New York in July 1980, only to be fined and sentenced to thirty days in jail in April 1981. In March 1982, he re-formed The Mamas and The Papas as a lounge act with Denny Doherty, daughter Mackenzie Phillips (born November 10, 1959), and Elaine "Spanky" McFarlane. Mackenzie was best known for her role in the CBS-TV situation comedy *One Day at a Time* (1975–1983), while McFarlane was the former lead vocalist for Spanky and Our Gang, who had major hits with "Sunday Will Never Be the Same," "Lazy Day," and "Like to Get to Know You" in 1967 and 1968. Scott McKenzie replaced Denny Doherty in 1987 and Mackenzie Phillips continued to tour with the group until 1992. Denny Doherty later took over the role as leader of The Mamas and Papas and was superceded by Scott McKenzie.

John Phillips shared songwriting credit with Scott McKenzie, Terry Melcher, and Beach Boy Mike Love on The Beach Boys' top 1988 hit "Kokomo." In 1989, John and Michelle's daughter Chynna Phillips (born February 12, 1968) formed the vocal group Wilson Phillips with Beach Boy Brian Wilson's daughters Carnie and Wendy. Their debut album produced five hits, including the top hits "Hold On," "Release Me," and "You're in Love," but *Shadows and Light* proved less successful. Wilson Phillips disbanded in 1993 and Chynna Phillips recorded *Naked and Sacred* for EMI Records in 1995.

THE MAMAS AND THE PAPAS BIBLIOGRAPHY

Phillips, John, with Jim Jerome. *Papa John: An Autobiography.* Garden City, NY: Doubleday, 1986.

Phillips, Michelle. *California Dreamin': The True Story of The Mamas and The Papas.* New York: Warner Books, 1986.

The Journeymen (with John Phillips and Scott McKenzie)

The Journeymen	Capitol	1629	'61	†
	Capitol	98536	'92	CS/CD†
Coming Attractions—Live!	Capitol	1770	'62	†
New Directions in Folk Music	Capitol	1951	'63	†

The Halifax Three (with Denny Doherty)

The Halifax Three	Epic	26038	'63	†
San Francisco Bay Blues	Epic	26060	'63	†

The Big Three (with Cass Elliot)

The Big Three	FM	307	'63	†
Live at the Recording Studio	FM	311	'64	†
The Big Three Featuring Cass Elliot	Roulette	42000	'69	†
The Big Three (Featuring Mama Cass Elliott)	Sequel	755	'96	CD
Distant Reflections	Accord	7180	'82	†

The Mugwumps (with Cass Elliot and Denny Doherty)

The Mugwumps	Warner Brothers	1697	'67	†

The Mamas and The Papas

If You Can Believe Your Eyes and Ears	Dunhill	50006	'66	†
	MCA	31042		CS/CD
The Mamas and The Papas	Dunhill	50010	'66	†
Deliver	Dunhill	50014	'67	†
	MCA	31044	'87	CD
Monterey International Pop Festival	Dunhill	50100	'71	†
	One Way	22033		CD
The Papas and The Mamas	Dunhill	50031	'68	†
	MCA	31335	'87	CD
People Like Us	Dunhill	50106	'71	†

Mamas and Papas Anthologies and Compilations

Book of Songs	Dunhill	50022	'67	†
Farewell to the First Golden Era	Dunhill	50025	'67	†
	MCA	709		CS
Golden Era, Volume 2	Dunhill	50038	'68	†
16 Greatest Hits	Dunhill	50064	'69	†
	MCA	1647		CS
	MCA	5701		CD
Anthology—A Gathering of Flowers	Dunhill	50073	'70	†
20 Golden Hits	Dunhill	50145	'73	†
California Dreamin'	Pickwick	3357		†
Monday, Monday	Pickwick	3380	'75	†
Biggest Hits	Pickwick	(2)2076	'75	†
Best	MCA	(2)6019	'82	LP/CS
Creeque Alley/The History of The Mamas and The Papas	MCA	(2)10195	'91	CD
Words of Love	Pair	1322	'93	CD

Cass Elliot

Dream a Little Dream	Dunhill	50040	'68	†
Bubblegum, Lemonade, and Something for Mama	Dunhill	50055	'69	†
Make Your Own Kind of Music	Dunhill	50071	'69	†
Mama's Big Ones (Her Greatest Hits)	Dunhill	50093	'70	†
	MCA	719		CS
	MCA	31147		CD
Dream a Little Dream: The Cass Elliot Collection	MCA	11523	'97	CD
Cass Elliot	RCA	4619	'72	†
The Road Is No Place for a Lady	RCA	4753	'72	†
Don't Call Me Mama Anymore	RCA	0303	'73	†
Her Best Music	Pickwick	(2)2075	'75	†
Dream a Little Dream	Pickwick	3359		†

Cass Elliot and Dave Mason

Dave Mason and Cass Elliot	Blue Thumb	8825	'71	†

John Phillips

John Phillips	Dunhill	50077	'70	†

Denny Doherty

Watcha Gonna Do	Dunhill	50096	'71	†
Waiting for a Sign	Ember	1036	'74	†

Michelle Phillips

Victim of Romance	A&M	4651	'77	†

Wilson Phillips

Wilson Phillips	SBK	93745	'90	CS/CD
Shadows and Light	SBK	98924	'92	CS/CD

Chynna Phillips

Naked and Sacred	EMI	35705	'95	CS/CD

BARRY MANN/CYNTHIA WEIL

Barry Mann (born Barry Iberman on February 9, 1939, in Brooklyn, New York) and Cynthia Weil (born October 18, 1937, in New York).

Another of the brilliant professional songwriting teams employed at New York's Brill Building during the '60s, Barry Mann and wife Cynthia Weil wrote dozens of hit songs for a variety of acts. Their songwriting credits included "Uptown" for The Crystals, "On Broadway" for The Drifters, "We Gotta Get Out of This Place" for The Animals, and "You've Lost That Lovin' Feelin'" and "(You're My) Soul and Inspiration" for The Righteous Brothers.

Barry Mann abandoned his architecture studies to become a songwriter in 1958. Achieving his first hit in collaboration with Mike Anthony in early 1959 with "She Say (Oom Dooby Doom)" as performed by The Diamonds, he was hired as a staff songwriter to Al Nevins and Don Kirshner's Aldon Music, housed at New York's famed Brill Building. Teaming with several other writers on a number of early '60s hits, Mann cowrote "Footsteps" for Steve Lawrence, "I Love How You Love Me" for The Paris Sisters, and the maudlin "Patches" for Dickey Lee. Encouraged by Don Kirshner, Mann recorded an album of his own for ABC Records in 1961 that yielded a near-smash hit with the novelty song "Who Put the Bomp (In the Bomp, Bomp, Bomp)," cowritten with Gerry Goffin.

Barry Mann's greatest success came in collaboration with Cynthia Weil, whom he married in 1961. Their early hit compositions included "Uptown" and "He's Sure the Boy I Love" for The Crystals, both from 1962. Mann-Weil hit songs from 1963 included "My Dad" for Paul Petersen, "Blame It on the Bossa Nova" for Eydie Gorme, "Only in America" for Jay and The Americans, and the classic "On Broadway" for The Drifters. Subsequent hit compositions were "I'm Gonna Be Strong" for Gene Pitney, "Saturday Night at the Movies" for The Drifters, and "We Gotta Get Out of This Place" for The Animals. In late 1964, the duo worked with songwriter-producer extraordinaire Phil Spector on "Walking in the Rain" for The Ronettes and the classic "You've Lost That Lovin' Feelin'" for The Righteous Brothers. During 1966, they provided The Righteous Brothers with "(You're My) Soul and Inspiration" and Paul Revere and The Raiders with "Kicks" and "Hungry." Other hit compositions with which they were associated through 1970 included Max Frost and The Troopers' "Shapes of Things to Come," Cass Elliot's "It's Getting Better" and "Make Your Own Kind of Music," and B. J. Thomas' "I Just Can't Help Believing."

By the late '60s, Barry Mann and Cynthia Weil had left Aldon Music and moved to the West Coast, where Mann unsuccessfully attempted to launch a solo recording career. Another attempt in 1975 yielded the minor hit "The Princess and the Punk." Later hits with which Barry Mann was associated included "Here You Come Again" by Dolly Parton and "Sometimes When We Touch" with Dan Hill, both from 1977. Barry Mann and James Horner composed the music for the 1986 animated film *An American Tail*.

Barry Mann

Who Put the Bomp	ABC	399	'61	†
Lay It All Out	New Design	30876	'72	†
Survivor	RCA	0860	'75	†
Barry Mann	Casablanca	7228	'80	†
Barry Mann and James Horner (Composers)				
An American Tail (music from '86 soundtrack)	MCA	39096	'87	CS/CD

MANFRED MANN

Manfred Mann (born Michael Lubowitz on October 21, 1940, in Johannesburg, South Africa), keyboards; Paul Jones (born Paul Pond on February 24, 1942, in Portsmouth, Hampshire, England), vocals; Michael Vickers (born April 18, 1941, in Southampton, Hampshire, England), guitar; Tom McGuinness (born December 2, 1941, in London, England), bass; and Mike Hugg (born August 11, 1942, in Andover, Hampshire, England), drums.

Later members included bassists Jack Bruce (born May 14, 1943, in Glasgow, Scotland) and Klaus Voorman (born April 29, 1942, in Berlin, Germany) and vocalist Mike D'Abo (born March 1, 1944, in Betchworth, Surrey, England).

The third British group to achieve a top American hit, Manfred Mann were important purveyors of British rhythm-and-blues, scoring more than a dozen British hits while managing only four major American hits (including one of the earliest versions of Bob Dylan's "The Mighty Quinn"). The group included, for a time, bassists Jack Bruce (Cream) and Klaus Voorman (The Plastic Ono Band). Disbanding the group in 1969, Manfred Mann subsequently formed the jazz-influenced Chapter Three and the hard rock Earth Band, who achieved a top hit with Bruce Springsteen's "Blinded by the Light" from the best-selling *The Roaring Silence* album in 1976.

Mike Lubowitz started studying piano at the age of six and moved to England from South Africa in 1961. In London, as Manfred Mann, he formed The Mann-Hugg Blues Brothers with drummer Mike Hugg in late 1962. Following the addition of vocalist Paul Jones, the group became Manfred Mann. Debuting at London's Marquee club in March 1963, the group quickly established themselves on the rhythm-and-blues club circuit, replacing their original bassist with Tom McGuinness at the beginning of 1964.

Signed to HMV Records (Ascot in the United States), Manfred Mann scored their first British hit with "5-4-3-2-1" in early 1964, followed by "Hubble Bubble Toil and Trouble" and Jeff Barry and Ellie Greenwich's "Do Wah Diddy Diddy," a top British and American hit. After the major hit "Sha La La," the group had a major British and minor American hit with "Come Tomorrow" and British-only hits with Carole King and Gerry Goffin's "Oh No Not My Baby" and Bob Dylan's "If You Gotta Go, Go Now."

In late 1965, Mike Vickers left Manfred Mann, as Tom McGuinness switched to guitar and Jack Bruce was recruited to play bass. Following the top British and major American hit "Pretty Flamingo," the group switched to Fontana Records (Mercury in the United States). By the end of July 1966, Paul Jones had left Manfred Mann for solo career and Jack Bruce had departed to form Cream. They were replaced by singer Mike D'Abo and German bassist Klaus Voorman. Jones starred in the 1967 movie *Privilege* and managed two smash British-only hits from the film with "High Time" and "I've Been a Bad Boy." Manfred Mann continued to achieve British-only hits through 1969, including "Semi-Detached Suburban Mr. Jones," "Ha! Ha! Said the Clown," and "Fox on the Run," but only Bob Dylan's previously unrecorded "The Mighty Quinn" proved a (top) British and (major) American hit.

Manfred Mann disbanded in the middle of 1969, and Mann and Mike Hugg soon regrouped as the jazz-styled Chapter Three for one album. Mike D'Abo coauthored "Build Me Up Buttercup" (a smash British and American hit for The Foundations in 1968 and 1969) and authored "Gladbags and Handrags" (a moderate hit for Rod Stewart in 1972) and recorded two solo albums for A&M Records in the early '70s. In 1971, Mann formed Manfred Mann's Earth Band, scoring a British-only hit with "Joybringer" in 1973 and a top American hit with Bruce Springsteen's "Blinded by the Light" from *The Roaring Silence,* their best-selling album, in 1976. Realigned in 1979, The Earth Band endured until 1986.

Manfred Mann

The Manfred Mann Album	Ascot	16015	'64	†
The Five Faces of Manfred Mann	Ascot	16018	'65	†
The Manfred Mann Album/The Five Faces of Manfred Mann	EMI	37067	'96	CD
My Little Red Book of Winners	Ascot	16021	'65	†
Mann Made	Ascot	16024	'66	†
Pretty Flamingo	United Artists	6549	'66	†
Up the Junction (soundtrack)	Mercury	61159	'68	†
The Mighty Quinn	Mercury	61168	'68	†

Manfred Mann Anthologies and Compilations

Greatest Hits	United Artists	6551	'66	†
The Best of the EMI Years	Griffin	(2)559	'96	CD
Second Chapter: Best of the Fontana (i.e., Mercury) Years	Fontana	522665	'94	CS/CD
Best	Janus	3064	'74	†
Greatest Hits	Capitol	11688	'77	†
Best	Capitol	16073		†
Best	EMI	96096	'92	CS/CD

Paul Jones

Sings Songs from *Privilege* and Others	Capitol	2795	'67	†
Crucifix in a Horseshoe	London	605	'70	†

Mike D'Abo

Down at Rachel's Place	A&M	4346	'72	†
Broken Rainbows	A&M	3634	'74	†

Manfred Mann's Chapter Three

Manfred Mann Chapter Three	Polydor	244013	'70	†

Manfred Mann's Earth Band

Manfred Mann's Earth Band	Polydor	5015	'72	†
Glorified, Magnified	Polydor	5031	'72	†
Get Your Rocks Off	Polydor	5050	'73	†
Solar Fire	Polydor	6019	'74	†
The Good Earth	Warner Brothers	2826	'74	†
Nightingales and Bombers	Warner Brothers	2877	'75	†
The Roaring Silence	Warner Brothers	2965	'76	†
	Warner Brothers	3055		CS
Watch	Warner Brothers	3157	'78	†
Angel Station	Warner Brothers	3302	'79	†
Chance	Warner Brothers	3498	'81	†
Best	Warner Archives	46231	'96	CS/CD
Somewhere in Afrika	Arista	8194	'83	†

MARTHA AND THE VANDELLAS

Martha Reeves (born July 18, 1941, in Eufaula, Alabama), Rosalind Ashford (born September 2, 1943, in Detroit, Michigan), and Annette Beard. Beard was replaced in late 1963 by Betty Kelly (born September 16, 1944, in Detroit).

One of Motown Records' earliest and most exciting female vocal groups, Martha and The Vandellas achieved two smash pop and rhythm-and-blues hits with "Heat Wave" and "Quicksand" before the ascendancy of The Supremes, who came to be regarded as the label's most important female act. Showcasing a raucous rhythm-and-blues style distinct from that of the less exuberant Supremes, Martha and The Vandellas scored numerous crossover hit singles with songs composed by Holland-Dozier-Holland between 1963 and 1967, including the classics "Dancing in the Streets" and "Nowhere to Run." The group endured until late 1971, after which Martha Reeves left Motown for an inauspicious solo career. Martha and The Vandellas were inducted into the Rock and Roll Hall of Fame in 1995.

Martha Reeves moved to Detroit as a teenager and helped form The Del-Phis in 1960, recording for Checkmate Records in 1961. Spotted performing solo by Motown executive Mickey Stevenson, Reeves became secretary in the company's A&R department. Recording the occasional demonstration tape as part of her job, she first came to the attention of Berry Gordy, Jr., as a substitute for an absent artist at a recording session. With high school friends Rosalind Ashford and Annette Beard, she backed Marvin Gaye's recording of "Stubborn Kind of Fellow," his first hit from 1962.

Signed to the newly formed Gordy label in September 1962 as Martha and The Vandellas, the group scored their first major pop and near-smash rhythm-and-blues hit in the spring of 1963 with the rather tame "Come and Get These Memories." Subsequently utilizing a harder-edged, brassy style propelled by Martha's dynamic lead vocals, Martha and The Vandellas achieved a smash pop and top rhythm-and-blues hit with Holland-Dozier-Holland's classic "Heat Wave" that summer. By year's end, Annette Beard had left the group, to be replaced by Betty Kelly, formerly with The Velvelettes. Martha and The Vandellas continued having smash crossover hits through early 1965 with Holland-Dozier-Holland's "Quicksand" and "Nowhere to Run," and Mickey Stevenson and Marvin Gaye's "Dancing in the Streets." Although Gordy was concentrating on the career development of The Supremes, Martha and The Vandellas achieved major pop and smash R&B hits with the less raunchy "My Baby Loves Me," "I'm Ready for Love," "Jimmy Mack" (a top R&B hit), and "Honey Chile" through 1967.

However, Martha Reeves and The Vandellas, as they were billed beginning in late 1967, never had another major hit. The group disbanded for two years, reforming in 1971 with Martha Reeves as the only original member to record *Black Magic,* which produced three moderate rhythm-and-blues hits. In late 1972, Martha Reeves launched a solo career, but her recordings for MCA, Arista, and Fantasy through 1980 failed to sell. The original trio reunited in 1989 for American engagements into the '90s. Martha and The Vandellas were inducted into the Rock and Roll Hall of Fame in 1995.

MARTHA REEVES BIBLIOGRAPHY

Reeves, Martha, and Mark Bego. *Dancing in the Streets: Confessions of a Motown Diva.* New York: Hyperion, 1994.

Martha and The Vandellas

Come and Get These Memories	Gordy	902	'63	†
	Motown	0366	'94	CS/CD
Heat Wave	Gordy	907	'63	†
	Motown	5145	'89	CS/CD
Dance Party	Gordy	915	'65	†
	Motown	5433	'89	CD†
Heat Wave/Dance Party	Motown	8149		CD†
Greatest Hits	Gordy	917	'66	†
	Motown	5204		CS/CD
Watch Out	Gordy	920	'66	†
	Motown	5265	'90	CS/CD†
Live!	Gordy	925	'67	†
Anthology	Motown	(2)778	'74	†
Motown Superstar Series, Volume 11	Motown	5111	'81	CS
Compact Command Performance	Motown	9057	'86	CD†
Live Wire! The Singles 1962–1972	Motown	6316	'93	CS/CD
Motown Milestones	Motown	0405	'95	CS/CD
Dancing in the Streets	Pickwick	3386	'75	†

Martha Reeves and The Vandellas

Ridin' High	Gordy	926	'68	†
Sugar and Spice	Gordy	944	'70	†
Natural Resources	Gordy	952	'70	†
Black Magic	Gordy	958	'72	†
	Motown	5477	'90	CS/CD†

Martha Reeves

Martha Reeves	MCA	414	'74	†
The Rest of My Life	Arista	4105	'76	†
We Meet Again	Fantasy	9549	'78	†
Gotta Keep Moving	Fantasy	9591	'80	†

JOHN MAYALL

Born November 29, 1933, in Macclesfield, Cheshire, England. In addition to luminaries Eric Clapton and Jack Bruce (Cream), Peter Green, John McVie, and Mick Fleetwood (Fleetwood Mac), and Mick Taylor (The Rolling Stones), Mayall's '60s bands included drummers Hughie Flint (born March 15, 1942), Aynsley Dunbar (born January 10, 1946, in Lancaster, Lancashire, England), Keef Hartley (born March 8, 1944, in Preston, Lancashire, England), and Jon Hiseman (born June 21, 1944, in Woolwich, London, England); guitarist Jon Mark (born Cornwall, England); and saxophonist Johnny Almond (born July 20, 1946, in Enfield, Middlesex, England).

Often labeled the "grandfather" of British blues, John Mayall, along with Alexis Korner, was a key figure in British rhythm-and-blues in the '60s, helping spark the British blues revival of the late '60s. A staunch defender and champion of neglected and exploited black American bluesmen, Mayall himself might have remained unrecognized (as was Alexis Korner) had not later-day "superstar" Eric Clapton been a member of his early Bluesbreakers. Supplying a loose, noncommercial format within which his band members could explore their proclivities for the blues, John Mayall provided the training ground for many of Britain's leading instrumentalists, including lead guitarists Clapton, Peter Green, and Mick Taylor, bassists John McVie and Jack Bruce, and drummer Mick Fleetwood. Disbanding The Bluesbreakers in 1968, Mayall achieved his greatest commercial success with 1969's *The Turning Point* and 1970's *U.S.A. Union*.

John Mayall became fascinated with the blues at the age of thirteen and eventually learned to play guitar, keyboards, and harmonica. Forming his first group, The Powerhouse Four, while in college during the mid-'50s, he assembled The Blues Syndicate in March 1962. At the urging of Alexis Korner, he moved to London in 1963, turning professional that February and forming The Bluesbreakers with bassist John McVie. By the time of Mayall's first British-only album, the band comprised Mayall, McVie, guitarist Roger Dean, and drummer Hughie Flint. During the spring of 1965, former Yardbird Eric Clapton replaced Dean, and McVie and Jack Bruce shared bass chores through June 1966. This aggregation recorded the classic *Bluesbreakers* album, one of the most compelling blues albums ever made in Great Britain.

When Jack Bruce and Eric Clapton departed to form Cream and Hughie Flint left, Mayall recruited guitarist Peter Green and drummer Aynsley Dunbar for *A Hard Road*. By the spring of 1967, Peter Green had left The Bluesbreakers to form Fleetwood Mac with on-again, off-again Mayall drummer Mick Fleetwood. Mayall subsequently recorded *Crusade* with John McVie, guitarist Mick Taylor, drummer Keef Hartley, and two saxophonists. He recorded *The Blues Alone* as a solo album, accompanied by only Hartley. By September

1967, McVie had left to join Fleetwood Mac, and Mayall reconstituted The Bluebreakers with Taylor, Hartley, saxophonists Chris Mercer and Dick Heckstall-Smith, bassist Tony Reeves, and drummer Jon Hiseman for *Bare Wires,* consisting entirely of Mayall compositions. The album was the last album to be issued under The Bluesbreakers moniker for eighteen years.

John Mayall next moved to Los Angeles, where he recorded *Blues from Laurel Canyon* with Mick Taylor. In 1969, Taylor dropped out to join The Rolling Stones. Mayall subsequently abandoned the loud electric format in favor of a revolutionary, acoustic, drummerless aggregation with string bassist Steve Thompson, guitarist Jon Mark, and tenor saxophonist-flutist Johnny Almond. This grouping recorded the live *Turning Point* album, the best-selling album of Mayall's career, for his new label, Polydor. It featured the favorite "Room to Move" and the nine-minute "California." The group's sole studio album, *Empty Rooms,* yielded Mayall's only (minor) hit, "Don't Waste My Time."

In 1970, John Mayall made yet another stylistic shift, employing American musicians Don "Sugarcane" Harris (violin), Harvey Mandel (guitar), and Larry Taylor (bass) for the jazz-oriented *U.S.A. Union. Back to the Roots,* recorded with various alumni, including Clapton, Green, Taylor, Dunbar, Hartley, and Hiseman, was later remixed and rerecorded and released as *Archives to Eighties.* Mayall continued to record for Polydor through 1974, subsequently switching to ABC, then DJM Records. He conducted a brief Bluesbreakers reunion tour of America and Australia with John McVie and Mick Taylor in 1982. By 1985, he had revived The Bluesbreakers name for *Behind the Iron Curtain* for GNP Crescendo and subsequent recordings for Island. In the '90s, John Mayall recorded for the Silvertone label.

John Mayall and Eric Clapton

Bluesbreakers	London	492	'67	†
	London	50009	'78	†
	Deram	800086		CS/CD
	Mobile Fidelity	00616	'94	CD

John Mayall's Bluesbreakers

A Hard Road	London	502	'67	†
	Deram	820474	'87	CD
Crusade	London	529	'68	†
	Deram	820537	'87	CD
Bare Wires	London	537	'68	†
	Deram	820538	'88	CD†
Looking Back (recorded 1964–1968)	London	562	'69	†
	Deram	820331		CD
Primal Solos (recorded 1966, 1968)	London	50003	'77	†
	Deram	820320		CD
London Blues (1964–1969)	Deram	(2)844302	'92	CD
Diary of a Band	London	570	'70	†
	Deram	844029	'94	CD
Live in Europe	London	589	'71	†
reissued as Diary of a Band, Volume Two	Deram	844030	'94	CD
Through the Years	London	(2)600/1	'71	†
	Deram	844028	'91	CD
The 1982 Reunion Concert	One Way	30008	'94	CD
Cross Country Blues	One Way	30009	'94	CD
Behind the Iron Curtain	GNP Crescendo	2184	'86	LP/CS/CD
Chicago Line	Island	842869	'88	CS/CD
A Sense of Place	Island	842795	'90	CS/CD

John Mayall and Others

Raw Blues	London	543	'68	†
	Polydor	820479	'88	CS/CD

John Mayall

The Blues Alone	London	534	'68	†
	Deram	820535	'88	CD
	Mobile Fidelity	662	'96	CD
Blues from Laurel Canyon	London	545	'69	†
	Deram	820539	'90	CD
The Turning Point	Polydor	244004	'69	†
	Deram	823305		CS/CD
Empty Rooms	Polydor	244010	'70	†
U.S.A. Union	Polydor	244022	'70	†
Back to the Roots	Polydor	(2)253002	'71	†
revised edition released as Archives to Eighties	Deram	837127	'88	CS/CD
Memories	Polydor	5012	'71	†
Jazz Blues Fusion	Polydor	5027	'72	†
Moving On	Polydor	5036	'72	†
Ten Years Are Gone	Polydor	(2)3005	'73	†
Best	Polydor	(2)3006	'74	†
The Latest Edition	Polydor	6030	'74	†
John Mayall Plays John Mayall	Polydor	820536	'88	CD†
Room to Move (1969–1974)	Polydor	(2)517291	'92	CD
New Year, New Band, New Company	Blue Thumb	6019	'75	†
	One Way	22072		CD
Notice to Appear	ABC	926	'76	†
	One Way	22070		CD
A Banquet of Blues	ABC	958	'76	†
	One Way	22075		CD
Lots of People	ABC	992	'77	†
	One Way	22073		CD
A Hard Core Package	ABC/MCA	1039	'77	†
	One Way	22071		CD
The Last of the British Blues	ABC/MCA	1086	'78	†
	One Way	22074		CD
Bottom Line	DJM	23	'79	†
No More Interviews	DJM	29	'79	†
Roadshow Blues Band	Accord	7209	'82	†
Road Show	Magnum America	62	'96	CD
Wake Up Call	Silvertone	41518	'93	CS/CD
Spinning Coin	Silvertone	41541	'95	CS/CD
Blues for the Lost Days	Silvertone	41605	'97	CS/CD
Silver Tones: The Best of John Mayall	Silvertone	41658	'98	CS/CD

MC5

Rob Tyner (born Robert Derminer on December 12, 1944, in Detroit, Michigan; died September 17, 1991, in Royal Oak, Michigan), vocals; Wayne Kramer (born April 30, 1948, in Detroit), guitar; Fred "Sonic" Smith (born August 14, 1949, in West Virginia; died November 4, 1994, in Detroit), guitar; Michael Davis, bass; and Dennis Thompson, drums.

One of the inspirations for the British punk rock movement of the late '70s, The MC5, along with The Velvet Underground and The Stooges, achieved a widespread reputation later that far outdistanced their popularity during their existence. Featuring a loud, fast, aggressive attack in their music, The MC5 projected a boldly confrontational antiestablishment political stance. Initially associated with radical polemicist John Sinclair, The MC5 appeared at the 1968 Democratic National Convention in Chicago and produced one acclaimed and controversial album, *Kick Out the Jams,* before their rapid descent into obscurity. Guitarist Fred "Sonic" Smith later married punk poet Patti Smith and contributed heavily to her "comeback" 1988 album *Dream of Life.*

In 1964, guitarists Wayne Kramer and Fred "Sonic" Smith formed The Bounty Hunters in Lincoln Park, Michigan. The two recruited vocalist Rob Tyner, bassist Michael Davis, and drummer Dennis Thompson, and changed the group's name to The Motor City Five, moving to Detroit in 1966. Recording two local singles, The MC5 became Detroit's leading underground group by 1967. They came under the management of John Sinclair, founder of the revolutionary White Panther Party and leader of the Trans Love Energies commune. Becoming the "house band" for the Party, The MC5 performed in Lincoln Park during the 1968 Chicago Democratic National Convention, which featured one of the most vicious police riots in the history of American politics.

Signed to Elektra Records, The MC5 recorded their debut album live at the Grande Ballroom in Detroit in October. Yielding a minor hit with the title song, *Kick Out the Jams* also included "I Want You Right Now," "Come Together," and "Motor City Is Burning." However, the title song featured prominent use of the word "motherfucker," which led to difficulties with Elektra and their eventual dismissal from the label. Sinclair, arrested three times for marijuana possession, began a ten-year sentence for possession of two "joints" in 1969 (the conviction was overturned in 1972 after John Lennon took up his cause). Sinclair later became a poet and blues and jazz scholar and, since the '80s, has performed poetry with his Blues Scholars band.

The MC5 moved to Atlantic Records, where rock critic (and later Bruce Springsteen associate) Jon Landau produced their second album, a studio effort that drew praise but sold poorly. Following 1970's *High Time,* comprising entirely original compositions, Atlantic dropped the band. They moved to England for a while, but broke up in 1972.

Mike Davis resurfaced in the late '70s with the Detroit-based band Destroy All Monsters with ex-Stooge Ron Asheton. Asheton later joined Dennis Thompson in the group New Race. Wayne Kramer, imprisoned for two years for dealing cocaine in the mid-'70s, returned to music around 1980, forming a short-term partnership with Johnny Thunders, one-time member of The New York Dolls, in Gang War. Kramer later led his own band, Air Raid, and eventually released a solo album on the independent label Epitaph in 1995, followed by 1996's *Dangerous Madness.* Fred "Sonic" Smith formed the band Sonic Rendezvous in the late '70s and married Patti Smith in 1980. He played a major role in writing, playing, and recording her 1988 comeback album, *Dream of Life.* Rob Tyner died of a heart attack on September 17, 1991, in Royal Oak, Michigan, and Fred "Sonic" Smith died from heart failure in Detroit on November 4, 1994.

JOHN SINCLAIR BIBLIOGRAPHY

Sinclair, John. *Guitar Army: Secret Writings, Prison Writings.* World Publishing, 1972.
Sinclair, John, and Robert Levin. *Music and Politics.* New York: World Publishing, 1971.

MC5

Babes in Arms (recorded 1966–1970)	ROIR	122	'83	CS/CD
Kick Out the Jams	Elektra	74042	'69	†
	Elektra	60894	'91	CS/CD

American Ruse (rehearsals for *Back in the USA*)	Total Energy	2001	'95	CD
Teen Age Lust (recorded live '70)	Total Energy	3008	'96	LP/CD
Back in the U.S.A.	Atlantic	8247	'70	†
	Rhino	71033	'92	CD
High Time	Atlantic	8285	'71	†
	Rhino	71034	'92	CD
Thunder Express: One Day Live in Studio (recorded 1972)	Skydog	62254	'94	CD
Power Trip	Alive	5	'94	CD
Gang War (with Wayne Kramer and Johnny Thunders)				
Street Fighting	Skydog	62258	'94	CD
Live at the Channel Club (recorded 1980)	RB Entertainment	9001	'95	CD
Wayne Kramer				
The Hard Stuff	Epitaph	86447	'95	CS/CD
Dangerous Madness	Epitaph	86458	'96	LP/CS/CD
Citizen Wayne	Epitaph	86488	'97	CD
LLMF	Epitaph		'98	CD
Wayne Kramer and John Sinclair				
If I Could Be with You	Schoolkids	2200	'96	CD
Patti Smith with Fred "Sonic" Smith				
Dream of Life	Arista	8453	'88	LP/CS/CD†
	Arista	18828	'96	CS/CD
Scots Pirates (with Fred "Sonic" Smith)				
Revolutionary Means	Schoolkids'	1539	'95	CD

MOBY GRAPE

Alexander "Skip" Spence (born April 18, 1946, in Windsor, Ontario, Canada), guitar, vocals; Jerry Miller (born July 10, 1943, in Tacoma, Washington), lead guitar, vocals; Peter Lewis (born July 15, 1945, in Los Angeles), guitar, vocals; Bob Mosley (born December 4, 1942, in Paradise Valley, California), bass, vocals; and Don Stevenson (born October 15, 1942, in Seattle, Washington), drums.

Often labeled as legendary, Moby Grape produced one of the classic albums of San Francisco's psychedelic era with their debut album. Playing structured songs rather than the free-form improvisations favored by most other area groups, *Moby Grape* featured three guitars and intriguing vocal harmonies, containing songwriting contributions from all five members. However, the album's popularity was mitigated by a massive Columbia Records promotional campaign and the simultaneous release of five singles. Although their second album sold quite well, Moby Grape soon devolved into dissension and drug use. Indeed, Moby Grape is sometimes regarded as the first major band to become a casualty of the psychedelic drug LSD.

Formed by Peter Lewis and Bob Mosley in August 1966 in San Francisco, Moby Grape added Don Stevenson and guitarists Jerry Miller and Skip Spence, the original drummer for The Jefferson Airplane. Debuting in November and playing the Fillmore in December, the group signed with Columbia Records and began recording their first album in Los Angeles in March. The album's June release was accompanied by an unprecedented wave of publicity from Columbia Records, as ten of the album's thirteen songs were issued as singles. The album included the haunting "Sitting by the Window" and the countrified "8:05," yet yielded only one minor hit with "Omaha."

Performing at the Monterey International Pop Festival, Moby Grape next recorded the double-record set *Wow/Grape Jam*. One record, *Wow,* was recorded in the studio and included Spence's "Motorcycle Irene," Mosley's "Murder in My Heart for the Judge," and Miller's "Can't Be So Bad." The other record, *Grape Jam,* was an improvisational recording made with the assistance of Al Kooper and Mike Bloomfield. (Columbia later issued each of the two records as single records.) Although the album sold quite well, Skip Spence soon left the group with drug problems. He later recorded *Oar* in Nashville for Columbia, playing all the instruments and handling all composing, arranging, and production chores. The group moved to Boulder Creek, near Santa Cruz, California, but Mosley soon departed, leaving the remaining three to record *Truly Fine Citizen,* their final album for Columbia.

By the summer of 1969, Moby Grape had broken up. Jerry Miller and Don Stevenson played for two years in The Rhythm Dukes, which included Sons of Champlin leader Bill Champlin. The five original members of Moby Grape reunited in 1971 to record *20 Granite Creek* for Reprise but never performed live. Bob Mosley recorded a solo album and Matthew Katz, owner of the Moby Grape name, assembled his own group to record *Great Grape* for Columbia.

The members of Moby Grape played in various aggregations around Santa Cruz, California, during the '70s. Mosley, Miller, and Lewis were members of another edition of Moby Grape from 1973 to 1975. In 1977, Mosley played in The Ducks, augmented by Neil Young that summer, while Miller, Lewis, and Spence formed The Grape for 1978's *Live Grape.* In 1991, the original lineup of Moby Grape (minus Skip Spence) reunited for Spring Tour West USA. By 1997, the group had won legal rights to the Moby Grape name.

Moby Grape

Moby Grape	Columbia	9498	'67	†
Wow/Grape Jam	Columbia	(2)3	'68	†
Wow	Columbia	9613		†
Grape Jam	Columbia	1		†
'69	Columbia	9696	'69	†
Truly Fine Citizen	Columbia	9912	'69	†
Great Grape	Columbia	31098	'72	†
Very Best	Columbia/Legacy	(2)53041	'93	CS/CD
Omaha	Harmony	30392	'71	†
20 Granite Creek	Reprise	6460	'71	†
Live Grape	Escape	1	'78	†

Skip Spence

Oar	Columbia	9831	'69	†
	Sony	9831		CS/CD†

Bob Mosley

Bob Mosley	Reprise	2068	'72	†

THE MONKEES

Michael Nesmith (born December 30, 1942, in Houston, Texas), guitar, vocals; Davy Jones (born December 30, 1945, in Manchester, England), tambourine, vocals; Peter Tork (born Peter Thorkelson on February 13, 1944, in Washington, D.C.), bass, vocals; and Michael "Mickey" Dolenz (born March 8, 1945, in Tarzana, California), drums, vocals.

A crassly manufactured American group of the late '60s, The Monkees were essentially actors hired to portray musicians for an NBC-TV situation comedy series modeled on The Beatles' *A Hard Day's Night.* Don Kirshner, head of the Brill Building professional songwriting "factory," masterminded the concept, using his staff to provide many of The Monkees' hits. Eventually allowed to play their own instruments with their third album, The Mon-

THE MONKEES (CORBIS-BETTMANN)

kees, though critically castigated, did produce several enduring pop singles, including "I'm a Believer," "Daydream Believer," and "Pleasant Valley Sunday." Nonetheless, the group dissolved after the cancellation of their television show and the release of the movie *Head*. The group re-formed several times in various configurations (without Michael Nesmith), most successfully in 1986, owing to the rebroadcast of their television show on MTV and the reissue of their albums on Rhino Records. Nesmith, the group's only accomplished musician and songwriter, subsequently recorded some of the earliest country-rock with his First National Band. He later formed his own Pacific Arts Records in 1977 and pioneered the production of music videos for the label in the early '80s. The concept was later popularized with enormous success by the MTV cable network.

The Monkees were created through auditions conducted by NBC television in September 1965. The principals were chosen from more than 400 applicants that included Stephen Stills and Jerry Yester. Mickey Dolenz had been a child actor, appearing in the TV series *Circus Boy,* using the name Mickey Braddock, from 1956 to 1958, and later was lead singer of The Missing Links. Davy Jones had been a racehorse jockey and appeared in the London and New York productions of the musical *Oliver!* before unsuccessfully attempting a solo singing career. Both Peter Tork and Michael Nesmith had performed music professionally. Tork had played Greenwich Village coffeehouses, whereas Nesmith had done sessions work in Memphis for Stax/Volt Records and played in the duo Mike and John with John London in Los Angeles.

The Monkees television series debuted in September 1966, with Don Kirshner as musical supervisor. His songwriting staff provided the group with many of their hits, starting with Tommy Boyce and Bobby Hart's top hit "Last Train to Clarksville." The series proved enormously successful as the group continued to record with sessions musicians such as James Burton, Leon Russell, Glen Campbell, and Hal Blaine, scoring smash hits with Neil Diamond's "I'm a Believer" (backed with the major hit "I'm Not Your Steppin' Stone") and "A Little Bit Me, A Little Bit You." The members, led by Nesmith, were finally allowed to play their own instruments beginning with *Headquarters.*

Touring the United States in 1967, briefly with Jimi Hendrix as the opening act, The Monkees' fourth album yielded a smash hit with Carole King and Gerry Goffin's wry "Pleasant Valley Sunday," backed by the major hit "Words." *The Birds, the Bees and the Monkees* produced the top hit "Daydream Believer" (written by John Stewart) and the smash "Valleri" (by Boyce and Hart). The final episode of the television show was broadcast in March 1968 and the show was canceled in June. Following the major hit "D. W. Washburn" (by Jerry Leiber and Mike Stoller), the group achieved only minor hits through 1970. The

Monkees' late 1968 comedy film *Head,* produced by their television producer Bob Rafelson and Jack Nicholson, proved a commercial failure, although the soundtrack album contained some of the members' finest offerings, including Nesmith's "Circle Sky" and Tork's "Can You Dig It." Tork quit The Monkees in early 1969 and Nesmith left following *The Monkees Present,* which included his minor hit, "Listen to the Band." Only Dolenz and Jones remained for 1970's *Changes.* Dolenz and Jones resurfaced in 1975 and 1976 with songwriters Tommy Boyce and Bobby Hart for one album and tour.

Of the four Monkees, only Michael Nesmith was able to establish himself as a solo artist. The Paul Butterfield Blues Band recorded his "Mary, Mary" on their *East-West* album, Linda Ronstadt and The Stone Poneys scored their first and only major hit with his "Different Drum" in 1967, and The Nitty Gritty Dirt Band managed a minor hit with his "Some of Shelly's Blues" in 1971. After producing and conducting an instrumental album of his own songs for Dot while still a member of The Monkees, he signed with RCA in 1970 and formed The First National Band with old associate John London and steel guitarist Orville "Red" Rhodes. Regarded as one of the finest country-rock bands to emerge from Los Angeles, the group recorded two albums and scored a major hit in 1970 with Nesmith's haunting "Joanne." They subsequently fell into disarray during the recording of their third album, which was completed with legendary guitarist James Burton and keyboardist Glen D. Hardin, who were later members of Emmylou Harris' Hot Band. Nesmith later formed the short-lived Second National Band and recorded the solo album *And the Hits Just Keep on Coming,* often regarded as his finest work, with stalwart Red Rhodes.

During 1972, Michael Nesmith founded his own label, Countryside, under the auspices of Elektra Records, but the label was later abandoned when David Geffen succeeded to the presidency of Elektra. After recording a final album for RCA with Red Rhodes, Nesmith allowed his contract to expire, purchased his old masters, and formed Pacific Arts Records in Carmel, California, in 1977. He recorded several albums for the label in the late '70s and expanded the company's operation into the production of videos. His award-winning 1981 television special *Elephant Parts* was one of the first to be specifically aimed at the home VCR market, and his *Pop Clips,* for cable television's Nickelodeon network, provided the prototype for MTV months before the music network was launched. Nesmith further expanded into feature-length movies with 1983's *Timerider,* scoring his biggest film success with the cult favorite *Repo Man* in 1984. Other film, television, and video projects followed, although none proved particularly successful.

In 1986, Davy Jones, Peter Tork, and Mickey Dolenz reunited as The Monkees for a surprisingly successful national tour. Spurred on by MTV's airing of the group's television show and the reissue of their first six albums (including *Head*) on Rhino Records, the group was introduced to a new generation and enjoyed renewed popularity. Dolenz and Tork even scored a major hit with "That Was Then, This Is Now." In 1987, the three toured again and recorded all new songs for Rhino on *Pool It!,* which produced a minor hit with "Heart and Soul." In the '90s, Mickey Dolenz recorded two children's albums and Nesmith returned to recording with Rio Records. Peter Tork recorded *Stranger Things Have Happened* for the small Beachwood label in 1994. All four original members of The Monkees reunited for 1996's *Justus* on Rhino Records and 1997's ABC-TV special *Hey, Hey It's the Monkees.* In the mid-'90s, Michael Nesmith's guitarist-son Jason was a member of Nancy Boy with Donovan's son Donovan Leitch, Jr.

THE MONKEES BIBLIOGRAPHY

Dolenz, Mickey, and Mark Bego. *I'm a Believer: My Life of Monkees, Music and Madness.* New York: Hyperion, 1993.

Jones, Davy. *They Made a Monkee Out of Me.* Dome Press, 1987.

Lefcowitz, Eric. *The Monkees' Tale.* Berkeley, CA: Last Gasp Press, 1985, 1989.

Reilly, Edward, Maggie McMannus, and Bill Chadwick. *The Monkees: A Manufactured Image.* Ann Arbor, MI: Pierian Press, 1987.

David Jones

David Jones	Colpix	493	'65	†

The Monkees

Album	Label	Number	Year	Format
The Monkees	Colgems	101	'66	†
	Rhino	70140	'86	†
	Arista	8524	'88	CS/CD†
	Rhino	71790	'94	CS/CD
	Sundazed	5045	'96	LP
More of The Monkees	Colgems	102	'67	†
	Rhino	70142	'86	†
	Arista	8525	'88	CS/CD†
	Rhino	71791	'94	CS/CD
	Sundazed	5046	'96	LP
Monkees' Headquarters	Colgems	103	'67	†
	Rhino	70143	'86	†
	Arista	8602	'89	CS/CD†
	Rhino	71792	'94	CS/CD
	Sundazed	5047	'96	LP
Live 1967	Rhino	70139	'87	CS/CD
Pisces, Aquarius, Capricorn and Jones, Ltd.	Colgems	104	'67	†
	Rhino	70141	'86	†
	Arista	8603	'89	CS/CD†
	Rhino	71793	'94	CS/CD
	Sundazed	5048	'96	LP
The Birds, The Bees and The Monkees	Colgems	109	'68	†
	Rhino	144	'86	†
	Rhino	71794	'94	CS/CD
	Sundazed	5049	'96	LP
Head (soundtrack)	Colgems	5008	'68	†
	Rhino	145	'86	†
	Rhino	71795	'94	CS/CD
Instant Replay	Colgems	113	'69	†
	Rhino	71796	'94	CS/CD
Greatest Hits	Colgems	115	'69	†
	Arista	4089	'76	†
	Arista	8313		CS/CD†
	Rhino	72190	'95	CS/CD
The Monkees Present	Colgems	117	'69	†
	Rhino	147	'85	†
	Rhino	71797	'94	CS/CD
Changes	Colgems	119	'70	†
	Rhino	70148	'86	†
	Rhino	71798	'94	CS/CD
Barrel Full	Colgems	(2)1001	'71	†
More Greatest Hits	Arista	8334	'82	CS/CD†
Monkee Flips	Rhino	113	'84	†

Missing Links	Rhino	70150	'87	CS/CD
Pool It!	Rhino	70706	'87	LP/CS/CD†
	Rhino	72154	'95	CS/CD
Missing Links, Volume 2	Rhino	70903	'89	CS/CD
Listen to the Band	Rhino	(4)70566	'91	CS/CD
Missing Links, Volume 3	Rhino	72153	'95	CD
Justus	Rhino	72542	'96	CS/CD
Anthology	Rhino	75269	'98	CD

Monkees Children's Album

Barrel Full of Monkees: Monkees 4 Kids	Kid Rhino	72406	'96	CS/CD

Davy Jones

Davy Jones	Bell	6067	'72	†

Dolenz, Jones, Boyce and Hart

Dolenz, Jones, Boyce and Hart	Capitol	11513	'76	†
Concert in Japan	Varèse Sarabande	5625	'96	CD

Mike Nesmith and The First National Band

Magnetic South	RCA	4371	'70	†
Loose Salute	RCA	4415	'70	†
Nevada Fighter	RCA	4497	'71	†
Michael Nesmith and The First National Band	Rio	(2)5066	'93	CS/CD

Michael Nesmith and The Second National Band

Tantamount to Treason	RCA	4563	'72	†

Michael Nesmith

The Wichita Train Whistle Sings	Dot	25861	'68	†
	Pacific Arts	113		†
And the Hits Just Keep on Comin'	RCA	4695	'72	†
	Pacific Arts	9439	'77	†
	Pacific Arts	116		†
Pretty Much Your Standard Ranch Trash	RCA	0164	'73	†
	Pacific Arts	9440	'77	†
	Pacific Arts	117		†
The Prison	Pacific Arts	9428	'74	†
	Pacific Arts	101		†
	Rio	5076	'94	CS/CD
	Rio	2009		CD
Compilation	Pacific Arts	9425	'77	†
	Pacific Arts	106		†
From a Radio Engine to a Photon Wing	Pacific Arts	9486	'77	†
	Pacific Arts	107		†
Live at the Palais	Pacific Arts	118	'78	†
Infinite Rider on the Big Dogma	Pacific Arts	130	'79	†
The Newer Stuff	Rhino	70168	'89	CS/CD†
The Older Stuff: The Best of Michael Nesmith (1970–1973)	Rhino	70763	'91	CS/CD†
Tropical Campfires	Rio	5000	'92	CS/CD
The Garden	Rio	5075	'94	CS/CD
	Rio	2001		CD

Nancy Boy (with Jason Nesmith)

Nancy Boy	Sire	61895	'96	CS/CD

Mickey Dolenz Children's Record				
Mickey Dolenz Puts You to Sleep	Kid Rhino	70413	'91	CS/CD
Broadway Mickey	Kid Rhino	71676	'94	CS/CD
Peter Tork				
Stranger Things Have Happened	Beachwood	2522	'94	CS/CD

THE MOODY BLUES

Denny Laine (born Brian Hines on October 29, 1944, in Birmingham, Warwickshire, England), guitar, vocals; Mike Pinder (born December 27, 1941, in Birmingham), keyboards, guitar; Clint Warwick (born Clinton Eccles on June 25, 1949, in Birmingham), bass; Ray Thomas (born December 29, 1942, in Stourport-on-Severn, Hertfordshire, England), bass; and Graeme Edge (born March 30, 1942, in Rochester, Kent, England), drums.

Laine and Warwick left in 1966, to be replaced by Justin Hayward (born October 14, 1946, in Swindon, Wiltshire, England), lead vocals, lead guitar, keyboards, sitar; and John Lodge (born July 20, 1945, in Birmingham), bass, vocals. In 1978, Pinder was replaced by Patrick Moraz (born June 24, 1948, in Morges, Switzerland), keyboards.

Starting out as one of Great Britain's finest rhythm-and-blues bands, The Moody Blues regrouped in the late '60s with a new sound for the landmark *Days of Future Passed* album, recorded with the London Festival Orchestra. Hailed for its fusion of rock and classical music (and censured as bombastic and pretentious), the album was one of the first albums of progressive rock as well as one of the first "concept" albums, and forever linked the group to psychedelic music for its mysticism. *Days of Future Passed* was also noteworthy for its introduction and popularization of the mellotron, then an advanced keyboard-synthesizer instrument capable of producing prerecorded sounds of non-keyboard instruments. *In Search of the Lost Chord,* recorded without orchestra but with multiple overdubs, continued the pattern The Moody Blues would follow through *Seventh Sojourn:* lush synthesized orchestration, cosmic lyrics, plaintive melodies, and haunting vocals by Justin Hayward. The group disbanded thereafter for a variety of other projects, reassembling in 1978 and briefly reestablishing themselves with 1986's *The Other Side of Life.*

The Moody Blues were formed in 1964 in Birmingham, England, by Denny Laine, Mike Pinder, Clint Warwick, Ray Thomas, and Graeme Edge. Thomas and Pinder had been in the Birmingham group El Riot and The Rebels, while Laine had led Denny Laine and The Diplomats between 1962 and 1964. The Moody Blues debuted in Birmingham in May 1964, later playing at London's famed Marquee club. Signed to British Decca (London/Deram in the United States), the group's second single, the blues-style "Go Now!" became a smash British and major American hit in early 1965. However, the initial lineup never again achieved even another moderate hit and, in 1966, both Laine and Warwick left, with Laine eventually joining Paul McCartney's Wings in 1971.

Adding Justin Hayward and John Lodge, The Moody Blues obtained a mellotron and embarked on a totally new musical direction under producer Tony Clarke. The lineup's debut album, *Days of Future Passed,* eschewed their blues backgrounds and was hailed both as a "concept" album and for its adventurous fusion of rock and classical music. Recorded with The London Festival Orchestra, the album yielded a major hit with "Tuesday Afternoon" and included the classic "Nights in White Satin," a smash hit upon rerelease in 1972. For their next album, *In Search of the Lost Chord,* The Moody Blues made extensive use of the mellotron and studio overdubbing, playing more than thirty different instruments to produce their characteristic lavish sound without an orchestra. The album contained the cosmic favorites "Legend of a Mind" and "Om" and produced a minor hit with the rocking "Ride My See-Saw."

On *the Threshold of a Dream* yielded a minor hit with "Never Comes the Day" in 1969, the year The Moody Blues formed Threshold Records. The group's first album release on the label, *To Our Children's Children's Children,* contained band favorites such as "Higher and Higher" and "I Never Thought I'd Live to Be a Hundred/Million." Abandoning multiple overdubs beginning with *A Question of Balance,* The Moody Blues scored major hits with "Question," "The Story in My Eyes," and "Isn't Life Strange" and "I'm Just a Singer (In a Rock and Roll Band)" from *Seventh Sojourn.*

After a nine-month world tour ended in the United States in early 1974, the members of The Moody Blues settled down to a variety of outside projects. The first and most successful of these, Justin Hayward and John Lodge's *Blue Jays,* yielded two minor hits with "I Dreamed Last Night" and "Blue Guitar." Other projects included solo albums by Thomas, Pinder, Hayward, and Lodge, and two albums by Edge with Adrian Gurvitz.

In July 1977, The Moody Blues announced their intention to reunite for yet another album. Following the release of *Octave,* which produced minor hits with "Steppin' in a Slide Zone" and "Driftwood," The Moody Blues conducted a successful worldwide tour with Patrick Moraz (formerly of Yes) substituting for Michael Pinder, who had moved to California. Moraz joined the band on a permanent basis in 1978. Pinder eventually reemerged in the mid-'90s, recording one music and two children's albums for his own label, One Step Records.

The Moody Blues' 1981 *Long Distance Voyager* produced two major hits, "Gemini Dream" and "The Voice," and 1986's *The Other Side of Life,* featuring guitar synthesizers and electronic drums, yielded their first near-smash hit in years with "Your Wildest Dreams." They conducted a world tour in 1986, switching to Polydor Records for *Sur La Mer* and its moderate hit "I Know You're Out There Somewhere." Patrick Moraz left The Moody Blues in early 1992 and, in 1994, the group toured America performing with local symphony orchestras. Polydor's 5-CD set *Time Traveler* compiled studio recordings from *Days of Future Passed* through *Keys to the Kingdom,* as well as Justin Hayward and John Lodge's *Blue Jays.*

The Moody Blues

Number 1	London	428	'65	†
In the Beginning	Deram	18051	'71	†
Early Blues	Compleat	(2)672008	'85	†
The Magnificent Moodies	Threshold	820758		CD†
Days of Future Passed	Deram	18012	'68	†
	Threshold	820006		CS/CD
	Mobile Fidelity	00512	'89	CD†
In Search of the Lost Chord	Deram	18017	'68	†
	Threshold	820168		CS/CD†
	Mobile Fidelity	00576	'93	CD†
On the Threshold of a Dream	Deram	18025	'69	†
	Threshold	820170		CS/CD
	Mobile Fidelity	215	'94	LP
	Mobile Fidelity	00612	'94	CD
To Our Children's Children's Children	Threshold	1	'70	†
	Threshold	820364		CS/CD
	Mobile Fidelity	253	'96	LP†
	Mobile Fidelity	671	'96	CD
A Question of Balance	Threshold	3	'70	†
	Threshold	820211		CS/CD
	Mobile Fidelity	737	'98	CD

Every Good Boys Deserves Favour	Threshold	5	'71	†
	Threshold	820160		CS/CD
	Mobile Fidelity	232	'95	LP
	Mobile Fidelity	00643	'95	CD
Seventh Sojourn	Threshold	7	'72	†
	Threshold	820159		CS/CD
	Mobile Fidelity	718	'98	CD
Caught Live Plus Five	London	(2)690/1	'77	†
	Threshold	820161		CS
Octave	London	708	'78	†
	Threshold	820329		CS/CD
Long Distance Voyager	Threshold	2901	'81	†
	Threshold	820105		CS/CD
	Mobile Fidelity	700		CD
The Present	Threshold	2902	'83	
	Threshold	810119		CS/CD
The Other Side of Life	Threshold	829179	'86	CS/CD
Prelude	Polydor	820517	'87	CD†
Sur La Mer	Polydor	835756	'88	CS/CD
Keys of the Kingdom	Polydor	849433	'91	CS/CD
A Night at Red Rock with The Colorado Symphony Orchestra	Polydor	517977	'93	CS/CD

Moody Blues Reissues

In Search of the Lost Chord/On the Threshold of a Dream	Threshold	810100		CS
A Question of Balance/To Our Children's Children's Children	Threshold	810101		CS

Moody Blues Anthologies and Compilations

This Is The Moody Blues	Threshold	(2)12/13	'74	†
	Threshold	820007		CS
	Threshold	(2)820007		CD
Voices in the Sky (Best)	Threshold	820155	'85	LP/CS/CD†
Greatest Hits (1967–1988)	Threshold	840659	'89	CS/CD
Time Traveller	Polydor	(5)516436	'94	CD
	Polydor	(4)5223	'96	CD
The Collection	Griffin	105		CD

Graeme Edge Band with Adrian Gurvitz

Kick Off Your Muddy Boots	Threshold	15	'75	†
Paradise Ballroom	London	686	'77	†

Ray Thomas

From Mighty Oaks	Threshold	16	'75	†
Hopes, Wishes and Dreams	Threshold	17	'76	†

Michael Pinder

The Promise	Threshold	18	'76	†
Among the Stars	One Step	432	'95	CS/CD

Mike Pinder Children's Albums

A Planet with One Mind	One Step	0434	'95	CS/CD
A People with One Heart	One Step	0435	'96	CS/CD

Justin Hayward and John Lodge

Blue Jays	Threshold	15	'75	†
	London	820491	'87	CD

Justin Hayward

Songwriter	Deram	18073	'77	†
	Deram	820492		CD†
Nightflight	Deram	4801	'80	†
	Polydor	820555	'90	CD†
Classic Blue	Griffin	215	'89	CD
The View from the Hill	CMC	86202	'96	CS/CD

John Lodge

Natural Avenue	London	683	'77	†
	London	820464	'87	CD†

THE MOTHERS OF INVENTION

Frank Zappa (born December 21, 1940, in Baltimore, Maryland; died December 4, 1993, in Los Angeles), lead guitar, vocals; Elliott Ingber, guitar; Ray Collins (born November 19, 1937), lead vocals; Roy Estrada (born April 17, 1943, in Santa Ana, California), bass, vocals; and Jimmy Carl Black (born February 1, 1938, in El Paso, Texas), drums. By 1967, Ingber had departed, and the group subsequently added Don Preston (born September 21, 1932, in Flint, Michigan), keyboards; Jim "Motorhead" Sherwood (born May 18, 1942), saxophone; John "Bunk" Gardner (born May 12, 1933), saxophone; and Billy Mundi, drums. Later members included Ian Underwood (born May 22, 1939, in New York City), keyboards, woodwinds; Art Tripp III (born September 10, 1939), percussion; Aynsley Dunbar (born January 10, 1946, in Lancaster, Lancashire, England), drums; George Duke (born January 12, 1946, in San Rafael, California), keyboards; Howard Kaylan (born Howard Kaplan on June 22, 1945, in New York City) and Mark Volman (born April 19, 1944, in Los Angeles), vocals; and Ruth Underwood, vibes, marimba.

THE MOTHERS OF INVENTION, WITH FRANK ZAPPA (HENRY DILTZ/CORBIS)

The Mothers of Invention, masterminded by Frank Zappa, were perhaps the first and only rock group to establish *and* sustain themselves as a strictly "underground" phenomenon. Their debut album, *Freak Out!,* was unique in '60s rock, incisively combining '50s parodies, cynical and acerbic social commentary, self-mocking and self-serving diatribes, and bizarre, extended free-form pieces. It was one of the first double-record sets in rock, certainly the first for a new, unknown group. Zappa and The Mothers flaunted the standard path to success and intentionally projected a group aura of flagrantly indelicate and contemptuous on-stage behavior that can be seen as the first instance of calculated theatrics in rock. Furthermore, The Mothers of Invention performed (and recorded) remarkably disciplined, precise, and technically demanding music, complete with intricate and complex changes of time and key signatures and unusual and difficult phrasings, directed by Zappa as composer, arranger, conductor, and lead guitarist. Exploring jazz-rock and scatalogical humor with various editions of The Mothers through 1975, Frank Zappa proved an amazingly prolific artist, recording over fifty albums while working with over 200 musicians during his thirty-year career. Beginning with 1968's *Lumpy Gravy,* issued under his own name, he revealed an ongoing proclivity for a unique fusion of modern classical and rock music, a penchant that may ultimately lead to Zappa's recognition as one of the most important composers of "serious" music in the twentieth century. Nonetheless, Zappa was never lumped with the progressive rock groups of the late '60s and '70s, since he composed and performed as a true devotee of classical music and not as a dilettante and usurper of the tradition.

Frank Zappa moved with his family to California at the age of ten and eventually they settled in Lancaster by 1956. Taking up drums at age twelve, he was fascinated with rhythm-and-blues, doo-wop, and the classical avant-garde music of Igor Stravinsky and Edgard Varèse as a teenager. He became a member of The Blackouts while still in high school, switching to guitar at eighteen. Zappa then studied music at Chaffey College in Alta Loma and manned The Omens (aka The Soots), with Don Van Vliet (aka Captain Beefheart), and The Muthers. In 1962, he wrote the '50s parody/tribute pastiche "Memories of El Monte" with Ray Collins for the doo-wop group The Penguins. After composing scores for the films *The World's Greatest Sinner* and *Run Home Slow,* Zappa bought a recording studio in Cucamonga in 1963. There he recorded unsuccessfully for a variety of obscure labels under a variety of names. In 1964, Zappa moved to Los Angeles and began working with the rhythm-and-blues band The Soul Giants, whose members included vocalist Ray Collins, bassist Roy Estrada, and drummer Jim Black (aka Jimmy Carl Black). Becoming The Mothers under Zappa's direction in May, the group included as its early members guitarists Alice Stuart, Henry Vestine (later with Canned Heat), and Jim Guercio (later the producer-manager of Chicago).

The Mothers signed with manager Herb Cohen in 1965 and were spotted by producer Tom Wilson at Los Angeles' Whiskey A-Go-Go. Comprising Zappa, Collins, Estrada, Black, and guitarist Elliott Ingber, the group was signed by Wilson to the Verve subsidiary of MGM as The Mothers of Invention. They issued their debut album as a double-record set, an unprecedented move for a new group. *Freak Out!* contained a wondrous mixture of '50s parodies ("How Could I Be Such a Fool," "You Didn't Try to Call Me"), social commentary ("Trouble Every Day," Zappa's response to the Watts riots, and "Who Are the Brain Police"), songs about the group ("Hungry Freaks, Daddy," "Motherly Love"), and bizarre and complex extended pieces ("Help, I'm a Rock," "The Return of the Son of Monster Magnet"), as well as the pop-style "Any Way the Wind Blows."

When Elliott Ingber left the group for Captain Beefheart's band, The Mothers of Invention added keyboardist Don Preston, saxophonists Bunk Gardner and Jim "Motorhead" Sherwood, and drummer Billy Mundi for *Absolutely Free.* The album included the socially conscious satires "Plastic People," "Brown Shoes Don't Make It," and "America Drinks and Goes Home," the classic "Call Any Vegetable," and the jam-style "Invocation and Ritual Dance of the Young Pumpkin." In late 1966, The Mothers began a six-month residency at the Garrick Theater in New York's Greenwich Village, where their shows had a decidedly theatrical bent, utilizing props and choreography and inviting crazy participation by audience members. After adding keyboard and woodwind player Ian Underwood, the group next recorded the Zappa-produced *We're Only in It for the Money,* which parodied The Beatles' *Sgt. Pepper's Lonely Hearts Club Band* album and derided The Mothers' followers and the so-called "hippie" movement. Jim Black returned to drums and Art Tripp was added on percussion with the departure of Billy Mundi, and the group next recorded the excellent

'50s parody, *Cruising with Ruben and The Jets,* which included "Jelly Roll Gumdrop," and rere-cordings of three songs from *Freak Out!,* "How Could I Be Such a Fool," "Anyway the Wind Blows," and "You Didn't Try to Call Me."

Earlier, Frank Zappa had recorded his solo debut, *Lumpy Gravy,* in New York City with a fifty-piece orchestra and the vocal assistance of several Mothers. A serious compositional work, the album explored classical influences such as those of Edgard Varèse and Igor Stravinsky within the rock format. During 1968 and 1969, Zappa produced albums for The GTOs and Wild Man Fischer and Captain Beefheart's *Trout Mask Replica.* In 1969, he formed Straight and Bizarre Records in conjunction with manager Herb Cohen under the aegis of Warner Brothers/Reprise Records. Alice Cooper's debut album and Tim Buckley's *Blue Af-ternoon* were issued on Straight, and Bizarre releases included The Mothers' *Uncle Meat* and Zappa's *Hot Rats. Uncle Meat* largely comprised instrumentals for an unfinished movie, and *Hot Rats* was recorded with the assistance of Lowell George, Don Preston, Ian Underwood, violinists Don "Sugarcane" Harris and Jean Luc Ponty, and Captain Beefheart. Sometimes re-garded as an early fusion album and usually considered to be one of Zappa's finest early solo albums, *Hot Rats* featured heavy use of synthesizers and included the classic "Willie the Pimp" (with vocals by Beefheart), plus "Peaches en Regalia" and "The Gumbo Variations."

MGM/Verve later issued four compilation sets by The Mothers, but, in the fall of 1969, Zappa disbanded the group. Subsequent releases for the early incarnation of the group were *Burnt Weenie Sandwich* and the live *Weasels Ripped My Flesh.* In late 1969, Lowell George and Roy Estrada formed Little Feat. Art Tripp joined Captain Beefheart's Magic Band. In the early '70s, Jim Sherwood formed Ruben and The Jets for two albums and Jimmy Carl Black assembled Geronimo Black with Bunk Gardner. In the early '80s, Sherwood, Black, Gardner, Don Preston, and Elliott Ingber reunited as The Grandmothers.

Frank Zappa composed and arranged *King Kong: Jean-Luc Ponty Plays the Music of Frank Zappa* for the violinist before forming a new edition of The Mothers in the spring of 1970 with Ian Underwood, keyboardist George Duke, drummer Aynsely Dunbar, and former Turtles vocalists Mark Volman and Howard Kaylan, initially billed as The Phlorescent Leech and Eddie and later shortened to Flo and Eddie. Following Zappa's solo album, *Chunga's Re-venge,* the group recorded the score to the surreal and psychedelic band-on-the-road movie *200 Motels,* which featured performances by Ringo Starr and Keith Moon, and included puerile Zappa songs such as "Shove It Right In" and "Penis Dimension." Written and filmed in London and released on United Artists, the film contained video explorations later adopted by MTV.

During 1970 and 1971, The Mothers toured extensively, producing the live albums *Fill-more East, June 1971* and *Just Another Band from L.A.,* which included the "mini-opera" "Billy the Mountain" and Flo and Eddie's "Eddie, Are You Kidding?" During their Fillmore East en-gagement, The Mothers jammed with John Lennon, in his first live performance since the Plastic Ono Band in 1969, and Yoko Ono. Released by Lennon and Ono as one-half of the double record set *Sometime in New York City* in 1972, the recordings were issued as part of *Playground Psychotics* in 1992.

Seriously injured when pushed from the stage of the Rainbow Theatre in London in De-cember 1971, Frank Zappa convalesced, as Kaylan, Volman, Preston, and Dunbar formed Flo and Eddie. Zappa reemerged in 1972 with the solo album *Waka Jawaka,* with its side-long "Big Swifty." He next recorded the jazz-style *The Grand Wazoo* with Preston, Duke, Dunbar, and additional horns and percussionists as The Mothers. A new edition of The Mothers, with Ian and Ruth Underwood and trombonist Bruce Fowler, recorded *Over-Nite Sensation* with Duke and Jean-Luc Ponty for DiscReet Records, Zappa's new label for Warner Brothers/Reprise. The live set *Roxy and Elsewhere,* with "Penguin in Bondage" and the instrumental "Don't You Ever Wash That Thing," and *One Size Fits All* were the final al-bums for The Mothers.

Frank Zappa's solo debut on DiscReet, *Apostrophe ('),* was recorded with a variety of former Mothers plus former Cream bassist Jack Bruce and yielded a minor hit with "Don't Eat the Yellow Snow." During May 1975, Zappa and old associate Captain Beefheart performed at the Armadillo World Headquarters in Austin, Texas, and live recordings from the shows were issued as *Bongo Fury.* In August 1975, Zappa regained ownership of his Verve masters, but, following *Zoot Allures,* he became entangled in another wrangle with his record label. Warner Brothers/Reprise refused to release his four-record set *Läther.* Zappa subsequently sued manager Herb Cohen and Warner Brothers, which parceled out the recordings on four albums: *Zappa in New York, Studio Tan, Sleep Dirt,* and *Orchestral Favorites,* the latter recorded with a thirty-seven-piece orchestra. *Läther* was eventually released by Rykodisc in 1996.

After touring in 1978 with a band that included guitarist Adrian Belew, keyboardist Peter Wolf, and drummer Terry Bozzio, Frank Zappa signed with Phonogram/Mercury, which issued his albums on Zappa Records. His debut for the label, *Sheik Yerbouti,* was his most accessible album in years and served to introduce a new generation to his unique vision. While containing more puerile material such as "Broken Hearts Are for Assholes" and the Peter Frampton parody "I Have Been in You," the album included the moderate hit "Dancin' Fool" (a parody of disco music) and the controversial "Jewish Princess." Originally intended as a triple-record set, the elaborate tale *Joe's Garage* was ultimately issued as a single record, *Act I,* and double-record, *Acts II and III. Act I* included more Zappa scatology such as "Crew Slut" and "Wet T-Shirt Nite," as well as the controversial "Catholic Girls," whereas *Acts II and III* were viewed as dreary and boring.

Frank Zappa's film *Baby Snakes* was premiered in early 1980 and, after Mercury refused to issue his single "I Don't Wanna Get Drafted," he severed relations with the company. Subsequent Zappa albums were issued on his own mail-order record company Barking Pumpkin and released nationally on the Rykodisc label begining in 1986. In the late '80s and early '90s, a number of albums by The Mothers of Invention and Frank Zappa on Barking Pumpkin were distributed nationally by Capitol Records.

Frank Zappa was amazingly prolific in the '80s. He issued three albums in 1981, including *Shut Up 'n' Play Yer Guitar,* on which he demonstrated his prowess as an electric guitarist, an overlooked facet of his career. *Ship Arriving Too Late to Save a Drowning Witch* produced his biggest hit with "Valley Girl," with vocals by his fourteen-year-old daughter Moon Unit. Conductor Pierre Boulez commissioned him to compose a symphonic work, *The Perfect Stranger,* which was issued on Angel Records in 1984. Zappa also recorded an album of the works of an obscure eighteenth-century classical composer named Francesco Zappa.

In 1985, Zappa took center stage at Senate subcommittee hearings considering the recommendations of the Parents Music Resource Center, staunchly opposing censorship in the recording industry and vociferously advocating the right of freedom of speech. His *Frank Zappa Meets the Mothers of Prevention* lampooned the PMRC and included the biting "Porn Wars." In 1986 and 1987, Rykodisc issued recordings of Zappa's symphonic compositions recorded by the 102-piece London Symphony Orchestra, conducted by Kent Nagano. Zappa composed and performed the Grammy Award–winning *Jazz from Hell* on the synclavier, a sophisticated instrument that was both synthesizer and computer.

In 1988, Frank Zappa conducted his final four-month tour of the United States and Europe, the Broadway the Hard Way tour. During the American portion of the tour, fans were encouraged to register to vote at facilities provided at concert sites. The tour produced three albums, *Broadway the Hard Way, The Best Band You Never Heard in Your Life,* and *Make a Jazz Noise Here.* Also in 1988, Frank Zappa anthologized his concert career with the twelve-CD set *You Can't Do That on Stage Anymore,* also available as six separate two-CD sets. Later, to circumvent the "bootlegging" of recordings of his live concerts, he issued the eight-CD set *Beat the Boots* in 1991 (also available as single CDs), followed by *Beat the*

Boots # 2 in 1992. In 1990, Zappa met with new Czechoslovakian president Vaclav Havel and briefly served as that country's cultural and trade emissary to the West. Zappa later formed the company So What? to link businesses in the Soviet Union and Eastern Europe with those in the West.

Diagnosed with prostate cancer, Frank Zappa died of complications from the disease on December 4, 1993, in his Laurel Canyon home. Recent recordings of his works include *The Yellow Shark,* performed by the German classical group Ensemble Modern, and *Zappa's Universe,* performed by a large stage cast that included guitarist Steve Vai, son Dweezil Zappa, and The Persuasions. His last and perhaps most ambitious work, *Civilization, Phaze III,* was initially available only by mail order through Barking Pumpkin Records. In 1994, Rykodisc acquired the rights to Frank Zappa's entire catalog, reissuing virtually all of his recordings in 1995.

Frank Zappa's eldest son Dweezil first played guitar with his father in 1982 at the age of twelve, cowriting "My Mother Is a Space Cadet" with guitarist Steve Vai in 1983. Dweezil began recording in the late '80s and served as a video jockey for MTV. In 1993, he and his younger brother Ahmet formed the group Z, recording *Shampoohorn* for Barking Pumpkin Records.

FRANK ZAPPA BIBLIOGRAPHY

Chevalier, Dominique. *Viva! Zappa.* New York: St. Martin's Press, 1986.

Lennon, Nigel. *Being Frank: My Time with Frank Zappa.* Los Angeles: California Classics Books, 1995.

Walley, David. *No Commercial Potential: The Saga of Frank Zappa and The Mothers of Invention.* New York: Outerbridge and Lazard, 1972.

————. *No Commercial Potential: The Saga of Frank Zappa, Then and Now.* New York: E. P. Dutton, 1980.

Watson, Ben. *Frank Zappa: The Negative Dialectics of Poodle Play.* New York: St. Martin's Press, 1995.

Zappa, Frank, with Peter Occhiogrosso. *The Real Frank Zappa Book.* New York: Poseidon Books, 1989.

The Mothers of Invention

Freak Out!	Verve	(2)65005	'66	†
	Barking Pumpkin/ Capitol	74208	'88	CS†
	Rykodisc	40062	'88	CD†
	Rykodisc	10501	'95	CS/CD
Absolutely Free	Verve	65013	'67	†
	Barking Pumpkin/ Capitol	74214	'88	CS†
	Rykodisc	10093		CD†
	Rykodisc	10502	'95	CS/CD
We're Only in It for the Money	Verve	65045	'68	†
	Rykodisc	10503	'95	LP/CS/CD
Cruising with Ruben and The Jets	Verve	65055	'68	†
	Barking Pumpkin/ Capitol	74209	'88	CS†
	Rykodisc	10063	'88	CD†
	Rykodisc	10505	'95	CD
Mothermania—The Best of The Mothers	Verve	65068	'69	†
The &?X! of The Mothers	Verve	65074	'69	†
The Mothers of Invention	MGM	112	'70	†

The Worst of The Mothers	MGM	4754	'71	†
Weasels Ripped My Flesh (recorded 1967–1969)	Bizarre/Reprise	2028	'70	†
	Rykodisc	10163	'90	CD†
	Rykodisc	10510	'95	CD
Ahead of Their Time (recorded October 1968 in London)	Barking Pumpkin/ Capitol	74246	'93	CD†
	Rykodisc	10559	'95	CD
Uncle Meat	Bizarre/Reprise	(2)2024	'69	†
	Barking Pumpkin/ Capitol	74210	'88	CS†
	Rykodisc	(2)10064/65	'88	CD†
	Rykodisc	10506	'95	CS
	Rykodisc	(2)10506/07	'95	CD
Burnt Weenie Sandwich	Reprise	6370	'70	†
	Barking Pumpkin/ Capitol	74239	'91	CS/CD†
	Rykodisc	10509	'95	CD
Jean Luc Ponty				
King Kong/Ponty Plays Zappa	World Pacific	20172	'70	†
	Pacific Jazz	89539	'93	CD
Geronimo Black (with Jimmy Carl Black and Bunk Gardner)				
Geronimo Black	Uni	73132	'72	†
	One Way	22114		CD
Welcome Black	Helios	4405	'80	†
Jimmy Carl Black and The Mannish Boys				
A Lil Dab'l Do Ya	Amazing	1013	'87	LP/CS
The Mannish Boys				
Satellite Rock	Amazing	1016		LP/CS
Jimmy Carl Black/Eugene Chadbourne				
Pachuco Cadaver: The Jack and Jim Show	Fire Ant/City Hall	1007	'96	CD
Ruben and The Jets (with Jim Sherwood)				
For Real	Mercury	659	'73	†
Con Safos	Mercury	694	'73	†
The Grandmothers				
The Grandmothers	Rhino	302	'81	†
Frank Zappa and The Mothers				
Fillmore East, June 1971	Reprise	2042	'71	†
	Rykodisc	10167	'90	CD†
	Rykodisc	10512	'95	CS/CD
Playground Psychotics	Barking Pumpkin/ Capitol	(2)74244	'92	CD†
	Rykodisc	(2)10557/58	'95	CD
200 Motels (soundtrack)	United Artists	(2)9956	'71	†
	MCA	(2)4183	'86	LP/CS
	Rykodisc	(2)10513	'98	CS/CD
Just Another Band from L.A.	Bizarre/Reprise	2075	'72	†
	Rykodisc	10161	'90	CD†
	Rykodisc	10515	'95	CD

The Grand Wazoo	Bizarre/Reprise	2093	'72	†
	Rykodisc	10026	'86	CD†
	Rykodisc	10517	'95	CD
Over-Nite Sensation	DiscReet/Reprise	2149	'73	†
	DiscReet	2288		†
	Barking Pumpkin/ Capitol	74221	'89	CS†
	Rykodisc	10518	'95	CS/CD
Roxy and Elsewhere	DiscReet	(2)2202	'74	†
	Barking Pumpkin/ Capitol	(2)74241	'91	CS/CD†
	Rykodisc	10520	'95	CS/CD
One Size Fits All	DiscReet	2216	'75	†
	Barking Pumpkin/ Capitol	74216	'88	CS†
	Rykodisc	10063		CD†
	Rykodisc	10521	'95	CD
	Rykodisc	80521	'96	CD
Frank Zappa/Captain Beefheart/The Mothers				
Bongo Fury	DiscReet	2234	'75	†
	Barking Pumpkin/ Capitol	74220	'89	CS†
	Rykodisc	10097	'89	CD†
	Rykodisc	10522	'95	CD
Frank Zappa				
Rare Meat: Early Works of Frank Zappa (recorded 1962–1963)	Del-Fi (EP)	70010		CD
Cucamonga (recorded 1963–1964)	Del-Fi	71261	'98	CD
The Lost Episodes (recorded 1958–1972, 1980, 1992)	Rykodisc	40573	'96	CD
Mystery Disc	Rykodisc	10580	'98	CD
Lumpy Gravy	Verve	68741	'67	†
	Rykodisc	10504	'95	CD
Hot Rats	Bizarre/Reprise	6356	'69	†
	Barking Pumpkin/ Capitol	74211	'88	CS†
	Rykodisc	10066	'88	CD†
	Rykodisc	10508	'95	CS/CD
Chunga's Revenge	Bizarre/Reprise	2030	'70	†
	Rykodisc	10164	'90	CD†
	Rykodisc	10511	'95	CD
Waka Jawaka	Bizarre/Reprise	2094	'72	†
	Barking Pumpkin/ Capitol	74215	'88	CS†
	Rykodisc	10094		CD†
	Rykodisc	10516	'95	CD
Apostrophe (')	DiscReet	2175	'74	†
	DiscReet	2289		†
	Barking Pumpkin/ Capitol	74222	'89	CS†
	Rykodisc	10519	'95	CS/CD
	Rykodisc	80519	'96	CD

Zoot Allures	Warner Brothers	2970	'76	†
	Rykodisc	10160	'90	CD†
	Rykodisc	10523	'95	CD
Läther (recorded 1973–1977)	Rykodisc	10574	'96	CD
Zappa in New York	DiscReet	(2)2290	'78	†
	Barking Pumpkin/ Capitol	74240	'91	CS/CD†
	Rykodisc	(2)10524/25	'95	CD
Studio Tan	DiscReet	2291	'78	†
	Barking Pumpkin/ Capitol	74237	'91	CS/CD†
	Rykodisc	10526	'95	CD
Sleep Dirt	DiscReet	2292	'79	†
	Barking Pumpkin/ Capitol	74238	'91	CS/CD†
	Rykodisc	10527	'95	CD
Orchestral Favorites	DiscReet	2294	'79	†
	Barking Pumpkin/ Capitol	74236	'91	CS/CD†
	Rykodisc	10529	'95	CD
Sheik Yerbouti	Zappa	(2)1501	'79	†
	Barking Pumpkin/ Capitol	74225	'91	CS†
	Rykodisc	40162	'90	CD†
	Rykodisc	10528	'95	CS/CD
Joe's Garage, Act I	Zappa	1603	'79	†
	Rykodisc	10530	'95	CS
Joe's Garage, Acts II and III	Zappa	(2)1502	'79	†
	Rykodisc	10531	'95	CS
Joe's Garage	Barking Pumpkin/ Capitol	(3)74206	'87	CS†
Joe's Garage, Acts I, II, and III	Rykodisc	(2)10060/61	'87	CD†
	Rykodisc	(2)10530/31	'95	CD
Tinsel Town Rebellion	Barking Pumpkin	(2)37336	'81	†
	Rykodisc	40166	'90	CD†
	Rykodisc	10532	'95	CD
Shut Up 'n' Play Yer Guitar	Barking Pumpkin	(3)38289	'81	†
	Rykodisc	(2)10028/29	'86	CD†
	Rykodisc	(3)10533-35	'95	CD
You Are What You Is	Barking Pumpkin	(2)37537	'81	†
	Rykodisc	40165	'90	CD†
	Rykodisc	10536	'95	CD
Ship Arriving Too Late to Save a Drowning Witch	Barking Pumpkin	38066	'82	†
	Barking Pumpkin/ Capitol	74235	'91	CS/CD†
	Rykodisc	10537	'95	CD
The Man from Utopia	Barking Pumpkin	38403	'83	†
	Barking Pumpkin/ Capitol	74245	'93	CD†
	Rykodisc	10538	'95	CD

Baby Snakes (soundtrack from 1979 movie)	Barking Pumpkin	1115	'82	†
	Barking Pumpkin/ Capitol	74219	'88	CS/CD†
	Rykodisc	10539	'95	CS/CD
Them or Us	Barking Pumpkin	(2)74200	'84	LP†
	Barking Pumpkin/ Capitol	74200		CS†
	Rykodisc	40027	'86	CD†
	Rykodisc	10543	'95	CD
Thing Fish	Barking Pumpkin	(3)74201	'84	†
	Rykodisc	(2)10020/21	'86	CD†
	Rykodisc	(2)10544/45	'95	CD
Frank Zappa Meets The Mothers of Prevention	Barking Pumpkin	74203	'85	†
	Rykodisc	10023	'86	CD†
	Rykodisc	10547	'95	CD
Does Humor Belong in Music (released in Europe in 1986)	Rykodisc	10548	'95	CD
Jazz from Hell	Barking Pumpkin/ Capitol	74205	'86	CS†
	Rykodisc	10030		CD†
	Rykodisc	10549	'95	CD
Guitar	Barking Pumpkin/ Capitol	(2)74212	'88	CS†
	Rykodisc	(2)10079/80	'88	CD†
	Rykodisc	(2)10550/51	'95	CD
Broadway the Hard Way	Barking Pumpkin/ Capitol	74218	'88	CS†
	Rykodisc	40096	'89	CD†
	Rykodisc	10552	'95	CD
The Best Band You Never Heard in Your Life	Barking Pumpkin/ Capitol	(2)74233	'91	CS/CD†
	Rykodisc	(2)10553/54	'95	CD
Make a Jazz Noise Here	Barking Pumpkin/ Capitol	(2)74234	'91	CS/CD†
	Rykodisc	(2)10555/56	'95	CD
Civilization, Phase III	Barking Pumpkin	(2)1	'94	CS/CD
Strictly Commercial: The Best of Frank Zappa	Rykodisc	40500	'95	LP/CS/CD

Reissues

We're Only In It for the Money/Lumpy Gravy	Rykodisc	40024	'86	CD†
Apostrophe/Over-Nite Sensation	Rykodisc	40025	'86	CD†

Beat the Boots

Beat the Boots	Foo-Eee	(8)70907	'91	CS
'Tis the Season to Be Jelly: The Mothers of Invention, Sweden 1967	Foo-Eee	70542	'91	CD
The Ark: The Mothers of Invention, Boston 1968	Foo-Eee	70538	'91	CD
Freaks and Motherfu*%!!@#: Fillmore East 1970	Foo-Eee	70539	'91	CD
Piquantique: Zappa, Stockholm and Sydney 1973	Foo-Eee	70544	'91	CD
Unmitigated Audacity: Zappa and The Mothers, Notre Dame University 1974	Foo-Eee	70540	'91	CD
Saarbrucken 1979	Foo-Eee	70543	'91	CD
Anyway the Wind Blows: Zappa, Paris 1979	Foo-Eee	70541	'91	CD
As An Am Zappa, New York 1981	Foo-Eee	70537	'91	CD

Beat the Boots # 2	Foo-Eee	(11)70372	'92	LP
	Foo-Eee	(7)70372	'92	CS
	Foo-Eee	(8)70372	'92	CD

You Can't Do That on Stage Anymore

(With a Box)	Rykodisc	(12)10092		CD
Sampler	Barking Pumpkin/ Capitol	74213	'88	CS†
Volume 1	Rykodisc	(2)10081/82	'88	CD†
	Rykodisc	10561/62	'95	CD
Volume 2	Barking Pumpkin/ Capitol	(3)74217	'88	CS†
	Rykodisc	(2)10083/84	'88	CD†
	Rykodisc	(2)10563/64	'95	CD
Volume 3	Rykodisc	(2)10085/86	'89	CD†
	Rykodisc	(2)10065/66	'95	CD
Volume 4	Barking Pumpkin/ Capitol	(2)74231	'91	CS†
	Rykodisc	(2)10087/88	'91	CD†
	Rykodisc	(2)10567/68	'95	CD
Volume 5	Rykodisc	(2)10089/90	'92	CD†
	Rykodisc	10569/70	'95	CD
Volume 6	Rykodisc	(2)10091/92	'92	CD†
	Rykodisc	(2)10571/72	'95	CD

Zappa Classical Recordings

Zappa, Vol. 1	Barking Pumpkin	38820	'83	†
reisssued as London Symphony Orchestra	Rykodisc	10022	'86	CD†
Boulez Conducts Zappa: The Perfect Stranger	Angel	38170	'84	†
	Barking Pumpkin/ Capitol	74242	'92	CS/CD†
	Rykodisc	10542	'95	CD
Francesco Zappa	Barking Pumpkin	74202	'84	†
	Rykodisc	10546	'95	CD
London Symphony Orchestra, Volume 2	Barking Pumpkin/ Capitol	74207	'87	CS†
London Symphony Orchestra, Volume I and II	Rykodisc	(2)10540/41	'95	CD
The Yellow Shark	Barking Pumpkin/ Capitol	71600	'93	CS/CD†
	Rykodisc	40560	'95	CS/CD

Various Artists

Zappa's Universe	Verve	513575	'93	CS/CD

Dweezil Zappa

Havin' a Bad Day	Rykodisc	10057	'87	CD†
My Guitar Wants to Kill Your Mama	Chrysalis	41633	'88	CS/CD†
Confessions	Barking Pumpkin/ Capitol	74232	'91	CS/CD†

Z (with Dweezil and Ahmet Zappa)

Shampoohorn	Barking Pumpkin/ Rhino	71760	'94	CS/CD†

LAURA NYRO

Born Laura Nigro on October 18, 1947, in the Bronx, New York; died April 9, 1997, in Danbury, Connecticut.

At the forefront of the female singer-songwriter movement in the late '60s, Laura Nyro received widespread critical acclaim for her second album *Eli and the Thirteenth Confession* and its follow-up *New York Tendaberry.* Nonetheless, she remained a cult favorite, as artists such as The Fifth Dimension, Blood, Sweat and Tears, Three Dog Night, and Barbra Streisand scored smash hits with pop-style renditions of her early compositions. Nyro retreated from the exigencies of the music business during the early '70s, reemerged several times later in the '70s and '80s, and recorded her first major label album in nine years in 1993.

Laura Nyro began playing piano at a very early age, ostensibly writing her first song at the age of eight. After attending Manhattan's High School of Music and Art, she signed with Verve Records in 1966 and made her first extended professional appearance at San Francisco's hungry i in early 1967. Her debut album, *More Than a New Discovery* (reissued by Columbia as *The First Songs*), contained "Wedding Bell Blues," "And When I Die," "Stoney End," "Blowin' Away," and "He's a Runner," yet was sorely overlooked by the record-buying public. At 1967's celebrated Monterey International Pop Festival, she played with a trio of black female backup singers as a soul revue, but the experiment proved less than successful and she was nearly booed off the stage.

Switching to Columbia Records, Laura Nyro's debut for the label, *Eli and the Thirteenth Confession,* was greeted by highly favorable critical reviews but barely sold despite the inclusion of "Sweet Blindness," "Eli's Coming," "Stoned Soul Picnic," and the overlooked "Woman's Blues." Although the public failed to recognize her exceptional songwriting, dynamic delivery, and fine piano accompaniment, a number of acts began recording her songs with astounding success. In 1968, The Fifth Dimension scored a smash with her "Stoned Soul Picnic," followed by "Sweet Blindness," the top hit "Wedding Bell Blues," and the major hits "Blowin' Away" and "Save the Country" through 1970. Blood, Sweat and Tears had a smash hit with "And When I Die" in 1969 and recorded "He's a Runner" on their third album. Three Dog Night hit with "Eli's Coming" and Barbra Streisand scored a smash with "Stoney End" in late 1970.

Laura Nyro's second Columbia album, *New York Tendaberry,* with "You Don't Love Me When I Cry" and "Sweet Lovin' Baby," became her best-selling album, yet *Christmas and the Beads of Sweat* sold less well despite yielding her only (minor) hit with a remake of Gerry Goffin and Carole King's "Up on the Roof." In 1971, under producers Kenny Gamble and Leon Huff, Nyro recorded *It's Gonna Take a Miracle,* an album of soul/rhythm-and-blues classics, with the Labelle trio, but she soon retired from the music business. She reemerged in 1975, recording the jazz-flavored *Smile* and touring again, but again withdrew in 1979. She recorded the neglected *Mother's Spiritual* for 1984 release and later wrote "Broken Rainbow," used as the title song to an award-winning documentary about the Native Americans' loss of their land. Nyro resumed touring in 1988, recorded *Live at the Bottom Line* for Cypress Records, and returned to Columbia Records for 1993's *Walk the Dog and Light the Light.* Laura Nyro died of ovarian cancer on April 9, 1997, in Danbury, Connecticut, at the age of 49.

Laura Nyro

More Than a New Discovery	Verve	3020	'67	†
reissued as The First Songs	Columbia	31410	'72	CD
Eli and the Thirteenth Confession	Columbia	9626	'68	CD
New York Tendaberry	Columbia	9737	'69	CD
Christmas and the Beads of Sweat	Columbia	30259	'70/'90	CD

It's Gonna Take a Miracle	Columbia	30987	'71	CD
Smile	Columbia	33912	'76/'91	CD
Season of Lights	Columbia	34331	'77	†
Nested	Columbia	35449	'78	†
Mother's Spiritual	Columbia	39215	'84	†
Live at the Bottom Line	Cypress	(2)6430	'89	LP†
	Cypress	6430	'89	CS/CD†
Walk the Dog and Light the Light	Columbia	52411	'93	CS/CD
Stoned Soul Picnic	Columbia/Legacy	(2)48880	'97	CD
Laura Nyro Tribute Album				
Time and Love	Astor Place	4007	'97	CD

PHIL OCHS

Born December 19, 1940, in El Paso, Texas; died April 9, 1976, in Far Rockaway, Queens, New York.

Author of some of the most potent and clever, topical and satirical songs of American folk music's "protest" era, Phil Ochs was regarded as Bob Dylan's only rival in the early '60s. Best remembered for his songs "I Ain't Marching Anymore," "There but for Fortune," and "Outside a Small Circle of Friends," Ochs never achieved mainstream success and was generally inactive during the '70s, ultimately committing suicide in 1976.

Phil Ochs studied journalism at Ohio State University, forming the folk duo The Sundowners with Jim Glover before dropping out to move to New York City in the early '60s. Ochs became involved with the *Broadside* magazine movement and debuted at Gerde's Folk City in Greenwich Village in August 1962. Signed to Elektra Records in 1964, his debut album contained "Talking Vietnam," "Too Many Martyrs," "The Power and the Glory," and his tribute to Woody Guthrie, "Bound for Glory." His second album, *I Ain't Marching Anymore,* established him at the forefront of the protest movement with its anthemic title song, "The Men Behind the Guns," and "Here's to the State of Mississippi," and included the satirical "Draft Dodger Rag." In the fall of 1965, Joan Baez scored a minor hit with Ochs' "There but for Fortune," included on his *In Concert* album, generally regarded as his finest acoustic work. The album also featured "Love Me, I'm a Liberal," "Cops of the World," "When I'm Gone," and the love song "Changes."

By 1966, the popularity of folk music was fading in favor of folk-rock, leading to a public rift between Phil Ochs and Bob Dylan, who had taken up electric guitar in 1965. Ochs moved to Los Angeles and switched to A&M Records, adapting elaborate arrangements for his debut for the label, *Pleasures of the Harbor,* which included his telling and satirical attack on apathy, "Outside a Small Circle of Friends." *Tape from California* contained "White Boots Marching in a Yellow Land" and one of the most potent antiwar songs of the '60s, "The War Is Over." Ochs appeared at protests during the 1968 Democratic Convention in Chicago. Following *Rehearsals for Retirement* and *Greatest Hits* (actually all new material, including "Chords of Fame" and the overlooked "Gas Station Women"), Ochs recorded *Gunfight at Carnegie Hall,* issued in Canada only.

During the early '70s, Phil Ochs lived in London and traveled extensively. He suffered damage to his vocal chords when assaulted in Africa and fell into fits of depression and bouts with alcoholism. Returning to New York, he organized a benefit for victims of the Chilean junta that had overthrown Salvador Allende in 1974, convincing Bob Dylan to appear. Phil Ochs last performed publicly in October 1975 and hanged himself to death at his sister's house in Far Rockaway, Queens, New York, on April 9, 1976, at the age of 35.

Still a revered and lamented figure, Phil Ochs' posthumous releases included early '60s recordings on Smithsonian/Folkways and Archives Alive, Elektra's *There but for Fortune,* A&M's *Chords of Fame* (which compiled his recordings for Elektra and A&M) and *The War Is Over,* and live sets on Rhino and Vanguard.

PHIL OCHS BIBLIOGRAPHY

Eliot, Marc. *Death of a Rebel.* Garden City, NY: Anchor Press, 1979; New York: Franklin Watts, 1989.

Schumacher, Michael. *There but for Fortune: The Life of Phil Ochs.* New York: Hyperion, 1996.

Phil Ochs

Songs for Broadside (Broadside #10)	Folkways	5320	'76	†
Broadside Tapes # 1 (Broadside #14)	Folkways	5362	'80	†
reissued as The Broadside Tapes, Volume 1 (recorded early '60s)	Smithsonian/Folkways	40008	'94	CS/CD
A Toast to Those Who Are Gone (recorded prior to 1964)	Archives Alive	70080	'89	CS/CD
Live at Newport (recorded 1963–1966)	Vanguard	77017	'96	CD
All the News That's Fit to Sing	Elektra	7269	'64	†
	Hannibal	4427	'94	CD
I Ain't Marching Anymore	Elektra	7287	'65	†
	Hannibal	4422	'94	CD
Phil Ochs Live in Concert	Elektra	7310	'66	†
	Rhino/Elektra	78007	'95	CD
There but for Fortune	Elektra	60832	'89	CS/CD
Pleasures of the Harbor	A&M	4133	'67	†
Tape from California	A&M	4148	'68	†
Rehearsals for Retirement	A&M	4181	'69	†
"Greatest Hits"	A&M	4253	'70	†
Gunfight at Carnegie Hall	A&M	9010	'74	†
	Mobile Fidelity	00794		CD†
Chords of Fame	A&M	(2)4599	'77	†
Greatest Hits	A&M	3125	'81	†
The War Is Over: The Best of Phil Ochs	A&M	5215	'88	CS/CD
There and Now: Live in Vancouver, 1968	Rhino	70778	'91	CS/CD
Farewells and Fantasies	Rhino	(3)73518	'97	CD

ROY ORBISON

Born April 23, 1936, in Vernon, Texas; died December 6, 1988, in Madison, Tennessee.

Achieving his first recognition as a rockabilly singer in the mid-'50s, Roy Orbison recorded for Sun Records alongside Elvis Presley, Carl Perkins, Johnny Cash, and Jerry Lee Lewis. Nonetheless, his greatest success came between 1960 and 1965 as a singles artist on Monument Records. There he recorded dramatic and emotional renditions of his own ballads delivered with a stunning tenor voice of extraordinary range and depth, certainly one of the most distinctive and engaging voices in the history of rock. Influencing artists such as Del Shannon, Bruce Springsteen, and Elvis Costello, Orbison scored more than fifteen major hits in the first half of the '60s, including "Only the Lonely," "Crying," and "Oh, Pretty Woman," his best-selling single and signature song. Little heard from after switching to MGM Records in 1965, Roy Orbison endured personal tragedies and diminished American popularity, rarely performing and recording from the late '60s to the mid-'80s. He eventually reemerged in 1986 to record *Class of '55* with former Sun labelmates Johnny Cash, Carl Perkins, and Jerry Lee Lewis. Thereby inspired to write and record again, Orbison recorded with the "supergroup" The Traveling Wilburys and recorded the most successful album of his career, *Mystery Girl*, in 1988.

ROY ORBISON (HULTON-DEUTSCH COLLECTION/CORBIS)

Roy Orbison was raised in Wink, Texas, where he took up guitar at the age of six and formed his own band, The Wink Westerners, in 1952. He attended North Texas University with Pat Boone and first recorded in early 1956 as leader of The Teen Kings at Norman Petty's studio in Clovis, New Mexico. Signed to the Memphis-based Sun label, Orbison's soaring voice was hardly suited to the "rockabilly" he recorded there, yet "Ooby Dooby" became a minor hit in the summer of 1956. He toured and recorded for Sun until 1958 without achieving another hit.

Roy Orbison moved to Nashville to concentrate on songwriting for Acuff-Rose Music, placing "Claudette," written for his wife, with The Everly Brothers in 1958. Briefly recording for RCA Records, he switched to Fred Foster's newly formed Monument label in late 1959. After the minor hit "Uptown," Orbison scored a smash with the classic "Only the Lonely," cowritten with Joe Melson. The song initiated a string of powerful, nearly operatic ballad hits cowritten with Melson such as "Blue Angel," "I'm Hurtin,'" and the top hit "Running Scared" (backed by Felice and Boudleaux Bryant's "Love Hurts"), recorded with string section, male backup voices, and a driving bolero-like crescendo. The smash hit "Crying" (again with Melson) was backed by the major hit "Candyman," written by Fred Neil, and Orbison's success continued with Cindy Walker's "Dream Baby," "Leah," "In Dreams," "Falling," and "Mean Woman Blues" (a near smash rhythm-and-blues hit) backed with "Blue Bayou." He first toured Great Britain in 1962 and, in 1963, he toured that country as headliner act to The Beatles and Gerry and The Pacemakers. The hits continued with Willie Nelson's "Pretty Paper," and two songs cowritten with Bill Dees, "It's Over" and the top hit classic "Oh, Pretty Woman."

After hits with "Goodnight" and "(Say) You're My Girl," Roy Orbison switched to MGM Records, but only "Ride Away" proved to be a major hit and, by 1968, he had dropped out of the charts. Dogged by personal problems (his wife was killed in a motorcycle accident on June 6, 1966; two of his three children died when his Nashville home burned on September 14, 1968), Orbison appeared in the silly 1967 movie *The Fastest Guitar Alive* and recorded entire albums of songs by Don Gibson and Hank Williams, as well as a duet effort with Hank Williams, Jr. Refusing to join rock 'n' roll "revival" shows and seldom touring the United States after the late '60s (although he continued to tour Europe and Great Britain regularly), Orbison eventually recorded new albums for Mercury, Monument, and

Elektra in 1975, 1977, and 1979, respectively. In 1977, he returned to American touring and saw Linda Ronstadt score a smash pop and country hit with "Blue Bayou."

In 1980, Roy Orbison achieved a minor pop and smash country hit in duet with Emmylou Harris on "That Lovin' You Feelin' Again" from the film *Roadie*. The following year, Don McLean scored a smash hit with his rendition of "Crying," and Van Halen achieved a near-smash with a remake of "Oh, Pretty Woman" in 1982. In 1986, he joined Sun Records alumni Johnny Cash, Carl Perkins, and Jerry Lee Lewis for *Class of '55*. The experience renewed his vigor for writing and recording, and he soon signed with Virgin Records and rerecorded nineteen of his hits for *In Dreams* under producer T-Bone Burnett. His rerecording of "In Dreams" was featured in the 1986 movie *Blue Velvet,* and, on September 30, he performed at an all-star tribute with Bruce Springsteen, Elvis Costello, Tom Waits, Bonnie Raitt, and others that was aired on the Cinemax cable network in December 1988 and released as an album one year later as *A Black and White Night Live*. He also scored a moderate country hit with k.d. lang on a remake of his "Crying" and later joined George Harrison, Bob Dylan, Jeff Lynne, and Tom Petty as Lefty Wilbury for The Traveling Wilburys' *Volume One* album, singing lead vocals on "Not Alone Any More."

Roy Orbison was inducted into the Rock and Roll Hall of Fame in 1987 and recorded a new album for Virgin Records in 1988. However, on December 6, 1988, he died of a heart attack in Madison, Tennessee, at the age of 52. The album, *Mystery Girl,* was released in early 1989 and became the best-selling album of his career. It featured "Careless Heart," "She's a Mystery to Me" (written by The Edge and Bono of U2), "In the Real World," and "A Love So Beautiful," and yielded a near-smash hit with "You Got It," written by Orbison, Jeff Lynne, and Tom Petty. Virgin Records later assembled *King of Hearts* for 1992 release.

ROY ORBISON BIBLIOGRAPHY

Amburn, Ellis. *Dark Star: The Roy Orbison Story*. New York: Carol Publishing Group, 1990.
Clayson, Alan. *Only the Lonely: Roy Orbison's Life and Legacy*. New York: St. Martin's Press, 1989.

Roy Orbison

At the Rock House	Sun	1260	'61	†
reissued as The Original Sound	Sun	113	'69	†
Sun Story, Volume 4	Sunnyvale	904	'77	†
The Sun Years	Rhino	70916	'89	CS/CD
Orbiting with Roy Orbison	Design	164		†
The RCA Days	RCA	9664		CS†
Early Orbison	Monument	18023	'64	†
Lonely and Blue	Monument	14002	'61	†
	Monument	21427		CS/CD†
	K-tel	75049	'95	CS/CD
Crying	Monument	14007	'62	†
	Monument	21428		CS/CD†
	Sony	75050	'95	CS/CD
In Dreams	Monument	18003	'63	†
	Monument	6620	'77	†
	Monument	21429		CS/CD†
	K-tel	75031	'95	CS/CD
There Is Only One Roy Orbison	MGM	4308	'65	†
	Polydor	841153	'89	CS†
	Polydor	841153	'89	CS†

The Orbison Way	MGM	4322	'66	†
	Polydor	841154	'89	CS†
Classic Roy Orbison	MGM	4379	'66	†
	Polydor	841155	'89	CS†
Roy Orbison Sings Don Gibson	MGM	4424	'66	†
	Polydor	841156	'89	CS†
Fastest Guitar Alive (soundtrack)	MGM	4475	'67	†
	CBS	45405		CS/CD†
Cry Softly, Lonely One	MGM	4514	'67	†
Many Moods	MGM	4636	'69	†
Great Songs	MGM	4659	'70	†
Roy Orbison and Hank Williams, Jr.	MGM	4683	'70	†
Hank Williams the Orbison Way	MGM	4835	'72	†
I'm Still in Love with You	Mercury	1045	'75	†
Regeneration	Monument	7600	'77	†
Laminar Flow	Elektra	198	'79/'89	CD
In Dreams	Virgin	(2)90604	'87	LP/CS/CD†
	Virgin	(2)86013		LP/CS/CD†
Mystery Girl	Virgin	91058	'89	LP/CS/CD†
	Virgin	86103		CS/CD
	Mobile Fidelity	00555	'91	CD†
A Black and White Night	Virgin	91295	'89	LP/CS/CD†
	Virgin	86133		CS/CD
King of Hearts	Virgin	86520	'92	CS/CD
The Great Roy Orbison—In Concert	Goldies	63122	'96	CD

Roy Orbison Anthologies and Compilations

Greatest Hits	Monument	14009	'62	†
	Monument	6619	'77	†
More of Roy Orbison's Greatest Hits	Monument	18024	'64	†
	Monument	6621	'77	†
Orbisongs	Monument	18035	'65	†
Very Best	Monument	18045	'66	†
	Monument	6622	'77	†
The All-Time Greatest Hits of Roy Orbison	Monument	(2)31484	'72	†
	Monument	(2)8600	'77	†
	Monument	44348	'88	CS/CD
The All-Time Greatest Hits of Roy Orbison, Volume 2	Monument	44349	'88	CS/CD
Our Love Song	Monument	45113	'89	CS/CD
Best-Loved Standards	Monument	45114	'89	CS/CD
Rare Orbison	Monument	45115	'89	CS/CD
The All-Time Greatest Hits of Roy Orbison, Volumes 1 and 2	Monument	45116	'89	CS/CD
Rare Orbison II	CBS	45404		†
	Sony	45404		CS/CD†
Roy Orbison Sings Lonely and Blue	Epic/Legacy	66219	'94	CD
Super Hits	Columbia/Legacy	67297	'95	CS/CD
For the Lonely: A Roy Orbison Anthology, 1956–1965	Rhino	(2)71493	'88	CS
	Rhino	71493	'88	CD
The Classic Roy Orbison (1965–1968)	Rhino	70711	'89	CS/CD
The Singles Collection (1965–1973)	Polydor	839234	'89	LP/CS/CD†
Ride Away	Polygram	847983		CS/CD

The Legendary Roy Orbison (1955–1985)	Sony	(4)46809	'90	CS/CD
Best of His Rare Classics	Curb/Warner Brothers 77481		'91	CS/CD
Greatest Hits "Live"	Remember	75031	'96	CD
The Legend	Hollywood/IMG	429		CS

Jerry Lee Lewis, Johnny Cash, Roy Orbison and Carl Perkins

Class of '55	Columbia	830002	'86	LP/CS/CD†
	Mercury Nashville	830002	'94	CS/CD

The Traveling Wilburys

Volume One	Wilbury	25796	'88	CS/CD

PENTANGLE

Bert Jansch (born November 3, 1943, in Glasgow, Scotland), acoustic guitar, vocals; John Renbourn (born in 1944 in London), acoustic guitar, sitar, vocals; Jacqui McShee, vocals; Danny Thompson (born April 1939), standup bass; and Terry Cox, drums.

One of the first British folk-rock bands, Pentangle performed exclusively on acoustic instruments until 1971, in contrast to their main competition, Fairport Convention. Formed in 1967, Pentangle featured the crystalline soprano voice of Jacqui McShee and the virtuoso guitar playing of Bert Jansch and John Renbourn. Their eclectic music encompassed traditional British folk songs, jazz instrumentals, blues songs, and contemporary original compositions. However, Pentangle attracted only a limited following in the United States, as virtually no British folk-rock band of the era achieved mass popularity in this country. Both Jansch and Renbourn recorded on their own while members of Pentangle and continued to do so after Pentangle's demise in 1973. At the beginning of the '90s, Pentangle reunited with McShee and Jansch for recordings on the Celtic label Green Linnet.

John Renbourn received his first guitar at the age of thirteen and became interested in folk music and the blues as a teenager. He performed around Guildford and moved to London in 1964, where he met guitarists Bert Jansch and Davy Graham. Jansch had performed in Edinburgh clubs before moving on to the London folk club circuit, recording an album of jazz-style instrumentals released on Vanguard Records in 1966. In late 1967, with bassist Danny Thompson, vocalist Jacqui McShee, and drummer Terry Cox, Renbourn and Jansch formed Pentangle. McShee had sung in folk clubs with her sister, while Thompson and Cox were experienced sessions musicians who had briefly played with Alexis Korner's Blues Incorporated.

Signed to Transatlantic Records (Reprise in the United States), Pentangle's debut album featured the outstanding playing of the guitarists and vocals dominated by McShee's crystalline soprano voice on traditional British folk songs, group-composed originals, plus The Staple Singers' "Hear My Call" and Jansch's "Mirage." Attracting a devoted cult following, the group's double-record set *Sweet Child,* comprising one record of studio recordings and the other of a 1968 concert, is often considered their finest work. Pentangle successfully toured the United States in 1969. *Basket of Light* produced the minor British hits "Once I Had a Sweetheart" and "Light Flight," whereas *Cruel Sister* introduced electric guitar to the group sound. In the meantime, Jansch and Renbourn recorded solo albums for Reprise and duet albums for Vanguard. After *Solomon's Seal,* Pentangle disintegrated in the spring of 1973.

Danny Thompson teamed with guitarist John Martyn for a while, as Bert Jansch recorded two albums in California that were released only in Great Britain. Jacqui McShee was a member of John Renbourn's band from 1974 to 1981. In the late '70s, Renbourn and Jansch hooked up with guitarist Stefan Grossman (a veteran of The Even Dozen Jug Band

and The Fugs), recording for Grossman's Kicking Mule label. In the early '80s, the original Pentangle reunited for *Open the Door,* with Jansch and McShee later recording *In the Round* for Varrick and two albums for the Celtic label Green Linnet. Renbourn began recording for the Flying Fish label in the early '80s and, by the mid-'80s, Renbourn and Grossman were recording for the Shanachie label. Jansch and Renbourn's *After the Dance* was released on Shanachie in 1992, and the following year Flying Fish issued *Wheel of Fortune,* recorded by Renbourn and multi-instrumentalist Robin Williamson of The Incredible String Band. Danny Thompson toured with Richard Thompson beginning in 1994, and the two recorded *Industry* for Hannibal Records, released in 1997.

Pentangle

Pentangle	Reprise	6315	'68	†
Sweet Child	Reprise	(2)6334	'69	†
Basket of Light	Reprise	6372	'70	†
	Transatlantic	205		CD†
Cruel Sister	Reprise	6430	'71	†
Reflection	Reprise	6463	'71	†
Solomon's Seal	Reprise	2100	'72	†
The Essential Pentangle, Volume 1	Transatlantic	602	'87	CD†
The Essential Pentangle, Volume 2	Transatlantic	606	'87	CD†
A Maid That's Deep in Love	Shanachie	79066	'87	CS/CD
Early Classics	Shanachie	79078	'92	CS/CD
Open the Door	Varrick	017	'85	CS
In the Round	Varrick	026	'86	CS/CD
So Early in the Spring	Green Linnet	3048	'90	CS/CD
Think of Tomorrow	Green Linnet	3057	'91	CS/CD

Bert Jansch

Lucky Thirteen	Vanguard	79212	'66	†
Birthday Blues	Reprise	6343	'69	†
Rosemary Lane	Reprise	6455	'71	†
Moonshine	Reprise	2129	'73	†
Strolling Down the Highway	Transatlantic	604		CD†
A Rare Conundrum	Kicking Mule	302	'78	†
Conundrum	Kicking Mule	303		CS
Best	Kicking Mule	334	'79	†
	Shanachie	99004	'92	CS/CD
Thirteen Down	Kicking Mule	309	'80	LP
Heartbreak	Hannibal	1312	'83	CS/CD
Sketches	Temple	2035	'90	CS/CD
When the Circus Comes to Town	Cooking Vinyl	092	'95	CD

Bert Jansch and John Renbourn

Stepping Stones	Vanguard	6506	'69	†
Jack Orion	Vanguard	6544	'71	†
After the Dance	Shanachie	99006	'92	CS/CD

John Renbourn

The Soho Years	Transatlantic	603	'87	CD†
John Renbourn (recorded 1965–1966)	Reprise	(2)6482	'73	†
Sir John Alot	Reprise	6344	'69	†
	Lost Lake	0084		†
	Shanachie	97021	'92	CS/CD

The Lady and the Unicorn	Reprise	6407	'71	†
	Lost Lake	0087		†
	Transatlantic	224		CD†
	Shanachie	97022	'92	CS/CD
Faro Annie	Reprise	2082	'72	†
A Maid in Bedlam	Shanachie	79004	'77	CS/CD
The Black Balloon	Kicking Mule	163	'79	†
	Shanachie	97009	'90	CS/CD
The Hermit	Transatlantic	336	'80	†
	Shanachie	97014	'91	CS/CD
The Enchanted Garden	Kicking Mule	312	'81	†
	Shanachie	79074	'90	CS/CD
Another Monday	Shanachie	95005		†
Live in America	Flying Fish	(2)27103	'82	LP†
	Flying Fish	90103		CS
	Flying Fish	70103		CD
The Nine Maidens	Flying Fish	378	'85	LP†
	Flying Fish	90378	'85	CS
	Flying Fish	70378	'86	CD
Ship of Fools	Flying Fish	466	'88	LP†
	Flying Fish	90466	'88	CS
	Flying Fish	70466	'88	CD
John Renbourn and Stefan Grossman				
Stefan Grossman and John Renbourn	Kicking Mule	152	'78	CS
Under the Volcano	Kicking Mule	162	'80	CS
Live	Shanachie	95001	'85	CS/CD
The Three Kingdoms	Shanachie	95006	'87	CS/CD
Snap a Little Owl	Shanachie	97003	'89	CS/CD
John Renbourn and Robin Williamson				
Wheel of Fortune	Flying Fish	90626	'93	CS
		70626	'93	CD
Richard Thompson and Danny Thompson				
Industry	Hannibal	1414	'97	CD

PETER, PAUL AND MARY

Peter Yarrow (born May 31, 1938, in New York City), guitar, tenor vocals; (Noel) Paul Stookey
(born November 30, 1937, in Baltimore, Maryland), guitar, baritone vocals; and Mary Travers
(born November 7, 1937, in Louisville, Kentucky), soprano vocals.

Scoring a series of major hits between 1962 and 1969, Peter, Paul and Mary became the
most popular and successful folk group of the '60s. Key figures in the ascension of folk music, Peter, Paul and Mary introduced and popularized the compositions of songwriters Bob
Dylan, Gordon Lightfoot, and John Denver. The trio's huge commercial success exposed
both the folk and protest movements to a mass audience and opened the way for the later
successes of Bob Dylan and "folk-rock" music. Disbanding in 1970, Peter, Paul and Mary
pursued individual projects until reuniting in 1978. Expanding their touring schedule in
1983, Peter, Paul and Mary returned to recording in the late '80s as folk music enjoyed a
renaissance with the likes of Tracy Chapman and Suzanne Vega.

PETER, PAUL AND MARY (UPI/CORBIS-BETTMANN)

Peter, Paul and Mary were brought together by manager Albert Grossman in New York City's Greenwich Village during 1961. Peter Yarrow was a Cornell University graduate in psychology who had worked for a time as a solo artist and appeared at the 1960 Newport Folk Festival. Noel Paul Stookey had led a high school rock band before pursuing a career around Greenwich Village as a standup comic. He encouraged former folk group member Mary Travers to return to singing after her appearance in the flop Broadway show, *The Next President*. Conducting intensive rehearsals for seven months, Peter, Paul and Mary debuted at The Bitter End in Greenwich Village and signed with Warner Brothers Records.

Peter, Paul and Mary's debut album became a top album hit, staying on the charts for well over three years. It included standard folk material such as Reverend Gary Davis' "If I Had My Way," Hedy West's "500 Miles," and Pete Seeger's "Where Have All the Flowers Gone," and original compositions by Yarrow and Stookey. It yielded a moderate hit with "Lemon Tree" and a near-smash hit with "If I Had a Hammer," coauthored by Seeger. Quickly thrust into the forefront of the folk movement, Peter, Paul and Mary became favorites on the college circuit and frequently performed at political rallies and protest marches. Their second album, *(Moving),* also became a best-seller, remaining on the album charts for nearly two years. It produced a smash hit with "Puff, The Magic Dragon," written by Yarrow and Leonard Lipton, moderate hits with "Stewball" and "Tell It on the Mountain," and contained Woody Guthrie's "This Land Is Your Land."

With *In the Wind,* Peter, Paul and Mary began featuring songs by then-unknown contemporary songwriters. The smash successes of "Blowin' in the Wind" and "Don't Think Twice, It's All Right" introduced Bob Dylan to a wider audience and bolstered the burgeoning "folk-protest" movement. Following the live double-record set *In Concert,* the trio recorded *A Song Will Rise,* which contained the first hit version of Gordon Lightfoot's "For Lovin' Me," and *See What Tomorrow Brings,* which included Lightfoot's "Early Morning Rain" and Tom Paxton's "Last Thing on My Mind."

The *Peter, Paul and Mary Album* featured Laura Nyro's "And When I Die" and Richard Farina's "Pack Up Your Sorrows" and was followed by perhaps their finest albums, *Album 1700* and *Late Again. Album 1700* produced a near-smash hit with Stookey's collaborative tongue-in-cheek "I Dig Rock and Roll Music" while containing John Denver's "Leaving on a Jet Plane" (a top pop and easy-listening hit when released as a single two years later) and some of the group's most memorable compositions, including the touching "House Song," Yarrow's antiwar "The Great Mandella (The Wheel of Life)," and the classic "The Song Is Love." *Late Again* included "Hymn" and "Rich Man, Poor Man," coauthored by Stookey and Yarrow, respectively, and Tim Hardin's "Reason to Believe," and yielded a moderate hit with Bob Dylan's "Too Much of Nothing."

Following *Peter, Paul and Mommy* and the major hit "Day Is Done," Peter Yarrow, Paul Stookey and Mary Travers went their separate ways in 1970. Stookey fared the best of the three as a solo artist, scoring a major hit with "Wedding Song (There Is Love)" from the excellent *Paul And* album in 1971. By the mid-'70s, Paul Stookey had retreated to Maine and Peter Yarrow had become involved in television and record production work, leaving Mary Travers as the only former member to perform extensively. In 1976, Yarrow produced Mary MacGregor's best-selling *Torn Between Two Lovers* album, coauthoring the top hit title song. He also coproduced the 1978 CBS animated television special, "Puff, The Magic Dragon," based on the song. He later supervised the soundtracks to two more animated television specials based on the song.

In 1978, Peter, Paul and Mary reunited at the Survival Sunday benefit show in California, subsequently recording *Reunion* for Warner Brothers. They performed thirty to fifty concerts a year until 1983, when they began playing around 100 engagements a year. Without a major label deal during most of the '80s, Peter, Paul and Mary eventually recorded *No Easy Walk to Freedom* for the small Gold Castle label, followed by the Christmas album *A Holiday Celebration*. Two Peter, Paul and Mary PBS television specials fared well in the late '80s and their Gold Castle recordings were reissued by Warner Brothers in 1992. By 1995, Peter, Paul and Mary had returned to their original label, Warner Brothers, for *Lifelines*, recorded with Pete Seeger, Ramblin' Jack Elliott, Holly Near, Judy Collins, and Emmylou Harris. *Lifelines Live,* from 1996, featured Odetta, Tom Paxton, and John Sebastian.

Peter, Paul and Mary

Peter, Paul and Mary (Moving)	Warner Brothers	1449	'62	CS/CD
	Warner Brothers	1473	'63	CD
In the Wind	Warner Brothers	1507	'63	†
	Warner Brothers	26224	'90	CD
In Concert	Warner Brothers	(2)1555	'64	†
	Warner Brothers	1555		CS
	Warner Brothers	(2)1555		CD
A Song Will Rise	Warner Brothers	1589	'65	†
	Warner Brothers	26225	'90	CD
See What Tomorrow Brings	Warner Brothers	1615	'65	†
	Warner Brothers	26654	'91	CD
Peter, Paul and Mary Album	Warner Brothers	1648	'66	†
	Warner Brothers	26653	'91	CD
Album 1700	Warner Brothers	1700	'67	CS/CD
Late Again	Warner Brothers	1751	'68	†
	Warner Brothers	26666	'92	CD
Peter, Paul and Mommy	Warner Brothers	1785	'69	CS/CD
Best (Ten Years Together)	Warner Brothers	2552	'70	†
	Warner Brothers	3105	'92	CS/CD
Reunion	Warner Brothers	3231	'78	CS
Such Is Love (recorded 1981)	Warner Brothers	47084	'98	CS/CD
No Easy Walk to Freedom	Gold Castle	71301	'87/'89	LP/CS/CD†
	Warner Brothers	45071	'92	CS/CD
A Holiday Celebration	Gold Castle	71316	'88/'89	LP/CS/CD†
	Warner Brothers	45070	'92	CS/CD
Flowers and Stones	Gold Castle		'90	†
	Warner Brothers	45069	'92	CS/CD
Peter, Paul and Mommy, Too	Warner Brothers	45216	'93	CS/CD
	Warner Brothers	45240	'93	CS

Lifelines	Warner Brothers	45851	'95	CS/CD
Lifelines Live	Warner Brothers	46298	'96	CS/CD
Mary Travers				
Mary	Warner Brothers	1907	'71	†
Morning Glory	Warner Brothers	2609	'72	†
All My Choices	Warner Brothers	2677	'73	†
Circles	Warner Brothers	2795	'74	†
It's in Every One of Us	Chrysalis	1168	'78	†
Paul Stookey				
Paul And	Warner Brothers	1912	'71	†
Noel—One Night Stand	Warner Brothers	2674	'73	†
Bodyworks	Gold Castle	71333	'90	CS/CD†
Peter Yarrow				
Peter	Warner Brothers	2599	'72	†
That's Enough for Me	Warner Brothers	2730	'73	†
Hard Times	Warner Brothers	2860	'75	†
Love Songs	Warner Brothers	2891	'75	†

WILSON PICKETT

Born March 18, 1941, in Prattville, Alabama.

One of the most popular male black singers of the '60s, comparable to only Otis Redding, Wilson Pickett helped introduce the aggressive rhythmic style of soul music. Aided immeasurably by the excellent studio bands backing him at the Stax Studio in Memphis, Tennessee, and the Fame Studios in Muscle Shoals, Alabama, Pickett scored a series of rhythm-and-blues and pop hits on Atlantic Records between 1963 and 1972, including the classics "In the Midnight Hour," "Mustang Sally," and "Funky Broadway." Recording for a variety of labels since leaving Atlantic Records in 1972, he failed to reestablish himself in the '80s and '90s. Wilson Pickett was inducted into the Rock and Roll Hall of Fame in 1991.

Raised in rural Prattville, Alabama, Wilson Pickett moved to Detroit at the age of sixteen and made his professional debut as lead singer of the gospel quartet The Violinaires in the late '50s. From 1961 to 1963, he manned the Detroit vocal group The Falcons, authoring and singing lead on their smash 1962 rhythm-and-blues hit "I Found a Love." Pickett subsequently went solo, joining Lloyd Price's Double L label, where he wrote and recorded "If You Need Me" (a smash R&B hit for Solomon Burke in 1963) and scored a near-smash R&B hit with "It's Too Late."

Signing with Atlantic Records in 1964, Wilson Pickett completed his early recordings in Memphis with Booker T. Jones and Steve Cropper of The MG's. Cropper coauthored three of his early hits, the classic "In the Midnight Hour" (a major pop and top rhythm-and-blues hit) and "Don't Fight It" (a smash R&B hit) from his debut Atlantic album, and "634-5789" (another major pop and top R&B hit) from *The Exciting Wilson Pickett,* the album that established him as a major soul star. That album also included the major R&B hit "Ninety-Nine and a Half (Won't Do)," Bobby Womack's "She's So Good to Me," and the top R&B and smash pop hit "Land of 1,000 Dances" (originally a minor hit for its author Chris Kenner in 1963), all recorded at the Fame Studios in Muscle Shoals, Alabama.

Wilson Pickett subsequently scored smash R&B and major pop hits with "Mustang Sally," a remake of "I Found a Love," and Dyke and The Blazers' "Funky Broadway," all recorded in Muscle Shoals. After the R&B smashes "I'm in Love" and "She's Lookin' Good," Pickett teamed with songwriter-producer Bobby Womack in 1968 for *Midnight Mover,* which yielded a smash R&B and major pop hit with Womack's title song. In 1969, Pickett achieved a major pop hit with The Beatles' "Hey Jude" (recorded with guitarist Duane Allman), followed in 1970 by the novelty crossover hit "Sugar Sugar." Later, in 1970, Pickett worked with producers Kenny Gamble and Leon Huff at Sigma Sound Studios in Philadelphia, and the resulting album *In Philadelphia* yielded two major crossover hits with "Engine Number Nine" and "Don't Let the Green Grass Fool You."

After the crossover hits "Don't Knock My Love—Part 1" and "Fire and Water," recorded in Muscle Shoals, Wilson Pickett left Atlantic Records for RCA, with minimal success. He later recorded for several different record companies, including his own Wicked label, but failed to achieve another major pop or rhythm-and-blues hit. Pickett joined Motown Records in 1987 and was inducted into the Rock and Roll Hall of Fame in 1991.

Wilson Pickett

It's Too Late	Double L	8300	'64	†
In the Midnight Hour	Atlantic	8114	'65	†
	Rhino	71275	'93	CS/CD
The Exciting Wilson Pickett	Atlantic	8129	'66	†
	Rhino	71276	'93	CS/CD
Wicked Pickett	Atlantic	8138	'67	†
The Sound of Wilson Pickett	Atlantic	8145	'67	†
Best	Atlantic	8151	'67	†
I'm in Love	Atlantic	8175	'68	†
	Rhino	72218	'95	CD
Midnight Mover	Atlantic	8183	'68	†
Hey, Jude	Atlantic	8215	'69	†
Right On	Atlantic	8250	'70	†
In Philadelphia	Atlantic	8270	'70	†
	Rhino	72219	'95	CD
Best, Volume 2	Atlantic	8290	'71	†
Don't Knock My Love	Atlantic	8300	'71	†
Greatest Hits	Atlantic	(2)501	'73	†
Best	Atlantic	81283	'85	LP/CS/CD†
	Rhino	81283		CS/CD†
Greatest Hits	Atlantic	81737	'87	CD†
	Rhino	81737		CD
Great Wilson Pickett Hits	Wand	672	'66	†
Wickedness	Trip	8010	'71	†
Mr. Magic Man	RCA	4858	'73	†
Miz Lena's Boy	RCA	0312	'73	†
Pickett in the Pocket	RCA	0495	'74	†
Join Me and Let's Be Free	RCA	0856	'75	†
	RCA	2149	'77	†
Chocolate Mountain	Wicked	9001	'76	†
A Funky Situation	Big Tree	76011	'78	†
I Want You	EMI-America	17019	'79	†
Right Track	EMI-America	17043	'81	†
American Soul Man	Motown	6244	'87	CD†
A Man and a Half: The Best of Wilson Pickett	Rhino	(2)70287	'92	CS/CD
Very Best	Rhino	71212	'93	CS/CD

PINK FLOYD

Roger "Syd" Barrett (born January 6, 1946, in Cambridge, England), lead guitar, vocals; Rick Wright (born July 28, 1945, in London, England), keyboards, vocals; Roger Waters (born September 6, 1944, in Great Bookham, Surrey, England), bass, piano, vocals; and Nick Mason (born January 27, 1945, in Birmingham, England), drums. Barrett was replaced in 1968 by David Gilmour (born March 6, 1944, in Cambridge).

PINK FLOYD (HULTON-DEUTSCH COLLECTION/CORBIS)

Generally regarded as the first "underground" group to emerge from the London music scene of the '60s, Pink Floyd was probably the first British psychedelic band, due in large part to the lead guitar playing and surrealistic, mystically obsessed lyrics of founder Syd Barrett. The first British band to utilize a light show in performance, Pink Floyd won a devoted following with their excellent debut album, *The Piper at the Gates of Dawn.* However, Barrett dropped out of the group in 1968, due to psychological problems and/or psychedelic drug abuse, after which he became a mysterious and inscrutable cult idol whose following persists to this day. With bassist Roger Waters assuming the role of principal songwriter, Pink Floyd became one of the first bands of the progressive rock movement, featuring elaborate productions with choirs and sophisticated orchestrations and the keyboard-synthesizer playing of Rick Wright. Developing a spectacular performance style perhaps unmatched in the history of rock, Pink Floyd used massive lighting and sound systems and presented their songs in highly theatrical form, complete with massive stage props. Pink Floyd eventually broke through into mass popularity with 1973's *The Dark Side of the Moon,* a monumental album concerned with lunacy and alienation as wrought by contemporary society. The album established the group as "superstars," selling thirteen million copies in the United States (thirty million worldwide) and remaining on the album charts a record fourteen years. Following their ambitious *The Wall* album and tour, Roger Waters left Pink Floyd acrimoniously in 1984 to pursue a modest solo career. Pink Floyd eventually regrouped without Waters in 1987 for *A Momentary Lapse of Reason* and massive concert tours in 1988 and 1994. Pink Floyd was inducted into the Rock and Roll Hall of Fame in 1996.

Roger "Syd" Barrett attended school with Roger Waters and David Gilmour in the early '60s in Cambridge. Barrett moved to London after school, where he took up guitar and played in several groups, including a folk duo with Gilmour. Waters moved to London to study architecture and met Rick Wright and Nick Mason in an architecture class. In 1964, Waters, Mason, and Wright formed Sigma 6, which later became The T-Set and The Abdabs. The Abdabs broke up in late 1965 and Mason, Wright, and Waters recruited guitarist Syd Barrett for a new group, dubbed Pink Floyd by Barrett. By March 1966, Pink Floyd had obtained their first regular engagement at London's Marquee club, where they experimented with feedback and lighting effects. In October, they moved to London's Sound/Light Workshop, where they were accompanied by a light show, the first of its kind in Great Britain. Becoming the house band at the UFO Club by year's end, Pink Floyd signed with EMI Records (the small, experimental Tower label in the United States) in March 1967.

Pink Floyd's first single, Barrett's "Arnold Layne," concerned a perverted transvestite and proved so controversial that even "underground" Radio London banned the song, yet it became a major British hit. Barrett's "See Emily Play" became a smash British hit in the spring and Pink Floyd's debut album was released in the United States near the end of 1967. Critically acclaimed as one of the most original albums of the '60s, *The Piper at the Gates of Dawn* was dominated by Barrett's surreal, mystical songwriting. However, the group's next three British singles fared poorly as Pink Floyd toured America for the first time in October 1967.

Barrett's behavior, already erratic, began to deteriorate and Dave Gilmour joined the group as second guitarist in early 1968. By April, Barrett had left amid rumors of drug abuse and bizarre stories of his unpredictable behavior. Between 1968 and 1970, Barrett recorded on several occasions, often with Gilmour and Wright. Two albums of his recordings were released in 1970 and eventually repackaged as a double-record set for United States release in 1974. Each album was issued in CD form in 1990 and 1989's *Opel* comprised alternate takes and unreleased material from the sessions. All three albums were included on 1994's *Crazy Diamond.* Inspiring a devoted cult following that persists to this day, Barrett's influence can be seen in the work of many '80s acts, most notably Robyn Hitchcock. Syd Barrett remains a mysterious and enigmatic figure, seldom appearing in public.

With Barrett's departure, Pink Floyd reverted to a quartet and Roger Waters began assuming the role of chief songwriter. *A Saucerful of Secrets* contained his "Let There Be More Light" and "Set Controls for the Heart of the Sun." In the summer of 1969, they first toured with a custom-built quadraphonic sound system as their soundtrack to the film *More* was released. At the beginning of 1970, Pink Floyd's double-record set *Ummagumma* was issued on EMI's new "underground" label Harvest (and later reissued on Capitol). Their first moderately successful album in the United States, *Ummagumma* comprised one live album and one studio album.

In 1970, Waters recorded a soundtrack album, *Music from "The Body,"* with electronics wizard Ron Geesin. Pink Floyd's *Atom Heart Mother* was debuted at the Bath Festival in England during June and the album featured choir, orchestra, and remarkably diverse sounds under the influence of Geesin. Pink Floyd's stage shows became more elaborate and, in the summer of 1971, an outdoor concert in London utilized a sixty-foot inflatable octopus. The group-produced *Meddle* included the instrumental "One of These Days" and the twenty-three-minute-plus "Echoes," one of their most popular songs.

Following the soundtrack to the film *Le Vallee* entitled *Obscured by Clouds,* Pink Floyd spent nine months recording their next album. Premiered live in London in 1972 using more than nine tons of equipment, *The Dark Side of the Moon* comprised entirely songs written by Roger Waters and became an instant best-seller, establishing Gilmour as a guitar hero and the group as "superstars." Dealing with alienation and madness as caused by the pressures of contemporary society, the album yielded Pink Floyd's first major American hit, "Money," and included group favorites such as "Brain Damage" and "Time." The album sold millions of copies worldwide and remained on the American album charts for *more than fourteen years.* The group spent much of 1973 performing the album in its entirety in an elaborately staged production.

Pink Floyd's *Wish You Were Here,* recorded for their new label Columbia, became a best-seller and featured Gilmour's title song, the classic "Welcome to the Machine," and Waters' tribute to Syd Barrett, "Shine on You Crazy Diamond." Continuing to explore the themes of repression, alienation, and loneliness, Pink Floyd's *Animals* depicted society as divided into three castes, dogs, pigs, and sheep, and the album included songs for each. Their massive tour in support of the album utilized tons of musical and lighting equipment and, in performance, featured a huge flying pig. Rick Wright and David Gilmour each recorded solo albums released in 1978 and Pink Floyd reconvened for new recordings in April 1979.

In late 1979, Pink Floyd issued their next album, *The Wall,* almost entirely composed by Roger Waters. Another bleak and gloomy view of modern society, the album was considered their most ambitious and personal work in years and stayed on the album charts for more than two years, selling more than ten million copies in the United States. The album contained group favorites such as "Is There Anybody Out There?" "Nobody Home," and "Comfortably Numb," and produced a minor hit with "Run Like Hell" and a top hit with the controversial "Another Brick in the Wall (Part II)." The 1980 tour in support of *The Wall* was so massive that it was performed in only three cities, London, New York, and Los Angeles. It was one of the most elaborate rock productions ever mounted, utilizing a thirty-foot-high, stage-wide wall of cardboard blocks that were toppled before the end of the shows. The production featured films, sophisticated lighting, and gigantic plastic inflatables in one of the most awesome and spectacular performances in rock history. The album later served as the basis for the grim, violent 1982 movie *The Wall,* starring Bob Geldof of The Boomtown Rats and directed by Alan Parker.

Rick Wright left Pink Floyd after the tour and Nick Mason recorded the solo album *Fictitious Sports* in 1981. Following 1983's desultory *The Final Cut,* essentially a Roger Waters solo album, Pink Floyd dissolved. Dave Gilmour and Roger Waters each recorded solo albums for Columbia Records in 1984. In 1986, Waters sued for formal dissolution of Pink Floyd, but, in 1987, Gilmour, Rick Wright, and Nick Mason reconstituted the group for *A Momentary Lapse of Reason,* entirely written by Gilmour. The album yielded a minor hit with "Learning to Fly" and remained on the album charts for more than a year. With eight-piece accompaniment, the three toured arenas in 1987 and stadiums in 1988. Waters countered with the concept album *Radio K.A.O.S.* and his own tour in 1987.

Pink Floyd toured internationally in 1989 and, in July 1990, *The Wall* was performed as a benefit for the Memorial Fund for Disaster Relief at the Berlin Wall by Roger Waters and a host of others, including Paul Carrack, Van Morrison, Sinead O'Connor, Joni Mitchell, and Levon Helm and Rick Danko of The Band. In 1991, David Palmer and The Royal Philharmonic Orchestra recorded *The Music of Pink Floyd: Orchestral Maneuvers,* and, in 1992, Waters recorded *Amused to Death* with guitarist Jeff Beck. In 1994, Pink Floyd issued *The Division Bell* on Sony and toured once again. The tour produced the 1995 live set *Pulse.* Pink Floyd was inducted into the Rock and Roll Hall of Fame in 1996.

PINK FLOYD BIBLIOGRAPHY

McDonald, Bruno (editor). *Pink Floyd: through the eyes of . . . the band, its fans, friends, and foes.* New York: Da Capo Press, 1997.

Miles. *Pink Floyd: Another Brick.* London: Omnibus Press, 1980.

Schaffner, Nicholas. *Saucerful of Secrets: The Pink Floyd Odyssey.* New York: Harmony Books, 1991.

Watkinson, Mike, and Pete Anderson. *Crazy Diamond: Syd Barrett and the Dawn of Pink Floyd.* London: Omnibus Press, 1990.

Syd Barrett

| The Madcap Laughs and "Barrett" | Harvest | (2)11314 | '74 | † |
| Barrett | Capitol | 46606 | '90 | CS†/CD |

The Madcap Laughs	Capitol	46607	'90	CS†/CD
Opel	Capitol	91206	'89	CS†/CD
Crazy Diamond	Capitol	(3)81412	'94	CD†
Octopus (The Best Of)	Cleopatra	5771	'92	CD
Roger Waters and Ron Geesin				
Music from "The Body"	Harvest	751	'70	†
	Restless/Retro	72395	'90	CS†/CD
Pink Floyd				
The Piper at the Gates of Dawn	Tower	5093	'67	†
	Capitol	46384	'87	CS/CD
A Saucerful of Secrets	Tower	5131	'68	†
	Capitol	46383	'87	CS/CD
A Nice Pair (reissue of the above two)	Harvest	(2)11257	'73	†
	Capitol	11257		CS†
More (soundtrack)	Tower	5169	'69	†
	Harvest	11198	'73	†
	Capitol	16230	'85	†
	Capitol	46386		CS†/CD
Relics (recorded 1967–1969)	Harvest	759	'71	†
	Capitol	16234	'83	CS
	Capitol	35603	'96	CD
Ummagumma	Harvest	(2)388	'69	†
	Capitol	46404		CS/CD
Atom Heart Mother	Harvest	382	'70	†
	Capitol	16337	'85	†
	Capitol	46381		CS/CD
	Mobile Fidelity	00595	'93	CD†
	Mobile Fidelity	202	'94	LP†
Meddle	Harvest	832	'71	†
	Capitol	46034		CS/CD
	Mobile Fidelity	00518		CD†
Obscured by Clouds	Harvest	11078	'72	†
	Capitol	16330	'85	†
	Capitol	46385		CS/CD
The Dark Side of the Moon	Harvest	11163	'73	†
	Capitol	46001		CS/CD
	Mobile Fidelity	00517	'88	CD†
The Dark Side of the Moon XX	Capitol	81479	'93	CD†
Works (recorded 1968–1973)	Capitol	12276	'83	CS
	Capitol	46478		CD
Gift Set	Capitol	91340		CS/CD†
Wish You Were Here	Columbia	33453	'75	CS/CD
	Columbia/Legacy	53753	'93	CD†
Animals	Columbia	34474	'77	CS/CD
The Wall	Columbia	(2)36183	'79	CS/CD
	Mobile Fidelity	(2)00537	'90	CD†
A Collection of Great Dance Songs (1975–1981)	Columbia	37680	'81	CS/CD
The Final Cut	Columbia	38243	'83	CS/CD
A Momentary Lapse of Reason	Columbia	40599	'87	CS/CD
Delicate Sound of Thunder	Columbia	(2)44484	'88	CS/CD

The Division Bell	Columbia	64200	'94	CS/CD
Pulse	Columbia	(2)67065	'95	CS/CD

David Palmer and The Royal Philharmonic Orchestra

The Music of Pink Floyd: Orchestral Maneuvers	RCA	57960	'91	CS/CD

London Philharmonic Orchestra

Us and Them: Symphonic Pink Floyd	Point Music	446623	'95	CS/CD

Tribute Album

A Saucerful of Pink: Tribute to Pink Floyd	Cleopatra	(2)9551	'95	CD

David Gilmour

David Gilmour	Columbia	35388	'78	CS/CD
About Face	Columbia	39296	'84	CS/CD

Richard (Rick) Wright

Wet Dream	Columbia	35559	'78	†

Nick Mason

Fictitious Sports	Columbia	37307	'81	†

Nick Mason and Rick Fenn

Profiles	Columbia	40142	'85	†
	K-tel	40142	'95	CS/CD

Roger Waters

The Pros and Cons of Hitchhiking	Columbia	39290	'84	CS/CD
Radio K.A.O.S.	Columbia	40795	'87	CS/CD
Amused to Death	Columbia	47127	'92	CS/CD
	Columbia/Legacy	64426	'94	CD
The Wall: Berlin 1990	Mercury	(2)846611	'90	CS/CD

GENE PITNEY

Born February 17, 1941, in Hartford, Connecticut.

Gene Pitney was a successful singles artist during the '60s, scoring numerous hits featuring his dramatic tenor voice on songs written by Burt Bacharach and Hal David and Barry Mann and Cynthia Weil. An accomplished songwriter, Pitney composed the hits "Rubber Ball" (Bobby Vee), "Hello Mary Lou" (Ricky Nelson), and "He's a Rebel" (The Crystals). Recording a diversity of material, including country-and-western albums with George Jones and Melba Montgomery, he also assisted The Rolling Stones in recording their *12 X 5* album, recorded the Jagger-Richards composition "That Girl Belongs to Yesterday," and made some of the earliest recordings of songs written by Randy Newman. Gene Pitney's popularity waned in the United States in the late '60s, yet he continued to tour Europe and England regularly while becoming involved in the world of finance.

Gene Pitney grew up in Rockville, Connecticut, and studied piano, drums, and guitar as a child. He began writing songs and performing with his group The Genials in high school and made his first recordings for Decca in 1959 with Ginny Arnell as Jamie and Jane. He also recorded as Billy Bryan for Blaze Records and under his own name for Festival Records in 1960. His first major success came as a songwriter, composing the smash hits "Rubber Ball" for Bobby Vee, "Hello Mary Lou" for Ricky Nelson, and "He's a Rebel" for The Crystals. In 1961, Pitney dropped out of college to concentrate on music, signing with Musicor Records and scoring his first moderate hit with his own "(I Wanna) Love My Life Away," followed by Carole King and Gerry Goffin's "Every Breath I Take," coproduced by Phil Spector. His *Only Love Can Break a Heart* album yielded major hits with "Town Without Pity," "Half Heaven—Half Heartache," and "True Love Never Runs Smooth," and smash hits with two Burt Bacharach—Hal David compositions, "(The Man Who Shot) Liberty Valance" and "Only Love Can Break a Heart." Pitney hit with "Mecca" and "Twenty Four Hours from Tulsa," another Bacharach-David composition, in 1963. He also toured Great Britain that year and met The Rolling Stones, subsequently scoring a moderate American and near-smash British hit with Mick Jagger and Keith Richards' "That Girl Belongs to Yesterday" and assisting The Rolling Stones in the recording of their *12 X 5* album.

In 1964, Gene Pitney had near-smash hits with "It Hurts to Be in Love" and "I'm Gonna Be Strong," the latter written by Barry Mann and Cynthia Weil, and began recording albums in foreign languages. In 1965 and 1966, he recorded country albums with George Jones and Melba Montgomery, scoring major country hits with "I've Got Five Dollars and It's Saturday Night" and "Louisiana Mama" with Jones and "Baby, Ain't That Fine" with Montgomery. Major pop hits for Pitney through 1968 included "Last Chance to Turn Around" and "She's a Heartbreaker," and the Mann-Weil compositions "Looking Through the Eyes of Love" and "Backstage," both smash British hits. He also recorded the Randy Newman songs "Nobody Needs Your Love," "Something's Gotten Hold of My Heart," and "Just One Smile," all smash British hits.

Gene Pitney never achieved another major pop hit in the United States and his popularity faded in this country in the late '60s. Nonetheless, he continued to tour Britain and Europe while avoiding the "oldies" revival circuit. In 1974, he cut his touring schedule to six months a year, as he became involved in real estate and stock market investments. Pitney later scored a British near-smash hit with a remake of "Something's Gotten Hold of My Heart" in duet with Marc Almond in 1988.

Gene Pitney

Many Sides of Gene Pitney	Musicor	3001	'62	†
Only Love Can Break a Heart	Musicor	3003	'62	†
Sings Just for You	Musicor	3004	'63	†
Blue Gene	Musicor	3006	'63	†
Meets the Fair Young Ladies of Folkland	Musicor	3007	'64	†
Italiano	Musicor	3015	'64	†
It Hurts to Be in Love	Musicor	3019	'64	†
I Must Be Seeing Things	Musicor	3056	'65	†
Looking Through the Eyes of Love	Musicor	3069	'65	†
Espanol	Musicor	3072	'65	†
Backstage I'm Lonely	Musicor	3095	'66	†
Nessuno Mi Puo Giudicare	Musicor	3100	'66	†
The Gene Pitney Show	Musicor	3101	'66	†
Greatest Hits of All Time	Musicor	3102	'66	†
The Country Side of Gene	Musicor	3104	'66	†
Young and Warm and Wonderful	Musicor	3108	'66	†
Just One Smile	Musicor	3117	'67	†
Pitney Espanol	Musicor	3154		†
Sings Burt Bacharach	Musicor	3161	'68	†
She's a Heartbreaker	Musicor	3164	'68	†
This Is Gene Pitney (Singing The Platter's Golden Platters)	Musicor	3183	'70	†

Gene Pitney Anthologies and Compilations

World-Wide Winners	Musicor	3005	'63	†
Big 16	Musicor	3008	'64	†
More Big 16, Volume 2	Musicor	3043	'65	†

More Big 16, Volume 3	Musicor	3085	'66	†
Golden Greats	Musicor	3134	'67	†
The Gene Pitney Story	Musicor	(2)3148	'68	†
Greatest Hits	Musicor	3174	'69	†
Superstar	Musicor	3193	'71	†
Ten Years After	Musicor	3206	'71	†
Golden Hits	Musicor	3250	'71	†
A Golden Hour of Gene Pitney	Musicor	3233	'72	†
Gene Pitney	Springboard Int'l	4057	'76	†
The Best	Piccadilly	3321	'82	†
Anthology (1961–1968)	Rhino	(2)1102	'84	†
	Rhino	5896		CS
Anthology (excerpts from above)	Rhino	75896	'86	CD
Best of Gene Pitney	K-tel	3028	'91	CS/CD
More Greatest Hits	Varèse Sarabande	5569	'95	CS/CD
The Ultimate Anthology	One Way	31368	'95	CD
The Great Recordings	Tomato	(2)71732	'95	CD
The Great Gene Pitney	Goldies	63132	'95	CD
Greatest Hits	Curb/Atlantic	77758	'95	CS/CD
Best of Easy Listening	Richmond	2145		CS
Town Without Pity	Richmond	2306		CS
20 Greatest Hits	Fest	4410		CS/CD
The Best of Gene Pitney	Impact	004		LP
The Collection	Griffin	369		CD

Gene Pitney and George Jones

Gene Pitney and George Jones	Musicor	3044	'65	†
It's Country Time Again	Musicor	3065	'65	†
Best of Country	Richmond	2223		CS
One Has My Name	Richmond	2239		CS

Gene Pitney and Melba Montgomery

Being Together	Musicor	3077	'66	†

Gene Pitney, George Jones and Melba Montgomery

Famous Country Duets	Musicor	3079	'65	†

PROCOL HARUM

Gary Brooker (born May 29, 1945, in London), piano, vocals; Keith Reid (born October 10, 1946, in London), lyrics; Matthew Fisher (born March 7, 1946, in London), organ; Ray Royer (born October 8, 1945, in England), guitar; Dave Knights (born June 28, 1945, in Islington, London), bass; and Bobby Harrison (born June 28, 1943, in East Ham, London), drums. After their first single, Royer and Harrison left, to be replaced by guitarist Robin Trower (born March 9, 1945, in London) and drummer Barry J. "B. J." Wilson (born March 18, 1947, in Middlesex, England; died in Oregon in 1989). Knights and Fisher left the group in 1969, to be replaced by organist-bassist Chris Copping (born August 29, 1945, in Southend, Essex). Trower departed in 1971. Procol Harum disbanded in 1977 and reunited in 1991 with Brooker, Reid, Fisher, and Trower.

One of the first '60s groups to regularly and prominently feature two keyboard instruments (piano and organ), Procol Harum burst onto the scene with 1967's smash hit "A Whiter Shade of Pale," certainly one of the classic singles of the decade. Essentially an album and live concert band thereafter, Procol Harum maintained a remarkably distinct and sophisticated sound during their career, incorporating the stirring organ, dynamic piano, and stunning lead guitar playing of Matthew Fisher, Gary Brooker, and Robin Trower, respectively. The group also featured the amazingly innovative free-form drumming of B. J. Wilson, one of the most overlooked drummers of the '60s and '70s, and showcased the scholarly lyrics of Keith Reid, the group's virtually unseen sixth member. With melodist Brooker favoring minor key tunes profoundly influenced by classical composers such as Bach, and Reid contributing stark and majestic lyrics alternately surreal, melancholic, mythic, and ominous, Procol Harum's first three albums were in the forefront of rock as literate and challenging music. Later emphasizing the powerful lead guitar playing of Trower, Procol Harum became far more popular in the United States than they were in their native England. Trower left the group in 1971 and enjoyed considerable success in America as leader of a power trio modeled after that of Jimi Hendrix. In the meantime, Procol Harum regrouped with several new members and enjoyed unexpected critical and commercial success with 1972's *Live with the Edmonton Symphony Orchestra.* Disbanding in 1977, Procol Harum reunited with Brooker, Reid, Fisher, and Trower in 1991.

Procol Harum began their evolution as The Paramounts, a rhythm-and-blues group formed in Essex, England, around 1961. The group comprised pianist Gary Brooker, guitarist Robin Trower, and bassist Chris Copping, later joined by drummer B. J. Wilson in 1963. Recording a series of unsuccessful British R&B singles, The Paramounts persevered until 1966, when Brooker formed a songwriting team with lyricist Keith Reid. Procol Harum was formed in April 1967, with Brooker, Reid, organist Matthew Fisher, guitarist Rob Royer, bassist Dave Knights, and drummer Bobby Harrison. Their debut single on Deram, "A Whiter Shade of Pale," featured Reid's mythic and surreal lyrics and the ominous organ playing of Fisher. It became a smash British and American hit and launched Procol Harum into international prominence. However, both Royer and Harrison soon departed, and Brooker recruited former Paramounts Robin Trower and B. J. Wilson for the completion of their debut album. *Procol Harum* served as an excellent first release, containing nine Brooker-Reid collaborations including "A Whiter Shade of Pale," the foreboding "Something Following Me," the raunchy "Mabel," "Conquistador," and the powerful five-minute tour de force, "(Outside the Gates of) Cerdes." Intellectually as well as emotionally stimulating, the album demonstrated that rock music could be intelligent and challenging.

Touring the United States for the first time in 1967 and 1968 as "Homburg" was becoming a moderate American hit single, Procol Harum next recorded *Shine on Brightly.* Issued in the United States on A&M Records, the album included "Skip Softly (My Moonbeams)," "Rambling On," and the title song, yet featured the eighteen-minute "In Held Twas in I," which depicted a stunning musical and lyrical journey from the depths of self-pity and depression to regal affirmation and renewed faith. Their next album, *A Salty Dog,* was their masterpiece, exploring a number of musical avenues enhanced by various dubbed-in sounds. It was filled with excellent songs, all with lyrics by Reid, such as the title song, "The Milk of Human Kindness," "Too Much Between Us," "All This and More," "Pilgrim's Progress," and the amusing but fateful "Boredom."

However, after producing *A Salty Dog,* Matthew Fisher left Procol Harum to become a producer and pursue a neglected solo career. Dave Knights also departed, and he and Fisher were replaced by a single new member, bassist-organist Chris Copping, another former member of The Paramounts. Reduced to a performing quartet, Procol Harum emphasized the forceful guitar playing of Robin Trower on *Home* and *Broken Barricades. Home* included two Trower-Reid collaborations, "Whisky Train" and "About to Die," as well as Brooker-Reid compositions such as "Still There'll Be More" and "Your Own Choice." *Broken Barricades* contained three more melodies provided by Trower, most significantly the tribute to Jimi Hendrix, "Song for a Dreamer," in addition to Brooker and Reid's "Simple Sister," "Power Failure," and the lurid "Luskus Delph."

In July 1971, Robin Trower departed Procol Harum. The group realigned with Brooker, Wilson, Copping (who switched to organ), guitarist Dave Ball, and bassist Alan Cartwright. While touring North America in late 1971, Procol Harum was invited to record with the Edmonton Symphony Orchestra in Canada. Live recordings of the concert became an instant surprise success, garnering the group critical acclaim and an expanded audience. The album, which compiled several of the group's early songs and the "In Held Twas in I" suite in full orchestral and choral treatment, yielded the group's third and final hit, "Conquistador," originally included on their debut album. Procol Harum then switched to Chrysalis Records for *Grand Hotel.* However, their fortunes began to fade with *Exotic Birds and Fruit,* a decidedly "hard rock" effort. *Procol's Ninth,* produced by legendary producers Jerry Leiber and Mike Stoller, included the favorite "Pandora's Box," but *Something Magic* fared poorly and Procol Harum disbanded in 1977. Gary Brooker subsequently recorded several solo albums before becoming a regular member of Eric Clapton's touring band in the late '80s.

Upon leaving Procol Harum, Robin Trower formed the short-lived group Jude with Scottish vocalist Frankie Miller, former Stone the Crows bassist Jim Dewar, and former Jethro Tull drummer Clive Bunker. Trower next formed his own powerhouse trio with Dewar (who performed vocals) and drummer Reg Isidore. Their debut album for Chrysalis, *Twice Removed from Yesterday,* sold marginally despite the stunning Jimi Hendrix—derived guitar playing of Trower on songs such as "Hannah" and "Man of the World." *Bridge of Sighs* became a best-seller, at least in the United States, where Trower consciously concentrated his efforts. Former Sly and The Family Stone drummer Bill Lordan replaced Isidore for the *For Earth Below* album. Subsequent Robin Trower albums through 1980 sold well, with *Long Misty Days* yielding Trower's only (minor) hit, "Caledonia." Dewar left in 1980 and Trower formed B.L.T. with Lordan and former Cream bassist Jack Bruce in 1981. Trower soon recorded *Truce* with Bruce before reforming his own band with Dewar for his final Chrysalis album *Back It Up.* In 1986, he recorded the independently released *Passion* and resumed touring, later switching to Atlantic Records.

In 1991, Procol Harum reunited with Gary Brooker, Keith Reid, Matthew Fisher, and Robin Trower for *The Prodigal Stranger* and a new round of touring, with Tim Renwick substituting for Trower. In 1993, Windsong U.K. issued the live BBC Radio One concert *Robin Trower* and, in 1995, Brooker, Fisher, and Trower recorded *The Long Goodbye* with the London Symphony Orchestra for RCA.

Procol Harum

The Early Years	Griffin	100		CD
Procol Harum	Deram	18008	'67	†
	A&M	2515	'87	CD
reissued as A Whiter Shade of Pale	A&M	4373	'73	†
	A&M	3136	'81	†
Shine on Brightly	A&M	4151	'68	CD†
A Salty Dog	A&M	4179	'69	†
	A&M	3123		CD
Home	A&M	4261	'70	†
	Mobile Fidelity	00793	'89	CD†
Broken Barricades	A&M	4294	'71	†
Live with the Edmonton Symphony Orchestra	A&M	4335	'72	†
	Mobile Fidelity	00788	'90	CD†

Best	A&M	4401	'73	†
	A&M	3259	'84	CS/CD
Greatest Hits	A&M	0523	'96	CD
Grand Hotel	Chrysalis	1037	'73	†
	Chrysalis	21037	'85	CD†
Exotic Birds and Fruit	Chrysalis	1058	'74	†
Procol's Ninth	Chrysalis	1080	'75	†
Something Magic	Chrysalis	1130	'77	†
The Chrysalis Years (1973–1977)	Chrysalis	21705	'89	CS/CD†
The Prodigal Stranger	Zoo	11011	'91	CS/CD
The Collection	Griffin	120		CD

London Symphony Orchestra

Symphonic Music of Procol Harum: The Long Goodbye	RCA	68029	'95	CS/CD

Matthew Fisher

Journey's End	RCA	0195	'73	†
I'll Be There	RCA	0325	'74	†
Matthew Fisher	A&M	4801	'80	†

Robin Trower

Twice Removed from Yesterday	Chrysalis	1039	'73	†
	Chrysalis	41039	'83	†
	Chrysalis	21039		CS/CD†
Bridge of Sighs	Chrysalis	1057	'74	†
	Chrysalis	21057	'86	CS/CD
	Mobile Fidelity	684		CD
For Earth Below	Chrysalis	1073	'75	†
	Chrysalis	41073	'83	†
	Chrysalis	21073		CS/CD†
Live	Chrysalis	1089	'76	†
	Chrysalis	41089	'83	†
	Chrysalis	21089		CS/CD†
Long Misty Days	Chrysalis	1107	'76	†
	Chrysalis	41107	'83	†
	Chrysalis	21107		CS/CD†
In City Dreams	Chrysalis	1148	'77	†
	Chrysalis	41148	'83	†
	Chrysalis	21148		CS/CD†
Caravan to Midnight	Chrysalis	1189	'78	†
	Chrysalis	41189	'83	†
	Chrysalis	21189		CS/CD†
Victims of the Fury	Chrysalis	1215	'80	†
	Chrysalis	41215	'83	†
Back It Up	Chrysalis	41420	'83	†
	Chrysalis	21420	'86	CS/CD†
Essential	Chrysalis	21853	'91	CS/CD
BBC Radio Live in Concert: Live at the Paris Theatre (recorded 1975)	Griffin	328		CD
In Concert (recorded 1977)	King Biscuit Flower Hour	88012	'96	CD
Passion	GNP Crescendo	2187	'86	LP/CS/CD
Take What You Need	Atlantic	81838	'88	CS/CD†

In the Line of Fire	Atlantic	82080	'90	CS/CD†
Robin Trower	Windsong U.K.	013	'93	CD
The Collection	Griffin	291		CD
Robin Trower, Jack Bruce and Bill Lordan				
B.L.T.	Chrysalis	1324	'81	†
	Chrysalis	41324	'83	†
	Chrysalis	21324	'91	CS/CD†
Robin Trower and Jack Bruce				
Truce	Chrysalis	1352	'82	†
	Chrysalis	41352	'83	†
	Chrysalis	21352		CD†
	One Way	17609		CD
Robin Trower and Others				
No Stopping Anytime (compilation of songs from above two albums)	Chrysalis	21704	'89	CS/CD
Gary Brooker				
No More Fear of Flying	Chrysalis	1224	'79	†
Lead Me to the Water	Mercury	4054	'82	†
Echoes in the Night	Mercury	824652	'85	LP/CS/CD†

QUICKSILVER MESSENGER SERVICE

John Cipollina (born August 24, 1943, in Berkeley, California; died May 29, 1989, in Greenbrae, California), lead guitar, vocals; Gary Duncan (born Gary Grubb on September 4, 1946, in San Diego, California), lead and rhythm guitar, vocals; David Freiberg (born August 24, 1938, in Boston), bass; and Greg Elmore (born September 4, 1946, in Coronado, California), drums. Songwriter-guitarist-vocalist Dino Valenti (born Chester Powers on November 7, 1943, in Danbury, Connecticut; died November 16, 1994, in Santa Rosa, California) was a member from 1970 to 1979.

Stalwarts of the "psychedelic" music scene in San Francisco during the second half of the '60s, The Quicksilver Messenger Service is often regarded as the scene's most representative band, given its extended improvisations featuring the twin lead guitars of John Cipollina and Gary Duncan. Folk singer Dino Valenti, originally intended as the band's frontman, did not join the band in 1965, yet he authored the oft-recorded "Hey Joe" and the love-and-peace anthem "Let's Get Together," recorded by The Jefferson Airplane and The Youngbloods. The Quicksilver Messenger Service eventually recorded an excellent debut album in 1968, but endured a variety of personnel changes following a second album, with Valenti finally joining in 1970. Quicksilver remained nominally intact through the '70s, while original bassist David Freiberg manned The Jefferson Starship from 1973 to 1985.

Formed in late 1964 in San Francisco by guitarist John Cipollina, bassist David Freiberg, and vocalist Jim Murray, The Quicksilver Messenger Service was conceived as a rock vehicle for folk singer Dino Valenti, who had been an important member of the Greenwich Village folk scene in the early '60s. As Chester Powers, Valenti wrote "Hey Joe" and "Let's Get Together," the classic psychedelic era song of fellowship. The Quicksilver lineup was completed with the June 1965 addition of Gary Duncan and Greg Elmore, but Valenti was imprisoned on drug charges. He eventually recorded a solo album released in 1968.

Debuting professionally in December 1965, The Quicksilver Messenger Service became a huge live attraction around the Bay Area. They performed at the Monterey International Pop Festival in June 1967, with Murray leaving the following October. Eventually signing with Capitol Records in late 1967, their debut album contained Hamilton Camp's "Pride of Man," Valenti's "Dino's Song," and the classic psychedelic instrumentals "The Fool" and "Gold and Silver."

The Quicksilver Messenger Service's second album included Dale Evans' title song "Happy Trails" and featured the side-long "Who Do You Love Suite," from which was extracted the minor hit "Who Do You Love." Gary Duncan left in January 1969 to form The Outlaws with Dino Valenti, but returned to the group in December with Valenti. In the meantime, the group had added British sessions keyboardist Nicky Hopkins for *Shady Grove*. He remained with the group for *Just for Love,* which yielded a moderate hit with "Fresh Air," and *What About Me.* John Cipollina left in October 1970 and formed Copperhead, which recorded one album for Columbia before disbanding in 1973. David Freiberg left in September 1971, to tour and record with The Jefferson Starship from 1973 to 1985.

Largely inactive in 1973 and 1974, Quicksilver reunited in March 1975 with Cipollina, Freiberg, Valenti, Duncan, and Elmore for the dismal *Solid Silver* album. The group remained nominally intact under Dino Valenti through 1979, as Cipollina pursued sessions work and various music projects around the Bay Area, including Thunder and Lightning with Nick Gravenites and the loosely structured Dinosaurs with other Bay Area music veterans. In 1986, Greg Duncan revived the Quicksilver name for the atrocious *Peace by Piece* album. John Cipollina died in Greenbrae, California, of emphysema on May 29, 1989, at the age of 45, and Dino Valenti died in Santa Rosa, California, on November 16, 1994, after a brief illness, at the age of 51.

Quicksilver Messenger Service

Quicksilver Messenger Service	Capitol	2904	'68	†
	Capitol	16089		†
	Capitol	91146	'94	CD
Happy Trails	Capitol	120	'69	†
	Capitol	16090		†
	Capitol	91215	'94	CD
Shady Grove	Capitol	391	'70	†
	Capitol	16094		†
	One Way	57339		CD
Just for Love	Capitol	498	'70	†
	Capitol	16093		†
	One Way	57821		CD†
What About Me	Capitol	630	'70	†
	Capitol	16092		†
	One Way	57820		CD†
Quicksilver	Capitol	819	'71	†
	Capitol	16091		†
	One Way	17411		CD
Comin' Thru	Capitol	11002	'72	†
	One Way	17412		CD
Anthology	Capitol	(2)11165	'73	†
Solid Silver	Capitol	11462	'75	†
	Capitol	11820	'78	†
Sons of Mercury (1968–1975)	Rhino	(2)70747	'91	CS/CD
Peace by Piece	Capitol		'86	†

Dino Valenti

Dino	Epic	26335	'68	†
	Lite Price	7954	'98	CD

Copperhead (with John Cipollina)

Copperhead	Columbia	32250	'73	†

THE RASCALS

Felix Cavaliere (born November 29, 1943, in Pelham, New York), organ, vocals; Eddie Brigati (born October 22, 1946, in Garfield, New Jersey), percussion, vocals; Gene Cornish (born May 14, 1945, in Ottawa, Ontario, Canada), guitar; and Dino Danelli (born July 23, 1945, in Jersey City, New Jersey), drums.

The Young Rascals, as they were initially known, began as a white rhythm-and-blues group, leading critics to devise the term "blue-eyed soul" to describe their work and that of The Righteous Brothers. Showcasing the amazingly soulful vocals of Felix Cavaliere, The Young Rascals scored a series of hit singles, primarily composed by Cavaliere and Eddie Brigati, from 1966 to 1969. One of the first white rock groups to record for Atlantic Records, The Rascals later shifted toward psychedelia and social consciousness following their smash hit "Groovin'." They eventually disbanded in 1972 and, after various solo and group projects, three of the four members reunited in 1988. The Rascals were inducted into the Rock and Roll Hall of Fame in 1997.

The Young Rascals were formed in Garfield, New Jersey, in 1964 by Dino Danelli and three former members of Joey Dee's Starliters, Felix Cavaliere, Gene Cornish, and Eddie Brigati. Cavaliere had performed with the high school group The Stereos and led Felix and The Escorts while attending Syracuse University. The Young Rascals debuted at the local Choo Choo Club in February 1965 and developed a reputation as an exciting live act. Playing rhythm-and-blues-style music centered around the vocals and organ playing of Cavaliere, the group graduated to Manhattan clubs by the fall of 1965.

Signed to Atlantic Records by Ahment Ertegun, The Young Rascals' second single, "Good Lovin'," a cover version of The Olympics' minor 1965 hit, became a top pop hit in early 1966 and was followed by the major hits "You Better Run" (written by Cavaliere and Brigati) and "I've Been Lonely Too Long" (by Cavaliere). Their first two rhythm-and-blues-styled albums became best-sellers, yet they adopted a lighter sound for *Groovin'*. The album yielded a top pop and smash R&B hit with the title song and smash pop hits with "A Girl Like You" and "How Can I Be Sure," all three written by Cavaliere and Brigati.

After another major hit with "It's Wonderful," The Young Rascals became simply The Rascals for the smash pop hit "A Beautiful Morning," by Cavaliere and Brigati. *Freedom Suite,* a double-record set that included an entire instrumental record entitled "Music Music," yielded the top pop and major rhythm-and-blues hit "People Got to Be Free" and the major hit "A Ray of Hope," both by Cavaliere and Brigati. "See" and "Carry Me" became major hits for The Rascals, but, by the time the group had switched to Columbia Records in 1971, only Cavaliere and Danelli remained. The group disbanded in 1972 after two poor-selling albums for the label. The Rascals were inducted into the Rock and Roll Hall of Fame in 1997.

In late 1972, Gene Cornish and Dino Danelli formed Bulldog, managing a moderate hit with "No." Later in the decade, they formed Fotomaker with Wally Bryson, former lead guitarist for The Raspberries. Felix Cavaliere surfaced as a solo artist on Bearsville Records in 1974 and manned the group Treasure in 1977. He eventually scored a moderate solo hit with "Only a Lonely Heart Sees" on Epic in 1980. Eddie Brigati joined his brother David, another former member of Joey Dee's Starliters, for a neglected album on Elektra Records in 1976.

In 1988, Felix Cavaliere, Gene Cornish, and Dino Danelli reunited as The Rascals for the fortieth anniversary concert of Atlantic Records and subsequently conducted a national tour. Danelli and Cornish began touring as The New Rascals in 1989. In 1994, Felix Cavaliere returned to recording with *Dreams in Motion* for producer Don Was' new Karambolage label.

The Young Rascals

The Young Rascals	Atlantic	8123	'66	†
	Rhino	70237	'88	LP/CS†
	Warner	27617		CD†
Collections	Atlantic	8134	'67	†
	Rhino	70238	'88	LP/CS†
	Warner	27618		CD†
Groovin'	Atlantic	8148	'67	†
	Rhino	70239	'88	LP/CS†
	Warner	27619		CD†

The Rascals

Once Upon a Dream	Atlantic	8169	'68	†
	Rhino	70240	'88	LP/CS†
Time Peace (The Rascals' Greatest Hits)	Atlantic	8190	'68	CS/CD†
Freedom Suite	Atlantic	(2)901	'69	†
	Rhino	70241	'88	LP/CS†
See	Atlantic	8246	'70	†
Search and Nearness	Atlantic	8276	'71	†
Peaceful World	Columbia	(2)30462	'71	†
The Island of Real	Columbia	31103	'72	†
Rock and Roll Treasures	Pair	1106	'86	CS
The Ultimate Rascals	Warner	27605	'86	CD
Searching for Ecstasy: The Rest of The Rascals, 1969–1972	Rhino	70242	'86	LP/CS†
Anthology 1965–1972	Rhino	(2)71031	'92	CS/CD
Anthology	Rhino	71077	'92	CS
Very Best	Rhino	71277	'93	CS/CD†

Bulldog (with Gene Cornish and Dino Danelli)

Bulldog	Decca	75370	'72	†
Smasher	Buddah	5600	'74	†

Fotomaker (with Gene Cornish and Dino Danelli)

Fotomaker	Atlantic	19165	'78	†
Vis-a-vis	Atlantic	19208	'78	†
Transfer Station	Atlantic	19246	'79	†
The Fotomaker Collection	Rhino	72221	'95	CD

Felix Cavaliere

Felix Cavaliere	Bearsville	6955	'74	†
Destiny	Bearsville	6958	'75	†
Castles in the Air	Epic	35990	'80	†
Dreams in Motion	Karambolage	11062	'94	CS/CD

Treasure (with Felix Cavaliere)

Treasure	Epic	34890	'77	†

Brigati

Lost in the Wilderness	Elektra	1074	'76	†

OTIS REDDING

Born September 9, 1941, in Dawson, Georgia; died December 10, 1967, near Madison, Wisconsin.

OTIS REDDING (UPI/CORBIS-BETTMANN)

Generally regarded as the single most important and influential male soul artist of the '60s, Otis Redding was one of the first black artists to broaden his appeal to white audiences with a raw, spontaneous style that bore a stark contrast to the smooth, sophisticated music of Motown. His intensely expressive yet gruff baritone, which was alternately seductive and agonized and exuded both gentleness and assertiveness, popularized the style and helped establish the Memphis-based Stax-Volt label. Aided immeasurably by Booker T. and The MGs and The Memphis Horns, Redding's initial success encouraged black artists such as Aretha Franklin and Wilson Pickett to record with the same Memphis backing group. Largely unrecognized as a songwriter, Otis Redding authored or coauthored most of his own hits, including "These Arms of Mine," "I've Been Loving You Too Long (To Stop Now)," and "I Can't Turn You Loose," as well as "Respect" and "Sweet Soul Music," hits for Aretha Franklin and Arthur Conley, respectively. With June 1967's powerful performance as the only soul artist to play at the Monterey International Pop Festival, Redding began to extend his popularity to rock audiences, but he was killed in a plane crash on December 10, 1967, at the age of 26. His posthumous top pop and R&B hit "(Sittin' On) The Dock of the Bay" revealed a more personal and introspective direction in his songwriting. Otis Redding was inducted into the Rock and Roll Hall of Fame in 1989.

Raised in Macon, Georgia, Otis Redding began singing in a local chuch choir. He dropped out of high school in the tenth grade and began touring the South with Johnny Jenkins and The Pinetoppers. With the group, he made his first recording in 1960 as Otis and The Shooters. He later recorded "Shout Bamalama" in a vocal style reminiscent of Little Richard, and the song was released nationally on the Bethlehem label.

In 1962, Otis Redding was allowed to record his own "These Arms of Mine" at a Johnny Jenkins session at the Stax studio in Memphis that was completed early. The song became a major rhythm-and-blues and minor pop hit in early 1963 on the newly formed Volt subsidiary of Stax Records, to which he was quickly signed. Recording thereafter in Memphis with the Stax house band of Booker T. and The MGs and The Memphis Horns (often augmented by keyboardist Isaac Hayes), Redding scored a number of modest crossover hits for Volt through 1964, including "That's What My Heart Needs," "Pain in My Heart," and "Chained and Bound." He managed his first moderate pop hit with the uptempo "Mr. Pitiful" (backed by "That's How Strong My Love Is") in early 1965. Redding toured regularly through 1967, accompanied by either Booker T. and The MGs or The Bar-Kays, developing a greater initial following for his raw, powerful music in Europe than at home.

In the spring of 1965, Otis Redding broke through into the pop market with the classic "I've Been Loving You Too Long (To Stop Now)," cowritten with Jerry Butler, and his emphatic "Respect." His outstanding *Otis Blue* album included the two hits, Sam Cooke's "Shake" and "A Change Is Gonna Come," and The Rolling Stones' "Satisfaction," which later became a crossover hit. Redding's "I Can't Turn You Loose"/"Just One More Day" became a major two-sided rhythm-and-blues hit at the end of 1965, and his *Dictionary of Soul* album yielded crossover hits with "My Lover's Prayer" (by Redding), "Fa-Fa-Fa-Fa-Fa (Sad Song)" (cowritten by Redding and The MGs' Steve Cropper), and the classic "Try a Little Tenderness."

In 1967, Arthur Conley scored a smash crossover hit with the Conley-Redding composition "Sweet Soul Music" and Aretha Franklin had a top pop and R&B hit with Redding's "Respect." Otis Redding recorded *King and Queen* with Carla Thomas and the album yielded smash R&B and major pop hits with Lowell Fulsom's "Tramp" and Eddie Floyd's "Knock On Wood."

Appearing as the only soul act at the June 1967 Monterey International Pop Festival, Otis Redding attained widespread recognition with his incendiary performance and began establishing himself with pop audiences. However, while touring, Redding's airplane crashed into Lake Monona near Madison, Wisconsin, on December 10, 1967, killing him and four members of The Bar-Kays, James King, Ronald Caldwell, Phalon Jones, and Carl Cunningham. In early 1968, Redding's recording of "(Sittin' On) The Dock of the Bay," cowritten with Steve Cropper, became a top pop and rhythm-and-blues hit. Posthumous crossover hits continued into 1969 with "The Happy Song (Dum Dum)," "Amen," "I've Got Dreams to Remember," "Papa's Got a Brand New Bag" and "Love Man." Redding's recording legacy was largely ignored in the '70s and '80s, but virtually all his albums were reissued in CD form by Rhino Records in the early '90s. Otis Redding was inducted into the Rock and Roll Hall of Fame in 1989.

In the late '70s, Otis Redding's sons Dexter and Otis III formed The Reddings with cousin Mark Locket for recordings on the Believe in a Dream label, distributed by Columbia. They scored a rhythm-and-blues smash with "Remote Control" in 1980 and eventually switched to Polydor Records in the late '80s.

OTIS REDDING BIBLIOGRAPHY

Schiesel, Jane. *The Otis Redding Story*. Garden City, NY: Doubleday, 1973.

Otis Redding

Pain in My Heart	Atco	33161	'64	†
	Rhino	80253	'91	CS/CD
The Great Otis Redding Sings Soul Ballads	Volt	411	'65	†
	Atco	33248		†
	Rhino	91706	'91	CS/CD
Otis Blue/Otis Redding Sings	Volt	412	'65	†
Soul	Atco	33284		†
	Rhino	80318	'91	CS/CD
	Mobile Fidelity	575	'93	CD†
The Soul Album	Volt	413	'66	†
	Atco	33285		†
	Rhino	91705	'91	CS/CD

Dictionary of Soul	Volt	415	'66	†
	Atco	33249		†
	Rhino	91707	'91	CS/CD
Live in Europe	Volt	416	'67	†
	Atco	33286		†
	Rhino	90395	'91	CS/CD
Dock of the Bay	Volt	419	'68	†
	Atco	33288		†
	Rhino	80254	'91	CS/CD
The Immortal Otis Redding	Atco	33252	'68	†
	Rhino	80270	'91	CS/CD
In Person at the Whiskey A-Go-Go	Atco	33265	'68	†
	Rhino	70380	'92	CS/CD
Recorded Live	Atlantic	19346	'82	†
	Rhino	19346		CS
Love Man	Atco	33289	'69	†
	Rhino	70294	'92	CS/CD
Tell the Truth	Atco	33333	'70	†
	Rhino	70295	'92	CS/CD†
Remember Me	Stax	8572	'92	CS/CD
Good to Me: Live at the Whiskey A-Go-Go, Volume 2	Stax	8579	'93	CS/CD
Otis Redding Anthologies and Compilations				
History	Volt	418	'67	†
	Atco	33261		†
Best	Atco	(2)801	'72	†
Best of Otis Redding	Atlantic	81282	'85	†
The Otis Redding Story	Atlantic	(4)81762	'87	CS†
	Atlantic	(3)81762	'87	CD†
	Rhino	(2)81762		CS†
	Rhino	(3)81762		CD†
Very Best	Rhino	71147	'92	CS/CD
Otis! The Definitive Otis Redding	Rhino	(4)71439	'93	CS/CD
Very Best, Volume 2	Rhino	71930	'95	CS/CD
Love Songs	Rhino	72955	'98	CD
Dreams to Remember: The Otis Redding Anthology	Rhino	(2)75471	'98	CD
The Legend of Otis Redding	Pair	(2)1062	'86	CS
The Ultimate Otis Redding	Warner	27608		CD
Otis Redding and Carla Thomas				
King and Queen	Stax	716	'67	†
	Rhino	82256	'91	CS/CD
Otis Redding/Jimi Hendrix Experience				
Historic Performances at the Monterey International Pop Festival	Reprise	2029	'70	†
Otis Redding and Little Joe Curtis				
Here Comes Soul	Stereo Fidelity	29200	'68	†
The Reddings				
The Awakening	Believe in a Dream	36875	'80	†
Class	Believe in a Dream	37175	'81	†
Steamin' Hot	Believe in a Dream	37974	'82	†
If Looks Could Kill	Polydor	823324	'85	†
The Reddings	Polydor	835292	'88	LP/CS/CD†

PAUL REVERE AND THE RAIDERS

Paul Revere (born January 7, 1942, in Boise, Idaho), keyboards; Mark Lindsay (born March 9, 1942, in Cambridge, Idaho), lead vocals, saxophone; Drake Levin, guitar; Mike Holiday, bass; and Mike Smith, drums. In 1964, Philip "Fang" Volk replaced Holiday. Freddie Weller (born September 9, 1947, in Atlanta, Georgia) was lead guitarist from 1967 to 1971.

The first rock group to sign with Columbia Records, Paul Revere and The Raiders, like The Monkees, were aided immeasurably by regular appearances on national television, owing to Dick Clark. Scoring a series of smash hit singles and best-selling albums in 1966 and 1967, Paul Revere and The Raiders faded from popularity in the '70s and established themselves on the oldies circuit under the directorship of Paul Revere. Lead vocalist Mark Lindsay also pursued a parallel solo career beginning in 1969.

Starting out in Idaho in 1959 as The Downbeats, with Paul Revere and Mark Lindsay, the group became Paul Revere and The Raiders in 1960. They achieved their first moderate hit with the instrumental "Like, Long Hair" on the Gardena label in 1961. Regrouping in Portland, Oregon, around 1962 with Revere, Lindsay, and Mike Smith, the group enjoyed considerable regional success and recorded an early version of the raunchy Richard Berry classic "Louie, Louie." Nonetheless, another local group, The Kingsmen, scored the national hit in 1963. Realigning with Revere, Lindsay, Smith, Drake Levin, and Mike "Doc" Holiday, the group secured a Columbia Records recording contract, replacing Holiday with Phil "Fang" Volk in 1964.

Moving to Los Angeles in 1965, Paul Revere and The Raiders' first big break came when they became the house band for Dick Clark's daily ABC-TV show *Where the Action Is* in June. That fall, they had a moderate hit with "Steppin' Out," followed by the major hit "Just Like Me," both written by Revere and Lindsay. They subsequently scored smash hits with two Barry Mann and Cynthia Weil songs, "Kicks" and "Hungry," and two songs written by Lindsay and producer Terry Melcher, "Good Thing" and "Him or Me—What's It Gonna Be?" "The Great Airplane Strike" and "Ups and Downs," cowritten by Melcher and Lindsay, became major hits. In 1967, Drake Levin, Mike Smith, and Phil Volk formed Brotherhood (later Friendsound), as Freddy Weller joined the Raiders on lead guitar. The group had their own Saturday morning ABC-TV show *Happening,* produced by Dick Clark, in 1968 and 1969 as the major hits continued with "I Had a Dream," "Talk Too Much," "Mr. Sun, Mr. Moon," and "Let Me." Lindsay's parallel solo career produced major hits with "Arizona" and "Silver Bird" around the same time.

Experiencing frequent personnel changes, the group became The Raiders in 1970 and managed a top hit with John D. Loudermilk's "Indian Reservation" and a major hit with "Birds of a Feather." Paul Revere and The Raiders subsequently remained nominally intact under the direction of Paul Revere, establishing themselves on the state fair and oldies circuit and securing a longstanding engagement at Harrah's Reno (Nevada). In 1988, Paul Revere and erstwhile Righteous Brother Bill Medley opened the oldies dance club Kicks in Reno.

Paul Revere and The Raiders

Like, Long Hair	Gardena	1000	'61	†
Paul Revere and The Raiders	Sande	1001	'63	†
In the Beginning	Jerden	7004	'66	†
Here They Come!	Columbia	9107	'65	†
	Columbia/Legacy	09107	'92	CD
Just Like Us!	Columbia	9251	'66	†
	Sundazed	6127		CD
Midnight Ride	Columbia	9308	'66	†
	Columbia/Legacy	09308	'92	CD

The Spirit of '67	Columbia	9395	'66	†
	Sundazed	6095		CD
Revolution!	Columbia	9521	'67	†
	Sundazed	6096		CD
Two All-Time Great Selling LPs (reissue of above two albums)	Columbia	(2)12	'69	†
Christmas Present . . . and Past	Columbia	9555	'67	†
Goin' to Memphis	Columbia	9605	'68	†
Something Happening	Columbia	9665	'68	†
	Sundazed	6097		CD
Hard 'n' Heavy	Columbia	9753	'69	†
Alias Pink Puzz	Columbia	9905	'69	†
Special Edition	Raider/America		'82	†

The Raiders

Collage	Columbia	9964	'70	†
Indian Reservation	Columbia	30768	'71	†
Country Wine	Columbia	31106	'72	†

Paul Revere and The Raiders Anthologies and Compilations

Greatest Hits	Columbia	9462	'67	†
	Columbia	35593	'79	CS/CD
Greatest Hits, Volume II	Columbia	30386	'71	†
All-Time Greatest Hits	Columbia	(2)31464	'72	†
The Legend of Paul Revere	Columbia	45311	'90	CS
	Columbia	(2)45311	'90	CD
Paul Revere and The Raiders	Harmony	30089	'70	†
Good Thing	Harmony	30975		†
Movin' On	Harmony	31183	'72	†
Paul Revere and The Raiders	Pickwick	3176		†
Good Things	Hollywood/IMG	701	'92	CS

The Brotherhood (with Phil Volk, Drake Levin and Mike Smith)

The Brotherhood	RCA	4092	'68	†
Brotherhood, Brotherhood	RCA	4228	'69	†

Friendsound (with Phil Volk, Drake Levin and Mike Smith)

Joyride	RCA	4114	'69	†

Mark Lindsay

Arizona	Columbia	9986	'70	†
Silverbird	Columbia	30111	'70	†
You've Got a Friend	Columbia	30735	'71	†

THE RIGHTEOUS BROTHERS

Bill Medley (born September 19, 1940, in Santa Ana, California), bass-baritone; and Bobby
Hatfield (born August 10, 1940, in Beaver Dam, Wisconsin), tenor.

Among the first to capitalize on what became known as "blue-eyed soul" (one of the more offensive terms coined to describe a genre of rock music), The Righteous Brothers achieved their greatest success in the mid-'60s under producer extraordinaire Phil Spector. His "wall-of-sound" technique, coupled with Bill Medley's booming bass vocals and Bobby Hatfield's soaring gospel-style tenor, yielded one of the finest singles of all time, "You've Lost That Lovin' Feelin.'" Following up with the similarly styled "Just Once in My Life" and

"(You're My) Soul and Inspiration," The Righteous Brothers broke up for the first time in 1968, reuniting for 1974's maudlin smash hit "Rock and Roll Heaven." Medley subsequently pursued a prolific solo career highlighted by the top 1987 pop and easy listening hit "(I've Had) The Time of My Life," rejoining Hatfield occasionally into the '90s.

Bill Medley and Bobby Hatfield formed a vocal duo in 1961 and recorded for Smash Records as The Paramours. They ostensibly received the name The Righteous Brothers from fans attending performances during a six-month engagement at The Black Derby in Santa Ana, California. Switching to the small Hollywood label Moonglow, the duo scored their first moderate hit with Medley's "Little Latin Lupe Lu" in 1963. Building a regional following, The Righteous Brothers reached a national audience through regular appearances on television's *Hullabaloo* and *Shindig* shows beginning in 1964.

In June 1964, Medley and Hatfield accepted an offer to record for producer Phil Spector, and, by early 1965, they had scored a top pop and British and smash rhythm-and-blues hit with "You've Lost That Lovin' Feelin,'" written by Spector, Barry Mann, and Cynthia Weil, on Spector's Philles label. A stunning recording featuring layers of orchestration and a near-orgasmic vocal performance by Medley and Hatfield, the single came to be regarded as one of the greatest ever recorded. Under Spector, The Righteous Brothers recorded three more smash crossover hits, "Just Once in My Life," written by Spector, Carole King, and Gerry Goffin, and the Tin Pan Alley standards "Unchained Melody" and "Ebb Tide."

By late 1965, The Righteous Brothers had switched to the Verve subsidiary of MGM Records, where they scored a top pop and major rhythm-and-blues hit with the Spector-styled "(You're My) Soul and Inspiration," written by Barry Mann and Cynthia Weil. After the major hit "He," The Righteous Brothers managed only moderate-to-minor hits through 1967, and, by 1968, the duo had broken up. Medley subsequently pursued a solo recording career on MGM, achieving moderate hits with "Brown Eyed Woman" and "Peace Brother Peace" in 1968. He recorded for MGM through 1970 and then switched to A&M Records. In the meantime, Hatfield recruited Jimmy Walker, a former member of The Knickerbockers (1965's "Lies"), for a sole Righteous Brothers album and recorded a solo album.

The duo reunited in 1974 on Dennis Lambert and Brian Potter's Haven label. Their debut album *Give It to the People* surprisingly yielded three hits, a smash hit with the rock-and-roll death song "Rock and Roll Heaven," the major hit title song, and the moderate hit "Dream On." A second album for the label failed miserably, and Medley resumed his solo career in the late '70s on United Artists. He eventually achieved success in the country field on RCA Records in 1984 with "Till the Memory's Gone," "I Still Do," and "I've Always Got the Heart to Sing the Blues." During the '80s, Medley opened two successful oldies dance clubs called The Hop in Orange County and, in 1988, joined Paul Revere in opening another, Kicks, in Reno, Nevada. In 1987, he scored a top pop and easy-listening hit in duet with Jennifer Warnes on "(I've Had) The Time of My Life" from the hit movie *Dirty Dancing*. The Righteous Brothers' "Unchained Melody" became a major hit from the movie *Ghost* in 1990. In 1991, the duo recorded *Reunion* and Bill Medley recorded *Blue Eyed Singer* for Curb/Warner Brothers Records. They duo has toured regularly during the summer since the mid-'90s.

The Righteous Brothers

Right Now!	Moonglow	1001	'63	†
Some Blue-Eyed Soul	Moonglow	1002	'65	†
This Is New	Moonglow	1003	'65	†
Best	Moonglow	1004	'66	†
The Moonglow Years	Verve	511157	'91	CS/CD
You've Lost That Lovin' Feelin'	Philles	4007	'65	†
Just Once in My Life	Philles	4008	'65	†
Back to Back	Philles	4009	'65	†

Soul and Inspiration	Verve	65001	'66	†
Go Ahead and Cry	Verve	65004	'66	†
Sayin' Something	Verve	65010	'67	†
Greatest Hits	Verve	65020	'67	†
Souled Out	Verve	65031	'67	†
Standards	Verve	65051	'68	†
One for the Road	Verve	65058	'68	†
Greatest Hits, Volume 2	Verve	65071	'69	†
Greatest Hits	Verve	823662	'90	LP/CS†
	Verve	823119	'90	CD†
The Very Best of The Righteous Brothers: Unchained Melody	Verve	847248	'90	CS/CD
The Righteous Brothers	MGM	102	'70	†
History	MGM	4885	'73	†
Give It to the People	Haven	9201	'74	†
The Sons of Mrs. Righteous	Haven	9203	'75	†
Anthology (1962–1974)	Rhino	(2)71488	'89	CS/CD
Unchained Melody	Curb/Warner Brothers	77381	'90	CS/CD
Reunion	Curb/Warner Brothers	77423	'91	CS/CD
Best of The Righteous Brothers, Volume 2: Then and Now	Curb/Warner Brothers	77522	'91	CS/CD
You've Lost That Lovin' Feelin'	Special Music	511078	'91	CD

Jimmy Walker and Bobby Hatfield as The Righteous Brothers

Re-birth	Verve	65076	'70	†

Bobby Hatfield

Messin' in Muscle	MGM	4727	'71	†

Bill Medley

100%	MGM	4583	'68	†
Soft and Soulful	MGM	4603	'69	†
Someone Is Standing Outside	MGM	4640	'70	†
Nobody Knows	MGM	4702	'70	†
Gone	MGM	4741	'71	†
A Song for You	A&M	3505	'71	†
Smile	A&M	3517	'73	†
Lay a Little Lovin' on Me	United Artists	929	'78	†
Sweet Thunder	United Artists	1024	'80	†
	Liberty	1097	'81	†
Right Here and Now	RCA	4434	'82	†
I Still Do	RCA	8519	'84	†
Still Hung Up on You	RCA	5352	'85	†
The Best of Bill Medley (rerecordings)	MCA/Curb	42257	'89	LP/CS/CD†
The Best of Bill Medley	Curb/Warner Brothers	77307	'90	CS/CD
Blue Eyed Singer	Curb/Warner Brothers	77409	'91	CS/CD

JOHNNY RIVERS

Born John Ramistella on November 7, 1942, in New York City.

Popularizer of the mid-'60s discotheque scene through his live recordings at Los Angeles' Whiskey A-Go-Go, Johnny Rivers successfully covered a number of rock and soul hits during the decade and had noteworthy hits with "Secret Agent Man," "Poor Side of Town," and, later, "Swayin' to the Music (Slow Dancin')." He enjoyed considerable success with The Fifth Dimension on his own record label, Soul City, formed in 1966, and helped advance the career of songwriter Jimmy Webb. His 1965 hit recording of Leadbelly's classic "Midnight Special" became the theme of the late-night television music show that ran from 1973 to 1981.

At the age of three, Johnny Rivers moved with his family to Baton Rouge, Louisiana, where he grew up. He took up guitar at age eight and formed his first music group at fourteen. In 1957, he met disc jockey Alan Freed, who suggested the name change to Johnny Rivers. Rivers made his first recordings, in a rockabilly style, in New York in 1958 and moved to Nashville at the age of seventeen to record demonstration records. In 1960, he moved to Los Angeles, where he recorded for a number of small labels through 1964. He also briefly performed at Nevada casinos as a member of Louis Prima's band. Playing regularly at Los Angeles discotheques, he began a long-running engagement at the newly opened Whiskey A-Go-Go in 1964. Signed to Imperial Records, Rivers recorded live albums at the club that sparked the discotheque craze and produced a number of cover hits beginning in 1964 with the smash hit "Memphis," written by Chuck Berry. In 1966, he scored a smash hit with P. F. Sloan and Steve Barri's television theme song "Secret Agent Man" and a top hit with "Poor Side of Town," cowritten with producer Lou Adler.

During 1966, Johnny Rivers formed Rivers Music, signing songwriter Jimmy Webb, and Soul City Records, signing The Fifth Dimension. The group scored a number of hits for the label through 1969, including the smash hits "Up, Up and Away" (by Webb), "Stoned Soul Picnic" and "Wedding Bell Blues" (by Laura Nyro), and the medley "Aquarius/Let the Sun Shine In" from the rock musical *Hair*. In 1968, Al Wilson had a major pop hit on Soul City with "The Snake." In 1967, Johnny Rivers performed at the Monterey International Pop Festival and successfully covered several Motown classics, achieving his final major hit for five years with James Hendricks' "Summer Rain." By the end of 1969, he had divested himself of interest in Soul City and ceased personal appearances. His biggest album success came with 1968's *Realization* on Imperial Records. He subsequently recorded for several different labels, scoring his final major hit in 1977 with "Swayin' to the Music (Slow Dancin')" on Big Tree Records. In the early '80s, he recorded the gospel album *Not a Through Street* for Priority Records and essentially retired from the music business.

Johnny Rivers

The Early Years	Sunset	5251	'69	†
The Sensational Johnny Rivers	Capitol	2161	'64	†
Go, Johnny, Go!	United Artists	6386	'64	†
At the Whiskey A-Go-Go	Imperial	12264	'64	†
Here We A-Go-Go Again!	Imperial	12274	'64	†
In Action!	Imperial	12280	'65	†
Meanwhile, Back at the Whiskey A-Go-Go	Imperial	12284	'65	†
Rocks the Folk	Imperial	12293	'65	†
And I Know You Wanna Dance	Imperial	12307	'66	†
Changes	Imperial	12334	'66	†
	Liberty	10121		†
Rewind	Imperial	12341	'67	†
Changes/Rewind	EMI	99900	'92	CS/CD†
Realization	Imperial	12372	'68	†
Slim Slo Slider	Imperial	16001	'70	†
Totally Live at the Whiskey A-Go-Go	EMI	32819	'95	CD
Home Grown	United Artists	5532	'71	†
L.A. Reggae	United Artists	5650	'72	†
Blue Suede Shoes	United Artists	075	'73	†
	Liberty	10154	'82	†

Wild Night	United Artists	486	'76	†
Road	Atlantic	7301	'74	†
Last Boogie in Paris	Atlantic		'74	†
	Varèse Sarabande	5580	'95	CD
New Lovers and Old Friends	Epic	33681	'75	†
Outside Help	Big Tree	76004	'77	†
Borrowed Time	RSO	3082	'81	†
Not a Through Street (religious)	Priority	38439	'83	†
	Epic	38439		LP/CS†
Greatest Hits (rerecordings)	MCA	917	'85	†

Johnny Rivers Anthologies and Compilations

Johnny Rivers	Pickwick	3022	'65	†
If You Want It, I Got It	Pickwick	3191		†
Golden Hits	Imperial	12324	'66	†
	Liberty	12324		†
A Touch of Gold	Imperial	12427	'69	†
	Liberty	12427		†
Best	Liberty	10120	'81	†
Whiskey A-Go-Go Revisited	Sunset	5157	'67	†
Superpak	United Artists	(2)93	'72	†
Very Best	United Artists	253	'74	†
	United Artists	444	'75	†
	EMI	90727		CS/CD†
Best	EMI America	92883	'87	CS/CD†
Anthology	Rhino	(2)70793	'91	CS/CD

SMOKEY ROBINSON AND THE MIRACLES

"Smokey" Robinson (born William Robinson on February 19, 1940, in Detroit), lead vocals; Emerson Rogers, tenor; Bobby Rogers (born February 19, 1940, in Detroit), tenor; Ronnie White (born April 5, 1939, in Detroit; died August 26, 1995, in Detroit), baritone; and Warren "Pete" Moore (born November 11, 1939, in Detroit), bass vocals; with guitarist Marvin Tarplin. Claudette Rogers (born in 1942) replaced Emerson Rogers in 1956 and retired in 1964.

Along with the Brian Holland–Lamont Dozier–Eddie Holland team, William "Smokey" Robinson was the songwriting and production mainstay of Berry Gordy's Detroit-based Tamla-Motown organization during the '60s. In fact, "Shop Around," written by Gordy and Robinson and recorded by Robinson's Miracles, effectively launched the company into national prominence. While providing such classic compositions as "My Guy," "My Girl," and "Ain't That Peculiar" to other Motown acts, Smokey Robinson wrote and sang lead on classics by The Miracles such as "You've Really Got a Hold on Me," "The Tracks of My Tears," and "I Second That Emotion." His emotion-laden tenor vocals, sung in a distinctive falsetto with impeccable phrasing and exquisite timing, were arguably the most expressive of any of the Motown singers and perhaps of any vocalist of the '60s. In early 1972, Robinson left The Miracles and assumed full-time executive duties at Motown. He pursued a parallel solo recording career and resumed touring in 1975, scoring impressive hits into the late '80s. Smokey Robinson was inducted into the Rock and Roll Hall of Fame in 1987.

William "Smokey" Robinson began writing songs as a child and formed The Matadors at Northern High School in Detroit with friends Bobby and Emerson Rogers, Ronnie White,

Warren "Pete" Moore, and guitarist Marv Tamplin in 1955. Established on the Detroit club circuit, the group added sister Claudette Rogers when Emerson Rogers enlisted in the Army in 1956. In 1957, Robinson met Berry Gordy, Jr., and the group became The Miracles, making their first recordings for End Records in 1958. Eventually signed to Tamla Records in 1959, they recorded Gordy and Robinson's "Bad Girl" and the song, leased to Chess Records, became a minor pop hit late in the year. The group's second nationally distributed release (on Tamla), "Shop Around," written by Robinson and Gordy, became a top rhythm-and-blues and smash pop hit at the end of 1960 and effectively introduced the Motown organization to the pop mainstream.

Moderate pop and major rhythm-and-blues hits continued for The Miracles into 1962, when Mary Wells scored crossover smashes with three songs composed and produced by Smokey Robinson, "The One Who Really Loves You," "You Beat Me to the Punch" (coauthored with Ronnie White), and "Two Lovers." In 1963, The Miracles achieved smash crossover hits with Robinson's "You've Really Got a Hold on Me" and Holland-Dozier-Holland's "Mickey's Monkey." Thereafter, The Miracles regularly placed singles in the middle level of the pop and R&B charts through 1964, as Robinson produced his own "The Way You Do the Things You Do" for The Temptations. Claudette Rogers, Smokey's wife since 1959, retired from performing at the beginning of 1964, although she continued to record with the group.

In early 1965, Smokey Robinson provided top pop and rhythm-and-blues hits to Mary Wells and The Temptations with "My Guy" and "My Girl," respectively. The Miracles *Going to A-Go-Go* album included four major pop and smash rhythm-and-blues hits with "Ooo, Baby, Baby," the classic "The Tracks of My Tears," "My Girl Has Gone," and "Going to A-Go-Go," all coauthored by Robinson. In 1965 and 1966, Robinson supplied Marvin Gaye with "I'll Be Doggone" and "Ain't That Peculiar," The Temptations with "My Baby" and "Get Ready," and The Marvelettes with "Don't Mess with Bill." Following another major pop and smash R&B hit with "(Come 'Round Here) I'm the One You Need," his group became Smokey Robinson and The Miracles in April 1967, the year he was appointed vice president in charge of artist development at Motown. The group continued to score crossover hits through 1968 with "The Love I Saw in You Was Just a Mirage," "More Love," the smash classic "I Second That Emotion," "If You Can Want," and "Special Occasion."

Although Smokey Robinson and The Miracles continued to achieve smash rhythm-and-blues hits, they had difficulty scoring major pop hits after early 1969's "Baby, Baby Don't Cry," perhaps due to the creative exhaustion of Robinson. The classic "Tears of a Clown," written with Stevie Wonder, became a belated top pop and rhythm-and-blues hit in late 1970 (it had been included on 1967's *Make It Happen* album) and was followed by the group's final major pop hit, "I Don't Blame You at All," in 1971. In January 1972, Motown announced the impending "retirement" of Smokey Robinson, and the group completed a six-month "farewell" tour, performing their final concert in Washington, D.C., on July 16.

Smokey Robinson subsequently assumed full-time duties as Motown vice president, as the other Miracles sought out a new lead vocalist, eventually recruiting William Griffin. They managed rhythm-and-blues smashes with "Do It Baby" (a major pop hit) and "Don't Cha Love It" in 1974 and achieved their biggest success with 1975's top pop and smash R&B hit, "Love Machine (Part 1)." The Miracles switched to Columbia Records in 1976, disbanding in the late '70s. Bobby Rogers reformed The Miracles in 1982.

Smokey Robinson's debut solo album, *Smokey,* yielded a major pop and smash R&B hit with "Baby Come Close" in late 1973. His masterpiece album of the '70s, *A Quiet Storm,* yielded the top rhythm-and-blues and major pop hit "Baby That's Backatcha," the R&B smash "The Agony and the Ecstasy," and the major R&B hit "Quiet Storm." Robinson resumed touring in 1975 and continued to score major rhythm-and-blues-only hits into 1978 with "Open," "There Will Come a Day (I'm Gonna Happen to You)," and "Daylight and Darkness."

In late 1979, Smokey Robinson's sensuous "Cruisin'" became a smash pop and R&B hit. The similarly seductive "Being with You," the title song to the most commercially successful album of his solo career, became a crossover smash in 1981. During 1983, Robinson recorded with High Energy's Barbara Mitchell ("Blame It on Love") and Rick James ("Ebony Eyes"), and reunited with The Miracles for the *Motown 25th Anniversary* NBC television special. He eventually achieved crossover smashes with 1987's "Just to See Her" and "One Heartbeat" from *One Heartbeat,* his best-selling latter-day album. Smokey Robinson was inducted into the Rock and Roll Hall of Fame in 1987. He resigned his Motown vice presidency in 1988 and left the organization in 1990, recording 1991's *Double Good Everything* for SBK Records. Ronnie White, an original member of The Miracles, died in Detroit on August 26, 1995, of leukemia at the age of 57.

SMOKEY ROBINSON BIBLIOGRAPHY

Robinson, Smokey, with David Ritz. *Smokey: Inside My Life.* New York: McGraw-Hill, 1989.

The Miracles

From the Beginning	Bell	1063		†
Hi, We're The Miracles	Tamla	220	'61	†
	Motown	5160		CS/CD†
Cookin' with The Miracles	Tamla	223	'62	†
	Motown	0368	'94	CS/CD
Shop Around	Tamla	224	'62	†
I'll Try Something New	Tamla	230	'62	†
Christmas with The Miracles	Tamla	236	'63	†
	Motown	5254	'87	CS/CD
The Fabulous Miracles	Tamla	238	'63	†
Miracles "Live" on Stage	Tamla	241	'63	†
Doin' Mickey's Monkey	Tamla	245	'63	†
	Motown	5439	'89	CD†
Tribute to the Great Nat King Cole	Tamla	261	'65	†
Going to A Go-Go	Tamla	267	'65	†
	Motown	5269	'89	CS/CD
Away We A Go-Go	Tamla	271	'66	†
	Motown	5136	'89	CD†

Smokey Robinson and The Miracles

Make It Happen	Tamla	276	'67	†
reissued as The Tears of a Clown	Tamla	276	'70	†
	Motown	9092		CD
	Motown	5156		CS/CD
Special Occasion	Tamla	290	'68	†
	Motown	5418	'89	CD†
Live!	Tamla	289	'69	†
Time Out for Smokey Robinson and The Miracles	Tamla	295	'69	†
	Motown	5437	'89	CD†
Four in Blue	Tamla	297	'69	†
What Love Has Joined Together	Tamla	301	'70	†

A Pocket Full of Miracles	Tamla	306	'70	†
The Season for Miracles	Tamla	307	'70	†
	Motown	3762	'91	CS†
	Motown	5253	'91	CS/CD
One Dozen Roses	Tamla	312	'71	†
Flying High Together	Tamla	318	'72	†

Anthologies, Compilations, and Reissues

Greatest Hits from the Beginning	Tamla	(2)254	'65	†
	Motown	(2)8238		†
Greatest Hits, Volume 2	Tamla	280	'68	†
	Motown	5210		CS/CD
1957–1972	Tamla	(2)320	'72	†
Anthology	Motown	(3)793	'74	†
	Motown	(2)6196		CD†
	Motown	(2)793		CD†
	Motown	(2)0472	'95	CS/CD
Compact Command Performance (18 Greatest Hits)	Motown	6071		CD†
	Motown	9041	'89	CD†
Compact Command Performances, Volume 2	Motown	6202	'86	CD†
Going to A Go-Go/The Tears of a Clown	Motown	8004	'86	CD†
Doin' Mickey's Monkey/Away We A Go-Go	Motown	8150		CD†
Time Out/Special Occasion	Motown	8143		CD†
What Love Has Joined Together	Motown	5282	'90	CS/CD†
Great Songs and Performances That Inspired the Motown 25th Anniversary TV Show	Motown	5316		LP/CS/CD
Motown Legends	Motown	5360		†
The 35th Anniversary Collection	Motown	(4)6334	'94	CS/CD
Tears of a Clown	Pickwick	3389	'75	†
Whatever Makes You Happy: More of the Best (1961–1971)	Rhino	71181	'93	CS/CD
Motown Legends	Esx	8259	'95	CS/CD

The Miracles

Renaissance	Tamla	325	'73	†
Do It Baby	Tamla	334	'74	†
Don't Cha Love It	Tamla	336	'75	†
City of Angels	Tamla	339	'75	†
The Power of Music	Tamla	344	'76	†
Greatest Hits	Tamla	357	'77	†
Love Crazy	Columbia	34460	'77	†
The Miracles	Columbia	34910	'78	†

Smokey Robinson

Smokey	Tamla	328	'73	†
	Motown	5134		CS/CD†
Pure Smokey	Tamla	331	'74	†
A Quiet Storm	Tamla	337	'75	†
	Motown	5197	'89	CS/CD
Smokey/A Quiet Storm	Motown	8128	'86	CD†
Smokey's Family Robinson	Tamla	341	'76	†
Deep in My Soul	Tamla	350	'77	†
Love Breeze	Tamla	359	'78	†
Smokin'	Tamla	363	'79	†

Where There's Smoke	Tamla	366	'79	†
	Motown	5267	'89	CS/CD†
Warm Thoughts	Tamla	367	'80	†
Being with You	Motown	375	'81	†
	Motown	5349	'89	CS/CD†
Being with You/Where There's Smoke	Motown	8101	'86	CD†
Yes It's You Lady	Tamla	6001	'82	†
Touch the Sky	Tamla	6030	'83	†
Blame It on Love and All the Great Hits	Tamla	6064	'83	†
	Motown	5401	'90	CS/CD
Essar	Tamla	6098	'84	†
Smoke Signals	Tamla	6156	'86	LP/CS/CD†
One Heartbeat	Motown	6226	'87	CS/CD
Love, Smokey	Motown	6268	'90	LP/CS/CD†
Motown Superstar Series, Volume 18	Motown	5118		CS
Motown Legends	Esx	8519	'95	CS/CD
Double Good Everything	SBK	97968	'91	CS/CD†

THE ROLLING STONES

Michael "Mick" Jagger (born July 26, 1943, in Dartford, Kent, England), lead vocals, harmonica; Keith Richards (born December 18, 1943, in Dartford), rhythm guitar; Brian Jones (born Lewis Brian Hopkin-Jones on February 28, 1942, in Cheltenham, Gloucestershire, England; died July 3, 1969, in Hartfield, Sussex), guitar, sitar, dulcimer, vocals; Bill Wyman (born William Perks on October 24, 1936, in Plumstead, London, England), bass; Charlie Watts (born June 2, 1941, in Islington, London), drums; and Ian Stewart (born July 18, 1938, in Pittenweem, Fife, Scotland; died December 12, 1985, in London), piano. Stewart was phased out of the band in 1963, although he continued to tour and record with the group, becoming known as the "sixth Rolling Stone." Brian Jones left the group in June 1969, to be replaced by guitarist Michael "Mick" Taylor (born January 17, 1949, in Welwyn Garden City, Hertfordshire, England). Taylor left in 1974 and was replaced by guitarist Ron Wood (born June 1, 1947, in Hillingdon, Middlesex, England). Bill Wyman left the group in 1992.

Initially the finest English interpreters of American rhythm-and-blues, The Rolling Stones developed into one of the most potent and popular rock 'n' roll bands of the '60s and '70s, sustaining their popularity into the '90s as the longest-lived rock 'n' roll band. With vocalist Mick Jagger adopting a flamboyant, boisterous, and ostentatious on-stage persona and the group cultivating an arrogant, rebellious, and outrageous image, The Rolling Stones were one of the most identifiable of the British groups and became the only genuine competition to The Beatles, beginning with their 1965 top pop hit classic "(I Can't Get No) Satisfaction." Jagger and Keith Richards developed into a powerful songwriting team that provided a number of classic '60s singles, including "Get Off My Cloud," "As Tears Go By," "19th Nervous Breakdown," "Paint It Black," and "Ruby Tuesday." Sparked by the singular versatility of Brian Jones, the group's initial leader and most talented instrumentalist, The Rolling Stones' *Aftermath* album became a classic of the era. Comprising entirely Jagger-Richards songs, the album initiated their penchant for songs ominous and demonic ("Paint It Black") and openly sexist ("Stupid Girl," "Under My Thumb"). Ably demonstrating the ability to record ballads and country-style songs, The Rolling Stones mimicked psychedelia with their unfortunate *Their Satanic Majesties Request* album. They returned to favor with 1968's "Jumpin' Jack Flash" single and *Beggar's Banquet* album, generally acknowledged as their most cohesive and compelling album, and sustained their popularity with their classic

<small>THE ROLLING STONES (HULTON-DEUTSCH COLLECTION/CORBIS)</small>

top hit single "Honky Tonk Women" and *Let It Bleed* album. However, Brian Jones soon departed (and died), and The Rolling Stones subsequently participated in the debacle at Altamont, California, a tragically vicious event that brought into question the group's wisdom, integrity, and credibility. With the loss of their most innovative musician (Brian Jones) and the breakup of their primary musical challenge (The Beatles), The Rolling Stones were relatively inactive for several years, as Jagger became the world's best known and most notorious rock performer and Keith Richards garnered renown as the world's most infamous drug abuser. Ascending to the self-ascribed status of "the world's greatest rock 'n' roll band," The Rolling Stones conducted their first American tour since Altamont in 1972, as their concerts became more cultural than musical events. *Exile on Main Street* came to be considered as their last significant effort, as subsequent albums seemed to be mere collections of mostly second-rate songs, some of which reflected contemporary trends such as disco and reggae. With the addition of guitarist Ron Wood, The Rolling Stones devolved into caricature and self-parody, as their reputation was brought into question through Keith Richards' 1977 heroin arrest, filmmaker Robert Frank's sordid tour film *Cocksucker Blues,* and former associate Tony Sanchez's sensationalistic 1979 *Up and Down with The Rolling Stones* book.

The group conducted one of the most successful rock tours to date in 1981 as "Start Me Up" and *Tattoo You* served to reestablish the band's credentials. However, the group members spent most of the '80s involved in solo projects, regrouping for 1989's *Steel Wheels* album and tour. Inducted into the Rock and Roll Hall of Fame that year, The Rolling Stones later conducted record-setting tours in support of *Voodoo Lounge* and *Bridges to Babylon* in an effort to sustain their reputation as "the world's greatest rock 'n' roll band."

Mick Jagger and Keith Richards first met in primary school and encountered each other again in 1960. Jagger, a student at the London School of Economics, was playing with mutual friend Dick Taylor in Little Blues and The Blue Boys, who subsequently added Richards. Brian Jones had been playing as a jazz saxophonist before briefly joining Alexis Korner's Blues Incorporated, which included Charlie Watts. Wanting to form his own rhythm-and-blues band, Jones recruited pianist Ian Stewart and guitarist Jeff Bradford, among others. Jones first met Jagger, Richards, and Taylor at the Ealing Jazz club, where Blues Incorporated held residency. Jagger and Richards were soon jamming there with Charlie Watts and harmonica player Cyril Davies. By 1961, Jagger was rehearsing with Jones, Bradford, and Stewart, to soon be joined by Richards and Taylor, as Bradford became the first departure. Jagger began singing with Blues Incorporated in late 1961, joining as permanent singer in early 1962, by which time the band had graduated to the Marquee club in London. Jagger, Jones, and Richards began sharing an apartment and recorded a demonstration tape that was rejected by EMI Records. Taylor became the next departure, later to form The Pretty Things.

After debuting at the Marquee club in July 1962 as Brian Jones and Mick Jagger and The Rollin' Stones, the group added bassist Bill Wyman through auditions in December 1962 and attempted to persuade drummer Charlie Watts also to join. He did join in January 1963 and the group (Jagger, Richards, Jones, Stewart, Watts, and Wyman) subsequently played the rhythm-and-blues club circuit and secured a residency at the Crawdaddy Club in Richmond, where they attracted a burgeoning following. In May, Andrew "Loog" Oldham became their manager and signed the group with Decca Records (London in the United States). He began cultivating a rebellious image for the group and demoted Ian Stewart, who continued to record and play with the band, eventually becoming their tour manager.

The Rolling Stones' first single, Chuck Berry's "Come On," became a minor British hit in June 1963. They conducted their first British tour in support of The Everly Brothers and Little Richard in September, scoring their first major British hit in December with "I Wanna Be Your Man," provided by Beatles songwriters John Lennon and Paul McCartney. Gene Pitney managed a minor American hit with Jagger and Richards' "That Girl Belongs to Yesterday" at the beginning of 1964 and The Rolling Stones soon achieved a smash British hit with Buddy Holly's "Not Fade Away," the group's first moderate American hit. Their debut American album was pervaded with American rhythm-and-blues songs such as "Walking the Dog," "I Just Want to Make Love to You," "Can I Get a Witness," and "Tell Me" (their first major American hit). The group first toured the United States in June, returning in October. The Rolling Stones' *12 X 5* included the top British and major American hit "It's All Over Now" (originally recorded by Bobby Womack's Valentinos) and the smash American hit "Time Is on My Side" (previously recorded by Irma Thomas). By year's end, Marianne Faithfull had scored a major American and near-smash British hit with Jagger and Richards' "As Tears Go By."

With *Now!* Jagger and Richards began writing songs for the group. The album produced a major American hit with their "Heart of Stone" in early 1965. *Out of Our Heads,* recorded primarily in Chicago, finally established The Rolling Stones in the United States. The album yielded a near-smash with Jagger and Richards' "The Last Time" (backed with "Play with Fire") and a top hit with their classic "(I Can't Get No) Satisfaction" (both top British hits). The album also included "The Spider and the Fly" and the satirical "Under Assistant West Coast Promotion Man." The Rolling Stones toured the United States twice in 1965, achieving a top British and American hit with "Get Off My Cloud" and a smash American hit with their version of "As Tears Go By" from *December's Children*. The psychedelic "19th Nervous Breakdown" became a smash British and American hit and the group conducted their last tour of America for three years in 1966. Otis Redding scored a moderate pop and smash rhythm-and-blues hit with "Satisfaction" in early 1966 and Chris Farlowe scored a top British hit with Jagger and Richards' "Out of Time" that summer.

Aftermath, the first Rolling Stones album consisting entirely of Jagger-Richards compositions, established the group as an album band. While including the top British and American hit "Paint It Black" (on which Brian Jones played sitar), the album contained the major American hit "Lady Jane" (Jones on dulcimer), the chauvinistic "Stupid Girl" and "Under My Thumb," and the eleven-minute "Goin' Home." During July, "Mother's Little Helper," backed by "Lady Jane," became a near-smash American hit, while "Have You Seen Your Mother, Baby, Standing in the Shadows," one of their most ambitious productions to date, proved a smash British and American hit in November.

After the live album *Got Live, If You Want It,* The Rolling Stones issued *Between the Buttons,* Andrew Oldham's final production for the group. It included the top American and smash

British hit "Ruby Tuesday"/"Let's Spend the Night Together," as well as the overlooked "Yesterday's Papers," "Amanda Jones," and "Something Happened to Me Yesterday." Appearing on CBS-television's *Ed Sullivan Show* in January 1967, the group performed "Let's Spend the Night Together" as "Let's Spend Some Time Together." Later Jagger and Richards, then Jones, were charged in the first big drug arrests in British rock, in response to which the stately *London Times* came to their defense. Their next album, *Flowers,* featured a number of their recent hits plus "Out of Time" and the country-styled "Back Street Girl" and "Sittin' on a Fence."

The Rolling Stones next attempted to capitalize on psychedelia and the success of The Beatles' *Sgt. Pepper's Lonely Hearts Club Band.* "Dandelion"/"We Love You" became a major British and American hit, but the self-produced *Their Satanic Majesties Request* was not well received critically, yet yielded a major American hit with "She's a Rainbow." During 1967, Brian Jones had ostensibly played very little on the recordings of The Rolling Stones, becoming estranged from the rest of the group and even requiring hospitalization in December. He was arrested again in May 1968, shortly before the release of "Jumpin' Jack Flash," often regarded as the group's most potent single since "Satisfaction" and their first top British and American hit in two years.

The much-delayed *Beggar's Banquet,* undoubtedly The Rolling Stones' finest and most coherent album, included the classic "Sympathy for the Devil," the anthemic "Salt of the Earth," the country-styled "No Expectations," and "Stray Cat Blues" and "Jigsaw Puzzle," as well as "Street Fighting Man," oddly only a minor hit as a single. After participating in the legendary never-to-be-seen (until 1996) television special "Rock and Roll Circus," Brian Jones quit the group in early July 1969, to be replaced by guitarist Mick Taylor from John Mayall's band. On July 3, Jones was found dead in the swimming pool of his Sussex home at the age of twenty-five, leading to later speculation that he was murdered. Two days later, Taylor debuted with The Rolling Stones at a free concert at London's Hyde Park, attended by 250,000 fans. Mick Jagger soon left for Australia to perform the title role in the movie *Ned Kelly,* released in 1970.

During the summer of 1969, another classic Rolling Stones single, "Honky Tonk Women," recorded with Mick Taylor, became a top British and American hit. The group subsequently embarked on an American tour in November. Concluding the tour, the group announced plans for a free concert in northern California, but the concert site was changed several times and eventually took place at Altamont Speedway. Held on December 6, the concert was a highly publicized tragedy. With the Hells Angels providing security in exchange for beer, the show was staged without adequate food services and health facilities and The Stones, demonstrating their aloofness from the audience, delayed more than an hour before appearing on the stage. Once they took the stage, the group worked the crowd into hysteria with unfortunate results. During "Under My Thumb," a fan near the front was stabbed to death (as graphically captured in the film *Gimme Shelter*) and the concert devolved into ugly chaos. Charges and counter charges by participants were later aired, and the leftist press denounced the event as the "death" of rock 'n' roll and the "Woodstock spirit."

Also in late 1969, The Rolling Stones released *Let It Bleed,* which contained Robert Johnson's "Love in Vain," "Gimme Shelter" (ironic in the light of Altamont), the classic "You Can't Always Get What You Want," and the menacing "Midnight Rambler," as well as the title song. A period of inactivity ensued for the group, as Jagger appeared as the ambisexual star of Nicholas Roeg's *Performance* film. The soundtrack album included a memorable Jagger solo single, "Memo from Turner." In March 1971, The Rolling Stones announced they were leaving England for tax purposes, yet they conducted their first British tour in five years, augmented by keyboardist Nicky Hopkins and saxophonist Bobby Keys. In April, they issued the sexist and racist "Brown Sugar" (a top American and smash British hit) on their newly formed record label, Rolling Stones Records, distributed by Atlantic in the United States. Their debut album for the label, *Sticky Fingers,* contained "Brown Sugar," the countrified "Wild Horses" (a major hit), "Dead Flowers," the jam-style "Can't You Hear Me Knocking," and "Sister Morphine," the latter coauthored (without credit) by Marianne Faithfull.

By the early '70s, concerts by The Rolling Stones were attended more as cultural events than as musical performances. Mick Jagger, in particular, was adopted by the so-called "jet set," especially after his much-publicized marriage to Bianca de Macias in May 1971. The double-record set *Exile on Main Street* was released to coincide with their massive 1972 tour accompanied by Nicky Hopkins and Bobby Keys. The album included "Rocks Off," "Rip This Joint," and "Sweet Virginia," and produced a near-smash British and American hit with "Tumbling Dice" and a major American hit with "Happy."

Conducting immensely successful tours of America and Europe in 1973, The Rolling Stones' next two albums, *Goat's Head Soup,* recorded in Jamaica, and *It's Only Rock 'n' Roll,* were considered minor works compared to previous albums, yet each contained several exceptional songs. *Goat's Head Soup* yielded a top American and smash British hit with the ballad "Angie" and a minor hit with "Doo Doo Doo Doo Doo (Heartbreaker)," while containing the notorious "Star Star," perhaps better known as "Starfucker." *It's Only Rock 'n' Roll,* the first Stones album produced by Jagger and Richards as "The Glimmer Twins," featured the major international hits "It's Only Rock 'n' Roll" and "Ain't Too Proud to Beg" (originally a hit for The Temptations), while including "Dance Little Sister" and "Time Waits for No One." In 1974, the in-concert film *Ladies and Gentlemen: The Rolling Stones,* filmed in Texas during the 1972 tour, was released.

During 1975, The Rolling Stones again mounted a huge, lavishly staged, and lucrative American tour, augmented by Billy Preston. Mick Taylor had quit the group the previous December, to be replaced by "guest artist" Ron Wood, guitarist for The Faces, for the grandiose tour. Their next album, *Black and Blue,* eventually appeared in 1976 to critical disapproval. The album's sexist promotional campaign later inspired a boycott by Women Against Violence Against Women (WAVAW) against the entire organization responsible for distribution of Rolling Stones Records, Warner Communications. The album yielded only one major hit, "Fool to Cry." Ron Wood finally became an official member of the group in June 1977. In the meantime, Bill Wyman had recorded two solo albums, and Mick Taylor had worked with The Jack Bruce Band and Gong before recording a solo album for Columbia Records in 1979 and touring and recording with Bob Dylan in the early '80s.

The Rolling Stones again toured the United States in 1978, this time without the elaborate staging and massive props of the 1975 tour, accompanied by keyboardists Ian McLagan (formerly of The Faces) and Ian Stewart. Performing at small and medium-sized halls as well as at huge outdoor concerts, the group broke the rock concert attendance record in July at the New Orleans Superdome, where more than 80,000 fans were present. *Some Girls* became the group's best-selling nonanthology album on the strength of the top American and smash British disco-style hit single "Miss You," the near-smash American hit "Beast of Burden," and the moderate American hit "Shattered." The album also contained "When the Whip Comes Down," "Far Away Eyes," and Richards' "Before They Make Me Run."

In February 1977, Keith Richards was arrested in Toronto on charges of possession of heroin for sale, yet he got off lightly in October 1978, being required to continue drug rehabilitation and perform a benefit concert. For the concert, performed in April 1979, Richards and Ron Wood assembled The New Barbarians with keyboardist Ian McLagan, saxophonist Bobby Keys, jazz bassist Stanley Clarke, and Meters drummer Joe Modeliste. The concert and subsequent American tour neatly coincided with the release of Wood's third solo album, *Gimme Some Neck,* which included eight originals by Wood and Bob Dylan's "Seven Days." During 1979, The Rolling Stones were the subject of controversy as the result of former associate Tony Sanchez's ghastly and lurid account of his eight-year tenure with The Rolling Stones, *Up and Down with The Rolling Stones.* Their reputation had also been tarnished by a film made by Robert Franks during the group's 1972 tour, *Cocksucker Blues.* The movie, completed in 1973 and shown several times during 1975 and 1976, was legally suppressed by the group and ultimately withdrawn from public viewing in 1988.

Finally, in 1980, another much-delayed Rolling Stones album was issued, *Emotional Rescue,* but it did little to dispel the allegation that the group was no longer the "world's greatest rock 'n' roll band." The album produced a smash British and American hit with the title song and a major American hit with "She's So Cold." In 1981, The Rolling Stones redeemed themselves with the unaffected *Tattoo You* album, the smash international hit "Start Me Up" and the major American hits "Waiting on a Friend" and "Hang Fire," and a massively successful tour conducted in the final four months of the year. However, despite signing a new distribution deal with Columbia Records in August 1983, the group recorded only two studio albums, 1983's *Undercover* and 1986's *Dirty Work,* over the next seven years. During that time, they scored a mere five hits, highlighted by the smash American and major British hits "Undercover of the Night" and "Harlem Shuffle," the latter a cover version of Bob and Earl's 1964 hit.

Much of the '80s was taken up by individual efforts by the members of The Rolling Stones, as Jagger and Richards became estranged from each other. In 1983, Bill Wyman and Charlie Watts toured as part of Ronnie Lane's brief benefit tour for Appeal for Actions Research Into Multiple Sclerosis. Mick Jagger shared lead vocals with Michael Jackson on The Jacksons' smash 1984 pop and R&B and major British hit "State of Shock." He recorded two lackluster solo albums, *She's the Boss* and *Primitive Cool,* managing major hits with "Just Another Night" and "Dancing in the Street" (recorded with David Bowie). In 1988, he became the first member of The Rolling Stones to tour solo and to tour Japan. Longtime associate Ian Stewart, who had recorded an album with his blues band Rocket 88 in 1980, died in London of a heart attack on December 12, 1985, at the age of forty-seven. Charlie Watts began performing with large bands in late 1985 and assembled the British jazz band The Charlie Watts Orchestra for one 1987 American album, *Live at Fulham Town Hall,* and two brief American tours. Ron Wood toured with Bo Diddley as The Gunslingers in 1987 and 1988.

In 1986, Keith Richards served as music director for the Chuck Berry concert film *Hail! Hail! Rock 'n' Roll* and produced Aretha Franklin's version of "Jumpin' Jack Flash," a major pop and R&B hit from the movie of the same name. Two years later, he assembled a group that came to be known as The X-Pensive Winos, with drummer and songwriting partner Steve Jordan, guitarist Waddy Wachtel, keyboardist Ivan Neville, and bassist Charlie Drayton. They recorded *Talk Comes Cheap,* which featured the bitter indictment of Jagger, "You Don't Move Me Anymore," and toured America in late 1988, with their December 15 show eventually being released as *Live at the Hollywood Palladium.* In May 1989, Bill Wyman opened the restaurant Sticky Fingers Cafe in the fashionable Kensington district of London.

Inducted into the Rock and Roll Hall of Fame in 1989, The Rolling Stones finally assembled that year to record the diverse *Steel Wheels* album and conduct a world tour, their first tour in eight years. The album sold more than two million copies, producing American hits with "Mixed Emotions" (a smash) and "Rock and a Hard Place," and the tour was the highest-grossing rock tour to date. In 1990, they toured about a dozen European cities with their "Urban Jungle" tour. "Highwire," which castigated international arms dealers, became a minor hit and was one of two studio cuts from the otherwise live *Flashpoint* album. In late 1991, The Rolling Stones signed a new record deal with Virgin Records that was to commence in 1993, but Bill Wyman soon quit the group.

Mick Jagger appeared in the 1992 science fiction thriller *Freejack* and later recorded his third solo album *Wandering Spirit.* In 1992, Ron Wood issued his solo album, *Slide on This,* and Keith Richards recorded a second solo album, *Main Offender,* and toured with The X-Pensive Winos into 1993. Bill Wyman and Charlie Watts recorded solo albums, released in Japan and Great Britain, respectively.

The Rolling Stones' debut album on Virgin Records, *Voodoo Lounge,* was issued shortly before the group conducted a three-month tour of American stadiums. Recorded with bassist Darryl Jones, the album produced only minor hits with "Love Is Strong" and "Out of Tears," yet it sold more than two million copies and seemed to reestablish the group after a five-year lapse. The well-received American tour grossed more than $120 million and continued in Central and South America and Australia in 1995. The tour ultimately grossed more than $300 million and appeared to confirm the group's reputation as the "world's greatest rock 'n' roll band," at least in live performance.

The Rolling Stones' 1995 live acoustic album *Stripped* yielded a major British hit with Bob Dylan's "Like a Rolling Stone." In September 1997, the group launched a year-long world tour in support of *Bridges to Babylon,* which featured "Anybody Seen My Baby?" and "Already Over Me." This tour produced 1998's live set *No Security,* used as the name of their 1999 world tour.

ROLLING STONES BIBLIOGRAPHY

Aeppli, Felix. *Heart of Stone: The Definitive Rolling Stones Discography, 1962–1983.* Ann Arbor, MI: Pierian Press, 1985.

Aftel, Mandy. *Death of a Rolling Stone: The Brian Jones Story.* New York: Delilah Books, 1982.

Andersen, Christopher. *Jagger Unauthorized.* New York: Delacorte Press, 1993.

Appleford, Steve. *The Rolling Stones: It's Only Rock and Roll: Song by Song.* New York: Schirmer Books, 1997.

Bockriss, Victor. *Keith Richards: The Biography.* New York: Poseidon Press, 1992.

Bonanno, Massimo. *The Rolling Stones Chronicle: The First Thirty Years.* New York: Holt, 1990.

Booth, Stanley. *Dance with the Devil: The Rolling Stones and Their Time.* New York: Random House, 1984.

————. *The True Adventures of The Rolling Stones.* London: Heinemann, 1985.

————. *Keith.* New York: St. Martin's Press, 1995.

Carr, Roy. *Rolling Stones: An Illustrated Record.* New York: Harmony Books, 1976.

Charone, Barbara. *Keith Richards: Life as a Rolling Stone.* London: Futura, 1979.

Dalton, David. *Rolling Stones: An Unauthorized Biography in Words, Pictures and Music.* New York: Amsco Music Publishing, 1972.

————. *Rolling Stones.* New York: Quick Fox, 1979.

————. *The Rolling Stones: The First Twenty Years.* New York: Alfred A. Knopf, 1981.

Dimmick, Mary Laverne. *The Rolling Stones: An Annotated Bibliography.* Pittsburgh: University of Pittsburgh Press, 1972, 1979.

Dowley, Tim. *The Rolling Stones.* New York: Hippocrene, 1983.

Elliott, Martin. *The Rolling Stones: Complete Recording Sessions 1963–1989.* New York: Sterling Publications, 1989.

Elman, Richard M. *Uptight with The Stones: A Novelist's Report.* New York: Scribner, 1973.

Fitzgerald, Nicholas. *Brian Jones: The Inside Story of the Original Rolling Stone.* New York: G. P. Putnam's Sons, 1985.

Flippo, Chet. *On the Road with The Rolling Stones: 20 Years of Lipstick, Handcuffs, and Chemicals.* Garden City, NY: Doubleday, 1985.

Giuliano, Geoffrey. *The Rolling Stones Album: Thirty Years of Music and Memorabilia.* New York: Viking Studio Books, 1993.

Goodman, Pete. *Our Own Story by The Rolling Stones.* New York: Bantam Books, 1965.

Greenfield, Robert. *A Journey Through America with The Rolling Stones.* New York: E. P. Dutton, 1974.

Hotchner, A. E. *Blown Away: The Rolling Stones and the Death of the Sixties.* New York: Simon and Schuster, 1990.

Jackson, Laura. *Golden Stone: The Untold Life and Tragic Death of Brian Jones.* New York: St. Martin's Press, 1993.

Jasper, Tony. *The Rolling Stones.* London: Octopus Books, 1976.

Karnbach, James, and Carol Bernson. *It's Only Rock 'n' Roll: The Ultimate Guide to The Rolling Stones.* New York: Facts on File, 1997.

Loewenstein, Dora (editor). *The Rolling Stones: A Life on the Road.* New York: Penguin, 1998.

Marks-Highwater, J. *Mick Jagger: The Singer, Not the Song.* New York: Popular Library, 1973.

McPhail, Jessica Holman Whitehead. *Yesterday's Paper: The Rolling Stones in Print, 1963–1984.* Ann Arbor, MI: Pierian Press, 1986.

Norman, Philip. *Symphony for the Devil: The Rolling Stone Story.* New York: Linden Press/Simon and Schuster, 1984.

————. *The Life and Good Times of The Rolling Stones.* New York: Harmony Books, 1989.

Palmer, Robert. *The Rolling Stones.* Garden City, NY: Doubleday, 1983.

Pascall, Jeremy. *The Rolling Stones.* London, New York: Hamlyn, 1977.

Rolling Stone. The Rolling Stones. San Francisco: Straight Arrow Books, 1975.

Sanchez, Tony. *Up and Down with The Rolling Stones: The Inside Story.* New York: William Morrow, 1979.

Sandford, Christopher. *Mick Jagger: Primitive Cool.* New York: St. Martin's Press, 1994.

Scaduto, Anthony. *Mick Jagger: Everybody's Lucifer.* New York: David McKay, 1974.

Seay, Davin. *Mick Jagger: The Story Behind The Rolling Stones.* Secaucus, NJ: Birch Lane Press, 1993.

Tremlett, George. *The Rolling Stones.* New York: Warner Books, 1974.

Weiner, Sue, and Lisa Howard. *The Rolling Stones A to Z.* New York: Grove Press, 1983.

Wyman, Bill, and Ray Coleman. *Stone Alone: The Story of a Rock 'n' Roll Band.* New York: Viking, 1990.

Studio Albums by The Rolling Stones

The Rolling Stones	London	375	'64	†
	Abkco	7375	'86	CS/CD
12 X 5	London	402	'64	†
	Abkco	7402	'86	CS/CD
Now!	London	420	'65	†
	Abkco	7420	'86	CS/CD
Out of Our Heads	London	429	'65	†
	Abkco	7429	'86	CS/CD
December's Children (and Everybody's)	London	451	'65	†
	Abkco	7451	'86	CS/CD
Aftermath	London	476	'66	†
	Abkco	7476	'86	CS/CD
Between the Buttons	London	499	'67	†
	Abkco	7499	'86	CS/CD
Their Satanic Majesties Request	London	2	'67	†
	Abkco	8002	'86	CS/CD
Beggar's Banquet	London	539	'68	†
	Abkco	7539	'86	CS/CD
Let It Bleed	London	4	'69	†
	Abkco	8004	'86	CS/CD

Sticky Fingers	Rolling Stones	59100	'71	†
	Rolling Stones	40488	'86	LP/CS/CD†
	Virgin	39504	'94	CD
	Virgin	39525	'94	CS/CD
Exile on Main Street	Rolling Stones	(2)2900	'72	†
	Rolling Stones	40489		CS/CD†
	Virgin	39503	'94	CD
	Virgin	39524	'94	CS/CD
Goat's Head Soup	Rolling Stones	59101	'73	†
	Rolling Stones	39106		†
	Rolling Stones	40492	'86	CS/CD†
	Virgin	39498	'94	CD
	Virgin	39519	'94	CS/CD
It's Only Rock 'n' Roll	Rolling Stones	79101	'74	†
	Rolling Stones	40493	'86	CS/CD†
	Virgin	39500	'94	CD
	Virgin	39522	'94	CS/CD
Black and Blue	Rolling Stones	79104	'76	†
	Rolling Stones	40495	'86	CS/CD†
	Virgin	39499	'94	CD
	Virgin	39520	'94	CS/CD
Some Girls	Rolling Stones	39108	'78	†
	Rolling Stones	40449	'86	CS/CD†
	Virgin	39505	'94	CD
	Virgin	39526	'94	CS/CD
Emotional Rescue	Rolling Stones	16015	'80	†
	Rolling Stones	40500	'88	CS/CD†
	Virgin	39501	'94	CD
	Virgin	39523	'94	CS/CD
Tattoo You	Rolling Stones	16052	'81	†
	Rolling Stones	40502	'88	CS/CD†
	Virgin	39502	'94	CD
	Virgin	39521	'94	CS/CD
Undercover	Rolling Stones	90120	'83	†
	Rolling Stones	40504	'86	CS/CD†
	Virgin	39649	'94	CS/CD
Dirty Work	Rolling Stones	40250	'86	CS/CD†
	Virgin	39648	'94	CS/CD
Steel Wheels	Rolling Stones	45333	'89	CS/CD†
	Virgin	39647	'94	CS/CD
Voodoo Lounge	Virgin	39782	'94	CS/CD
Bridges to Babylon	Virgin	44712	'97	CS/CD

"Live" Albums by The Rolling Stones

Got Live if You Want It	London	493	'66	†
	Abkco	7493	'87	CS/CD
Rock and Roll Circus (filmed and recorded December 1968)	Abkco	1268	'96	CS/CD
Get Yer Ya-Ya's Out (recorded November 1969)	London	5	'70	†
	Abkco	8005	'86	CS/CD

Love You Live (recorded 1975–1977)	Rolling Stones	(2)9001	'77	†
	Atco	(2)9001		†
	Rolling Stones	40496		CS/CD†
	Virgin	(2)45671	'98	CD
Still Life (American Concert '81)	Rolling Stones	39113	'82	†
	Rolling Stones	40503	'88	CS/CD†
	Virgin	45674	'98	CD
Flashpoint (recorded 1989–1990)	Rolling Stones	47456	'91	LP/CS/CD†
	Virgin	45670	'98	CD
Stripped	Virgin	41040	'95	CS/CD
No Security	Virgin	46740	'98	CS/CD
Rolling Stones Anthologies and Compilations				
Big Hits (High Tide and Green Grass)	London	1	'66	†
	Abkco	8001	'86	CS/CD
Flowers	London	509	'67	†
	Abkco	7509	'86	CS/CD
Through the Past Darkly (Big Hits, Volume 2)	London	3	'69	†
	Abkco	8003	'86	CS/CD
Hot Rocks: 1964–1971	London	(2)606/7	'72	†
	Abkco	6667	'86	CS
	Abkco	(2)6667	'86	CD
More Hot Rocks (Big Hits and Fazed Cookies)	London	(2)626/7	'72	†
	Abkco	6267	'86	CS
	Abkco	(2)6267	'86	CD
Metamorphosis	Abkco	1	'75	†
The Singles Collection: The London Years	Abkco	1218	'89	CS/CD
The Singles Collection: The London Years	Abkco	(3)1231	'91	CD
Made in the Shade	Rolling Stones	79102	'75	†
	Rolling Stones	40495	'86	CD†
Sucking in the Seventies	Rolling Stones	16028	'81	†
Rewind (1971–1984)	Rolling Stones	90176	'84	†
	Rolling Stones	40505	'86	CD†
The London Symphony Orchestra				
Symphonic Music of The Rolling Stones	RCA	62526	'94	CS/CD
The London Symphonic Orchestra				
Plays the Music of The Rolling Stones	Esx	7067	'95	CS/CD
Brian Jones				
Brian Jones Presents the Pipes of Pan at Joujouka	Rolling Stones	49100	'71	†
	Point	446487	'95	CD†
	Point	(2)446612	'96	CD
Wyman, Watts, Jagger, Ry Cooder and Nicky Hopkins				
Jammin' with Edward	Rolling Stones	39100	'72	†
Bill Wyman				
Monkey Grip	Rolling Stones	79100	'74	†
Stone Alone	Rolling Stones	79103	'76	†
Drinkin' TNT 'n' Smokin' Dynamite	Blind Pig	1182	'82	†
Mick Taylor				
Mick Taylor	Columbia	35076	'79/'92	CD
Coastin' Home	Shattered	007	'96	CD

Mick Taylor and Carla Olson				
Too Hot for Snakes	Razor & Tie	1987	'91	CS/CD
Ron Wood				
I've Got My Own Album to Do	Warner Brothers	2819	'74	†
	Warner Brothers	45692	'94	CD
Now Look	Warner Brothers	2872	'75	†
	Warner Brothers	45693	'94	CD
Gimme Some Neck	Columbia	35702	'79	CD
1234	Columbia	37473	'81	†
Slide on This	Continuum	19210	'92	CS/CD
Slide on Live	Koch	8002	'98	CD
Ron Wood and Ronnie Lane				
Mahoney's Last Chance (soundtrack)	Atco	36126	'76	†
Rocket 88 (with Ian Stewart)				
Rocket 88	Atlantic	19293	'81	†
Mick Jagger				
Performance (soundtrack)	Warner Brothers	1846	'70	†
	Warner Brothers	2554	'72	†
	Warner Brothers	26400	'90	CD
Ned Kelly (soundtrack)	United Artists	5213	'70	†
She's the Boss	Columbia	39940	'85	CS/CD†
	Atlantic	82553	'93	CS/CD
Primitive Cool	Columbia	40919	'87	LP/CS/CD†
	Atlantic	82554	'93	CS/CD
Wandering Spirit	Atlantic	82436	'93	CS/CD
Keith Richards				
Talk Is Cheap	Virgin	90973	'88	CS/CD†
	Virgin (3 minis)	91047	'89	CD†
	Virgin	86079		CD
	Mobile Fidelity	00557	'92	CD†
Keith Richards and The X-Pensive Winos				
at the Hollywood Palladium (recorded December 1988)	Virgin	91808	'91	CS/CD†
	Virgin	86262		CS/CD
Main Offender	Virgin	86499	'92	CS/CD
Charlie Watts				
Long Ago and Far Away	Pointblank/Virgin	41695	'96	CS/CD

THE RONETTES

Veronica "Ronnie" Bennett (born August 10, 1943, in New York City), Estelle Bennett (born July 22, 1944, in New York City), and Nedra Talley (born January 27, 1946, in New York City).

Perhaps the best remembered of the so-called "girl groups" of the early '60s, The Ronettes achieved their biggest success under producer Phil Spector. Featuring his revolutionary "wall-of-sound" production technique, their classic "Be My Baby" became a smash rhythm-and-blues and pop hit in the fall of 1963. They followed up with several more hits, but quickly faded from popularity with Spector's withdrawal from the music business in 1966 and the demise of his Philles label in 1967. Lead singer Ronnie Bennett was married to Spector from 1968 to 1974 and attempted several comebacks with songs written by

THE RONETTES (HULTON-DEUTSCH COLLECTION/CORBIS)

George Harrison, Harry Nilsson, and Billy Joel during the '70s. During the '80s, she recorded albums for Genya Ravan's Polish Records and Columbia Records.

Formed in New York City in 1958 as the dance act The Dolly Sisters, the group comprised sisters Estelle and Veronica "Ronnie" Bennett and cousin Nedra Talley. Performing as resident dancers at the Peppermint Lounge in New York City in 1961, the group signed with Don Kirshner's Colpix label, initially recording as Ronnie and The Relatives. Becoming The Ronettes in 1962, they recorded several singles and an album's worth of material released in 1965. They attracted the attention of producer Phil Spector, who signed them to his Philles label. In 1963, they scored a smash pop, R&B, and British hit with "Be My Baby," written by Spector, Jeff Barry, and Ellie Greenwich. Through 1964 they achieved major pop hits with "Baby, I Love You," written by Spector, Barry and Greenwich, and "Walking in the Rain," written by Barry Mann and Cynthia Weil, and moderate pop hits with "Do I Love You?" and "(The Best Part Of) Breaking Up." They achieved their last (minor) hit in late 1966 as The Ronettes Featuring Veronica with "I Can Hear Music," a major hit for The Beach Boys in 1969.

The Ronettes continued to record for Philles Records with only minor success through 1966, when they broke up. In 1968, Ronnie Bennett married Phil Spector and she spent the next four years with him ensconced in his Beverly Hills mansion. In 1969, he unsuccessfully attempted to revive The Ronettes' career on A&M Records with "You Came, You Saw, You Conquered." On her own, Ronnie Spector managed a minor hit with George Harrison's "Try Some, Buy Some" on Apple Records in 1971. In 1973, she separated from Spector and formed a new edition of The Ronettes that lasted three years and recorded two unsuccessful singles for Buddah Records. Late '70s releases for Ronnie Spector included 1976's "Paradise," written by Phil Spector and Harry Nilsson and produced by Spector, and 1977's "Say Goodbye to Hollywood," written by Billy Joel and produced by "Miami" Steven Van Zandt. In 1980, she recorded *Siren* for Genya Ravan's New York–based Polish Records, and the album included The Ramones' "Here Today, Gone Tomorrow" and "Happy Birthday, Rock and Roll," dedicated to Phil Spector. In 1986 she sang the lead line from "Be My Baby" behind Eddie Money's smash pop hit "Take Me Home Tonight." Ronnie Spector recorded *Unfinished Business* for Columbia Records in 1987, and Harmony Books published her book *Be My Baby* in 1990.

RONNIE SPECTOR BIBLIOGRAPHY

Spector, Ronnie, with Vince Waldron. *Be My Baby: How I Survived Mascara, Miniskirts and Madness, Or My Life as a Fabulous Ronette.* New York: Harmony Books, 1990.

The Ronettes				
The Ronettes Featuring Veronica	Colpix	486	'65	†
The Early Years, 1961–1962	Rhino	70524	'92	CD
Presenting the Fabulous Ronettes	Philles	4006	'64	†
Best	Abkco	7212	'92	CS/CD
Ronnie Spector				
Siren	Polish	808	'80	†
Unfinished Business	Columbia	40620	'87	†

SAM AND DAVE

Sam Moore (born October 12, 1935, in Miami, Florida) and Dave Prater (born May 9, 1937, in Ocilla, Georgia; died April 9, 1988, near Sycamore, Georgia).

One of the most exciting live soul acts of the '60s and soul music's most popular duo, Sam and Dave scored a series of hits from 1966 to 1968, highlighted by the classics "Hold On! I'm Comin'" and "Soul Man." Working with producer-songwriters Isaac Hayes and Dave Porter and recording at the Stax studio in Memphis, Sam and Dave provided a raw, dynamic sound that contrasted sharply with the smoother sound of Motown. Sam and Dave broke up in 1969 and reunited twice between 1972 and 1981, enjoying renewed popularity as a result of The Blues Brothers' 1978 hit recording of "Soul Man." Sam and Dave were inducted into the Rock and Roll Hall of Fame in 1992.

Sam Moore and Dave Prater, veterans of the gospel groups The Melionaires and The Sensational Hummingbirds, respectively, met at the King of Hearts club in Miami in 1961. They teamed up as a duet and recorded for Roulette Records in the early '60s with little success. Signed to Atlantic Records by Jerry Wexler in 1965, with singles and albums issued on the Stax label, the duo recorded at the Stax studio in Memphis under songwriter-producers Isaac Hayes and Dave Porter, who wrote virtually all their hits. Usually recording with Hayes on piano and backed by Booker T. and The MGs and the raw-sounding Memphis Horns, Sam and Dave scored a smash rhythm-and-blues hit with "You Don't Know Like I Know" at the beginning of 1966. Their classic "Hold On! I'm Comin'" became a top R&B and major pop hit, followed by the rhythm-and-blues smashes "Said I Wasn't Gonna Tell Nobody," "You Got Me Hummin,'" and "When Something Is Wrong with My Baby." They later scored pop and rhythm-and-blues smashes with the classic "Soul Man" and "I Thank You."

In 1968, Sam and Dave's recording contract reverted to Atlantic Records when Stax Records was sold to Gulf-Western. Their subsequent success was largely restricted to the rhythm-and-blues field, most notably with "You Don't Know What You Mean to Me" and "Soul Sister, Brown Sugar." Disbanding for solo careers in late 1969, Sam and Dave reunited from 1972 to 1975, recording *Back at 'Cha* for United Artists. They again separated, reactivating the duo after the success of The Blues Brothers' late 1978 recording of "Soul Man" to tour through 1981. In 1986, Sam Moore rerecorded "Soul Man" with Lou Reed for the film of the same name. Dave Prater was killed in an automobile accident near Sycamore, Georgia, on April 9, 1988. Sam Moore appeared with Junior Walker in the 1988 movie *Tapeheads* and enjoyed a renewed solo career in 1994 when his duet with Conway Twitty on "Rainy Night in Georgia" appeared on the smash crossover album *Rhythm, Country and Blues.* Sam and Dave were inducted into the Rock and Roll Hall of Fame in 1992.

SAM AND DAVE BIBLIOGRAPHY

Moore, Sam. *Sam and Dave: An Oral History.* New York: Avon Books, 1998.

Sam and Dave

Sam and Dave	Roulette	25323	'67	†
Hold On! I'm Comin'	Stax	708	'66	†
	Atlantic	80255	'91	CS/CD
Double Dynamite	Stax	712	'67	†
	Atlantic	80305	'91	CS/CD
Soul Men	Stax	725	'67	†
	Atlantic	81718	'87	CS†
	Rhino	70296	'92	CS/CD
I Thank You	Atlantic	8205	'68	†
	Rhino	71012	'92	CS/CD
Best	Atlantic	8218	'69	CS
Best	Atlantic	81279	'85	CS/CD
Greatest Songs	Curb/Atlantic	77740	'95	CS/CD
Back at 'Cha	United Artists	524	'75	†
The Best Soul	Sound	920	'91	CD
Soothe Me	Rhino	71232	'93	CS/CD
Sweat 'n' Soul: Anthology	Rhino	(2)71253	'93	CS/CD
Very Best	Rhino	71871	'95	CS/CD
Soul Man	Remember	75015	'96	CD
The Soul of Sam and Dave	Dominion	408		CS/CD
Sweet and Funky Gold	Hollywood/IMG	188		CS/CD

SANTANA

Carlos Santana (born July 20, 1947, in Autlan de Navarro, Jalisco, Mexico), lead guitar, vocals; Gregg Rolie (born June 17, 1947, in Seattle, Washington), keyboards, vocals; David Brown (born February 15, 1947, in New York City), bass; Mike Carabello (born November 18, 1947, in San Francisco), congas, percussion; Jose "Chepito" Areas, timbales, percussion; and Michael Shrieve (born July 6, 1949, in San Francisco), drums. Later members included guitarist-vocalist Neal Schon (born February 27, 1954, in San Mateo, California); lead vocalists Leon Patillo, Greg Walker, Alex Ligertwood, and Buddy Miles; percussionists Coke Escovedo, Armando Peraza (timbales), and Raul Rekow (conga); keyboardists Tom Coster and Chester Thompson; bassists Alphonso Johnson and Benny Reitveld; and drummers Leon "Ndugu" Chancler and Graham Lear. Gregg Rolie and Neal Schon departed in 1972 and formed Journey in 1973.

One of the few unknown groups to appear at 1969's Woodstock Festival, Santana was immediately launched into international prominence with their landmark debut album. As the first group to successfully blend Latin and African rhythms with rock instrumentation, Santana was the first and only Latin group to achieve mainstream popularity until the rise of Los Lobos in the mid-'80s. Showcasing the stunning lead guitar playing of Carlos Santana, generally regarded as one of the most intensely emotional and technically disciplined rock lead guitar players, Santana prominently featured virtuoso Latin percussionists who propelled the group's sound. The success of Santana's first three albums spawned a number of less auspicious imitators and fostered the adoption of Latin, African, and exotic percussion instruments by soul, rock, and jazz groups. Touring more extensively than perhaps any other rock band in the history of rock music, Santana became the most popular American

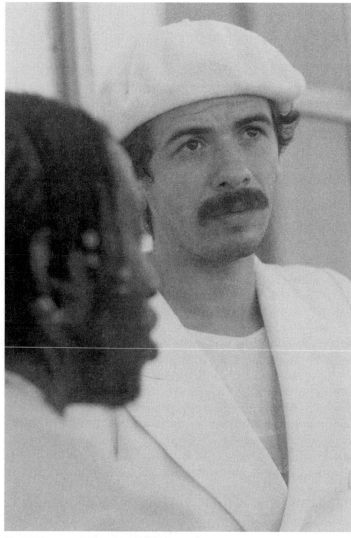

CARLOS SANTANA (HENRY DILTZ/CORBIS)

band in the world by playing engagements on virtually every continent. However, following *Abraxas,* their most cohesive album and esteemed as their masterpiece, and *Santana III,* the group began to disassemble as Carlos Santana began exploring spiritual concerns and jazz-style music with *Caravanserai.* Beginning in 1972, Carlos Santana started recording outside the band and, with the 1975 departure of drummer Michael Shrieve, Santana became the only original member to still play in the band. With varying personnel, Santana continued to record best-selling albums of Latin-style rock into the early '80s, when the group's popularity began to wane. Santana was inducted into the Rock and Roll Hall of Fame in 1998.

Encouraged to learn violin by his father at the age of five, Carlos Santana moved with his family to Tijuana, Mexico, in 1952. He discovered guitar at the age of eight and emigrated with his family to San Francisco in 1962. After high school graduation, Santana returned to Tijuana to play local bars and clubs for two years, returning to San Francisco in 1966. He soon formed The Santana Blues Band with keyboardist Gregg Rolie and bassist David Brown to play local engagements, including the Fillmore Auditorium. He gained his first recognition as a guest guitarist on *The Live Adventures of Mike Bloomfield and Al Kooper* and began exploring Latin and African rhythms in his music with the 1969 additions of conga player Mike Carabello, timbales player Jose "Chepito" Areas, and drummer Michael Shrieve. The group's name was subsequently shortened to Santana.

As one of the few unknown acts to appear at the Woodstock Festival in August 1969, Santana electrified the crowd with a stunning extended performance of the band's "Soul Sacrifice," featuring one of the most famous drum solos in the history of rock by Michael Shrieve. Signed to Columbia Records, Santana's debut album came out barely a month after Woodstock. It featured layers of exotic percussion and Carlos Santana's passionate lead guitar playing (replete with his signature sustained-note style) and became an instant success, staying on the album charts for more than two years. The album included "Soul Sacrifice," a minor hit version of Olatunji's "Jingo," and the near-smash hit "Evil Ways." *Abraxas,* usually regarded as their finest work, yielded a smash hit with Peter Green's "Black Magic Woman" and a major hit with Tito Puente's "Oye Como Va," while containing Carlos' own "Samba Pa Ti." For their third album, variously referred to as *New Album* and *Santana III,* the group added guitarist Neal Schon and percussionist Coke Escovedo. The album produced a major hit with "Everybody's Everything" and a moderate hit with "No One to Depend On."

Internal disputes within Santana had become rife in 1971 and the group disbanded for a time in 1972. In the meantime, Carlos Santana recorded a best-selling live album with powerhouse drummer-vocalist Buddy Miles from The Electric Flag. Santana formed a new edition of the group in the fall of 1972, by which time he had embraced the teachings of guru Sri Chinmoy and taken on the spiritual name "Devadip." The new group's lineup included holdovers Neal Schon, Gregg Rolie, Chepito Areas, and Michael Shrieve plus keyboardist Tom Coster and aging Latin percussionist Armando Peraza, among others. Shrieve had introduced Carlos Santana to the music of Miles Davis and John Coltrane, and this aggregation recorded Santana's first departure from Latin-style rock, *Caravanserai,* which revealed a decided jazz orientation. Gregg Rolie and Neal Schon subsequently departed to form Journey with bassist Ross Valory in 1973.

In 1973, Carlos Santana toured and recorded *Love, Devotion, Surrender* with guitarist "Mahavishnu" John McLaughlin, the man who had introduced him to the philosophy of Sri Chinmoy. Santana later recorded *Illuminations* with fellow devotee "Turiya" Alice Coltrane, the keyboard and harp-playing widow of jazz saxophonist John Coltrane. The Santana group's next album, *Welcome,* recorded with jazz vocalist Leon Thomas, continued to exhibit the group leader's spiritual bent and jazz orientation. Yet another edition of the band, with vocalist Leon Patillo and drummers Michael Shrieve and Leon "Ndugu" Chancler (Shrieve's subsequent replacement), recorded *Borboletta.* During 1975, Santana, rejoined by original bassist David Brown, toured the United States with Eric Clapton and, at mid-year, impresario Bill Graham became the group's manager.

Eventually, in 1976, Santana returned to its Latin-style sound with the highly acclaimed *Amigos* album, which featured "Europa," "Dance, Sister, Dance," and "Gitaro." The members included Tom Coster (utilizing synthesizer for the first time), vocalist Greg Walker, Armando Peraza, and Leon Chancler. Walker, Peraza, and Chancler left before the release of *Festival,* but Walker and Chepito Areas returned for the double-record set *Moonflower,* along with newcomers Raul Rekow (congas) and Graham Lear (drums). The live album yielded a major hit with a cover version of The Zombie's "She's Not There," whereas *Inner Secrets* provided hits with cover versions of Buddy Holly's "Well All Right" and The Classics IV's "Stormy." In 1979, Carlos Santana issued the mostly instrumental solo album *Oneness: Silver Dreams—Golden Reality. Marathon* featured new vocalist Alex Ligertwood and yielded a moderate hit with "You Know That I Love You." By early 1980, Santana included Ligertwood, Armando Peraza, Graham Lear, and Raul Rekow, among others. During the year, Carlos Santana recorded *The Swing of Delight* with jazz musicians Herbie Hancock, Wayne Shorter, and Ron Carter.

The Santana group scored a major hit with Russ Ballard's "Winning" and a minor hit with J. J. Cale's "The Sensitive Kind" from *Zebop!,* the band's last best-selling album. They managed their final major hit in 1982 with "Hold On" from *Shango.* Carlos next recorded the diverse solo album *Havana Moon* with Booker T. Jones, The Fabulous Thunderbirds, and Willie Nelson, who sang lead vocals on "They All Went to Mexico." Santana began playing Nevada casinos in 1984, by which time the group included vocalists Greg Walker and Alex Ligertwood, drummer Graham Lear, and later-day mainstays Chester Thompson (keyboards) and Alphonso Johnson (bass). The group toured with Bob Dylan in 1985 and added Buddy Miles for the *Freedom* album and tour. After the *Blues for Salvador* album and tour, Carlos Santana toured the United States and Europe with jazz saxophonist Wayne Shorter.

During 1988, Santana reunited with Carlos Santana, Gregg Rolie, Chepito Areas, and Michael Shrieve, joined by Armando Peraza, Chester Thompson, and Alphonso Johnson, for a tour, but a promised reunion album was never recorded, and the veterans soon went their separate ways. In 1989, Carlos Santana formed his own record label, Guts and Grace Records. The Santana group recorded two more albums for Columbia before switching to Polydor Records in 1992. In 1993, they toured with Bob Dylan and recorded *Sacred Fire,* for which the group added Carlos' guitar playing brother Jorge, a veteran of the '70s Latin rock group Malo (1972's major hit "Suavecito"). In 1994, Santana performed at the Woodstock II Festival and Island Records issued *The Santana Brothers,* recorded by Carlos and Jorge Santana with their nephew Carlos Hernandez. Carlos Santana toured with Jeff Beck in 1995. In 1998, Gregg Rolie, Neal Schon, Mike Shrieve, Mike Carabello, and Chepito Areas reunited to record *Abraxas Pool* for Miramar Records, eventually released in 1997. Santana was inducted into the Rock and Roll Hall of Fame in 1998.

Santana

Santana	Columbia	9781	'69	CD
	Columbia	00692		CS
	Columbia/Legacy	64212	'94	CD
Abraxas	Columbia	30130	'70/'85	CS/CD
	Mobile Fidelity	00552	'91	CD†
Santana III	Columbia	30595	'71	CS/CD
Caravanserai	Columbia	31610	'72	CS/CD
Welcome	Columbia	32445	'73	CS
Lotus (recorded 1973 in Japan)	Columbia	(2)46764	'91	CS/CD
Borboletta	Columbia	33135	'74	†
	Columbia/Legacy	33135		CS/CD
Amigos	Columbia	33576	'76	CS/CD
Festival	Columbia	34423	'76	†
	Columbia/Legacy	34423	'90	CS/CD
Moonflower	Columbia	(2)34914	'77	†
	Columbia	34914		CS/CD
Inner Secrets	Columbia	35600	'78	CS/CD
Marathon	Columbia	36154	'79	CS/CD
Zebop!	Columbia	37158	'81/'84	CS/CD
Shango	Columbia	38122	'82	CS/CD
Beyond Appearances	Columbia	39527	'85	CS/CD
Freedom	Columbia	40272	'87	CS/CD
Spirits Dancing in the Flesh	Columbia	46065	'90	CS/CD
Milagro	Polydor	513197	'92	CS/CD
Sacred Fire: Live in South America	Polydor	521082	'93	CS/CD

Santana Anthologies and Compilations

Greatest Hits	Columbia	33050	'74/'84	CS/CD
Viva Santana!	Columbia	(2)44344	'88	CS/CD
The Sound of Carlos Santana	Pair	1246		CS/CD
Doin' It	Pair	1286	'90	CS/CD
Early Magic!	Special Music	4809		CS/CD
Soul Sacrifice	Special Music	4821		CS/CD

Carlos Santana and Buddy Miles

Live!	Columbia	31308	'72	CS
	Columbia/Legacy	66416	'94	CD

Carlos Santana and John McLaughlin

Love, Devotion, Surrender	Columbia	32034	'73	CS/CD

Devadip Carlos Santana and Turiya Alice Coltrane

Illuminations	Columbia	32900	'74	†

Carlos Santana

Oneness/Silver Dreams—Golden Reality	Columbia	35686	'79	†

The Swing of Delight	Columbia	(2)36590	'80	†
	Columbia	36590	'90	CD†
Havana Moon	Columbia	38642	'83	CS/CD
Blues for Salvador	Columbia	40875	'87	CS/CD

The Santana Brothers

Brothers	Island	523677	'94	CS/CD

Abraxas Pool (with Gregg Rolie, Neal Schon, Michael Shrieve, Mike Carabello, and Chepito Areas)

Abraxas Pool	Miramar	23082	'97	CS/CD

DEL SHANNON

Born Charles Westover on December 30, 1934, in Coopersville, Michigan; died February 8, 1990, in Santa Clarita, California.

One of the few early rock-and-roll artists to write his own songs, Del Shannon's biggest and best-remembered hit, "Runaway," featured an instrumental break by coauthor Max Crook performed on the musitron, a keyboard instrument that preceded the synthesizer. Continuing to achieve major American hits through 1964, Del Shannon enjoyed greater popularity in Great Britain than in the United States, a fate he shared with Gene Vincent and others. In fact, he was the first American artist to record a Beatles' song ("From Me to You") and wrote "I Go to Pieces" for Peter and Gordon. With his career in eclipse for nearly fifteen years, Del Shannon attempted a comeback with 1981's *Drop Down and Get Me,* produced by Tom Petty.

Charles Westover took up guitar and singing as an early teenager and adopted his stage name, Del Shannon, after graduating from high school. He first performed on the Army's *Get Up and Go* radio show in Germany in 1958 while serving in the Army. Following his discharge in 1959, he returned to Battle Creek, Michigan, and performed in local clubs with pianist Max Crook. In 1960, he signed with the Detroit-based Big Top label, achieving his most celebrated hit (a top pop and British hit) with "Runaway," cowritten with Crook, in 1961. He followed up with the smash hit "Hats Off to Larry" and the major hit "So Long Baby." First touring Great Britain in the fall of 1962, Shannon met The Beatles and won a devoted following. Touring Great Britain again in the spring of 1963, he performed with The Beatles in May. Scoring smash British hits with "The Swiss Maid" and "Two Kinds of Teardrops," Shannon had a major American hit with "Little Town Flirt" in 1963, followed by the minor hit "From Me to You," the first song written by John Lennon and Paul McCartney to make the American charts.

In late 1962, Del Shannon left Big Top amidst legal disputes with the label and his managers, forming the short-lived label, Berlee, on which he managed a minor hit on with "Sue's Gotta Be Mine" in late 1963. Switching to Amy Records in 1964, he scored a major hit with Otis Blackwell's "Handy Man," a near-smash with the classic "Keep Searchin' (We'll Follow the Sun)," and a moderate hit with "Stranger in Town" through 1965. In early 1965, Peter and Gordon had a near-smash American hit with Shannon's "I Go to Pieces." By 1966, he had moved to Los Angeles and signed with Liberty Records. He enjoyed little success with the label and left it in 1969, later arranging The Smith's smash hit "Baby It's You" and producing Brian Hyland's smash hit "Gypsy Woman."

Del Shannon toured Great Britain regularly in the '60s and '70s, recording *Live in England* in 1972. He later recorded singles with Jeff Lynne ("Cry Baby Baby Cry") and Dave Edmunds ("And the Music Plays On") in England. He met Tom Petty in 1978 and, over the next three years, recorded *Drop Down and Get Me,* with Petty as producer. The album produced a moderate hit with a remake of Phil Phillips' 1959 smash hit "Sea of Love," but Shannon was unable to sustain a career outside the oldies revival circuit. Del Shannon was nearing completion of a new album with Lynne and Petty (later released as *Rock On*) when he shot himself to death on February 8, 1990. Shannon was inducted into the Rock and Roll Hall of Fame in 1999.

Del Shannon

Runaway	Big Top	1303	'61	†
Little Town Flirt	Big Top	1308	'63	†
	Rhino	70983	'90	CS/CD
Handy Man	Amy	8003	'64	†
Sings Hank Williams	Amy	8004	'65	†
	Rhino	70982	'90	CS/CD
1,661 Seconds	Amy	8006	'65	†
This Is My Bag	Liberty	7453	'66	†
Total Commitment	Liberty	7479	'66	†
Further Adventures of Charles Westover	Liberty	7539	'68	†
Live in England	United Artists	151	'74	†
Drop Down and Get Me	Elektra	568	'81	†
	Varèse Sarabande	5927		CD
Rock On!	Gone Gator	10296	'91	CS/CD

Del Shannon Anthologies and Compilations

Best	Dot	25824	'67	†
Del Shannon Sings	Post	9000		†
Vintage Years	Sire	(2)3708	'75	†
Best	Pickwick	3595	'78	†
Runaway Hits	Rhino	71056	'86	LP/CS†
Greatest Hits	Rhino	70977	'90	CS/CD
Runaway	Pair	1293	'91	CS/CD
The Liberty Years	EMI	95842	'91	CS/CD†
Greatest Hits	Curb/Atlantic	77756	'95	CS/CD
At His Best	Special Music	4823		CS/CD

THE SHIRELLES

Shirley Owens (born June 10, 1941), Beverly Lee (born August 3, 1941), Doris Coley (born August 2, 1941), and Addie "Micki" Harris (born January 22, 1940; died June 10, 1982, in Atlanta, Georgia), all born in Passaic, New Jersey.

One of the most popular and enduring girl groups (preceded, most significantly, only by The Chantels), The Shirelles recorded excellent material in the early '60s provided by Carole King and Gerry Goffin, Burt Bacharach and Hal David, and their producer Luther Dixon. Their success, beginning with the classic "Will You Love Me Tomorrow," helped establish Scepter Records, an independent record company run by Florence Greenberg. Scoring a series of hits with such songs as "Dedicated to the One I Love," "Baby It's You," and their best-remembered song, "Soldier Boy," The Shirelles enjoyed only modest success after the 1964 departure of Luther Dixon for Capitol Records. The Shirelles were inducted into the Rock and Roll Hall of Fame in 1996.

Formed in 1957 while Shirley Owens, Beverly Lee, Doris Coley, and Addie "Micki" Harris were in high school in Passaic, New Jersey, The Shirelles were convinced to record for Florence Greenberg's tiny Tiara label. Their first recording, "I Met Him on a Sunday (Ronde, Ronde)," written by the four, became a moderate pop hit when leased to Decca

Records in 1958. Florence Greenberg and songwriter Luther Dixon subsequently formed Scepter Records. With Greenberg as manager and Dixon as producer, The Shirelles scored a minor hit in 1959 with "Dedicated to the One I Love," written by Lowman Pauling of The Five Royales. In 1960, "Tonight's the Night," cowritten by Owens and Dixon, became a moderate pop and major rhythm-and-blues hit. Their next single included as its B-side "Boys," later recorded by The Beatles, and their subsequent single, "Will You Love Me To-morrow," written by Carole King and Gerry Goffin, became a top pop and smash R&B hit. The song's success established the Scepter label and made The Shirelles one of the most popular girl groups of the early '60s.

In 1961, The Shirelles scored pop and rhythm-and-blues smashes with "Dedicated to the One I Love" (upon rerelease) and "Mama Said," coauthored by Dixon. After the major pop hit "Big John" (a smash R&B hit), the group achieved smash crossover hits with "Baby It's You," written by Burt Bacharach, Hal David, and Bernie Williams, and the maudlin "Soldier Boy," cowritten by Dixon and Greenberg. "Welcome Home Baby" and "Everybody Loves a Lover" became major pop and R&B hits, and were followed by the crossover smash "Foolish Little Girl," coauthored by Neil Sedaka's songwriting partner Howie Greenfield. After their final major pop hit, "Don't Say Goodnight and Mean Goodbye," The Shirelles worked on the movie *It's a Mad, Mad, Mad, Mad World*. Their minor 1964 crossover hit "Sha-La-La" soon became a major hit for England's Manfred Mann.

Luther Dixon subsequently left Scepter for Capitol Records and The Shirelles never again scored a major hit. Doris Coley, by then Doris Kenner, left the group in 1968 and the remaining three attempted a comeback on RCA Records in the early '70s. In 1975, Kenner returned, as Shirley Owens, by then Shirley Alston, left for a solo career. Micki Harris, Beverly Lee, and Doris Kenner toured as The Shirelles in the early '80s, but, on June 10, 1982, Harris died of a heart attack at the age of 42 after a performance in Atlanta. The three surviving original members subsequently agreed that each could assemble groups using The Shirelles' name. The Shirelles were inducted into the Rock and Roll Hall of Fame in 1996.

The Shirelles

Tonight's the Night	Scepter	501	'60	†
Sing to Trumpets and Strings	Scepter	502	'61	†
	Sundazed	6016	'93	CD
Baby It's You	Scepter	504	'62	†
	Sundazed	6012	'93	CD
Foolish Little Girl	Scepter	511	'63	†
	Sundazed	6017	'93	CD
Sing Their Songs in the Great Movie				
"It's a Mad, Mad, Mad, Mad World" and Others	Scepter	514	'63	†
Sing Golden Oldies	Scepter	516	'64	†
Spontaneous Combustion	Scepter	562	'67	†
Happy and in Love	RCA	4581	'71	†
The Shirelles	RCA	4698	'72	†

Shirelles Anthologies and Compilations

Greatest Hits	Scepter	507	'63	†
Greatest Hits, Volume 2	Scepter	560	'65	†
Remember When	Scepter	(2)599	'72	†
Swing the Most	Pricewise	4001		†
Here and Now	Pricewise	4002		†
Sing Their Best	Springboard Int'l	4006	'73	†

Very Best	United Artists	340	'75	†
	Rhino	71807	'94	CS/CD
To Know Him Is to Love Him	Piccadilly	3318	'82	†
Anthology 1959–1967	Rhino	(2)1101	'84	†
Anthology 1959–1965	Rhino	75897	'86	CD
Sha La La La La	Impact	003		LP
Lost and Found	Impact	010	'87	LP
Greatest Hits	Impact	011	'87	LP/CD
Dedicated to You	Pair	1241	'91	CS/CD
The World's Greatest Girl Group	Tomato	(2)71731	'95	CD
Greatest Hits	Curb/Atlantic	77782	'95	CS/CD
Greatest Hits	Remember	75040	'96	CD
Soulfully Yours	Kent	032		†
16 Greatest Hits	Deluxe	7904		CS
16 Greatest Hits	Fest	4414		CS/CD
Greatest Hits	Special Music	4805		CS/CD
Original Golden Hits	Hollywood/IMG	114		CS/CD
The Fabulous Shirelles	Ace	011		CS/CD
Best	Ace	356		CD
The Shirelles and King Curtis				
Give a Twist Party	Scepter	505	'62	†
	Sundazed	6013	'93	CD
Eternally Soul	Scepter	569	'68	†
Shirley Alston				
Shirley Alston	Prodigal	10008	'76	†
Lady Rose (Shirley Alston)				
Lady Rose	Strawberry	6004	'77	†
Sings The Shirelles' Greatest Hits	Strawberry	6006	'77	†

SIMON AND GARFUNKEL

Paul Simon (born October 13, 1941, in Newark, New Jersey), guitar and tenor vocals; and
Art Garfunkel (born November 5, 1941, in Forest Hills, New York), tenor vocals.

The most successful American vocal duo since The Everly Brothers, Simon and Garfunkel started out as a rock 'n' roll duet in the late '50s but established themselves in the mid-'60s with Simon's classic "The Sounds of Silence," to which producer Tom Wilson had added rock instrumentation in their absence. Thus, thrust into the forefront of folk-rock, Simon and Garfunkel helped open the way for soft rock with their beautiful overdubbed harmonies and the use of strings on Simon's exquisitely melodic songs of isolation and alienation. Later becoming more personal, compassionate, and diversified in his songwriting, Simon wrote some of the most literate, honest, and finely crafted songs of the second half of the '60s, opening the way for the singer-songwriter movement of the '70s. Simon and Garfunkel's career culminated with the masterful *Bridge Over Troubled Water,* but, at the height of their popularity, they parted company. While Art Garfunkel established himself as an interpretive singer in the soft-rock field, Paul Simon gradually established himself as America's premier contemporary songwriter with best-selling albums and smash hits such as "Mother and Child Reunion," "Kodachrome," "50 Ways to Leave Your Lover," and "Slip Slidin' Away." However, Simon's career began to falter in the late '70s, yet he regained his stature as a music artist

SIMON AND GARFUNKEL (CORBIS-BETTMANN)

with 1986's engrossing *Graceland* album. Introducing the rhythms and music of South Africa to America and the world, the album, along with Peter Gabriel's *So* album, served to expose and generate interest in the music of diverse non-Western cultures around the world and led to the popularization of so-called "world beat" music. He reaffirmed his passion and determination to introduce the music of exotic cultures with 1990's *The Rhythm of the Saints* album, which featured the rhythms of West Africa and Brazil. However, Simon's next project, the Broadway musical *Capeman* proved an unfortunate failure. Simon and Garfunkel were inducted into the Rock and Roll Hall of Fame in 1990.

Paul Simon grew up in Queens, New York, where he met Art Garfunkel at the age of eleven. They began singing and writing songs together in 1955 and, in late 1957, scored a moderate hit with "Hey, Schoolgirl" as Tom and Jerry on Big Records. They appeared on Dick Clark's *American Bandstand,* but subsequent singles for Big, including "Teenage Fool," recorded by Simon as True Taylor, proved unsuccessful. These recordings for Big Records were later included on Pickwick Records' *The Hit Sounds of Simon and Garfunkel.* The two split up after high school to attend different colleges. Garfunkel went to Columbia University, whereas Simon attended Queens College, where he met Carole King. Simon began writing songs and working as a song promoter for E. B. Marks Publishing while recording demonstration tapes (including one with Carole King, "Just to Be with You," that became a minor pop hit for The Passions in 1959). In the early '60s, he worked as a songwriter-producer at Amy Records and recorded under a variety of pseudonyms, including Tico and The Triumphs ("Motorcycle"), Jerry Landis ("The Lone Teen Ranger"), and Paul Kane ("He Was My Brother"). Around the same time, Art Garfunkel was recording as Artie Garr on Octavia and Warwick Records.

Paul Simon performed in Greenwich Village folk clubs such as Gerde's Folk City in 1963 and was joined by Garfunkel later in the year. The duo eventually won an audition with Tom Wilson of Columbia Records after Simon returned from Europe in 1964. The audition led to Simon and Garfunkel's debut album, *Wednesday Morning, 3 A.M.,* recorded and released in late 1964. In January 1965, Simon left for England, where he played folk clubs and recorded the British-only album *Paul Simon Songbook.* While there, Simon and Bruce Woodley of The Seekers collaborated on "Someday One Day," a major British hit for The Seekers in 1966, and "Red Rubber Ball," a smash American hit for The Cyrkle in 1966.

A vacationing Art Garfunkel joined Paul Simon in England in the summer of 1965, and, in their absence, Wilson overdubbed rock instrumentation onto "Sounds of Silence" from their debut album. With the advent of folk-rock, the song became a top hit in late 1965. Returning to New York, the two hastily recorded *Sounds of Silence* and began touring the college circuit. The album, pervaded by the duo's precise, overdubbed, close-harmony singing, was released as "Homeward Bound" (included on their next album) was becoming a smash hit and yielded a smash hit with the alienated "I Am a Rock."

Over the next five years, Simon and Garfunkel were one of the most successful acts in popular music, recording some of the most artistically and commercially successful albums of the era. Strings were utilized for *Parsley, Sage, Rosemary and Thyme,* which included the self-consciously poetic major hit "The Dangling Conversation," the ditty "The 59th Street Bridge Song (Feelin' Groovy)," the satiric "A Simple Desultory Philippic," and the depressing but moving "7 O'Clock News"/"Silent Night." Like its predecessor, *Parsley, Sage, Rosemary and Thyme* remained on the album charts for nearly three years. The duo subsequently scored major hits with "A Hazy Shade of Winter," "At the Zoo," and "Fakin' It," and performed at the Monterey International Pop Festival in June 1967.

Simon and Garfunkel next worked on the soundtrack to the Mike Nichols' movie *The Graduate.* The album included six instrumental songs by David Grusin, the hit "Scarborough Fair" (based on a seventeenth-century folk ballad), and the top hit classic "Mrs. Robinson." *Bookends,* their first self-produced album, was perhaps the masterpiece of their career. It included the hits "A Hazy Shade of Winter," "At the Zoo," "Fakin' It," and "Mrs. Robinson" as well as "Save the Life of My Child" and "America." In 1969, Simon and Garfunkel achieved a near-smash hit with the classic "The Boxer," later included on *Bridge Over Troubled Water.* The album also yielded the smash hit "Cecilia," the major hit "El Condor Pasa," recorded with the Peruvian group Los Incas, and included "Keep the Customer Satisfied," "So Long, Frank Lloyd Wright," and "Baby Driver." The album ultimately sold over five million copies in the United States. "Bridge Over Troubled Water," a top pop, easy-listening, and British hit, was eventually recorded by more than 200 artists.

In early 1970, the Simon and Garfunkel team separated. By then, Art Garfunkel had worked in the Mike Nichols' films *Catch-22* (1969) and *Carnal Knowledge* (1970). In early 1972, Columbia Records issued Paul Simon's debut solo album. Coproduced by Simon, *Paul Simon* confirmed his reputation as one of the consummate songwriting craftsmen of '70s rock with compositions such as "Duncan" and "Run That Body Down" and the hits "Mother and Child Reunion" (recorded in Jamaica) and "Me and Julio Down by the Schoolyard." He recorded *There Goes Rhymin' Simon* primarily in Muscle Shoals, Alabama, and the album contained the smash hits "Loves Me Like a Rock" (recorded with the gospel group The Dixie Hummingbirds) and "Kodachrome," as well as "Something So Right" and "Take Me to the Mardi Gras." Conducting his first solo tour of America and Europe in 1973, Simon's next album was recorded on the tour.

In the meantime, Art Garfunkel had recorded his debut solo album, *Angel Claire,* which featured easy-listening material such as Jimmy Webb's "All I Know" (a near-smash pop hit) and Van Morrison's "I Shall Sing" (a moderate hit). In 1974, he scored a moderate pop hit with "Second Avenue," and *Breakaway,* produced by Richard Perry, yielded top easy-listening hits with a remake of The Flamingos' 1959 hit "I Only Have Eyes for You," "Break Away," and the duet with Paul Simon, "My Little Town." Garfunkel's 1977 *Watermark* album comprised primarily Jimmy Webb songs, yet yielded a major pop and top easy-listening hit with Sam Cooke's "(What A) Wonderful World," recorded with Paul Simon and James Taylor. Garfunkel conducted his only tour in 1977 and 1978, scored a minor pop hit with a remake of The Skyliners' 1959 hit "Since I Don't Have You," and costarred in the disconcerting and explicit Nicholas Roeg movie *Bad Timing—A Sexual Obsession. Scissors Cut* produced a top British hit with "Bright Eyes," but yielded only a minor American hit with "A Heart in New York." In 1986, Garfunkel appeared in the movie *Good to Go* and recorded the Christmas album *The Animals' Christmas* with Amy Grant.

Paul Simon coproduced his 1975 top album hit *Still Crazy After All These Years,* which yielded a top pop and easy-listening hit with "50 Ways to Leave Your Lover" and a moderate pop hit with the title song. It also included "I Do It for Your Love," "Have a Good Time," a duet with Phoebe Snow on "Gone at Last," and the near-smash pop and top easy-listening duet with Art Garfunkel, "My Little Town." Simon conducted a major international tour in 1975 and 1976 and appeared in Woody Allen's Academy Award–winning 1977 movie *Annie Hall.* Late that year, Columbia issued *Greatest Hits, Etc.,* which compiled many of his hits and included the bonus songs "Slip Slidin' Away" (a smash pop hit) and "Stranded in a Limousine."

By early 1979, Paul Simon had switched to Warner Brothers Records. He subsequently became involved in legal disputes with his former label Columbia while working on his first feature film, *One-Trick Pony,* for Warner. He wrote, scored, and starred in the movie as a musician seeking another hit record after years on the road. Eventually released in October 1980, the movie featured performances by The B-52's, Sam and Dave, and the reunited Lovin' Spoonful, with Lou Reed appearing as Simon's unsympathetic producer. The film proved a commercial failure, but the soundtrack album produced a smash hit with "Late in the Evening" and a moderate hit with the title song.

On September 19, 1981, Paul Simon and Art Garfunkel reunited for a free concert in New York's Central Park. The performance drew an estimated crowd of 500,000 and resulted in a live double-record and HBO cable television special for the duo. The two began recording an album together and toured for the first time in twelve years in 1982 and 1983. Simon ultimately decided to erase Garfunkel's vocals and release the album as a solo album. Despite the inclusion of the moderate hit "Allergies" and excellent songs such as "Think Too Much" and "The Late Great Johnny Ace," *Hearts and Bones* sold only moderately.

Never a prolific writer, Paul Simon became interested in the music of South Africa in the summer of 1984. In February 1985, he flew to Johannesburg to investigate the music of black South Africans. Using the recorded music of South African groups as a starting point, he began composing lyrics. He formed a basic trio of musicians with guitarist Chikapa "Ray" Phiri, bassist Baghiti Khumalo, and drummer Isaac Mthsli and flew the trio to New York for recordings. Over the next year, he recorded the material for *Graceland* with the trio, the vocal group Ladysmith Black Mambazo, and the band Stimela, among others. With the accordion as the common link, he also recorded "That Was Your Mother" with the zydeco band Rockin' Dopsie and The Twisters and "All Around the World" with Los Lobos. The album produced a major hit with "You Can Call Me Al" and two minor hits with "Graceland" and "Boy in the Bubble" and, amazingly, sold spectacularly, remaining on the album charts for nearly two years and eventually selling over four million copies in the United States. Although the album reinvigorated Simon's career, it also stirred controversy, inasmuch as Simon had recorded in South Africa during a United Nations cultural boycott of the country.

In 1987, Paul Simon toured internationally with Ladysmith Black Mambazo, Stimela, and South African expatriates Hugh Masekela and Miriam Makeba. Their concert in Zimbabwe, the country's biggest musical event since Bob Marley and The Wailers performed at that country's Independence Day celebration in 1980, resulted in a Showtime cable television special in May.

Paul Simon next immersed himself in the rhythms of Brazil and West Africa. As with *Graceland,* the rhythms preceded the songs for *The Rhythm of the Saints* in an inductive style of songwriting, with poet Derek Walcott as the lyrical inspiration. Regarded as even more ambitious than *Graceland, The Rhythm of the Saints* was recorded over a two-year period and featured "Born at the Right Time," "The Cool, Cool River," and "She Moves On," and yielded a minor hit with "The Obvious Child." Simon toured in support of the album and performed a free solo concert in New York's Central Park that drew 750,000 and was broadcast live on the HBO cable television network. The concert also produced a live album that was issued in 1991. With the lifting of the cultural boycott of South Africa in late

1991, Simon became the first international star to perform in the country in early 1992, although one of the tour's offices was bombed and protesters picketed the concert.

Simon and Garfunkel were inducted into the Rock and Roll Hall of Fame in 1990. They reunited occasionally during the '90s for benefit concerts and performed at New York's Paramount Theater in the fall of 1993. In May 1992, Paul Simon married Edie Brickell, vocalist of The New Bohemians from 1986 to 1991. In 1994, he coproduced her *Picture Perfect Morning* album. Simon next enlisted Derek Walcott to cowrite the book and lyrics for the musical *Capeman,* based on the true story of a teenage Puerto Rican who murdered two people in New York in 1959. Eventually staged on Broadway in January 1998, the $11 million production closed less than two months later after being panned by critics who nonetheless appreciated the show's mix of pop, salsa, rock, and doo-wop music.

SIMON AND GARFUNKEL BIBLIOGRAPHY

Humphries, Patrick. *Paul Simon, Still Crazy After All These Years.* New York: Doubleday, 1989.

Kingston, Victoria. *Simon and Garfunkel: The Biography.* New York: Fromm International, 1998.

Leigh, Spencer. *Paul Simon: Now and Then.* Liverpool: Raven Books, 1973.

Luftig, Stacey (editor). *The Paul Simon Companion: Four Decades of Commentary.* New York: Schirmer Books, 1997.

Marsh, Dave. *Paul Simon.* New York: Quick Fox, 1978.

Morella, Joseph, and Patricia Barey. *Simon and Garfunkel: Old Friends, A Dual Biography.* New York: Birch Lane Press, Carol Publishing Group, 1991.

Simon and Garfunkel

The Hit Sounds of Simon and Garfunkel	Pickwick	3059	'67	†
Wednesday Morning, 3 A.M.	Columbia	9049	'64	CS/CD
Sounds of Silence	Columbia	9269	'66	CS/CD
Parsley, Sage, Rosemary and Thyme	Columbia	9363	'66	CS/CD
The Graduate (soundtrack)	Columbia	3180	'68	CD
	Columbia	20030		CS
Bookends	Columbia	9529	'68	CS/CD
	Mobile Fidelity	732	'98	CD
Bridge Over Troubled Water	Columbia	9914	'70	CS/CD
	Columbia/Legacy	53444	'93	CD
	Columbia/Legacy	64421	'94	CD
Greatest Hits	Columbia	31350	'72/'85	CS/CD
Collected Works	Columbia	(5)37587	'81	†
	Columbia/Legacy	(3)45322	'90	CS/CD
Old Friends	Columbia/Legacy	(3)64780	'97	CS/CD
The Concert in Central Park	Warner Brothers	(2)3654	'82	CS
	Warner Brothers	3654		CD
Paul Simon				
Paul Simon	Columbia	30750	'72	†
	Warner Brothers	25588	'87	CS/CD
There Goes Rhymin' Simon	Columbia	32280	'73	†
	Warner Brothers	25589	'87	CS/CD
Live Rhymin'	Columbia	32855	'74	†
	Warner Brothers	25590	'87	CS/CD
Still Crazy After All These Years	Columbia	33540	'75	†
	Warner Brothers	25591	'87	CS/CD

Greatest Hits, Etc.	Columbia	35032	'77/'85	LP/CS/CD†
Collected Works	Columbia	(5)37581	'81	†
One-Trick Pony (soundtrack)	Warner Brothers	3472	'80/'87	CS/CD
Hearts and Bones	Warner Brothers	23942	'83/'84	CS/CD
Graceland	Warner Brothers	25447	'86	CS/CD
Negotiations and Love Songs, 1971–1986	Warner Brothers	(2)25789	'88	CS
	Warner Brothers	25789	'88	CD
The Rhythm of the Saints	Warner Brothers	26098	'90	CS/CD
Paul Simon's Concert in the Park	Warner Brothers	(2)26737	'91	CS/CD
1964–1993	Warner Brothers	(3)45394	'93	CD
Songs from *The Capeman*	Warner Brothers	46814	'97	CS/CD
Art Garfunkel				
Angel Claire	Columbia	31474	'73	CS/CD
Breakaway	Columbia	33700	'75	CS/CD
Watermark	Columbia	34975	'77	†
	Columbia/Legacy	34975		CD
Fate for Breakfast	Columbia	35780	'79	†
	Columbia/Legacy	35780	'90	CD
Scissors Cut	Columbia	37392	'81	†
	Columbia/Legacy	37392		CD
Lefty	Columbia	40942	'88	CD†
Garfunkel	Columbia	45008	'88	CS/CD
Up Until Now	Columbia	47113	'93	CS/CD
Art Garfunkel and Amy Grant				
The Animals' Christmas	Columbia	40212	'86/'90	CS/CD

THE SIR DOUGLAS QUINTET

Doug Sahm (born November 6, 1941, in San Antonio, Texas), guitar, fiddle, vocals; Augie Meyer (born May 31, 1940, in San Antonio), organ; Francisco "Frank" Morin (born August 13, 1946), saxophone, vocals; Jack Barber, bass, replaced by Harvey Kagan (born April 18, 1946); and John Perez (born November 8, 1942), drums.

Led by Doug Sahm, already a popular music veteran as a country music prodigy and '50s rock 'n' roll artist, The Sir Douglas Quintet, like The Beau Brummels, achieved their greatest acclaim as a San Francisco–based band with a British sound. Formed with organist Augie Meyer, The Sir Douglas Quintet's *Mendocino* album is regarded as a landmark album in the field of country-rock. Sahm later introduced Tex-Mex accordionist Flaco Jimenez through recordings for Atlantic Records in the early '70s and ultimately helped popularize Tex-Mex music in the '90s with The Texas Tornados, comprising Sahm, Meyer, Jimenez, and Freddie Fender.

Doug Sahm began singing at the age of five and took up pedal steel guitar at the age of six. He performed on radio station KMAC in San Antonio and soon began making personal appearances with Webb Pierce and Faron Young, becoming a featured player on the *Louisiana Hayride* by the age of eight. Sahm made his first recordings as Little Doug in 1955 and, by 1958, he was leading a rock 'n' roll group, The Pharoahs. He recorded a series of singles for Texas-based record companies such as Warrior, Harlem, and Renner Records from 1959 to 1964.

In 1964, Doug Sahm assembled The Sir Douglas Quintet with organist Augie Meyer, saxophonist Frank Morin, bassist Jack Barber, and drummer John Perez. Signed to Huey

Meaux's Houston-based Tribe label, the group scored a major hit with Sahm's "She's About a Mover" in 1965, followed by the moderate hit "The Rains Came" and the oddly titled debut album *The Best of the Sir Douglas Quintet.* Sahm relocated to San Francisco in 1966, switching to the Smash subsidiary of Mercury Records for *Honkey Blues,* recorded with Morin as part of a four-piece horn section. Reconstituted with Sahm, Meyer, Perez, Morin, and bassist Harvey Kagan, The Sir Douglas Quintet recorded *Mendocino.* The album included Delbert McClinton's "If You Really Want Me to I'll Go" and the Sahm compositions "Mendocino" (a moderate hit) and "I Wanna Be Your Mama Again," soon recorded by Tracy Nelson and Mother Earth. The group later recorded two eclectic albums of country, Tex-Mex, blues, and rock songs before Sahm disbanded the group to return to San Antonio.

Moving to Austin in late 1972, Doug Sahm signed with Atlantic Records. Recording with Augie Meyer, Bob Dylan, Doctor John, and Tex-Mex accordionist Flaco Jimenez, the Atlantic sessions (issued on CD in 1992) produced the albums *Doug Sahm and Band* and *Texas Tornado.* The former album featured Dylan's "Wallflower" and Sahm's "(Is Anybody Going To) San Antone." Sahm soon switched to Warner Brothers for *Groover's Paradise,* recorded with Stu Cook and Doug Clifford of Creedence Clearwater Revival. He then formed The Texas Tornados with Meyer, Morin, and Kagan for *Texas Rock for Country Rollers* on Dot Records. Sahm reunited The Sir Douglas Quintet in 1976, recording *Live Love* for Meyer's Texas Re-Cord label. By 1980, Sahm had moved to John Fahey's Takoma label. There he recorded the solo album *Hell of a Spell* and *Border Wave,* recorded as a Sir Douglas Quintet album with Meyer, Perez, guitarist-vocalist Alvin Crow, and bassist "Speedy" Sparks.

For much of the '80s, Doug Sahm and The Sir Douglas Quintet toured and recorded in northern Europe. In 1987, Sahm teamed with guitarist Amos Garrett and former Blasters pianist Gene Taylor for *Return of the Formerly Brothers,* initially issued on Canada's Stony Plain label. Returning to the United States, Doug Sahm toured with blues singer Angela Strehli in 1989 as Antone's Texas Rhythm-and-Blues Revue, with Flaco Jimenez as special guest. Later in the year, he performed at Slim's in San Francisco with Jimenez, Augie Meyer, and singer Freddy Fender. Fender's career had faded after he had scored top country and smash pop hits with "Before the Next Teardrop Falls" and "Wasted Days and Wasted Nights" in 1975. Jimenez had been playing Tex-Mex music on accordion for thirty-five years. As The Texas Tornados, the four signed with Reprise Records, recording their debut album in English and Spanish versions. Those and two subsequent albums sold remarkably well and helped popularize Tex-Mex music. However, in 1994, Doug Sahm left the group, reforming The Sir Douglas Quintet with Augie Meyer, Doug Clifford, and sons Shawn and Shandon to record *Daydreaming at Midnight.* In late 1995, The Texas Tornados re-formed and recorded *Four Aces,* which featured Sahm's "Little Bit Better Than Nada."

Sir Douglas Quintet

The Best of The Sir Douglas Quintet	Tribe	47001	'66	†
She's About a Mover — The Tribe Masters	Mercury			CS/CD†
Honkey Blues	Smash	67108	'68	†
Mendocino	Smash	67115	'69	†
Together After Five	Smash	67130	'70	†
Rough Edges (recorded 1969)	Mercury	655	'72	†
1 + 1 + 1 = 4	Philips	600344	'70	†
The Return of Doug Saldana	Philips	600383	'71	†
The Best of Doug Sahm and The Sir Douglas Quintet (1968–1975)	Mercury	846586	'90	CD
Texas Rock for Country Rollers	Dot	2057	'76	†
Live Love	Texas Re-Cord	1007	'78	†
Best	Takoma	7086	'80	†
	Takoma	72786	'87	LP/CS/CD†

Border Wave	Takoma	7088	'81	†
	Takoma	72788	'88	LP/CS†
Live	Takoma	72795	'87	LP/CS/CD†
Quintessence	Varrick	004	'83	CS
·Day Dreaming at Midnight	Elektra/Nonesuch	61474	'94	CS/CD

Doug Sahm/Augie Meyer

Get on Up	Collectables	669		CD

Doug Sahm

The Early Years	Collectables	5559		CD
Doug Sahm and His Band	Atlantic	7254	'73	†
Texas Tornado	Atlantic	7287	'73	†
The Best of Doug Sahm's Atlantic Sessions	Rhino	71032	'92	CS/CD
Groover's Paradise	Warner Brothers	2810	'74	†
Hell of a Spell	Takoma	7075	'80	†
	Takoma	72775		LP/CS†
Live Texas Tornado	Takoma	72795	'83	CS/CD†
Juke Box Music	Antone's	0008	'89	LP/CS/CD
The Last Real Texas Blues Band	Antone's	74212	'95	CS/CD
Get a Life	Watermelon	11076	'98	CD

Augie Meyer

Western Head Music Co.	Polydor	244069	'73	†
You Ain't Rollin' Your Roll Rite	Paramount		'73	†
California Blues	Paramount	6065	'74	†
Live at the Longneck	Texas Re-Cord	1002	'76	†
Finally in Lights	Texas Re-Cord	1005	'77	†
My Main Squeeze	Atlantic America	90856	'88	LP/CS†

Doug Sahm/Amos Garrett/Gene Taylor

Return of The Formerly Brothers (recorded 1987)	Rykodisc	10127	'89	CS/CD
Live in Japan	Mobile Fidelity	757	'92	CD†

The Texas Tornados

The Texas Tornados	Reprise	26251	'90	CS/CD
Los Texas Tornados	Reprise	26472	'91	CS/CD
Zone of Our Own	Reprise	26683	'91	CS/CD
Hangin' by a Thread	Reprise	45058	'92	CS/CD†
Best	Reprise	45511	'94	CS/CD
4 Aces	Reprise	46197	'96	CS/CD

SLY AND THE FAMILY STONE

Sly Stone (born Sylvester Stewart on March 15, 1944, in Dallas, Texas), lead vocals, keyboards, guitar; Rosemary Stewart (born March 21, 1945, in Vallejo, California), piano, vocals; Freddie Stewart (born June 5, 1946, in Dallas, Texas), guitar, vocals; Larry Graham (born August 14, 1946, in Beaumont, Texas), bass, vocals; Jerry Martini (born October 1, 1943, in Boulder, Colorado), saxophone, clarinet, piano, accordion; Cynthia Robinson (born January 12, 1946, in Sacramento, California), trumpet, vocals; and Greg Errico (born September 1, 1946, in San Francisco), drums.

Sylvester Stewart, later-day leader of Sly and The Family Stone, first came to prominence as producer for San Francisco disc jockey Tom Donahue's Autumn label in the mid-'60s, supervising hit recordings by Bobby Freeman, The Mojo Men, and The Beau Brummels. Under Stewart's directorship beginning in 1967, Sly and The Family Stone were rock music's first fully integrated group and one of the first groups to successfully combine elements of rhythm-and-blues and rock. Incorporating psychedelic lead guitar, the resounding funk bass of Larry Graham, and jazz-style horn arrangements, Sly and The Family Stone were the first psychedelic soul group and one of the first funk groups, influencing later artists such as George Clinton, Rick James, and Prince. Initially favoring self-affirming, socially optimistic lyrics composed by Stewart such as "Everyday People," "Stand!," and "Thank You (Falettinme Be Mice Elf Agin)," Sly and The Family Stone benefited from both AM and "underground" FM radio airplay and enjoyed popularity with both black and white audiences. Larry Graham helped popularize funk music after his departure from the group in 1972, but Sly and The Family Stone experienced diminished popularity in the mid-'70s, as Stewart became mired in concert cancellations, legal disputes, and drug

SLY STONE (HULTON-DEUTSCH COLLECTION/CORBIS)

problems. Sly and The Family Stone were inducted into the Rock and Roll Hall of Fame in 1993.

As a child, Sylvester Stewart moved to Vallejo, California, where he sang with siblings Rose and Freddie in the gospel group The Stewart Four, who recorded "On the Battlefield of My Lord" when Sylvester was four. By then, he was already playing drums and guitar and he eventually taught himself a number of other instruments, including piano and organ. In 1960, he scored a local hit with "Long Time Ago" and later manned The Stewart Brothers (with Freddie) and The Viscanes, who achieved another local hit with "Yellow River" when he was a high school senior. After graduation, he attended junior college and radio broadcasting school and secured disc jockey positions on San Francisco Bay Area black radio stations KSOL and KDIA. In 1964, Stewart met disc jockey Tom Donahue and soon became staff producer for Donahue's Autumn label. There he wrote and produced Bobby Freeman's smash crossover dance hit "C'mon and Swim" and produced the early hits of The Beau Brummels ("Laugh, Laugh," "Just a Little") while recording local groups such as The Vejtables ("I Still Love You"), The Mojo Men ("Dance with Me"), and The Great Society (with Grace Slick). Brother Freddie formed the soul band The Stone Souls in the mid-'60s, while Sylvester led The Stoners, with trumpeter Cynthia Robinson.

Around 1966, The Stoners and The Stone Souls merged to form Sly and The Family Stone. Developing a regional reputation as a live act, the group was joined by the Stewarts' cousin Larry Graham, a veteran multi-instrumentalist, in 1967. Signed with Epic Records, the group's debut album, *A Whole New Thing,* featured shared and contrasted lead vocals, psychedelic lead guitar, complex horn arrangements, and a funky rhythm sound rooted in Graham's bass playing. *Dance to the Music* produced a near-smash pop and rhythm-and-blues hit with the title song, but *Life* fared poorly. Early 1969's *Stand!,* sometimes labeled as soul music's first concept album and regarded as one of the most influential albums of the era, firmly established the group with black and white audiences. It included the classic "I Want to Take You Higher," "Don't Call Me Nigger, Whitey," the ominous "Somebody's Watching You," and "You Can Make It if You Try." The album yielded a major crossover hit with "Stand!" and a top crossover hit with "Everyday People," backed by the funk classic "Sing a Simple Song."

Sly and The Family Stone scored a smash pop and rhythm-and-blues hit with "Hot Fun in the Summertime" just days before their appearance at the Woodstock Festival in August 1969. One of the most dynamic and electrifying acts at the festival, the group next scored a top pop and R&B hit with "Thank You (Falettinme Be Mice Elf Agin)," backed with "Everybody Is a Star." However, Stewart became mired in legal and drug-related problems and, by 1971, the group had developed a reputation for failing to show up at scheduled concerts, a circumstance that occasionally led to riots, as it did in Chicago. Their next album of new material, the ironically titled *There's a Riot Goin' On,* came more than two years after the release of *Stand!* and revealed a darker, disillusioned side to Sly's songwriting. The album yielded a top pop and rhythm-and-blues hit with "Family Affair" and a major crossover hit with "Runnin' Away."

Sly and The Family Stone subsequently suffered the departures of bassist Larry Graham and drummer Greg Errico. Their next album, 1973's *Fresh,* produced a major pop and smash R&B hit with "If You Want Me to Stay." Sylvester Stewart married Kathy Silva in June 1974 during a concert at Madison Square Garden attended by 23,000 fans. Sly and The Family Stone achieved their last important hit soon thereafter with "Time for Livin,'" a moderate pop and near-smash rhythm-and-blues hit.

Upon departure, Larry Graham formed Hot Chocolate and the group evolved into Graham Central Station. Signed to Warner Brothers Records, the group became one of the era's most popular funk bands, scoring a moderate pop and near-smash R&B hit with "Can You Handle It" in 1974. *Ain't No 'Bout-A-Doubt It,* the group's best-selling album, yielded a moderate pop and top rhythm-and-blues hit with "Your Love" and major R&B hits with "It's Alright" and "The Jam." Subsequent albums sold progressively less well as the group scored rhythm-and-blues hits with "Love," "Now Do-U-Wanta Dance," and "My Radio Sure Sounds Good to Me" through 1978. In 1980, Graham went solo, achieving his biggest success with his debut album *One in a Million You* and its two smash R&B hits "One in a Million You" (a near-smash pop hit) and "When We Get Married." After the 1981 R&B smash "Just Be My Lady," Graham's popularity waned. In 1987, he dueted with Aretha Franklin on her minor R&B hit "If You Need My Love Tonight." Graham Central Station reassembled for a brief Japanese tour in 1992 and ultimately reunited with five of its six original members in 1995 to tour and once again record for Warner Brothers.

By 1978, Jerry Martini had joined Rubicon with Jack Blades and Brad Gillis, scoring a major hit with "I'm Gonna Take Care of Everything." In the meantime, Sylvester Stewart's career was in serious trouble. He filed for bankruptcy in 1976 and switched record labels in 1979. In the early '80s, he toured and recorded with George Clinton's Funkadelic, appearing on 1981's *The Electric Spanking of War Babies.* He recorded his final Sly and The Family Stone album in 1983. Thereafter better known for his legal and drug problems, Stewart unsuccessfully attempted comebacks with Bobby Womack in 1984 and 1987. He managed a minor pop and smash R&B hit in 1986 with "Crazay," recorded with Jesse Johnson of The Time. Sly and The Family Stone were inducted into the Rock and Roll Hall of Fame in 1993.

Sly and The Family Stone

A Whole New Thing	Epic	26324	'67	†
	Epic	30335	'71	†
	Epic/Legacy	66424	'95	CD
Dance to the Music	Epic	26371	'68	†
	Epic	30334	'71	†
	Epic/Legacy	66427	'95	CD
Life	Epic	26397	'68	†
	Epic	30333	'71	†
	Epic/Legacy	66423	'95	CD
Stand!	Epic	26456	'69/'86	CS/CD
	Epic/Legacy	53410	'93	CD
	Epic/Legacy	64422	'94	CD
Greatest Hits	Epic	30325	'70	CS/CD
There's a Riot Goin' On	Epic	30986	'71	CS/CD
Fresh	Epic	32134	'73	†
	Epic/Legacy	32134	'91	CD
Small Talk	Epic	32930	'74	†
High Energy	Epic	(2)33462	'75	†
Heard Ya Missed Me, Well, I'm Back	Epic	34348	'76	†
Ten Years Too Soon	Epic	35974	'79	†
Anthology	Epic	(2)37071	'81	†
	Epic	37071		CS/CD
Back on the Right Track	Warner Brothers	3303	'79	†
Ain't but the One Way	Warner Brothers	23942	'83	†
Best	Hollywood/IMG	717	'92	CS
Slyest Freshest Funkiest Rarest Cuts	City Hall	00002	'96	CD
The Masters	Eagle Rock	365	'98	CD

Sly Stone

High on You	Epic	33835	'75	†

Graham Central Station

Graham Central Station	Warner Brothers	2763	'73/'91	CD†
	Warner Archives	2763	'96	CS/CD
Release Yourself	Warner Brothers	2814	'74/'91	CD†
Ain't No 'Bout-A-Doubt It	Warner Brothers	2876	'75	†
Mirror	Warner Brothers	2937	'76	†
Now Do U Wanta Dance	Warner Brothers	3041	'77	†
My Radio Sure Sounds Good to Me	Warner Brothers	3175	'78	†
Star Walk	Warner Brothers	3322	'79	†
Graham Central Station	Warner Brothers	26339	'96	CS/CD
The Best of Larry Graham and Graham Central Station	Black Music 'O Skool	46043	'96	CS/CD

Larry Graham

One in a Million You	Warner Brothers	3447	'80	†
Just Be My Lady	Warner Brothers	3554	'81	†
Sooner or Later	Warner Brothers	3668	'82	†
Victory	Warner Brothers	23878	'83	†
Fired Up	Warner Brothers	25307	'85	†

Rubicon

Rubicon	20th Century	552	'78	†

SMALL FACES

Steve Marriott (born January 30, 1947, in Bow, London, England; died April 20, 1991, in Saffron Walden, Essex, England), lead guitar, lead vocals; Jimmy Winston (born James Langwith on April 20, 1945, in Stratford, London), keyboards, replaced by Ian McLagan (born May 12, 1945, in London, England), keyboards, guitar, vocals; Ronnie Lane (born April 1, 1946, in Plaistow, London; died June 4, 1997, in Trinidad, CO [USA]), bass, guitar, vocals; and Kenny Jones (born September 16, 1948, in Stepney, London), drums.

THE FACES

Rod Stewart (born January 10, 1945, in Highgate, London), vocals; Ron Wood (born June 1, 1947, in Hillingdon, Middlesex, England), rhythm guitar, bass; Ian McLagan, Ronnie Lane, and Kenny Jones.

HUMBLE PIE

Peter Frampton (born April 22, 1950, in Beckenham, Kent, England), guitar, vocals; Greg Ridley (born October 23 circa 1947 in Carlisle, Cumberland, England), bass, vocals; Jerry Shirley (born February 4, 1952, in England), drums; and Steve Marriott. Frampton left in October 1971, replaced by David "Clem" Clempson (born September 5, 1949, in Tamworth, Staffordshire, England).

The seminal British singles band of the latter half of the '60s, The Small Faces, along with The Who, were favorites of England's young Mods with their stylish dress and energetic performances. Hugely popular in England, The Small Faces were perhaps the most accomplished English band to never enjoy similar success in the United States. In 1968, they issued one of the oddest-packaged albums in rock history, their masterpiece *Ogden's Nut Gone Flake,* in a round rather than square jacket. Leader Steve Marriott left The Small Faces in 1969 to form Humble Pie with Peter Frampton, who stayed with the group until late 1971, when he launched his own enormously successful solo career, topped by 1976's *Frampton Comes Alive.* The remaining Small Faces regrouped as The Faces with Rod Stewart and Ron Wood from The Jeff Beck Group, achieving their biggest album success with late 1971's *A Nod Is as Good as a Wink . . . To a Blind Horse.* Rod Stewart recorded both solo and with The Faces through 1975, after which he also pursued a hugely successful career as a solo artist. Steve Marriott reformed The Small Faces in 1976 and Humble Pie in 1980, as Ron Wood joined The Rolling Stones and Kenny Jones joined The Who.

Formed in London as a British rhythm-and-blues band in June 1965, The Small Faces comprised Steve Marriott, Ronnie Lane, Kenny Jones, and Jimmy Winston. Marriott had played the Artful Dodger in the London production of *Oliver!* at age twelve and recorded a solo single for Decca in 1963. Signed to British Decca, The Small Faces recorded one major British-only hit single, "Whatcha Gonna Do About It," before Winston left in late 1965, to be replaced by Ian McLagan. Effervescent and well dressed in performance, The Small Faces quickly became favorites of England's young Mods, scoring smash British-only hits through 1966 with "Sha-La-La-La-Lee," and Marriott and Lane's "Hey Girl," "All or Nothing," and "My Mind's Eye."

The Small Faces began recording for Immediate Records, the new label of Rolling Stones' manager-producer Andrew "Loog" Oldham, in the spring of 1967 and came under his management that summer. Veering toward psychedelia, they achieved a British-only hit with "Here Comes the Nice" and finally penetrated into the American market with "Itchycoo Park," made distinctive through the manipulation of phasing. Although Small Faces' al-

bums had been issued in Great Britain on Decca in 1966 and 1967, their first American release did not come until 1968 on Immediate. British-only hits continued with "Tin Soldier,"
"Lazy Sunday," and "Universal," but, following *Ogden's Nut Gone Flake,* regarded as one of the
great albums of the late '60s, Steve Marriott quit the group to form Humble Pie in April
1969 with guitarist Peter Frampton, formerly with The Herd.

Humble Pie signed with Oldham's Immediate label, recording two rather pastoral albums and the smash British-only hit "Natural Born Bugie" for the label before switching to
A&M Records in 1970. More effective live than on recordings, the group's first American
success came with 1971's live double-record set *Rockin' the Fillmore,* which yielded a minor
hit with "I Don't Need No Doctor." Marriott's hard-rock orientation overwhelmed Frampton's more gentle, romantic leanings and, as a consequence, Frampton left the group in
October 1971. He was replaced by David "Clem" Clempson, previously with Colosseum.
The group's first album with Clempson, *Smokin',* became their best-seller, containing the
favorite "30 Days in the Hole" and producing a minor hit with "Hot 'n' Nasty." Subsequent
albums sold progressively less well and the group disbanded in 1975. At the beginning of
the '80s, Marriott reconstituted Humble Pie with guitarist-vocalist Bobby Tench, bassist
Anthony Jones, and original Jerry Shirley for two albums on Atlantic Records.

With the dissolution of the first edition of The Small Faces, former members Ronnie
Lane, Ian McLagan, and Kenny Jones recruited guitarist Ron Wood and vocalist Rod Stewart from The Jeff Beck Group in June 1969. Signing with Warner Brothers Records, they
shortened their name to The Faces, although their debut album, *First Step,* was credited to
The Small Faces. Touring America successfully several times in 1970, The Faces broke
through with late 1971's *A Nod Is as Good as a Wink . . . To a Blind Horse.* The album yielded a
major hit with "Stay with Me" two months after Stewart's "(I Know) I'm Losing You," recorded with The Faces, became a major hit from his *Every Picture Tells a Story* album.

Following his departure from The Jeff Beck Group, Rod Stewart had secured a solo
recording contract with Mercury Records. Thus, he recorded both solo and with The Faces,
but his popularity as a solo artist became paramount with *Every Picture Tells a Story.* Stewart
continued to record and tour with The Faces through 1975, becoming one of the most popular live bands of the time, but they managed only one more moderate hit with "Cindy Inci-
dentally" in 1973. Ronnie Lane played his final engagement with The Faces that May, to be
replaced on bass by Tetsu Yamauchi, formerly with Free. Lane later formed Slim Chance,
which recorded three British albums (one released in the United States) and scored one
British hit with "How Come?" before disbanding in 1977.

In 1974, Ron Wood recorded his first solo album, *I've Got My Own Album to Do,* with Ian
McLagan and Rolling Stones guitarist Keith Richards. During the summer of 1975, Wood
toured with both The Rolling Stones (as Mick Taylor's replacement) and Rod Stewart and
The Faces. Wood's second solo album was released that July. Given the apparent conflicts
with Ian McLagan, Wood's increasing involvement with The Rolling Stones, and his own
rising popularity, Rod Stewart announced his departure from The Faces in December
1975, effectively ending the career of The Faces.

Steve Marriott recorded a solo album in 1975 and reconstituted The Small Faces with Ian
McLagan, Kenny Jones, and bassist-vocalist Rick Wills in June 1976 for two overlooked albums for Atlantic. The Small Faces dissolved in the spring of 1978. By 1979, Kenny Jones
had joined The Who and Rick Wills had joined Foreigner. Ian McLagan recorded two solo albums for Mercury and subsequently became a member of The Rolling Stones' touring band.

In 1976, Ronnie Lane reunited with Ron Wood for the soundtrack to the movie *Ma-
honey's Last Chance,* later recording *Rough Mix* with Pete Townshend of The Who. Wood, an
official member of The Rolling Stones since July 1977, released another solo set, *Gimme
Some Neck,* recorded with McLagan, Richards, Charlie Watts, and Mick Fleetwood, in the
spring of 1979. The album included eight Wood originals and "Seven Days," written for

Wood by Bob Dylan. Wood later briefly toured with The New Barbarians, which comprised Richards, McLagan, and jazz bassist Stanley Clarke.

In 1983, Ronnie Lane, diagnosed with multiple sclerosis in 1976, recruited Eric Clapton, Jeff Beck, Jimmy Page, Joe Cocker, Paul Rodgers, and others for a brief tour in support of his Appeal for Action Research Into Multiple Sclerosis organization. He then moved to Texas and toured once again in 1987 and 1990. Steve Marriott's *30 Seconds to Midnight* was released in 1989. On April 20, 1991, after returning from the United States where he had been working with Peter Frampton, Marriott died in a house fire at his Saffron Walden cottage in Essex at the age of 44. By then, Kenny Jones had formed The Law with former Bad Company vocalist Paul Rodgers.

SMALL FACES BIBLIOGRAPHY

Pidgeon, John. *Rod Stewart and the Changing Faces.* St. Albans, England: Panther, 1976.

The Small Faces

The Small Faces	Polydor	820572		CD†
From the Beginning	Polydor	820766		CD†
	Deram	844633		CD
There Are but Four Small Faces	Immediate	1252002	'68	†
	Immediate	47895	'91	CD†
Ogden's Nut Gone Flake	Immediate	1252008	'68	†
	Abkco	4225	'73	†
	Compleat	675003	'85	†
	Immediate	46964	'91	CD†
All or Nothing	Immediate	52427	'92	CD†
Immediate Story, Volume 2	Sire	(2)3709	'76	†
Early Faces	Pride	0001	'72	†
History of The Small Faces	Pride	0014		†
Archetypes	MGM	4955	'74	†
By Appointment	Accord	7157	'82	†
The Small Faces	Compleat	672004	'84	†
Playmates	Atlantic	19113	'77	†
78 in the Shade	Atlantic	19171	'78	†
20 Greatest Hits	Big Time		'88	CD†
Greatest Hits	Griffin	001		CD
Greatest Hits	Griffin	146		CD

Humble Pie

Town and Country	Immediate	207	'69	†
	Immediate	47349	'91	CS/CD†
	Griffin	0836		CD
As Safe as Yesterday	Immediate	101	'69	†
	Immediate	47899	'91	CS/CD†
Lost and Found—Town and Country/Safe as Yesterday	A&M	(2)3513	'72	†
Humble Pie	A&M	4270	'70	†
	A&M	3127		†
	A&M	2512	'87	CD
Rock On	A&M	4301	'71	CD†
Rockin' the Fillmore	A&M	3506	'71	†
	A&M	6008		CS/CD

Smokin'	A&M	4342	'72	†
	A&M	3132		CD
Eat It	A&M	(2)3701	'73	†
Thunderbox	A&M	3611	'74	†
Street Rats	A&M	4514	'75	†
Best	A&M	3208	'82	CS/CD
Hot 'n' Nasty: The Anthology	A&M	(2)540164	'94	CD
Humble Pie (recorded at Winterland, May 1973)	King Biscuit Flower Hour	88015	'96	CD
On to Victory	Atlantic	38122	'80	†
	Atco	38122	'91	CD
Go for the Throat	Atlantic	38131	'81	†
	Atco	38131	'91	CD
The Scrubbers Sessions	Archive	80001	'97	CD
Best	Griffin	503		CD

Steve Marriott

Marriott	A&M	4572	'76	†
30 Seconds to Midnight	Griffin	214	'89	CD
Live at Dingwall's (recorded June 1984)	Cleopatra	330	'98	CD

The Faces

First Step	Warner Brothers	1851	'70/'93	CD
	Warner Brothers	26376	'93	CD
Long Player	Warner Brothers	1892	'71/'93	CD
	Warner Brothers	26191	'93	CD
A Nod Is as Good as a Wink . . . To a Blind Horse	Warner Brothers	2574	'71/'93	CD
	Warner Brothers	25929	'93	CD
Ooh La La	Warner Brothers	2665	'73/'93	CD
	Warner Brothers	26368	'93	CD
Snakes and Ladders: Best	Warner Brothers	2897	'76	†

Rod Stewart and The Faces

Live	Warner Brothers	2572		†
Coast to Coast: Overture and Beginners	Mercury	697	'73	†
	Mercury	832128		CD†
Rod Stewart and The Faces	Springboard Int'l	4030	'75	†
Early Session	Richmond	2305		CS

Ron Wood

I've Got My Own Album to Do	Warner Brothers	2819	'74	†
	Warner Brothers	45692	'94	CD
Now Look	Warner Brothers	2872	'75	†
	Warner Brothers	45693	'94	CD
Gimme Some Neck	Columbia	35702	'79	CD
1234	Columbia	37473	'81	†
Slide on This	Continuum	19210	'92	CS/CD
Slide on Live	Koch	8002	'98	CD

Ron Wood and Bo Diddley

Live at the Ritz	Victory	480008	'92	CS/CD

Ronnie Lane/Slim Chance

Ronnie Lane/Slim Chance	A&M	3638	'75	†

Ronnie Lane and Ron Wood

Mahoney's Last Chance (soundtrack)	Atco	36126	'76	†

Ronnie Lane and Pete Townshend

Rough Mix	MCA	2295	'77	†
	Atco	90097	'83	CS/CD

Ian McLagan

Troublemaker	Mercury	3786	'80	†
Bump in the Night	Mercury	4007	'81	†

The Law (with Kenny Jones)

The Law	Atlantic	82195	'91	CS/CD

SONNY AND CHER

Salvatore "Sonny" Bono (born February 16, 1935, in Detroit; died January 5, 1998, near South Lake Tahoe, California) and Cher (born Cherilyn Sarkisian LaPierre on May 20, 1946, in El Centro, California).

Sonny and Cher were one of the most famous and successful couples in rock music in the mid-'60s, owing to hits such as "I Got You Babe" and "Baby Don't Go." Mistakenly identified with the Los Angeles folk-rock movement, Sonny and Cher scored one of their biggest successes in 1967 with the classic "The Beat Goes On," as Cher launched a solo career with such hits as "Bang Bang (My Baby Shot Me Down)." In the early '70s, Cher established herself as a popular Las Vegas performer and easy-listening artist with such hits as "Gypsys, Tramps and Thieves" and "Half Breed," while the couple enjoyed mainstream exposure with their CBS television variety show from 1971 to 1974. After the couple divorced in 1974, Cher returned to performing in Las Vegas, eventually becoming the city's highest paid entertainer. During the '80s, Cher became the *only* rock star to consistently demonstrate talent as an actor, as evidenced by the films *Silkwood, Mask, Suspect,* and *Moonstruck.* Sonny later entered Republican party politics, while Cher's musical career blossomed in the late '80s.

Sonny Bono moved to Hollywood in 1954 and began his musical career as a songwriter at Specialty Records. Bono's "High School Dance" was recorded as the flip-side of Larry Williams' 1957 smash hit "Short Fat Fannie" and Williams later recorded "She Said Yeah," cowritten by Bono and later covered by The Rolling Stones. As a consequence, Bono became an apprentice producer at Specialty while recording unsuccessfully as Don Christy, Sonny Christy, and Ronny Sommers. When Specialty curtailed operations in 1960, he continued to write and record unsuccessfully, although his "Needles and Pins," cowritten with Jack Nitzche, did become a major hit for The Searchers in 1964. In 1962, through Nitzche, Bono met Phil Spector and became his assistant.

Born to Armenian and Cherokee Indian parents, Cher moved to Hollywood as a teenager to pursue an acting career, supplementing her income by singing background vocals on sessions for Phil Spector's Philles label. There she met Bono in 1963 and the couple soon married, later recording as Sonny and Cher for Vault Records and as Caesar and Cleo for Reprise Records. Cher also recorded as Bonnie Jo Mason for Annette Records and as Cherilyn for Imperial Records.

Signed to Atco Records in 1965, Sonny and Cher scored a top pop hit with "I Got You Babe," written, produced, and arranged by Sonny, and a major pop hit with "Just You" from their debut album *Look at Us.* Sonny's "Laugh at Me" and the couple's "But You're Mine" became major hits on Atco, as Reprise reissued "Baby Don't Go," a near-smash hit for the couple. Cher, recording solo for Imperial Records, scored major hits with Bob Dylan's "All I

Really Want to Do" and "Where Do You Go" in 1965, followed by the smash "Bang Bang (My Baby Shot Me Down)," written by Sonny, in the spring of 1966.

Sonny and Cher became prominent members of Los Angeles' elite hippie set and continued to achieve major hits with "What Now My Love," "Little Man," and Sonny's classic "The Beat Goes On." They appeared in the films *Good Times* (1967) and *Chastity* (1969), and Cher scored a near-smash hit with "You Better Sit Down Kids" in late 1967. Their daughter Chastity was born in Los Angeles on March 4, 1969. Cher switched to Atco Records in 1968 and Sonny and Cher moved to Kapp Records (later MCA Records) in 1971. In 1970, Cher began modeling for *Vogue,* becoming a fashion queen and international celebrity.

In 1970, Sonny and Cher moved to the Las Vegas club circuit, later hosting their own variety show on CBS television from 1971 to 1974. Thereby leaving the rock audience behind in favor of the easy-listening crowd, Sonny and Cher scored near-smash pop and smash easy-listening hits with "All I Ever Need Is You" and "A Cowboy's Work Is Never Done." Cher achieved a succession of pop and easy-listening hits through 1974, including the top pop and smash easy-listening hits "Gypsys, Tramps and Thieves," "Half-Breed," and "Dark Lady."

Sonny and Cher divorced in 1974 and each had their own short-lived network television show in 1974 and 1975, respectively. By 1975, Cher had switched to Warner Brothers Records for the Jimmy Webb–produced *Stars,* but the album and two subsequent for the label failed to produce any major hits. She married Gregg Allman in the summer of 1975, but the relationship lasted all of nine days, and the couple eventually divorced in 1977. The liaison produced one dismal album, *Two the Hard Way.* Sonny and Cher resumed their professional relationship from 1976 to 1977 for *The Sonny and Cher Show* on CBS television.

Cher returned to performing in Las Vegas casinos and moved to Casablanca Records in 1979, scoring a near-smash pop hit with the disco-style "Take Me Home." Late in the year, she formed the new wave–style band Black Rose with guitarist Les Dudek, but their album failed to sell and the group soon disbanded. In 1979, Sonny moved to Palm Springs, where he opened his own Italian restaurant. He appeared in the 1988 film *Hairspray* with Debbie Harry and served as mayor of Palm Springs from 1988 to 1992. Unsuccessfully campaigning for the Republican Party nomination for the U.S. Senate seat vacated by retiring Alan Cranston, Sonny won election as the Representative from California's 44th District in 1994. Reelected in 1996, he died in a skiing mishap near South Lake Tahoe, California, on January 5, 1998, at the age of 62.

In February 1982, Cher returned to her first career pursuit, acting, by appearing in the Broadway production of *Come Back to the Five and Dime, Jimmy Dean, Jimmy Dean.* She won praise for her straight dramatic role and later starred with Sandy Dennis and Karen Black in the film version. She garnered critical acclaim and an Academy Award nomination for her role in the 1983 film *Silkwood* with Meryl Streep and Kurt Russell and, in 1985, enjoyed well-deserved recognition of her demanding role in *Mask,* with Sam Elliott and Eric Stoltz. She starred in three 1987 films, *Suspect* with Dennis Quaid; *The Witches of Eastwick* with Jack Nicholson; and *Moonstruck* with Nicholas Cage, Danny Aiello, and Olympia Dukakis. In 1988, Cher achieved the pinnacle of any acting career, an Oscar, for her performance in *Moonstruck.*

In 1987, David Geffen convinced Cher to return to recording, and her debut for his label produced major hits with "I Found Someone," written and produced by Michael Bolton, and "We All Sleep Alone," cowritten and coproduced by Jon Bon Jovi. Her 1989 album, *Heart of Stone,* became the best-selling album of her career, selling more than two million copies. It yielded two smash pop and top easy-listening hits with "After All," sung in duet with Peter Cetera, and "If I Could Turn Back Time," plus the near-smash "Just Like Jesse James," and the major hit "Heart of Stone." Cher toured North America in 1990, but that year's film *Mermaids,* with Cher and Winona Ryder, was not well received. Cher's 1991 *Love Hurts* album produced only one major hit with "Love and Understanding." In 1992 and

1994, Cher joined ensemble casts for the films *The Player* and *Ready to Wear*. In 1995, Cher switched to Reprise Records, where she scored hits with "Walking in Memphis" and "One by One." She made her directing debut in 1996 with one of the three short films of HBO's *If These Walls Could Talk* abortion trilogy.

In the '90s, Sonny and Cher's daughter Chastity formed the pop band Ceremony with longtime friend Heidi Shink, using the name Chance, for *Hang Out Your Poetry* on Geffen Records. In 1996, Chastity was appointed media entertainment director for the Gay and Lesbian Alliance Against Defamation. In 1998, Little, Brown published Chastity's book *Family Outing,* which told stories of the "coming out" (as a homosexual) process that she and others had experienced. By the late '90s, Cher's son by Gregg Allman, Elijah Blue (born July 10, 1977), was singer for the band Deadsy, which released its debut album in 1997.

SONNY AND CHER BIBLIOGRAPHY

Bono, Chastity, with Billie Fitzpatrick. *Family Outing.* Boston: Little, Brown, 1998.

Bono, Sonny. *And the Beat Goes On.* New York: Pocket Books, 1991.

Cher, with Jeff Coplon. *The First Time.* New York: Simon Schuster, 1998.

Pellegrino, Vicki. *Cher!* New York: Ballantine Books, 1975.

Quirk, Lawrence J. *Totally Uninhibited: The Life and Wild Times of Cher.* New York: William Morrow, 1991.

Taraborrelli, J. Randy. *Cher: A Biography.* New York: St. Martin's Press, 1986.

Sonny and Cher

Baby, Don't Go	Reprise	6177	'65	†
Look at Us	Atco	33-177	'65	†
	Sundazed	6139	'98	CD
The Wondrous World of Sonny and Cher	Atco	33-183	'66	†
	Sundazed	6140	'98	CD
At Their Best (compilation of the above two albums)	Pair	(2)1140	'86	CS
In Case You're in Love	Atco	33-203	'67	†
	Sundazed	6141	'98	CD
Good Times (soundtrack)	Atco	33-214	'67	†
Best	Atco	33-219	'67	†
The Two of Us	Atco	(2)804	'72	†
The Beat Goes On — The Best of Sonny and Cher	Atco	11000	'76	†
	Rhino	91796	'91	CS/CD
Sonny and Cher Live	Kapp	3654	'71	†
	Kapp	5554	'72	†
	MCA	2009		†
All I Ever Need Is You	Kapp	3660	'72	†
	Kapp	5560	'72	†
	MCA	2021		†
Mama Was a Rock 'n' Roll Singer, Papa Used To Write All Her Songs	MCA	2102	'73	†
Live in Las Vegas, Volume 2	MCA	(2)8004	'73	†
Greatest Hits	MCA	2117	'74	†
All I Ever Need: The Kapp/MCA Anthology	MCA	(2)11300	'95	CS/CD
I Got You Babe	Rhino	71233	'93	CS/CD

Sonny

Inner Views	Atco	33-229	'67	†

Cher

All I Really Want to Do	Imperial	12292	'65	†
The Sonny Side of Cher	Imperial	12301	'66	†
All I Really Want to Do/The Sonny Side of Cher	EMI	80241	'92	CS/CD†
Cher	Imperial	12320	'66	†
With Love	Imperial	12358	'67	†
Backstage	Imperial	12373	'68	†
Golden Greats	Imperial	12406	'68	†
This Is Cher	Sunset	5276	'70	†
Superpak	United Artists	(2)88	'72	†
Superpak, Volume 2	United Artists	(2)94	'72	†
Very Best	United Artists	237	'74	†
	United Artists	377	'75	†
Very Best, Volume 2	United Artists	435	'75	†
Best, Volume 1	Liberty	10110	'81	†
Best, Volume 2	Liberty	10111	'81	†
Best of Cher	EMI	91836	'89	CS/CD†
Bang Bang: The Best of Cher	EMI	92773	'90	CS/CD†
3614 Jackson Highway	Atco	33-298	'69	†
Chastity (soundtrack)	Atco	33-302	'69	†
Cher	Kapp	3649	'71	†
reissued as Gypsys, Tramps and Thieves	Kapp	5549	'72	†
	MCA	2020		†
	MCA	624		†
	MCA	31376	'90	CD
Foxy Lady	Kapp	5514	'72	†
Bittersweet White Light	MCA	2101	'73	†
Half-Breed	MCA	2104	'73	†
Dark Lady	MCA	2113	'74	†
Greatest Hits	MCA	2127	'74	†
	MCA	37028		†
	MCA	922	'90	CS/CD
Cher Sings the Hits	Springboard Int'l	4029	'75	†
Stars	Warner Brothers	2850	'75	†
I'd Rather Believe in You	Warner Brothers	2898	'76	†
Cherished	Warner Brothers	3046	'77	†
Take Me Home	Casablanca	7133	'79	†
Prisoner	Casablanca	7184	'79	†
The Casablanca Years	Casablanca	320	'96	CS/CD
Outrageous	Polygram	838644		CS
I Paralyze	Columbia	38096	'82/'90	CS/CD†
Cher	Geffen	24164	'87	CS/CD†
Heart of Stone	Geffen	24239	'89	CS/CD
Love Hurts	Geffen	24369	'91	CS/CD
	Geffen	24421	'91	CD
It's a Man's World	Reprise	46179	'96	CS/CD
Believe	Warner Brothers	47121	'98	CD

Gregg Allman and Cher (Allman and Woman)

Two the Hard Way	Warner Brothers	3120	'77	†

Black Rose				
Black Rose	Casablanca	7234	'80	†
Ceremony (with Chastity and Chance)				
Hang Out Your Poetry	Geffen	24523	'93	CS/CD†
Deadsy (with Elijah Blue)				
Deadsy	Sire	62011	'97	CS/CD

PHIL SPECTOR

Born December 26, 1940, in the Bronx, New York.

Undoubtedly the single most important and influential producer in the history of rock music, Phil Spector devised his trademark "wall-of-sound" technique for a series of smash hit records between 1962 and 1966 for The Crystals, The Ronettes, The Righteous Brothers, and others on his own label, Philles Records. Integrating numerous guitars, massive string and horn sections, and dozens of background voices to produce a dense, murky sound that emphasized only the lead vocals and the drums, Spector's production style brought an unprecedented level of sophistication and complexity to record production. The youngest-ever head of a record label at the age of twenty-one with Philles Records, Spector produced smash hit classics on the label such as "He's a Rebel" for The Crystals, "Be My Baby" for The Ronettes, and, for The Righteous Brothers, "You've Lost That Lovin' Feelin,'" generally regarded as one of the ten classic singles in the entire history of rock. Spector astutely utilized the services of some of the best songwriters of the day (Jeff Barry and Ellie Greenwich, Barry Mann and Cynthia Weil, Carole King and Gerry Goffin) and many of Los Angeles' finest sessions musicians (keyboardists Harold Battiste and Leon Russell; guitarists Barney Kessel, Herb Ellis, and Joe Pass; horn players Steve Douglas and Jim Horn; and drummers Hal Blaine and Earl Palmer). He was the most successful independent producer in rock music when, in 1966, the dismal American showing of Ike and Tina Turner's "River Deep—Mountain High" led to his withdrawal from the music business for several years and the closure of Philles Records. One of rock's most enigmatic and perplexing figures, Spector eventually reemerged with productions for The Beatles, John Lennon, and George Harrison in the early '70s, but these efforts paled in comparison to his earlier work, still acknowledged as classics some thirty years after their original release. The compilation set *Back to Mono* forms an essential foundation for contemporary rock that has influenced virtually every contemporary producer. Phil Spector was inducted into the Rock and Roll Hall of Fame in 1989.

Phil Spector moved to Los Angeles at the age of thirteen with his mother and sister. He studied guitar and piano in high school and formed The Teddy Bears in 1958 with Annette Kleinbard and Marshall Leib. Signed to Dore Records, the trio soon scored a top pop and near-smash rhythm-and-blues hit with Spector's own "To Know Him Is to Love Him," but subsequent recordings for Imperial fared poorly and the group disbanded in 1959. After unsuccessfully recording with The Spectors Three for Trey Records, Spector worked on the West Coast under Lester Sill and Lee Hazlewood and subsequently served as understudy to Jerry Leiber and Mike Stoller in New York. He coauthored Ben E. King's solo debut pop and R&B hit "Spanish Harlem" with Leiber and produced the hits "Corinna, Corinna" for Ray Peterson, "Pretty Little Angel Eyes" for Curtis Lee, and "I Love How You Love Me" for The Paris Sisters.

Phil Spector formed Philles Records with Lester Sill in late 1961. The Crystals were the label's first signing and they soon had pop and rhythm-and-blues hits with "There's No Other" and "Uptown." The so-called "wall-of-sound" technique devised by Spector was launched into international prominence with The Crystals' top pop and smash R&B hit "He's a Rebel," written by Gene Pitney. Following "He's Sure the Boy I Love," The Crystals had smash crossover hit classics with "Da Doo Ron Ron" and "Then He Kissed Me," both cowritten by Spector, Jeff Barry, and Ellie Greenwich.

In late 1962, Phil Spector bought out Lester Sill and assumed total control of Philles Records. Bob B. Soxx and The Blue Jeans (with Darlene Love) followed their near-smash crossover hit "Zip-A-Dee Doo-Dah" with the moderate pop hit "Why Do Lovers Break Each Other's Hearts," while Darlene Love scored moderate pop hits with "(Today I Met) The Boy I'm Gonna Marry" and "Wait 'Til My Bobby Gets Home," all produced by Spector. In mid-1963, Spector signed The Ronettes to Philles Records and they soon had a smash pop and R&B hit with "Be My Baby," written by Spector, Barry, and Greenwich. Other major crossover hits for The Ronettes through 1964 were "Baby, I Love You" and "Walking in the Rain." In late 1963, Philles issued the celebrated Christmas album *A Christmas Gift for You,* featuring Philles artists performing seasonal standards plus Darlene Love's "Christmas (Baby Please Come Home)," written by Spector, Greenwich, and Barry. The album was included as part of 1991's anthology set *Back to Mono.*

During 1964, Phil Spector signed The Righteous Brothers and, at year's end, the duo scored a top pop and smash rhythm-and-blues hit with "You've Lost That Lovin' Feelin'," written by Spector, Barry Mann, and Cynthia Weil. The recording came to be regarded as one of rock's all-time classic singles. The Righteous Brothers subsequently achieved smash pop hits with "Just Once in My Life" (by Spector, Carole King, and Gerry Goffin), "Unchained Melody," and "Ebb Tide" before switching to Verve Records, where their top pop hit "(You're My) Soul and Inspiration" mimicked Spector's production style.

In the spring of 1966, Philles Records issued the Spector-Barry-Greenwich epic "River Deep—Mountain High" as recorded by Ike and Tina Turner, but the single failed to become anything more than a minor American pop hit (it was a smash hit in Great Britain), much to Spector's chagrin, as he ostensibly considered it his consummate production effort. Thus rebuffed by the American public, Spector withdrew from the record business and soon closed Philles Records, ending a stellar chapter in the history of rock music. He married Veronica "Ronnie" Bennett of The Ronettes in 1968, but the couple divorced in 1974.

During the rest of the '60s, Phil Spector was largely inactive, although he did make a cameo appearance in the film *Easy Rider* and worked for a time at A&M Records, producing one album by The Checkmates. He later salvaged The Beatles' *Let It Be* album and produced George Harrison's *All Things Must Pass* and four albums for John Lennon, including *Imagine.* He left Apple Records in 1973 and formed Warner-Spector Records under the aegis of Warner Brothers Records. The label reissued his *Christmas Album* and issued the two-record set *Greatest Hits,* but productions for Cher ("A Woman's Story"), Cher and Nilsson ("A Love Like Yours Don't Come Knocking Every Day"), and Ronnie Spector (Spector and Nilsson's "Paradise") fared poorly. Forming Phil Spector International in Great Britain in conjunction with Polydor Records, Spector produced Dion's *Born to Be with You* (unreleased in the United States) for the label. Spector's later productions for Leonard Cohen (*Death of a Ladies' Man*) and The Ramones (*End of the Century*) failed to reestablish him. Since coproducing Yoko Ono's *Season of Glass* in 1981, Spector has remained largely in seclusion. Inducted into the Rock and Roll Hall of Fame in 1989, Phil Spector emerged to assemble 1991's four-disc set *Back to Mono,* which included the entire *Christmas Album.*

PHIL SPECTOR BIBLIOGRAPHY

Fitzpatrick, John J., and James E. Fogerty. *Collecting Phil Spector: The Man, the Legend, and His Music.* St. Paul: Spectacle Press, 1991.

Ribowsky, Mark. *He's a Rebel.* New York: E. P. Dutton, 1989.

Williams, Richard. *Out of His Head: The Sound of Phil Spector.* New York: Outerbridge and Lazard; distributed by E. P. Dutton, 1972.

The Teddy Bears

The Teddy Bears	Imperial	9067	'59	†

Phil Spector

The Early Productions, 1958–1961	Rhino	203		LP†
Today's Hits	Philles	4004	'63	†
A Christmas Gift to You	Philles	4005	'63	†
reissued as Phil Spector's Christmas Album	Apple	3400	'72	†
	Warner-Spector	9103	'75	†
	Pavillion	37686	'81	†
reissued as A Christmas Gift for You	Rhino	70235		LP/CS/CD†
	Abkco	4005		CS/CD
Phil Spector's Greatest Hits	Warner-Spector	9104	'77	†
Phil Spector: Back to Mono (1958–1969)	Abkco	(4)7118	'91	LP/CS/CD

SPIRIT

Jay Ferguson (born May 10, 1947, in Burbank, California), lead vocals; Randy California (born Randolph Wolfe on February 20, 1951, in Los Angeles; died January 2, 1997, off Molokai, Hawaii), guitar, vocals; John Locke (born September 25, 1943, in Los Angeles), keyboards; Mark Andes (born February 19, 1948, in Philadelphia, Pennsylvania), bass; and Ed Cassidy (born May 4, 1931 [although some claim May 4, 1923], in Chicago), drums.

Acclaimed as one of the West Coast's finest and most unusual groups of the late '60s, Spirit never progressed beyond a cult status with their engaging songs and improvisatory stylings. Recording classics such as "Mechanical World" and "Nature's Way" and hitting with "I've Got a Line on You," Spirit fragmented after recording their masterpiece *The Twelve Dreams of Dr. Sardonicus.* Lead vocalist-songwriter Jay Ferguson and bassist Mark Andes later formed Jo Jo Gunne, but the group scored only one hit, and Ferguson subsequently pursued a solo career that culminated in the pop-style near-smash "Thunder Island" in late 1977. Spirit reunited a number of times with principals Randy California and Ed Cassidy until California's death in 1997.

The evolution of Spirit began with the formation of The Red Roosters in 1965. The members included guitarist Randy California, his drummer stepfather Ed Cassidy, vocalist-keyboardist Jay Ferguson, and bassist Mark Andes. Cassidy was a veteran jazz drummer, having previously worked with Julian "Cannonball" Adderley, Gerry Mulligan, and Thelonious Monk. Cassidy had also played in The Rising Sons with Ry Cooder and Taj Mahal. California started playing guitar at the age of five and frequented his uncle Ed Pearl's Ash Grove folk club in Los Angeles as a teenager. Jay Ferguson studied piano as a child and played with Mark Andes in high school. The Red Roosters broke up in 1966, and, that summer, California played with Jimi Hendrix's Blue Flames in New York's Greenwich Village.

Formed in Los Angeles in late 1966 with California, Cassidy, and keyboardist John Locke as Spirits Rebellious, the group shortened their name to Spirit in the summer of 1967 with the additions of former Red Roosters Ferguson and Andes. Developing a respectable following through engagements in West Coast clubs, Spirit signed with Ode Records, the new label of Lou Adler, who produced their first three albums. Their debut album featured Andes and Ferguson's neglected classic "Mechanical World," Ferguson's "Fresh-Garbage" and "Uncle Jack," and Locke's instrumental "Elijah." Their second album yielded the group's only major hit with California's "I Got a Line on You" and *Clear Spirit* included the favorite "Dark Eyed Woman."

Spirit switched to Epic Records in 1970 for their best selling album, *The Twelve Dreams of Dr. Sardonicus.* The album yielded a minor hit with Ferguson's "Animal Zoo" and included Ferguson's "Mr. Skin" (a minor hit in 1973), and California's "Morning Will Come," "Nothin' to Hide," and his neglected classic "Nature's Way." However, in mid-1971, California left to undertake a solo career and Jay Ferguson and Mark Andes departed to form the hard-rock group Jo Jo Gunne with Mark's guitarist brother Matthew. California recorded the experimental *Kaptain Kopter and The Fabulous Twirly Birds,* while Jo Jo Gunne, one of the first signings to newly formed Asylum Records, recorded four albums for the label, managing only one major hit, "Run Run Run," from their debut album and eventually breaking up in 1974. By 1976, Ferguson had initiated a solo career that produced a near-smash hit with "Thunder Island" in late 1977.

John Locke and Ed Cassidy persevered with brothers Al and Chris Staehly for *Feedback,* but, by 1973, no original members remained in Spirit. In early 1974, Cassidy and California reformed Spirit with bassist Barry Keene, signing with Mercury Records. They recorded *Spirit of '76* with John Locke and *Son of Spirit* and *Farther Along* with Locke and Andes brothers Mark and Matthew. Mark Andes soon joined Firefall, staying until 1980. John Locke was a member of Nazareth from 1981 to 1982 and Andes later manned Heart (1982–1986) and Whitesnake (1986–1987).

Ed Cassidy and Randy California persevered with Spirit, recording *Live Spirit* in Germany for their own Potato label, while California recorded several albums in Europe. In 1984, the two reunited briefly with Ferguson, Locke, and Andes for *Spirit of '84,* but they soon went their separate ways. Cassidy and California subsequently teamed up to tour and record for I.R.S. By the mid-'90s, Spirit comprised Randy California, Ed Cassidy, and keyboardist Scott Monahan. Randy California drowned off Molokai, Hawaii, on January 2, 1997, at the age of 45.

Spirit

Spirit	Ode	44004	'68	†
	Epic	31547	'92	CD†
The Family That Plays Together	Ode	44014	'69	†
	Epic	31461	'72	†
Clear Spirit	Ode	44016	'69	†
Spirit/Clear Spirit	Epic	(2)31457	'73	†
Twelve Dreams of Dr. Sardonicus	Epic	30267	'70	CS/CD
	Mobile Fidelity	00800		CD†
Feedback	Epic	31175	'72	†
The Family That Plays Together/Feedback	Epic	(2)33761	'75	†
Best	Epic	32271	'73	CS/CD
Time Circle (1968–72)	Epic/Legacy	(2)47363	'91	CD

Randy California

Kaptain Kopter and The Fabulous Twirly Birds	Epic	31755	'72	†

Jo Jo Gunne

Jo Jo Gunne	Asylum	5053	'72	†
Bite Down Hard	Asylum	5065	'73	†
Jumpin' the Gunne	Asylum	5071	'73	†
So . . . Where's the Show?	Asylum	1022	'74	†

Jay Ferguson

All Alone in the End Zone	Asylum	1063	'76	†

Thunder Island	Asylum	1115	'77		†
Real Life Ain't This Way	Asylum	158	'79		†
Terms and Conditions	Capitol	12083	'80		†
White Noise	Capitol	12196	'82		†
Randy California and Ed Cassidy					
Spirit of '76	Mercury	(2)804	'75		†
Son of Spirit	Mercury	1053	'75		†
Spirit					
Farther Along	Mercury	1094	'76		†
Future Games	Mercury	1133	'77		†
Live Spirit	Potato	2001	'78		†
Journey to Potatoland	Rhino	303	'81		†
Spirit of '84	Mercury	818514	'84		†
Rapture in the Chamber	IRS/MCA	82007	'88		LP/CS/CD†
Tent of Miracles	Caroline	22001	'90		CD†

DUSTY SPRINGFIELD

Born Mary O'Brien on April 16, 1939, in Hampstead, London, England.

THE SPRINGFIELDS

Dusty Springfield, Tom Springfield (born Dion O'Brien on July 2, 1934, in Hampstead, London), and Tim Feild.

Starting out with the British folk-style trio The Springfields with her brother, Dusty Springfield scored a series of smash British hits from 1963 to 1968. Managing smash American hits with "Wishin' and Hopin'" and "You Don't Have to Say You Love Me," she established herself as perhaps the only female British soul artist with her classic *Dusty in Memphis* album. Seldom recording after two early '70s albums for Dunhill, Dusty Springfield staged a modest comeback with late 1987's "What Have I Done to Deserve This" with The Pet Shop Boys. Her songs were featured in several mid-'90s movies. Springfield was inducted into the Rock and Roll Hall of Fame in 1999.

After singing with The Lana Sisters, Dusty Springfield formed The Springfields with Tim Feild and brother Tom in 1960 to perform on England's folk club circuit. Signed to Philips Records, the group scored a major American pop and country-and-western hit with "Silver Threads and Golden Needles" in 1962. Replacing Feild with Mike Pickworth (also known as Mike Hurst), the group achieved British smashes with "Island of Dreams" and "Say I Won't Be There" in early 1963. The Springfields disbanded in the fall of 1963 and Tom Springfield later wrote the top British hit "The Carnival Is Over" and the smash British and American hit "Georgy Girl" for The Seekers.

Dusty Springfield subsequently pursued a solo career on Philips, quickly managing a smash British and major American hit with Burt Bacharach and Hal David's "I Only Want to Be with You." Over the next five years, she was consistently successful in Great Britain, scoring smash hits with Bacharach and David's "I Just Don't Know What to Do with Myself," "Losing You" (cowritten by Tom Springfield), "In the Middle of Nowhere," Gerry Goffin and Carole King's "Some of Your Lovin'" and "Goin' Back," and "I Close My Eyes," and major hits with "Stay Awhile," "Little by Little," "I'll Try Anything," and "Give Me Time." Bacharach and David's "Wishin' and Hopin'" was a major American hit in 1964, "You Don't

Have to Say You Love Me" became a top British and smash American hit in 1965, and "All I See Is You" proved a near-smash British and major American hit in 1966. "The Look of Love," from the film *Casino Royale,* became a major American hit in 1967.

Debuting on the American night club circuit in late 1966, Dusty Springfield had switched to Atlantic Records by 1968. She traveled to the United States to record *Dusty in Memphis* under producer Jerry Wexler. A masterful recording, the album included four Goffin-King songs and Randy Newman's "I Don't Want to Hear It Anymore," and yielded four American hits, including the near-smash "Son of a Preacher Man" and the moderate hit "The Windmills of Your Mind," featured in the film *The Thomas Crown Affair.* The title song to *A Brand New Me,* recorded under Philadelphia soul producers Kenny Gamble and Leon Huff, proved her last major American hit for eighteen years.

Dusty Springfield permanently relocated to Los Angeles in the early '70s and became a successful sessions singer. She ceased performing in 1972 and signed with Dunhill Records for two albums. She returned to recording on United Artists in 1978 and performing briefly in 1980. Following 1982's *White Heat* on Casablanca Records, she recorded and made public appearances only occasionally, later scoring a smash British and American hit with "What Have I Done to Deserve This" with The Pet Shop Boys in 1987. In the mid-'90s, Dusty Springfield recorded *A Very Fine Love* in Nashville and her songs were featured in the films *Pulp Fiction, While You Were Sleeping,* and *Muriel's Wedding.* She was inducted into the Rock and Roll Hall of Fame in 1999.

The Springfields

Silver Threads and Golden Needles	Philips	600052	'62	†
Folksongs from the Hills	Philips	600076	'63	†

Dusty Springfield

Stay Awhile/I Only Want to Be with You	Philips	600133	'64	†
	Wing	16353	'67	†
Dusty	Philips	600156	'64	†
Oooooo Weeeee!!!	Philips	600174	'65	†
You Don't Have to Say You Love Me	Philips	600210	'66	†
Golden Hits	Philips	600220	'66	†
	Polydor	824467	'85	CS
The Look of Love	Philips	600256	'67	†
Everything's Coming Up Dusty	Philips	600303	'67	†
Casino Royale (soundtrack)	Colgems	5005	'67	†
	Varèse Sarabande	5265	'90	CS/CD
Just Dusty	Mercury	16380	'69	†
Something Special	Mercury	(2)120	'69	†
Dusty in Memphis	Atlantic	8214	'69	†
	Rhino	71035	'92	CS/CD
A Brand New Me	Atlantic	8249	'70	†
	Rhino	71036	'92	CS/CD
Cameo	Dunhill	50128	'73	†
Longing	Dunhill	50186	'74	†
Wishin' and Hopin'	Pickwick	3232		†
It Begins Again	United Artists	791	'78	†
	Liberty	10024		†
Living Without Your Love	United Artists	936	'79	†
	Liberty	10026		†
White Heat	Casablanca	7271	'82	†
A Very Fine Love	Columbia	67053	'95	CS/CD

STEPPENWOLF

John Kay (born Joachim Krauledat on April 12, 1944, in Tilsit, East Germany), guitar, vocals; Goldy McJohn (born May 2, 1945), keyboards; Michael Monarch (born July 5, 1950, in Los Angeles), lead guitar; John Morgan, bass; and Jerry Edmonton (born October 24, 1946, in Canada; died November 28, 1993, near Santa Barbara, California), drums. Later members included bassists Nick St. Nicholas (born September 28, 1942, in Hamburg, Germany) and George Biondo (born September 3, 1945, in Brooklyn, New York), and guitarist Larry Byrom (born December 27, 1948).

Led by one-time folk singer John Kay, Steppenwolf scored two smash hits with the classics "Born to Be Wild" and "Magic Carpet Ride" in the late '60s while recording Kay's decidedly existential and politically oriented songs such as "Desperation," "The Ostrich," and 'Don't Step on the Grass, Sam." "Born to Be Wild" featured the phrase "heavy metal thunder," later shortened to denote an entire genre of rock music. Fading from popularity in the '70s, Steppenwolf disbanded for a time, only to be reconstituted by Kay in 1974.

Born near-blind, John Kay fled East Germany with his mother in 1958, settling in Canada. He performed as a folk singer in Toronto's Yorkville district in the early '60s, and moved to New York in 1963 and Santa Monica, California, in 1964, to tour the folk club circuit. Back in Toronto in 1966, he and organist Goldy McJohn joined The Sparrow, originally formed in 1965 by Jerry and Dennis Edmonton (also known as Mars Bonfire) and bassist Nick St. Nicholas. Traveling to New York, then Los Angeles, The Sparrow signed with Columbia Records, which eventually released an album of their recordings after the success of Steppenwolf. Dennis Edmonton/Mars Bonfire later recorded a neglected album for Columbia Records.

In 1967, John Kay, Goldy McJohn, and Jerry Edmonton moved to Los Angeles and formed Steppenwolf with lead guitarist Michael Monarch and, later, bassist John Morgan. Developing a reputation as a live act on the West Coast, Steppenwolf signed with Dunhill Records. Their debut album yielded a smash hit with the classic biker song, "Born to Be Wild," and included Hoyt Axton's "The Pusher" and Kay's existential "Desperation" and "The Ostrich." "Born to Be Wild" and "The Pusher" were featured in the 1969 cult classic Peter Fonda–Dennis Hopper movie *Easy Rider*. *Steppenwolf the Second* produced another smash hit with the psychedelic "Magic Carpet Ride" and contained Mars Bonfire's "Faster Than the Speed of Life" and Kay's satirical "Don't Step on the Grass, Sam."

At Your Birthday Party yielded a near-smash hit with "Rock Me" and a minor hit with "It's Never Too Late," but subsequent singles by Steppenwolf proved moderate hits at best, and personnel defections began in 1969. Monarch and Morgan left in April, to be replaced by guitarists Larry Byrom and Nick St. Nicholas from the group T.I.M.E. for *Monster*. Nick St. Nicholas left in mid-1970, to be replaced by George Biondo. Steppenwolf disbanded in 1972. John Kay subsequently recorded two overlooked solo albums for Dunhill before reviving Steppenwolf with McJohn, Jerry Edmonton, and Biondo in 1974. They scored a major hit with "Straight Shootin' Woman" on Mums Records. The group disbanded again around 1976, with Kay reconstituting the group as its sole original member in 1980 for touring and recordings on DBX, Qwil, and I.R.S. Records.

The Sparrow

The Sparrow	Columbia	9758	'69	†
Tighten Up Your Wig: The Best of John Kay and The Sparrow	Columbia/Legacy	53044	'93	CS/CD

T.I.M.E. (with Larry Byrom and Nick St. Nicholas)

12 Originals	Liberty	7558	'68	†
Smooth Ball	Liberty	7605	'69	†

Mars Bonfire

Faster Than the Speed of Life	Columbia	9834	'69	†

Steppenwolf

Early Steppenwolf	Dunhill	50060	'69	†
	MCA	31356	'90	CD
Steppenwolf	Dunhill	50029	'68	†
	MCA	37045		†
	MCA	1596		CS
	MCA	31020		CD
	Mobile Fidelity	714		CD
Steppenwolf the Second	Dunhill	50037	'68	†
	MCA	37046		†
	MCA	1597		CS
	MCA	31021		CD
Steppenwolf/Steppenwolf The Second	MCA	(2)6933		CS
At Your Birthday Party	Dunhill	50053	'69	†
	MCA	1668		CS/CD†
Monster	Dunhill	50066	'69	†
	MCA	31328	'88	CS/CD
Live	Dunhill	(2)50075	'70	†
	MCA	(2)6013	'89	CS
	MCA	6013	'89	CD
Seven	Dunhill	50090	'70	†
	MCA	37047		†
	MCA	1598	'89	CS/CD
Gold	Dunhill	50099	'71	†
For Ladies Only	Dunhill	50110	'71	†
	MCA	31354	'89	CD
Rest in Peace	Dunhill	50124	'72	†
16 Greatest Hits	Dunhill	50135	'73	†
	MCA	1599		CS
	MCA	37049		CD
16 Great Performances	ABC	4011	'75	†
	Pickwick	3603	'78	†
Born to Be Wild: A Retrospective	MCA	(2)10389	'91	CS/CD
Slow Flux	Mums	33093	'74	†
Hour of the Wolf	Epic	33583	'75	†
Skullduggery	Epic	34120	'76	†
Reborn to Be Wild	Epic	34382	'76	CS

John Kay

Forgotten Songs and Unsung Heroes	Dunhill	50120	'72	†
My Sportin' Life	Dunhill	50147	'73	†
Lone Steppenwolf	MCA	31178	'88	CD†
All in Good Time	Mercury	3715	'78	†

John Kay and Steppenwolf

Wolftracks	DBX	1084	'84	†
	Allegiance	72854		LP/CS†
Rock and Roll Rebels	Qwil	1560	'87	†
Rise and Shine	I.R.S./MCA	82046	'90	CS/CD†
Live at Twenty-Five	ERA	5030	'94	CS/CD

THE SUPREMES

Diana Ross (born March 26, 1944, in Detroit), Florence Ballard (born June 30, 1943, in Detroit; died February 22, 1976, in Detroit), Mary Wilson (born March 6, 1944, in Greenville, Mississippi), and Barbara Martin. Martin left the group in 1962 and Ballard departed in 1967. Ballard was replaced by Cindy Birdsong (born December 15, 1939, in Camden, New Jersey). Later members included Jean Terrell, Lynda Lawrence, Scherrie Payne, and Susaye Green.

THE SUPREMES (UPI/CORBIS-BETTMANN)

Undoubtedly Motown's most successful female group, scoring ten top pop hits between 1964 and 1967, The Supremes were challenged in terms of sales success as a vocal group by only The Temptations, who recorded for the company's Gordy label. Certainly one of the most popular vocal groups of all time, The Supremes challenged the popularity of Elvis Presley and The Beatles during the '60s. Prime purveyors of the sophisticated, highly commercial, and sometimes bland black vocal group sound of Motown, The Supremes were one of the first black groups to achieve massive popularity with both black and white audiences, as six of their songs topped both the pop and rhythm-and-blues charts during their heyday, while numerous additional songs became crossover smashes. Certainly much of their popularity was based on their insistent promotion by Berry Gordy, Jr., and the production and songwriting of the Holland-Dozier-Holland team, who seemingly reserved much of their finest material for the group. The H-D-H team provided The Supremes with the classics "Where Did Our Love Go," "Baby Love," "Come See About Me," "Stop! In the Name of Love," "Back in My Arms Again," "You Can't Hurry Love," and "You Keep Me Hangin' On," among others. Even before the change of billing to Diana Ross and The Supremes in 1967, Berry Gordy was making a determined effort to elevate Ross to the forefront of the Motown spotlight, as Florence Ballard and Mary Wilson, both better singers, were relegated to the role of backup vocalists by as early as 1964. Although challenged by the rise of the grittier, rougher, and more openly erotic sound of artists recording for Stax and Atlantic Records by 1966 and suffering the loss of the Holland-Dozier-Holland team in 1968, Diana Ross and The Supremes nonetheless retained their status as the world's most widely recognized black group with hits such as "Love Child," one of Motown's earliest attempts at social consciousness, and "Someday We'll Be Together," Diana Ross' last hit with the group. Ross subsequently embarked on a successful solo career, as Gordy worked tirelessly to establish her as a multimedia star. She became the most popular black female singer of the '70s while appearing on Broadway and in Las Vegas as well as on television, as the reconstituted Supremes endured until 1977. With her well-received portrayal of Billie Holiday in the film *Lady Sings the Blues,* Ross was launched as a movie star, transcending her legacy as leader of The Supremes. Scoring her last significant successes in the early '80s, Ross remained one of the world's most popular touring performers, although her glamorous, patronizing shows were little more than exercises in self-aggrandizement. Switching to RCA Records for 1981's *Why Do Fools Fall in Love* album, Ross returned to Motown Records in 1989, but her albums failed to produce any enduring hits. The Supremes were inducted into the Rock and Roll Hall of Fame in 1988.

Diana Ross, Florence Ballard, Mary Wilson, and Betty McGlown began singing together while still in high school in 1959 as The Primettes, the companion group to The Primes, whose members Otis Williams and Eddie Kendricks later formed The Temptations. In 1960, Barbara Martin replaced McGlown and the group made their first recording for Lupine Records. They auditioned for Berry Gordy, Jr., while still in high school, but he insisted they finish high school. Signed to Tamla Records in January 1961, the group changed their name to The Supremes and recorded two unsuccessful singles for the label before switching to Motown in 1962. Barbara Martin left the group in 1962, and they continued as a trio, working as backup vocalists for other Motown artists until 1964. With Florence Ballard on lead vocals, The Supremes scored their first minor pop hit in 1962 with Smokey Robinson's "Your Heart Belongs to Me" and were subsequently placed with songwriter-producers Brian Holland, Lamont Dozier, and Eddie Holland. After Diana Ross supplanted Ballard as lead vocalist, they finally achieved their first major pop and rhythm-and-blues hit with "When Your Lovelight Starts Shining Through His Eyes" in late 1963.

In the summer of 1964, The Supremes' "Where Did Our Love Go" marked their breakthrough and initiated a string of five top pop hits with "Baby Love," "Come See About Me," "Stop! In the Name of Love," and "Back in My Arms Again." Only "Come See About Me" and "Stop! In the Name of Love" failed to top the rhythm-and-blues charts. In the spring of 1965, they toured Europe, performing at New York's Copacabana night club in July. Further top pop and R&B hits provided by Holland-Dozier-Holland through the spring of 1967 were "You Can't Hurry Love," "You Keep Me Hangin' On," and "Love Is Here and Now You're Gone." "I Hear a Symphony" and the psychedelic- sounding "The Happening" became top pop and smash rhythm-and-blues hits, and "Nothing but Heartaches," "My World Is Empty Without You," and "Love Is Like an Itching in My Heart" were smash pop and rhythm-and-blues hits.

In 1967, Florence Ballard quit or was forced out of The Supremes, to be replaced by Cindy Birdsong, a former member of Patti Labelle and The Blue Belles. Ballard briefly attempted a solo career on ABC Records and eventually died impoverished of cardiac arrest on February 22, 1976, at the age of thirty-two. The group was subsequently billed as Diana Ross and The Supremes, scoring a pop and rhythm-and-blues smash with another pyschedelic soul song, "Reflections." After the near-smash pop and major R&B hit "In and Out of Love," the Holland-Dozier-Holland team left Motown Records. In 1968, Diana Ross and The Supremes scored a top pop and smash R&B hit with "Love Child," one of Motown's few attempts at socially conscious lyrics, followed by the crossover smash "I'm Gonna Make You Love Me," recorded with The Temptations. In 1969, "I'm Livin' in Shame" became a crossover smash and "I'll Try Something New," recorded with The Temptations, became a major pop and R&B hit, as did "The Composer." Diana Ross' final single with The Supremes, "Someday We'll Be Together," was a top crossover hit.

At the beginning of 1970, Diana Ross left The Supremes for a solo career. Mary Wilson and Cindy Birdsong persevered with new member Jean Terrell. Over the next two years, they scored major pop and smash rhythm-and-blues hits with "Up the Ladder to the Roof," "River Deep—Mountain High" (with The Four Tops), "Nathan Jones," and "Floy Joy," with the smash pop and top R&B hit "Stoned Love" intervening. Birdsong left the group in 1972 (replaced by Lynda Lawrence), returned in 1974, and left again in 1976. Terrell left in 1973, replaced by Scherrie Payne, sister of Freda Payne (1970's pop smash "Band of Gold"). They scored their last major R&B and moderate pop hit with "I'm Gonna Let My Heart Do the Walking" in the summer of 1976. By late 1976, The Supremes comprised Wilson, Payne, and Susaye Greene. The group essentially disbanded in 1977, although Wilson toured England with two new members in 1978. In 1979, Payne and Greene recorded a duet album and Mary Wilson recorded a solo album for Motown. Wilson subsequently sustained her own career largely in Europe, returning to the American cabaret circuit in the '90s.

Diana Ross made her solo performing debut in March 1970 and initially worked with songwriter-producers Nicholas Ashford and Valerie Simpson. They provided her with the top pop and rhythm-and-blues hit "Ain't No Mountain High Enough" and the major crossover hits "Reach Out and Touch (Somebody's Hand)," and "Remember Me." Ross' next major pop hit came in 1973 with the top pop and smash R&B hit "Touch Me in the Morning," cowritten by Michael Masser. In the meantime, she had begun regularly appearing on television and made the movie *Lady Sings the Blues,* portraying Billie Holiday. The soundtrack album became a best-seller, remaining on the album charts for more than a year.

In 1973, Diana Ross teamed with Marvin Gaye for *Diana and Marvin.* The album yielded three hits, including the major pop hits "You're a Special Part of Me" (a rhythm-and-blues smash) and "My Mistake (Was to Love You)." In 1975, Ross starred in the film *Mahogany* and the movie's theme (also known as "Do You Know Where You're Going To"), written by Michael Masser and Gerry Goffin, became a top pop and major R&B hit. Her most successful album in years, *Diana Ross,* produced a top pop and R&B hit with the disco-sounding "Love Hangover" and a major pop and R&B hit with "One Love in My Lifetime."

In June 1976, Ross brought her *Evening with Diana Ross* stage show to Broadway, later touring the country with the show and appearing in the first one-woman, prime-time television special in March 1977. After the crossover hit "Gettin' Ready for Love," Ross appeared in the film version of the hit play *The Wiz* with Michael Jackson, Nipsey Russell, and Richard Pryor. Probably the most expensive all-black film ever made ($20 million), the film was visually spectacular, utilizing stunning costuming, elaborate special effects, and massive production numbers, but, despite a $6 million promotional campaign, it proved a relative failure.

Diana Ross was using producers outside the Motown organization by the late '70s. *The Boss,* produced by Richard Perry, included the major crossover hit title song, written by Nicholas Ashford and Valerie Simpson, and 1980's *Diana,* written and produced by Niles Rodgers and Bernard Edwards of Chic, yielded a top crossover hit with "Upside Down" and a crossover smash with "I'm Coming Out." "It's My Turn," from the movie of the same name, became a major crossover hit and, in 1981, her collaboration with Lionel Richie, "Endless Love" (again from the movie with the same title), became a top pop, easy-listening, *and* rhythm-and-blues hit.

In 1981, Diana Ross switched to RCA Records for a reported $20 million, recording six albums for the label through 1987. Smash rhythm-and-blues and major pop hits through 1985 included a remake of Frankie Lymon and The Teenagers' "Why Do Fools Fall in Love," "Mirror Mirror," "Muscles" (written and produced by Michael Jackson), "Swept Away" (written and produced by Daryl Hall), and "Missing You" (written and produced by Lionel Richie and dedicated to Marvin Gaye). Her final major R&B hits came with "Telephone," "Eaten Alive," and "Dirty Looks." She scored a top British hit in 1986 with "Chain Reaction," written and coproduced by Barry Gibb. In 1989, she conducted a world tour and returned to Motown Records, but Berry Gordy, Jr., was by then no longer involved with the company. Neither *Workin' Overtime,* produced by Niles Rodgers, nor *The Force Behind the Power,* largely produced by Peter Asher, sold well. In 1993, Villard Books published Diana Ross' evasive, self-serving autobiography *Secrets of a Sparrow.*

In December 1981, the musical *Dreamgirls,* ostensibly based on the career of The Supremes, began a long run on Broadway and later went into repertoire. Although Diana Ross disavowed the show and refused to see it, Mary Wilson endorsed it. In 1983, The Supremes (Ross, Wilson, and Cindy Birdsong) reunited for the twenty-fifth anniversary Motown television special, but tales of Ross' untoward behavior at the ceremony were confirmed with Wilson's best-selling book *Dreamgirl: My Life as a Supreme,* published by St. Martin's Press in 1986. Having persevered with regular tours of Europe in the '80s, Wilson experienced a revitalization of her career with the publication of *Dreamgirl.* She later wrote the sequel *Supreme Faith.* From 1986 to 1993, Jean Terrell, Scherrie Payne, and Lynda Lawrence toured as The FLOs (Former Ladies of the Supremes). The Supremes were inducted into the Rock and Roll Hall of Fame in 1988.

THE SUPREMES BIBLIOGRAPHY

Berman, Connie. *Diana Ross: Supreme Lady.* New York: Popular Library, 1978.

Brown, Geoff. *Diana Ross.* New York: St. Martin's Press, 1981.

Haskins, James. *I'm Gonna Make You Love Me: The Story of Diana Ross.* New York: Dial Press, 1980.

————. *Diana Ross: Star Supreme.* New York: Viking Kestrel, 1985.

Itzkowitz, Leonore K. *Diana Ross.* New York: Random House, 1974.

Ross, Diana. *Secrets of a Sparrow.* New York: Villard Books, 1993.

Taraborrelli, J. Randy. *Diana.* Garden City, NY: Doubleday, 1985.

————. *Call Her Miss Ross.* Secaucus, NJ: Birch Lane Press, Carol Publishing Group, 1989.

Turner, Tony, with Barbara Aria. *All That Glittered: My Life with The Supremes.* New York: Dutton, 1990.

Wilson, Mary, with Patricia Romanowski. *Supreme Faith: Someday We'll Be Together.* New York: HarperCollins, 1990.

Wilson, Mary, with Patricia Romanowski and Ahrgus Juilliard. *Dreamgirl: My Life as a Supreme.* New York: St. Martin's Press, 1986.

The Supremes

Meet The Supremes	Motown	606	'63	†
	Motown	5253		CS/CD†
Where Did Our Love Go	Motown	621	'65	†
	Motown	5270		CS/CD†
A Bit of Liverpool	Motown	623	'64	†
	Motown	5249	'89	CD†
Country, Western and Pop	Motown	625	'65	†
	Motown	0327	'94	CS/CD†
More Hits	Motown	627	'65	†
	Motown	5440	'89	CS/CD†
We Remember Sam Cooke	Motown	629	'65	†
	Motown	5495	'91	CS/CD†
At the Copa	Motown	636	'65	†
	Motown	5162	'90	CS/CD†
Merry Christmas	Motown	638	'65	†
	Motown	5252		CS/CD

I Hear a Symphony	Motown	643	'66	†
	Motown	5147		CS/CD
Supremes A Go-Go	Motown	649	'66	†
	Motown	5138	'89	CS/CD
Sing Holland-Dozier-Holland	Motown	650	'67	†
	Motown	5182	'89	CS/CD†
Sing Rodgers and Hart	Motown	659	'67	†
The Rodgers and Hart Collection	Motown	9074	'87	CD†
Greatest Hits	Motown	(2)663	'67	†
Greatest Hits, Volumes 1 and 2	Motown	(2)237		CS†
	Motown	237		CD†
Greatest Hits, Volume 1	Motown	5357	'89	CS/CD
Greatest Hits, Volume 2	Motown	5358		CS/CD

Diana Ross and The Supremes

Reflections	Motown	665	'68	†
	Motown	5494	'91	CS/CD
Love Child	Motown	670	'68	†
	Motown	5245	'89	CS/CD†
Funny Girl	Motown	672	'68	†
Live at London's Talk of the Town	Motown	676	'68	†
	Motown	530328	'94	CS/CD
Let the Sunshine In	Motown	689	'69	†
	Motown	5305		CS/CD†
Cream of the Crop	Motown	694	'69	†
	Motown	5435	'89	CS/CD†
Greatest Hits, Volume 3	Motown	702	'69	†
	Motown	5203		CS/CD
Farewell	Motown	708	'70	†
Anthology	Motown	(3)794	'74	LP/CS
	Motown	(2)794		CD
Motown Superstar Series, Volume 1	Motown	101		†
	Motown	5101		CS
Compact Command Performance (18 Greatest Hits)	Motown	6073		CD†
Captured Live on Stage	Motown	(2)5278		CS/CD
Great Songs and Performances That Inspired the Motown 25th Anniversary TV Show	Motown	5313	'85	CS/CD
Supremes Sing Motown	Motown	5371	'86	†
25th Anniversary	Motown	(3)5381	'86	CS†
	Motown	(2)5381	'86	CD†
Every Great No. 1 Hit	Motown	9038	'87	CD†
	Motown	5498		CS/CD
Never-Before-Released Masters	Motown	9075	'87	CD†
More Hits by The Supremes	Motown	5440	'89	CS/CD†
Anthology	Motown	(2)0511	'95	CS/CD
The Ultimate Collection	Motown	0827	'97	CS/CD
Motown Legends	Esx	8520	'95	CS/CD

The Supremes/Diana Ross and The Supremes Reissues

Where Did Our Love Go/I Hear a Symphony	Motown	5270	'86	CD†
Love Child/Supremes A Go-Go	Motown	8121	'86	CD†
Let the Sunshine In/Cream of the Crop	Motown	8132	'86	CD†

More Hits by The Supremes/Sing Holland-Dozier-Holland	Motown	8151		CD†
The Supremes and The Temptations				
The Supremes Join The Temptations	Motown	679	'68	†
	Motown	5139		CS/CD
T.C.B.	Motown	682	'68	†
	Motown	5171		CS/CD†
Together	Motown	692	'69	†
	Motown	5436	'89	CS/CD†
The Supremes Join The Temptations/Together	Motown	8138		CD†
On Broadway	Motown	699	'69	†
Motown Legends	Motown	5368		†
The Supremes and The Four Tops				
The Magnificent Seven	Motown	717	'70	†
	Motown	5123		CS/CD†
The Return of The Magnificent Seven	Motown	736	'71	†
Dynamite	Motown	745	'71	†
Best	Motown	5491	'91	CS/CD
The Supremes (without Diana Ross)				
Right On	Motown	705	'70	†
	Motown	5442	'89	CS/CD†
New Ways, but Love Stays	Motown	720	'70	†
	Motown	5497	'91	CS/CD†
Touch	Motown	737	'71	†
	Motown	5447		CS/CD†
Floy Joy	Motown	751	'72	†
	Motown	5441	'89	CS/CD†
The Supremes	Motown	756	'72	†
The Supremes	Motown	828	'75	†
High Energy	Motown	863	'76	†
Mary, Scherrie and Susaye	Motown	873	'77	†
At Their Best (1973–1978)	Motown	904	'78	†
Greatest Hits and Rare Classics	Motown	5487	'91	CS/CD
Motown Legends: Stoned Love	Esx	8523	'95	CS/CD
Mary Wilson				
Mary Wilson	Motown	927	'79	†
Scherrie Payne and Susaye Greene				
Partners	Motown	920	'79	†
Diana Ross				
Diana Ross	Motown	711	'70	†
Diana!	Motown	719	'71	†
	Motown	5155		CS/CD†
Everything Is Everything	Motown	724	'70	†
Surrender	Motown	723	'71	†
	Motown	5423	'89	CD†
Lady Sings the Blues	Motown	(2)0758	'72	CS
	Motown	0758		CD
Touch Me in the Morning	Motown	772	'73	†
	Motown	5163		CS/CD
The Last Time I Saw Him	Motown	812	'73	†

Live at Caesar's Palace	Motown	801	'74	†
	Motown	5169		CS/CD
Mahogany (soundtrack)	Motown	858	'75	†
Diana Ross	Motown	861	'76	†
	Motown	5294	'89	CS/CD
Greatest Hits	Motown	869	'76	CS
	Motown	869	'91	CD
An Evening with Diana Ross	Motown	(2)877	'77	†
	Motown	(2)5268		CS
	Motown	5268		CD
Baby, It's Me	Motown	890	'77	†
	Motown	5434		CD†
Ross	Motown	907	'78	†
The Boss	Motown	923	'79	†
	Motown	5198		CS/CD†
Diana	Motown	936	'80	†
	Motown	5383	'87	CS/CD
Diana/The Boss	Motown	8102	'86	CD†
To Love Again	Motown	951	'81	†
All the Great Hits	Motown	(2)960	'81	†
	Motown	960		CS/CD
Ain't No Mountain High Enough	Motown	5135	'89	CS/CD
Ain't No Mountain High Enough/Surrender	Motown	8142		CD†
Anthology	Motown	(2)6049	'83	CS/CD
Diana's Duets	Motown	5214	'87	CS/CD
Compact Command Performance (14 Greatest Hits)	Motown	6072		CD†
All the Great Love Songs	Motown	6105		CD†
Why Do Fools Fall in Love	RCA	4153	'81	†
	RCA	5162	'84	CS†
Silk Electric	RCA	4384	'82/'90	CS/CD†
Ross	RCA	4677	'83	LP/CS/CD†
Swept Away	RCA	5009	'84	CS/CD†
Eaten Alive	RCA	5422	'85	CD†
Red Hot Rhythm and Blues	RCA	6388	'87	LP/CS/CD†
Endless Love	RCA	61136	'92	CS/CD
Workin' Overtime	Motown	6274	'89	CS/CD†
The Force Behind the Power	Motown	6316	'91	CS/CD
Anthology: The Best of Diana Ross (updated through 1991)	Motown	(2)0520	'95	CS/CD
Stolen Moments: The Lady Sings . . . Jazz and Blues	Motown	6340	'93	CS/CD
Musical Memoirs, Forever	Motown	(4)6357	'93	CS/CD
The Remixes	Motown	6377	'94	CS/CD
One Woman: The Ultimate Collection	Motown	0428	'94	CS/CD
Take Me Higher	Motown	0586	'95	CS/CD†

Diana Ross and Marvin Gaye

Diana and Marvin	Motown	803	'73	†
	Motown	5124	'87	CS/CD

Diana Ross and Others

The Wiz (soundtrack)	MCA	(2)14000	'78	†
	MCA	(2)6010		†

THE TEMPTATIONS

Eddie Kendricks (born December 17, 1939, in Birmingham, Alabama; died October 5, 1992, in Birmingham), tenor; Otis Williams (born Otis Miles on October 30, 1941, in Texarkana, Texas), baritone; Melvin Franklin (born David English on October 12, 1942, in Montgomery, Alabama; died February 23, 1995, in Los Angeles), bass vocals; Paul Williams (born July 2, 1939, in Birmingham; died August 17, 1973, in Detroit), baritone; and Eldridge Bryant. Bryant left in late 1963, to be replaced by David Ruffin (born January 18, 1941, in Meridian, Mississippi; died June 1, 1991, in Philadelphia), baritone.

David Ruffin left the group in 1968, to be replaced by Dennis Edwards (born February 3, 1943, in Birmingham, Alabama). David Ruffin's brother Jimmy Ruffin (born May 7, 1939, in Collinsville, Mississippi) was a solo artist for Motown. Eddie Kendricks and Paul Williams left The Temptations in 1971, to be replaced by Richard Street (born October 5, 1942, in Detroit) and Damon Harris (born July 3, 1950, in Baltimore, Maryland). Later members included Glenn Leonard, Louis Price, Ali Ollie Woodson, Ron Tyson, Theo Peoples, and Ray Davis.

Motown's most popular and longest enduring male vocal group, The Temptations were one of the most successful black vocal groups of all time. One of the first groups to feature two lead singers, David Ruffin and Eddie Kendricks, The Temptations achieved their initial success under the direction of songwriter-producer Smokey Robinson, who cowrote most of their early hits. Known for their precise on-stage dance routines, The Temptations scored a dozen major crossover hits featuring the brilliant combination of Ruffin's rich, earthy baritone and Kendricks' plaintive near-falsetto tenor under producer-songwriter Norman Whitfield beginning in 1966. With the departure of Ruffin in 1968, Whitfield experimented with the musical advances of Sly and The Family Stone and the developing social consciousness of lyrics in black music. Thus, in collaboration with Barrett Strong, Whitfield advanced The Temptations into the forefront of psychedelic soul with such smash hits as "Cloud Nine," "Psychedelic Shack," "Ball of Confusion," and the classic "Papa Was a Rolling Stone." Remarkably versatile, The Temptations provided a consistently engaging sound despite numerous personnel changes and were one of the few Motown groups to continue successfully recording in the '70s. Ruffin and Kendricks reunited with the surviving Temptations for an album and tour in 1982. The Temptations were inducted into the Rock and Roll Hall of Fame in 1989.

The evolution of The Temptations began during the late '50s with two Detroit-based groups, The Primes and The Distants. The Distants, with Otis Williams, Melvin Franklin, Richard Street, and Eldridge Bryant, had been formed by members of The Questions and The Elegants. The Primes (whose companion group The Primettes later became The Supremes) had formed in Birmingham, Alabama, and included Eddie Kendricks and Paul Williams. In 1960, Kendricks and Paul Williams joined Bryant, Franklin, and Otis Williams to become The Elgins, signing with Berry Gordy's Miracle label. They changed their name to The Temptations in 1961 and switched to the Gordy label in 1962, scoring their first rhythm-and-blues hit with "Dream Come Home." In 1963, choreographer Cholly Atkins started teaching the group intricate synchronized dance routines that became their in-performance trademark. Late that year, Bryant quit the group and was replaced by David Ruffin.

In early 1964, The Temptations achieved their first major pop hit with "The Way You Do the Things You Do," cowritten and produced by William "Smokey" Robinson and featuring the lead vocals of Eddie Kendricks. After the major pop hit "Girl (Why You Wanna Make Me Blue)," written by Eddie Holland and Norman Whitfield, the group scored a top pop and rhythm-and-blues hit with the classic "My Girl," cowritten (with Ronald White) and produced by Robinson, with Ruffin on lead vocals. Subsequent major pop and smash R&B

hits for The Temptations produced by Robinson included "It's Growing," "Since I Lost My Baby," and "My Baby" (cowritten by Robinson and Warren Moore) and Robinson's "Get Ready."

The Temptations next recorded primarily under songwriter-producer Norman Whitfield, who produced (and coauthored with Eddie Holland) the top rhythm-and-blues and smash pop hits "Ain't Too Proud to Beg," "Beauty Is Only Skin Deep," and "(I Know) I'm Losing You." Frank Wilson coauthored and produced the crossover smash "All I Need," and Whitfield produced and coauthored the crossover smashes "You're My Everything," "(Loneliness Made Me Realize) It's You That I Need," the classic "I Wish It Would Rain," and "I Could Never Love Another (After Loving You)." In July 1968, David Ruffin left the group for a solo career and was replaced by Dennis Edwards of The Contours. By then, former Distant and Monitor member Richard Street had begun filling in for an ailing Paul Williams.

David Ruffin's brother Jimmy had been recording for Berry Gordy's Soul label since 1964. He scored a near-smash pop and rhythm-and-blues hit with "What Becomes of the Brokenhearted" in 1966 and subsequent major crossover hits with "I've Passed This Way Before" and "Gonna Give Her All the Love I've Got." David Ruffin managed a smash pop and rhythm-and-blues hit with "My Whole World Ended (The Moment You Left Me)" in 1969, followed by the major R&B hits "I've Lost Everything I Ever Loved" and "I'm So Glad I Fell for You." A 1970 duet album yielded a major R&B hit with "Stand by Me," but, by 1972, Jimmy Ruffin had left the Motown organization. David Ruffin stayed on, eventually scoring a top rhythm-and-blues and near-smash pop hit with "Walk Away from Love" and near-smash R&B hits with "Heavy Love" and "Everything's Coming up Love" in 1975 and 1976. In 1980, Jimmy Ruffin scored a near-smash pop hit with "Hold on to My Love," cowritten and produced by Bee Gee Robin Gibb.

The reconstituted Temptations were teamed with The Supremes in 1968 and 1969. They scored a smash crossover hit with a remake of Dee Dee Warwick's late 1966 hit "I'm Gonna Make You Love Me" and a major crossover hit with "I'll Try Something New." Beginning in late 1968, Norman Whitfield began experimenting with psychedelic soul and social consciousness for The Temptations. With this new style, The Temptations scored a top pop and rhythm-and-blues hit with the classic "I Can't Get Next to You" and smash R&B and pop hits with "Cloud Nine," "Run Away Child, Running Wild," "Psychedelic Shack," and "Ball of Confusion," all cowritten by Whitfield and Barrett Strong.

The Temptations returned to their mellow ballad style in 1971 for the top pop and R&B hit classic "Just My Imagination (Running Away with Me)" with Eddie Kendricks on lead vocals. That summer, Kendricks left the group for a solo career and was permanently replaced by Damon Harris. Around the same time, Paul Williams retired from touring due to illness and was replaced by stand-in Richard Street. On August 17, 1973, Paul Williams was found dead in his car in Detroit, an apparent suicide at the age of 34.

In 1973, Eddie Kendricks' solo career took off. The disco-style songs "Keep on Truckin' (Part 1)" and "Boogie Down" became top rhythm-and-blues and pop hits and were followed by seven R&B smashes, including the major pop hits "Son of Sagittarius" and "Shoeshine Boy." In 1978, he switched to Arista Records, where he managed one major R&B hit, "Ain't No Smoke Without Fire."

From late 1971 to 1974, The Temptations scored numerous smash rhythm-and-blues hits for Motown. Of these, "Superstar (Remember How You Got Where You Are)" and "Let Your Hair Down" became major pop hits, the classic "Papa Was a Rolling Stone" was a top pop hit, and "Masterpiece" proved a near-smash pop hit. After Norman Whitfield left the Motown organization, The Temptations achieved top R&B hits with "Happy People" (cowritten by Lionel Richie) and "Shakey Ground" (their last major pop hit) and the R&B smash "Keep Holding On" in 1975 and 1976. In 1975, Glenn Leonard replaced Damon

Harris, who returned to his former group (which later became Impact) before attempting a solo career in late 1978. Dennis Edwards left the group from 1977 to 1979, replaced by Louis Price.

The Temptations switched to Atlantic Records in May 1977, but were back at Gordy by 1980, by which time Edwards had returned to replace Price. In 1982, The Temptations reunited with David Ruffin and Eddie Kendricks for one album and tour. The reunion album yielded a rhythm-and-blues smash with "Standing on the Top—Part 1," featuring Rick James. Ron Tyson replaced Glenn Leonard in 1983, the year The Temptations toured internationally with The Four Tops. In 1983, Ali Ollie Woodson replaced Edwards and the group managed another R& B smash with "Treat Her Like a Lady." However, they would not achieve another major pop hit until 1991. Between 1986 and 1987, The Temptations had smash rhythm-and-blues hits with "Lady Soul, " "I Wonder Who She's Seeing Now," and "Look What You Started."

In May 1985, David Ruffin and Eddie Kendrick (he had shortened his name) joined white soul singers Daryl Hall and John Oates for the reopening of the Apollo Theater in Harlem. The four scored a major pop hit with "The Apollo Medley," which comprised "The Way You Do the Things You Do" and "My Girl." Ruffin and Kendrick subsequently toured together and later recorded a duet album that yielded a major rhythm-and-blues hit with "I Couldn't Believe It." On June 1, 1991, David Ruffin died in Philadelphia of a drug overdose at the age of 50. On October 5, 1992, Eddie Kendricks died in Birmingham, Alabama, of lung cancer at the age of 52.

In 1989, The Temptations scored a smash R&B hit with "Special," and, in 1991, they accompanied Rod Stewart on the near-smash pop hit "The Motown Song" from his *Vagabond Heart* album. By 1992, The Temptations were regularly touring with The Four Tops. The group continued to record for Motown in the '90s, but, on February 23, 1995, Melvin Franklin died in Los Angeles of heart failure at the age of 52. By the late 1998 broadcast of the NBC-TV miniseries "The Temptations" and the release of *Phoenix Rising,* The Temptations were anchored by Ron Tyson and original member Otis Williams.

THE TEMPTATIONS BIBLIOGRAPHY

Turner, Tony, with Barbara Aria. *Deliver Us from Temptation: The Tragic and Shocking Story of The Temptations and Motown.* New York: Thunder's Mouth Press, 1992.

Williams, Otis, with Patricia Romanowski. *Temptations.* New York: G. P. Putnam's Sons, 1988.

The Temptations

Meet The Temptations	Gordy	911	'64	†
	Motown	5140	'89	CS/CD
The Temptations Sing Smokey	Gordy	912	'65	†
	Motown	5205	'89	CS/CD
Temptin' Temptations	Gordy	914	'65	†
	Motown	5374	'90	CS/CD
Gettin' Ready	Gordy	918	'66	†
	Motown	5373	'89	CS/CD
Live!	Gordy	921	'67	†
With a Lot O' Soul	Gordy	922	'67	†
	Motown	5299	'89	CS/CD†
In a Mellow Mood	Gordy	924	'67	†
	Motown	5235	'89	CS/CD

I Wish It Would Rain	Gordy	927	'68	†
	Motown	5276	'89	CS/CD
Live at the Copa	Gordy	938	'68	†
	Motown	5306	'89	CS/CD†
Cloud Nine	Gordy	939	'69	†
	Motown	5159		CS/CD
The Temptations Show (TV)	Gordy	933	'69	†
Puzzle People	Gordy	949	'69	†
	Motown	5172	'89	CS/CD
Christmas Card	Gordy	951	'69	†
	Motown	5251		CS/CD
Psychedelic Shack	Gordy	947	'70	†
	Motown	5164		CS/CD
At London's Talk of the Town	Gordy	953	'70	†
Sky's the Limit	Gordy	957	'71	†
	Motown	5474	'90	CS/CD†
Solid Rock	Gordy	961	'72	†
	Motown	5480	'90	CS/CD†
All Directions	Gordy	962	'72	†
	Motown	5417	'89	CD
Masterpiece	Gordy	965	'73	†
	Motown	5144	'89	CS/CD
1990	Gordy	966	'73	†
The Temptations	Gordy	967	'74	†
A Song for You	Gordy	969	'75	†
	Motown	5272	'89	CS/CD
House Party	Gordy	973	'75	†
Wings of Love	Gordy	971	'76	†
The Temptations Do The Temptations	Gordy	975	'76	†
Hear to Tempt You	Atlantic	19143	'77	†
Bare Back	Atlantic	19188	'78	†
Power	Gordy	994	'80	†
Give Love at Christmas	Gordy	998	'80	†
	Motown	5279		CS/CD
The Temptations	Gordy	1006	'81	†
Reunion	Gordy	6008	'82	†
	Motown	0304	'94	CS/CD
Surface Thrills	Gordy	6032	'83	†
Back to Basics	Gordy	6085	'83	†
Truly for You	Gordy	6119	'84	†
	Motown	6119	'88	CS/CD
Touch Me	Gordy	6164	'86	†
To Be Continued . . .	Gordy	6207	'86	†
	Motown	6207		CS/CD
Together Again	Motown	6246	'87	LP/CS/CD†
Special	Motown	6275	'89	LP/CS/CD†
Milestone	Motown	6331	'91	CS/CD
For Lovers Only	Motown	0568	'95	CS/CD
Phoenix Rising: Temptations 4Ever	Motown	0937	'98	CS/CD

Temptations Reissues

Cloud Nine/Puzzle People	Motown	8116	'86	CD†
Psychedelic Shack/All Directions	Motown	8122	'86	CD†
A Song for You/Masterpiece	Motown	8135	'86	CD†
Live at the Copa/With a Lot O' Soul	Motown	8137	'86	CD†
I Wish It Would Rain/In a Mellow Mood	Motown	8154		CD†
Meet The Temptations/The Temptations Sing Smokey	Motown	8160		CD†

Temptations Anthologies and Compilations

Greatest Hits, Volume 1	Gordy	919	'66	†
	Motown	5411	'88	CS/CD
Greatest Hits, Volume 2	Gordy	954	'70	†
	Motown	5412	'88	CS/CD
Anthology	Motown	(3)782	'73	LP/CS†
	Motown	(2)782		CD†
Compact Command Performance (15 Greatest Hits)	Motown	6125	'85	CD†
All the Million Sellers	Motown	5212	'81	CS/CD
Great Songs and Performances That Inspired the Motown 25th Anniversary TV Show	Motown	5315		CS/CD
25th Anniversary	Motown	(2)5389	'86	CS/CD†
Emperors of Soul	Motown	(5)0338	'94	CS/CD
Anthology: The Best of The Temptations	Motown	(2)0524	'95	CS/CD
Anthology: The Temptations One by One (David Ruffin, Dennis Edwards, Eddie Kendricks and Paul Williams)	Motown	0615	'96	CS/CD
Puzzle People	Pickwick	3396		†
Hum Along and Dance: More of the Best (1963–1974)	Rhino	71180	'93	CS/CD
Motown Legends	Esx	8524	'95	CS/CD
Motown Legends	Esx	8525	'95	CS/CD

The Temptations and The Supremes

The Supremes Join The Temptations	Motown	679	'68	†
	Motown	5139	'89	CS/CD
T.C.B.	Motown	682	'68	†
	Motown	5171	'89	CS/CD†
Together	Motown	692	'69	†
	Motown	5436	'89	CS/CD†
The Supremes Join The Temptations/Together	Motown	8138		CD†
On Broadway	Motown	699	'69	†
Motown Legends	Motown	5368		CS†

Jimmy Ruffin

Top Ten	Soul	704	'67	†
	Motown	5445		CS/CD†
Ruff 'n Ready	Soul	708	'69	†
	Motown	5459	'90	CS/CD†
Groove Governor	Soul	727	'70	†
Sunrise	RSO	3078	'80	†

David and Jimmy Ruffin

I Am My Brother's Keeper	Soul	728	'70	†
Motown Superstar Series, Volume 8	Motown	108		†
	Motown	5108		CS†

David Ruffin

My Whole World Ended	Motown	685	'69		†
Doin' His Thing—Feelin' Good	Motown	696	'69		†
David Ruffin	Motown	762	'73		†
Me 'n Rock 'n Roll Are Here to Stay	Motown	818	'74		†
Who I Am	Motown	849	'75		†
Everything's Coming Up Love	Motown	866	'76		†
In My Stride	Motown	885	'77		†
At His Best	Motown	895	'78		†
	Motown	5211		CS/CD	
Motown Legends	Esx	8521	'95	CS/CD	
So Soon We Change	Warner Brothers	3306	'79		†
Gentleman Ruffin	Warner Brothers	3416	'80		†

Daryl Hall and John Oates with David Ruffin and Eddie Kendrick

Live at the Apollo	RCA	7035	'85	CS/CD†	

David Ruffin and Eddie Kendrick

Family	RCA	6765	'87	CS/CD	

Eddie Kendricks

All By Myself	Tamla	309	'71		†
People . . . Hold On	Tamla	315	'72		†
	Motown	5280		CS/CD	
Eddie Kendricks	Tamla	327	'73		†
Boogie Down	Tamla	330	'74		†
For You	Tamla	335	'74		†
The Hit Man	Tamla	338	'75		†
He's a Friend	Tamla	343	'75		†
Goin' Up in Smoke	Tamla	346	'76		†
Slick	Tamla	356	'77		†
At His Best	Tamla	354	'78		†
	Motown	5481	'90	CS/CD	
Motown Superstar Series, Volume 19	Motown	5119		CS†	
Vintage '78	Arista	4170	'78		
	Razor & Tie	2149	'97	CD	
Something More	Arista	4250	'79		†
Love Keys	Atlantic	19294	'81		†

Monitors (with Richard Street)

Greetings! We're The Monitors	Soul	714	'69		†

True Reflection (with Glenn Leonard)

Where I'm Coming From	Atco	7031	'73		†

Impact (with Damon Harris)

Impact	Atco	36-135	'76		†
The 'Pac Is Back	Fantasy	9359	'77		†

Damon Harris

Damon	Fantasy	9567	'78		†

Dennis Edwards

Don't Look Any Further	Gordy	6057	'84		†
	Motown	5404		CS/CD†	
Coolin' Out	Gordy	6148	'85	LP/CS†	

THREE DOG NIGHT

Danny Hutton (born September 10, 1942, in Buncrana, Ireland), vocals; Cory Wells (born February 5, 1942, in Buffalo, New York), vocals; Chuck Negron (born June 8, 1942, in the Bronx, New York), vocals; Mike Allsup (born March 8, 1947, in Modesto, California), lead guitar; Jimmy Greenspoon (born February 7, 1948, in Los Angeles), keyboards; Joe Schermie (born February 12, 1945, in Madison, Wisconsin), bass; and Floyd Sneed (born November 22, 1943, in Calgary, Alberta, Canada), drums.

One of the most popular American rock bands of the late '60s and early '70s, Three Dog Night featured three lead vocalists who also supplied tight three-part harmony. Scoring ten smash hits and a dozen best-selling albums between 1969 and 1974, Three Dog Night explored no new musical ground but did provide the first recorded success for songwriters Harry Nilsson, Laura Nyro, Randy Newman, and John Hiatt.

Danny Hutton was raised in the United States and began his musical career in his teens as a producer, songwriter, and, eventually, vocalist. In 1965, he had a minor hit with "Roses and Rainbows" on the HBR (Hanna-Barbera) label. Envisioning a group fronted by three singers who would share lead vocals and perform three-part harmony, Hutton enlisted Cory Wells from a group he was producing, The Enemys, and Chuck Negron. Wells had manned a Texas band called The Satellites before moving to Los Angeles with The Enemys, while Negron was a solo artist for Columbia Records. The three assembled a band and took the name Three Dog Night in 1968. After successful engagements in West Coast clubs and a long-term stand at Los Angeles' Whiskey A-Go-Go, the group signed with Dunhill Records.

Working with producer Gabriel Mekler, Three Dog Night launched its career with three albums that remained on the album charts for more than a year. The first included a major hit version of Otis Redding's classic "Try a Little Tenderness" and the smash hit, "One," written by Harry Nilsson. Yielding the smash hit "Easy to Be Hard" (from the rock musical *Hair*), their second album provided major hits with "Celebrate" and Laura Nyro's "Eli's Coming," and also contained Elton John and Bernie Taupin's obscure "Lady Samantha." Subsequently recording under producer Richard Podolor, Three Dog Night next recorded *Captured Live at the Forum*.

It Ain't Easy included the top hit "Mama Told Me Not to Come," written by Randy Newman, and the major hit "Out in the Country," written by Paul Williams and Roger Nichols. *Naturally* produced three hits with "One Man Band," Hoyt Axton's "Joy to the World" (a top hit), and Russ Ballard's "Liar" (a near-smash hit), originally recorded by Argent. The hits continued with Paul Williams' "An Old Fashioned Love Song" (a top easy-listening hit), Hoyt Axton's "Never Been to Spain," and "The Family of Man" from *Harmony*. *Seven Separate Fools* produced the top pop and easy-listening hit "Black and White" and the major hit "Pieces of April," whereas *Cyan* included the smash hit "Shambala" and the major hit "Let Me Serenade You." *Hard Labor* yielded a smash hit with Leo Sayer's "The Show Must Go On" and a major hit with John Hiatt's "Sure as I'm Sittin' Here."

Personnel changes for Three Dog Night began in 1973 with the departure of Joe Schermie. They scored their final moderate hits with Allen Toussaint's "Play Something Sweet (Brickyard Blues)" in 1974 and "Til the World Ends" in 1975. Recording for ABC Records after it absorbed Dunhill in 1975, Three Dog Night realigned briefly after Danny Hutton's departure in 1976. Cory Wells recorded a solo album for A&M in 1978 and Three Dog Night reunited for touring in 1981, recording 1983's *It's a Jungle* under Richard Podolor. They continued to tour, replacing Chuck Negron with guitarist-vocalist Paul Kingery at the beginning of 1986. With Danny Hutton and Cory Wells as mainstays, Three Dog Night toured into the '90s on the oldies circuit. Chuck Negron returned to recording with 1995's *Am I Still in Your Heart* on Viceroy Records.

THREE DOG NIGHT BIBLIOGRAPHY

Cohen, Joel. *Three Dog Night and Me.* Pasadena: Open Horizon, 1971.

Greenspoon, Jimmy, with Mark Bego. *One Is the Loneliest Number: On the Road and Behind the Scenes with the Legendary Rock Band, Three Dog Night.* New York: Pharos Books, 1991.

Danny Hutton

Pre-Dog Night	MGM	4664	'70	†
Three Dog Night				
Three Dog Night	Dunhill	50048	'69	†
	MCA	31045	'85	CD†
Suitable for Framing	Dunhill	50058	'69	†
	MCA	31046	'87	CD†
Captured Live at the Forum	Dunhill	50068	'69	†
	MCA	31342	'89	CD
It Ain't Easy	Dunhill	50078	'70	†
	MCA	31047	'87	CD†
Naturally	Dunhill	50088	'70	†
	MCA	31355	'89	CD†
Golden Biscuits	Dunhill	50098	'71	†
Harmony	Dunhill	50108	'71	†
	MCA	31329	'88	CD†
Seven Separate Fools	Dunhill	50118	'72	†
	MCA	31339	'89	CD†
Around the World	Dunhill	(2)50138	'73	†
Cyan	Dunhill	50158	'73	†
	MCA	31366	'90	CD
Hard Labor	Dunhill	50168	'74	†
	MCA	31362	'90	CD
Joy to the World—Their Greatest Hits	Dunhill	50178	'74	†
	MCA	1466		CS/CD
Dog Style	Dunhill	50198	'74	†
Coming Down Your Way	ABC	888	'75	†
American Pastime	ABC	928	'76	†
Best	MCA	(2)6018	'82	LP/CS
	MCA	6018		CD
Celebrate: The Three Dog Night Story 1965–1975	MCA	(2)10956	'93	CS/CD
It's a Jungle	Passport	5001		
Cory Wells				
Touch Me	A&M	4673	'78	†
Chuck Negron				
Am I Still in Your Heart	Viceroy	8024	'95	CS/CD

TRAFFIC

Steve Winwood (born May 12, 1948, in Birmingham, Warwickshire, England), keyboards, guitar, vocals; Chris Wood (born June 24, 1944, in Birmingham; died July 12, 1983, in London), flute, saxophone; and Jim Capaldi (born August 24, 1944, in Evesham, Worcestershire, England), drums, keyboards, vocals. Multi-instrumentalist Dave Mason (born May 10 circa 1946, in Worcester, Worcestershire, England) was in and out of the group from the spring of 1967 to the fall of 1968.

SPENCER DAVIS GROUP

Spencer Davis (born July 17, 1937, in Swansea, West Glamorgan, Wales), guitar; Steve Winwood, guitar, keyboards, vocals; Muff Winwood (born Mervyn Winwood, on June 14, 1943, in Birmingham), bass; and Pete York (born August 15, 1942, in Redcar, Cleveland, England), drums.

BLIND FAITH

Eric Clapton (born Eric Clapp on March 30, 1945, in Ripley, Surrey, England), lead guitar, vocals; Steve Winwood, keyboards, vocals; Rick Grech (born November 1, 1945, in Bordeaux, France; died March 17, 1990, in Leicester, England), bass; and Peter "Ginger" Baker (born August 19, 1939, in Lewisham, London), drums.

Amassing one of the most impressive bodies of work in rock history during his thirty-year career, Steve Winwood gained his first recognition with The Spencer Davis Group, one of the vanguard groups of the British rhythm-and-blues movement, as a teenager, singing, playing on, and cowriting the group's near-smash hits "Gimme Some Lovin'" and "I'm a Man." Joining drummer-songwriter Jim Capaldi, reed player Chris Wood (one of the first horn players to be an integral part of a major British rock band), and intermittent member Dave Mason, Winwood recorded three fascinating albums with Traffic characterized by surreal lyrics, a jazz-style sound, and his distinctive compelling voice. England's premier psychedelic band, Traffic provided Winwood the means to explore his existential and spiritual concerns in song, a penchant he maintained throughout his career. Traffic endured a chaotic history of breakups, re-formations, and personnel changes, with Mason establishing himself as an excellent songwriter with 1970's *Alone Together* album. Traffic regrouped following Winwood's brief stint with the ready-made "supergroup" Blind Faith to record the best-selling folk-style *John Barleycorn Must Die* album. Never achieving a major American hit, Traffic nonetheless proved themselves a popular album band, particularly with the classic jazz-style *Low Spark of High Heeled Boys,* perhaps the group's finest album and Winwood's most lyrically incisive. After Traffic disbanded in 1974, Winwood largely retreated from the music scene. In 1981, he formed a longstanding songwriting partnership with Will Jennings that launched his solo career with "While You See a Chance" and yielded top pop hits with "Higher Love" and "Roll with It." Established as a solo artist with 1986's *Back in the High Life* and 1988's *Roll with It,* Steve Winwood rejoined Jim Capaldi as Traffic for a 1994 tour and album.

Steve Winwood gained his first musical experience with a skiffle band at the age of eleven. An accomplished multi-instrumentalist, he and his brother Muff formed the Muff Woody Jazz Band in Birmingham in 1962. Adding Spencer Davis and Peter York, they became the Rhythm and Blues Quartet, changing their name to The Spencer Davis Group by 1963. Featuring Steve on organ, lead guitar, and lead vocals, they broke through with two top British hits composed by Jamaican Jackie Edwards, "Keep on Running" and "Somebody Help Me." Winwood soon cowrote their smash British and American hit "Gimme Some Lovin'" with Muff and Davis, and the near-smash British and American hit "I'm a Man" with producer Jimmy Miller.

Wanting to form his own group, Steve Winwood left The Spencer Davis Group in April 1967 and retreated to a Berkshire cottage for six months of rehearsals with Dave Mason, Chris Wood, and Jim Capaldi. Capaldi and Mason had played in the Birmingham-based groups the Hellions and Deep Feeling, and Chris Wood had jammed with the other three in Birmingham clubs before Winwood's departure from The Spencer Davis Group. Signed to Island Records (United Artists in the United States) and named Traffic, the group's debut album, *Mr. Fantasy,* featured Winwood and Capaldi's "Paper Sun," with Mason on sitar, and

Mason's "Hole in My Shoe," both smash British hits. The remarkably diverse and experimental album also contained "Coloured Rain," "Heaven Is in Your Mind," "Dear Mr. Fantasy," and "Smiling Phases," all cowritten by Winwood, Capaldi, and Wood.

Dave Mason's penchant for pop-style melodies conflicted with the jazz orientation of the others and he left Traffic in December 1967, playing with Delaney and Bonnie. Nonetheless, he was back for *Traffic*, which included his "You Can All Join In" and the classic "Feelin' Alright?" as well as Winwood and Capaldi's "Pearly Queen" and their surreal "Forty Thousand Headmen," later covered by Blood, Sweat and Tears. Traffic first toured America in 1968, but, in October, Mason left again. In January 1969, Traffic split up and *Last Exit* featured one live side and one studio side, which included "Medicated Goo" and "Shanghai Noodle Factory."

Steve Winwood joined Ginger Baker, Eric Clapton, and bassist Rick Grech for Blind Faith in February. Lasting seven months, the group debuted at London's Hyde Park in June and conducted one sellout American tour. Their best-selling album contained three Winwood songs, including "Sea of Joy" and the classic "Can't Find My Way Back Home." After the group broke up in September, Winwood joined Ginger Baker's Air Force, with Baker, Grech, Chris Wood, and Denny Laine, for one live album.

In January 1970, Steve Winwood began recording his solo debut album *Mad Shadows,* but the project became a Traffic endeavor when Chris Wood and Jim Capaldi joined. Issued as *John Barleycorn Must Die,* the album combined elements of jazz, rock, and folk and served as a fine testament to Winwood's versatility, becoming Traffic's best-selling album to date. In addition to the title song, it included the instrumental "Glad," Winwood and Capaldi's "Freedom Rider" and "Stranger to Himself," and the minor hit "Empty Pages." The group toured again in 1970, augmented by Rick Grech, and their brief British tour in the summer of 1971 with Dave Mason resulted in the live set *Welcome to the Canteen.*

Dave Mason had already recorded the excellent *Alone Together* album, initially released on multicolored vinyl (the album later became a valued collectors' item). The album featured seven outstanding compositions by Mason, including "World in Changes," "Sad and Deep as You," "Shouldn't Have Took More Than You Gave," and "Look at You Look at Me," yet it produced only one moderate hit with "Only You Know and I Know." The album, however, overshadowed much of Mason's subsequent career. He recorded a duet album with Mama Cass Elliot and permanently settled in America in 1973, making solo recordings for Columbia from 1973 to 1980. *Let It Flow* yielded a minor hit with "So High (Rock Me Baby and Roll Me Away)" and a moderate hit with "Let It Go, Let It Flow," but the album's big hit, "We Just Disagree," was written by his guitar accompanist, Jim Krueger. Dave Mason maintained a low profile in the '80s, recording only one album, and eventually joined Fleetwood Mac in late 1993.

In 1971, Steve Winwood, Chris Wood, and Jim Capaldi recorded *The Low Spark of High Heeled Boys,* perhaps the crowning achievement of their career, for Island Records. In addition to the twelve-minute title song, the album contained "Many a Mile to Freedom," Grech and drummer Jim Gordon's "Rock and Roll Stew," and Capaldi's "Light Up or Leave Me Alone." Jim Capaldi recorded his debut solo album for Island Records at Muscle Shoals, Alabama, with Winwood, Dave Mason, and studio veterans David Hood (bass) and Roger Hawkins (drums). Hood and Hawkins joined Traffic in Jamaica to record *Shoot Out at the Fantasy Factory,* which featured Winwood and Capaldi's "(Sometimes I Feel So) Uninspired." Joined by Muscle Shoals' associate Barry Beckett (keyboards), the aggregation conducted a world tour in 1973, recording the live *On the Road* album. The Muscle Shoals recruits departed after the tour, and Traffic completed their final British and American tours in 1974 and recorded the keyboard-dominated *When the Eagle Flies* album.

Traffic disbanded and Jim Capaldi resumed his solo recording career for Island, scoring a smash British hit with a revival of Boudleaux Bryant's "Love Hurts," originally recorded by Roy Orbison in 1961. Steve Winwood retired to his Gloucestershire home, where he built his own studio, emerging for a "jam" album for Antilles and recording with Japanese percussionist-keyboardist Stomu Yamashta in the ambitious "Go" group. Winwood recorded his debut solo album for Island in 1977 and began collaborating with Nashville songwriter Will Jennings in 1981. Winwood's *Arc of a Diver* album, recorded entirely on his own, yielded a near-smash hit with "While You See a Chance," but, after 1982's *Talking Back to the Night,* he was not to record another album for four years. In the meantime, Capaldi had recorded for RSO, then Atlantic, where he scored a major hit in 1983 with "That's Love." Chris Wood died in London of liver failure on July 12, 1983, at the age of 39.

Steve Winwood eventually reemerged in 1986 with the best-selling *Back in the High Life* album. It yielded four hits, the top hit "Higher Love," the near-smash "The Finer Things," and the major hits "Freedom Overspill" and "Back in the High Life Again." "The Finer Things" and "Back in the High Life Again" also became top easy-listening hits. Reestablished as a solo artist, Winwood toured in 1986 and scored a near-smash with a new version of "Valerie" (originally released in 1982) from the compilation set *Chronicles.* Jim Capaldi returned to Island Records in 1988 and assisted Winwood on his next two albums. Winwood's 1988 *Roll with It* album, on his new label Virgin Records, produced a top pop and easy-listening hit with "Roll with It," a smash hit with "Don't You Know What the Night Can Do?" and a major pop and top easy-listening hit with "Holding On." Winwood toured again in 1988 and next recorded *Refugees of the Heart,* which yielded a major hit with "One and Only Man," cowritten with Jim Capaldi.

In 1994, Steve Winwood and Jim Capaldi revived Traffic for *Far from Home,* with Winwood singing and playing guitar, keyboards, bass, and synthesized reeds. The album featured "Here Comes a Man" and "Nowhere Is Their Freedom." Recruiting four backup musicians, Winwood and Capaldi toured extensively in the United States as Traffic in 1994, appearing at the Woodstock II festival in August.

STEVE WINWOOD BIBLIOGRAPHY

Welch, Chris, with Steve Winwood. *Steve Winwood—Roll with It.* New York: Perigee Books, 1990.

Spencer Davis Group (with Steve Winwood)

Gimme Some Lovin'	United Artists	6578	'67	†
I'm a Man	United Artists	6589	'67	†
Greatest Hits	United Artists	6641	'68	†
Best	EMI	91834	'89	CS/CD†
	EMI	46598		CS/CD
Best (1964–1967)	Rhino	70172	'87	CS

Traffic

Mr. Fantasy	United Artists	6651	'68	†
	Island	90060		LP/CS/CD†
	Island	842783		CS/CD
	Mobile Fidelity	00572	'93	CD†
Traffic	United Artists	6676	'68	†
	Island	90059		LP/CS/CD†
	Island	842590		CS/CD
	Mobile Fidelity	00629	'95	CD†
Last Exit	United Artists	6702	'69	†
	Island	90925	'88	LP/CS/CD†
	Island	842787	'88	CS/CD

Best	United Artists	5500	'69	†
John Barleycorn Must Die	United Artists	5504	'70	†
	Island	90058		LP/CS/CD†
	Island	842780		CS/CD
Welcome to the Canteen	United Artists	5550	'71	†
	Island	90924	'88	LP/CS/CD†
	Island	842417	'88	CS/CD
Heavy Traffic	United Artists	421	'75	†
More Heavy Traffic	United Artists	526	'75	†
The Low Spark of High-Heeled Boys	Island	9306	'71	†
	Island	9180		†
	Island	90026		LP/CS/CD†
	Island	842779		LP/CS/CD
	Mobile Fidelity	209	'94	LP
	Mobile Fidelity	00609	'94	CD†
Shoot Out at the Fantasy Factory	Island	9323	'73	†
	Island	9224		†
	Island	90027		LP/CS/CD†
	Island	842781		CS/CD
	Mobile Fidelity	669	'96	CD
On the Road	Island	(2)9336	'73	†
	Island	(2)2		†
	Island	90028		CS/CD†
	Island	842893		CS/CD
Smiling Phases	Island	(2)510553	'91	CD
When the Eagle Flies	Asylum	1020	'74	†
Far from Home	Virgin	39490	'94	CD
Blind Faith				
Blind Faith	Atco	33-304	'69	†
	RSO	3016	'77	†
	RSO	825094	'86	LP/CS/CD†
	Polydor	825094		CS/CD
	Mobile Fidelity	00507	'89	CD†
Ginger Baker's Air Force				
Ginger Baker's Air Force	Atco	(2)703	'70	†
	Polydor	837349	'89	CD†
Dave Mason and Cass Elliot				
Dave Mason and Cass Elliot	Blue Thumb	8825	'71	
	MCA	31340	'89	CD
Dave Mason				
Alone Together	Blue Thumb	19	'70	†
	MCA	27035		CS
	MCA	31170		CD
	Mobile Fidelity	00573	'93	CD†
	Heavy Vinyl	11319	'95	LP
Headkeeper	Blue Thumb	34	'72	†
	MCA	31326	'88	CD†
Dave Mason Is Alive	Blue Thumb	54	'73	†
Best	Blue Thumb	6013	'74	†
	MCA	800	'82	†

Very Best	Blue Thumb	6032	'78	†
	MCA	715		CS
	MCA	31169		CD
At His Best	ABC/MCA	880	'75	†
It's Like You Never Left	Columbia	31721	'73	†
	One Way	26077	'95	CD
Dave Mason	Columbia	33096	'74	†
	One Way	26080	'95	CD
Split Coconut	Columbia	33698	'75	†
	One Way	26079	'95	CD
Certified Live	Columbia	(2)34174	'76	†
	One Way	26078	'95	CD
Let It Flow	Columbia	34680	'77	†
	Columbia/Legacy	34680	'90	CS/CD
Mariposa de Oro	Columbia	35285	'78	†
Old Crest on a New Wave	Columbia	36144	'80	†
Best	Columbia	37089	'81	†
reissued as Greatest Hits	Columbia	37089		CS/CD
Two Hearts	MCA	42086	'88	LP/CS/CD†
Jim Capaldi				
Oh, How We Danced	Island	9314	'72	†
	Island	9187		†
Whale Meat Again	Island	9254	'74	†
Short Cut Draw Blood	Island	9336	'76	†
	Antilles	7050		LP†
Daughter of the Night	RSO	3037	'78	†
Fierce Heart	Atlantic	80059	'83	†
One Man Mission	Atlantic	80182	'84	†
Some Come Running	Island	91024	'88	LP/CS/CD†
	Island	842606		CS/CD†
Steve Winwood/Remi Kabaka/Abdul Lasisi Amao				
Mdash-Aiye-Keta	Antilles	7005	'76	†
Stomu Yamashta's Go (with Steve Winwood)				
Go	Island	9358	'76	†
	Island	9387		†
Go Live from Paris	Island	(2)10	'78	†
Steve Winwood				
Winwood	United Artists	(2)9950	'71	†
	United Artists	(2)9964	'72	†
Steve Winwood	Island	9494	'77	†
	Island	842774	'89	CS/CD
	Mobile Fidelity	691	'97	CD
Arc of a Diver	Island	9576	'81	†
	Island	842365	'90	CS/CD
	Mobile Fidelity	579	'93	CD†
Talking Back to the Night	Island	9777	'82	†
	Island	842366	'90	CS/CD
	Mobile Fidelity	674	'96	CD

Back in the High Life	Island	25448	'86	LP/CS/CD†
	Island	830148	'90	CS/CD
	Mobile Fidelity	00611	'94	CD†
Chronicles	Island	25660	'87	LP/CS/CD†
	Island	842364	'90	CS/CD
The Finer Things	Island	(4)516870	'95	CS/CD
Roll with It	Virgin	90946	'88	CS/CD†
	Virgin	86069		CS/CD
Refugees of the Heart	Virgin	91405	'90	LP/CS/CD†
	Virgin	86189		CS/CD

IKE AND TINA TURNER

Ike Turner (born Izear Turner on November 5, 1931, in Clarksdale, Mississippi), piano, guitar, vocals; and Tina Turner (born Anna Mae Bullock on November 26, 1939, in Brownsville, Tennessee), vocals.

IKE AND TINA TURNER (HULTON-DEUTSCH COLLECTION/CORBIS)

Bandleader, songwriter, arranger, producer, and multi-instrumentalist Ike Turner achieved his first success in 1951 with his Kings of Rhythm behind Jackie Brenston's top rhythm-and-blues hit "Rocket 88," often regarded as the first "rock 'n' roll" record. He later worked as a talent scout for Modern Records, ostensibly producing B. B. King, Howlin' Wolf, and Elmore James. Devising a revue format for his Kings of Rhythm in St. Louis, Turner added vocalist and wife-to-be Tina in 1957. Touring the so-called "chitlin'" circuit for a decade, Ike and Tina Turner developed a gutsy and ribald stage act, with Tina, the show's focal point, performing in an overtly sexual manner, complete with feigned orgasms and provocative verbal exchanges with Ike. One of the most exciting musical acts of its time, The Ike and Tina Turner Revue was rivaled by only James Brown and The Fabulous Flames in terms of musical spectacle. Perhaps on the strength of their smash British hit, "River Deep—Mountain High," produced by the legendary Phil Spector, Ike and Tina Turner became far more popular in Great Britain than in the United States. They eventually attained the first massive exposure of their stage act on The Rolling Stones' 1969 American tour and subsequently looked to the world of rock music for material and an expanded audience, which they achieved with their smash crossover hit, "Proud Mary," in 1971. Ike and Tina Turner were inducted into the Rock and Roll Hall of Fame in 1991.

Tina Turner, long abused by Ike physically and psychologically, walked out on him in 1976 and subsequently spent nearly a decade trying to establish herself as a solo recording and performing artist, while retaining her fierce, flamboyant style. She finally achieved her breakthrough with 1984's *Private Dancer* album and its three smash crossover hits, "What's Love Got to Do with It," "Better Be Good to Me," and "Private Dancer." Her popularity was enhanced by the 1986 publication of her autobiography *I, Tina,* and the subsequent film biography *What's Love Got to Do with It,* released in 1993. Celebrated by feminists for her successful struggle to escape an abusive relationship and establish herself independently, Tina Turner saw her success wane in the United States in the mid-'90s, although she retained an enormous following in Europe and around the world.

Ike Turner started playing piano at the age of five and initiated his musical career at age eleven as piano accompanist to Sonny Boy Williamson (Aleck Ford) and Robert Nighthawk. By 1945, he was working as a disc jockey at WROX in Clarksdale, Mississippi, forming The Rhythm Kings in the late '40s. The group backed Jackie Brenston's top 1951 rhythm-and-blues hit "Rocket 88," recorded at the Sun Studio in Memphis with Ike on piano. Mastering guitar, Turner was hired as a songwriter and talent scout by Modern Records, ostensibly "discovering" B. B. King and Howlin' Wolf and playing sessions for King, Wolf, Elmore James, and Johnny Ace. Around 1954, he moved to East St. Louis, Missouri, where he became a rhythm-and-blues star with The Rhythm Kings.

Tina Turner grew up in Knoxville, Tennessee, and sang in a local church choir as a child. She moved to St. Louis around 1954 and met Ike Turner at the age of seventeen. She eventually succeeded in joining Ike Turner's revue in 1957. The couple soon married and Ike developed an exciting stage act billed as "The Ike and Tina Turner Revue" in 1960 based around Tina as lead vocalist, accompanied by his Kings of Rhythm and a female backing vocal trio dubbed The Ikettes. Recording for the Midwestern rhythm-and-blues label Sue, Ike and Tina Turner scored a series of R&B smashes in the early '60s with "A Fool in Love" (a major pop hit), "I Idolize You," "It's Gonna Work Out Fine" (another major pop hit), "Poor Fool," and "Tra La La La La."

In 1962, The Ikettes had a smash rhythm-and-blues and major pop hit with "I'm Blue (The Gong-Gong Song)" on Atco Records. In 1965, The Ikettes, with Vanetta Fields, Jessie Smith, and Robbie Montgomery, scored a moderate pop and R&B hit with "Peaches 'n' Cream" and a major R&B hit with "I'm So Thankful" on Modern Records. By 1968, this edition of The Ikettes had left the Turners, recording as The Mirettes and achieving a major R&B hit with "In the Midnight Hour" on Revue Records. Later lineups of The Ikettes included P. P. Arnold, Claudia Lennear, and Bonnie Bramlett (later of Delaney and Bonnie).

Relocating to Los Angeles in 1962, The Ike and Tina Turner Revue toured the "chitlin'" circuit of rhythm-and-blues clubs with their raunchy stage act and recorded for a variety of labels, including Warner Brothers, Loma, Pompeii, Blue Thumb, and Minit. They met songwriter-producer Phil Spector while working on the film *The T 'n' T Show* and he coauthored and produced their "River Deep—Mountain High" single, regarded as one of the finest singles of all time, in 1966. Although the song became a smash hit in Great Britain, it fared dismally in the United States and led to Spector's withdrawal from the music business.

The Ike and Tina Turner Revue toured Great Britain with The Rolling Stones in 1966 and received their first widespread American exposure in support of The Rolling Stones' 1969 tour of North America. They soon began recording contemporary material such as The Beatles' "Come Together," The Rolling Stones' "Honky Tonk Women," and Sly Stone's "I Want to Take You Higher." They finally broke through with the mainstream audience with a dynamic reworking of Creedence Clearwater Revival's "Proud Mary," a smash pop and rhythm-and-blues hit from *Workin' Together,* the best-selling album of their career, on Liberty Records. They conducted a hugely successful European tour in 1971, recording the live set *What You Hear Is What You Get* for United Artists, which had absorbed Liberty

Records. They scored another major pop hit in 1973 with Tina's autobiographical "Nutbush City Limits." Ike and Tina Turner were inducted into the Rock and Roll Hall of Fame in 1991.

Tina Turner launched her solo recording career on United Artists Records in 1974. She appeared in the equivocal film *Tommy* as the Acid Queen in 1975, singing The Who song of the same name. In July 1976, in the face of contractual obligations for albums and tours, Tina Turner walked out on her abusive husband Ike. Over the next eight years, she struggled to survive and establish herself in a solo career. She divorced Ike and developed a slick but ribald lounge act for Las Vegas casinos and later the Fairmont hotel chain. She recorded the last of three solo albums for United Artists in 1978. Ike Turner recorded an album for Fantasy Records in 1980 and later became mired in legal and drug-related problems that led to his incarceration for eighteen months in 1990 and 1991.

In 1979, Tina Turner met Australian promoter Roger Davies, who became her manager the next year. She moved away from easy-listening material and toured the United States with The Rolling Stones in 1981. She began a concerted comeback effort in 1982 at London's Hammersmith Odeon and later performed showcase dates at the Ritz Hotel in New York City. In 1983, she signed with Capitol Records, recording her debut for the label, *Private Dancer,* in Great Britain.

Private Dancer launched Tina Turner into international prominence. It produced five hits, including a smash rhythm-and-blues and major pop hit with her version of Al Green's "Let's Stay Together," the top pop and smash R&B hit "What's Love Got to Do with It," and the pop and rhythm-and-blues smashes "Better Be Good to Me" and "Private Dancer," the latter written by Mark Knopfler. The album stayed on the charts for more than two years and sold ten million copies worldwide (five million in the United States). She conducted a world tour of more than 100 cities in 1985, as the third *Mad Max* film, *Beyond Thunderdome,* costarring Turner, became one of the year's hit movies. The soundtrack album included her crossover smash "We Don't Need Another Hero" and the major pop hit "One of the Living." During the year, she also helped record USA for Africa's "We Are the World" and performed at Live Aid with Mick Jagger.

In 1986, Tina Turner recorded the best-selling *Break Every Rule* album and William Morrow published her autobiography, *I, Tina.* Although not as consistent as *Private Dancer, Break Every Rule* yielded four hits, including the crossover smash "Typical Male" and the major pop hit "What You Get Is What You See." Tina Turner conducted a world tour from March 1987 to March 1988 and her *Live in Europe* album included Robert Palmer's "Addicted to Love" and her own "Nutbush City Limits." *Foreign Affair* produced a major pop hit with "The Best." She again toured the United States in 1993 as the movie *What's Love Got to Do with It,* based on her autobiography, became one of the year's most highly acclaimed hits. As well as serving as a dynamic musical movie and yielding the near-smash hit "I Don't Wanna Fight," the film celebrated Tina's ability to survive and reestablish herself with pride and dignity in the face of domestic violence. Tina Turner performed the title song to the James Bond film *Goldeneye* in 1995 and recorded her first entirely new studio album in seven years, *Wildest Dreams,* featuring a remake of John Waite's top 1984 hit "Missing You," for Virgin Records in 1996. She toured North America again in 1997.

TINA TURNER BIBLIOGRAPHY

Fissinger, Laura. *Tina Turner.* New York: Ballantine Books, 1985.

Mills, Bart. *Tina.* New York: Warner Books, 1985.

Turner, Tina, with Kurt Loder. *I, Tina.* New York: Morrow, 1986.

Wynn, Ron. *Tina: The Tina Turner Story.* New York: Macmillan, 1985; Collier Books, 1985.

Ike Turner and His Kings of Rhythm

Volume 1	Ace	22	'88	†
Volume 2	Ace	146		†

Ike Turner

Rocks the Blues	Crown	367	'63	†
A Black Man's Soul	Pompeii	6003	'69	†
Blues Roots	United Artists	5576	'72	†
Confined to Soul	United Artists	051	'73	†
Bad Dreams	United Artists	087	'73	†
The Edge	Fantasy	9597	'80	†
I Like Ike: Best	Rhino	71819	'94	CS/CD
Rhythm Rockin' Blues	Ace	553	'95	CD

Ike and Tina Turner

The Sound of Ike and Tina Turner	Sue	2001	'61	†
Dance with Ike and Tina Turner	Sue	2003	'62	†
Dynamite	Sue	2004	'63	†
Don't Play Me Cheap	Sue	2005	'63	†
It's Gonna Work Out Fine	Sue	2007	'63	†
Greatest Hits	Sue	1038	'65	†
The Soul of Ike and Tina Turner	Kent	519		†
	Kent	014		†
	United	7740		†
Festival of Live Performances	Kent	538		†
	United	7755		†
Please, Please, Please	Kent	550		†
	United	7765		†
Revue Live	Kent	5014		†
	United	7735		†
The Ike and Tina Sessions	Kent	065	'87	LP/CS/CD†
The Dynamic Duo	Crown	004		†
The Ike and Tina Show Live	Warner Brothers	1579	'65	†
Live	Loma	5904	'67	†
Greatest Hits	Warner Brothers	1810	'69	†
River Deep–Mountain High	Philles	4011	'66	†
	A&M	4178	'69	†
	A&M	3179	'82	LP/CS/CD†
In Person	Minit	24018	'68	†
So Fine	Pompeii	6000	'68	†
Cussin', Cryin' and Carryin' On	Pompeii	6004	'69	†
Outta Season	Blue Thumb	5	'69	†
The Hunter	Blue Thumb	11	'69	†
The Hunter/Outta Season	Blue Moon	4001	'93	CD
Best	Blue Thumb	49	'73	†
Her Man . . . His Woman	Capitol	571	'70	†
Come Together	Liberty	7637	'70	†
Workin' Together	Liberty	7650	'70	†
Get Back	Liberty	51156	'85	†
What You Hear Is What You Get	United Artists	(2)9953	'71	†
'Nuff Said	United Artists	5530	'71	†
Feel Good	United Artists	5598	'72	†

Let Me Touch Your Mind	United Artists	5660	'72	†
Greatest Hits	United Artists	5667	'73	†
The World of Ike and Tina Turner	United Artists	(2)064	'73	†
Nutbush City Limits	United Artists	180	'73	†
The Gospel According to Ike and Tina Turner	United Artists	203	'74	†
Greatest Hits	United Artists	592	'76	†
Airwaves	United Artists	917	'78	†
Workin' Together	EMI America	10311	'86	CS†
Best	EMI America	46599	'87	CD†
Proud Mary: The Best of Ike and Tina Turner	EMI	95846	'91	CS/CD
What You Hear Is What You Get: Live At Carnegie Hall	EMI	38309	'96	CS/CD

Various Albums by Ike and Tina Turner

The Fantastic Ike and Tina Turner	Sunset	5265	'69	†
Ike and Tina Turner's Greatest Hits	Sunset	5286	'69	†
Ooh Poo Pah Doo	Harmony	11360	'69	†
	Harmony	30400		†
Something's Got a Hold of Me	Harmony	30567		†
16 Great Performances	ABC	4014	'71	†
Too Hot to Hold	Springboard Int'l	4011		†
	Pickwick	3284		†
Workin' Together	Pickwick	3032	'78	†
	Pickwick	3606	'79	†
Get It—Get It!	Pickwick	3328		†
Hot 'n' Sassy	Accord	7147	'81	†
Golden Empire	Striped Horse	2001	'86	LP/CS†
Golden Classics	Collectables	5107	'88	LP/CS/CD
It's Gonna Work Out Fine	Collectables	5137		LP/CS/CD
Greatest Hits, Volume 1	Saja	91223	'89	CS/CD
Greatest Hits, Volume 2	Saja	91224	'89	CS/CD
Greatest Hits, Volume 3	Saja	91228	'89	CS/CD
Greatest Hits	Curb/Warner Brothers	77332	'90	CS/CD
The Great Rhythm and Blues Sessions	Tomato	70382	'91	CD
Workin' It Out	Pair	1292	'91	CS/CD
The Ike and Tina Turner Collection	Mogull	35830	'93	CS/CD
Legendary Superstars: Ike and Tina Turner Featuring The Ikettes	Original Sound	9323	'94	CS/CD
Rock and Roll	Richmond	2233		CS
So Fine!	Special Music	4826		CS/CD

The Ikettes

Soul Hits	Modern	102	'65	†
(G)Old and New	United Artists	190	'74	†
Fine, Fine, Fine	Kent	063	'87	LP/CD

Tina Turner

Turns the Country On	United Artists	200	'74	†
Acid Queen	United Artists	495	'75	†
	Razor & Tie	1985	'91	CD
Rough	United Artists	919	'78	†
Private Dancer	Capitol	12330	'84	†
	Capitol	46041		CS/CD
Break Every Rule	Capitol	12530	'86	†
	Capitol	46323		CS/CD

Tina Live in Europe	Capitol	(2)90126	'88	CS/CD
Foreign Affair	Capitol	91873	'89	CS/CD
	Capitol	91329		CD†
Simply the Best	Capitol	97152	'91	CS/CD
The Collected Recordings: Sixties to Nineties	Capitol	(3)29724	'94	CD
Tina Turner	Bella Musica	89926	'90	CD†
Tina Turner, Volume 2	Bella Musica	89941	'91	CD†
What's Love Got to Do	Virgin	88189	'93	CS/CD
Wildest Dreams	Virgin	41920	'96	CS/CD
Tina Turner Goes Country	Playback	12331		CS

THE TURTLES

Mark Volman (born April 19, 1944, in Los Angeles), guitar, saxophone, lead vocals; Howard Kaylan (born Howard Kaplan on June 22, 1945, in New York City), keyboards, saxophone, backing and harmony vocals; Al Nichol (born March 31, 1945), keyboards, guitar, bass, vocals; Jim Tucker (born October 17, 1946, in Los Angeles), guitar; Charles "Chuck" Portz (born March 28, 1945, in Santa Monica, California), bass; and Don Murray (born November 8, 1945, in Los Angeles), drums. Later members included drummers John Barbata (born April 1, 1946, in New Jersey) and John Seiter (born August 17, 1944, in St. Louis, Missouri), and bassist Jim Pons (born March 14, 1943, in Santa Monica).

Mistakenly identified with the folk-rock movement as a result of their near-smash hit version of Bob Dylan's "It Ain't Me, Babe" in 1965, The Turtles evolved from a surf band and enjoyed their greatest success with pop-style songs such as "Happy Together," "She'd Rather Be with Me," and "Elenore." The last hit was taken from their 1968 album *The Turtles Present the Battle of the Bands,* one of the oddest collections of songs from the late '60s. With the demise of The Turtles in 1970, the group's two masterminds, Mark Volman and Howard Kaylan, joined Frank Zappa's Mothers of Invention as Phlorescent Leech and Eddie, later shortened to Flo and Eddie. Touring extensively and recording four albums with Zappa, Flo and Eddie later recorded four brilliant yet overlooked albums of rock parody and satire. In the '80s, they pursued sessions work, wrote commercials, and scored and recorded children's cartoons. In the latter half of the '80s, Mark Volman and Howard Kaylan reconstituted The Turtles for national tours and club appearances.

Mark Volman and Howard Kaylan met at Westchester High School in Los Angeles in 1961, the year Kaylan formed the surf group The Nightriders with Al Nichol, Chuck Portz, and Don Murray. Adding Volman on saxophone in 1963, the group became The Crossfires, releasing two local singles. In 1965, they signed with White Whale Records and changed their name to The Turtles, adding second guitarist Jim Tucker. Capitalizing on the burgeoning folk-rock movement, The Turtles' debut album included "Eve of Destruction" and three Bob Dylan songs, including the near-smash hit "It Ain't Me, Babe." They next scored major hits with P. F. Sloan's "Let Me Be" and Sloan and Steve Barri's "You Baby." In mid-1966, Murray and Portz departed, to be replaced by John Barbata and Jim Pons, a founding member of The Leaves ("Hey Joe").

The Turtles subsequently achieved their most successful year in 1967 with the top pop hit "Happy Together" (backed by Warren Zevon's "Like The Seasons"), the smash hit "She'd Rather Be with Me," and the major hits "You Know What I Mean" and "She's My Girl," all written by Gary Bonner and Alan Gordon. In mid-1968, The Turtles scored a moderate hit with Harry Nilsson's "The Story of Rock and Roll," next recording *The Turtles Present the Battle of the Bands.* The album yielded smash hits with the group's "Elenore" and "You Showed Me," written by Gene Clark and Jim McGuinn of The Byrds. For the album, the group recorded under a variety of different names in different styles, showcasing a developing satirical bent with songs such as "Surfer Dan," "I'm Chief Kamanananalea (We're the Royal Macadamia Nuts)," and "Chicken Little Was Right." After *Turtle Soup,* produced by The Kinks' Ray Davies, The Turtles disbanded in mid-1970. John Barbata joined Crosby, Stills and Nash for a time, later joining The Jefferson Airplane in 1972.

Mark Volman and Howard Kaylan (and later Jim Pons) subsequently joined Frank Zappa's Mothers of Invention as the Phlorescent Leech and Eddie. Touring Europe and America extensively with Zappa, Mark "Flo" Volman and Howard "Eddie" Kaylan performed their own feature spot in concert and recorded two live albums with the group. They also helped record *Chunga's Revenge* and the soundtrack to the movie *200 Motels,* in which they appeared. Volman and Kaylan also recorded as background vocalists for Marc Bolan/T. Rex in 1971 and 1972 (including the major hit "Bang a Gong"). With the dissolution of the current edition of The Mothers of Invention at the end of 1971, Flo and Eddie recorded two outstanding yet neglected albums of rock satire for Reprise Records and toured in support of Alice Cooper's "Billion Dollar Babies" tour in 1973.

Howard Kaylan and Mark Volman later wrote the screenplay to the X-rated animated movie *Cheap,* wrote satirical articles for the American rock press, and hosted their own successful syndicated radio show originating from Los Angeles' KROQ. Signed to Columbia Records in 1975, the duo recorded two more excellent yet overlooked albums of rock parody and satire before moving into sessions and television work. They recorded a silly reggae album in 1981, wrote radio and television commercials (including all of the commercials for David Bowie's RCA albums), and wrote and recorded music for the children's cartoons *Strawberry Shortcake* and *The Care Bears.* In 1984 and 1985, with a reconstituted Turtles, they headlined two "Happy Together Tours" with other '60s groups, subsequently touring independently as The Turtles.

The Crossfires

Out of Control	Rhino	019	'81	†
	Sundazed	6062	'95	CD

The Turtles

It Ain't Me Babe	White Whale	7111	'65	†
	Rhino	151	'82	LP/CS†
	Sundazed	6035	'95	CD
You Baby	White Whale	7112	'66	†
	Rhino	153	'83	LP/CS†
	Sundazed	6036	'95	CD
Happy Together	White Whale	7114	'67	†
	Rhino	152	'83	LP/CS†
	Sundazed	6037	'95	CD
Golden Hits	White Whale	7115	'67	†
The Turtles Present the Battle of the Bands	White Whale	7118	'68	†
	Rhino	70156	'86	LP/CS†
	Sundazed	6038	'95	CD
Turtle Soup	White Whale	7124	'69	†
	Rhino	70157	'86	LP/CS†
	Sundazed	6086		CD
More Golden Hits	White Whale	7127	'70	†
Wooden Head	White Whale	7133	'70	†
	Rhino	154	'84	LP/CS†
	Sundazed	6087		CD
Happy Together Again — Greatest Hits	Sire	(2)3703	'74	†
Greatest Hits	Rhino	160	'82	†

Best (1965–1969)	Rhino	70177	'86	CS
Chalon Road	Rhino	70155	'87	LP/CS†
Shell Shock	Rhino	70158	'87	LP/CS†
Turtle Wax: Best, Volume 2	Rhino	70159	'88	CS/CD
Captured Live	Rhino	71153	'92	CS/CD
Love Songs	Rhino	71873	'95	CS/CD
20 Greatest Hits	Rhino	75160		CD

Flo and Eddie with Frank Zappa and The Mothers of Invention

Chunga's Revenge	Bizarre/Reprise	2030	'70	†
	Rykodisc	10164	'90	CD†
	Rykodisc	10511	'95	CD
Fillmore East, June 1971	Bizarre/Reprise	2042	'71	†
	Rykodisc	10167	'90	CD†
	Rykodisc	10512	'95	CS/CD
Just Another Band from L.A.	Bizarre/Reprise	2075	'72	†
	Rykodisc	10161	'90	CD†
	Rykodisc	10515	'95	CD
Playground Psychotics	Barking Pumpkin/ Capitol	(2)74244	'92	CD†
	Rykodisc	(2)10557/58	'95	CD
200 Motels (soundtrack)	United Artists	(2)9956	'71	†
	MCA	(2)4183	'86	LP/CS
	Rykodisc	(2)10513	'98	CS/CD

Flo and Eddie

The Phlorescent Leech and Eddie	Reprise	2099	'72	†
Flo and Eddie	Reprise	2141	'73	†
Illegal, Immoral and Fattening	Columbia	33554	'75	†
	One Way	22673		CD
Moving Targets	Columbia	34262	'76	†
Best (from the above four albums)	Rhino	70134	'86	CS†
Rock Steady with Flo and Eddie	Epiphany	4010	'81	†
Best	Rhino	71097	'92	CD

THE VELVET UNDERGROUND

Lou Reed (born Louis Firbank on March 2, 1943, in Freeport, Long Island, New York), vocals, keyboards, guitar; John Cale (born December 5, 1940, in Crynant, West Glamorgan, Wales), vocals, viola, keyboards, bass; Sterling Morrison (born August 29, 1942, in East Meadow, Long Island, New York; died August 30, 1995, in Poughkeepsie, New York), guitar, bass; Nico (born Christa Paffgen on October 16, 1938, in Cologne, West Germany; died July 18, 1988, on Ibiza, Spain), vocals; and Maureen "Mo" Tucker (born 1945 in New Jersey), drums. Nico left after the first album and John Cale after the second. He was replaced by Doug Yule.

A seminal late '60s New York band whose influence was not recognized until years after their disbandment, The Velvet Underground recorded overpowering, desperate songs of contemporary street life concerning sadomasochism, prostitution, and drug addiction (the classic "Heroin") that bore a stark contrast to the then-popular psychedelic and folk-rock music. The Velvet Underground featured the harsh, sinister, and real-life songs of Lou Reed, the avant-garde musical innovations of John Cale, the thin but sensual voice of Nico, and the drumming of Maureen Tucker, one of the few female drummers in rock music.

Launched in association with artist Andy Warhol, The Velvet Underground toured with his "total environment" show, The Exploding Plastic Inevitable, perhaps the first multimedia show complete with music, dancers, films, lights, and projections. The Velvet Underground became the vehicle for Reed's eerie visions of life after the departures of Nico (after the first album) and Cale (after the second album). Serving as an inspiration to late '70s punk and new-wave acts such as Patti Smith, The Sex Pistols, and Talking Heads and '80s groups such as R.E.M. and Sonic Youth, The Velvet Underground was inducted into the Rock and Roll Hall of Fame in 1996. While Nico's solo career remained relatively undistinguished and John Cale retained a limited following among critics and avant-garde fans, Lou Reed became the most successful, if erratic, of the former members as a solo artist. Breaking through with his David Bowie–produced *Transformer* album (and its surprise hit with "Walk on the Wild Side"), Reed scored his biggest album success with the live *Rock 'n' Roll Animal* album. During the early '80s, Reed recorded mellower rock for adults, returning to his harsher thematic styles with 1989's *New York*. In 1990, he teamed with John Cale for *Songs for Drella,* a tribute album to their one-time mentor Andy Warhol, and later recorded the moody examination of life and the spirit, *Magic and Loss.*

Lou Reed first played professionally while in his early teens with Long Island bands such as Pasha and The Prophets and The Jades. Studying journalism and creative writing at Syracuse University, he worked as a journalist and as a songwriter for Pickwick Records and met John Cale in 1964. Cale had studied classical viola and piano in London, and his compositions had been broadcast by the BBC when he was eight years old. Cale came to the United States in 1963 on a Leonard Bernstein fellowship but abandoned his classical studies to pursue his interest in avant-garde music, joining LaMonte Young's experimental group The Dream Syndicate on electric viola. Reed teamed with Cale and classically trained guitarist Sterling Morrison in bands such as The Ostriches and The Primitives, adding female drummer Maureen Tucker in 1965. Becoming The Velvet Underground, the group enjoyed a residency at Cafe Bizarre in Greenwich Village in the winter of 1966 and immediately sparked controversy for their unorthodox music and stage demeanor.

The Velvet Underground came to the attention of artist Andy Warhol, who was looking for a rock group to add to his multimedia outfit, The Factory. Among the members of The Factory was Nico, who had been a European model since the age of sixteen. She had moved to New York in 1959 and studied acting with Lee Strasberg before appearing in Warhol's 1966 *Chelsea Girls* film. Augmented by Nico, The Velvet Underground joined Warhol's "total environment" show, The Exploding Plastic Inevitable, which opened in New York and subsequently toured Canada and the United States.

Signed to MGM/Verve Records, The Velvet Underground recorded their debut album with Andy Warhol as nominal producer. Packaged in a jacket that featured Warhol's famous peelable banana cover, *The Velvet Underground and Nico* comprised music and lyrics the likes of which had not yet appeared in rock music. Propelled by John Cale's innovative musical experimentation and Lou Reed's disarmingly realistic and sinister lyrics, the album included the startling "Heroin," with its screeching, electronic drugged-out crescendo, the sadomasochistic "Venus in Furs," the gritty "I'm Waiting for the Man," "There She Goes Again," and the gentle "Sunday Morning" and "I'll Be Your Mirror," the latter sung by Nico. Garnering virtually no radio airplay, the album failed to sell, yet it was eventually recognized as one of the most influential albums of the '60s.

Nico subsequently left The Velvet Underground to pursue a solo career and, with the attendant loss of interest by Warhol and the press, the group's *White Light/White Heat* was largely ignored by the public, yet it contained the lurid seventeen-minute classic "Sister Ray." The group toured to diminishing audiences and Cale left in March 1968. He was replaced by multi-instrumentalist Doug Yule for the subtle *The Velvet Underground* album, which featured the ballad "Pale Blue Eyes." Recordings made for a fourth (unreleased) MGM/Verve album surfaced in 1985 on *VU.* The group switched to Cotillion Records for their final studio album, *Loaded,* which included "Rock and Roll" and "Sweet Jane." Following a summer's residency at Max's Kansas City in New York, Reed left The Velvet Underground in August 1970. Morrison left in March 1971, soon followed by Tucker, after which the group maintained with new members through 1973.

Nico was the first former member of The Velvet Underground to record a solo album, but *Chelsea Girl* failed to sell despite the inclusion of Jackson Browne's "These Days" and Bob Dylan's "I'll Keep It with Mine." *The Marble Index,* for Elektra, featured her own morose songwriting and harmonium playing, and her two subsequent albums, *Desertshore* and *The End,* were produced by John Cale. By the mid-'70s, her career had fallen into disarray, although she continued to record until her death on July 18, 1988, of a cerebral hemorrhage incurred in a bicycle accident on the Spanish island of Ibiza.

In the meantime, John Cale had produced The Stooges' debut album, launched his own recording career on Columbia with *Vintage Violence,* and recorded *Church of Anthrax* with minimalist saxophonist-keyboardist Terry Riley. Cale switched to Reprise for *The Academy in Peril* and the critically-acclaimed *Paris 1919,* recorded with Lowell George and Ritchie Hayward of Little Feat. However, by 1974, Cale had returned to England.

By 1972, Lou Reed had signed a solo contract with RCA Records, recording his debut album in London. His second, *Transformer,* produced in London by David Bowie and Mick Ronson, yielded a major hit with "Walk on the Wild Side," and served as his breakthrough album. However, the *Berlin* album sold poorly, so Reed assembled a touring band to record *Rock 'n' Roll Animal* at New York's Academy of Music. The album became the best-seller of his career and included "Heroin," "Sweet Jane," and the classic "Rock 'n' Roll." *Sally Can't Dance* also sold quite well despite its air of parody and Reed's career reached its nadir with 1975's *Metal Machine Music,* which consisted of little more than feedback, electronic beeps, and tape hiss.

In 1974, Nico and John Cale performed a concert at London's Rainbow Theatre with synthesizer player Brian Eno (of Roxy Music) and bassist Kevin Ayers and percussionist Robert Wyatt (of Soft Machine) that produced the live album *June 1, 1974.* Cale recorded *Fear* (regarded as one of his finest solo albums) and *Slow Dazzle* with Eno and guitarist Phil Manzanera, another veteran of Roxy Music, and toured Europe in the spring of 1975. He produced Patti Smith's stunning debut *Horses* and The Modern Lovers' debut album, switching to A&M Records for *Sabotage Live.*

Following the sedate *Coney Island Baby,* Lou Reed switched to Arista Records for a number of poor-selling mediocre albums, save perhaps *Street Hassle,* through 1980. That year he appeared in a cameo role in Paul Simon's *One Trick Pony* movie. Returning to RCA Records, he recorded more accessible and mature albums for the label beginning with 1982's acclaimed *The Blue Mask.* He helped record the "Sun City" single, toured with the first Amnesty International tour, and performed a number of benefits for the homeless. Reed returned to his anxious style of songwriting on Sire Records with the politicized *New York* album, hailed as his most vital album in fifteen years. In 1990, Reed joined John Cale for the first time in twenty years to compose and perform the tribute album to the late Andy Warhol, *Songs for Drella.*

John Cale recorded several albums in the '80s, most notably *Music for a New Society,* assisting Brian Eno in the recording of 1990's *Wrong Way Up.* Maureen Tucker reemerged with 1981's *Playin' Possum* and later recorded for the independent label 50 Skidillion Watts. Reed recorded the moving yet demanding *Magic and Loss,* inspired by the deaths of two friends, one of whom was songwriter Doc Pomus. In January 1993, Lou Reed performed at President Bill Clinton's inaugural ball, later joining Sterling Morrison, Maureen Tucker, and John Cale as The Velvet Underground for a European tour and *Live MCMXCIII,* recorded at L'Olympia Theatre in Paris. On August 30, 1995, Sterling Morrison died of non-Hodgkins lymphoma in Poughkeepsie, New York, at the age of 53. By 1996, the year The Velvet Underground was inducted into the Rock and Roll Hall of Fame, Reed had switched to Warner Brothers for *Set the Twilight Reeling,* recorded entirely in his home studio. Cale recorded the music for the film *I Shot Andy Warhol* and the album *Walking on Locusts* for Hannibal/Rykodisc in 1996, the year Maureen Tucker joined songwriter-guitarist Mark Goodman in Magnet.

THE VELVET UNDERGROUND BIBLIOGRAPHY

Bockris, Victor. *The Velvet Underground Story.* New York: Quill, 1983.
————. *Transformer: The Lou Reed Story.* New York: Simon and Schuster, 1994.
Young, James. *Nico: The End.* Woodstock, NY: Overlook Press, 1993.

Original Velvet Underground Studio Albums

The Velvet Underground and Nico	Verve	65008	'67	†
	Verve/Polydor	823290	'85	CS/CD
	Mobile Fidelity	695	'97	CD
White Light/White Heat	Verve	65046	'68	†
	Verve	825119	'85	CS/CD
	Mobile Fidelity	724	'98	CD
The Velvet Underground	MGM	4617	'69	†
	Verve/Polydor	815454	'85	CS/CD
Loaded	Cotillion	9034	'70	†
	Warner	27613		CD

Later Velvet Underground Albums

1969 Live	Mercury	(2)7504	'74	†
	Mercury	826284		CS
also available as Live With Lou Reed, Volumes I & II	Verve/Polydor	834823/4	'88	CD
Live at Max's Kansas City (recorded August 1970)	Cotillion	9500	'72	CS/CD
The Velvet Underground	MGM	131	'71	†
Archetype	MGM	4950	'74	†
Lou Reed with The Velvet Underground	Pride	0022	'73	†
VU	Verve	823721	'85	CS/CD
Another View	Verve	829405	'86	CS/CD
Best of The Velvet Underground: Words and Music of Lou Reed	Verve	841164	'89	CS/CD
Peel Slowly and See (remastered versions of 4 original studio albums plus previously unreleased material recorded 1965–1970)	A&M	(5)7887	'95	CD
Live MCMXCIII	Sire	(2)45464	'93	CS/CD
(abridged version)	Sire	45465	'93	CS/CD
(limited edition)	Sire	45434	'93	CD

Nico

Chelsea Girl	Verve	65032	'67	†
	Polydor	835209	'88	CD
The Marble Index	Elektra	74029	'68/'91	CD†
Desertshore	Reprise	6424	'70	†
	Warner Archives	6424	'93	LP/CS/CD
The End	Island	9311	'74	†
	Island	518892	'96	CD
	Polydor	314518	'96	CD
Icon (recorded 1980, 1981)	Cleopatra	9709	'96	CD
Drama of Exile (recorded 1981)	Aura	715	'83	†
(original version)	Buda/Allegro	926472	'96	CD
	Cleopatra	1079	'93	CS/CD

Chelsea Girl Live	Cleopatra	6108	'95	CD
Do or Die	ROIR	117		CS/CD
Live Heroes	Performance	385		LP/CS/CD
Hanging Gardens	Restless	72383	'88	CS/CD†
John Cale				
Vintage Violence	Columbia	1037	'70	†
	Columbia/Legacy	01037	'90	CD
The Academy in Peril	Reprise	2079	'72	†
	Warner Archives	2079	'93	LP/CD
Paris 1919	Reprise	2131	'73	†
	Reprise	25926	'93	CD†
Fear	Island	9301	'75	†
Slow Dazzle	Island	9317	'75	†
Guts	Island	9459	'77	†
	Antilles	7063		†
Music for a New Society	Island		'82	†
	Rhino	71743	'94	CD
The Island Anthology	Island/ Chronicles	(2)524235	'96	CD
Even Cowgirls Get the Blues (recorded 1978, 1979)	ROIR	196	'91	CS/CD
Sabotage Live	A&M	004	'79	†
Honi Soit	A&M	4849	'81	†
Caribbean Sunset	Antilles	8401	'84	†
John Cale Comes Alive	Antilles	8402	'84	†
Words for the Dying	Opal/ Warner Brothers	26024	'89	CS/CD†
Fragments of a Rainy Season	Hannibal	1372	'92	CS/CD
Walking on Locusts	Hannibal	1395	'96	CD
Eat/Kiss: Music for the Films by Andy Warhol	Hannibal	1407	'97	CD
Seducing Down the Door: A Collection 1970–1990	Rhino	(2)71685	'94	CD
I Shot Andy Warhol (music from soundtrack)	Tag	92690	'96	CS/CD
Nico	Detour	22122	'98	CD
John Cale and Terry Riley				
Church of Anthrax	Columbia	30131	'71	†
John Cale, Kevin Ayers, Brian Eno and Nico				
June 1, 1974	Island	9291	'74	†
John Cale and Brian Eno				
Wrong Way Up	Opal/ Warner Brothers	26421	'90	CS†/CD
John Cale and Bob Neuwirth				
Last Day on Earth	MCA	11037	'94	CS/CD
Lou Reed				
Lou Reed	RCA	4701	'72	†
Transformer	RCA	4807	'72	CD†
	RCA	3806		LP/CS†
	RCA	66600	'95	CD
Berlin	RCA	0207	'73/'89	CS/CD†
	RCA	4388		†
	RCA	67489	'98	CD

Rock 'n' Roll Animal	RCA	0472	'74	†
	RCA	3664	'80	CS/CD
Sally Can't Dance	RCA	0611	'74/'89	CS/CD†
Live	RCA	0959	'75	†
	RCA	3752		CS/CD
Metal Music Machine: The Amine Beta Ring	RCA	(2)1101	'75	†
Coney Island Baby	RCA	0915	'76/'89	CS/CD†
	RCA	2480	'77	†
Walk on the Wild Side: The Best of Lou Reed	RCA	2001	'77	†
	RCA	7653	'88	CS
	RCA	3753	'88	CD
Different Times: Lou Reed in the '70s	RCA	66864	'96	CS/CD
Rock and Roll Heart	Arista	4100	'76	†
Street Hassle	Arista	4169	'78	†
	Arista	18499	'87	CS†/CD
Live . . . Take No Prisoners	Arista	(2)8502	'78	†
The Bells	Arista	4229	'79	†
Growing Up in Public	Arista	9522	'80	†
Rock 'n' Roll Diary, 1967–1980	Arista	8603	'80	†
	Arista	8434		CS
The Blue Mask	RCA	4221	'82	
Legendary Hearts	RCA	4568	'83/'90	CS/CD†
New Sensations	RCA	4998	'84	CS/CD†
Mistrial	RCA	7190	'86	CS/CD†
Walk on the Wild Side and Other Hits	RCA	52162	'90	CS/CD
Between Thought and Expression: The Lou Reed Anthology	RCA	(3)2356	'92	CS/CD
Wild Child	Pair	1024	'86	CD
New York	Sire	25829	'89	CS/CD
Magic and Loss	Sire	26662	'91	CS/CD
Set the Twilight Reeling	Warner Brothers	46159	'96	CS/CD
Perfect Night	Warner Brothers	46917	'98	CS/CD
Lou Reed and John Cale				
Songs for Drella	Sire	26140	'90	CS/CD
	Sire	26205	'90	CD
Maureen Tucker				
Playin' Possum			'81	†
Life in Exile After Abdication	50 Skidillion	7	'89	LP/CS/CD
I Spent a Week There the Other Night	Young God		'91	†
	Sky	3104	'94	CD
Dogs Under Stress	New Rose		'93	†
	Sky	3103	'94	CD
Magnet				
Don't Be a Penguin	PC Music	03	'97	CD

JUNIOR WALKER AND THE ALL STARS

Junior Walker (born Autry DeWalt, Jr., in 1942 in Blytheville, Arkansas; died November 23, 1995, in Battle Creek, Michigan), saxophone, vocals; Willie Woods, guitar; Vic Thomas, organ; and James Graves, drums.

The only Motown instrumentalist to make recordings under his own name, Junior Walker (and The All Stars) scored a number of hits between 1965 and 1970 featuring Walker's dynamic tenor saxophone solos. Initially hitting with uptempo dance tunes such as "Shotgun" and "(I'm A) Roadrunner," Junior Walker and The All Stars later achieved success with ballads like "What Does It Take (To Win Your Love)."

Autry DeWalt grew up in South Bend, Indiana, where he took up saxophone in high school and played in local jazz and rhythm-and-blues clubs with bands such as The Jumping Jacks and The Stix Nix. Moving to Battle Creek, Michigan, in the late '50s, he formed Junior Walker and The All Stars in 1961 to play the local club circuit. The following year, the group was spotted by Johnny Bristol (half of the duo Johnny and Jack, who recorded the original version of "Someday We'll Be Together" in 1961). Bristol recommended the group to Harvey Fuqua, who signed them to his own Harvey label. Fuqua's labels Tri-Phi and Harvey were absorbed by Motown Records in 1963, and Junior Walker and The All Stars began recording for the subsidiary label Soul in 1964.

In early 1965, Junior Walker and The All Stars scored a top rhythm-and-blues and smash pop hit with Walker's classic "Shotgun." Following the uptempo "Do the Boomerang" and "Shake and Fingerpop" (moderate pop and major R&B hits), the group achieved hits with the instrumental "Cleo's Mood" and the Holland-Dozier-Holland classic "(I'm A) Roadrunner," a smash R&B and major pop hit. All these hits were contained on the group's debut album *Shotgun*. Subsequent hits included a cover of Marvin Gaye's smash 1965 pop and R&B hit "How Sweet It Is (To Be Loved by You)" and "Pucker Up Buttercup."

Home Cookin' yielded four hits with the title song, Holland-Dozier-Holland's "Come See About Me" (a top pop and smash rhythm-and-blues hit for The Supremes in 1965), "Hip City—Pt. 2," and "What Does It Take (To Win Your Love)," a smash pop and top R&B hit. Subsequently working with Johnny Bristol as producer, Junior Walker and The All Stars scored smash rhythm-and-blues and major pop hits with a cover of The Guess Who's "These Eyes," "Gotta Hold on to This Feeling," and "Do You See My Love (For You Growing)."

Junior Walker and The All Stars continued to record for Soul Records with moderate success into the '70s, scoring their last major rhythm-and-blues hit with the instrumental "Walk in the Night" in 1972. In 1976, Walker began recording solo for Soul Records, moving to Norman Whitfield's Whitfield Records in 1979. He provided the saxophone solo for Foreigner's 1981 smash pop hit "Urgent" and returned to Motown in 1983. Junior Walker and The All Stars toured into the '90s. Junior Walker died in Battle Creek, Michigan, of cancer on November 23, 1995.

Junior Walker and The All Stars

Shotgun		Soul	701	'65	†
		Motown	5141	'89	CS/CD†
Soul Session		Soul	702	'66	†
Roadrunner		Soul	703	'66	†
		Motown	5427	'89	CD†
Shotgun/Road Runner		Motown	8123	'86	CD†
Live!		Soul	705	'67	†
		Motown	5465	'90	CS/CD†
Home Cookin'		Soul	710	'69	†
		Motown	530402	'94	CS/CD
Greatest Hits		Soul	718	'69	†
		Motown	5208		CS/CD
What Does It Take to Win Your Love		Soul	721	'70	†
Live		Soul	725	'70	†
A Gasssss		Soul	726	'70	†

Rainbow Funk	Soul	732	'71	†
Moody Jr.	Soul	733	'72	†
Hot Shot	Soul	745	'76	†
Anthology	Motown	(2)786	'74	LP/CS†
Motown Superstar Series, Volume 5	Motown	5105		†
All the Great Hits	Motown	9012		CD†
	Motown	5297		CS/CD
Compact Command Performances	Motown	6203	'86	CD†
Gotta Hold on to This Feeling	Motown	5460	'90	CS/CD†
Nothing but Soul: The Singles 1962–1983	Motown	(2)6270	'94	CS/CD
The Ultimate Collection	Motown	0828	'97	CS/CD
Shotgun	Pickwick	3391	'75	†
Junior Walker				
Sax Appeal	Soul	747	'76	†
Whopper Bopper Show Stopper	Soul	748	'76	†
Smooth	Soul	750	'78	†
Back Street Boogie	Whitfield	3331	'79	†
Blow the House Down	Motown	6053	'83	†
Shake and Fingerpop	Magnum	49	'96	CD

DIONNE WARWICK

Born Marie Dionne Warrick on December 12, 1940, in East Orange, New Jersey.

In perhaps the most successful hit-making partnership of the '60s, singer Dionne Warwick, lyricist Hal David, and producer-arranger-composer Burt Bacharach registered more than thirty-five hits between 1962 and 1971 on Scepter Records. Featuring Warwick's svelte, light, and perfectly phrased vocals, Bacharach's precise, complex orchestral arrangements, and David's anguished pop-style lyrics, their songs brought a new level of sophistication to soul music with hits such as "Anyone Who Had a Heart," "Walk on By," and "Message to Michael." However, by 1967, Bacharach and David's material had become geared to the white adult audience, and Warwick's most consistent success occurred in the easy-listening arena. Suffering diminished popularity after leaving Scepter Records and separating from the Bacharach-David team in 1971, Warwick reestablished herself with 1979's *Dionne* album and sustained her '80s career with such hits as "Heartbreaker," "That's What Friends Are For," and "Love Power." Helping immeasurably along the way were producers such as Thom Bell, Barry Manilow, Barry Gibb, and Luther Vandross.

Dionne Warwick was born into a family of gospel singers and began singing in the New Hope Baptist Church choir in Newark, New Jersey, at the age of six. She played piano with the gospel group The Drinkard Singers and later was a member of The Gospelaires with sister Dee Dee and aunt Cissy Houston (Whitney's mother). Dionne graduated from Hart Music College in Connecticut and the Warwick sisters, Cissy Houston, and Doris Troy began singing together at recording sessions in New York in the late '50s. During the session for The Drifters' "Mexican Divorce" in 1961, Dionne met songwriter-producer-arranger Burt Bacharach, who helped secure her sessions work and a recording contract with Scepter Records.

With Bacharach and lyricist Hal David producing and writing the songs, Dionne Warwick scored her first major pop and smash rhythm-and-blues hit with her debut single, "Don't Make Me Over," at the end of 1962. Subsequent successes for the team through 1966 included the smash pop, rhythm-and-blues, and easy-listening hits "Anyone Who Had a Heart,"

"Walk on By," and "Message to Michael," and the major pop and R&B hits "Reach Out for Me," "Trains and Boats and Planes," and "I Just Don't Know What to Do with Myself."

By 1964, sister Dee Dee Warwick was pursuing her own solo career, recording "You're No Good" for Jubilee Records. She signed with the Blue Rock subsidary of Mercury Records, scoring a major rhythm-and-blues hit "We're Doing Fine" in 1965. Moving to the parent label in 1966, she achieved major rhythm-and-blues hits with "I Want to Be with You" (a moderate pop hit), "I'm Gonna Make You Love Me" (a smash pop and rhythm-and-blues hit for The Supremes and The Temptations in 1968 and 1969), and "Foolish Fool" through 1969. She subsequently recorded for Atco Records, managing a near-smash rhythm-and-blues hit with "She Didn't Know (She Kept on Talking)" in 1970. She continued to record into the '80s for Private Stock and RCA.

Debuting on the cabaret circuit by 1967 and fully established as an international recording artist, Dionne Warwick began recording less dynamic Bacharach-David songs as the team began working on movie scores and stage musicals. Through 1968, she scored a smash crossover hits with "I Say a Little Prayer" and "(Theme From) The Valley of the Dolls," and major crossover hits with "Alfie," "Do You Know the Way to San Jose," and "Promises, Promises." "This Girl's in Love with You" became a pop and rhythm-and-blues smash in 1969 and "I'll Never Fall in Love Again" became a pop smash in 1970. The rest of her smash hits through 1971, including "Who Is Gonna Love Me," "Let Me Go to Him," "Make It Easy on Yourself," and "Who Gets the Guy," came in the easy-listening field.

By 1971, Dionne Warwick had switched to Warner Brothers Records, but after a single album with Burt Bacharach and Hal David, the duo and the singer parted company. She used the last name Warwicke from late 1971 to 1975, achieving her only major pop hit until 1979 with 1974's "Then Came You." Recorded in Philadelphia with The Spinners and produced by Thom Bell, the song became a top pop and smash rhythm-and-blue and easy-listening hit. Bell produced her *Track of the Cat* album, which yielded a rhythm-and-blues smash with "Once You Hit the Road," and she next toured and recorded the live *A Man and a Woman* with Isaac Hayes.

In 1979, Dionne Warwick switched to Arista Records, where her debut, simply *Dionne,* was produced by Barry Manilow. It yielded three hits, including the smash pop hit "I'll Never Love This Way Again" and the major pop hit "Deja Vu," and became the best-selling album of her career. "No Night So Long" became a top easy-listening and major pop/R&B hit in 1980, and Bee Gee Barry Gibb produced her *Heartbreaker* album, which yielded a top easy-listening and major pop/R&B hit with the title tune. Luther Vandross produced Warwick's *How Many Times Can We Say Goodbye,* and the title song, sung as a duet, became a smash rhythm-and-blues and major pop hit.

In 1980 and 1981 and again in 1985 and 1986, Dionne Warwick hosted the syndicated variety television series *Solid Gold.* She reunited with Burt Bacharach for 1984's *Finder of Lost Loves.* In 1985, she took part in the recording of USA for Africa's "We Are the World," scoring a top pop, rhythm-and-blues, and easy-listening hit with "That's What Friends Are For" late in the year. Written by Bacharach and his wife Carole Bayer Sager, the song was recorded with "Friends" Elton John, Gladys Knight, and Stevie Wonder, and, at the request of Elizabeth Taylor, profits from the song were donated to the cause of AIDS research. Frequently appearing at benefit and tribute concerts throughout the '80s and '90s, Warwick managed her last major pop/R&B (and top easy-listening) hit with "Love Power," in duet with Jeffrey Osborne, in 1987.

Dionne Warwick toured with Burt Bacharach in 1992 and reunited with Bacharach *and* Hal David for *Friends Can Be Lovers.* In 1994, she recorded a collection of Brazilian songs, *Aquarela Do Brasil,* for Arista and *Celebration in Vienna* with opera singer Placido Domingo for Sony Classical. She subsequently became perhaps better known for her "infomercials" for the *Psychic Friends Network.*

Dionne Warwick on Scepter Records

Presenting Dionne Warwick	Scepter	508	'63	†
Anyone Who Had a Heart	Scepter	517	'64	†
Make Way for Dionne Warwick	Scepter	523	'64	†
The Sensitive Sound of Dionne Warwick	Scepter	528	'65	†
Here I Am	Scepter	531	'65	†
In Paris	Scepter	534	'66	†
Here, Where There Is Love	Scepter	555	'66	†
On Stage and at the Movies	Scepter	559	'67	†
The Windows of the World	Scepter	563	'67	†
Golden Hits, Volume 1	Scepter	565	'67	†
Magic of Believing	Scepter	567		†
Valley of the Dolls	Scepter	568	'68	†
Promises, Pomises	Scepter	571	'68	†
Soulful	Scepter	573	'69	†
Greatest Motion Picture Hits	Scepter	575	'69	†
Golden Hits, Volume 2	Scepter	577	'69	†
I'll Never Fall in Love Again	Scepter	581	'70	†
Very Dionne	Scepter	587	'70	†
The Dionne Warwick Story—A Decade of Gold	Scepter	(2)596	'71	†
From Within	Scepter	598	'72	†

Dee Dee Warwick

I Want to Be with You	Mercury	61100	'67	†
Dee Dee Warwick	Mercury	61221	'69	†
Turnin' Around	Atco	33-337	'70	†
She Didn't Know: The Atco Sessions (recorded 1970–1972)	Soul Classics	2111	'96	CS/CD

Later Dionne Warwick

Dionne	Warner Brothers	2585	'71	†
Just Being Myself	Warner Brothers	2658	'73	†
Then Came You	Warner Brothers	2846	'75	†
Track of the Cat	Warner Brothers	2893	'75	†
Love at First Sight	Warner Brothers	3119	'77	†
Dionne	Arista	4230	'79	†
	Arista	9512		†
No Night So Long	Arista	9526	'80	†
Hot! Live and Otherwise	Arista	(2)8605	'81	†
	Arista	(2)8111		CS/CD†
Friends to Love	Arista	9585	'82	†
Heartbreaker	Arista	9609	'82	†
How Many Times Can We Say Goodbye	Arista	8104	'83	†
Finder of Lost Loves	Arista	8262	'84	†
Dionne Warwick and Friends	Arista	8398	'85	CS/CD
Reservations for Two	Arista	8446	'87	CS/CD†
Greatest Hits 1979–1990	Arista	8540	'89	CS/CD
Sings Cole Porter	Arista	8573	'90	CS/CD
Friends Can Be Lovers	Arista	18682	'92	CS/CD
Aquarela Do Brasil	Arista	18777	'94	CS/CD
Dionne Sings Dionne	River North	161431	'98	CS/CD

Dionne Warwick and Isaac Hayes

A Man and a Woman	ABC	(2)996	'77	†
	MCA	(2)10012	'83	†

Dionne Warwick and Placido Domingo

Celebration in Vienna	Sony Classical	64304	'94	CS/CD

Various Dionne Warwick Anthologies and Compilations

Dionne Warwick	Pickwick	(2)2056	'73	†
Make It Easy on Yourself	Pickwick	3338		†
Golden Voice	Springboard Int'l	4001	'73	†
Sings Her Very Best	Springboard Int'l	4002	'73	†
One Hit After Another	Springboard Int'l	4003	'73	†
Greatest Hits, Volume 2	Springboard Int'l	4032	'75	†
Very Best	United Artists	337	'75	†
	United Artists	388	'75	†
Only Love Can Break a Heart	Musicor	2501	'77	†
Anthology 1962–1971	Rhino	(2)1100	'84	†
Anthology	Rhino	75898	'86	CD†
Collection	Rhino	71100	'89	CS/CD
Hidden Gems: The Best of Dionne Warwick, Volume 2	Rhino	70329	'92	CS/CD
The Dynamic Dionne Warwick (Greatest Hits)	Pair	(2)1043	'86	LP/CS†
Masterpieces	Pair	(2)1098	'86	LP/CS†
At Her Very Best	Pair	1243		CS/CD
From the Vaults (recorded 1963–1965)	Soul Classics	2104	'95	CS/CD
Her Classic Songs, Vol. 2: Say a Little Prayer	Curb	77894	'98	CS/CD
Her Greatest Hits	Special Music	4929		CS/CD
Her Greatest Hits, Volume 2	Special Music	4930		CS

JANN WENNER/ROLLING STONE MAGAZINE

Born January 7, 1946, in New York City.

With *Rolling Stone* magazine, editor and mastermind Jann Wenner created a viable alternative to trade magazines and fan magazines in the coverage of contemporary popular music in the late '60s. Quickly becoming a commercial success and earning a reputation as an authority within the music business, *Rolling Stone* employed some of the finest music writers in the business, including Lester Bangs, Greil Marcus, and Jon Landau. Attaining respectability with the "straight" press through award-winning articles on the Altamont debacle of The Rolling Stones and the Charles Manson family, the magazine later drew considerable mainstream attention for the writings of "Doctor" Hunter S. Thompson, the creator of the so-called "gonzo" style of journalism. At the height of its editorial power and influence by 1972, *Rolling Stone* later began emphasizing investigative reporting and coverage of aspects of popular culture to the detriment of rock music coverage. The magazine's enormous success served to encourage the proliferation of rock magazines such as *Circus, Creem,* and *Crawdaddy,* yet, by the mid-'70s, *Rolling Stone* was only nominally a music magazine. Wenner abandoned San Francisco for New York in 1977 and began broadening the magazine's popularity with writers such as Dave Marsh, Tom Wolfe, and Joe Eszterhas, and photographers Annie Leibovitz and Richard Avedon. *Rolling Stone* again started emphasizing music coverage in the mid-'80s, but, by the '90s, it had been clearly superseded as a cutting-edge music publication by *Spin* magazine.

Jann Wenner was raised in suburban Marin County, north of San Francisco, California. He attended the University of California at Berkeley during the Free Speech Movement, which he covered for the campus publication the *Daily Californian*. He met *San Francisco Chronicle* music critic Ralph Gleason in 1965 and dropped out of college in 1966 to work as

JANN WENNER (UPI/CORBIS-BETTMANN)

a freelance writer and arts editor for the local radical magazine *Sunday Ramparts.* In 1967, Wenner and Gleason formulated a plan to publish a professional, journalistic periodical that would serve as an alternative to music trade magazines, fan magazines, and "underground" journals in its coverage of contemporary popular music and the youth culture.

By borrowing $7,500 from friends and relatives, persuading a printer to provide credit and free office space, and employing a part-time volunteer staff, Jann Wenner published the first issue of *Rolling Stone* with a cover date of November 9, 1967. Although most of the issue's press run was returned, the publication was remarkably professional. However, Wenner's mercurial management style soon led to the departure of early staff members and the recruitment of Jon Landau. Eschewing psychedelic art and obtaining newsstand distribution, *Rolling Stone* was a financial success by 1969, and increased revenues allowed Wenner to expand and professionalize his staff. Supported by record company advertising since its eighth issue, *Rolling Stone* moved to a new, expensive location in 1970, opened offices in Los Angeles and New York, and unsuccessfully attempted to launch a British edition in conjunction with Mick Jagger.

As *Rolling Stone* expanded rapidly, Jann Wenner spent money extravagantly and failed at establishing two new magazines, *New York Scenes* and the environmentally minded *Earth Times.* On the verge of financial collapse, the magazine was ostensibly bailed out by major record companies. A 1970 cover article on American politics, published in Wenner's absence, led to the dismissal of many staff members, including managing editor John Burks (who was largely responsible for the magazine's success) and the end of political coverage. Nonetheless, award-winning articles on Altamont and the Charles Manson family brought *Rolling Stone* respectability with the "straight" press, and the publication's heretofore chaotic front-office operation was stabilized under self-made millionaire–investor Max Palevsky.

With *Rolling Stone* at perhaps the height of its fame in 1970, Jann Wenner employed writer Hunter S. Thompson, a cult figure largely on the basis of his book, *The Hell's Angels.* Practicing a writing style that became known as "gonzo" journalism, a careful and precise yet rambling stream-of-consciousness style complete with accounts of fortifying drug use, Thompson soon made an impact with the critically acclaimed two-part article, "Fear and Loathing in Las Vegas." He subsequently produced perhaps the most discerning coverage of the 1972 presidential campaign, which encouraged Wenner to expand the magazine's political coverage, hire first-rate reporters such as Joe Klein and Richard Goodwin, and expand the provinces of cultural critic Jonathon Cott and investigative reporter Joe Eszterhas. In 1975, *Rolling Stone* eliminated nudity and four-letter words and actively sought mainstream advertisers of cigarettes, liquor, and automobiles.

The decline of Hunter Thompson's writing and the death of Ralph Gleason in June 1975 marked a difficult period for *Rolling Stone.* Celebrities such as Truman Capote, Andy Warhol, and John Dean were hired to write articles. Jon Landau departed and the quality of the magazine's music coverage began to suffer, as the magazine presented long, in-depth articles concerned with established artists. Although *Rolling Stone* gained notoriety for its investigative reporting, as evidenced by articles on Karen Silkwood and Patty Hearst, the magazine was "scooped" by the "straight" press on reports of music industry "drugola" and endured a declining reputation for its music coverage.

In September 1976, Jann Wenner announced that he was moving *Rolling Stone* to New York City, where he sought to shake the magazine's counterculture image and establish a new legitimacy as a general-interest magazine with cover stories on personalities such as Jane Fonda, Johnny Carson, and Robert Redford. In 1977, Wenner bought *Outside* magazine, selling it in 1979 during a difficult financial period. In 1981, he expanded *Rolling Stone*'s coverage of motion pictures and signed a film deal with Paramount Pictures that produced the facile and self-aggrandizing *Perfect* film in 1985. In late 1981, Wenner launched the magazine *Record* to cover exclusively contemporary rock music, but the venture ended in 1986.

Rolling Stone adopted a slick-paper format in 1983 and the magazine began again emphasizing music coverage in 1984. In 1985, Wenner and his wife bought up outstanding shares of Straight Arrow Press, the parent company of *Rolling Stone,* thus securing total control of the magazine. That year, Wenner also bought fifty percent interest in *Us* magazine and launched an offensive two-year advertising campaign to divorce *Rolling Stone* from its hippie origins. By the '90s, *Rolling Stone* had been superseded by *Spin* magazine as the most daring and adventurous periodical covering contemporary popular music. In 1992, Jann Wenner launched the outdoor magazine *Men's Journal,* inaugurating the family magazine *Family Life* in 1993.

JANN WENNER/ROLLING STONE BIBLIOGRAPHY

Anson, Robert Sam. *Gone Crazy and Back Again: The Rise and Fall of The* Rolling Stone *Generation.* Garden City, NY: Doubleday, 1981.

Draper, Robert. Rolling Stone *Magazine: The Uncensored History.* New York: Doubleday, 1990.

THE WHO

Pete Townshend (born May 19, 1945, in Chiswick, London, England), lead and rhythm guitar, vocals; Roger Daltrey (born March 1, 1944, in Hammersmith, London), lead vocals; John Entwhistle (born October 9, 1944, in Chiswick), bass, French horn, vocals; and Keith Moon (born August 23, 1947, in Wembley, London; died September 7, 1978, in London), drums. Keith Moon was replaced by Kenny Jones (born September 16, 1948, in Stepney, East London).

Extremely popular in their native England by 1966 as perhaps the finest British rhythm-and-blues band of its time, The Who, like The Beatles and perhaps The Rolling Stones, comprised distinct and immediately recognizable personalities. Along with The Kinks' Ray

Davies, Pete Townshend was one of the era's greatest songwriters as well as one of rock music's all-time great guitarists and showmen, providing the group's powerful guitar riffs and performing feats such as rapid windmill guitar strokes, acrobatic leaps, and knee drops on stage. Keith Moon, one of rock music's most flamboyant and maniacally colorful figures, played drums with incredible energy and melodic style, influencing an entire generation of rock drummers. Roger Daltrey, one of rock music's most distinctive voices, melodic even at high volume, added his own touches by madly twirling his microphone and vigorously prancing on stage. John Entwhistle played his bass with a rapid virtuoso technique as perhaps rock music's most influential bassist, performing unmoved and stock-still as the group's apparent center of gravity. Regarded as rock music's first auto-destructive group, The Who's Townshend and Moon regularly demolished their equipment in performance, retaining the expensive practice until 1969. Moreover, Pete Townshend was one of the first guitarists to popularize the creative use of feedback, and, coupled with Moon's furious drumming, led to The Who's identification as one of the earliest heavy-metal bands. Additionally, on the basis of songs such as "My Generation" (regarded as one of the greatest rock singles of the '60s), The Who influenced a generation of punk bands that developed in the latter half of the '70s.

Along with The Small Faces, The Who became musical representatives of the "Mod" movement with their flashy pop-art stage apparel. They eventually broke through in the United States with their celebrated appearance at the Monterey International Pop Festival in June 1967. Their *Sell Out* album was one of the first "concept" albums and the album's hit, "I Can See for Miles," was an early example of psychedelic music. Nonetheless, The Who's greatest claim to fame came with 1969's *Tommy* album. Although arguably not the first "rock opera," it was the first successful one and brought fortune, international fame, and artistic respectability to The Who. Along with The Beatles' *Sgt. Pepper's Lonely Hearts Club Band,* it was one of the landmark albums of the '60s and drew the favorable attention of "serious" drama, opera, and classical music critics. Its success finally led to the recognition of rock music as something other than trivial, cacaphonous, and youth-oriented music, and to the legitimization of rock as a valid art form.

Although *Tommy* overshadowed the rest of the career of The Who, their *Live at Leeds* album was one of the finest live albums made in the history of rock and their *Who's Next* album demonstrated and popularized the creative use of synthesizers. Seriously challenging The Rolling Stones' claim of being "the world's greatest rock 'n' roll band," The Who was one of rock music's longest-lived bands until Keith Moon's death in September 1978. Persevering until 1982 and reuniting in 1989, The Who was inducted into the Rock and Roll Hall of Fame in 1990. In 1991, Townshend helped transform *Tommy* into a stage musical and the show proved enormously successful, reinvigorating a staid New York stage musical scene and introducing the medium to a new audience.

In 1959, Pete Townshend and classically trained John Entwhistle formed The Confederates while still in grammar school. Three years later, Roger Daltrey invited Entwhistle to join his band, The Detours, soon adding Townshend and drummer Doug Sanden. Daltrey functioned as the leader, lead guitarist, and lead singer with the group but eventually assumed the sole role of lead vocalist. Under manager Peter Meaden, the group adopted a colorful "mod" image, became The High Numbers, and issued their first single, "I'm the Face," in mid-1964. By October 1964, they had replaced Sanden with Keith Moon from the surf band The Beachcombers. The group became The Who under new managers Kit Lambert and Chris Stamp, who encouraged Townshend to develop his songwriting. The two urged the group to display open aggression on stage and cultivated the group's mod image with flashy clothes, including Townshend's renowned Union Jack jacket. In 1965, during a performance at the Railway Tavern, Pete Townshend inadvertently broke the neck of his guitar on a low ceiling. Townshend and Keith Moon subsequently destroyed their equipment, an expensive practice the group reenacted at virtually every performance for the next four years.

Enjoying a highly successful residency at London's Marquee club, the Who signed to American Decca (Brunswick and later Reaction and Track in Great Britain) on the recommendation of American producer Shel Talmy. They scored four consecutive smash hits in Britain through the spring of 1966 with Talmy as producer: "I Can't Explain," the archetypal heavy metal "Anyway, Anyhow, Anywhere," the instant classic "My Generation," and "Substitute." "I Can't Explain" and "My Generation" became minor American hits. Their debut album contained "My Generation," "The Kids Are Alright," and the satiric "A Legal Matter," all by Townshend, plus the manic instrumental "The Ox," but it failed to sell in the United States. "I'm A Boy" and "Happy Jack" became smash British hits and their second album, *Happy Jack,* yielded their first major American hit with the title song, while including Entwhistle's "Boris the Spider" and "Whiskey Man," and Townshend's first attempt at an extended piece, "A Quick One While He's Away."

Launched in America with their frenetic performance at the Monterey International Pop Festival in June 1967 (later chronicled in the D. A. Pennebaker film) and subsequent late summer tour in support of Herman's Hermits, The Who issued one of the earliest concept albums, *The Who Sell Out,* a tribute to Britain's pirate radio stations, at year's end. Featuring a bizarre album cover and satiric radio station commercials between songs, the album contained the near-smash British and American hit "I Can See for Miles," "Armenia City in the Sky," and the gentle "Rael." The Who quickly became a major concert attraction in the United States and next released the anthology set *Magic Bus,* which included Townshend's "Call Me Lightning," "Magic Bus" (a major American hit), and "Pictures of Lily" (a smash British hit in 1967), and a remake of the surf song "Bucket T.," featuring Entwhistle's humorous French horn solo.

The Who's next album was the highly influential "rock opera" *Tommy.* Although not the first work of its kind, the album proved hugely successful, remaining on the album charts for more than two years and yielding a major hit with "Pinball Wizard." An odd and elaborate tale of lost innocence, redemption, and contrition, *Tommy* featured a number of instrumental interludes and Sonny Boy Williamson's "Eyesight to the Blind," as well as the psychedelic "Acid Queen," the inspiring "Sensation," the liberating "I'm Free," and Tommy's final rejection and plea for acceptance, "We're Not Gonna Take It"/"See Me, Feel Me." Performed in its entirety only twice—once in London and once in New York—*Tommy* drew the attention and praise of "serious" drama, opera, and classical music critics as well as fans and rock critics.

Tommy was performed in excerpted form by The Who for nearly two years and inspired both an all-star London stage production and an excessive and frankly unfortunate film by Ken Russell. The stage production, released on album in late 1972, featured the London Symphony Orchestra and Chamber Choir and performances by Rod Stewart, Merry Clayton, Steve Winwood, Sandy Denny, Richie Havens, Ringo Starr, and The Who. Director, screenwriter, and coproducer Ken Russell's 1975 film version, an extravagant and bizarre production replete with repulsive, inane, and tedious scenes, featured Roger Daltrey as Tommy and performances by Eric Clapton, Tina Turner, Elton John, and the members of The Who. It also contained the decidedly shallow acting and poor musical performances of Ann-Margret, Oliver Reed, and Jack Nicholson.

Seriously challenging The Rolling Stones' claim to being "the world's greatest rock-and-roll band," particularly after their celebrated appearance at the Woodstock Music and Art Fair (and subsequent film) in August 1969, The Who next recorded *Live at Leeds,* one of the most exciting live albums ever issued. The album produced a major American hit with Eddie Cochran's "Summertime Blues" and contained Johnny Kidd's "Shakin' All Over" and extended versions of both "My Generation" and "Magic Bus." The 1995 CD reissue doubled the length of the original album.

Who's Next, their first studio album in two years, was another milestone in the history of rock, showcasing Townshend's outstanding and innovative use of synthesizers. The album included several finely crafted and brilliantly performed extended pieces such as "Baba O'Riley," "Song Is Over," and the disillusioned "Won't Get Fooled Again" (a near-smash British and major American hit), as well as the menacing "Behind Blue Eyes" (a moderate American hit) and Entwhistle's "My Wife." The Who soon issued the anthology set *Meaty, Beaty, Big and Bouncy,* which Townshend reviewed in *Rolling Stone.* The album successfully collected the singles of The Who through "Pinball Wizard" and "The Magic Bus," and included Townshend's overlooked "The Seeker." In the summer of 1972, The Who scored a near-smash British and major American hit with "Join Together."

The Who's next album of new material was the double-record set *Quadrophenia.* Although greeted by equivocal reviews, the album was perhaps even more ambitious and personal than *Tommy* and every bit its equal in musical and dramatic terms. Concerned with the early history of The Who and the Mod movement through its protagonist Jimmy, *Quadrophenia's* title referred to Jimmy's double schizophrenia, the four members of The Who as representatives of the four sides of his personality, and the four recurrent musical themes of the album. Oddly criticized for its lack of unity, the album was heavily orchestrated and lavishly produced. It included "I'm the One," "5:15," "Is It in My Head," and "Drowned," plus the minor hits "Love, Reign O'er Me" and "The Real Me." For the first time in two years, The Who toured in support of the album.

In the meantime, the members of The Who had pursued individual projects. Keith Moon appeared in Frank Zappa's film *200 Motels* (1971) and the David Essex films *That'll Be the Day* (1973) and *Stardust* (1974). John Entwhistle recorded three solo albums, including a brilliant debut, through 1973. Pete Townshend supported Eric Clapton's "comeback" at London's Rainbow Theatre in January 1973 and recorded his solo debut for fellow devotees of guru Meher Baba. *Who Came First* proved so popular that it was issued as a regular commercial release. With Townshend handling virtually every musical instrument and engineering chore, the album included "Pure and Easy," "Nothing Is Everything (Let's See Action)," and an adaptation of Meher Baba's Universal Prayer, "Parvardigar." Roger Daltrey's debut solo album proved the most successful of the group member's outside releases. Produced by David Courtney and former pop star Adam Faith, *Daltrey* featured the collaborative compositions of Courtney, Faith, and Leo Sayer. The album yielded a smash British and minor American hit with "Giving It All Away" and contained outstanding existential songs such as "The Way of the World," "You Are Yourself," and "Hard Life," plus "One Man Band."

During 1974, John Entwhistle assembled a remarkable collection of mostly unreleased Who material as *Odds and Sods.* An excellent summation of the career of The Who, the album included their first single release, "I'm the Face," a dynamic and superior version of "Pure and Easy," the menacing and moving "Naked Eye," and the neglected rock anthem, "Long Live Rock." John Entwhistle toured and recorded with the band Ox in 1975, as Keith Moon issued his first solo album and Daltrey his second. Daltrey's *Ride a Rock Horse* included "Oceans Away" and yielded a minor hit with Russ Ballard's "Come and Get Your Love."

The Who's next album, *The Who by Numbers,* was recorded during a relatively inactive period that lasted until 1977, but it was perhaps the group's weakest effort to date, producing a major hit with "Squeeze Box." The Who conducted a major American tour in 1975 and 1976 (including a joint performance with The Grateful Dead in October 1976), but Townshend, suffering permanent hearing loss and desirous of spending more time with his family, withdrew from the public eye. Daltrey appeared in Ken Russell's equivocal *Lisztoma-*

nia movie as composer Franz Liszt in 1975 and Moon moved to Los Angeles in 1976. Daltrey recorded his third solo album in 1977 and Townshend reemerged triumphantly with *Rough Mix,* recorded with Ronnie Lane of The Faces.

In 1978, The Who returned with their first album in nearly three years, *Who Are You.* It contained "Had Enough," "Sister Disco," and "Music Must Change" and produced a major hit with the title song, but, on September 7, 1978, Keith Moon was found dead in his London flat at the age of 31, the victim of a drug overdose. By the beginning of 1979, former Small Faces drummer Kenny Jones had replaced Moon. The group toured in the summer of 1979, augmented by keyboardist John "Rabbit" Bundrick, a former member of Free. During the year, The Who released two feature-length films and double-record soundtrack albums, the excellent documentary *The Kids Are Alright* and the fictional *Quadrophenia,* based on their 1973 album. *The Kids Are Alright* included the first offical release from the legendary 1968 television special *The Rolling Stones Rock and Roll Circus* and the soundtrack yielded a minor hit with "Long Live Rock." Perhaps due to American audiences unfamiliarity with the Mod movement, *Quadrophenia* failed at the box office. The soundtrack album featured remixes from the original album, three new songs, and an entire side of "oldies" such as James Brown's "Night Train" and The Ronettes' "Be My Baby."

The Who toured America again in late 1979, but, at a performance at Cincinnati's Riverfront Stadium on December 3, eleven people were killed in the crush of callous fans outside the stadium, an unfortunate legacy to the career of one of rock music's most talented and exciting acts. By 1980, The Who had switched to Warner Brothers for their American releases, and Townshend had recorded *Empty Glass,* with its near-smash hit "Let My Love Open the Door," as his debut for his new label, Atco. Roger Daltrey starred in the title role of the film *McVicar,* based on the life of bank robber John McVicar, widely known in Great Britain for his repeated escapes from prison. The soundtrack album, credited to Daltrey and Russ Ballard, featured all the members of The Who, producing a major hit with "Without Your Love." In 1981, The Who toured again and released *Face Dances,* which yielded a major hit with "You Better You Bet."

In 1982 and 1983, The Who conducted their "Farewell Tour" of stadiums with The Clash as their opening act, officially disbanding in December 1983. The tour produced the live set *Who's Last.* Atco issued Townshend's *All the Best Cowboys Have Chinese Eyes* and Townshend joined the prestigious publishing firm Faber and Faber as an editor in 1983. Townshend's *Scoop* compiled his demo recordings, as would *Another Scoop* in 1987. Roger Daltrey appeared in the BBC production of *The Beggar's Opera* as McHeath and later costarred in the BBC-Time-Life production of Shakespeare's *Comedy of Errors.* He switched to Atlantic for *Parting Should Be Painless,* followed in 1985 by *Under the Raging Moon.* During 1985, Pete Townshend published his first book, the collection of poetry and prose *Horse's Neck,* and recorded the ambitious *White City — A Novel* with Pink Floyd guitarist David Gilmour, among others. The album yielded a major hit with "Face the Face."

The Who reunited for the Live Aid concert in July 1985, but immediately went their separate ways. Townshend toured England with Deep End, which included David Gilmour, and the tour produced both a concert video and album released in 1986. John Entwistle toured on his own in 1988 and Townshend composed and recorded songs for the musical *The Iron Man,* based on a children's story by Ted Hughes. The album included The Who's "Dig" and "Fire" and John Lee Hooker's "Over the Top" and "I Eat Heavy Metal."

Townshend, Daltrey, and Entwistle reunited for a Who stadium tour in 1989 sponsored by Budweiser and Miller Lite beers. For the tour, the three were augmented by guitarist Steve Bolton, keyboardist John "Rabbit" Bundrick, drummer Simon Phillips, a five-piece horn section, and three backup vocalists. The tour included two full performances of *Tommy,* one in New York and one in Los Angeles. The Los Angeles show, the highlight of the tour, was offered as a pay-per-view cable televison show and featured guest performances by Steve Winwood, Elton John, Billy Idol, Phil Collins, and Patti Labelle. However, the tour was viewed cynically by critics. The Who were inducted into the Rock and Roll Hall of Fame in 1990.

In November 1991, Pete Townshend began working with Des McAnuff, the artistic director of the La Jolla (California) Playhouse to transform *Tommy* into a stage musical. The setting was changed, connecting dialogue was added, and Townshend composed one new song, "I Believe My Own Eyes." The show opened at the La Jolla Playhouse in July 1992, debuted on Broadway in April 1993, and won five Tony Awards. The show went on national tour in October.

In the meantime, Roger Daltrey starred in the 1990 film *Mack the Knife* with Raul Julia and recorded *Rocks in the Head*. In 1994, he conducted a "Daltrey Sings Townshend" tour with a thirty-two-piece orchestra. Pete Townshend composed and recorded the ambitious *PsychoDerelict* and toured the show with three actors and an eight-piece band in 1993. The August performance at the Brooklyn Academy of Music was later broadcast as part of PBS television's *Great Performances* series. In 1995, John Entwhistle toured as a member of Ringo Starr's All-Starr Band.

In June 1996, Pete Townshend, Roger Daltrey, and John Entwhistle reunited to perform *Quadrophenia* at the Prince's Trust benefit show in London's Hyde Park with Billy Idol, Gary Glitter, and drummer Zak Starkey (Ringo's son). They subsequently performed the show five times at New York's Madison Square Garden in July and toured North America with the show for five weeks in the fall. In 1998, Townshend's keyboardist daughter Emma recorded her debut album *Winterland*.

THE WHO BIBLIOGRAPHY

Barnes, Richard. *The Who: Maximum R&B*. London: Eel Pie, 1982; New York: St. Martin's Press, 1983; London: Plexus, 1996.

Benson, Joe. *Uncle Joe's Record Guide: Eric Clapton, Jimi Hendrix, The Who*. Glendale, CA: J. Benson Unlimited, 1987.

Butler, Dougal, with Chris Trengrove and Peter Lawrence. *Full Moon: The Amazing Rock & Roll Life of Keith Moon*. New York: William Morrow, 1981.

Clarke, Steve (compiler). *The Who in Their Own Words*. New York: Quick Fox, 1979.

Guiliano, Geoffrey. *Behind Blue Eyes: The Life of Pete Townshend*. New York: Dutton, 1996.

Herman, Gary. *The Who*. New York: Macmillan, 1972.

Marcus, Greil. "The *Rolling Stone* Interview: Pete Townshend." *Rolling Stone*, no. 320 (June 26, 1980), pp. 34–39.

Marsh, Dave. *Before I Get Old: The Story of The Who*. New York: St. Martin's Press, 1983.

Rolling Stone. *The Who*. San Francisco: Straight Arrow Books, 1975.

Stein, Jeff, and Chris Johnston. *The Who*. New York: Stein and Day, 1973.

Swenson, John. *The Who: Britain's Greatest Rock Group*. New York: Tempo, 1979.

Townshend, Pete. "Meaty, Beaty, Big and Bouncy." *Rolling Stone*, no. 97 (December 9, 1971), pp. 36–37.

———. "The Punk Meets the Godfather." *Rolling Stone*, no. 252 (November 17, 1977), pp. 54–59.

———. *Horse's Neck*. Boston: Houghton Mifflin, 1985.

Tremlett, George. *The Who*. New York: Warner Books, 1975.

Wolter, Stephen, and Karen Kimber. *The Who in Print: An Annotated Bibliography, 1965 Through 1990*. Jefferson, NC: McFarland and Co., 1992.

Early Albums by The Who

The Who Sings My Generation	Decca	74664	'66	†
	MCA	2044		†
	MCA	31330		CD
Happy Jack	Decca	74892	'67	†
	MCA	2045		†
reissued as A Quick One	MCA	31331		CD†
	MCA	11267	'95	CS/CD
The Who Sell Out	Decca	74950	'67	†
	MCA	2046		†
	MCA	31332		CD†
	MCA	11268	'95	CS/CD

Tommy

Tommy	Decca	(2)7205	'69	†
	MCA	(2)10005		†
	MCA	10801	'93	CS/CD
	MCA	11417	'96	CS/CD
	Mobile Fidelity	00533	'90	CD†
Tommy—1972 Studio Cast with London Symphony Orchestra and Chambre Choir	Ode	(2)99001	'72	†
	Rhino	71113	'89	CS/CD
Tommy—Studio Cast (excerpts)	Pickwick	3339		†
Tommy (highlights from studio cast)	Griffin	340		CD
Tommy (music from soundtrack)	Polydor	(2)9502	'75	†
	Polydor	(2)841121	'94	CD
The Who's Tommy (music from 1993 Broadway original cast musical)	RCA	(2)61874	'93	CS/CD
The Who's Tommy (excerpts from original cast musical)	RCA	62522	'94	CS/CD

The Who

Live at Leeds	Decca	79175	'70	†
	MCA	2022		†
	MCA	3023		†
	MCA	37000		†
	MCA	11215	'95	CS/CD
	MCA	11230	'95	CD†
Who's Next	Decca	79182	'71	†
	MCA	2023		†
	MCA	3024		†
	MCA	1691		CS†
	MCA	37217		CD†
	MCA	11269	'95	CS/CD
	MCA	11312	'95	CD
	Heavy Vinyl	11164	'95	LP
Quadrophenia	MCA	(2)10004	'73	†
	MCA	(2)6895		CS/CD
	MCA	(2)11463	'96	CS/CD
	Mobile Fidelity	(2)20550	'91	CD†

The Who by Numbers	MCA	2161	'75	†
	MCA	3026		†
	MCA	37002		†
	MCA	1579		CS
	MCA	31197		CD
	MCA	11493	'97	CD
Who Are You	MCA	3050	'78	†
	MCA	1580		CS
	MCA	37003		CD
	Mobile Fidelity	561	'92	CD†
The Kids Are Alright (soundtrack)	MCA	(2)11005	'79	†
	MCA	(2)6899		CS
	MCA	6899		CD
Face Dances	Warner Brothers	3516	'81	†
	MCA	25987	'89	CS/CD
It's Hard	Warner Brothers	23731	'82	†
	MCA	25986	'89	CS/CD
Who's Last	MCA	(2)8018	'84	CS/CD†
Join Together	MCA	(2)19501	'90	CS/CD†

Who Anthologies and Compilations

Magic Bus	Decca	75064	'68	†
	MCA	2047		†
	MCA	31333		CD†
Meaty, Beaty, Big and Bouncy	Decca	79184	'71	†
	MCA	2025		†
	MCA	3025		†
	MCA	1578		CS
	MCA	37001		CD†
Odds and Sods	MCA	2126	'74	†
	MCA	37169	'82	†
	MCA	1659		CS/CD
Hooligans	MCA	(2)12001	'81	CS/CD†
Greatest Hits	MCA	5408	'83	†
	MCA	1496		CS/CD
Who's Missing (recorded 1965–1972)	MCA	25982	'86	CS
	MCA	31221	'86	CD†
Two's Missing (recorded 1964–1973)	MCA	5712	'87	CS†
	MCA	31222	'87	CD†
Who's Better Who's Best	MCA	(2)8031	'88	CS
	MCA	8031	'88	CD†
30 Years of Maximum R&B: The Gift Set	MCA	(4)11150	'94	CD
My Generation—The Very Best of The Who	MCA	11462	'96	CS/CD

Who Reissues

A Quick One/The Who Sell Out	MCA	(2)4067	'74	CS†
Magic Bus/The Who Sings My Generation	MCA	(2)4068	'74	CS†
Who Are You/Live at Leeds	MCA	(2)6913	'78	CS†
Meaty, Beaty, Big and Bouncy/The Who by Numbers	MCA	(2)6914	'75	CS†
Who's Next/Odds and Sods	MCA	(2)6939	'74	CD†

The Who and Various Artists

Quadrophenia (music from soundtrack)	Polydor	(2)6235	'79	†
	Polydor	519999	'94	CD

London Philharmonic Orchestra

Who'serious: Symphonic Music of The Who	RCA	6311	'98	CS/CD

John Entwhistle

Smash Your Head Against the Wall	Decca	79183	'71	†
	MCA	2024		†
	Sundazed	6116		CD
Whistle Rhymes	Decca	79190	'72	†
	MCA	2027		†
	Sundazed	6117		CD
Rigor Mortis Sets In	MCA	321	'73	†
Mad Dog (with Ox)	MCA	2129	'75	†
Too Late the Hero	Atco	38-142	'81	†
The Rock	Griffin	615	'96	CD
John Entwhistle (recorded 1974)	King Biscuit Flower Hour	8030	'97	CD

Roger Daltrey

Daltrey	MCA	328	'73	†
	MCA	2349		†
	MCA	37032		†
Ride a Rock Horse	MCA	2147	'75	†
	MCA	37030		†
One of the Boys	MCA	2271	'77	†
	MCA	37031		†
Best Bits	MCA	5301	'82	†
Parting Should Be Painless	Atlantic	80128	'84	†
Under a Raging Moon	Atlantic	81269	'85	CS†/CD
Rocks in the Head	Atlantic	82359	'92	CS†/CD

Roger Daltrey/Rick Wakeman

Lisztomania (soundtrack)	A&M	4546	'75	†
	Saga	9042	'92	CD

Roger Daltrey/Russ Ballard

McVicar (soundtrack)	Polydor	6284	'80	†

Pete Townshend

Who Came First	Decca	79189	'72	†
	MCA	2026		†
	Rykodisc	10246	'92	CS/CD
Empty Glass	Atco	32100	'80	CS/CD†
	Atlantic	82544	'94	CD
	Atlantic	82811	'95	CS/CD
All the Best Cowboys Have Chinese Eyes	Atco	38149	'82	CS/CD†
	Atlantic	82812	'95	CS/CD
Scoop	Atco	(2)90063	'83	†
	Atco	90063		CS†/CD
White City: A Novel	Atco	90473	'85	CS/CD
Another Scoop (recorded 1964–1984)	Atco	(2)90539	'86	CD

Pete Townshend's Deep End Live!	Atco	90553	'86	CD
The Iron Man (A Musical by Pete Townshend)	Atlantic	81996	'89	CD
PsychoDerelict	Atlantic	82494	'93	CS†/CD
PsychoDerelict (edited vesion)	Atlantic	82535	'93	CS†/CD
Coolwalkingsmoothtalking-straightsmokingfirestoking:				
The Best of Pete Townshend	Atlantic	82712	'96	CS/CD
Pete Townshend and Ronnie Lane				
Rough Mix	MCA	2295	'77	†
	Atco	90097	'83	CS/CD
Emma Townshend				
Winterland	EastWest America	62174	'98	CS/CD

STEVIE WONDER

Born Steveland Morris on May 13, 1950, in Saginaw, Michigan.

Achieving his first recognition as a child prodigy with the top hit instrumental "Fingertips" in 1963, Stevie Wonder languished for several years at Motown before establishing himself as a singles artist in the mid-'60s with "Uptight (Everything's Alright)." Through 1970, he scored a series of crossover smashes with pop-style songs such as "A Place in the Sun," "I Was Made to Love Her," "For Once in My Life," and "My Cherie Amour." A multitalented musician, Wonder's first self-produced album, *Signed, Sealed and Delivered,* initiated a series of albums that he performed, recorded, and produced entirely by himself. Wonder subsequently experimented with synthesizers and other electronic keyboard instruments and negotiated a new contract with Motown that granted him artistic control of his recordings, thus making him, along with Marvin Gaye, one of the few Motown artists to achieve such independence. Established as a serious composer with *Music of My Mind,* the first album recorded after signing his new contract, Stevie Wonder broke through to the mass white audience without abandoning his black fans with 1972's *Talking Book* album. The album yielded two top hit classics, "Superstition" and "You Are the Sunshine of My Life," and included a number of outstanding songs, making him, along with Marvin Gaye, one of the first black artists to become recognized as an album artist. With *Innervisions,* Wonder added songs of pointed social commentary (the classic "Higher Ground," among others) to his repertoire of pop-style songs and romantic ballads. *Fulfillingness' First Finale* completed a remarkable quartet of excellent albums and his next, *Songs in the Key of Life,* came to be regarded as his masterpiece. Although Stevie Wonder's productivity has been sporadic since the late '70s, he continued to score smash crossover hits well into the '80s, with "I

Just Called to Say I Love You" becoming the best-selling single of his career in 1984. Stevie Wonder was inducted into the Rock and Roll Hall of Fame in 1989.

Afflicted by blindness as a newborn, Steveland Morris moved with his family to Detroit in 1954. Playing harmonica by the age of five, he started piano lessons at six and took up drums at eight. Writing his first song by the age of ten, Wonder was spotted in 1961 by The Miracles' Ronnie White, who took him to Brian Holland. Holland arranged an audition with Motown Records' Berry Gordy, Jr., and Wonder was immediately signed to the Tamla label and assigned the name "Little" Stevie Wonder. Working primarily with songwriter-producer Henry Cosby until 1970, Wonder scored a surprising top pop and rhythm-and-blues hit in 1963 with the raucous harmonica instrumental, "Fingertips—Part 2," recorded live at Chicago's Regal Theater, complete with mistakes, musical puns, and a shouting stage manager. The following year he enrolled in the Michigan School for the Blind, studied classical piano, and managed moderate pop hits with the harmonica-based songs "Workout, Stevie, Workout" and "Harmonica Man." He also appeared in the 1964 films *Bikini Beach* and *Muscle Beach Party.*

Dropping the "Little" appellation in the summer of 1964, Stevie Wonder emerged in 1965 and 1966 with the energetic dance-style smash hit "Uptight (Everything's Alright)" (which he cowrote with Henry Cosby and Sylvia Moy), the major hit "Nothing's Too Good for My Baby," and a near-smash hit version of Bob Dylan's "Blowin' in the Wind" from *Uptight*. While recording a wide variety of material on his albums, Wonder quickly established himself as a popular crossover singles artist with romantic ballads and uptempo pop-style songs such as "A Place in the Sun," "Trav'lin' Man," the top rhythm-and-blues and pop smash "I Was Made to Love Her," and "I'm Wondering," the latter two cowritten with Cosby and Moy. Following an album of Christmas material and an instrumental album released under the name Rednow Eivets, Wonder's *For Once in My Life* yielded five hits, including the top R&B and smash pop hit "Shoo-Be-Doo-Be-Doo-Da-Day" and the crossover smash hit title song. *My Cherie Amour* produced two smash hits with the title song and "Yester-Me, Yester-You, Yesterday."

Stevie Wonder's first self-produced album, *Signed Sealed and Delivered,* contained four hits, including the top R&B and smash pop hit title song and the crossover smash "Heaven Help Us All." Unjustly criticized for the easy-listening nature of his songs (only "My Cherie Amour" proved a smash easy-listening hit), Wonder certainly did record pop-style material and his flexible vocal style was unlike any other Motown act. He began experimenting with various rhythmic and musical textures and different electric keyboard instruments, including the synthesizer, with *Where I'm Coming From*. The album included the crossover smash "If You Really Love Me" and the neglected ballad "Never Dreamed You'd Leave in Summer," both written by Wonder and then-wife Syreeta Wright.

In 1971, at the age of 21, Stevie Wonder negotiated a new contract with Motown that gave him artistic control over his recordings and provided for the unprecedented formation of his own music publishing company, Black Bull Music, and production company, Taurus Productions. For his first album under the new contract, *Music of My Mind,* he played every instrument, coauthored the songs with Syreeta Wright, and produced. The album sold remarkably well despite yielding only one hit, "Superwoman (Where Were You When I Needed You)." The album began to establish Wonder as an album artist, and, as a consequence of a well-received summer 1972 tour with The Rolling Stones, he attracted a huge following among the white rock audience while retaining his black fans.

Stevie Wonder's growing popularity and recognition was immeasurably bolstered by the exceptional *Talking Book* album, one of the finest albums of the '70s. In addition to producing two top pop hits with the mellow "You Are the Sunshine of My Life" (a smash R&B hit) and the seminal "Superstition" (a top R&B hit), the album contained three other excellent songs, "You've Got It Bad Girl," "Blame It on the Sun," and "I Believe (When I Fall in Love It

Will Be Forever)." For his next album, Wonder performed virtually all the instrumental chores and solely composed all the songs. The monumental *Innervisions* yielded two top rhythm-and-blues and smash pop hits with the socially conscious "Higher Ground" and "Living for the City," and the smash R&B and major pop hit "Don't Worry 'Bout a Thing." The album also included favorites such as "Too High," "Golden Lady," and "All in Love Is Fair."

Working with other artists, Stevie Wonder cowrote The Miracles' 1970 top pop and rhythm-and-blues hit "The Tears of a Clown," wrote and produced The Spinners' 1970 smash R&B and major pop hit "It's a Shame," and wrote Rufus's 1974 smash pop and R&B hit "Tell Me Something Good." He produced Syreeta Wright's first and second albums and Minnie Riperton's *Perfect Angel,* which included her top pop and smash R&B hit "Lovin' You." However, on August 6, 1973, he was involved in a serious auto accident near Durham, North Carolina, that left him in a coma for four days.

Stevie Wonder staged a remarkable recovery and recorded yet another outstanding album, *Fulfillingness' First Finale.* It debuted at the top of the album charts and produced the top pop and R&B hit "You Haven't Done Nothin'" (ostensibly an indictment of Richard Nixon) and the seminal crossover smash "Boogie on, Reggae Woman," while including the religious "Heaven Is 10 Million Years Away." Following a tour in the winter of 1974, Wonder essentially retired from the road to work on his epic, *Songs in the Key of Life.* Eventually issued in the fall of 1976 accompanied by a four-song EP, the album included two top crossover hits, "I Wish" and the tribute to Duke Ellington, "Sir Duke." The album also contained the moderate crossover hits "Another Star" and "As," as well as "Isn't She Lovely" and other captivating songs. Earlier, in April, Wonder had signed a contract renewal with Motown valued at $13 million, the largest such contract to date.

Film producer Michael Braun subsequently approached Stevie Wonder about composing a song for a documentary on plant life. Wonder ultimately composed and recorded an entire score, later returning to the studio to add more songs and lyrics and overdub the sounds of nature. Eventually issued as *Journey Through the Secret Life of Plants,* the album was criticized as esoteric, inaccessible, and tedious, yet it yielded a crossover smash with "Send One Your Love." Wonder toured in 1980 and recorded *Hotter Than July,* which produced a top rhythm-and-blues and smash pop hit with "Master Blaster (Jammin')," inspired by Bob Marley, and the smash R&B and major pop hit "I Ain't Gonna Stand for It." The album also contained his tribute to Martin Luther King, Jr., "Happy Birthday," the ballad "Lately," and uptempo songs such as "Let's Get Serious" and "Always."

Stevie Wonder has maintained a relatively low profile since the early '80s. In 1982, he scored a top rhythm-and-blues and smash pop hit with "That Girl" from his anthology set *Original Musiquarium,* which also provided hits with "Do I Do" and "Ribbon in the Sky." His duet with Paul McCartney on "Ebony and Ivory" also became a top R&B and smash pop hit in 1982. He participated in the campaign to establish Martin Luther King, Jr.'s birthday as a national holiday and hosted a 1986 television special marking its first celebration. He provided seven original songs to the soundtrack to the 1984 film *The Woman in Red,* including the maudlin top pop and rhythm-and-blues hit "I Just Called to Say I Love You" and the major crossover hit "Love Light in Flight." The soundtrack album also included the didactic "Don't Drive Drunk," but the song did not appear in the movie.

Touring in 1983 and 1986, Stevie Wonder issued his first album of new material in five years, *In Square Circle,* in 1985. The album yielded four hits, including the top pop and rhythm-and-blues hit "Part-Time Lover" and the crossover smash "Go Home." He participated in the recording of USA for Africa's "We Are the World" in 1985 and later recorded with Elton John and Gladys Knight as Dionne Warwick's "friends" on the top pop and rhythm-and-blues hit, "That's What Friends Are For." *Characters,* from 1987, produced two top R&B hits with "Skeletons" (a major pop hit) and "You Will Know," and the R&B smash duet with Michael Jackson, "Get It." Stevie Wonder was inducted into the Rock and Roll

Hall of Fame in 1989. He composed and recorded eleven songs for the soundtrack to Spike Lee's provocative film *Jungle Fever,* released in 1991. He eventually toured in support of 1995's *Conversation Piece,* recording the live *Natural Wonder* album with the Tokyo Philharmonic Orchestra.

STEVIE WONDER BIBLIOGRAPHY

Dragonwagon, Crescent. *Stevie Wonder.* New York: Flash Books, 1977.
Elsner, Constance. *Stevie Wonder.* New York: Popular Library, 1977.
Haskins, James. *The Stevie Wonder Scrapbook.* New York: Grosset and Dunlap, 1978.

Stevie Wonder

Tribute to Uncle Ray	Tamla	232	'63	†
The Jazz Soul of Little Stevie Wonder	Tamla	233	'63	†
	Motown	5219		CS/CD
The 12-Year-Old Genius	Tamla	240	'63	†
Workout, Stevie, Workout	Tamla	248	'63	†
With a Song in My Heart	Tamla	250	'64	†
	Motown	5150		CS/CD
Stevie at the Beach	Tamla	255	'64	†
Uptight—Everything's Alright	Tamla	268	'66	†
	Motown	5183		CS/CD†
Down to Earth	Tamla	272	'66	†
	Motown	5166	'89	CS/CD
I Was Made to Love Her	Tamla	279	'67	†
	Motown	5273	'89	CS/CD
Someday at Christmas	Tamla	281	'67	†
	Tamla	362	'78	†
	Motown	9081		CD†
	Motown	5255		CS/CD
Eivets Rednow	Gordy	932	'68	†
reissued as Alfie	MoJazz	0549	'95	CS/CD
For Once in My Life	Tamla	291	'69	†
	Motown	9032		CD†
	Motown	5234		CS/CD
My Cherie Amour	Tamla	296	'69	†
	Motown	9083		CD†
	Motown	5179		CS/CD
Live	Tamla	298	'70	†
Signed, Sealed and Delivered	Tamla	304	'70	†
	Motown	9029		CD†
	Motown	5176		CS/CD
Where I'm Coming From	Tamla	308	'71	†
	Motown	5247	'90	CS/CD
Music of My Mind	Tamla	314	'72	†
	Motown	9076	'87	CD†
	Motown	0314		CS/CD
Talking Book	Tamla	319	'72	†
	Motown	9051		CD†
	Motown	0319		CS/CD

Innervisions	Tamla	326	'73	†
	Motown	9052	'87	CD†
	Motown	0326		CS/CD
	Mobile Fidelity	00554	'91	CD
Fulfillingness' First Finale	Tamla	332	'74	†
	Motown	9077	'87	CD†
	Motown	0332		CS/CD
Songs in the Key of Life	Tamla	(2)340	'76	†
	Tamla	6115		CD†
	Motown	(2)0340		CS/CD
Journey Through the Secret Life of Plants	Tamla	(2)371	'79	†
	Tamla	(2)6127		CD†
	Motown	(2)6127		CS/CD
Hotter Than July	Tamla	373	'80	†
	Tamla	6205	'86	CD†
	Motown	9064	'87	CD†
	Motown	6205		CS/CD
The Woman in Red (music from soundtrack)	Motown	6108	'84	CS/CD
In Square Circle	Tamla	6134	'85	LP/CS/CD†
	Motown	6134		CS/CD
Characters	Motown	6248	'87	CS/CD
Jungle Fever (music from soundtrack)	Motown	6291	'91	CS/CD
Conversation Piece	Motown	0238	'95	CS/CD
Natural Wonder (live)	Motown	(2)0546	'95	CS/CD

Stevie Wonder Reissues

My Cherie Amour/Signed, Sealed and Delivered	Tamla	8106	'86	CD†
For Once in My Life/Uptight	Tamla	8125	'86	CD†
Down to Earth/I Was Made to Love Her	Tamla	8153		CD†

Stevie Wonder Anthologies and Compilations

Greatest Hits	Tamla	282	'68	†
	Motown	0282		CS/CD
Greatest Hits, Volume 2	Tamla	313	'71	†
	Motown	0313		CS/CD
Love Songs: 20 Classic Hits	Tamla	6144		CD†
	Motown	9050	'85	CD†
Looking Back	Motown	(3)804	'77	†
Original Musiquarium I (Greatest Hits)	Tamla	(2)6002	'82	†
	Motown	(2)6002		CS/CD
Motown Legends	Motown	5362		†
Motown Legends	Esx	8527	'95	CS/CD

THE YARDBIRDS

Keith Relf (born March 22, 1943, in Richmond, Surrey, England; died May 14, 1976, in West London), vocals, harmonica; Chris Dreja (born November 11 circa 1946, in Surbiton, Surrey), rhythm guitar; Paul Samwell-Smith (born May 8, 1943, in London), bass; Jim McCarty (born July 25, 1943, in Liverpool, Lancashire, England), drums; and Anthony "Top" Topham, lead guitar. Topham was replaced by Eric Clapton (born Eric Clapp on March 30, 1945, in Ripley, Surrey) in October 1963. Clapton was replaced by Jeff Beck (born June 24, 1944, in

Wallington, Surrey) in March 1965. Samwell-Smith was replaced by Jimmy Page (born January 9, 1944, in London) in June 1966.

JEFF BECK'S YARDBIRDS (HULTON-DEUTSCH COLLECTION/CORBIS)

The Yardbirds are best remembered as the British group that introduced three of rock music's most celebrated lead guitar players, Eric Clapton, Jeff Beck, and Jimmy Page. Nonetheless, The Yardbirds were one of England's most influential groups, comparable in importance (but not popularity) to The Beatles, The Rolling Stones, and The Who. Despite the fact that they were more proficient and innovative musicians than The Rolling Stones, The Yardbirds failed to become "superstars," perhaps because The Stones were better performers and lead vocalist Keith Relf lacked Mick Jagger's charisma. Certainly The Yardbirds' chaotic career of personnel and managerial hassles interfered with their success. With Clapton as a member, The Yardbirds were one of the finest British rhythm-and-blues bands, but they adopted a more innovative yet commercial pop style under Jeff Beck. Along with The Who's Pete Townshend, Beck was one of the first electric guitarists to use feedback effectively and creatively in his playing, thus presaging the development of heavy-metal music. After sessions guitarist Jimmy Page joined in June 1966, The Yardbirds briefly utilized the twin-lead guitar format. Although Page's arrival marked the beginning of the end for The Yardbirds, the group did record one prototypical heavy-metal hit with Beck and Page on lead guitars, "Happenings Ten Years Time Ago" (which was actually predated by The Who's "Anyway, Anyhow, Anywhere"). With Beck's departure in November 1966, The Yardbirds endured a dismal period under producer Mickie Most before evolving into Led Zeppelin, the first group specifically described as heavy metal, in October 1968. The Yardbirds were inducted into the Rock and Roll Hall of Fame in 1992.

Keith Relf, Chris Dreja, Paul Samwell-Smith, and Jim McCarty, formed the Metropolitan Blues Quartet in the spring of 1963, adding lead guitarist Tony "Top" Topham in June. They played engagements in Richmond area clubs and took over residency of the Crawdaddy Club from the Rolling Stones. Topham was replaced by Eric Clapton, a former member of The Roosters and Casey Jones and The Engineers, in October. Developing a devoted following with their dynamic "rave-ups" (extended instrumental passages) of blues material, The Yardbirds first recorded behind bluesman Sonny Boy Williamson and later moved to London's Marquee club, where they recorded their debut album, *Five Live Yardbirds,* for Britain's Columbia Records. Their debut American album for Epic Records, *For Your Love,* produced a smash hit with Graham Gouldman's title song, already a smash British hit. However, disillusioned by the seemingly commercial and pop direction the group was taking, Clapton had already left in March 1965 in favor of John Mayall's Bluesbreakers, to be replaced by Jeff Beck of the Tridents.

The Yardbirds enjoyed their most creative and successful period during the tenure of Jeff Beck. Their second American album, *Having a Rave Up with The Yardbirds,* contained one live side of blues material, such as Howlin' Wolf's "Smokestack Lightning" and Bo Diddley's "I'm a Man," recorded with Eric Clapton, and a studio side featuring Jeff Beck. The studio side comprised two Graham Gouldman songs, "Heart Full of Soul" and "Evil-Hearted You," the socially conscious "You're a Better Man Than I," the Gregorian chant-like "Still I'm Sad," Johnny Burnette and The Rock 'n' Roll Trio's "The Train Kept A-Rollin,'" recorded at the Sun Studios in Memphis, and "I'm a Man." "Heart Full of Soul" and "Evil Hearted You"/"Still I'm Sad" were smash British hits, while "Heart Full of Soul" and the studio version of "I'm a Man" proved major American hits.

Garnering an enhanced reputation for Beck's creative use of feedback and their experimentation with unusual musical scales and instrumentation, The Yardbirds next recorded the British-only *Roger the Engineer.* Many of the cuts were contained on the American album *Over Under Sideways Down,* which yielded the major American hits "Over Under Sideways Down" and "Shapes of Things" (smash British hits), and included the exotic-sounding "Hot-House of Omagarashid" and "Ever Since the World Began," as well as the favorites "Lost Woman" and "Jeff's Boogie."

In 1966, Chris Dreja recorded two unsuccessful solo singles and, that June, Paul Samwell-Smith departed The Yardbirds to become a producer, most notably for Cat Stevens. Sessions guitarist Jimmy Page was recruited to take up bass, but switched to lead guitar when Jeff Beck became ill in September. With Dreja moving to bass and Beck's return, Beck and Page played twin lead guitars until November, when Beck quit the group. This lineup recorded only two songs, "Happenings Ten Years Time Ago" (a moderate American hit) and "Stroll On," performed in the movie *Blow Up.* With Beck's departure, the remaining four continued to perform and record as The Yardbirds under producer Mickie Most. Achieving minor American hits with "Little Games," "Ha Ha Said the Clown," and Nilsson's "Ten Little Indians," the aggregation recorded one American album, *Little Games.*

In the summer of 1968, Keith Relf and Jim McCarty dropped out of The Yardbirds to form the short-lived duo Together, and Page and Dreja unsuccessfully attempted to recruit guitarist Terry Reid and drummer B. J. Wilson for The New Yardbirds. With Dreja's departure to become a photographer, Page enlisted three new members to meet the group's contractual obligations that fall and, in October, the group changed its name to Led Zeppelin. The Yardbirds were inducted into the Rock and Roll Hall of Fame in 1992.

Keith Relf and Jim McCarty subsequently formed the progressive group Renaissance with Relf's vocalist sister Jane in 1969, but after one album produced by Paul Samwell-Smith, Relf and McCarty left. Entirely reconstituted with vocalist Annie Haslam, Renaissance enjoyed considerable album success in the '70s. Relf later played with Medicine Head, featuring vocalist John Fiddler, and eventually formed Armageddon around 1975. The group recorded one album for A&M Records, but, on May 14, 1976, Relf was found dead in his West London home at the age of 33, apparently electrocuted while playing guitar. McCarty formed Shoot in 1970 and later joined Illusion with Jane Relf. Chris Dreja, Paul Samwell-Smith, and McCarty reunited for live engagements in 1983 and later formed Box of Frogs with former Medicine Head vocalist John Fiddler for two albums for Epic. In 1989, McCarty formed the British Invasion All-Stars.

Original Yardbirds Albums

Five Live Yardbirds (recorded 1964)	Rhino	70189	'88	CS/CD
Live with Sonny Boy Williamson	Mercury	61071	'66	†
reissued as Clapton's Cradle: The Early Yardbirds Recordings	Evidence	26072	'95	CD
For Your Love	Epic	26167	'65	†

Having a Rave Up	Epic	26177	'65	†
Roger the Engineer	Warner Archives	45734	'97	CD
Over Under Sideways Down	Epic	26210	'66	†
reissued as The Yardbirds	Epic	38455	'83	†
Little Games	Epic	26313	'67	†
	EMI	54102	'96	CD
Little Games Sessions and More	EMI	(2)98213	'92	CD
Live at The BBC (recorded 1965–1968)	Warner Archives	46694	'97	CD
Yardbirds Anthologies and Compilations				
Greatest Hits	Epic	26246	'67	†
The Yardbirds Featuring Performances by Beck, Clapton and Page	Epic	(2)30135	'70	†
The Yardbirds with Jimmy Page—Live!	Epic	30615	'71	†
Favorites	Epic	34490	'77	†
Great Hits	Epic	34491	'77	†
Eric Clapton and The Yardbirds	Springboard Int'l	4036	'75	†
Jeff Beck and The Yardbirds	Springboard Int'l	4039	'75	†
For Your Love	Accord	7143	'81	†
Afternoon Tea	Rhino	253	'82	†
Greatest Hits, Volume 1	Rhino	70128	'86	CS
	Rhino	75895	'87	CD
Best of The Yardbirds	Rhino	71025	'94	CS/CD
Compleat Collection	Compleat	(2)2002	'84	†
The Best of British Rock	Pair	1151	'87	CD
Volume 1: Smokestack Lightning	Sony	(2)48655	'91	CD
Volume 2: Blues, Backtrack's and Shapes of Things	Sony	(2)48658	'91	CD
The Yardbirds with Eric Clapton	ROIR	4010	'96	CD
Eric Clapton and The Yardbirds—Rarities	LaserLight	12990	'98	CD
Where the Action Is!	Caroline	0132	'97	CD
The Best of British Rock	Special Music	4902		CS
The Yardbirds Featuring Eric Clapton and Jeff Beck	Special Music	4928		CD
The Yardbirds Featuring Eric Clapton—For Your Love	Griffin	1145		CD
Eric Clapton, Jeff Beck and Jimmy Page				
Guitar Boogie	RCA	4624	'72	†
	RCA	3768		†
Blue Eyed Blues	Griffin	20		CD
Clapton, Page, Beck	Dressed to Kill	(3)249	'98	CD
Renaissance (with Keith Relf)				
Renaissance	Elektra	74068	'70	†
Armageddon (with Keith Relf)				
Armageddon	A&M	4513	'75	†
Shoot (with Jim McCarty)				
On the Frontier	EMI	11229	'73	†
Illusion (with Jim McCarty)				
Out of the Mist	Island	9489	'77	†
Illusion	Island	9519	'78	†
Box of Frogs				
Box of Frogs	Epic	39327	'84	†
Strange Land	Epic	39923	'86	†
The Yardbirds Experience (with Jim McCarty)				
British Thunder	Griffin	580	'96	CD

THE YOUNGBLOODS

Jesse Colin Young (born Perry Miller on November 11, 1944, in New York City), vocals, guitar, bass; Jerry Corbitt (born in 1946 in Tifton, Georgia), guitar, bass, vocals; Lowell "Banana" Levinger (born in 1946 in Cambridge, Massachussetts), keyboards, guitar, banjo, mandolin, piano; and Joe Bauer (born September 26, 1941, in Memphis, Tennessee; died 1988), drums.

Favorably compared to The Lovin' Spoonful as purveyors of "good time" music in the late '60s, The Youngbloods helped popularize Dino Valenti's anthemic "Let's Get Together," a West Coast hit in 1967 and a smash national hit in 1969. Fronted by singer-songwriter-guitarist Jesse Colin Young, The Youngbloods recorded their finest album, *Elephant Mountain,* as a trio before disbanding in 1972. Jesse Colin Young established himself as a purveyor of mellow acoustic songs for RCA Records, particularly with *Song for Juli* and *Light Shine.*

Jesse Colin Young dropped out of college and assumed his stage name in 1963 to play East Coast folk clubs. He recorded one album for Capitol before switching to Mercury, where he recorded *Jesse Colin Young and The Youngbloods* with Peter Childs and John Sebastian. During 1965, he formed a duet with Jerry Corbitt, adding Lowell "Banana" Levinger and Joe Bauer by year's end. As the Youngbloods, the group performed as the house band at New York's Cafe Au-Go-Go and signed with RCA Records, achieving their first minor hit with the silly dance ditty "Grizzly Bear" by Corbitt. Their RCA debut album included "Get Together" by Chester Powers (aka Dino Valenti), a minor hit in 1967 and a smash hit upon rerelease in 1969. *Earth Music,* recorded in New York City, contained Young's "All My Dreams Blue" and "The Wine Song," the ditty "Euphoria," and an excellent version of Tim Hardin's "Reason to Believe."

In late 1967, Corbitt left The Youngbloods for a solo career, and the others continued as a trio, moving to the San Francisco Bay area. *Elephant Mountain,* recorded in Hollywood with Charlie Daniels as principal producer, came to be regarded as their finest album. It included "Rain Song," several gentle Young songs such as "Sunlight," "Beautiful," and "Ride the Wind," and two rather ominous Young songs, "Darkness, Darkness" and "Quicksand." In 1970, The Youngbloods signed with Warner Brothers Records and formed their own label, Raccoon. However, none of the albums for the label by the Youngbloods, Bauer, Young, and two spinoff groups featuring Bauer and Banana sold particularly well and, by 1972, the group had broken up.

Jesse Colin Young's first solo album for Warner Brothers, *Song for Juli,* contained idyllic songs such as "Morning Sun," "High on a Ridgetop," and "Country Home," as well as the title song, written for his daughter. The album became the best-selling album of his solo career, although he continued to record for Warner Brothers through 1977. He switched to Elektra for *American Dreams* and eventually recorded *The Highway Is for Heroes* for Cypress Records. In the '90s, he reemerged with *Swept Away* on his own Ridgetop label.

Jesse Colin Young

The Soul of a City Boy	Capitol	2070	'64	†
	Capitol	11267	'74	†
	Capitol	16129		†
	One Way	17526	'95	CD
Jesse Colin Young and The Youngbloods	Mercury	61005	'65	†
Two Trips with Jesse Colin Young	Mercury	61273	'70	†
Together	Raccoon	2588	'72	†
Song for Juli	Warner Brothers	2734	'73	†
Light Shine	Warner Brothers	2790	'74	†
Songbird	Warner Brothers	2845	'75	†

On the Road	Warner Brothers	2913	'76	†
Love on the Wing	Warner Brothers	3033	'77	†
American Dreams	Elektra	157	'78	†
The Highway Is for Heroes	Cypress	0103	'87	LP/CS/CD†
Best: The Solo Years	Rhino	70767	'91	CS/CD
Swept Away	Ridgetop	1035	'94	CS/CD

The Youngbloods

The Youngbloods	RCA	3724	'67	†
Earth Music	RCA	3865	'67	†
Elephant Mountain	RCA	4150	'69	†
	Mobile Fidelity	00792	'89	CD†
Best	RCA	4399	'70	†
	RCA	3680	'80	CS/CD
Ride the Wind	RCA	4465		†
	Raccoon	2563	'71	†
Sunlight	RCA	4561	'71	†
This Is The Youngbloods	RCA	(2)6051	'72	†
Rock Festival	Raccoon	1878	'70	†
Good and Dusty	Raccoon	2566	'71	†
High on a Ridgetop	Raccoon	2653	'72	†

Jerry Corbitt

Corbitt	Polydor	244003	'69	†
Jerry Corbitt	Capitol	771	'71	†

Joe Bauer

Moonset	Raccoon	1901	'71	†

Noggins

Crab Tunes	Raccoon	1944		†

Banana and The Bunch

Mid-Mountain Ranch	Raccoon	2626	'72	†

BIBLIOGRAPHY

ALMANACS

Bego, Mark. *The Rock & Roll Almanac*. New York: Macmillan, 1996.

Best, Kenneth. *Eight Days a Week: An Illustrated Record of Rock 'n' Roll*. San Francisco: Pomegranate Artbooks, 1992.

Formento, Dan. *Rock Chronicle: A 365 Day-by-Day Journal of Significant Events in Rock History*. New York: Delilah Communications, 1982.

Laufenberg, Frank. (Hugh Gregory, editor). *Rock and Pop Day by Day: Birthdays, Deaths, Hits and Facts*. London: Blandford, 1992.

Marchbank, Pearce, and Miles. *The Illustrated Rock Almanac*. New York: Paddington Press, 1977.

Tobler, John. *This Day in Rock: Day by Day Record of Rock's Biggest News Stories*. New York: Carroll and Graf Publishers, 1993.

DISCOGRAPHIES, RECORD CHARTS, AND RECORD GUIDES

Albert, George, and Frank Hoffman (compilers). *The Cash Box Country Singles Charts, 1958–1982*. Metuchen, NJ: Scarecrow Press, 1984.

————. *The Cash Box Black Contemporary Singles Charts, 1960–1984*. Metuchen, NJ: Scarecrow Press, 1986.

————. *The Cash Box Album Charts, 1955–1974*. Metuchen, NJ: Scarecrow Press, 1988.

————. *The Cashbox Country Album Charts, 1964–1988*. Metuchen, NJ: Scarecrow Press, 1989.

Benson, Joe. *Uncle Joe's Record Guide: Hard Rock, The First Two Generations*. Glendale, CA: J. Benson Unlimited, 1987.

————. *Uncle Joe's Record Guide: Eric Clapton, Jimi Hendrix, The Who*. Glendale, CA: J. Benson Unlimited, 1987.

Berry, Peter E. *. . . And the Hits Just Keep on Comin.'* Syracuse, NY: Syracuse University Press, 1977.

Bridgerman, Chuck. *Record Collector's Fact Book: Handbook of Rock & Roll, Rhythm & Blues, and Rockabilly Originals and Reproductions, Vol. 1 45 RPM 1952–1965*. Westminster, MD: Dis Publishing; Cockeysville, MD: distributed by Liberty Publishing Company, 1982.

Bronson, Fred. *The Billboard Book of Number One Hits*. New York: Billboard Publications, 1988.

————, and Adam White. *The Billboard Book of Number One Rhythm and Blues Hits*. New York: Billboard Books, 1993.

Brooks, Elston. *I've Heard These Songs Before: The Weekly Top Ten Tunes for the Past Fifty Years*. New York: Morrow Quill Paperbacks, 1981.

Clayson, Alan. *The Best of Rock: The Essential CD Guide*. San Francisco: Collins San Francisco, 1993.

Cowley, John, and Paul Oliver (editors). *The New Blackwell Guide to Recorded Blues*. Oxford, England; Cambridge, MA: Blackwell, 1995.

DeCurtis, Anthony, and James Henke. *The Rolling Stone Album Guide*. New York: Random House, 1992.

Docks, L. R. *1915–1965 American Premium Record Guide*. Florence, AL: Books Americana, 1980, 1982.

Duxbury, Janell R. *Rockin' the Classics and Classicizin' the Rock: A Selectively Annotated Discography*. Westport, CT: Greenwood Press, 1985.

Eddy, Chuck. *Stairway to Hell: The 500 Best Heavy Metal Albums in the Universe*. New York: Harmony Books, 1991.

Edwards, John W. *Rock 'n' Roll Through 1969: Discographies of All Performers Who Hit the Charts, Beginning in 1955*. Jefferson, NC: McFarland, 1992.

Edwards, Joseph. *Top 10's and Trivia of Rock & Roll and Rhythm & Blues, 1950–1973*. St. Louis: Blueberry Hill Publishing Company, 1974.

Elliott, Paul, and John Hotten. *The Best of Metal: The Essential CD Guide*. San Francisco: Collins San Francisco, 1993.

Emerson, Lucy. *The Gold Record*. New York: Fountain, 1978.

Erlewine, Michael, Chris Woodstra, Vladimir Bogdanov, and Cub Koda. *All Music Guide to the Blues: The Experts' Guide to the Best Blues Recordings*. San Francisco: Miller Freeman Books, 1996.

Erlewine, Michael, Vladimir Bogdanov, Chris Woodstra, and Stephen Thomas Erlewine (editors). *All Music Guide: The Experts' Guide to the Best CDs, Albums & Tapes*. San Francisco: Miller Freeman Books, 1992, 1994, 1997.

———. *All Music Guide to Country: The Experts' Guide to the Best Recordings in Country Music*. San Francisco: Miller Freeman Books, 1997.

Erlewine, Michael, Vladimir Bogdanov, and Chris Woodstra. *All Music Guide to Rock: The Best CDs, Albums and Tapes: Rock, Pop, Soul, Rhythm and Blues and Rap*. San Francisco: Miller Freeman Books, 1995.

Gambaccini, Paul (compiler). *Rock Critics Choice: The Top 200 Albums*. New York: Quick Fox, 1978.

———. *The Top 100 Rock 'n' Roll Albums of All Time*. New York: Harmony Books, 1987.

George, Nelson. *Top of the Charts: The Most Complete Listings Ever*. Piscataway, NJ: New Century Publishers, 1983.

Gillett, Charlie, and Stephen Nugent (editors). *Rock Almanac: Top Twenty Singles, 1955–73, and Top Twenty Albums, 1964–73*. New York: Doubleday, 1976.

———. *Rock Almanac: Top Twenty American and British Singles and Albums of the 50's, 60's and 70's*. Garden City, NY: Anchor Press, 1978.

——— and Simon Frith (editors). *The Beat Goes On: The Rock File Reader*. London; East Haven, CT: Pluto Press, 1996.

Goldstein, Stewart, and Alan Jacobson. *Oldies but Goodies: The Rock 'n' Roll Years*. New York: Mason/Charter, 1977.

Gonzalez, Fernando L. *Disco-File: The Discographical Catalog of American Rock and Roll and Rhythm and Blues Vocal Harmony Groups*. Flushing, NY: Gonzalez, 1977.

Guterman, Jimmy, and Owen O'Donnell. *The Worst Rock and Roll Records of All Time: A Fan's Guide to the Stuff You Love to Hate*. Secaucus, NJ: Carol Publishing Group, 1991.

Hadley, Frank-John. *The Grove Press Guide to the Blues on CD*. New York: Grove Press, 1993.

Hall, Doug. *Country on CD: The Essential Guide*. London: Kyle Cathie Limited, 1993.

Heggeness, Fred. *Goldmine Country & Western Record & CD Price Guide*. Iola, WI: Krause Publications, 1996.

Helander, Brock. *The Rock Who's Who: A Biographical Dictionary and Critical Discography Including Rhythm-and-Blues, Soul, Rockabilly, Folk, Country, Easy Listening, Punk, and New Wave*. New York: Schirmer Books, 1982.

———. *The Rock Who's Who* (second edition). New York: Schirmer Books, 1996.

Hill, Randall C. *The Official Price Guide to Collectible Rock Records*. Orlando, FL: House of Collectibles, 1980.

Hounsome, Terry. *New Rock Record*. New York: Facts on File, 1983.

————. *Rock Record: A Collectors' Directory of Rock Albums and Musicians*. New York: Facts on File, 1987.

————. *The Illustrated Book of Rock Records: A Book of Lists*. New York: Delilah Books, distributed by Putnam, 1982.

Hounsome, Terry, and Tim Chambre. *Rock Record*. New York: Facts on File, 1981.

Jasper, Tony. *The International Encyclopedia of Hard Rock and Heavy Metal*. New York: Facts on File, 1983.

———— (compiler). *The Top Twenty Book: The Official British Record Charts, 1955–1982*. Poole, Dorset: Blandford Press, 1983.

Leadbitter, Mike, and Neil Slaven. *Blues Records: 1943–1966*. New York: Oak Publications, 1968.

————. *Blues Records: 1943–1970*. London: Record Information Services, 1987.

Leibowitz, Alan. *The Record Collector's Handbook*. New York: Everest House, 1980.

Marsh, Dave. *The Heart of Rock & Soul: The 1001 Greatest Singles Ever Made*. New York: Plume, 1989.

Marsh, Dave, and John Swenson (editors). *The* Rolling Stone *Record Guide*. New York: Random House, 1979.

————. *The New* Rolling Stone *Record Guide*. New York: Random House/Rolling Stone Press, 1983.

McAleer, Dave. *The All Music Book of Hit Albums*. San Francisco: Miller Freeman Books; Emeryville, CA: distributed by Publishers Group West, 1994.

————. *The All Music Book of Hit Singles*. San Francisco: Miller Freeman Books; Emeryville, CA: distributed by Publishers Group West, 1994.

Miron, Charles. *Rock Gold: All the Hit Charts from 1955 to 1976*. New York: Drake Publishers, 1977.

Murray, Charles Shaar. *Blues on CD: The Essential Guide*. London: Kyle Cathie Limited, 1993.

Murrels, Joseph (compiler). *The Book of Golden Discs*. London: Barrie and Jenkins, 1974, 1978.

————. *Million Selling Records from the 1900s to the 1980s: An Illustrated Directory*. New York: Arco, 1985.

Music Master, *The 45 RPM Record Directory: 35 Years of Recorded Music 1947 to 1982*. Allison Park, PA: Record-Rama, 1983.

Naha, Ed (compiler). *Lillian Roxon's Rock Encyclopedia*. New York: Grosset and Dunlap, 1978.

Neely, Tim. *Goldmine Price Guide to Alternative Records*. Iola, WI: Krause Publications, 1996.

The Official Price Guide to Records. Orlando, FL: House of Collectibles, 1983.

Osborne, Jerry. *Record Album Price Guide*. Phoenix, AZ: O'Sullivan Woodside, 1977.

————. *Record Albums, 1948–1978*. Phoenix, AZ: O'Sullivan Woodside, 1978.

————. *Popular & Rock Records, 1948–1978*. Phoenix, AZ: distributed by O'Sullivan Woodside, 1978.

————. *Popular & Rock Price Guide for 45's: The Little Record With the Big Hole* (second edition). Phoenix, AZ: O'Sullivan Woodside, 1981.

————. *Rock, Rock & Roll 45's* (third edition). Phoenix, AZ: O'Sullivan Woodside, 1983.

————. *A Guide to Record Collecting*. Phoenix, AZ: O'Sullivan Woodside, 1979.

————. *Blues, Rhythm & Blues, Soul*. Phoenix, AZ: O'Sullivan Woodside, 1980.

Propes, Steve. *Golden Oldies: A Guide to 60's Record Collecting*. Radnor, PA: Chilton Book Company, 1974.

————. *Golden Goodies: A Guide to 50's and 60's Popular Rock and Roll Record Collecting*. Radnor, PA: Chilton Book Company, 1975.

Pruter, Robert (editor). *The Blackwell Guide to Soul Recordings*. Cambridge, MA: Blackwell Publishers, 1993.

Rees, Dafydd, and Luke Crampton. *Encyclopedia of Rock Stars.* New York: DK Publishing, 1996.

Rees, Tony. *Rare Rock: A Collector's Guide.* Poole, Dorset: Blandford Press; New York: distributed by Sterling Publishing, 1985.

Robbins, Ira A. (editor). *The Trouser Press Guide to New Wave Records.* New York: Charles Scribner's Sons, 1983, 1985; New York: Collier Books, 1989, 1991.

Rohde, H. Kandy. *The Gold of Rock and Roll: 1955–1967.* New York: Arbor House, 1970.

Rolling Stone. The Rolling Stone Record Review. San Francisco: Straight Arrow Books, 1971.

————. *The Rolling Stone Record Review,* Volume II. New York: Pocket Books, 1974.

————. *The Rolling Stone Album Guide.* New York: Random House, 1992.

Rosen, Craig. *The Billboard Book of Number One Albums: The Inside Story Behind Pop Music's Blockbuster Records.* New York: Billboard Books, 1996.

Roxon, Lillian. *Rock Encyclopedia.* New York: Grosset and Dunlap, 1969.

St. Pierre, Roger. *The Best of the Blues: The Essential CD Guide.* San Francisco: Collins San Francisco, 1993.

Scott, Frank. *The Down Home Guide to the Blues.* Pennington, NJ: A Cappella Books, 1991.

Scott, Frank, and Al Ennis. *The Roots & Rhythm Guide to Rock.* Pennington, NJ: A Cappella Books, 1993.

Shapiro, Bill. *The CD Rock & Roll Library: 30 Years of Rock & Roll on Compact Disc.* Kansas City: Andrews and McMeel, 1988.

Strong, M. C. *The Great Rock Discography.* Edinburgh: Canongate Press, 1995.

Tee, Ralph. *The Best of Soul: The Essential CD Guide.* San Francisco: Collins San Francisco, 1993.

Tudor, Dean. *Popular Music, An Annotated Guide to Recordings.* Littleton, CO: Libraries Unlimited, 1983.

Tudor, Dean, and Nancy Tudor. *Contemporary Popular Music.* Littleton, CO: Libraries Unlimited, 1979.

————. *Grass Roots Music.* Littleton, CO: Libraries Unlimited, 1979.

————. *Black Music.* Littleton, CO: Libraries Unlimited, 1979.

Umphred, Neal. *Goldmine's Price Guide to Collectible Record Albums 1949–1989.* Iola, WI: Krause Publications, 1991.

————. *Goldmine's Rock 'n' Roll 45 RPM Record Price Guide.* Iola, WI: Krause Publications, 1992, 1994.

Walters, Neal, and Brian Mansfield (editors). *MusicHound Folk: The Essential Album Guide.* Detroit: Visible Ink, 1998.

Weisbard, Eric, with Craig Marks. *Spin Alternative Record Guide.* New York: Vintage Books, 1995.

Whitburn, Joel. *The Billboard Book of Top 40 Hits, 1955 to Present.* New York: Billboard Publications, 1983.

————. *The Billboard Book of Top 40 Hits* (sixth edition). New York: Billboard Books, 1996.

————. *Billboard Top 1000 Singles, 1955–1987.* Milwaukee, WI: H. Leonard Books, 1988.

————. *Billboard Top 1000 Singles, 1955–1990.* Milwaukee, WI: H. Leonard Books, 1991.

————. *The Billboard Book of Top 40 Albums.* New York: Billboard Publications, 1987; New York: Billboard Books, 1995.

————. *Record Research Collection* (includes Top Pop Singles 1955–1993; Top Albums 1955–1992; Top R&B Singles 1942–1988; Top Country Singles 1944–1993; Top Adult Contemporary 1961–1993; Pop Memories 1890–1954; Pop Annual 1955–1994; plus yearly supplements entitled Music Yearbook). Menomenee Falls, WI: Record Research, 1988, 1989, 1990, 1991, 1992, 1993, 1994, 1995, 1996, 1997.

Williams, Paul. *Rock and Roll: The 100 Best Singles.* New York: Carroll and Graf Publishers, 1993.

ENCYCLOPEDIAS, DICTIONARIES, AND GENERAL REFERENCE

Aquila, Richard. *That Old Time Rock & Roll: A Chronicle of an Era 1954–1963.* New York: Schirmer Books, 1989.

Baggelar, Kristin, and Donald Milton. *Folk Music: More Than a Song.* New York: Crowell, 1976.

Bane, Michael. *Who's Who in Rock.* New York: Facts on File, 1981.

————. *White Boy Singin' the Blues.* New York: Penguin Books, 1982.

Bartis, Peter, Barbara Fertog, and Hillary Glatt. *Folklife Sourcebook: A Directory of Folklife Resources in the United States.* Washington, DC: Library of Congress, 1994.

Belz, Carl. *The Story of Rock.* New York: Oxford University Press, 1969, 1972; New York: Harper Colophon Books, 1973.

Benjaminson, Peter. *The Story of Motown.* New York: Grove Press, 1979.

Benson, Dennis C. *The Rock Generation.* Nashville: Abingdon, 1976.

Bernard, Shane K. *Swamp Pop: Cajun and Creole Rhythm and Blues.* Jackson: University Press of Mississippi, 1996.

Berry, Jason, Jonathan Foose, and Tad Jones. *Up from the Cradle of Jazz: New Orleans Music since World War II.* Athens: University of Georgia Press, 1986.

Betrock, Alan. *Girl Groups: The Story of a Sound.* New York: Delilah Books, distributed by Putnam, 1982.

Boeckman, Charles. *And the Beat Goes On: A Survey of Pop Music in America.* Washington, DC: Robert B. Luce, Inc., 1972.

Booth, Stanley. *Rhythm Oil: A Journey Through the Music of the American South.* New York: Pantheon Books, 1991.

Bowman, Robert M. J. *Soulsville, U.S.A.: The Story of Stax Records.* New York: Schirmer Books, 1997.

Broven, John. *Walking to New Orleans: Rhythm and Blues in New Orleans.* Gretna, LA: Pelican, 1988.

Brown, Len, and Gary Friederich. *Encyclopedia of Rock and Roll.* New York: Tower Publications, 1970.

Bufwack, Mary A., and Robert K. Oermann. *Finding Her Voice: The Saga of Women in Country Music.* New York: Crown Publishers, 1993.

Burt, Rob. *Surf City, Drag City.* Poole, Dorset; New York: Blandford, 1986.

Busnar, Gene. *It's Rock 'n' Roll.* New York: Wanderer Books, distributed by Simon and Schuster, 1979.

————. *The Superstars of Rock: Their Lives and Their Music.* New York: J. Messner, 1980.

Cackett, Alan. *The Harmony Illustrated Encyclopedia of Country Music.* New York: Crown Trade Paperbacks, 1991, 1994.

Cantwell, Robert. *When We Were Good: The Folk Revival.* Cambridge, MA: Harvard University Press, 1996.

Carlin, Richard. *The Big Book of Country Music: A Biographical Encyclopedia.* New York: Penguin, 1995.

Carr, Joe, and Alan Munde. *Prairie Nights to Neon Lights: The Story of Country Music in West Texas.* Lubbock, TX: Texas Tech University Press, 1995.

Cash, Anthony. *Anatomy of Pop.* London: British Broadcasting Corporation, 1970.

Chapple, Steve, and Reebee Garofalo. *Rock 'n' Roll Is Here to Pay: The History and Politics of the Music Industry.* Chicago: Nelson-Hall, 1977.

Christgau, Robert. *Any Old Way You Choose It: Rock and Other Pop Musics, 1967–1973.* Baltimore: Penguin Books, 1973.

Clarke, Donald (editor). *The Penguin Encyclopedia of Popular Music.* London: Viking; New York: Viking Penguin, 1989.

————. *The Rise and Fall of Popular Music.* New York: St. Martin's Press, 1996.

Clifford, Mike. *The Harmony Illustrated Encyclopedia Of Rock* (fifth edition). New York: Harmony Books, 1986; sixth edition, New York: Harmony Books, 1988.

Cohn, Nik. *Rock from the Beginning.* New York: Stein and Day, 1969.

Coleman, Ray (editor). *Today's Sound.* London, New York: Hamlyn, 1973.

Corvette, Nikki. *Rock 'n' Roll Heaven.* New York: Boulevard Books, 1997.

Country Music Foundation. *Country: The Music and the Musicians.* New York: Abbeville Press, 1988.

————. *Country: The Music and the Musicians: From the Beginnings to the '90s.* New York: Abbeville Press, 1994.

Country Music Magazine. The Comprehensive Country Music Encyclopedia. New York: Times Books, 1994.

Crenshaw, Marshall. *Hollywood Rock.* New York: HarperPerennial, 1994.

Curtis, James M. *Rock Eras: Interpretations of Music & Society, 1954–1984.* Bowling Green, OH: Bowling Green State University Popular Press, 1987.

Dachs, David. *Anything Goes: The World of Popular Music.* Indianapolis: Bobbs-Merrill, 1964.

————. *Inside Pop: America's Top Ten Groups.* New York: Scholastic, 1968.

————. *American Pop.* New York: Scholastic, 1969.

————. *Inside Pop 2.* New York: Scholastic, 1970.

————. *Encyclopedia of Pop/Rock.* New York: Scholastic, 1972.

Dalton, David, and Lenny Kaye. *Rock 100.* New York: Grosset and Dunlap, 1977.

Dannen, Fredric. *Hit Men: Power Brokers and Fast Money Inside the Music Business.* New York: Times Books, 1990.

David, Andrew. *Rock Stars: People at the Top of the Charts.* New York: Exeter Books, 1979.

Davis, Clive, with James K. Willwerth. *Clive: Inside the Record Business.* New York: William Morrow, 1975.

Davis, Francis. *The History of the Blues.* New York: Hyperion, 1995.

Dawidoff, Nicholas. *In the Country of Country: People and Places in American Music.* New York: Pantheon Books, 1997.

Deffa, Chip. *Blue Rhythms: Six Lives in Rhythm and Blues.* Urbana: University of Illinois Press, 1996.

Dellar, Fred, Alan Cackett, Ray Thompson, and Douglas B. Green. *The Harmony Illustrated Encyclopedia of Country Music.* New York: Harmony Books, 1987.

Denisoff, R. Serge. *Great Day Coming: Folk Music and the American Left.* Urbana: University of Illinois Press, 1971.

————. *Solid Gold: The Record Industry, Its Friends and Enemies.* New Brunswick, NJ: Transaction Books, 1975.

————. *Tarnished Gold: The Record Industry Revisited.* New Brunswick, NJ: Transaction Books, 1986.

————, and William D. Romanowski. *Risky Business: Rock in Film.* New Brunswick, NJ: Transaction Books, 1991.

DeRogatis, Jim. *Kaleidoscope Eyes: Psychedelic Rock From the '60s to the '90s.* Secaucus, NJ: Carol Publishing Group, 1996

DeTurk, David A., and A. Poulin, Jr. (editors). *The American Folk Scene.* New York: Dell, 1967.

Dickerson, James. *Goin' Back to Memphis: A Century of Blues, Rock 'n' Roll, and Glorious Soul.* New York: Schirmer Books, 1996.

DiMartino, Dave. *Singer-Songwriters: Pop Music's Performer-Composers from A to Zevon.* New York: Billboard Books, 1994.

Doukas, James N. *Electric Tibet.* Hollywood: Dominican Publishing Company, 1969.

Ehrenstein, David, and Bill Reed. *Rock on Film.* New York: Delilah Books, distributed by G. P. Putnam's Sons, 1982.

Eichenlaub, Frank. *The All American Guide to Country Music.* Castine, ME: Country Roads Press, 1992.

Eisen, Jonathan (editor). *The Age of Rock—Sounds of the American Cultural Revolution: A Reader.* New York: Random House, 1969.

————. *The Age of Rock 2.* New York: Random House, 1970.

————. *Twenty Minute Fandangos and Forever Changes.* New York: Random House, 1971.

Eliot, Marc. *Rockonomics: The Money Behind the Music.* New York: Watts, 1989; New York: Carol Publishing Group, 1993.

Elson, Howard. *Early Rockers.* London: Proteus, 1982.

Escott, Colin. *Tattooed on Their Tongues: A Journey Through the Backrooms of American Music.* New York: Schirmer Books, 1996.

Farr, Jory. *Moguls and Madmen: The Pursuit of Power in Popular Music.* New York: Simon and Schuster, 1994.

Fawcett, Anthony. *California Rock, California Sound; The Music of Los Angeles and Southern California.* Los Angeles: Reed Books, 1978.

Felton, Gary S. *The Record Collector's International Directory.* New York: Crown Publishers, 1980.

Flattery, Paul. *The Illustrated History of British Pop.* New York: Drake Publishers, 1975.

Fong-Torres, Ben (editor). *The* Rolling Stone *Rock 'n' Roll Reader.* New York: Bantam Books, 1975.

————. *What's That Sound? The Contemporary Music Scene from the Pages of* Rolling Stone. Garden City, NY: Anchor Press, 1976.

————. *The Hits Just Keep on Coming: The History of Top 40 Radio.* San Francisco: Miller Freeman Books, 1998.

Fornatale, Peter. *The Story of Rock 'n' Roll.* New York: William Morrow, 1987.

Frame, Peter. *Rock Family Trees.* New York: Quick Fox, 1980.

————. *Rock Family Trees 2.* New York: Quick Fox, 1983.

Fredericks, Vic (editor). *Who's Who in Rock 'n' Roll.* New York: Frederick Fell, 1968.

Friedlander, Paul. *Rock and Roll: A Social History.* Boulder, CO: Westview Press, 1996.

Gabree, John. *The World of Rock.* Greenwich, CT: Fawcett Publications, 1968.

Gaines, Steve. *Who's Who in Rock 'n' Roll.* New York: Popular Library, 1975.

Gammond, Peter. *The Oxford Companion to Popular Music.* Oxford, England; New York: Oxford University Press, 1991.

Garland, Phyl. *The Sound of Soul.* Chicago: Henry Regnery Company, 1969; New York: Pocket Books, 1971.

Garofalo, Reebee. *Rockin' the Boat: Mass Music and Mass Movements.* Boston: South End Press, 1992.

————. *Rockin' Out: Popular Music in the USA.* Boston: Allyn and Bacon, 1997.

Gentry, Linnell. *A History and Encyclopedia of Country, Western and Gospel Music.* Nashville: McQuiddy Press, 1961; Nashville: Clairmont Corp., 1969.

George, Nelson. *The Death of Rhythm & Blues.* New York: Pantheon Books, 1988.

Gillett, Charlie. *The Sound of the City: The Rise of Rock 'n' Roll.* New York: Outerbridge and Dienstfry; distributed by E. P. Dutton, 1970; London: Souvenir Press, 1971, 1983; New York: Dell, 1972.

————. *The Sound of the City: The Rise of Rock and Roll.* New York: Pantheon Books, 1983, 1984.

————. *Making Tracks: Atlantic Records and the Growth of a Multi-Billion-Dollar Industry.* New York: E. P. Dutton, 1974.

———— (editor). *Rock File.* London: New English Library, 1972.

Goldman, Albert H. *Freakshow: The Rocksoulbluesjazzsickjewblackhumorsexpoppsych Gig and Other Scenes of the Counter-Culture.* New York: Atheneum, 1971.

————. *Sound Bites.* New York: Turtle Bay Books, 1992.

Goldsmith, Peter David. *Making People's Music: Moe Asch and Folkways Records.* Washington, DC: Smithsonian Institution Press, 1998.

Goldstein, Richard. *Goldstein's Greatest Hits.* Englewood Cliffs, NJ: Prentice-Hall, 1970.

Goldsworthy, Jay (editor). *Casey Kasem's American Top 40 Yearbook.* New York: Target Books, 1979.

Goodman, Fred. *The Mansion on the Hill: Dylan, Young, Geffen, Springsteen, and the Head-on Collision of Rock and Commerce.* New York: Times Books, 1997.

Gordon, Robert. *It Came from Memphis.* Winchester, MA: Faber and Faber, 1995.

Gracyk, Theodore. *Rhythm and Noise: An Aesthetics of Rock.* Durham, NC: Duke University Press, 1996.

Gray, Andy. *Great Pop Stars.* London, New York: Hamlyn, 1973.

Green, Douglas B. *Country Roots: The Origins of Country Music.* New York: Hawthorn Books, 1976.

Green, Jonathon (editor). *The Book of Rock Quotes.* London, New York: Omnibus Press, 1978.

Gregory, Hugh. *Soul Music A–Z.* London: Blandford; New York: distributed by Sterling Publishing, 1991.

————. *Who's Who in Country Music.* London: Weidenfeld and Nicolson, 1993.

————. *1000 Great Guitarists.* San Francisco: GPI Books, 1994.

Grissim, John. *Country Music: White Man's Blues.* New York: Paperback Library, 1970.

Grossberg, Lawrence. *Dancing in Spite of Myself: Essays on Popular Culture.* Durham, NC: Duke University Press, 1997.

Grossman, Lloyd. *A Social History of Rock Music: From the Greasers to Glitter Rock.* New York: McKay, 1976.

Guitar Player. Rock Guitarists. Saratoga, CA: Guitar Player Productions, 1974.

————. *Rock Guitarists,* Volume II. Saratoga, CA: Guitar Player Productions, 1977.

Guralnick, Peter. *Feel Like Going Home: Portraits in Blues and Rock 'n' Roll.* New York: Outerbridge and Dienstfrey, 1971.

————. *Lost Highway: Journeys and Arrivals of American Musicians.* Boston: D. R. Godine, 1979.

————. *Sweet Soul Music: Rhythm and Blues and the Southern Dream of Freedom.* New York: Harper and Row, 1986.

Haislop, Neil, Ted Lathrop, and Harry Sumrall. *Giants of Country Music.* New York: Billboard Books, 1995.

Hale, Mark. *HeadBangers: The Worldwide Megabook of Heavy Metal Bands.* Ann Arbor, MI: Popular Culture, 1993.

Hall, Douglas K., and Sue C. Clark. *Rock: A World as Bold as Love.* New York: Cowles Book Company, 1970.

Hampton, Wayne. *Guerrilla Minstrels: John Lennon, Joe Hill, Woody Guthrie, and Bob Dylan.* Knoxville: University of Tennessee Press, 1986.

Haralambos, Michael. *Right On: From Blues to Soul in Black America.* London: Eddison Press, 1974; New York: Drake Publishers, 1975; New York: Da Capo Press, 1979.

Hardy, Phil, and Dave Laing (editors). *The Encyclopedia of Rock, Volume 1: The Age of Rock 'n' Roll.* St. Albans: Aquarius, 1976.

————. *The Encyclopedia of Rock, Volume 2: From Liverpool to San Francisco.* St. Albans: Aquarius, 1976.

————. *The Encyclopedia of Rock: 1955–1975.* St. Albans: Panther, 1977.

————. *Encyclopedia of Rock.* New York: Schirmer Books, 1988.

————. *The Faber Companion to 20th-Century Popular Music.* London; Boston: Faber and Faber, 1990.

Harrigan, Brian, and Malcolm Dome. *Encyclopedia Metallica*. London, New York: Bobcat Books, 1980.

Harris, Craig. *The New Folk Music*. Crown Point, IN: White Cliffs Media, 1991.

Heatley, Michael. *The Ultimate Encyclopedia of Rock: The World's Most Comprehensive Illustrated Rock Reference*. New York: HarperPerennial, 1993.

Helander, Brock. *The Rock Who's Who: A Biographical Dictionary and Critical Discography Including Rhythm-and-Blues, Soul, Rockabilly, Folk, Country, Easy Listening, Punk, and New Wave*. New York: Schirmer Books, 1982.

————. *The Rock Who's Who* (second edition). New York: Schirmer Books, 1996.

Hemphill, Paul. *The Nashville Sound: Bright Lights and Country Music*. New York: Simon and Schuster, 1970.

Henry, Tricia. *Break All Rules!: Punk Rock and the Making of a Style*. Ann Arbor, MI: UMI Research Press, 1989.

Herzhaft, Gerard. *Encyclopedia of the Blues*. Fayetteville: University of Arkansas Press, 1992, 1997.

Heylin, Clinton (editor). *The Penguin Book of Rock & Roll Writing*. London; New York: Viking, 1992.

————. *From the Velvets to the Voidoids: A Pre-Punk History for A Post-Punk World*. New York: Penguin, 1993.

————. *Bootleg: The Secret History of the Other Recording Industry*. New York: St. Martin's Griffin, 1996.

Hildebrand, Lee. *Stars of Soul and Rhythm & Blues*. New York: Billboard Books, 1994.

Hill, Randal C. *Superstars of Rock*. Austin, TX: Steck-Vaughn Company, 1986.

————. *Superstars of Soul*. Austin, TX: Steck-Vaughn Company, 1986.

Hirshey, Gerri. *Nowhere to Run: The Story of Soul Music*. New York: Times Books, 1984; New York: Penguin Books, 1985; New York: Da Capo Press, 1994.

Hoare, Ian (editor). *The Soul Book*. New York: Dell, 1976.

Hodenfield, Chris. *Rock '70*. New York: Pyramid Publications, 1970.

Holzman, Jac, and Gavan Daws. *Follow the Music: The Life and High Times of Elektra Records in the Great Years of American Pop Culture*. Santa Monica, CA: FirstMedia Books, 1998.

Hopkins, Jerry. *The Rock Story*. New York: New American Library, 1970.

————. *Festival! The Book of American Music Celebrations*. New York: Macmillan, 1970.

Jackson, Rick. *Encyclopedia of Canadian Rock, Pop and Folk Music*. Kingston, Ontario: Quary Press, 1994.

Jacobs, Philip. *Rock 'n' Roll Heaven*. New York: Gallery Books, 1990.

Jahn, Mike. *Rock: From Elvis to The Rolling Stones*. New York: Quadrangle/New York Times Book Company, 1973.

Jancik, Wayne. *The Billboard Book of One-Hit Wonders*. New York: Billboard Books, 1990.

————, and Ted Lathrop. *Cult Rockers*. New York: Simon and Schuster, 1995.

Jasper, Tony. *Understanding Pop*. London: S.C.M. Press, 1972.

Jenkinson, Philip, and Alan Warner. *Celluloid Rock: Twenty Years of Movie Rock*. London: Lorrimer, 1974.

Kelly, Michael Bryan. *The Beatle Myth: The British Invasion of American Popular Music*. Jefferson, NC: McFarland, 1991.

Kienzle, Rich. *Great Guitarists: The Most Influential Players in Blues, Country Music, Jazz and Rock*. New York: Facts on File, 1985.

Kiersh, Edward. *Where Are You Now Bo Diddley?: The Stars Who Made Us Rock and Where They Are Now*. Garden City, NY: Doubleday, 1986.

Kingsbury, Paul (editor). *Country on Compact Disc*. New York: Grove Press, 1993.

Knoedelseder, William. *Stiffed: A True Story of MCA, The Music Business, and The Mafia*. New York: HarperCollins, 1993.

Koster, Rick. *Texas Music: An Encyclopedia.* New York: St. Martin's Press, 1998.

Krebs, Gary M. *The Rock and Roll Reader's Guide.* New York: Billboard Books, 1997.

Laing, Dave. *The Sound of Our Time.* London: Sneed and Ward, 1969; Chicago: Quadrangle Books, 1970.

————. *The Electric Muse: The Story of Folk Into Rock.* London: Methuen, 1975.

Landau, Jon. *It's Too Late to Stop Now: A Rock 'n' Roll Journal.* San Francisco: Straight Arrow Books, 1972.

Larkin, Colin (editor). *The Guinness Encyclopedia of Popular Music* (6 volumes). New York: Stockton Books, 1996.

Larkin, Colin. *The Billboard Illustrated Encyclopedia of Rock.* New York: Billboard Books, 1998.

Larkin, Rochelle. *Soul Music.* New York: Lancer Books, 1970.

Lazell, Barry (editor). *Rock Movers and Shakers.* New York: Billboard Publications, 1989.

Lifton, Sarah. *The Listener's Guide to Folk Music.* New York: Facts on File, 1983.

Lissauer, Robert. *Lissauer's Encyclopedia of Popular Music in America: 1888 to the Present* (3 volumes). New York: Paragon House, 1991; New York: Facts on File, 1996.

Logan, Nick, and Bob Woffinden. *The Illustrated New Musical Express Encyclopedia of Rock.* London: Salamander Books, 1977; New York: Hamlyn, 1977.

———— (compilers). *The Illustrated Encyclopedia of Rock.* New York: Harmony Books, 1977.

————. *The Harmony Illustrated Encyclopedia of Rock.* New York: Harmony Books, 1982.

Lornell, Kip. *Introducing American Folk Music.* Madison, WI: Brown and Benchmark, 1993.

Love, Robert (editor). *The Best of* Rolling Stone: *25 Years of Journalism on the Edge.* New York: Doubleday, 1993.

Lydon, Michael. *Rock Folk: Portraits from the Rock 'n' Roll Pantheon.* New York: Dial Press, 1971.

————. *Boogie Lightnin'.* New York: Dial Press, 1974.

Mabey, Richard. *Behind the Scene.* London: Penguin Books, 1968.

————. *The Pop Process.* London: Hutchinson, 1969.

Macken, Bob, Peter Fornatale, and Bill Ayres. *The Rock Music Source Book.* Garden City, NY: Anchor Press, 1980.

Marcus, Greil. *Rock and Roll Will Stand.* Boston: Beacon Press, 1969.

————. *Mystery Train: Images of America in Rock 'n' Roll Music.* New York: E. P. Dutton, 1975, 1990.

———— (editor). *Stranded: Rock and Roll for a Desert Island.* New York: Knopf; distributed by Random House, 1979.

Marre, Jeremy, and Hannah Charlton. *Beats of the Heart: Popular Music of the World.* New York: Pantheon Books, 1985.

Marsh, Dave. *The First Rock & Roll Confidential Report: Inside the Real World of Rock & Roll.* New York: Pantheon Books, 1985.

————. *Fortunate Son: Criticism and Journalism by America's Best-Known Rock Writer.* New York: Random House, 1985.

————. *Sun City by Artists United Against Apartheid, The Struggle for Freedom in South Africa: The Making of the Record.* New York: Penguin Books, 1985.

————. *Louie Louie: The History and Mythology of the World's Most Famous Rock 'n' Roll Song.* New York: Hyperion, 1993.

————, and Kevin Stein. *The Book of Rock Lists.* Garden City, NY: A Dell/Rolling Stone Press Book, 1981.

————, and James Bernard. *The New Book of Rock Lists.* New York: Simon and Schuster, 1994.

May, Chris, and Tim Phillips. *British Beat.* London: Socion Books, n.d.

McCall, Michael, Dave Hoekstra, and Janet Williams. *Country Music Stars: The Legends and the New Breed.* Lincolnville, IL: Publications International, 1992.

McCloud, Barry. *Definitive Country: The Ultimate Encyclopedia of Country Music and Its Performers.* New York: Berkley Publishing Group, 1995.

McDonnell, Evelyn, and Ann Powers (compilers). *Rock She Wrote.* New York: Delta, 1995.

McDonough, Jack. *San Francisco Rock: The Illustrated History of San Francisco Rock Music.* San Francisco: Chronicle Books, 1985.

Melhuish, Martin. *Heart of Gold: 30 Years of Canadian Pop Music.* Toronto: CBC Enterprises, 1983.

Meltzer, Richard. *The Aesthetics of Rock.* New York: Something Else Press, 1970.

Merlis, Bob, and Davin Seay. *Heart & Soul: A Celebration of Black Music Styles in America, 1930–1975.* New York: Stewart, Tabori and Chang, 1997.

Millard, Bob. *Country Music: 70 Years of America's Favorite Music.* New York: HarperPerennial, 1993.

Miller, Jim (editor). *Rolling Stone Illustrated History of Rock & Roll.* New York: Rolling Stone Press, 1976, 1980.

Miller, Terry. *Folk Music in America: A Reference Guide.* New York: Garland Publishing, 1986.

Monnery, Steve, and Gary Herman. *Rock 'n' Roll Chronicles 1955–1963.* Stamford, CT: Longmeadow Press, 1991.

Morse, David. *Motown and the Arrival of Black Music.* New York: Macmillan, 1971.

Morse, Tim. *Classic Rock Stories.* New York: St. Martin's Griffin, 1998.

Muirhead, Bert. *The Record Producers File: A Directory of Rock Album Record Producers 1962–1984.* Dorset, England: Blandford Press, 1984.

Murray, Charles Shaar, and Neil Spencer. *Shots from the Hip.* New York: Penguin, 1991.

Nager, Larry. *Memphis Beat: The Story of America's Music Crucible.* New York: St. Martin's Press, 1998.

Naha, Ed (compiler). *Lillian Roxon's Rock Encyclopedia.* New York: Grosset and Dunlap, 1978.

Nanry, Charles (editor). *American Music: From Storyville to Woodstock.* New Brunswick, NJ: Transaction Books, distributed by E. P. Dutton, 1972.

Nettl, Bruno. *Folk Music in the United States: An Introduction.* Detroit: Wayne State University Press, 1976.

Nicholson, Stuart. *Jazz Rock: A History.* New York: Schirmer Books, 1998.

Nite, Norm N. *Rock On: The Illustrated Encyclopedia of Rock 'n' Roll: The Solid Gold Years.* New York: Thomas Y. Crowell, 1974.

———. *The Illustrated Encyclopedia of Rock 'n' Roll* (3 volumes). New York: Thomas Y. Crowell, 1974.

———. *Rock On: The Illustrated Encyclopedia of Rock 'n' Roll* (3 volumes). New York: Harper and Row, 1982.

———. *Rock On: The Illustrated Encyclopedia of Rock 'n' Roll, Volume II: The Modern Years, 1964–Present.* New York: Thomas Y. Crowell, 1978.

———. *Rock On Almanac: The First Four Decades of Rock 'n' Roll: A Chronology.* New York: Perennial Library, 1989; New York: Harper and Row, 1989; New York: HarperPerennial, 1992.

O'Brien, Lucy. *She Bop: The Definitive History of Women in Rock, Pop and Soul.* New York: Penguin Books, 1996.

Obstfeld, Raymond. *Jabberrock!: The Ultimate Book of Rock 'n' Roll Quotations.* New York: H. Holt, 1997.

Ochs, Michael. *Rock Archives: A Photographic Journey Through the First Two Decades of Rock & Roll.* Garden City, NY: Doubleday, 1984.

O'Donnell, Jim. *The Rock Book.* New York: Pinnacle Books, 1975.

Oermann, Robert K., with Douglas B. Green. *The Listener's Guide to Country Music*. New York: Facts on File, 1983.

————. *America's Music: The Roots of Country*. Atlanta: Turner Publishing, 1996.

Orloff, Katherine. *Rock 'n' Roll Woman*. Los Angeles: Nash Publishing, 1974.

Palmer, Robert. *Deep Blues*. New York: Viking Press, 1981; New York: Penguin Books, 1982.

————. *Rock & Roll: An Unruly History*. New York: Harmony Books, 1995.

Palmer, Tony. *All You Need Is Love: The Story of Popular Music*. New York: Grossman Publishers, 1976.

Paraire, Philippe. *50 Years of Rock Music*. New York: W. & R. Chambers, 1992.

Pareles, Jon, and Patricia Romanowski (editors). *The Rolling Stone Encyclopedia of Rock & Roll*. New York: Rolling Stone Press/Summit Books, 1983.

Pascall, Jeremy. *The Illustrated History of Rock Music*. New York: Galahad Books, 1978.

Pascall, Jeremy, and Rob Burt. *The Stars and Superstars of Black Music*. Secaucus, NJ: Chartwell Books, 1977.

Passman, Arnold. *The Dee Jays*. New York: Macmillan, 1971.

Peck, Ira (editor). *The New Sound/Yes!* New York: Four Winds Press, 1966.

Petrie, Gavin (editor). *Black Music*. London: Hamlyn, 1974.

————. *Rock Life*. London; New York: Hamlyn, 1974.

Phoebus. *The Stars and Superstars of Rock*. London: Phoebus Publishing/Octopus Books, 1974.

————. *Country Music*. London: Phoebus Publishing, 1976.

————. *The Stars and Superstars of Black Music*. London: Phoebus Publishing, 1977.

————. *West Coast Story*. London: Phoebus Publishing, 1977; Secaucus, NJ: Chartwell Books, 1977.

Pike, Jeff. *The Death of Rock 'n' Roll: Untimely Deaths, Morbid Preoccupations, and Premature Forecasts of Doom in Pop Music*. Boston: Faber and Faber, 1993.

Pollock, Bruce. *In Their Own Words*. New York: Macmillan, 1975.

————. *When Rock Was Young: A Nostalgic Review of the Top 40 Era*. New York: Holt, Rinehart and Winston, 1981.

————. *When Music Mattered: Rock in the 1960's*. New York: Holt, Rinehart and Winston, 1984.

————. *Hipper Than Our Kids: A Rock & Roll Journal of the Baby Boom Generation*. New York: Schirmer Books, 1993.

Prown, Pete, and Harvey P. Newquist. *Legends of Rock Guitar: The Essential Reference to Rock's Greatest Guitarists*. Milwaukee, WI: H. Leonard Books, 1997.

Pruter, Robert. *Chicago Soul*. Urbana: University of Illinois Press, 1991.

Redd, Lawrence N. *Rock Is Rhythm and Blues: The Impact of Mass Media*. East Lansing, MI: Michigan University Press, 1974.

Reid, Jan. *The Improbable Rise of Redneck Rock*. Austin, TX: Heidelberg Publishers, 1974.

Reyes, David. *Land of a Thousand Dances: Chicano Rock 'n' Roll from Southern California*. Albuquerque: University of New Mexico Press, 1998.

Reynolds, Simon. *Blissed Out: The Raptures of Rock*. London, New York: Serpent's Tail, 1990.

Rivelli, Pauline, and Robert Levin (editors). *The Rock Giants*. New York: World Publishing Company, 1970.

———— (editors). *The Black Giants*. New York: World Publishing Company, 1970.

Robinson, Richard (editor). *Rock Revolution*. New York: Popular Library, 1976.

————, and Andy Zwerling. *The Rock Scene*. New York: Popular Library, 1971.

Rock and Roll Hall of Fame Museum. *I Want to Take You Higher: The Psychedelic Era 1965–1969*. San Francisco: Chronicle Books, 1997.

Rolling Stone. The Rolling Stone Interviews. New York: Paperback Library, 1971.

————. *The Rolling Stone Interviews*, Volume 2. New York: Paperback Library, 1973.

—————. *The* Rolling Stone *Reader.* New York: Warner Paperback Library, 1974.

—————. *The* Rolling Stone *Interviews: Talking with the Legends of Rock & Roll, 1967–1980.* New York: St. Martin's Press/Rolling Stone Press, 1981.

Romanowski, Patricia, and Holly George-Warren (editors). *The New* Rolling Stone *Encyclopedia of Rock & Roll.* New York: Fireside, 1995.

Rosenberg, Neil V. *Transforming Tradition: Folk Music Revivals Examined.* Urbana: University of Illinois Press, 1993.

Roxon, Lillian. *Rock Encyclopedia.* New York: Grosset and Dunlap, 1969.

Russell, Tony. *The Blues: From Robert Johnson to Robert Cray.* New York: Schirmer Books, 1997.

St. Michael, Mick. *Heavy Metal.* Stamford, CT: Longmeadow Press, 1992.

Sandahl, Linda J. *Rock Films: A Viewer's Guide to Three Decades of Musicals, Concerts, Documentaries and Soundtracks, 1955–1986.* New York: Facts on File, 1987.

Sandberg, Larry, and Dick Weissman. *The Folk Music Sourcebook.* New York: Da Capo Press, 1989.

Sander, Ellen. *Trips: Rock Life in the Sixties.* New York: Scribner, 1973.

Santelli, Robert. *The Big Book of Blues: A Biographical Encyclopedia.* New York: Penguin, 1993.

Santoro, Gene. *Dancing in Your Head: Jazz, Blues, Rock and Beyond.* New York: Oxford University Press, 1994.

Sarig, Roni. *The Secret History of Rock: The Most Influential Bands You Never Heard.* New York: Billboard Books, 1998.

Sarlin, Bob. *Turn It Up! (I Can't Hear the Words): The Best of the New Singer/Songwriters.* New York: Simon and Schuster, 1974.

Schafer, William J. *Rock Music: Where It's Been, What It Means, Where It's Going.* Minneapolis: Augsburg Publishing, 1972.

Schaffner, Nicholas. *The British Invasion: From the First Wave to the New Wave.* New York: McGraw-Hill, 1982.

Schicke, Charles A. *Revolution in Sound: A Biography of the Recording Industry.* Boston: Little, Brown, 1974.

Scoppa, Bud. *The Rock People.* New York: Scholastic, 1973.

Sculatti, Gene. *San Francisco Nights: The Psychedelic Music Trip, 1965–1968.* New York: St. Martin's Press, 1985.

Selvin, Joel. *Monterey Pop: June 16–18, 1967.* San Francisco: Chronicle Books, 1992.

—————. *Summer of Love: The Inside Story of LSD, Rock & Roll, Free Love and High Times in the Wild West.* New York: Dutton, 1994; New York: Plume, 1995.

Shapiro, Nat, and Bruce Pollock. *Popular Music, 1920–1979: A Revised Cumulation.* Detroit: Gale Research Company, 1985.

Shaw, Arnold. *The Rock Revolution.* New York: Crowell-Collier Press, 1969.

—————. *The World of Soul: Black America's Contribution to the Pop Music Scene.* New York: Cowles Book Company, 1970.

—————. *Dictionary of American Pop/Rock.* New York: Schirmer Books, 1982.

—————. *Black Popular Music in America.* New York: Schirmer Books, 1986.

Sia, Joseph J. *Woodstock '69: Summer Pop Festivals.* New York: Scholastic, 1970.

Silver, Caroline. *The Pop Makers.* New York: Scholastic, 1966.

Smith, Joe, and Mitchell Fink (editors). *Off the Record: An Oral History of Popular Music.* New York: Warner Books, 1988.

Smith, Wes. *The Pied Pipers of Rock 'n' Roll: Radio Deejays of the 50s and 60s.* Marietta, GA: Longstreet Publishing, 1989.

Somma, Robert (editor). *No One Waved Goodbye: A Casualty Report on Rock and Roll.* New York: Outerbridge and Dientsfrey, 1971.

Sonnier, Austin M. *A Guide to the Blues: History, Who's Who, Research Sources.* Westport, CT: Greenwood Press, 1994.

Spitz, Robert Stephen. *The Making of Superstars: Artists and Executives of the Rock Music Business.* Garden City, NY: Anchor Press, 1978.

Stambler, Irwin. *Encyclopedia of Popular Music.* New York: St. Martin's Press, 1965.

————. *Guitar Years: Pop Music from Country and Western to Hard Rock.* Garden City, NY: Doubleday, 1970.

————. *Encyclopedia of Pop, Rock, and Soul.* New York: St. Martin's Press, 1975, 1989.

————, and Grelun Landon. *Encyclopedia of Folk, Country, and Western Music.* New York: St. Martin's Press, 1969, 1983.

————. *Country Music: The Encyclopedia.* New York: St. Martin's Press, 1997.

Stuessy, Joe. *Rock & Roll: Its History and Stylistic Development.* Englewood Cliffs, NJ: Prentice Hall, 1990.

Sumrall, Harry. *Pioneers of Rock and Roll: 100 Artists Who Changed the Face of Rock.* New York: Billboard Books, 1994.

Suter, Paul. *HM A-Z.* London: Omnibus, 1985.

Szatmary, David P. *A Time to Rock: A Social History of Rock 'n' Roll.* New York: Schirmer Books, 1996.

Taylor, Derek. *It Was Twenty Years Ago Today.* New York: Simon and Schuster, 1987.

Tee, Ralph. *Soul Music: Who's Who.* Rocklin, CA: Prima Publishing, 1992.

Thomson, Liz (editor). *New Women in Rock.* New York: Delilah/Putnam, 1984.

Tobler, John. *Guitar Heroes.* New York: St. Martin's Press, 1978.

————. *30 Years of Rock.* New York: Exeter Books: distributed by Bookthrift, 1985.

————, (editor). *Who's Who in Rock & Roll.* New York: Crescent Books, 1991.

Tobler, John, and Stuart Grundy. *The Record Producers.* New York: St. Martin's Press, 1982.

————. *The Guitar Greats.* New York: St. Martin's Press, 1984.

Tosches, Nick. *Country: The Biggest Music in America.* New York: Stein and Day, 1977.

Unterberger, Richie. *Unknown Legends of Rock 'n' Roll: Psychedelic Unknowns, Mad Geniuses, Punk Pioneers, Lo-Fi Mavericks, and More.* San Francisco: Miller Freeman Books, 1998.

Van Der Horst, Brian. *Rock Music.* New York: Watts, 1973.

Vassal, Jacques. *Electric Children: Roots and Branches of Modern Folk-Rock.* (Translation: Paul Barnett.) New York: Taplinger Publishing Company, 1975.

Vaughan, Andrew. *The World of Country Music.* Stamford, CT: Longmeadow Press, 1992.

Vincent, Rickey. *Funk: The Music, the People, and the Rhythm of One.* New York: St. Martin's Griffin, 1996.

Vinson, Lee. *Encyclopedia of Rock.* New York: Drake Publishers, 1976.

von Schmidt, Eric, and Jim Rooney. *Baby, Let Me Follow You Down: The Illustrated Story of the Cambridge Folk Years.* Garden City, NY: Anchor Books, 1979.

Walser, Robert. *Running with the Devil: Power, Gender, and Madness in Heavy Metal Music.* Hannover, NH: University Press of New England, 1993.

Ward, Ed, Geoffrey Stokes, and Ken Tucker. *Rock of Ages: The* Rolling Stone *History of Rock and Roll.* New York: Rolling Stone Press: Summit Books, 1986.

Warner, Jay. *Billboard Book of American Singing Groups: A History, 1940–1990.* New York: Billboard Books, 1992.

————. *Billboard's American Rock & Roll in Review.* New York: Schirmer Books, 1997.

Wexler, Jerry, and David Ritz. *Rhythm and the Blues: A Life in American Music.* New York: Knopf, 1993.

White, Timothy. *Rock Stars.* New York: Stewart, Tabori and Chang, 1984.

————. *Rock Lives: Profiles and Interviews.* New York: Henry Holt, 1989.

Williams, Paul. *Outlaw Blues: A Book of Rock Music.* New York: E. P. Dutton, 1969.

Wolliver, Robbie. *Bringing It All Back Home: 25 Years of American Folk Music at Folk City.* New York: Pantheon Books, 1986.

————. *Hoot!: A Twenty-Five-Year History of the Greenwich Village Music Scene*. New York: St. Martin's Press, 1994

Wood, Graham. *An A—Z of Rock and Roll*. London: Studio Vista, 1971.

York, William (editor). *Who's Who in Rock Music*. Seattle: Atomic Press, 1978; New York: Scribner, 1982.

Yorke, Ritchie. *Axes, Chops & Hot Licks: The Canadian Rock Music Scene*. Edmonton: M. G. Hurtig, 1971.

————. *The History of Rock 'n' Roll*. Toronto: Methuen/Two Continents, 1976.

Young, Jean, and Michael Lang. *Woodstock Music Festival Remembered*. New York: Ballantine Books, 1979.

INDEX